D1738105

The Psychology of Conflict
and Conflict Management
in Organizations

The Organizational Frontiers Series

The Organizational Frontiers Series is sponsored by the Society for Industrial and Organizational Psychology (SIOP). Launched in 1983 to make scientific contributions to the field, the series has attempted to publish books on cutting edge theory, research, and theory-driven practice in industrial/organizational psychology and related organizational science disciplines.

Our overall objective is to inform and to stimulate research for SIOP members (students, practitioners, and researchers) and people in related disciplines including the other subdisciplines of psychology, organizational behavior, human resource management, and labor and industrial relations. The volumes in the Organizational Frontiers Series have the following goals:

1. Focus on research and theory in organizational science, and the implications for practice.
2. Inform readers of significant advances in theory and research in psychology and related disciplines that are relevant to our research and practice.
3. Challenge the research and practice community to develop and adapt new ideas and to conduct research on these developments.
4. Promote the use of scientific knowledge in the solution of public policy issues and increased organizational effectiveness.

The volumes originated in the hope that they would facilitate continuous learning and a continuing research curiosity about organizational phenomena on the part of both scientists and practitioners.

The Organizational Frontiers Series

SIOP Organizational Frontiers Series

Series Editor

Robert D. Pritchard
University of Central Florida

The Psychology of Conflict and Conflict Management in Organizations
Carsten K. W. De Dreu and Michele J. Gelfand, Editors, 2008

Perspectives on Organizational Fit
Cheri Ostroff and Timothy A. Judge, Editors, 2007

The Psychology of Entrepreneurship
J. Robert Baum, Michael Frese, and Robert A. Baron, Editors, 2007

Situational Judgment Tests: Theory, Measurement, and Application
Jeff A. Weekley and Robert E. Ployhart, Editors, 2006

Discrimination at Work: The Psychological and Organizational Bases
Robert L. Dipboye and Adrienne J. Colella, Editors, 2005

The Dark Side of Organizational Behavior
Ricky W. Griffin and Anne O'Leary-Kelly, Editors, 2004

Health and Safety in Organizations
David A. Hofmann and Lois E. Tetrick, Editors, 2003

Managing Knowledge for Sustained Competitive Advantage
Susan E. Jackson, Michael A. Hitt, and Angelo S. DeNisi, Editors, 2003

Personality and Work: Reconsidering the Role
of Personality in Organizations
Murray R. Barrick and Ann Marie Ryan, Editors, 2003

Emotions in the Workplace
Robert G. Lord, Richard J. Klimoski, and Ruth Kanfer, Editors, 2002

Measuring and Analyzing Behavior in Organizations:
Advances in Measurement and Data Analysis
Fritz Drasgow and Neal Schmitt, Editors, 2002

The Psychology of Conflict
and Conflict Management
in Organizations

Edited by

Carsten K. W. De Dreu • Michele J. Gelfand

Lawrence Erlbaum Associates
Taylor & Francis Group

New York   London

Lawrence Erlbaum Associates
Taylor & Francis Group
270 Madison Avenue
New York, NY 10016

Lawrence Erlbaum Associates
Taylor & Francis Group
2 Park Square
Milton Park, Abingdon
Oxon OX14 4RN

© 2008 by Taylor & Francis Group, LLC
Lawrence Erlbaum Associates is an imprint of Taylor & Francis Group, an Informa business

Printed in the United States of America on acid-free paper
10 9 8 7 6 5 4 3

International Standard Book Number-13: 978-0-8058-5516-6 (Hardcover)

Visit the Taylor & Francis Web site at
http://www.taylorandfrancis.com

and the LEA and Routledge Web site at
http://www.routledge.com

Contents

Series Foreword

This is the 26th book in the Organizational Frontiers Series of books initiated by the SIOP. The overall purpose of the series volumes is to promote the scientific status of the field. Ray Katzell first edited the series. He was followed by Irwin Goldstein, Sheldon Zedeck, and Neal Schmitt. The topics of the volumes and the volume editors are chosen by the editorial board, or individuals propose volumes to the editorial board. The series editor and the editorial board then work with the volume editor(s) in planning the volume.

The success of the series is evident in the high number of sales (now over 50,000). Volumes have also received excellent reviews and individual chapters as well as volumes have been cited frequently.

This volume, edited by Carsten K. W. De Dreu and Michele J. Gelfand, is important because it presents current thinking and research on conflict. Conflict in organizations is pervasive and a necessary aspect of social interactions between people. The editors point out that conflict has substantial consequences for individuals, teams, and organizations in areas such as absenteeism, creativity, communication, social climate, and the quality of group decision making. They also argue there is a close connection between conflict and collaborative work and this connection has become more important with the growing emphasis on collaboration and teams.

The volume has other important strengths. Aside from being a truly comprehensive overview of the field, the editors and authors stress repeatedly that conflict in organizations is a multilevel phenomenon, and individual, group, and organizational antecedents and consequences must be considered to truly understand it. The editors do a masterful job of identifying communalities and differences across these levels of analysis. This multilevel emphasis continues throughout the volume. It also presents multiple approaches and disciplines to broaden our perspective on conflict. Finally, it identifies future research needs that will have a significant impact on conflict research for years to come.

The editors and chapter authors deserve our gratitude for clearly communicating the nature, application, and implications of the theory and research described in this book. Production of a volume such as this involves the hard work and cooperative effort of many individuals. The editors, the chapter authors, and the editorial board all played important roles in this endeavor. As all royalties from the series volumes are used

to help support SIOP, none of the editors or authors receives any remu-
neration. The editors and authors deserve our appreciation for engaging a
difficult task for the sole purpose of furthering our understanding of organizational science. We also want to express our gratitude to Anne Duffy,
our editor at Lawrence Erlbaum Associates, who has been a great help in
the planning and production of the volume.

Robert D. Pritchard
University of Central Florida
Series Editor

Contributors

Catherine E. Amiot is Assistant Professor of Psychology at the Université du Québec à Montréal. Her research focuses on intergroup dynamics, social identity change, and the motivations underlying social identification. She has published in *Personality and Social Psychology Bulletin, Journal of Management, British Journal of Social Psychology,* and *European Journal of Social Psychology.*

Julian Barling is Queen's Research Chair and Associate Dean (Ph.D., M.Sc., and Research programs) in the Queen's School of Business. Dr. Barling is the author/editor of several books, including most recently the *Handbook of Work Stress* (with Kevin Kelloway and Mike Frone, 2005) and the *Handbook of Workplace Violence* (with Kevin Kelloway and Joe Hurrell, 2006). He is currently editing the *Handbook of Organizational Behavior,* with Cary Cooper. Dr. Barling was the editor of the American Psychological Association's *Journal of Occupational Health Psychology* and serves on the editorial boards of the *Journal of Applied Psychology, Leadership and Organizational Development Journal,* and *Stress Medicine.* In 2001, Dr. Barling received the *National Post*'s Leaders in Business Education Award, and in 2002, he was elected a Fellow of the Royal Society of Canada.

Bianca Beersma is Assistant Professor in the Department of Work and Organizational Psychology at the University of Amsterdam, the Netherlands. Her research focuses on the effects of social and epistemic motivation on conflict, negotiation, and team processes and performance. She also studies the effects of personality and culture on conflict management. Her work has been published in *Academy of Management Journal,* the *Journal of Personality and Social Psychology, Journal of Applied Psychology, Organizational Behavior and Human Decision Processes, Social Justice Research,* and *International Journal of Conflict Management.*

Lehman Benson III is The McCoy/Rogers Fellow of Management and Associate Professor at the University of Arizona and is currently a visiting professor at Duke University. His ongoing research examines the effect of stress, time constraints, and feedback on judgment and decision making. Professor Benson has published numerous articles and book chapters in many journals such as *Organizational Behavior and Human Decision Pro-*

cesses, *Group Decision and Negotiation,* and *Psychological Research Bulletin.* He is on the editorial boards of the *Journal of Behavior Decision-Making* and *The Journal of Management.* He is also the CEO of Lehman Benson Consulting (LehmanBenson.com), which specializes in negotiation, diversity, and time-management training.

Katerina Bezrukova is Assistant Professor of Psychology at Rutgers University. Her current research interests include workplace diversity and group faultlines, organizational conflict and performance, intergroup and interorganizational relations, ethnopolitical conflict and peacekeeping, and diversity training. Her work has appeared in the *Journal of Organizational Behavior, Human Resource Management Journal,* and Best Paper *Proceedings of the Academy of Management.* She was a co-recipient of the Ulrich & Lake Award for Excellence for 2004 for her co-authored article titled "The Effects of Diversity on Business Performance: Report of the Diversity Research Network."

Wendy R. Boswell is Associate Professor and Mays Research Fellow in the Department of Management, Mays Business School, Texas A&M University. She is also the Director of the Center for Human Resource Management at Texas A&M. Her research focuses on employee attraction and retention, job search behavior, conflict management, and work stress. Professor Boswell's work has appeared in such journals as *Academy of Management Journal, Journal of Applied Psychology, Personnel Psychology, Human Resource Management, Journal of Vocational Behavior,* and *Journal of Management.* She serves on the editorial boards of *Personnel Psychology* and *Journal of Managerial Issues,* and serves as an Associate Editor for *Human Resource Management.*

Arthur P. Brief is the David S. Eccles Chair in Business Ethics and Presidential Professor at the University of Utah. His research focuses on the moral dimensions of organizational life (e.g., ethical decision making, race relations, and worker well-being). In addition to dozens of journal articles, Dr. Brief is the author of several books including *Attitudes In and Around Organizations* (1998). He is a past editor of *The Academy of Management Review.* He now co-edits *Research in Organizational Behavior* and the new *Academy of Management Annals.* He is a Fellow of the Academy of Management, American Psychological Society, and the American Psychological Association. He has been a Fulbright Fellow, a Batten Fellow at the Darden Graduate School of Business at the University of Virginia, and the Thomas S. Murphy Distinguished Professor of Research at the Harvard Business School.

Valentina Bruk-Lee is an Industrial/Organizational Psychology consultant. Her research focus is on the impact of interpersonal conflict on health and well-being, occupational stressors and strains, and personality. Her work has been published in *Journal of Occupational Health Psychology, Comprehensive Handbook of Psychological Assessment,* and *Encyclopedia of Industrial/Organizational Psychology.* She has presented at various national conferences and received funding from the National Institute for Occupational Safety and Health for her research on social stressors. Her applied experience spans the areas of selection, promotional testing, performance appraisal, and job analysis in both the public and private sectors.

Peter J. Carnevale is Professor of Psychology at New York University with an appointment in the Department of Management and Organizations at the Stern School of Business. His research focuses on the interplay of cognition, motivation, emotion, and culture in negotiation and mediation of conflicts. He was the inaugural recipient of the Jeffrey Z. Rubin Theory-to-Practice Award, 2002, awarded by the International Association for Conflict Management; and he is co-editor (with Carsten K. W. De Dreu) of the eclectic collection *Methods of Negotiation Research* (2006).

Ying Chen is a doctoral student in organizational studies at Vanderbilt University. Her research focuses on conflict management, diversity, and the effects of social/cultural contexts on interpersonal processes within organizations. Her current research projects include empirical studies of the effects of family-friendly HR policies on employee well-being, multinational companies' union strategies, and the relationship between leaders' strategic displays of negative emotions and employees' job performance.

Donald E. Conlon is the Eli Broad Professor of Management and Chairperson of the Department of Management at the Eli Broad College of Business, Michigan State University. His research focuses on organizational justice, negotiation and dispute resolution, and managerial decision making. Dr. Conlon has published in a variety of journals including *Administrative Science Quarterly, Academy of Management Journal, The Academy of Management Review, Journal of Applied Psychology,* and *Organizational Behavior and Human Decision Processes.* He received his Ph.D. from the organizational behavior group at the University of Illinois at Urbana-Champaign.

Russell Cropanzano is the Brien Lesk Professor of Organizational Behavior at the University of Arizona's Eller College of Management. Dr. Cropanzano's primary research areas include perceptions of organizational justice as well as the experience and impact of workplace emotion. He has edited four books, presented over 60 papers, and published roughly 80 scholarly articles and chapters. He is a co-author (with Robert Folger) of the book *Organizational Justice and Human Resources Management,* which won the 1998 Book Award from the International Association of Conflict

Management. Dr. Cropanzano was a winner of the 2000 Outstanding Paper Award from the *Consulting Psychology Journal*. He is currently editor of the *Journal of Management*, a fellow in the Society for Industrial/Organizational Psychology, and Representative-at-Large for the Organizational Behavior Division of the Academy of Management.

Carsten K. W. De Dreu is Professor and Chair of the Organizational Psychology Program at the University of Amsterdam, the Netherlands. He was president of the International Association for Conflict Management and is scientific director of the Kurt Lewin Graduate School for Social and Organizational Psychology. His research interests center on group processes and performance (including conflict and negotiation, and creativity and innovation). His research, which has been published in the major journals in psychology and organizational behavior, relies on a mixture of laboratory experiments, organizational field studies, and meta-analytic reviews. He has edited several books, including *Using Conflict in Organizations* (with Evert van de Vliert, 1997), *Group Consensus and Minority Influence* (with Nanne de Vries, 2001), and *Methods of Negotiation Research* (with Peter J. Carnevale, 2006).

Ray Friedman is the Brownlee O. Currey Professor of Management at the Owen Graduate School of Management, Vanderbilt University. His research focuses on conflict management, justice, and negotiation, with a special focus on labor negotiations, race (black–white perceptions of justice), and culture (U.S.–Chinese differences in dispute resolution). He has published one book, *Front Stage, Backstage: The Dramatic Structure of Labor Negotiations*, and numerous articles in journals such as *Academy of Management Journal, Administrative Science Quarterly, Journal of Applied Psychology, Organization Science, Journal of International Business Studies*, and *Human Resource Management*. Professor Friedman is past chair of the Conflict Management Division of the Academy of Management, and President of the International Association for Conflict Management.

Michele J. Gelfand is Professor in the Department of Psychology at the University of Maryland, College Park. Her research explores cultural influences on conflict, negotiation, justice, and revenge; workplace diversity and discrimination; and theory and methods in cross-cultural psychology. Her work has been published in such outlets as *Journal of Applied Psychology, Journal of Personality and Social Psychology, Organizational Behavior and Human Decision Processes, The Academy of Management Review, Academy of Management Journal*, and the *Annual Review of Psychology*. She co-edited (with Jeanne Brett) *The Handbook of Negotiation and Culture*. Professor Gelfand received the Ernest J. McCormick Award for Early Career Contributions from the Society for Industrial and Organizational Psychology and the LL Cummings Scholar Award from the Organizational Behavior of the Academy of Management. She is the Division Chair of the Conflict Management Division of the Academy of Management, past treasurer of the International Association for Cross-Cultural Psychology (2001–2005), and past program chair of the International Association for Conflict Management.

Barry M. Goldman is Associate Professor of Management and Policy at the Eller College of Management at the University of Arizona. His primary area of research involves dispute resolution and justice at work, particularly legal-claiming. His current focus is on mediation of work-related disputes. He has published in *Academy of Management Journal, Journal of Applied Psychology, Personnel Psychology, Journal of Management,* and *Journal of Organizational Behavior,* among other outlets. He is on the editorial boards of the *Journal of Applied Psychology, Journal of Management,* and *Negotiations and Conflict Management Research.* He teaches M.B.A. courses and doctoral seminars in negotiations and human resource management.

John R. Hollenbeck is currently the Eli Broad Professor of Management at the Eli Broad College of Business at Michigan State University. Dr. Hollenbeck served as the acting editor of *Organizational Behavior and Human Decision Processes* in 1995, the associate editor of *Decision Sciences* from 1999 to 2004, and the editor of *Personnel Psychology* from 1996 to 2002. He has published over 60 articles and book chapters on the topics of team decision making and work motivation, much of which was funded by the Office of Naval Research and the Air Force Office of Scientific Research.

Larry Hunter is Procter & Gamble Bascom Associate Professor of Management and Human Resources at the School of Business of the University of Wisconsin–Madison. He studies the effects of firms' employment practices on both individuals and organizations, and how those practices are related to choices in technology, to business strategies, to managerial decisions, and to the influence of consultants. His work has appeared in journals including *Industrial & Labor Relations Review, Strategic Management Journal,* and *Work and Occupations.* He was named Outstanding Young Scholar by the Labor and Employment Relations Association in 2001.

David Jaffee is Professor of Sociology and Assistant Vice President for Undergraduate Studies at the University of North Florida. His research interests have included social and economic development, deindustrialization and job loss, gender inequality in organizations, organization and management theory, pedagogy and instructional technology, the social dynamics of the college classroom, and the organizational and administrative dynamics of higher education. He is the author of *Levels of Socio-Economic Development Theory* and *Organization Theory: Tension and Change.*

Karen A. Jehn is Professor of Social and Organizational Psychology at Leiden University, the Netherlands. Her research focuses on intragroup conflict, group composition and performance, and lying in organizations. Professor Jehn has authored numerous scholarly publications in these areas, including articles in *Academy of Management Journal, Administrative Science Quarterly, Journal of Personality and Social Psychology, International Journal of Conflict Management, Research in Organization Behavior, Journal of Business Ethics, Business Ethics Quarterly*, and *Group Decision and Negotiation*. She has served on the editorial boards of *Administrative Science Quarterly, The Academy of Management Review, Journal of Organizational Behavior*, and *International Journal of Conflict Management* where she was an associate editor. She was also an associate director of the Solomon Asch Center for the Study of Ethnopolitical Conflict, the Research Director of the Alfred P. Sloan Foundation's Diversity Research Network, and the Chair of the Conflict Management Division of the Academy of Management.

Deborah M. Kolb is the Deloitte Ellen Gabriel Professor for Women and Leadership at Simmons School of Management. From 1991 to 1994, she was Executive Director of the Program on Negotiation at Harvard Law School and is currently co-director of The Negotiations in the Workplace Project. Her current research focuses on gender issues in negotiation and leadership. Her book *The Shadow Negotiation* was named a best business book by *Harvard Business Review* and received the Best Book Award from the International Association of Conflict Management in 2001. Professor Kolb is the co-author of *Everyday Negotiation: Navigating the Hidden Agendas of Bargaining* and *Her Place at the Table: A Woman's Guide to Negotiating Five Challenges to Leadership Success*. Her other books include *The Mediators, Hidden Conflict in Organizations: Uncovering Behind-the-Scenes Disputes, Making Talk Work*, and *Negotiation Eclectics*.

Laurie Metcalf is Assistant Professor at the University of Arkansas at Little Rock and a Ph.D. candidate at Texas A&M University. Her research focuses on conflict in a variety of contexts, including interpersonal deception in conflict, alternative views of mediation, and a framing approach to collegiate living-wage movements.

Andreas Mojzisch is Assistant Professor in the Economic and Social Psychology Unit at Georg-August-University Goettingen. He received his Ph.D. at Ludwig-Maximilians-University Munich. His main research interest is group decision making. He has focused on biased information pooling and biased information evaluation during group discussion, the effect of prediscussion dissent on confirmatory information search after group discussion, and the effect of social validation on the greater decisional impact of shared compared with unshared information. He has published in *The Academy of Management Review, Journal* *of Personality and Social Psychology, European Journal of Social Psychology,* and several other journals.

Mara Olekalns is Professor of Management (Negotiation) at the Melbourne Business School, University of Melbourne. Her research focuses on modeling the relationships between communication sequences and outcomes in negotiation. Professor Olekalns' more recent research also examines trust, deception, and turning points in negotiation. Her research has published in *Academy of Management Journal, Journal of Applied Psychology, Human Communication Research, Journal of Experimental Social Psychology,* and *Personality and Social Psychology Bulletin.* She is on the editorial boards of *Group Decision and Negotiation, Journal of Organizational Behavior,* and *Negotiation and Conflict Management Research.*

Julie B. Olson-Buchanan is Professor of Management and Chair of the Department of Management, Craig School of Business, California State University, Fresno. She earned her Ph.D. from the University of Illinois where she was a National Science Foundation fellow. Her research interests include conflict in organizations, technology-based selection, and virtual teams. Professor Olson-Buchanan's work has appeared in such journals as *Journal of Applied Psychology, Academy of Management Journal, Personnel Psychology,* and *Journal of Vocational Behavior.* She is co-editor of the book *Innovations in Computerized Assessment* and has authored several SIOP Frontiers chapters. She currently holds a Craig Fellowship and was Program Chair for the Society for Industrial and Organizational Psychology Conference (2006).

Dean G. Pruitt is Distinguished Scholar in Residence at the Institute for Conflict Analysis and Resolution at George Mason University and SUNY Distinguished Professor Emeritus in the Department of Psychology at the University at Buffalo: State University of New York. He has received the Lifetime Achievement Award from the International Association for Conflict Management and the Harold D. Lasswell Award for Distinguished Scientific Contribution to Political Psychology from the International Society of Political Psychology. He is author or co-author of *Social Conflict: Escalation, Stalemate, and Settlement; Negotiation in Social Conflict;* and *Negotiation Behavior.*

Linda L. Putnam is the George T. and Gladys H. Abell Professor in the Department of Communication at Texas A&M University. Her research focuses on negotiation and organizational conflict, discourse and negotiation, and language analysis in organizations. She is the co-editor of six books, including *The Sage Handbook of Organizational Discourse, The New Handbook of Organizational Communication,* and *Communication and Negotiation.* She has published over 100 journal articles and book chapters on organization communication, conflict management, discourse and organizations, and negotiation. She is a past president of the International Communication Association and the International Association for Conflict Management, and a past board member of the Academy of Management.

Jana L. Raver is Assistant Professor and E. Marie Shantz Research Fellow in Organizational Behaviour at Queen's School of Business. She completed her Ph.D. at the University of Maryland. Her work has been published in *Academy of Management Journal, The Academy of Management Review, Journal of Applied Psychology,* and several other journals and book chapters. Honors for her research include best paper and best publication awards from the Academy of Management and the International Association of Conflict Management. Her research focuses on interpersonal relations and group processes, with an emphasis upon examining helpful (i.e., citizenship behaviors) versus counterproductive (e.g., aggression, harassment, relationship conflicts) actions. Professor Raver's work also includes investigations of work group diversity, cross-cultural variation, and multilevel theory. She is currently on the editorial board of *Negotiation and Conflict Management Research.*

Stefan Schulz-Hardt is Professor of Industrial, Economic, and Social Psychology at Georg-August-University Goettingen. He has taught at the Universities of Kiel and Munich and was Professor of Social and Financial Psychology at Dresden University of Technology. His main research interests are group decision making and group performance, social information processing, price perception, and financial loss escalations. He has published in *The Academy of Management Review, Journal of Applied Psychology, Journal of Personality and Social Psychology, Organizational Behavior and Human Decision Processes,* and several other journals, and he has written numerous book chapters.

Kristin Smith-Crowe is Assistant Professor of Organizational Behavior in the David Eccles School of Business of the University of Utah. Her research focuses on ethics in organizations (especially antecedents of and reactions to wrongdoing) as well as worker safety training and research methods. She has published in *American Journal of Public Health, Journal of Applied Psychology,* and *Personnel Psychology.*

Paul E. Spector is a distinguished university professor of industrial/organizational (I/O) psychology and the I/O doctoral program director at the University of South Florida. His more than 100 articles have appeared in many journals, including *Academy of Management Journal, Journal of Applied Psychology, Journal of Management, Journal of Organizational Behavior, Journal of Occupational and Organizational Psychology, Journal of Vocational Behavior, Organizational Behavior and Human Decision Processes, Personnel Psychology,* and *Psychological Bulletin*. At present Professor Spector is the Point/Counterpoint editor for *Journal of Organizational Behavior* and is on the editorial boards of *Journal of Occupational and Organizational Psychology*, *Organizational Research Methods*, and *Personnel Psychology*. In 1991 the Institute for Scientific Information listed him as one of the 50 highest impact contemporary researchers (out of over 102,000) in psychology worldwide.

Jordan Stein is a doctoral student in the Department of Management and Organizations at the University of Arizona at Tucson. Her research focuses on organizational justice and conflict. She has published in the *Journal of Management*.

Deborah J. Terry is Professor of Social Psychology and Executive Dean of the Faculty of Social and Behavioural Sciences at the University of Queensland. Her primary research interests are attitudes, social influence, persuasion, group processes, and intergroup relations. She also has applied research interests in organizational and health psychology. She has published widely in these areas, is co-editor of *Social Identity Processes in Organizational Contexts* (2001) and *Attitudes, Behavior, and Social Context: The Role of Group Norms and Group Membership* (1999), and holds editorial positions with the *British Journal of Psychology* and the *European Journal of Social Psychology*.

Sherry Thatcher is Assistant Professor in the Management Information Systems Department at the Eller College of Management, University of Arizona. Her research focuses on the implications of diversity, faultlines, and identity on conflict, communication, and performance. She has published in *The Academy of Management Review, Group Decision and Negotiation*, and *International Journal of Conflict Management*.

Dean Tjosvold is the Henry Y. W. Fong Chair Professor, Management Department, Lingnan University, Hong Kong. He has also taught at Pennsylvania State University and Simon Fraser University, and has held several visiting professorships. He is a past president of the International Association of Conflict Management and was elected to the Academy of Management Board of Governors in 2004. He has published over 200 articles, 20 books, 30 book chapters, and 100 conference papers on managing conflict, cooperation and competition, decision making, power, and other management issues. He has served on several editorial boards, including *The Academy of Management Review, Journal of Organizational Behavior, Journal of Occupational and Organizational Psychology*, and *Journal of Management*, and is now Asian editor for the *Journal of World Business*. With colleagues, he has written books on teamwork, leadership, and conflict management in China published in Chinese. He is a partner in his family's health care business, which has 900 employees, and is based in Minnesota.

Elizabeth E. Umphress is an assistant professor in the Mays Business School at Texas A&M University. Her research focuses on three related themes: organizational justice, ethical behavior, and diversity. Her work has appeared in journals such as *Academy of Management Journal, Journal of Applied Psychology, Organization Science,* and *Organizational Behavior and Human Decision Processes.* Professor Umphress also serves on the editorial board of *The Academy of Management Review.*

Frank Vogelgesang is Assistant Professor in the Economic and Social Psychology Unit at Georg-August-University Goettingen. He received his Ph.D. from Dresden University of Technology. His research interests center on communication and decision making in groups and on the formation of false beliefs as a consequence of social hypothesis testing (especially in legal contexts). As a qualified trainer, Dr. Vogelgesang transports research findings in the fields of communication, decision making, conflict management and resolution, and team work from lab to life. He is author/co-author of several journal articles and chapters in edited books.

Laurie R. Weingart is Professor of Organizational Behavior and Director of the Center for Interdisciplinary Research on Teams at the David A. Tepper School of Business, Carnegie Mellon University, Pittsburgh, Pennsylvania. Her research focuses on conflict management in work groups and the tactical behavior and cognitive processes of negotiators in both dyads and groups. Her research has been published in *Academy of Management Journal, The Academy of Management Review, Journal of Applied Psychology, Journal of Personality and Social Psychology, Journal of Experimental Social Psychology, Cognitive Science, International Journal of Conflict Management,* and *Research in Organizational Behavior,* among others. She currently serves on the editorial boards of *Journal of Personality and Social Psychology, The Academy of Management Review, Organizational Behavior and Human Decision Processes,* and *Group Dynamics.*

I

Introduction:
Setting the Stage

1

Conflict in the Workplace: Sources, Functions, and Dynamics Across Multiple Levels of Analysis

CARSTEN K. W. DE DREU
University of Amsterdam

MICHELE J. GELFAND
University of Maryland

Conflict is a social phenomenon that occurs across species, time periods, and cultures. Conflict has been frequently studied among bees, ants, and other insect communities (Trivers & Hare, 1976), among crayfish (Huber, Panksepp, Yue, Delago, & Moore, 2001), and among chimpanzees (de Waal, 1989), to name but a few. Evidence of conflict among humans dates to the appearance of humankind itself (Keeley, 1996). Perhaps not surprisingly, given its complexity, the study of conflict is a multidisciplinary and multilevel scholarly enterprise. Conflict scholars can be found in most scientific disciplines, including physics, mathematics, biology, anthropology, psychology, sociology, economics, political science, organizational behavior, and communication studies. Although theories and methods across these disciplines are quite varied (De Dreu & Carnevale, 2005), they all focus on the same fundamental question; namely, "How do individuals and groups manage their interdependence with one another?" Whether examining a brain scan, a Petri dish, a fish tank, a beehive, small groups in the laboratory, or organizational decision-making teams, understanding the antecedents, processes, and outcomes of conflict is of critical theoretical and practical importance in many sciences; indeed, few areas of scholarly inquiry have attracted as much attention across disciplines as the study of conflict.

In the specific area of organizational behavior and industrial/organizational psychology, the study of conflict has a long history. In their seminal work on the social psychology of organizations, Katz and Kahn (1978) observed that "every aspect of organizational life that creates order and coordination of effort must overcome tendencies to action, and in that fact lies the potentiality for conflict" (p. 617). Every "school of organizational thought"—from Weber's bureaucracy and scientific management, to human relations and cooperative systems, to open systems theory—has as its central basis the question of how employees manage their mutual interdependencies and ensuing conflicts (see Jaffee, chapter 2, this volume, for a review). Indeed, conflict, work, and organizations are so strongly intertwined that some have concluded that organizations without conflict do not exist, and that conflict cannot exist without people being interdependent for their task achievements (e.g., Pfeffer, 1997; Pondy, 1967).

This close connection between conflict and collaborative work has become even stronger due to a variety of changes in the world of work and organizations. First, conflicts are more likely to emerge because of the increasing pressures to change, adapt, and innovate with concomitant increases in workload, job insecurity, role conflict, misunderstandings, and related grievances (e.g., Anderson, De Dreu, & Nijstad, 2004; Janssen, 2003; Peterson & Behfar, 2003). Second, due to globalization of economies and immigration at an increasingly larger scale, organizations face an exceedingly diverse workforce. Diversity may manifest itself in many different forms, some being more readily visible than others, and some being tied to task-relevant issues more than others. One way or the other, however, diversity is associated with conflict (Jehn, Bezrukova, & Thatcher, chapter 6, this volume). Third, the growing use of Internet and noncollocated interactions in which employees no longer work and communicate face-to-face puts increasing demands on communication processes and easily evokes misunderstanding and irritation (Friedman & Currall, 2003; see also Olekalns, Putnam, Weingart, & Metcalf, chapter 3, this volume). Fourth, and finally, the tendency to organize work in (semiautonomous) teams creates greater interdependency among employees, undermines the traditional power relations and hierarchical command–control typical of traditional organizations, and requires higher levels of self-management and self-regulation, including negotiation and conflict management skills (Pfeffer, 1997).

CONFLICT AND CONFLICT MANAGEMENT IN ORGANIZATIONS: THE PURPOSE OF THIS BOOK

Despite the critical importance of the study of conflict in organizations, surprisingly few comprehensive volumes focus exclusively on this phenomenon in organizational behavior and industrial and organizational psychology. In part this is because in (organizational) psychology, conflict is often treated in isolation rather than in connection with other social or organizational phenomena. For example, the *Annual Review of Psychology* chapters on I/O Psychology by Rousseau (1997), Wilpert (1995), O'Reilly (1991), Ilgen and Klein (1988), and Staw (1984) do not treat conflict management and dispute resolution at all, and only the more topical reviews touch on workplace conflict when they review literatures on mood (Brief & Weiss, 2002) or culture (Gelfand, Erez, & Aycan, in press). At the same time, reviews on negotiation and mediation by Carnevale and Pruitt (1992); Greenhalgh (1987); Lewicki, Weiss, and Lewin (1992); Levine and Thompson (1996); Pruitt (1998); Bazerman, Curhan, Moore, and Valley (2000); and De Dreu, Beersma, Steinel, and Van Kleef (2007) discuss conflict management and negotiation in isolation from the broader context of organizational structure, work-related attitudes, and performance.

In this volume, we aim to achieve two interrelated goals. First, we attempt to bring together and integrate classic and contemporary insight in conflict origins, conflict processes, and conflict consequences. Authors were charged with providing critical reviews of how their topics have evolved over time, and with new and promising directions for conflict research in organizations. Recognizing that conflict has multiple functions, some of which are negative and some of which are primarily positive (cf. Coser, 1956; De Dreu & Van de Vliert, 1997; Jehn, 1995), authors were also charged with highlighting both positive and negative consequences of conflict in their chapters and the multiple context factors that shape its occurrence and outcomes. Second, in designing this book, we started out with the fundamental premise that conflict in organizations is a multilevel phenomenon, and that to truly grasp the roots, dynamics, and consequences of conflict at work, we need to consider multiple levels within organizations, as well as their cross-level influences. Accordingly, we organized the book in terms of antecedents and consequences at the individual, group, and organizational levels.

Whereas each of the chapters in this volume focuses on distinct territory located at a specific level of analysis, in this chapter we provide a "bird's-eye" view of conflict across levels. We organized our chapter around two fundamental questions. First, we ask about the isomorphism of conflict: "What commonalities and differences do we find across levels of analysis, both in terms of antecedent root causes, dynamics, and consequences and functions?" Subsequently, we ask how much cross-level research is being done on conflict in organizations, and where new and exciting research questions can be identified. Accordingly, we integrate many aspects discussed in greater depth in the various chapters in this volume, connected them where possible, and generated new areas for future research.

In what follows, we first define the very phenomenon about which this volume is concerned—conflict—and note important distinctions that are relevant throughout the book. We then differentiate four levels of analysis that are relevant for understanding conflict in organizations: (a) individual, (b) group, (c) organization, and (d) national culture. After differentiating these levels, we begin to synthesize what is common and different across levels in terms of conflict antecedents, processes, and outcomes. We then turn to research that examines interactions across levels and discuss areas for future research.

DEFINING CONFLICT

Because conflict at work can take many forms, one may shy away from providing an encompassing and comprehensive definition of *conflict*. Throughout this book, chapter authors have implicitly or explicitly defined *conflict* as a process that begins when an individual or group perceives differences and opposition between itself and another individual or group about interests and resources, beliefs, values, or practices that matter to them (e.g., De Dreu, Harinck, & Van Vianen, 1999; Thomas, 1992; Van de Vliert, 1997; Wall & Callister, 1995). This process view dates back to the original work by Pondy (1967), who differentiated between latent and manifest conflict. Latent conflict includes perceived and felt conflict, and refers to within-person or within-group states. Manifest conflict, in contrast, includes constructive negotiations as well as outbursts of violence, and thus refers to between-person or between-group dynamics.

The transfers from within-party latent conflict to between-party manifest conflict is mediated by communication processes, such as verbal and nonverbal, and technology mediated or not (see Olekalns et al., chapter 3, this volume). In other words, the process view of conflict is multilevel in its orientation and well suited to examine cross-level influences and interaction, an issue we return to below. Furthermore, we can apply the process view to all kinds of parties, including (a) entire organizations, (b) formal or informal groups within organizations, or (c) individual employees. Finally, the process view leaves open how parties manage their conflicts, or how formal or informal parties intervene, as well as what outcomes the conflict has. This will become important when we discuss conflict processes and the functions conflict at work may have. Notably, conflict is distinct from other "dark-side" constructs that exist in the literature, including aggression, incivility, deviance, and bullying. Although these constructs share the fact that parties are interdependent and have opposing interests, values, or beliefs, conflict need not involve intent to harm another party and need not cause negative outcomes (see Raver & Barling, chapter 7, this volume). As will be evident throughout this book, conflict can have positive outcomes across multiple levels of analyses in organizations.

COMMONALITIES AND DIFFERENCES ACROSS LEVELS OF ANALYSIS

Organizations can be decomposed into different levels of analysis—the individual, the group level, the organizational level, and the local and national culture in which organizations are embedded. At the *individual level of analysis*, conflict antecedents and triggering events may relate to predisposition (e.g., dogmatism, agreeableness, power motivation) or job characteristics (e.g., role ambiguity, job autonomy), conflict processes involve individual motivation, cognition, and affective states as well as individual differences in tendencies to manage conflict in certain ways, and conflict consequences include individual well-being and health, absenteeism, and turnover (Spector & Bruk-Lee, chapter 9, this volume), as well as learning potential, cognitive flexibility, and creativity (e.g., Schulz-Hardt, Mojzisch, & Vogelgesang, chapter 5, this volume).

At the *group level of analysis* conflict may be rooted in power differences and leadership style (De Dreu & Van Kleef, 2004) or in heterogeneity in group composition (Jehn et al., chapter 6, this volume). Conflict processes relate to interaction patterns in managing conflict, negotiation, and small group communication (Olekalns et al., chapter 3, this volume), and conflict consequences involve aggression and escalation (Raver & Barling, chapter 7, this volume; Pruitt, chapter 8, this volume) as well as team innovation, team performance, and team member satisfaction and commitment (Beersma, Conlon, & Hollenbeck, chapter 4, this volume; Schulz-Hardt et al., chapter 5, this volume).

At the *organizational level of analysis*, conflict occurs as a result of mergers and acquisitions, and systems of conflict management can be analyzed. In this section of the book, authors provide critical insight into the history and current directions of union–management conflict (Friedman, Hunter, & Chen, chapter 12), organizational dispute–resolution systems (Olson-Buchanan & Boswell, chapter 11), the role of third parties in managing conflict in organizations (Goldman, Cropanzano, Stein, & Benson, chapter 10), and conflict in mergers and acquisitions (Terry & Amiot, chapter 13).

Finally, organizations are open systems and are embedded in local community contexts (Brief et al., 2005), institutional contexts (e.g., industry), and more distal national cultural contexts (Gelfand & Brett, 2004). Only recently has research begun to systematically explore how these contexts affect conflict in organizations. In this chapter, we discuss cultural influences on the antecedents, functions, and outcomes of conflict. We review some of the key findings on culture and conflict across multiple levels, discuss what might be universal versus culture-specific in terms of conflict in organizations, and highlight new frontiers of research.

SOURCES OF WORKPLACE CONFLICT ACROSS LEVELS OF ANALYSIS

Adopting a perspective that includes multiple levels of analysis neither clarifies the origins of conflict at work nor reveals whether and in what form these origins exist at each level. To explore these questions we discuss three broad classes of origins or sources of workplace conflict that can be found across levels. Acknowledging that there are myriad factors that affect conflict at different levels, we provide some parsimony of antecedents by examining three leading theoretical perspectives that can be, but to date have not been, applied to understand conflict at the individual, group, and organization levels of analysis. We then conclude this section with a discussion of how national culture affects sources of workplace conflict, and whether the sources discussed at other levels may or may not be applicable across national cultures.

In the sections that follow, we distinguish three root causes of conflict that are present across levels: (a) scarce resources, (b) a search for maintaining and promoting a positive view of the self, and (c) a desire to hold consensually shared and socially validated opinions and beliefs. Consecutively, we discuss the mixed-motive nature of social interdependencies in organizations that give rise to *resource conflicts* (sometimes referred to as conflicts of interest, or conflicts over outcomes) at different levels; the need to maintain and develop a positive view of oneself and the group to which one belongs, which gives rise to *ideological and value conflicts* (sometimes referred to as relationship, or affective conflict) at different levels; and the desire to hold a socially validated and consensually shared understanding of the world and the tasks that need to be done, which may give rise to *socio-cognitive conflict of understanding* (sometimes referred to as cognitive, or task-related conflict) at different levels (for similar taxonomies, see e.g., Coombs, 1987; De Dreu et al., 1999; Rapoport, 1960; Thibaut & Kelley, 1959; and Thomas, 1992).

Source #1: Scarce Resources and Conflicts of Interest

Resources within organizations are scarce and finite, and the access to—as well as the availability and distribution of—scarce resources constitutes one major cause of conflict at all levels of analysis. Individuals within a team negotiate time off-task, employees demand a greater share of the team bonus because they perceive their inputs exceed those of some colleagues, organizations negotiate access to new markets, and so on.

To appreciate and understand resource conflicts, it is useful to use as a starting point Interdependence Theory (Kelley & Thibaut, 1978; Rusbult &

Van Lange, 2003). The theory builds on rational choice theories designed by economists and mathematicians in the late 1940s and early 1950s and includes important insights from Realistic Conflict Theory (Sherif & Sherif, 1953), the theory of Cooperation and Competition (Deutsch, 1949, 1973; Stanne, Johnson, & Johnson, 1999; Tjosvold, 1998), and work on negotiation and bargaining (Pruitt, 1981).

In essence, Interdependence Theory assumes that participants within any social system—a dyad, a group, or an entire organization—depend on one another to obtain positive outcomes, and to avoid negative outcomes. The way participants' interests relate to one another, or are perceived to be related, then has important implications for their subsequent behavioral choices, the emerging interaction patterns, and the extent to which participants reach their desired end-state. Within the theory, the options and outcomes of interaction can be represented using a tool from classic game theory, the outcome matrix. An outcome matrix describes interdependence patterns involving two participants (individuals or groups A and B), each of whom can enact one of two behaviors, yielding four combinations representing the consequences of the participants' choices in terms of outcomes for A and B (Kelley & Thibaut, 1978).

Figure 1.1 provides an example of an outcome matrix. The matrix in Fig. 1.1 is a social dilemma (also called the Prisoner's Dilemma). It reflects the situation in which participants are better off individually by choosing D (the noncooperative choice), whereas both are better off by choosing C (the cooperative choice) than when they both choose D. From a selfish point of view, each player is motivated to choose D because no matter what the other player chooses, personal outcomes are maximized. This is sometimes referred to as individual rationality. From a collective point of view, however, each player is motivated to choose C because no matter what the other player chooses, collective outcomes are maximized. This is sometimes referred to as collective rationality. Interestingly, individual rationality is collectively irrational, and collective rationality is individually irrational. The dilemma facing participants in this situation thus is to be individually or collectively rational (Colman, 2003).

Mixtures of Motives as the Foundation of Resource Conflicts. The social dilemma depicted in Fig. 1.1 reflects that in most organizations, each individual employee is better off defecting (e.g., showing up late, not performing, stealing company property, laying low) when colleagues cooperate (e.g., work hard, help out, voice opinions), yet all employees are worse off when all defect and nothing gets produced at all (Katz & Kahn, 1978; Weber, Kopelman, & Messick, 2004). We note that social dilemmas can take different forms (e.g., public good vs. resource dilemmas), and that these different forms can have substantial impact on behavioral choices and the emergence of resource-based conflict of interest. Discussing this in greater depth, however, is beyond the scope of this chapter.

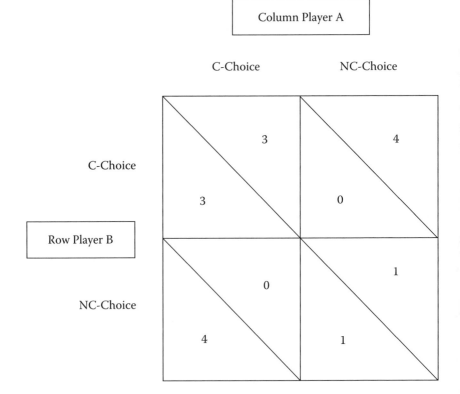

FIGURE 1.1. Schematic representation of a two-player social dilemma.

When we adopt social dilemmas as representative of interdependencies within organizations, we limit ourselves to two levels of analysis: (a) the individual and group level, when we see participants as individuals choosing between individual and group interests, and (b) the group and the organization level, when we see participants as groups choosing between group and organization interests (e.g., Wit & Kerr, 2002). This obvious shortcoming can be tackled in two ways. First, we may conceive of organizations, and the interdependence structures therein, as "nested social dilemmas" (e.g., Polzer, Stewart, & Simmons, 1999; Wit & Kerr, 2002). Second, we may identify the way interdependencies within as well as between groups are structured and drive behavior (Bornstein, 2003). We discuss each possibility in more detail.

Nested Social Dilemmas. In nested social dilemmas, three levels are identified: the (a) individual, (b) group, and (c) organization levels. An example, based on Wit and Kerr (2002), is the situation in which an R&D

department has succeeded in winning board approval to launch new projects and to recruit the necessary personnel. The R&D department has two equally sized subunits, one specializing in antidepressants and the other in pain relievers. Each senior researcher within the subunits now has to decide how to spend his or her own resources—in time, in effort, by calling in favors, and so forth. Focusing on a project proposal that nicely fits within their private interests—let us call it Proposal P(ersonal)—would offer each senior researcher the greatest possibility of fruitful collaboration with new colleagues and would result in the greatest personal benefit. Contributing resources to increase the chances of alternative project proposals from colleagues (Proposal C[olleague]) within one's subunit would be of less benefit personally, but would bring recognition to one's own subunit and could translate into a greater share of departmental resources for one's subunit as well as some potential for fruitful collaboration with newly recruited colleagues. Finally, trying to get Proposal O(rganization) awarded would be of little direct benefit either to oneself or to one's subunit, but would clearly yield the greatest benefit of any of the three proposals for the entire R&D department as a whole—it might increase the chances of the department acquiring even more and larger grants that would improve the department's prestige and financial situation, from which all employees, including the one submitting Proposal P, benefit.

The example shows that resource-based conflicts of interest emerge not only between individuals within the same unit, but also between individuals belonging to different subunits located within the same organization. Individuals as well as groups thus have overarching, common interests, and both individuals and groups can face the dilemma of being individually (or group) rational versus being collectively rational. Interestingly, as this example clarifies, being rational vis-à-vis the interests of one's subgroup is irrational vis-à-vis one's personal as well as one's overarching organization's interests. Likewise, pursuing personal benefits is at odds with group as well as with organization goals, and serving organizational goals hurts both one's group and one's personal interests. As Wit and Kerr (2002) explained, "The question is, 'How vigorously would you pursue your private interest, your own subgroup interest, or the collective interest?' In other words, would your primary concern be for 'me,' for 'just us,' or for 'us all'?" (p. 616).

Taken together, because conflicts of interests exist between individuals, their group, and the overarching organization, conflict over the access to and distribution of resources is likely to emerge. Conflicts are built into any organizational structure and will become manifest for one of two reasons. First, by pursuing their immediate and short-term self-interests, individuals or groups deliberately or inadvertently hurt collective interests including those of interdependent others. Such selfish choices are unlikely to be condoned—"a substantial proportion of the population is . . . willing to punish non-cooperators (or individuals who do not make fair offers) at a cost to themselves" (Ostrom, 1998,

p. 12)—and latent conflict of interest is turned into manifest conflict over resources. Our discussion of the nested social dilemma demonstrates that such conflicts are *inevitable* because no matter what participants do, they always hurt another participant's interests, being located at either the individual, the group, or the organization level.

Second, within nested social dilemmas conflicts over resources emerge because of premature suspicion, misunderstanding, incomplete information, or lack of insight. That is, conflict over resources may be the result of (own and others') misinterpretation of (other's and own) intentions and actions. For example, work on "noise" in social dilemmas shows that sometimes people's failure to cooperate is erroneously attributed to malevolent intent instead of to endogenous factors—as is the case when you forget to respond to an important and very urgent e-mail from your supervisor, not because you intentionally ignored the request, but because it arrived in your spam box, where you overlooked it (Van Lange, Ouwerkerk, & Tazelaar, 2002). This second reason why conflicts of interest turn into manifest conflict over resources is rooted in imperfect trust among organizational participants; a grain of doubt suffices to bring about conflict over resources.

Team Games. A second contribution to a multilevel theory of interdependencies and resource conflicts in organizations derives from an analysis of the ways interdependencies within as well as between groups are structured and drive behavior (Bornstein, 2003). Many models, theories, and descriptions—including the nested social dilemma analysis discussed above—treat organizations, firms, and social groups as unitary actors. These actors, however, are obviously not unitary. Decisions are made—or emerge—within a complex internal structure of governance (election, delegation, representation, leadership, networks). Moving to the (inter)group level increases the number of interdependencies among participants, which manifests itself in the need to use decision rules (e.g., majority rule vs. unanimity rule; see Beersma & De Dreu, 2002), in increased cognitive load (e.g., Kramer, 1991), and in the possibility of forming coalitions (Murnighan, 1978).

In intergroup relations, it is typically neither feasible nor desirable for all those concerned to be present at the bargaining table, and usually representatives conduct the negotiations (Walton & McKersie, 1965). Representatives are often accountable to their constituents, either for the outcomes they achieve or for the process of making decisions (Tetlock, 1992). Accountable representatives are motivated to impress constituents (Wall, 1991), and this often translates into a competitive stance toward their counterparts (e.g., Carnevale, Pruitt, & Seilheimer, 1981; O'Connor, 1997; but see Gelfand & Realo, 1999; Peterson & Thompson, 1997). In other words, representatives face a double social dilemma. First, their choices are cast within the intergroup context where benefiting their ingroup hurts the interests of the outgroup, and vice versa. At the same time, their choices are cast within the in-group context, where benefiting oneself hurts the interests of other individuals within the team, and vice versa.

Bornstein (2003) argued that when parties are groups rather than individuals, individuals experience mixed-motive interdependence within their in-group, as well as with the out-group. Consider a group of soldiers waiting to surprise attack their enemy. On both sides, each group is best off when all its group members fight hard and heroicly, thus increasing the probability of total victory and fending off the chances of total defeat. Within each group, however, individual members are better off playing hide-and-seek while their in-group members take the lead and fight hard and heroicly; the individual benefits from his or her group members' heroic actions yet minimizes the personal risk of injury. Obviously, when all group members think and act this way, they become collectively vulnerable, and each individual is worse off by not fighting than by fighting collectively.

The team-game analysis reveals that hostility toward the out-group is often perceived as cooperative, loyal behavior by members of one's in-group, and vice versa, cooperative and conciliatory behavior toward an outgroup may be perceived, by one's fellow ingroup members, as disloyal behavior that jeopardizes the in-group's fate. Consequently, groups tend to less cooperative with one another than individuals are in an interpersonal situation (Mikolic, Parker, & Pruitt, 1997; Robert & Carnevale, 1997; Wildschut, Pinter, Vevea, Insko, & Schopler, 2003). This reveals the double-edged-sword character of mixed-motive interdependencies within and between groups. On the one hand, intergroup conflicts tend to escalate more easily into cycles of exceedingly hostile exchanges, but on the other hand, within groups, cooperation is stimulated and team members are more motivated to work hard (Bornstein & Erev, 1997).

Summary and Synthesis. Resource conflicts emerge when and because individual, group, and organizational interests are misaligned, so that choices that benefit interests at one level hurt the interests at another level. This follows from a basic social dilemma analysis, but also from a more sophisticated analysis of organizations as nested social dilemmas, and of mixed-motive interdependencies in team games. By applying and extending interdependency theory, we can thus understand where resource conflicts come from and predict that they will be more complex, and more likely to escalate, as one moves up from the individual, to the group, to the organization level of analysis. The chapters in this volume illustrate this insight. For example, resource conflicts are the source of frustration and stress at the individual level (Spector & Bruk-Lee, chapter 9, this volume), the source of competition and escalation at the dyad and group levels (Pruitt, chapter 8, this volume), and the driving force behind union–management relations over the last century (Friedman et al., chapter 12, this volume). Moving up a level, research has shown that competition over resources in the community context can also affect negative attitudes within organizational contexts as well (Brief et al., 2005). In all, resource conflicts or conflicts of interest are powerful sources of conflict that traverse multiple levels of analysis.

Source #2: The Need for Positive (Social) Identity: Value and Relationship Conflicts

Apart from the fundamental need among most species to acquire and protect resources, higher-order animals, including chimpanzees and humans, also have a basic need to develop, maintain, and protect a positive view of the self. Work in social psychology has pointed out that the self-concept can be decomposed into individual and group level components, and that both individual and group-based aspects of the self-concept drive conflict at the individual and (inter)group level, respectively. In this section, we discuss this work in some detail. We begin with the individual level of analysis and discuss self-esteem and the stability of the self-concept. We then move on to discuss social identity theory (SIT) and the role of the self-concept in intergroup relations.

The types of conflicts that emerge because of participants' need to develop and maintain a positive identity often are ideological and value-laden. Ideologically based disputes, such as those involving societal issues (e.g., environment, gender equity, civil rights, abortion, and poverty), are conflicts in which one or more parties represent—or believe they represent—deeper ideological values. Value-related conflicts, such as those involving issues concerning morality or right and wrong, are conflicts in which one or more parties defend or promote their personal or group identity in terms of moral issues, social standing and reputation, likeability, and so on. Jehn (1994) has referred to these as "affective conflicts"; others refer to these ideological and value-related conflicts as "relationship conflicts" (e.g., De Dreu & Weingart, 2003a).

Ideological and value-related conflicts can be differentiated from resource conflicts in a number of ways. Perhaps the most important one is that parties may believe that mutually beneficial outcomes will require tradeoffs and compromises that strike at the core of their moral identity (Druckman & Zechmeister, 1973; Harinck & De Dreu, 2004; Harinck, De Dreu, & Van Vianen, 2000). For example, a prochoice/prolife value conflict cannot be settled by a 50–50 compromise that a random 50% of the requests for euthanasia and abortion are granted, or by an integrative solution in which the right to euthanasia is traded for the right to abortion. No party in a value conflict would perceive these types of solutions—which are typical in resource conflicts—as acceptable or defendable. Similarly, a "bad chemistry" conflict within a specific department of an organization cannot be solved by sprinkling nice odors or by instructing parties to behave and become friends. In other words, ideological and value-related conflicts require different types of management strategies and solutions.

But where do these ideological, value-related, and relationship types of conflicts come from? In the remainder of this section, we argue that at the individual, group, and organizational levels people strive for positive identity and self-view, and that in the process of developing, maintaining, and restoring a positive self-view, they deliberately or inadvertently hurt the positive self-view of proximal others—putting people together in an organization, group, or interpersonal interaction means exposure to (latent or manifest) ego-threat, and herein lies the second source of workplace conflict. We first consider this idea at the individual level of analysis, and discuss work on the self, on self-esteem, and on self-concept clarity. We then consider this idea at the group level of analysis and discuss work on social identity and self-categorization theory. We also discuss ideological and value conflicts at the organizational level, especially as they relate to organizational mergers and acquisitions.

Self-Esteem, Ego-Threat, and the Emergence of Value-Related Conflicts.   The self can be defined as the totality of interrelated yet distinct psychological phenomena that either underlie, causally interact with, or depend upon reflexive consciousness (Sedikides & Strube, 1997). Because humans generally strive for a positive self-view, they seek to affirm the self through promotion, enhancement, and protection of the self-view (Sedikides & Strube, 1997; Steele, 1988). People are motivated to convince themselves and relevant others that they are worthwhile, attractive, competent, and moral individuals, and to achieve this, a variety of cognitive and behavioral tactics and strategies are employed (Greenwald, 1980; Taylor & Brown, 1988; Tesser, Martin, & Cornell, 1996). For example, people are unrealistically optimistic that good things will happen to them (Weinstein, 1980); they are prone to an illusion of control (Langer, 1975); they overestimate their standing on a number of valued attributes such as leadership ability, logical reasoning, or athletic prowess (Kruger & Dunning, 1999); and they value objects they own more than identical objects they do not own (Beggan, 1992; Kahneman, Knetsch, & Thaler, 1990).

    The habitual ability or inability to satisfy the self-enhancement motive is reflected in someone's self-esteem—an attitude toward oneself that associates with numerous self-beliefs pertaining to the self as a whole or to its particular attributes (Sedikides & Strube, 1997; see also Banaji & Prentice, 1994; Markus & Wurf, 1987). When people are successful at self-enhancing, their self-esteem is positive and high; when they are unsuccessful, their self-esteem is negative and low. Although self-esteem is relatively stable and can be seen as a positive trait, positive feedback and flattery, or negative feedback and criticism, can lead to temporary positive or negative departures, respectively (Heatherton & Ambady, 1993). Especially when negative feedback or criticism is received and a drop in positive affect and self-esteem is experienced (Jussim, Yen, & Aiello, 1995), will people become motivated to self-enhance and to restore a positive self-view (Baumeister, Smart, & Boden, 1996; W. K. Campbell & Sedikides, 1999; De Dreu & Van Knippenberg, 2005). For example, self-threat produces less constructive and more hostile interaction than self-affirmation (Cohen & Sherman, 2002).

Recent work has pointed out that individual differences in the stability and clarity of the self-concept play a critical role in the extent to which ego-defensive tendencies are enacted. Put simply, the less stable and the more unclear the self-concept is, the less well the individual deals with hostility and negative feedback, and since hostility and negative feedback are part and parcel of social conflict, the more likely the conflict is to escalate (e.g., Bushman & Baumeister 1998; De Dreu & Van Knippenberg, 2005; Stucke & Sporer, 2002). For example, individuals with high explicit self-esteem but low implicit self-esteem tend to be more hostile and prone to prejudice compared with individuals in whom explicit and implicit self-esteem correspond (Jordan, Spencer, Zanna, Hoshino-Browne, & Correll, 2003). Kernis, Granneman, and Barclay (1989) found that persons with unstable, high self-esteem had the highest propensity for anger, as assessed by self-report, whereas those with stable, high self-esteem had the lowest (see also Bushman & Baumeister, 1998). Similar findings have been obtained in work on the individual's self-concept clarity—the extent to which the contents of an individual's self-concept are clearly and confidently defined, internally consistent, and temporally stable (J. D. Campbell, 1990). Ratings on the self-concept clarity scale negatively correlate with ratings on the Buss–Perry Aggression Questionnaire (Von Collani & Werner, 2005). Likewise, there is evidence that those with low rather than high self-concept clarity tend toward more aggressive responses following negative feedback (Stucke & Sporer, 2002) and toward greater hostility after being provoked by their conflict counterpart (De Dreu & Van Knippenberg, 2005).

Because individuals desire to develop, improve, and maintain a positive sense of themselves, in conflict situations, they tend to develop an inflated view of their own cooperativeness and their counterpart's hostility. This self-serving bias increases the likelihood of impasse in labor–management disputes (Babcock, Loewenstein, Issacharoff, & Camerer, 1995), increases negative perceptions and evaluations of counterparts and their conflict resolution behavior in intergroup conflicts (Mo'az, Ward, Katz, & Ross, 2002), and reduces the quality of settlements in interpersonal negotiations (De Dreu, Nauta, & Van de Vliert, 1995; Thompson & Loewenstein, 1992). Moreover, this general and quite fundamental human tendency leads individuals to react with hostility and competitiveness to any real or imagined threat to their positive self-view (Baumeister, 1998; see also Pruitt, chapter 8, this volume). Because conflict inherently involves a threat to the self-concept, increasing levels of hostility and competitiveness in response to one's counterpart are more likely than de-escalatory and constructive conflict behaviors (e.g., De Dreu & Van Knippenberg, 2005; Exline, Baumeister, Bushman, Campbell, & Finkel, 2004).

Social Identity Theory and Group-Level Value Conflict.   The central assumption underlying social identity theory (SIT; Tajfel, 1978) is that while people may think of themselves as independent individuals and define themselves on the basis of personal characteristics or preferences, there are many social settings in which people primarily think of themselves and others in terms of particular group memberships (e.g., in terms of their professional roles). Tajfel and Turner (1979) specified three processes that underlie such group-based thinking: (a) social categorization, (b) social comparison, and (c) social identification (Ellemers, Spears, & Doosje, 2002). Social categorization refers to the notion that people categorize individuals into groups, which enables them to focus on collective properties that are relevant to the situation at hand (e.g., marketing vs. production), while neglecting differences in age or clothing style that occur among individuals within the same group. Generally, a particular categorization is more likely to be used when group memberships are relatively invariable over time, whereas any category becomes less useful as an information-organizing principle to the extent that individuals are likely to change from one group to another (e.g., Ellemers, 1993).

Social comparison is the process by which a social categorization is invested with meaning. While people may have a relatively clear idea of the range of properties that apply to a particular group, proponents of the social identity approach maintain that social comparisons with other groups (e.g., salespersons versus customers in a store/salespersons versus production workers in the organization) determine which features or behavioral norms help to define the group in a particular situation. Generally, these features are those that distinguish the group from relevant comparison groups (e.g., Spears, Doosje, & Ellemers, 1997; Van Rijswijk & Ellemers, 2002). Thus, which different possible group memberships will become salient depends on the so-called comparative and normative fit of a particular categorization to the situation at hand (Haslam & Turner, 1992).

Social identification, finally, is the process by which information about social groups is related to the self. That is, it refers to the inclination of individuals to perceive themselves as representative of a particular group, which makes them perceive characteristic group features as self-descriptive and leads them to adopt distinctive group norms as guidelines for their own behavior. While most of us belong to multiple groups simultaneously, people are relatively willing to identify with groups that seem to contribute to a positive sense of self, such as high-status or high-power groups (Ellemers, 1993; Spears et al., 1997).

The cognitive tool of social categorization and the evaluative implications of social comparison processes can elicit a person's emotional involvement with a particular social group (Tajfel, 1978; see also Ellemers, Kortekaas, & Ouwerkerk, 1999): their sense of social identification. Because people seek to develop and maintain a positive identity, as well as engage in social comparison processes, one group's positive identity is cast in relative terms vis-à-vis other individuals or groups within or between organizations. Striving for a positive identity thus goes hand in hand with feeling better and superior to others, and it readily forms the basis for prejudice, competition, and hostility toward those seen as different from oneself or one's own group or community (Ellemers et al., 2002; Van Knippenberg, De Dreu, & Homan, 2004). This is clearly seen at the group level, where social category diversity leads to more value-related and relationship conflicts than social category homogeneity (Jehn, North-craft, & Neale, 1999). It is also seen at the intergroup level, where fault-line research shows that when individuals in a collective can be categorized into separated social entities, intergroup hostility and value-related conflicts emerge (e.g., Homan, Van Knippenberg, Van Kleef, & De Dreu, in press; Lau & Murnighan, 1998; also see Jehn et al., chapter 6, this volume).

Summary and Synthesis. Identity-related conflicts often take the form of value conflicts, or relationship conflicts (e.g., Jehn, 1995; see also Jehn et al., chapter 6, this volume). Importantly, conflicts rooted in threatened self-views appear at both the individual level and the intergroup level. Social identity theory provides clues as to whether identity conflicts emerge at the individual, within-team, or intergroup level; it depends on which level is made salient through incentive structures, categorization principles, and so on. Research by Wit and Kerr (2002) on nested social dilemmas showed, for example, that when the individual level was made salient—it was empha-sized that individuals differed from one another—participants more often made choices that served their personal interests and not those of their group or the overarching organization. However, when the group (organi-zation) level was made salient—it was emphasized that individuals within the group (organization) shared important features—participants sacrificed their personal interests to serve those of their group (organization). Thus, this work shows how social categorization processes can lead individuals to identity at the personal, group, or organizational level, and that identification subsequently drives strategic choices in resource-based conflicts of interest.[1]

It is important to note that social identity theory—and its core princi-ples—allows one to understand conflicts at any level. Whereas our discus-sion thus far emphasized the interindividual and the intergroup level, the theoretical predictions can be equally well applied to conflicts between entire organizations. A good example here is the work on mergers and acquisitions discussed by Terry and Amiot (chapter 13, this volume), who have applied social identity theory to understand conflicts between indi-viduals and groups who belonged to different organizations now being merged. Their work also highlights that many of the interpersonal and intergroup conflicts that arise out of identity issues are latent rather than manifest—they exemplify themselves in prejudice, feelings of superiority, implicit tendencies to serve one's ingroup at the expense of the outgroup, and so forth.

---

[1] It is worthwhile noting that in contrast to controlled laboratory experiments where resource-based conflicts of interest can be separated from identification-based value conflicts, such clean-cut distinctions cannot be made in the context of organizations where participants are outcome-interdependent by definition.

Source #3: Cognitive Consistency, Social Validation, and Sociocognitive Conflicts

The third theoretical perspective on conflict that can be applied to multiple levels of analysis is rooted in work around so-called sociocognitive conflict. It combines early thinking by developmental and child psychologists (e.g., Doise, Mugny, & Perret-Clermont, 1975; see also Levine, Resnick, & Higgins, 1993) with social psychological thinking about the individual's need for cognitive consistency and socially validated knowledge about oneself and the (immediate) surroundings (e.g., Festinger, 1954). Sociocognitive conflict theory is not about scarce resources and opposing interests, or about opposing values and the search for a positive identity. Instead, it addresses incompatible or diverging understanding and interpretation of facts and figures, and concerns the way people manage these conflicts of information, as well as the consequences of such conflicts for learning, understanding, and perceptual accuracy (e.g., Brehmer, 1976).

Sociocognitive conflict theory proceeds on the basis of three fundamental assumptions. First, it is assumed that people are motivated to hold accurate perceptions and insights about themselves, about others, and about the nonsocial world around them, including the (joint) tasks they are facing. Second, it is assumed that people are bounded in their rationality and lack both relevant information and information-processing capacities. As a result, different people develop distinct, diverging insights, beliefs, and understandings of otherwise identical objects of perception. Third, it is assumed that people seek cognitive consistency and social validation of their beliefs, insights, and understandings, and that divergence vis-à-vis others' perceptions, insights, and understandings creates tension that needs to be resolved.

Sociocognitive conflicts can be about intellective and judgmental problems. Intellective issues have correct solutions according to commonly accepted standards. Examples are "What is the shortest way from A to B?" and "Which procedure is most efficient?" Judgmental issues, however, have no correct solution and are a matter of taste. Examples are the question of how to get from A to B, and whether efficiency should be the prevailing criterion in selecting a procedure (cf. Baron, Kerr, & Miller, 1993; Kaplan & Miller, 1987). Intellective issues are associated with the influence to accept information about reality from another person (informational influence), while judgmental problems are associated with the influence to conform with the positive expectations of another person (normative influence; Deutsch & Gerard, 1955). Either way, divergent viewpoints regarding intellective or judgmental problems—sociocognitive conflict—create cognitive dissonance that needs to be resolved by (a) persuading the opponent, (b) changing one's own perspective or opinion, (c) integrating seemingly opposing viewpoints, or (d) dissolving the relationship.

Taken together, an important third source of conflict in organizations involves opinions, insights, and beliefs that are not consensually shared and that trigger opposition and debate (Brehmer, 1976; De Dreu et al., 1999;

see also Schulz-Hardt et al., chapter 5, this volume). These types of conflict are sometimes referred to as cognitive or information conflicts and have much in common with so-called task-related conflicts (De Dreu & Weingart, 2003; see also Jehn et al., chapter 6, this volume). Sociocognitive, task-related conflicts emerge out of preference or belief diversity in groups. Work on minority dissent and devil's advocacy has shown, for example, that when a minority faction opposes the majority view in the group, group members are more likely to doubt their fundamental assumptions, to search for new information, and to consider the task from multiple perspectives (Nemeth & Staw, 1989; Schulz-Hardt et al., chapter 5, this volume). Similarly, work by Jehn, Northcraft, and Neale (1999) showed that informational diversity in groups increased sociocognitive, task-related conflicts within those groups (also see Jehn et al., chapter 6, this volume).

There is quite some work on sociocognitive conflict at the individual and small-group level, primarily looking at its effects on learning and creative decision making. This work is reviewed in several chapters in this volume. Far less—if any—work has been done on the intergroup and organization levels of analysis. Although there seems to be no reason a priori to assume that sociocognitive conflicts are absent at the inter-group and organization level, research and theory development is clearly needed. For example, the ambiguous context of mergers between organizations would purportedly trigger opposition and debate among beliefs, opinions, and ideas, in addition to social identity conflicts discussed in Terry and Amiot's chapter (chapter 13, this volume). Also, as Friedman et al. (chapter 12, this volume) noted, a major component of labor–management relations involves the initial formation of preferences within groups (e.g., "attitudinal structuring"; Walton & McKersie, 1965) and fundamental transformations of the problem definition over time between groups (e.g., Putnam, 1997). Thus, sociocognitive conflict is relevant to the organizational level as well.

Cross-Cultural Variation in Sources of Conflicts

Last, we consider another level of analysis—national culture—and its influence on the antecedents of conflicts in organizations. Surprisingly little research has been done on sources of conflict and whether they are universal or culture-specific. Broadly speaking, universals are likely to occur when a phenomenon is influenced by a common biological process, a common social process, or a common ecological process (Pepitone & Triandis, 1987). We would speculate that the aforementioned sources of conflict (e.g., conflicts of interest, ideological and value conflicts, and sociocognitive conflicts) are likely universal; that is, they are likely to exist across many, if not all, national cultures. For example, we can surmise that in all national cultures, there is bound to be a scarcity of resources, producing conflicts of interest. Likewise, the need to defend one's values or identity is likely to be a fundamental need that traverses national cultures (thus producing affective or value-based conflicts). Finally, differences in viewpoints are perhaps inevitable regardless of the national culture conflict, suggesting that our third source of conflict—cognitive conflict—is also a universal antecedent of conflict.

At the same time, although these are likely broad universal sources of conflict, cross-cultural variation exists in the specific triggers of conflicts within each category. For example, what is perceived to be a threat to one's values can clearly vary across national cultures. Shteynberg, Gelfand, and Kim (2005) argued that conflict processes are "sparked" or initiated when core *cultural focal concerns* are violated, and thus, different events elicit conflict in different cultural contexts. Consistent with this, they found that violations to rights were perceived to be much more harmful and incited anger to a much greater degree in the United States, whereas violations to duties and face caused much more harm and incited anger to a greater degree in Korea. Individuals can project their values onto identical situations and perceive different "cultural slights" that are salient in their own cultural contexts. For example, Gelfand and colleagues (2001) found that identical conflict situations were perceived differently in the United States and Japan: Americans perceived conflicts to be more about winning and violations to individual rights, whereas Japanese perceived the same conflicts to be about compromise and violations to duties and obligations.

The processes that lead to value conflicts can also vary across cultures. For example, self-serving biases and self-enhancement—processes we have argued are facilitating factors in value conflicts—have been found to be more pronounced in individualistic cultures as compared with collectivistic cultures (Gelfand et al., 2002; see also Heine, Lehman, Markus, & Kitayama, 1999). Other self-processes—such as self-esteem and self-concept clarity, previously discussed—may also play a more powerful role in the production of conflict in individualistic cultures. On the other hand, given that individuals in collectivistic cultures focus on group identity, group-level constructs—group enhancement, group esteem, group concept clarity—will play a more powerful role in the elicitation of conflict in collectivistic cultures. This is consistent with research that has shown that samples from collectivistic cultures are much more competitive in intergroup or outgroup negotiations (Chen & Li, 2005; Probst, Carnevale, & Triandis, 1999; Triandis et al., 2001).

We would also argue that although resource and cognitive-based conflicts are likely universal, there is likely cultural variation in the nature and extent of these antecedents. Given that individuals are socialized to develop, express, and affirm their own ideas and seek to maximize their own outcomes in individualistic cultures, resource and cognitive-based conflicts might be more rampant at the individual level in these contexts. By contrast, in collectivistic cultures, individuals are socialized to subject their own interests and opinions to the group (and in high-power distance cultures, to the authority), suggesting that at the individual level, resource and cognitive conflicts might be more suppressed in these contexts. Yet again, because of higher group-level identity and associated processes, resource and cognitive conflicts may be even more acute in collectivist cultures at the between-group level, as compared with individualistic cultures. In all, while the general categories we have identified are likely universal, the specific triggers of conflict can be culturally variable.

Conclusions About the Sources of Conflict

In keeping with previous work, we defined conflict as a process that begins when one party perceives its interests, norms and values, or opinions and viewpoints being opposed, hurt, or countered by another party. We argued that within work settings, conflict may arise because of mixed-motive interdependencies (conflicts of interest, resource conflicts), because of the need to develop and maintain a positive identity vis-à-vis others (value conflicts), and because of the need to develop and maintain cognitive consistency and to hold socially validated and consensually shared understandings (information conflicts). In contrast to past work, we explicitly located these various sources of conflict at the individual, group, and organization levels of analysis and uncovered that at each of these levels conflict can be traced back to these fundamental sources. We also noted that little work has been done to integrate these levels; with regard to sociocognitive, information conflicts, there has been very little work even at the intergroup and organization level of analysis. The commonalities in explanatory mechanisms within each of these broad classes of theories, however, allow one to develop a more complex yet also more accurate understanding of the sources of workplace conflict and the ways they come about—that is, turn from latent into manifest conflicts. We also noted the potential cross-cultural universality of these sources of conflict, along with possible culture-specific triggers of conflict.

Before moving on, we should emphasize that it would be wrong to assume that workplace conflict involves only one of these three sources. Conflicts are not about access to scarce resources, or about the striving for positive and distinct identity, or about interpretations of reality. More often than not, workplace conflicts are about a mixture of opposing interests, clashing values, and incompatible beliefs. For example, De Dreu and Van Knippenberg (2005) showed that people anticipating a debate about judgmental issues ("Should economic growth be sacrificed to preserve the natural environment?") quickly identified with their position in the debate and the arguments supporting that position. As a result, identity striving became part of the conflict, and ego-threats were experienced. Work by Carnevale (2004) showed that groups (e.g., Israeli settlers) ascribe symbolic value to scarce resources (e.g., parts of Jerusalem) and that having versus not having access to these resources becomes affirmation versus threat of their social identity. Work by Jehn and Mannix (2001) showed that different types of conflict (e.g., relationship, task, process) emerge at different stages of group work.

The specific combination of various sources may have important effects on the ways these conflicts are managed, about the effectiveness of intervention techniques, and about the ultimate consequences these conflicts may have for individual well-being, team effectiveness, or organizational survival. For example, sociocognitive conflicts may be quite functional and promote the quality of group decision making but only when conflicts of interest are absent. That is, when participants perceive their goals to be cooperatively linked, they engage in constructive controversy and benefit from sociocognitive conflict. When they perceive their goals to be competitive linked, as in conflicts of interest, however, they do not engage in constructive controversy, and cognitive conflict hinders rather than helps team performance (e.g., Tjosvold, 1998). We believe herein lies an important question for future research and theory development: "How do mixtures of conflict sources affect conflict dynamics and ultimate outcomes?"

CONSEQUENCES OF WORKPLACE CONFLICT ACROSS LEVELS OF ANALYSIS

Conflict in organizations has multiple functions; it influences a number of outcome-related parameters and it does so in a variety of ways. Conflict outcomes can be seen in terms of the utility gained or lost by participants alone and together. Utility can be narrowly defined in economic, monetary terms or broadly defined in terms of both material (money) and nonmaterial (love, respect) value. Traditionally, conflict research has focused on material outcomes in terms of individual and collective gains and losses. For example, much of the work on interpersonal and small-group negotiation concentrates on predicting the joint gain parties realize in so-called integrative, win–win agreements that reconcile seemingly opposed aspirations (Bazerman et al., 2000; Carnevale & Pruitt, 1992; De Dreu et al., 2007).

The quality of agreement following dispute resolution has a variety of important influences on subsequent interaction processes and performance-related issues. For example, the party who gains the upper hand in the conflict sees its power-base strengthened and thus can operate more effectively in future endeavours. Integrative, win–win solutions create order and stability, foster social harmony, increase feelings of self-efficacy, reduce the probability of future conflict, and stimulate economic prosperity. Poor agreements, or failures to agree, leave parties dissatisfied, create frustration and annoyance, disrupt social order, drive new conflict, and fuel disharmony (De Dreu, Beersma, Stroebe, & Euwema, 2006; Rubin, Pruitt, & Kim, 1994).

Apart from these indirect effects, conflict can have more direct effects that are not necessarily mediated by the quality of the negotiated agreement. Alternative functions of workplace conflict can include health, well-being, life and/or job satisfaction, relationship commitment, community values, justice, and so forth. In studying other consequences of conflict and conflict management, the *time horizon* of short- versus longer-term effects becomes critical (Thomas, 1992). Conflict may increase or decrease the likelihood of short-term achievement of a shared goal such as making profit. In the longer run, the positive or negative effects may persist, become stronger, or disappear. For example, an intense but relatively short-lived conflict in a hospital between the head of operations and the nursing staff may lead to inefficiencies and medical errors in the short run but, in the long run, result in better working conditions, more participative decision making, and improved health care. In other words, conflict consequences may be found at the individual, group, and organization levels of analysis, but also across time. We discuss the issue of time in more depth at the end of this chapter.

In the sections below, we discuss four functions in more detail—the creating force of conflict, the influence on health and well-being, the effects on in-role and extra-role work performance, and the shaping of social structures. The creating force of conflict and the influence on health and well-being are treated extensively by Schulz-Hardt et al. (chapter 5, this volume) and Spector and Bruk-Lee (chapter 9, this volume). We will therefore devote more space to the effects on performance and on the shaping of social structures. In each section, however, and in keeping with our overarching goal in this chapter, we link our discussions to different levels of analysis and argue that effects are "quasi-isomorphic" at different levels of analysis. We also discuss whether and when these outcomes are likely to be invariant across national cultures.[2]

---

[2] It is important to note that when discussing the consequences of conflict, a distinction needs to be made between two classes of comparison. The first is that different ways of managing conflict can have different effects on individual well-being, creativity and innovation, performance, and so forth. Most research on conflict and conflict management is concerned with this analysis, and many of the insights gleaned from this work are reviewed in the chapters in this volume. For example, Beersma and colleagues (chapter 4, this volume) review the quality of negotiated agreement when conflict parties adopt a prosocial instead of a proself motivation. The second type of analysis implicitly or explicitly compares situations in which there is (intense) conflict with situations in which there is no (or mild) conflict. Obviously, both types of analyses are highly complementary. For example, compared with a no-conflict situation in which there is harmony, conflict may promote decision quality when the conflict is managed through cooperative problem solving and undermine decision quality when the parties withdraw and remain inactive. More elaborate discussions of the ways different conflict strategies influence decision quality and negotiated agreement can be found elsewhere (De Dreu, Harinck, & Van Vianen, 1999; De Dreu & Weingart, 2003b; Jehn & Bendersky, 2003; Tjosvold, 1991, 1998) and in other chapters in this volume (e.g., Olekalns et al., chapter 3; Beersma et al., chapter 4; Schulz-Hardt et al., chapter 5).

Conflict and Performance

Perhaps the most obvious area for organizational scientists to look for conflict's consequences is the impact conflict has, or can have, on individual, group, and organizational performance. Performance may be operationalized in many different ways, such as the productivity relative to one's most salient competitor, as the supervisor's evaluation of her employees' commitment, or as the quality of group decisions (e.g., Pritchard, 1992). Several scholars further argue that individual, group, and organizational performance can be decomposed into task-related performance and organizational citizenship behavior—compliance with collective goals, taking initiatives, and coordinating activities. Organizational citizenship behavior, sometimes referred to as extra-role or contextual performance, involves behaviors of a discretionary nature that are not part of the employee's formal role requirements, but nevertheless promote the effective functioning of the organization (Borman & Motowidlow, 1993; Organ, 1988; Podsakoff, Ahearne, & MacKenzie, 1997). Thus, first of all, conflict may influence *individual-level effectiveness*—personal development of skills, abilities, and knowledge, as well as the motivation to work hard and to achieve one's goals. In other words, conflict may impact task-related performance because through conflict people learn new skills and acquire new insights or because conflict undermines their motivation to perform and contribute.

Second, conflict may influence interpersonal, or *group-level effectiveness*—learning to work together, developing relationships, or reaching high-quality group decisions. Group performance may be undermined because conflict hurts efficient coordination or undermines the trust needed to communicate effectively and to share task-relevant information (De Dreu & Van Vianen, 2001). Conflict may increase group performance, however, because it leads people to reevaluate their working assumptions, to correct errors, and to approach decision problems from multiple perspectives (see also Schulz-Hardt, Jochims, & Frey, 2002; Schulz-Hardt et al., chapter 5, this volume). In particular, moderate compared with low levels of sociocognitive, task-related conflict contribute to team effectiveness (Jehn, 1995) and team innovation (De Dreu, 2006).

At the *intergroup and organization level*, conflict may influence performance in a number of ways as well. Consider, for example, the field experiment by Erev, Bornstein, and Galili (1993). They compared three conditions. In an individual incentive condition, workers had to pick oranges and were paid on the basis of their individual performance. In a team incentive condition, workers had to pick oranges and were paid on the basis of their team's task performance. In an intergroup competition condition, workers were paid on the basis of their team's outperforming the competitor. Results showed that the intergroup competition condition led to a higher task performance than the team condition, with the individual incentive condition being intermediate. The idea behind these findings is that resource-based conflicts of interest between groups strengthen within-group cohesion and individual work motivation to contribute to the group's success.

Other work on resource-based conflicts between groups points toward the same conclusion. Putnam (1997) analyzed teacher–board negotiations and concluded that active confrontation through negotiation promotes intergroup communication, increases mutual understanding, and results in greater acceptance of agreements and decisions than more tacit coordination. Finally, Walton, Cutcher-Gershenfeld, and McKersie (1994, pp. 72–73) reported both the negative and the positive consequences of union–management negotiations in the auto-supply, the pulp and paper, and the railroad industries. Inspection of their data reveals that within the pulp and paper industry, 20% of the negotiations resulted in negative consequences only, such as costly strikes, while 20% of the negotiations improved organizational effectiveness parameters. For the auto supply and the railroad industries, these percentages were 30 and 60, and 25 and 50, respectively. Apparently, active confrontation between competing groups—teams picking oranges, teacher and board representatives, or union and management—influences distal task performance at the overarching organizational level in a sometimes fairly positive way. As we will discuss below, however, the national culture context is likely a key moderator of the impact of active confrontation on performance in teams.

Conflict and Well-Being

Workplace conflict has important consequences for health and well-being (De Dreu, Van Dierendonck, & Dijkstra, 2004; Spector & Jex, 1998; see also Spector & Bruk-Lee, chapter 9, this volume). Conflict is a social stressor, bringing about stress responses such as elevated heart rate, increased respiration, dry mouth, and increased alertness. These responses are, in principle, functional and reflect the individual's readiness to cope with the stressful situation. When the stressor continues to be present and responses continue to be in effect, however, psychic and physical exhaustion may lead to deteriorated health and well-being.

Although all types of conflict may elicit stress, it seems reasonable to assume that resource-based conflicts of interest and sociocognitive task conflicts produce less severe and less intense stress than identity-based value and relationship conflicts. The idea behind this is that identity-related conflicts are more fundamental and emotional (De Dreu et al., 2004). Prolonged exposure to conflict may therefore result in behavioral consequences such as absenteeism, accident proneness, and drug abuse; psychological consequences such as lowered self-esteem and self-efficacy; psychosomatic complaints (Spector & Jex, 1998); or burnout (Dijkstra, Van Dierendonck, Evers, & De Dreu, 2005).

Reduced health and well-being is likely to manifest itself at higher levels of analysis. A unit with frequent conflicts between leaders and employees is likely to have a relatively large number of employees with lowered well-being and, thus, will be exemplified by high levels of absenteeism and turnover. In addition, such units are likely to have negative group affective tone, which in turn lowers group effectiveness and unit members' job satisfaction (George, 1991). In short, workplace conflicts influence employee health and well-being, and this in turn affects group affective tone and organization-level absenteeism and turnover rates.

Conflict and Change

Ample research indicates that conflict serves as a key driver of change at the individual, the group, and the organization level—without conflict no change, and no change without conflict (e.g., Coser, 1956; Moscovici, 1980). For example, at the individual level, moderately intense conflicts stimulate employee performance more than harmonious, peaceful settings (e.g., Van de Vliert & De Dreu, 1994) and promote individual creativity and cognitive flexibility (Carnevale & Probst, 1998; Nemeth, 1986). At the group level, sociocognitive task conflict within work teams increases members' innovative capacity, helping them to solve problems, and leads them to make better decisions (De Dreu, 2006; Jehn, 1995). Also, at the organization level, external threat and resource scarcity have been linked to organizational innovation in both primary studies and meta-analytic reviews (Anderson et al., 2004). For example, at the organizational level of analysis, there is evidence that budget deficiency and lower "slack" resources stimulate organizations to be more innovative in marketing and product development. Also, at the organizational level, Zaltman, Duncan, and Holbeck (1973) suggested that an organization innovates in order to cope with work overload or changing circumstances beyond their immediate control. Thus, at the organizational level, it seems that resource-based conflicts of interest may actually stimulate innovativeness.

Conflict and Social Structure

A final function of workplace conflicts is that they help define boundaries and clarify who and what belongs where. Conflict leads to (re)defined social identities, but also to the disappearance of certain group characteristics, institutions, languages, or specific subcultures and their expressions. A good example of this function is seen in work on mergers and acquisitions (Terry & Amiot, chapter 13, this volume), where conflict between groups shapes and sometimes redefines the relative status positions of formerly separate groups or organizations within the new constellation. Conflict also contributes to the shaping of group identity and organizational culture by implicitly or explicitly stimulating some members to leave the organization and by fostering turnover among peripheral group members more than among those seen as core (cf. work on attraction, selection, and attrition; Schneider, 1987). We return to this when we discuss cross-level influences of workplace conflict.

Cross-Cultural Variation in Outcomes of Conflict

Much, if not all, of the previous synthesis of conflict and organizational outcomes is based on research conducted in the United States or Western Europe. Cross-cultural influences on outcomes of conflict at the individual, team, and organization levels has received scant attention, yet we would expect that national culture is a highly relevant factor in considering the impact of conflict on outcomes in organizations. Using Jehn and Bendersky's (2003) parlance, national culture might serve as an *ameliorating* factor; that is, it might ameliorate the *negative* impact of conflict in organizations. For example, as chapters by Pruitt (chapter 8, this volume) and Spector and Bruk-Lee (chapter 9, this volume) attest, attributions to other parties is a critical determinant of when conflict will have a negative impact on individuals' health and escalation processes. At the same time, research has long demonstrated that culture plays a key role in attributional processes (see Choi, Nisbett, & Norenzayan, 1999, for a review). In general, individuals in collectivistic cultures are more likely to make situational attributions, whereas individuals in individualistic cultures are more likely to make dispositional attributions across numerous situations (Miller, 1984; Morris & Peng, 1994) and in conflict situations in particular (Morris, Leung, & Iyegnar, 2004; Valenzuela, Srivastava, & Lee, 2005). This suggests that the negative effect of conflict on individual health and escalation may be less pronounced in collectivistic cultures, especially with ingroup members.

Yet at the same time, culture might play a *suppressor* role; that is, it might suppress the *positive* effects of conflict. For example, the preceding discussion and numerous chapters in this volume highlight the fact that conflict and dissent can have a positive effect on innovation and creativity at multiple levels of analysis, yet this assumption has been rarely put to the cross-cultural test (Anderson et al., 2004). Research has shown that conformity pressures are stronger in collectivistic cultures (Bond & Smith, 1996), and heightened concerns for harmony might suggest that conflict is less likely to translate into creativity in collectivistic cultures (cf. Goncalo & Staw, 2006). Indeed, Nibler and Harris (2003) found that that high levels of debate benefited U.S., but not necessarily Chinese, groups. Similarly, Adair, Okumura, and Brett (2001) showed that among collectivistic groups, high joint gain was achieved through indirect (and not direct) communication (see Olekalns et al., chapter 3, this volume, for further discussion). Research has shown, however, that certain contextual conditions can enable open dissent to have positive effects in collectivistic cultures. For example, Tjosvold and Sun (2002) found that open discussion of conflict can be beneficial for relationships in China by it is complemented by nonverbal expressions of interpersonal warmth, and Tjosvold, Poon, and Yu (2005) showed that in China conflict can have positive consequences, so long as social face is confirmed during the process. Ng and Van Dyne (2001) also showed that dissent (minority influence) can have a positive impact on decision quality in collectivistic groups, particularly when individuals who express dissent occupy a high-status position. In all, culture is likely to moderate the impact of conflict on both positive and negative outcomes, and the situational context is likely crucial in helping to understand whether and when conflict has positive or negative effects across cultures.

Conclusions About the Consequences of Conflict Across Levels

Several functions of workplace conflicts other than economic and material outcomes can be identified. Some of these transcend various levels of analysis, such as the effects of conflict on creativity, innovation, and change, and the effects of conflict on health, well-being, workplace stress, and withdrawal responses. Other functions are located at some levels but not at others, and relate to the shaping and (re)definition of social boundaries, group membership, and cultural expression. Thus, an important payoff of taking a multilevel perspective on workplace conflict is that new functions can be identified, functions that go unnoticed when the analysis remains focused on one single level of analysis and functions that might change when moving across national cultures as discussed.

It seems that some sources of conflict discussed earlier are likely to be associated with some functions more than with others. For example, conflicts rooted in ego-threat and the need to defend and restore a positive (social) identity may be more likely to relate to lowered well-being and health complaints than information conflicts rooted in divergent interpretations of facts and figures, and vice versa, the creative force of conflict seems to be tied especially to sociocognitive conflicts and less to resource and identity conflicts.

When taking multiple functions into account, it becomes clear that conflict may have positive effects on some aspects located at one level (e.g., group cohesion and cooperation, individual work motivation) yet negative effects on aspects located at other levels (e.g., intergroup hostility, organizational effectiveness). Whether workplace conflicts benefit or hurt the organization as a collective thus heavily depends on where, how, and how intensely conflicts impact individual-, group-, and organization-level functions. Researchers and practitioners alike should be aware of this when concluding that conflicts are detrimental, or beneficial, and designing strategies to counter, or stimulate and preserve the situation—clearly, there often is more than meets the eye.

The Management of Conflict Across Levels of Analysis

In principle, the sources of conflict reviewed above say little about the particular outcomes conflict has, and in and by itself specific sources of conflict do not have certain outcomes. As mentioned earlier, the critical moderator between the emergence of conflict and the outcomes it has is the way conflict is managed. Broadly defined, conflict management is what parties—individuals, groups, or organizations—who experience conflict intend to do as well as what they actually do (Van de Vliert, 1997).

Although an infinite number of conflict management strategies may be conceived, one useful way to organize our thinking is by means of a three-way system distinguishing among unilateral action, joint action, and third-party decision making. Unilateral action involves those strategies and tactics that can be implemented by one conflict party and thus do not need the counterpart(s) to consent or work along. It includes (a) withdrawal and inaction, (b) yielding and giving in, and (c) dominating and forcing. Joint action refers to those strategies and tactics that cannot be implemented by one conflict party alone and that need the counterpart(s) to consent or work along. It includes negotiation, searching for a compromise, and mediation. Third-party decision making refers to those strategies aimed at handing over to a third party with the discretionary control to make a decision. Examples of third-party decision making include arbitration, adjudication, and mediation.

The three classes of conflict management are not mutually exclusive: Strategies may be used simultaneously or sequentially. Van de Vliert and colleagues (e.g., Van de Vliert, Euwema, & Huismans, 1995; Van de Vliert, Nauta, Euwema, & Janssen, 1997) have argued and shown that joint problem solving may be performed in close conjunction with unilateral forcing. As an example of sequential use of strategies from different classes, consider the famous tit-for-tat strategy (Axelrod & Hamilton, 1981) and the classic good-cop/bad-cop strategy, in which a conflict party seeks joint cooperative action after a period in which he or she (or some ally) has performed forceful and competitive unilateral pressure tactics (Hilty & Carnevale, 1992).

Olekalns et al. (chapter 3, this volume) provide a state-of-the art review of this and related work on sequences in conflict management and negotiation. In this and related work, several conflict phases have been identified. For example, following an in-depth analysis of labor-management negotiations, Walton and McKersie (1965) suggested that negotiations often begin in quite a harsh and competitive way. After a series of competitive exchanges, parties come to realize that this leads nowhere but to a costly impasse, that a change in behavior is needed, and that mutual problem solving is a viable alternative for safeguarding and promoting self-interest. This so-called "differentiation-before-integration" pattern is not limited to the ritual dance of labor–management negotiations. A laboratory study by Brett, Shapiro, and Lytle (1998) showed that procedural remarks—statements that refer to the process of the negotiation itself—changed the focus from contentious, distributive communication to more constructive, integrative communication. Harinck and De Dreu (2004) coded temporary impasses—points in the negotiation where parties deadlocked on some issues and remained stuck for a while. Higher levels of contending early in the negotiation were related to temporary impasses, and temporary impasses were, in turn, related to problem solving late in the negotiation. Stepping back from and reflecting upon the negotiation during a temporary impasse appears to facilitate a switch from competitive contending to more cooperative problem solving (see also Olekalns, Brett, & Weingart, 2003), especially when competitive strategizing during such breaks is avoided (Harinck & De Dreu, in press).

Because various chapters in the current volume treat conflict management in great detail, here we selectively highlight that there appears to be quite some consistency in tactics and strategies across levels of analysis. We briefly discuss several more or less related taxonomies of conflict management strategies that have been applied to the individual, group, and organization levels of analysis. We then discuss the relationship between the three sources of conflict identified earlier—(a) resource scarcity, (b) need for a positive identity, and (c) need for a correct and socially shared understanding—and the effectiveness of conflict management. Finally, as in previous sections, we end with a discussion of research on culture and conflict management, and whether the taxonomies and findings discussed in this section are universal or subject to culture-specificity.

Individual and Small Group Level

An important theory about conflict management is Deutsch's Theory of Cooperation and Competition (Deutsch, 1949, 1973). In brief, the theory argues that disputants may perceive their ultimate goals to be positively linked (cooperative interdependence), negatively linked (competitive interdependence), or not linked (independence). Cooperative versus competitive goal-interdependences, and their origins, are closely related to the concept of prosocial versus proself motives, discussed by Beersma and colleagues (chapter 4, this volume). In the case of competitive interdependence (or to a lesser extent, independence) disputants try to maximize their own outcomes, with no (or negative) regard for the outcomes obtained by their counterparts. In contrast, in the case of cooperative interdependency, disputants try to maximize both own and other's outcomes. Competitive interdependence leads to distrust, hostile attitudes, and negative interpersonal perceptions. Disputants use persuasive arguments, positional commitments, threats, bluffs, and coercive power to get their way. Cooperative interdependence, in contrast, leads to trust, positive attitudes and perceptions, and constructive exchange of information. Parties listen and seek to understand one another's perspective, which is what Tjosvold (1991, 1998) referred to as "constructive controversy." The theory has been tested in experimental game situations, as well as in a variety of field studies, and has generally received good support (for a review, see Tjosvold, 1998). This work has also shown that constructive controversy yields desirable outcomes to disputants and their collective alike. It promotes learning and innovation, team effectiveness, and the quality of group decision making, to name but a few.

Another important theory about conflict management is Dual Concern Theory (Pruitt & Rubin, 1986; also see Blake & Mouton, 1964; Olekalns et al., chapter 3, this volume). In a nutshell, it argues that conflict management is a function of high or low concern for self combined with high or low concern for other. A high concern for self and low concern for other results in a preference for forcing focused on imposing one's will on the other side (unilateral action). Forcing involves threats and bluffs, persuasive arguments, and positional commitments. Low concern for self and high concern for other results in a preference for yielding, which is oriented toward accepting and incorporating other's will. It involves unilateral concessions, unconditional promises, and offering help (unilateral action). Low concern for self and other results in a preference for avoiding, which involves reducing the importance of the issues and attempts to suppress thinking about the issues (unilateral action). High concern for self and other produces a preference for problem solving, which is oriented toward an agreement that satisfies both own and other's aspirations as much as possible (joint action). It involves an exchange of information about priorities and preferences, showing insights, and making tradeoffs between important and unimportant issues.

Recently, some authors have suggested that intermediate concern for self paired with intermediate concern for other results in a preference for compromising. Some see compromising as "half-hearted problem solving" (e.g., Pruitt & Rubin, 1986). Others, however, see it as a distinct strategy that involves the matching of other's concessions, the making of conditional promises and threats, and an active search for a middle ground (e.g., Van de Vliert, 1997). Empirically, the debate seems to be settled in favor of those viewing compromise as a separate strategy, although more work needs to be done (De Dreu, Evers, Beersma, Kluwer, & Nauta, 2001).

Ury, Brett, and Goldberg (1993) differentiated forcing and dominating into two subcategories—rights and power—in their taxonomy of approaches to dispute resolution. When using a rights-based approach, parties attempt to resolve the dispute by applying some standard of fairness, precedent, contract, or law. A focus on rights is likely to lead to agreements in which each party has to give up something in order to reach an agreement, with the possibility of one party giving more than receiving. A power-based approach results in the dispute being resolved by determining which party is able to force his or her desired outcome—who is stronger, has higher status, is able to coerce the other, or can force a concession from the other party. A power-based approach usually leads to agreements that have greater potential to escalate due to feelings of resentment and a desire for revenge (Brett et al., 1998; Tinsley, 2001; also see Friedman et al., chapter 12, this volume; Goldman et al., chapter 10, this volume; Pruitt, chapter 8, this volume). While either a rights-based or power-based approach can lead to concessions from the other party, rights-based concessions are usually evidenced when there is agreement about a standard, whereas power-based concessions reflect submission to a greater force.

Between-Group and Organizational Level

At the between-group and organization level of analysis, much effort has been invested in understanding (the effectiveness of) systems of conflict management. Rather than analyzing what individual parties or small groups do, researchers focusing on the organizational level of analysis have examined grievance-filing systems and their effectiveness (Olson-Buchanan & Boswell, chapter 11, this volume), formal and informal mediation and related forms of third-party intervention (Bendersky, 2003; Goldman et al., chapter 10, this volume), and the more or less ritualized labor–management conflict resolution process (Friedman et al., chapter 12, this volume). A common theme across all of these chapters is the importance of creating *structures* in organizations that help foster positive conflict-management strategies.

We would also add that at a more macro level of analysis, organizations can also create *conflict cultures* that are more or less effective in their approach to conflict (De Dreu, Van Dierendonck & Dijkstra, 2004). That is, although specific situational influences may cause individuals to adopt different conflict-management strategies across time, work settings are often highly stable and quite predictable. Employees interact with the same coworkers, incentive structures do not change overnight, employees do the same kinds of work for longer periods of time, and they face the same (interpersonal) problems on a recurring basis. In addition, individuals within the same unit, team, or department tend to influence one another (Salancik & Pfeffer, 1978), thus creating their own social environment with, most likely, rather stable and socially shared preferences for, and views about, the tasks to be done and the ways of dealing with one another.

An implication of these notions is that work teams and work units are likely to develop a *conflict culture*. Units within organizations, or even entire organizations, develop over time a relatively stable set of orientations toward, and strategies to manage conflict within that unit or between that unit and relevant outsiders such as other units within the organization, clients, and the like. Thus, in some units or in some organizations employees may develop a shared tendency to view conflict as negative and annoying, whereas in other units or other organizations employees may develop a shared tendency to view conflict as exciting and providing opportunity. Likewise, in some units or in some organizations employees may develop a shared tendency to approach and manage conflict through problem solving and open-minded debate, whereas in other units or other organizations employees may develop a shared tendency to approach and manage conflict by assuming a passive stance (De Dreu et al., 2004). Identifying the antecedents and consequences of conflict cultures in organizations is an important area for future research.

SOURCES OF CONFLICT AND CONFLICT MANAGEMENT

Earlier we noted a critical difference between resource-based conflict of interest and identity-based value and relationship conflicts: the fact that trade-offs and compromise solutions are unacceptable in the latter type of conflict. Indeed, Druckman and colleagues (Druckman, 1994; Druckman & Zechmeister, 1973) have shown repeatedly that negotiating a compromise solution becomes much more difficult when interests are tied to ideological values, and Harinck and colleagues (Harinck & De Dreu, 2004; Harinck, De Dreu, & Van Vianen, 2000) have shown that participants in a resource-conflict more easily switch from ineffective forcing to more effective and constructive problem solving than participants in value conflicts. In other words, resource-based conflicts of interest seem to lend themselves better to problem solving and compromise than identity-based value conflicts, and rights-based forms of forcing may lend themselves better to identity-related value conflicts (Jehn & Bendersky, 2003).

Whereas negotiation and problem solving may not be suitable for identity-based value conflicts, avoidance and withdrawal may be. Several studies found that teams with value and relationship conflicts functioned better to the extent that the members of these teams avoided these conflicts and did not attempt to manage them proactively (De Dreu & Van Vianen, 2001; Jehn, 1997; Murnighan & Conlon, 1991). In sociocognitive conflicts, where some truth-finding and learning takes place, forcing and persuasive bolstering one's position may be a much more acceptable and effective strategy than it is in resource-based conflicts of interest or in identity-based value conflicts. Indeed, group-decision-making research has shown time and time again that adding task-related dissent and devil's advocates to the team improves creativity, innovation, and decision quality (Janis, 1972; Nemeth & Staw, 1989; also see Schulz-Hardt et al., chapter 5, this volume).

Cross-Cultural Variation in Conflict Management

As in other areas that we have reviewed, most of the typologies of conflict management strategies were developed in the United States and Western Europe. Compared with research on antecedents and outcomes of conflict, however, there have been numerous studies of culture and conflict management strategies, which have most typically examined cultural differences in preferences for different strategies (see Gelfand & Brett, 2004;

Gelfand et al., in press). In general, research has shown that in individual-istic cultures, individuals tend to prefer forcing conflict resolution styles (Holt & DeVore, 2005) along with integrating interests (Tinsley, 2001). By contrast, individuals in collectivistic cultures tend to prefer power strate-gies (Tinsley, 2001) or styles of avoidance and withdrawal (Friedman, Chi, & Liu, 2006; Holt & DeVore, 2005; Morris et al., 1998; Oetzel et al., 2001), especially in intense disputes and disputes with ingroup members and superiors (Brew & Cairns, 2004; Derlega, Cukur, Kuang, & Forsyth, 2002; Friedman et al., 2006; Pearson & Stephan, 1998).

Fewer studies have examined whether the basic assumptions under-lying these taxonomies (e.g., the dual concern model, interest–rights–power theory) are applicable in other cultural contexts. Gabrielidis, Stephan, Ybarra, Pearson, and Villareal (1997), for example, showed that avoidance reflects a *concern for others*, rather than a lack thereof, as origi-nally conceived in the dual concern model (see also Cai & Fink, 2002). Similarly, Brett and Gelfand (2005) argued that while silence and avoid-ance are strategies that are viewed negatively in Western cultures, they are viewed quite positively in Eastern cultures. As discussed in Tsjovold and Sun (2002), the motives and strategies for avoidance in East Asian cul-tures range from passive strategies to highly proactive strategies, which often involve working through third parties (Tinsley & Brett, 2001). Thus, research on avoidance needs to capture this complexity in order to cap-ture cross-cultural variation in the construct. Additionally, while basic tenets of interest–rights–power framework are likely universal, the theory also likely needs to be expanded to capture conflict management strate-gies in other contexts. For example, power strategies might be more likely to include the interests and well-being of subordinates when used in high power distance and paternalistic cultures. In line with this, Tinsley (2004) argued that theory and research would benefit from examining not only individual but also collective rights, interests, and power as foci of con-flict strategies, to better capture conflict management strategies in East Asian cultures. In sum, although the typologies discussed previously are applicable to other cultures, they need to be expanded and/or refined to adequately reflect cross-cultural variation in conflict management.

Conclusions About Conflict Management at Different Levels of Analysis

Across levels of analysis, conflict management strategies can be mean-ingfully classified as unilateral actions (e.g, forcing, avoiding, yielding), as joint actions (e.g, negotiation, problem solving, mediation), or as third-party intervention (e.g., arbitration, going to court, fate). At the organiza-tion level, these tendencies to manage conflict are less fluid and subject to exogenous influences such as the fundamental sources of the conflict, and more ingrained in organizational structures, rules and regulations, and perhaps, organizational culture. Finally, national culture also plays an important role in the preferences and functions of different conflict management styles.

NEGLECTED LEVELS AND CROSS-LEVEL INFLUENCES: THE NEXT GENERATION OF CONFLICT RESEARCH

Collectively, the chapters in this volume highlight conflict anteced-ents, processes, and functions at the individual, group, organization, and cultural levels of analysis. We conclude this chapter with a discussion of important areas of future research on conflict in organizations from a lev-els of analysis perspective. We first focus on the importance of incorpo-rating issues of *time* into research on conflict in organizations. We then discuss the importance of cross-level organizational research, including top-down and bottom-up processes on conflict in organizations.

Time: A Neglected Dimension of Conflict

Although thinking in terms of individual, group, and organization levels of analysis is increasingly common in the organizational sciences (e.g., Klein & Kozlowski, 2000), scholars sometimes overlook other levels of analysis that have to do with the fluidity of change over *time*. Conflict is clearly a dynamic phenomenon that unfolds over time (Pondy, 1967), and thus issues of time are by definition critical for the study of conflict. For example, research on time and conflict can illustrate *when* different types of conflict are particularly impactful for later performance. Jehn and Man-nix (2001) showed that the time period in which conflict occurs and the patterns of conflict over time are critical for understanding group perfor-mance. Groups that had low to moderate levels of process conflict in early stages, moderately high levels of task conflict during middle and later stages, and low levels of relationship conflict across all stages were more successful than groups with other conflict profiles over time. Beersma and De Dreu (2005) found that groups with individualistically motivated negotiators achieved lower joint outcomes than groups with prosocially motivated negotiators, but subsequently performed better on tasks that required high levels of creative and innovative thinking.

Research on time and conflict can also call into question age-old assump-tions about causal relationships of conflict and organizational outcomes. For example, Peterson and Behfar (2003) found that negative performance feed-back increased task and relationship conflict in groups, and Janssen (2003) showed that organizational innovations caused (rather than predicted) rela-tionship conflicts among team members. Both studies thus illustrate that the conflict-to-outcome linkage discussed previously can have a reverse causal-ity. Although studies of time and conflict such as these are relatively rare, they clearly illustrate that time is of the essence in the study of conflict.

In highlighting frontiers of research on time and conflict, we turn to historians such as Braudel (1947) and propose that conflicts at all three levels are dynamic and embedded in different layers of time—structure, conjuncture, and events—as they each have different implications for conflict in organizations. Figure 1.2 provides a summary of our discussion below.

Structure refers to those aspects of the context that are fixed and hardly change. Workplace conflicts are embedded in *geographical contexts* within which organizations are located and this context influences conflict dynamics in organizations (Brief et al., 2005; Dietz, Robinson, Folger, Baron, & Schultz, 2003). For example, levels of community violence are significant predictors of workplace aggression, above and beyond organizational norms for fairness (Dietz et al., 2003). Interethnic conflict in communities also affects the dynamics of conflict within organizations (Brief et al., 2005). Other factors in the immediate geographical context that influence conflict include thermodynamic features, including ambient temperature. Van de Vliert, Huang, and Parker (2004) have shown that temperature has notable and quite stable influences on the emergence and management of conflicts. As we have noted throughout this chapter, the *national cultural context* within which organizations operate influences the emergence, outcomes, and management of workplace conflicts. A third and final example is the *historical context,* which provides a relatively stable

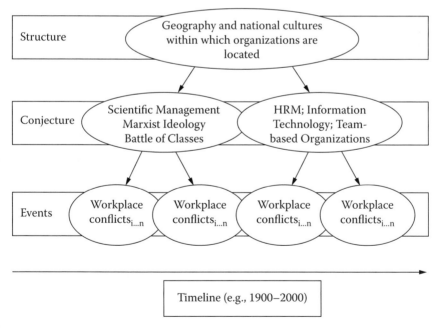

FIGURE 1.2. Conflict in and around organizations across different layers of time.

background—worker relations between U.S. citizens and Japanese managers, or between Dutch managers and German employees, are likely to be influenced by and interpreted in light of World War II, and although the impact of such historical events weakens over time, it does so at an exceedingly slow pace.

As can be seen in Fig. 1.2, thermodynamics, national culture, and history constitute the structural layer of time, within which conjunctures emerge. *Conjuncture* refers to those aspects of the situation that do change, but at a relatively slow pace. One may think about organizational culture, or about the fads and fashions that infatuate organizational life and dominate practices for relatively long stretches of time before fading out and being replaced by other, seemingly superior fads and fashions (Pfeffer, 1997; see also Jaffee, chapter 2, this volume). An example of conjuncture is the system installed by organizations to manage conflict and to assist third-party dispute resolution (see Goldman et al., chapter 10, this volume; Olson-Buchanan & Boswell, chapter 11, this volume).

Finally, another level of time that is relevant is *Events*, which refer to those aspects of the situation that change rapidly. Examples include the hefty debate within a cross-functional team that emerges and dissolves within a month's time, the fight between a supervisor and her employee about a particular task assignment, or the two-week strike called by unions to pressure management into an agreement. Within this level of analysis, scholars are interested in analyzing the temporal unfolding of discrete acts, and the situational and personal factors that affect bilateral conflict escalation and de-escalation (see Pruitt, chapter 8, this volume; Raver & Barling, chapter 7, this volume).

It is important to note that the four levels of analysis identified earlier— (a) individual, (b) group, (c) organization, and (d) national culture—are theoretically independent of the three layers of time. Across all levels, we can identify structures, conjunctures, and events. For example, at the individual level, employee behavior is a complex function of genetic make up (structure); life cycles, including career phases and family situation (conjunctures); and specific situational demands and opportunities that present themselves (events). Although organizations tend to be more stable than groups and individuals, dramatic and catastrophic "events" can occur at the organizational level as well. Even the climatic aspects of the national environment are subject to disruptive events such as volcanic eruptions, hurricanes, wars (see also the following discussion of how organizational events trigger conflict).

Figure 1.2 shows that distinguishing between various layers of time, each with a different pace, allows one to view relatively fluent and rapidly changing conflict events that emerge between individuals or between members of opposing groups and take place within a context characterized by particular conflict-management and dispute-resolution tools installed by the overarching organization. These systems and perspectives do not change overnight, and they provide an important background against which more fluid and emerging workplace conflicts take place. Finally, grievance-filing and dispute-resolution systems are embedded in, and legitimized by, nationwide judicial arrangements, longstanding traditions in labor–management exchanges, and perhaps national or regional culture. Again, while these may change, they do so at a slower pace than organization-specific, dispute-resolution systems.

Future research needs to explicitly incorporate these three layers of time into theories and research on conflict management. This will ultimately require the development of cross-level theories, which link more distal and relatively fixed aspects of the context (e.g., national culture, history) with organizational practices, cultures, and systems (conjunctures), with more dynamic and fluid interactions (events) at the micro-level of analysis. In the following, we highlight illustrative examples of the type of cross-level research that draws upon the previously made temporal distinctions.

Cross-Level Influences of Conflict in Organizations

In this chapter, we discussed antecedents and consequences of conflict at multiple levels, yet the frontiers of research on conflict will inevitably involve examining how factors at higher levels of analysis have cross-level influences on conflict at lower levels of analysis (top-down processes) and how factors at lower levels influence conflict at higher levels of analysis (bottom-up processes). We discuss each in turn.

Top-Down Processes and Conflict in Organizations. From a levels perspective, conflicts always occur in an organizational context, features of which can influence the nature and outcomes of conflict that occurs at lower levels. We note two distinct "roads" for this frontier: (a) top-down antecedents to different types of conflict at lower levels, and (b) top-down moderators of the conflict-to-outcome relationship.

First, future research would benefit from examining how factors at higher levels affect the emergence of different types of conflict among individuals and groups. Keeping in mind the previously made temporal distinctions, we can theorize that higher-level factors that are largely *structural or conjunctural* (e.g., national and organizational culture) affect the nature of conflict at lower levels, but also higher-level dynamic *events* (e.g., downsizing, restructuring, changes in leadership) can serve as facilitators of conflict at lower levels. For example, higher-level factors might facilitate or inhibit the extent to which there are conflicts at lower levels in organizations. Value and resource conflicts might be activated more in organizations where there are competitive organizational cultures with clear factions versus those that have cooperative organization cultures and superordinate organizational identities. Future research should also examine how community demographic composition and fault-lines filter down to affect the types of conflicts that occur in organizations (Brief et al., 2005). As another example, higher-level factors are also likely to affect the *co-occurrence* of different types of conflict at lower levels. For example, in organizational contexts where there is a lack of trust, task and relationship conflict are more highly related than in contexts where there is trust among employees (Simons & Peterson, 2000).

While the previous discussion focused on how factors at higher levels that are relatively stable (e.g., structure and conjuncture) affect conflict and lower levels, top-down effects on conflict types at lower levels may also occur due to highly dynamic *events* that occur at higher levels of analysis. For example, events such as organizational downsizing and restructuring, organizational changes in leadership, and/or changes in composition of workgroup can also affect conflict at lower levels of analysis. Terry and Amiot (chapter 13, this volume), for example, discuss how organizational merger and acquisitions can affect social identity conflicts at lower levels in organizations. Organizational changes, such as new leadership, might also facilitate resource-based conflicts in organizations because they result in increased ambiguity regarding resource allocations and increased competition. More generally, research needs to examine how both stable structures and dynamic events at higher organizational levels affect the incidence and type of conflict that occurs at lower levels of analysis.

Previously, we discussed how phenomena at higher levels of analysis can trigger and shape conflict at lower levels. Another important area for cross-level research on conflict is the examination of how factors at higher levels moderate the effects that different types of conflict have on outcomes. De Dreu and Weingart's (2003b) contingency approach to task conflict and outcomes suggested the need to examine moderators of the conflict-outcome relationship. Likewise, in their conflict-outcome moderated model (COM), Jehn and Bendersky (2003) similarly suggested that features of the group context (e.g., task interdependence, routineness of the task, group diversity, openness norms) as well as features of the organizational context (e.g., use of rights- versus interest-based third parties and dispute systems) can moderate the impact of task, relationship, and process-related conflict on outcomes. Chapters in this volume also attest to the importance of context as a moderator of the conflict-to-outcome relationship. For example, Jehn and colleagues (chapter 6) discuss the importance of context as a moderator of diversity effects on conflict in organizations.

Emergent, Bottom-Up Cross-Level Influences. Previously, we discussed top-down processes related to conflict in organizations, yet from a level of analysis perspective, it is equally important to examine bottom-up influences of conflict at lower levels on higher levels of analysis. Several chapters in this volume point to the importance of bottom-up processes. For example, drawing upon Schneider's (1987) attraction–selection–attrition model, we would argue that people with certain personalities (e.g., competitive, aggressive) self-select into organizations and create teams and organizations that have more resource based conflicts and competitive norms for managing conflict. In a related way, Jehn and colleagues (chapter 6, this volume) demonstrate how individual characteristics compile into group diversity structures that may have qualitatively different effects on the types of conflicts that emerge and the ways these conflicts are managed. Olekalns et al. (chapter 3, this volume) highlight how individual utterances and statements feed into distinct patterns of exchange that relate to meaningful outcomes at the group level.

An area not covered extensively in this volume that provides a good example of bottom-up, emergent cross-level influences is work on motivation and information processing in interpersonal and group negotiation. Building on behavioral decision theory (Neale & Bazerman, 1991) and dual concern theory (Rubin et al., 1994; see also Olekalns et al., chapter 3, this volume), De Dreu and colleagues (De Dreu, 2004, 2005; De Dreu & Carnevale, 2003; De Dreu et al., 2006; De Dreu, Weingart, & Kwon, 2000) proposed a motivated information-processing model of strategic choice in conflict and negotiation. Focusing primarily on negotiation in resource conflicts, they argued that interpersonal and group agreement is the result of a complex interplay between individual parties' cognitions and motivations—to reach high joint outcomes, negotiators need a deep understanding of the task, which requires them to exchange information and to systematically process new information. All this depends on their prosocial versus proself motivation, their high versus low motivation to engage in systematic information processing (so-called epistemic motivation), and the interaction between these social and epistemic motives.

Conclusions About Neglected Levels and Cross-Level Influences in Workplace Conflict

Conflict is a dynamic phenomenon and occurs within a multilevel organizational system. Cross-level and temporal theorizing on conflict in organizations is in its infancy, and we noted several exciting frontiers of future research. We discussed the importance of modeling how structural and conjectural factors affect conflict events and, thereafter, discussed how phenomena at macro levels of analysis affect conflict dynamics at lower levels, or how microlevel factors might affect conflict at higher levels of analysis. Fortunately, the advancement of complex statistical tools, such as hierarchical linear modeling and latent growth modeling, is uniquely situated to help develop this tradition in conflict research. For example, the former discussion of top-down influences on conflict types at lower levels can be seen within an *"intercepts-as-outcomes model"* (Hofmann, Griffin, & Gavin, 2000), wherein higher-level factors are predictors of the amount and nature of conflict at lower levels. By contrast, the discussion of top-down moderators of the conflict-to-outcome relationship is consistent with a *"slopes-as-outcomes"* model, wherein higher-level factors moderate the impact of conflict on outcomes (Hofmann et al., 2000).

CONCLUSION

Multilevel theory and techniques are relatively new to organizational behavior and industrial and organizational psychology (Klein & Kozlowski, 2000). Conflict research and theory has a strong tradition in multilevel thinking, but this has remained implicit. Throughout this chapter, we have highlighted the (quasi)isomorphism of conflict at the individual, group, and organization levels of analysis, showing that at each of these levels, conflict can be traced back to similar sources—resources, identity formation and maintenance, reality checking—and many functions of conflict can be found at each of these three levels. We also provided examples of work on bottom-up and top-down influences that cross levels of analysis, where conflicts at one level may have consequences for performance, innovation, or health and well-being at higher or lower levels.

Whereas the multilevel revolution is taking place in other areas in the field, conflict scholars and researchers seem to continue to work multilevel implicitly. In this chapter, we made this multilevel perspective explicit to provide a basis for further understanding, integration, and new research into cross-level influences in workplace conflicts.

REFERENCES

Adair, W. L., Okumura, T., & Brett, J. M. (2001). Negotiation behavior when cultures collide: The United States and Japan. *Journal of Applied Psychology, 86,* 371–385.
Anderson, N. R., De Dreu, C. K. W., & Nijstad, B. A. (2004). The routinization of innovation research: A constructively critical review of the state-of-the-science. *Journal of Organizational Behavior, 25,* 147–174.
Axelrod, R., & Hamilton, W. (1981). The evolution of cooperation. *Science, 211,* 1390–1396.
Babcock, L., Loewenstein, G., Issacharoff, S., & Camerer, C. (1995). Biased judgments of fairness in bargaining. *American Economic Review, 85,* 1337–1343.
Banaji, M. R., & Prentice, D. A. (1994). The self in social contexts. *Annual Review of Psychology, 45,* 297–332.
Baron, R. S., Kerr, N., & Miller, N. (1993). *Group process, group decision, group action.* London: Open University Press.
Baumeister, R. F. (1998). The self. In D. T. Gilbert, S. T. Fiske, & G. Lindzey (Eds.), *The handbook of social psychology* (Vol. 1, 4th ed., pp. 680–740). New York: McGraw-Hill.

Baumeister, R. F., Smart, L., & Boden, J. M. (1996). Relation of threatened egotism to violence and aggression: The dark side of high self-esteem. *Psychological Review, 103*, 5–33.

Bazerman, M. H., Curhan, J. R., Moore, D. A., & Valley, K. L. (2000). Negotiation. *Annual Review of Psychology, 51*, 279–314.

Beersma, B., & De Dreu, C. K. W. (2002). Integrative and distributive negotiation in small groups: Effects of task structure, decision rule, and social motive. *Organizational Behavior and Human Decision Processes, 87*, 227–252.

Beersma, B., & De Dreu, C. K. W. (2005). Conflict's consequences: Effects of social motives on postnegotiation creative and convergent group functioning and performance. *Journal of Personality and Social Psychology, 89*, 358–374.

Beggan, J. K. (1992). On the social nature of nonsocial perception: The mere ownership effect. *Journal of Personality and Social Psychology, 62*, 229–237.

Bendersky, C. (2003). Organizational dispute resolution systems: A complementarities model. *Academy of Management Review, 28*, 643–656.

Blake, R., & Mouton, J. S. (1964). *The managerial grid*. Houston: Gulf.

Bond, R., & Smith, P. B. (1996). Culture and conformity: A meta-analysis of studies using Asch's (1952b, 1956) line judgment task. *Psychological Bulletin, 119*, 111–137.

Borman, W. C., & Motowidlow, S. J. (1993). Expanding the criterion domain to include elements of contextual performance. In N. Schmitt & W. Borman (Eds.), *Personnel selection in organizations* (pp. 71–98). New York: Jossey-Bass.

Bornstein, G. (2003). Intergroup conflict: Individual, group, and collective interests. *Personality and Social Psychology Review, 7*, 129–145.

Bornstein, G., & Erev, I. (1997). The enhancing effect of intergroup competition on group performance. In C. K. W. De Dreu & E. Van de Vliert (Eds.), *Using conflict in organizations* (pp. 116–128). London: Sage.

Braudel, F. (1947). *Mémoires de la Méditerranée*. Paris: Livres de Poches.

Brehmer, B. (1976). Social judgement theory and the analysis of interpersonal conflict. *Psychological Bulletin, 83*, 985–1003.

Brett, J. M., & Gelfand, M. J. (2005). A cultural analysis of the underlying assumptions of negotiation theory. In L. Thompson (Ed.), *Frontiers of social psychology: Negotiations* (pp. 173–201). New York: Psychology Press.

Brett, J. M., Shapiro, D. L., & Lytle, A. L. (1998). Breaking the bonds of reciprocity in negotiations. *Academy of Management Journal, 41*, 410–424.

Brew, F. P., & Cairns, D. R. (2004). Do culture or situational constraints determine choice of direct or indirect styles in intercultural workplace conflicts? *International Journal of Intercultural Relations, 28*, 331–352.

Brief, A. P., Umpress, E. E., Dietz, J., Burrows, J. W., Butz, R. M., & Scholten, L. (2005). Community matters: Realistic group conflict theory and the impact of diversity. *Academy of Management Journal, 48*, 830–844.

Brief, A. P., & Weiss, H. M. (2002). Organizational behaviour: Affect in the workplace. *Annual Review of Psychology, 53*, 279–307.

Bushman, B. J., & Baumeister, R. F. (1998). Threatened egotism, narcissism, self-esteem, and direct and displaced aggression: Does self-love or self-hate lead to violence? *Journal of Personality and Social Psychology, 75*, 219–229.

Cai, D. A., & Fink, E. L. (2002). Conflict style differences between individualists and collectivists. *Communication Monographs, 69*, 67–87.

Campbell, J. D. (1990). Self-esteem and clarity of the self-concept. *Journal of Personality and Social Psychology, 59,* 538–549.

Campbell, W. K., & Sedikides, C. (1999). Self-threat magnifies the self-serving bias: A meta-analytic integration. *Review of General Psychology, 3,* 23–43.

Carnevale, P. J. (2004). *Ownership and identification in social conflict.* Paper presented at the annual meeting of the Society for Experimental Social Psychology, Columbus, OH.

Carnevale, P. J., & Probst, T. M. (1998). Social values and social conflict in creative problem solving and categorization. *Journal of Personality and Social Psychology, 74,* 1300–1309.

Carnevale, P. J., & Pruitt, D. G. (1992). Negotiation and mediation. *Annual Review of Psychology, 43,* 531–82.

Carnevale, P. J., Pruitt, D. G., & Seilheimer, S. (1981). Looking and competing: Accountability and visual access in integrative bargaining. *Journal of Personality and Social Psychology, 40,* 111–120.

Chen, X., & Li, S. (2005). Cross-national differences in cooperative decision-making in mixed-motive business contexts: The mediating effect of vertical and horizontal individualism. *Journal of International Business Studies, 36,* 622–636.

Choi, I., Nisbett, R. E., & Norenzayan, A. (1999). Causal attribution across cultures: Variation and universality. *Psychological Bulletin, 125,* 47–63.

Cohen, G. L., & Sherman, D. K. (2002). Accepting threatening information: Self-affirmation and the reduction of defensive biases. *Current Directions in Psychological Science, 11,* 119–123.

Colman, A. M. (2003). Cooperation, psychological game theory, and limitations of rationality in social interaction. *Behavioral and Brain Sciences, 26,* 139–198.

Coombs, C. H. (1987). The structure of conflict. *American Psychologist, 42,* 355–363.

Coser, L. A. (1956). *The functions of social conflict.* New York: The Free Press.

De Dreu, C. K. W. (2004). Motivation in negotiation: A social psychological analysis. In M. J. Gelfand & J. M. Brett (Eds.), *The handbook of negotiation and culture* (pp. 114–135). Stanford, CA: Stanford University Press.

De Dreu, C. K. W. (2005). A PACT against conflict escalation in negotiation and dispute resolution. *Current Directions in Psychological Science, 14,* 149–152.

De Dreu, C. K. W. (2006). When too much and too little hurts: Evidence for a curvilinear relationship between task conflict and innovation in teams. *Journal of Management, 32,* 83–107.

De Dreu, C. K. W., Beersma, B., Steinel, W., & Van Kleef, G. A. (2007). The psychology of negotiation: Principles and basic processes. In A. W. Kruglanski & E. T. Higgins (Eds.), *Handbook of basic principles in social psychology* (2nd ed.). New York: Guilford.

De Dreu, C. K. W., Beersma, B., Stroebe, K., & Euwema, M. C. (2006). Motivated information processing, strategic choice, and the quality of negotiated agreement. *Journal of Personality and Social Psychology, 90*(6), 927–943.

De Dreu, C. K. W., & Carnevale, P. J. (2005). Disparate methods and common findings in the study of negotiation. *International Negotiation, 10,* 193–203.

De Dreu, C. K. W., & Carnevale, P. J. D. (2003). Motivational bases of information processing and strategy in conflict and negotiation. In M. P. Zanna (Ed.), *Advances in Experimental Social Psychology* (Vol. 35, pp. 235–291). New York: Academic Press.

De Dreu, C. K. W., Evers, A., Beersma, B., Kluwer, E. S., & Nauta, A. (2001). A theory-based measure of conflict management strategies in the workplace. *Journal of Organizational Behavior, 22,* 645–668.

De Dreu, C. K. W., Harinck, F., & Van Vianen, A. E. M. (1999). Conflict and performance in groups and organizations. In C. L. Cooper & I. Robertson (Eds.), *International Review of Industrial and Organizational Psychology* (Vol. 14, pp. 369–414). Chichester, UK: Wiley.

De Dreu, C. K. W., Nauta, A., & Van de Vliert, E. (1995). Self-serving evaluation of conflict behavior and escalation of the dispute. *Journal of Applied Social Psychology, 25,* 2049–2066.

De Dreu, C. K. W., & Van de Vliert, E. (Eds.). (1997). *Using conflict in organizations.* London: Sage.

De Dreu, C. K. W., Van Dierendonck, D., & Dijkstra, M. T. (2004). Looking back, looking ahead: Conflict at work and individual health and well-being. *International Journal of Conflict Management, 15,* 1–18.

De Dreu, C. K. W., & Van Kleef, G. A. (2004). Power, social categorization, and social motivation in negotiation: Implications for managers and organizational leaders. In D. Van Knippenberg & M. A. Hogg (Eds.), *Leadership and power* (pp. 153–168). London: Sage.

De Dreu, C. K. W., & Van Knippenberg, D. (2005). The possessive self as a barrier to constructive conflict management: Effects of mere ownership, process accountability, and self-concept clarity on competitive cognitions and behavior. *Journal of Personality and Social Psychology, 89,* 345–357.

De Dreu, C. K. W., & Van Vianen, A. E. M. (2001). Managing relationship conflict and the effectiveness of organizational teams. *Journal of Organizational Behavior, 22,* 309–328.

De Dreu, C. K. W., & Weingart, L. R. (2003a). Task versus relationship conflict, team perfomance and team member satisfaction: A meta-analysis. *Journal of Applied Psychology, 88,* 741–749.

De Dreu, C. K. W., & Weingart, L. R. (2003b). Toward a contingency theory of conflict and performance in groups and organizational teams. In M. A. West, D. Tjosvold, & K. Smith (Eds.), *International handbook of organizational teamwork and cooperative working* (pp. 151–166). Chichester, UK: Wiley.

De Dreu, C. K. W., Weingart, L. R., & Kwon, S. (2000). Influence of social motives on integrative negotiation: A meta-analytical review and test of two theories. *Journal of Personality and Social Psychology, 78,* 889–905.

Derlega, V. J., Cukur, C. S., Kuang, J. C., & Forsyth, D. R. (2002). Independent construal of self and the endorsement of conflict resolution strategies in interpersonal, intergroup and international disputes. *Journal of Cross-Cultural Psychology, 33,* 610–625.

Deutsch, M. (1949). A theory of cooperation and competition. *Human Relations, 2,* 129–151.

Deutsch, M. (1973). *The resolution of conflict: Constructive and destructive processes.* New Haven, CT: Yale University Press.

Deutsch, M., & Gerard, H. (1955). A study of normative and informational social influences upon individual judgment. *Journal of Abnormal and Social Psychology, 51,* 629–636.

de Waal, F. B. M. (1989). *Peacemaking among primates.* Cambridge, MA: Harvard University Press.

Dietz, J., Robinson, S. L., Folger, R., Baron, R. A., & Schultz, M. (2003). The impact of community violence and an organization's procedural justice climate on workplace aggression. *Academy of Management Journal, 46,* 317–326.

Dijkstra, M. T. M., Van Dierendonck, D., Evers, A., & De Dreu, C. K. W. (2005). Conflict and well-being: The moderating role of personality. *Journal of Managerial Psychology, 20,* 87–104.

Doise, W., Mugny, G., & Perret-Clermont, A. N. (1975). Social interaction and the development of cognitive operations. *European Journal of Social Psychology, 5,* 367–383.

Druckman, D. (1994). Determinants of compromising behavior in negotiation: A meta-analysis. *Journal of Conflict Resolution, 38,* 507–556.

Druckman, D., & Zechmeister, K. (1973). Conflict of interest and value dissensus: Propositions in the sociology of conflict. *Human Relations, 26,* 449–466.

Ellemers, N. (1993). Influence of socio-structural variables on identity enhancement strategies. *European Review of Social Psychology, 4,* 27–57.

Ellemers, N., Kortekaas, P., & Ouwerkerk, J. (1999). Self-categorization, commitment to the group and social self-esteem as related but distinct aspects of social identity. *European Journal of Social Psychology, 28,* 371–98.

Ellemers, N., Spears, R., & Doosje, B. (2002). Self and social identity. *Annual Review of Psychology, 53,* 161–186.

Erev, I., Bornstein, G., & Galili, R. (1993). Constructive intergroup competition as a solution to the free rider problem: A field experiment. *Journal of Experimental Social Psychology, 29,* 463–478.

Exline, J. J., Baumeister, R. F., Bushman, B. J., Campbell, W. K., & Finkel, E. J. (2004). Too proud to let go: Narcissistic entitlement as a barrier to forgiveness. *Journal of Personality and Social Psychology, 87,* 894–912.

Festinger, L. (1954). A theory of social comparison processes. *Human Relations, 7,* 117–140.

Friedman, R., Chi, S., & Liu, L. A. (2006). An expectancy model of Chinese-American differences in conflict-avoiding. *Journal of International Business Studies, 37,* 76–91.

Friedman, R. A., & Currall, S. C. (2003). Conflict escalation: Dispute exacerbating elements of e-mail communication. *Human Relations, 56,* 1325–1427.

Gabrielidis, C., Stephan, W. G., Ybarra, O., Pearson, V. M., & Villareal, L. (1997). Preferred styles of conflict resolution: Mexico and the United States. *Journal of Cross-Cultural Psychology, 28,* 661–677.

Gelfand, M. J., & Brett, J. (Eds.). (2004). *The handbook of negotiation and culture.* Stanford, CA: Stanford University Press.

Gelfand, M. J., Erez, M., & Aycan, Z. (in press). Cross-cultural organizational behaviour. *Annual Review of Psychology.*

Gelfand, M. J., Higgins, M., Nishii, L., Raver, J., Dominguez, A., Yamaguchi, S., et al. (2002). Culture and egocentric biases of fairness in conflict and negotiation. *Journal of Applied Psychology, 87,* 833–845.

Gelfand, M. J., Nishii, L. H., Holcombe, K., Dyer, N., Ohbuchi, K., & Fukumo, M. (2001). Cultural influences on cognitive representations of conflict: Interpretations of conflict episodes in the U.S. and Japan. *Journal of Applied Psychology, 86,* 1059–1074.

Gelfand, M. J., & Realo, A. (1999). Individualism-collectivism and accountability in intergroup negotiations. *Journal of Applied Psychology, 84,* 721–736.

George, J. M. (1991). State or trait: Effects of positive mood on prosocial behaviours at work. *Journal of Applied Psychology, 76,* 299–307.

Goncalo, J. A., & Staw, B. M. (2006). Individualism-collectivism and group creativity. *Organizational Behavior & Human Decision Processes, 100,* 96–109.

Greenhalgh, L. (1987). Interpersonal conflicts in organizations. In C. L. Cooper & I .T. Robertson (Eds.), *International review of industrial and organizational psychology* (pp. 229–272). Chichester, UK: Wiley.

Greenwald, A. (1980). The totalitarian ego: Fabrication and revision of personal history. *American Psychologist, 35,* 603–618.

Harinck, F., & De Dreu, C. K. W. (2004). Negotiating interests or values and reaching integrative agreements: The importance of time pressure and temporary impasses. *European Journal of Social Psychology, 34,* 595–612.

Harinck, F., & De Dreu, C. K. W. (in press). Does taking a break help or hinder negotiation? Effects of mind set and cognitive activity. *Journal of Experimental Social Psychology.*

Harinck, F., De Dreu, C. K. W., & Van Vianen, A. E. M. (2000). The impact of conflict issues on fixed-pie perceptions, problem solving, and integrative outcomes in negotiation. *Organizational Behavior and Human Decision Processes, 81,* 329–358.

Haslam S. A., & Turner J. C. (1992). Context-dependent variation in social stereotyping 2: The relationship between frame of reference, self-categorization and accentuation. *European Journal of Social Psychology, 22,* 251–277

Heatherton, T. F., & Ambady, N. (1993). Self-esteem, self-prediction, and living up to commitments. In R. F. Baumeister (Ed.), *Self-esteem: The puzzle of low self-regard* (pp. 131–145). New York: Plenum Press.

Heine, S. J., Lehman, D. R., Markus, H. R., & Kitayama, S. (1999). Is there a universal need for positive self-regard? *Psychological Review, 106,* 766–794.

Hilty, J. A., & Carnevale, P. J. (1992). Black-hat/white-hat strategy in bilateral negotiation. *Organizational Behavior and Human Decision Processes, 55,* 444–469.

Hoffman, D. A., Griffin, M. A., & Gavin, M. B. (2000). The application of hierarchical linear modeling to organizational research. In K. J. Klein & S. W. J. Kozlowski (Eds.) *Multilevel theory, research, and methods in organizations* (pp. 467–511). San Francisco, CA: Jossey-Bass, Inc.

Holt, J. L., & De Vore, C. J. (2005). Culture, gender, organizational role, and styles of conflict resolution: A meta-analysis. *International Journal of Intercultural Relations, 29,* 165–196.

Homan, A. C., Van Knippenberg, D., Van Kleef, G. A., & De Dreu, C. K. W. (in press). Bridging faultlines by valuing diversity: The effects of diversity beliefs on information elaboration and performance in diverse workgroups. *Journal of Applied Psychology.*

Huber, R., Panksepp, J. B., Yue, Z., Delago, A., & Moore, P. (2001). Dynamic interactions of behavior and amine neurochemistry in acquisition and maintenance of social rank in crayfish. *Brain, Behavior and Evolution, 57,* 271–282.

Ilgen, D. R., & Klein, H. J. (1988). Organizational behavior. *Annual Review of Psychology, 40,* 327–351.

Janis, I. L. (1972). *Victims of groupthink: A psychological study of foreign-policy decisions and fiascos.* Boston: Houghton Mifflin.

Janssen, O. (2003). Innovative behaviour and job involvement at the price of conflict and less satisfactory relations with co-workers. *Journal of Occupation and Organizational Psychology, 76,* 347–364.

Jehn, K. (1994). Enhancing effectiveness: An investigation of advantages and disadvantages of value-based intragroup conflict. *International Journal of Conflict Management, 5*, 223–238.

Jehn, K. (1995). A multimethod examination of the benefits and detriments of intragroup conflict. *Administrative Science Quarterly, 40*, 256–282.

Jehn, K. (1997). Affective and cognitive conflict in work groups: Increasing performance through value-based intragroup conflict. In C. K. W. De Dreu & E. Van de Vliert (Eds.), *Using conflict in organizations* (pp. 87–100). London: Sage.

Jehn, K., & Mannix, E. (2001). The dynamic nature of conflict: A longitudinal study of intragroup conflict and group performance. *Academy of Management Journal, 44*, 238–251.

Jehn, K., Northcraft, G. B., & Neale, M. A. (1999). Why differences make a difference: A field study of diversity, conflict, and performance in workgroups. *Administrative Science Quarterly, 44*, 741–763.

Jehn, K. A., & Bendersky, C. (2003). Intragroup conflict in organizations: A contingency perspective on the conflict-outcome relationship. In B. Staw & R. Kramer (Eds.), *Research in organizational behavior* (Vol. 25, pp. 187–242). Oxford, UK: Elsevier Science, Inc.

Jordan, C. H., Spencer, S. J., Zanna, M. P., Hoshino-Browne, E., & Correll, J. (2003). Secure and defensive high self-esteem. *Journal of Personality and Social Psychology, 85*, 969–978.

Jussim, L., Yen, H., & Aiello, J. R. (1995). Self-consistency, self-enhancement, and accuracy in reactions to feedback. *Journal of Experimental Social Psychology, 31*, 322–356.

Kahneman, D., Knetsch, J. L., & Thaler, R. H. (1990). Experimental tests of the endowment effect and the Coase Theorem. *Journal of Political Economy, 98*, 1325–1348.

Kaplan, M. F., & Miller, C. E. (1987). Group decision making and normative versus informational influence: Effects of type of issue and assigned decision rule. *Journal of Personality and Social Psychology, 53*, 306–313.

Katz, D., & Kahn, D. (1978). *The social psychology of organizing.* New York: McGraw Hill.

Keeley, L. H. (1996). *War before civilization: The myth of the peaceful savage.* New York: Oxford University Press.

Kelley, H. H., & Thibaut, J. W. (1978). *Interpersonal relations: A theory of interdependence.* New York: Academic Press.

Kernis, M. H., Grannemann, B. D., & Barclay, L. C. (1989). Stability and level of self-esteem as predictors of anger arousal and hostility. *Journal of Personality and Social Psychology, 56*, 1013–1022.

Klein, K. L., & Kozlowski, S. W. J. (Eds.). (2000). *Multilevel theory, research, and methods in organizations: Foundations, extensions, and new directions.* San Francisco: Jossey-Bass.

Kramer, R. M. (1991). The more the merrier? Social psychological aspects of multiparty negotiations in organizations. In R. Lewicki, B. Sheppard, & M. Bazerman (Eds.), *Research on negotiation in organizations* (Vol. 3, pp. 307–332). Greenwich, CT: JAI Press.

Kruger, J., & Dunning, D. (1999). Unskilled and unaware of it: How difficulties in recognizing one's own incompetence lead to inflated self-assessments. *Journal of Personality and Social Psychology, 77*, 1121–1134.

Langer, E. (1975). The illusion of control. *Journal of Personality and Social Psychology, 32*, 311–328.

Lau, D. C., & Murnighan, J. K. (1998). Demographic diversity and faultlines: The compositional dynamics of organizational groups. *Academy of Management Review, 23*, 325–340.

Levine, J. M., Resnick, L. B., & Higgins, E. T. (1993). Social foundations of cognition. *Annual Review of Psychology, 44*, 586–612.

Levine, J. M., & Thompson, L. L. (1996). Conflict in groups. In E. T. Higgins, and A. W. Kruglanski (Eds.), *Social psychology: Handbook of basic principles* (pp. 745–776). New York: Guilford.

Lewicki, R. J., Weiss, S. E., & Lewin, D. (1992). Models of conflict, negotiation, and third party intervention: A review and synthesis. *Journal of Organizational Behavior, 13*, 209–252

Markus, H., & Wurf, E. (1987). The dynamic self-concept: A social psychological perspective. *Annual Review of Psychology, 38*, 299–337.

Mikolic, J. M., Parker, J. C., & Pruitt, D. G. (1997). Escalation in response to persistent annoyance: Groups versus individuals and gender effects. *Journal of Personality and Social Psychology, 72*, 151–163.

Miller, J. G. (1984). Culture and the development of everyday social explanation. *Journal of Personality and Social Psychology, 46*, 961–978.

Mo'az, I., Ward, A., Katz, M., & Ross, L. (2002). Reactive devaluation of an "Israeli" vs. "Palestinian" peace proposal. *Journal of Conflict Resolution, 46*, 515–546.

Morris, M. W., Leung, K., & Iyengar, S. S. (2004). Person perception in the heat of conflict: Negative trait attributions affect procedural preferences and account for situational and cultural differences. *Asian Journal of Social Psychology, 7*, 127–147.

Morris, M. W., & Peng, K. (1994). Culture and cause: American and Chinese attributions for social and physical events. *Journal of Personality and Social Psychology, 67*, 949–971.

Morris, M. W., Williams, K. Y., Leung, K., Larrick, R., Mendoza, M. T., et al. (1998). Conflict management style: Accounting for cross-national differences. *Journal of International Business Studies, 29*, 729–747.

Moscovici, S. (1980). Toward a theory of conversion behavior. In L. Berkowitz (Ed.), *Advances in experimental social psychology* (Vol. 13, pp. 209–239). New York: Academic Press.

Murnighan, J. K. (1978). Models of coalition behavior: Game theoretic, social psychological and political perspectives. *Psychological Bulletin, 85*, 1130–1153.

Murnighan, J. K., & Conlon, D. E. (1991). The dynamics of intense work groups: A study of British string quartets. *Administrative Science Quarterly, 36*, 165–186.

Neale, M. A., & Bazerman, M. H. (1991). *Rationality and cognition in negotiation.* New York: Free Press.

Nemeth, C. (1986). Differential contributions of majority and minority influence processes. *Psychological Review, 93*, 10–20.

Nemeth, C. J., & Staw, B. M. (1989). The tradeoffs of social control and innovation in groups and organizations. In L. Berkowitz (Ed.), *Advances in Experimental Social Psychology* (Vol. 22, pp. 175–210). New York: Academic Press.

Ng, K. Y., & Van Dyne, L. (2001). Individualism-collectivism as a boundary condition for effectiveness of minority influence in decision making. *Organizational Behavior & Human Decision Processes, 84,* 198–225.

Nibler, R., & Harris, K. L. (2003). The effects of culture and cohesiveness on intragroup conflict and effectiveness. *Journal of Social Psychology, 142,* 613–631.

O'Connor, K. (1997). Motives and cognitions in negotiation: A theoretical integration and empirical test. *International Journal of Conflict Management, 8,* 114–131.

Oetzel, J. G., Ting-Toomey, S., Masumoto, T., Yokochi, Y., Pan, X., et al. 2001. Face and facework in conflict: A cross-cultural comparison of China, Germany, Japan, and the United States. *Communication Monographs, 68,* 235–258.

Olekalns, M., Brett, J. M., & Weingart, L. R. (2003). Phases, transitions, and interruptions. Modelling processes in multi-party negotiations. *International Journal of Conflict Management, 14,* 191–211.

O'Reilly, C. (1991). Organizational behavior: Where we've been, where we're going. *Annual Review of Psychology, 42,* 427–458.

Organ, D. W. (1988). *Organizational citizenship behavior: The good soldier syndrome.* Lexington, MA: Lexington Books.

Ostrom, E. (1998). A behavioral approach to the rational choice theory of collective action. *The American Political Science Review, 92,* 1–22.

Pearson, V. M. S., & Stephan, W. G. (1998). Preferences for styles of negotiation: A comparison of Brazil and the U.S. *International Journal of Intercultural Relations, 22,* 67–83.

Pepitone, A., & Triandis, H. C. (1987). On the universality of social psychological theories. *Journal of Cross-Cultural Psychology, 18,* 471–498.

Peterson, E., & Thompson, L. L. (1997). Negotiation teamwork: The impact of information distribution and accountability on performance depends on the relationship among team members. *Organizational Behavior and Human Decision Processes, 72,* 364–383.

Peterson, R. B., & Behfar, K. J. (2003). The dynamic relationship between performance feedback, trust and conflict in groups: A longitudinal study. *Organizational Behavior and Human Decision Processes, 92,* 102–112.

Pfeffer, J. (1997). *New directions in organizational behavior.* Oxford, UK: Oxford University Press.

Podsakoff, P. M., Ahearne, M., & MacKenzie, S. B. (1997). Organizational citizenship behavior and the quantity and quality of work group performance. *Journal of Applied Psychology, 82,* 262–270.

Polzer, J., Stewart, K., & Simmons, J. (1999). A social categorization explanation for framing effects in nested social dilemmas. *Organizational Behavior & Human Decision Processes, 79,* 154–178.

Pondy, L. R. (1967). Organizational conflict: Concepts and models. *Administrative Science Quarterly, 12,* 296–320.

Pritchard, R. D. (1992). Organizational productivity. In M. D. Dunnette & L. M. Hough (Eds.), *Handbook of industrial and organizational psychology* (2nd ed., Vol. 3, pp. 443–471). Palo Alto, CA: Consulting Psychologists Press.

Probst, T. M., Carnevale, P. J., & Triandis, H. C. (1999). Cultural values in intergroup and single-group social dilemmas. *Organizational Behavior & Human Decision Processes, 77,* 171–91.

Pruitt, D. G. (1981). *Negotiation behavior.* New York: Academic Press.

Pruitt, D. G. (1998). Social conflict. In D. T. Gilbert, S. T. Fiske, & G. Lindzey (Eds.), The handbook of social psychology (Vol. 2, 4th ed., pp. 470–503). New York: McGraw-Hill.

Pruitt, D. G., & Rubin, J. Z. (1986). *Social conflict: Escalation, stalemate, and settlement.* New York: Random House.

Putnam, L. L. (1997). Productive conflict: Negotiation as implicit coordination. In C. K. W. De Dreu zand E. Van de Vliert (Eds.), *Using conflict in organizations* (pp. 147–160). London: Sage.

Rapoport, A. (1960). *Fights, games, and debates.* Ann Arbor: University of Michigan Press.

Robert, C., & Carnevale, P. J. (1997). Group choice in ultimatum bargaining. *Organizational Behavior and Human Decision Processes, 72,* 256–279.

Rousseau, D. M. (1997). Organizational behavior in the new organizational era. *Annual Review of Psychology, 48,* 515–546.

Rubin, J. Z., Pruitt, D. G., & Kim, S. H. (1994). *Social conflict: Escalation, stalemate, and settlement.* New York: McGraw-Hill.

Rusbult, C. E., & Van Lange, P. A. M. (2003). Interdependence, interaction and relationships. *Annual Review of Psychology, 54,* 351–375.

Salancik, G. R., & Pfeffer, J. (1978) A social information processing approach to job attitudes and task design. *Administrative Science Quarterly, 23,* 224–253.

Schneider, B. (1987). The people make the place. *Personnel Psychology, 40,* 437–453.

Schulz-Hardt, S., Jochims, M., & Frey, D. (2002). Productive conflict in group decision making: Genuine and contrived dissent to as strategies to counteract biased information seeking. *Organizational Behavior and Human Decision Processes, 88,* 563–586.

Sedikides, C., & Strube, M. J. (1997). Self evaluation: To thine own self be good, to thine own self be sure, to thine own self be true, and to thine own self be better. In M. P. Zanna, (Ed.), *Advances in experimental social psychology* (Vol. 29, pp. 209–269). San Diego, CA: Academic Press.

Sherif, M., & Sherif, C. W. (1953). *Groups in harmony and tension; an integration of studies of intergroup relations.* New York: Harper and Brothers.

Shteynberg, G., Gelfand, M. J., & Kim, H. G. (2005, April). *The cultural psychology of revenge.* Paper presented at the annual conference of the Society for Industrial and Organizational Psychology, Los Angeles, CA.

Simons, T. L., & Peterson, R. S. (2000). Task conflict and relationship conflict in top management teams: The pivotal role of intragroup trust. *Journal of Applied Psychology, 85,* 102–111.

Spears, R., Doosje, B., & Ellemers, N. (1997). Self-stereotyping in the face of threats to group status and distinctiveness: The role of group identification. *Personality and Social Psychology Bulletin, 23,* 538–53

Spector, P. E., & Jex, S. M. (1998). Development of four self-report measures of job stressors and strain: Interpersonal Conflict at Work Scale, Organizational Constraints Scale, Quantitative Workload Inventory, and Physical Symptoms Inventory. *Journal of Occupational Health Psychology, 3,* 356–367.

Stanne, M. B., Johnson, D. W., & Johnson, R. T. (1999). Does competition enhance or inhibit motor performance: A meta-analysis. *Psychological Bulletin, 125,* 133–154.

Staw, B. M. (1984). Organizational behavior: A review and reformulation of the field's outcome variables. *Annual Review of Psychology, 35,* 627–666.

Steele, C. M. (1988). The psychology of self-affirmation: Sustaining the integrity of the self. In L. Berkowitz (Ed.), *Advances in experimental social psychology* (Vol. 21, pp. 261–302). San Diego, CA: Academic Press

Stucke, T., & Sporer, S. L. (2002). When a grandiose self-image is threatened: Narcissism and self-concept clarity as predictors of negative emotions and aggression following ego-threat. *Journal of Personality, 70*, 509–532.

Tajfel, H. (1978). *Differentiation between social groups: Studies in the social psychology of intergroup relations.* New York: Academic Press.

Tajfel, H., & Turner, J. (1979). The social identity of intergroup behavior. In W. A. S. Worchel (Ed.), *Psychology and intergroup relations.* Chicago: Nelson-Hall.

Taylor, S. E., & Brown, J. D. (1988). Illusion and well-being: A social psychological perspective on mental health. *Psychological Bulletin, 103*, 193–210.

Tesser, A., Martin, L. L., & Cornell, D. P. (1996). On the substitutability of self-protective mechanisms. In P. M. Gollwitzer & J. A. Bargh (Eds.), *The psychology of action: Linking cognition and motivation to behavior* (pp. 48–68). New York: Guilford Press.

Tetlock, P. E. (1992). The impact of accountability on judgment and choice: Toward a social contingency model. In L. Berkowitz (Ed.), *Advances in experimental social psychology* (Vol. 25, pp. 331–376). New York: Academic Press.

Thibaut, J. W., & Kelley, H. H. (1959). *The social psychology of groups.* New York: John Wiley & Sons, Ltd.

Thomas, K. W. (1992). Conflict and negotiation processes in organizations. In M. D. Dunnette & L. M. Hough (Eds.), *Handbook of industrial and organizational psychology* (2nd ed., pp. 651–717). Palo Alto, CA: Consulting Psychologists Press.

Thompson, L., & Loewenstein, G. (1992). Egocentric interpretations of fairness and interpersonal conflict. *Organizational Behavior and Human Decision Processes, 51*, 176–197.

Tinsley, C. H. (2001). How negotiators get to yes: Predicting the constellation of strategies used across cultures to negotiate conflict. *Journal of Applied Psychology, 86*, 583–593.

Tinsley, C. H. (2004). Culture and conflict: Enlarging our dispute resolution framework. In M. J. Gelfand, & J. M. Brett (Eds.) *The Handbook of Negotiation and Culture* (pp. 193–212). Stanford, CA: Stanford University Press.

Tinsley, C. H., & Brett, J. M. (2001). Managing workplace conflict in the United States and Hong Kong. *Organizational Behavior & Human Decision Processes, 85*, 360–381.

Tjosvold, D. (1991). *The conflict-positive organization.* Reading, MA: Addison-Wesley.

Tjosvold, D. (1998). Cooperative and competitive goal approach to conflict: Accomplishments and challenges. *Applied Psychology: An International Review, 47*, 285–342.

Tjosvold, D., Poon, M., & Yu, Z. (2005). Team effectiveness in China: Cooperative conflict for relationship building. *Human Relations, 58*, 341–367.

Tjosvold, D., & Sun, H. F. (2002). Understanding conflict avoidance: Relationship, motivations, actions, and consequences. *International Journal of Conflict Management, 13*, 143–164.

Triandis, H. C., Carnevale, P., Gelfand, M. J., et al. (2001). Culture and deception in business negotiations: A multilevel analysis. *International Journal of Cross-Cultural Management, 1*, 73–90.

Trivers, R. L., & Hare, H. (1976). Haploidploidy and the evolution of the social insect. *Science, 191*, 249–263.

Ury, W. L., Brett, J. M., & Goldberg, S. B. (1993). *Getting disputes resolved: Designing systems to cut the costs of conflict.* Cambridge, MA: PON.

Valenzuela, A., Srivastava, J., & Lee, S. (2005). The role of cultural orientation in bargaining under incomplete information: Differences in causal attributions. *Organizational Behavior & Human Decision Processes, 96,* 72–88.

Van de Vliert, E. (1997). *Complex interpersonal conflict behavior: Theoretical frontiers.* Hove, UK: Psychology Press.

Van de Vliert, E., & De Dreu, C. K. W. (1994). Optimizing performance by stimulating conflict. *International Journal of Conflict Management, 5,* 211–222.

Van de Vliert, E., Euwema, M. C., & Huismans, S. E. (1995). Managing conflict with a subordinate or a superior: Effectiveness of conglomerated behavior. *Journal of Applied Psychology, 80,* 271–281.

Van de Vliert, E., Huang, X., & Parker, P. M. (2004). Do colder and hotter climates make richer societies more, but poorer societies less happy and altruistic? *Journal of Environmental Psychology, 24,* 17–30.

Van de Vliert, E., Nauta, A., Euwema, M. C., & Janssen, O. (1997). The effectiveness of mixing problem solving and forcing. In C. K. W. De Dreu & E. Van de Vliert (Eds.), *Using conflict in organizations* (pp. 38–52). London: Sage.

Van Knippenberg, D., De Dreu, C. K. W., & Homan, A. C. (2004). Work group diversity and performance: An integrative review and research agenda. *Journal of Applied Psychology, 89,* 1008–1022.

Van Lange, P. A. M., Ouwerkerk, J. W., & Tazelaar, M. J. A. (2002). How to overcome the detrimental effects of noise in social interaction: The benefits of generosity. *Journal of Personality and Social Psychology, 82,* 768–780.

Van Rijswijk, W., & Ellemers, N. (2002). Context effects on the application of stereotype content to multiple categorizable targets. *Personality and Social Psychology Bulletin, 28.*

Von Collani, G., & Werner, R. (2005). Self-related and motivational constructs as determinants of aggression. An analysis and validation of a German version of the Buss-Perry Aggression Questionnaire. *Personality and Individual Differences, 38,* 1631–1643

Wall, J., & Callister, R. (1995). Conflict and its management. *Journal of Management, 21,* 515–558.

Wall, J. A., Jr. (1991). Impression management in negotiations. In R. A. Giacalone & P. Rosenfeld (Eds.), *Applied impression management: How image-making affects managerial decisions* (pp. 133–156). Thousand Oaks, CA: Sage.

Walton, R. E., Cutcher-Gershenfeld, J. E., & McKersie, R. B. (1994). *Strategic negotiations: A theory of change in labor-management relations.* Boston: Harvard Business School Press.

Walton, R. E., & McKersie, R. B. (1965). *A behavioral theory of labor negotiations: An analysis of a social interaction system.* New York: McGraw Hill.

Weber, M. J., Kopelman, S., & Messick, D. M. (2004). A conceptual review of decision making in social dilemmas. *Personality and Social Psychology Review, 8,* 281–307.

Weinstein, N. D. (1980). Unrealistic optimism about future life events. *Journal of Personality and Social Psychology, 39,* 806–820.

Wildschut, T., Pinter, B., Vevea, J. L., Insko, C. A., & Schopler, J. (2003). Beyond the group mind: A quantitative review of the interindividual-intergroup discontinuity effect. *Psychological Bulletin, 129,* 698–722.

Wilpert, B. (1995). Organizational behavior. *Annual Review of Psychology, 46,* 59–90.

Wit, A. P., & Kerr, N. L. (2002). "Me versus just us versus us all" categorization and cooperation in nested social dilemmas. *Journal of Personality and Social Psychology, 83,* 616–637.

Zaltman, G., Duncan, R., & Holbeck, J. (1973). *Innovations and organizations.* New York: Wiley.

2

Conflict at Work Throughout the History of Organizations

DAVID JAFFEE
University of North Florida

This chapter provides a metatheoretical analysis of the sources of conflict in organizations, and the role of conflict in organization theory, throughout the past century and a half. The history of organizational conflict will be conceptualized as a history of tension and change in both organizations and the theoretical literature. Tension is created by the human capacity to resist structural constraints and to strive for a more congenial organizational environment. Change is generated by the dialectical interplay between these organizational structures and human reactions. This interchange has produced continuous changes within organizations and has driven the evolution of organizational theories and managerial strategies. There is no final resolution to the organizational tensions and conflicts. They are permanent features of all organizational systems populated by the human factor. The evolution of management strategy and organization theory can be chronicled as a history of trial and error in developing methods and techniques for managing and conceptualizing these tensions.

The first section of this chapter develops the outlines of a theoretical approach explaining organizational conflict and a metatheoretical framework for understanding the evolution of organization and management theory. This sets the stage for the subsequent sections of the chapter that apply the framework to the historical sweep of theoretical developments in the study of organizations. The starting point for this analysis of organizational conflict is the rise of the factory system and the early effort of industrial owners to recruit, control, and extract human labor power. The second critical phase involves the development of scientific management as a formal systematic method for managing organizational conflict and controlling factory workers. This is followed by the shift toward a more humanistic approach to human conflict management in organizations in the form of human relations theory and practice. Rational bureaucracy represents the fourth theoretical approach and organizational strategy for ensuring predictable control of the human factor. This has prompted a fifth phase of organizational theorizing described as "postbureaucratic." All of these approaches to organizational study are designed to understand and manage the human resource. The final section of the chapter considers the most recent literature aimed at further conceptualizing various modes of organizational conflict.

THE FUNDAMENTAL TENSIONS GENERATING ORGANIZATIONAL CONFLICT

All organizations embody two interrelated conflict-generating tensions with which almost every organization theory has had to grapple. The first—originating at the individual level—is based on the unique capacities of humans, as opposed to other organizational inputs or factors of production, to assess, subjectively evaluate, and act to change or resist their environments. The second—operating at the organizational level—is the structural differentiation of tasks, both vertically and horizontally, that produces identification and loyalty to parts rather than the whole. These two fundamental organizational tensions, often working in tandem, are not only responsible for the historical legacy of organizational conflict, but have also stimulated organizational theorizing and managerial strategizing.

Individual-Level Tension

At the most fundamental and general level, organizational conflict stems from the unique capacities of humans. Humans, unlike other "factors of production" or organizational inputs, have the capacity to assess subjectively their environments and act to resist, alter, or counter perceived constraints. When humans are embedded in organizational structures, there is an inherent tension between the goals and objectives of organizational owners and the valued discretion and autonomy of human agents. This human factor tension has manifested itself in forms of conflict that have shaped the history and evolution of organization theories and management practices. Put another way, this tension both produces and is the product of the structures and processes that we call "organization" or "administration."

Two further examples of the human factor tension are worth noting. First, Pondy's (1967) widely applied stage model of organizational conflict included the notion of "latent conflict," defined as the "drive for autonomy." He further explained, "Autonomy needs form the basis of a conflict when one party either seeks to exercise control over some activity that another party regards as his own province or seeks to insulate itself from such control" (p. 297). This is regarded here as an ever-present condition in all organizations; that is, there is always a potential for resistance, noncompliance, and recalcitrance, given the inherent controlling nature of organizational life. This creates a constant state of uncertainty that precludes predictable control, thus requiring theories and practices aimed at conceptualizing and managing the human factor of production.

A second approach to "latent conflict" was identified by S. S. Brehm and J. W. Brehm (1981) in their theory of "psychological reactance." The theory argued that a "threat to or loss of freedom motivates the individual to restore that freedom . . . individuals will sometimes be motivated to resist or act counter to attempted social influence" (p. 4). Organizations are constraining structures that threaten and compromise human freedom, and as such, they generate reactance and resistance.

Organizational Level Tension

A second inherent tension in all organizations is based on the division of work and authority. Differentiation, divisions of labor, hierarchy, and specialization are fundamental organizational principles. In almost all organizations, workers are assigned to particular jobs, departments, levels, and units. Such a differentiated and specialized division of labor can undermine organizational unity and stimulate organizational conflict.

There are two obvious and common divisions of labor within organizations. First, there is the *horizontal division of labor*, where humans carry out different kinds of tasks at the same level of the organization. Second is the *vertical division of labor*, involving differences in power, authority, rewards, and decision making. Differentiation on both dimensions can produce organizational conflict.

Together, these individual and organizational level tensions have contributed to the history of organizational conflict and, in turn, the evolution of organizational and management theories (see Jaffee, 2001). In this context, organizational conflict is viewed as a progressive force that draws attention to organizational problems, encourages critical reflection about the theoretical assumptions informing organizational systems, and drives changes in management practice.

ORGANIZATIONAL CONFLICT AND THE RISE OF THE FACTORY SYSTEM

The emergence of a factory system of production during the early stages of industrial capitalist development in Europe and the United States presaged the beginning of organizational conflict. The perpetual challenge posed by the human factor of production revealed itself even before workers had entered the factory. Capitalist production required that human labor be concentrated under one roof for the purpose of economic activity. However, the would-be workers, anticipating a loss of freedom and autonomy entailed in a subordinate wage–labor relationship with factory owners, engaged in resistance and rebellion. This new relationship posed a threat to roles and identities. A traditional way of life and labor was disrupted. This provoked intense resistance, opposition, and conflict over the emerging organization of factory production (see Bendix, 1956; Gutman, 1975; Montgomery, 1979; Pollard, 1965; Thompson, 1963).

One necessary condition for instituting a factory system of production is the "formal subordination of labor" (Harvey, 1982). In this process, those who might have owned or had access to productive property, providing an independent means of subsistence—such as peasants, small producers, farmers, craftsmen, and artisans—gradually lose control or access to their property. As increasingly larger portions of the population are forced into the labor market, where they must sell their labor power for a wage, the proletariat or working class is created. A large mass of workers is now organizationally constrained within a hierarchical factory system.

However, the establishment of the factory and wage labor system did not signal the end of the battle with labor—only a shift in terrain. The struggle over the formal subordination of labor eventually subsided and was replaced by conflicts between workers and owners over the "real subordination of labor" (Harvey, 1982), entailing various managerial strategies designed to control labor and extract work effort. Since there is no final solution, or one best way, to achieve this objective, it is an ongoing struggle and process in all organizations. A large part of the evolution of organization theory and management strategy can be chronicled as a history of trial and error in developing methods and techniques for this control and extraction.

At the time, however, the monumental challenge of coordinating and controlling large numbers of workers within a single factory had never been confronted on such a scale. During this period, one of the most significant sources of conflict, according to Reinhard Bendix (1956), was "traditionalism"—the ideological way of life among labor-prescribing precapitalist customs, norms, routines and work habits. This stood as the major obstacle to the enforcement of the "new discipline" within the factory. In the United States, the heterogeneity of the labor factor, fueled by the constant flow of immigrants, resulted in a variety of cultural habits that did not fit smoothly into the emerging industrial machine (Gutman, 1975; Montgomery, 1979).

Thus, the factory organization was characterized by an array of competing forces—traditional work habits, an emerging production system, managerial strategies to break traditions and impose discipline, and the reaction and resistance of labor. This produced an equally wide range of strategies to manage and contain the inevitable organizational conflicts. In the early stages, the primary strategy was to develop techniques that could accommodate the traditional culture carried into the factory. The system of "corporate welfare" (Montgomery, 1979), for example, involved a personalized system of labor employment, recruitment, and control within a familial-like environment. Over time, the system of paternalism gave way to a "subcontracting system" (see Clawson, 1980; Littler, 1982). This strategy was utilized not only because it retained the familial relationships between workers and, in this case, the subcontractor or middleman (Bendix, 1956), but also because owners continued to lack sufficient knowledge about production techniques and the labor process (Clawson, 1980). Thus, the subcontractor, who often hired friends and relatives, assumed the managerial tasks of organization and motivation. Among the other, less paternalistic methods designed to overcome problems of factory discipline were physical beating of children, the firing of workers or the threat of dismissal, and monetary fines for lateness, absenteeism, and insubordination (Pollard, 1965). Payment by results and piecework was also used as a means to entice labor to maximize work effort.

Conflict stemmed not just from the reorganization of work life, and the human reaction to it, but the hierarchical managerial command structure inherent in most organizational forms. This new system—in which some command and others obey—had to be bolstered with a legitimizing rationale. Here we find the initial development of "managerial ideology" (Bendix, 1956), which remains a powerful analytic tool for conceptualizing managerial efforts to the present day. As defined by Bendix, managerial ideologies

> interpret the facts of authority and obedience so as to neutralize or eliminate the conflict between the few and many in the interest of a more effective exercise of authority. To do this, the exercise of authority is either denied altogether on the grounds that the few merely order what the many want; or it is justified with the assertion that the few have qualities of excellence which enable them to realize the interests of the many. (p. 13)

The increasingly important ideological strategy of control was a recognition that compliance could not be assured by either the wage labor relationship or the formal authority system, exclusively. There remained the human capacity for subjective and behavioral resistance. As Bendix (1956) put it, "Beyond what commands can effect and supervision control, beyond what incentives can induce and penalties prevent, there exists an exercise of discretion important even in relatively menial jobs, which managers of economic enterprises seek to enlist for the achievement of managerial ends" (p. 251). This residual discretion always allows workers to retain some control over the exertion of mental and physical energy.

In these early stages of developing a factory system of production, we discover the historical legacy of the dialectical interplay involving efforts at organizational control, reactions of human resistance, and modified systems of organizational control to accommodate and contain the resistance (Braverman, 1972; Clawson, 1980; Edwards, 1979; Marglin, 1974). No single method or strategy ensures perpetual organizational harmony. This is clearly illustrated by Edwards' identification of organizations as "contested terrain" yielding a proliferation of managerial control strategies. He analyzed three major forms of control: direct, technical, and bureaucratic.

Direct control involves the personal exercise of authority by bosses over their workers. *Technical control* involves the application of technologies, such as the assembly line, that control and monitor the pace of the labor process. *Bureaucratic control* ties the control of workers to the formal structure and social relations of the bureaucratic organization. Each new form of control is developed and implemented in response to the resistance against, and failure of, its predecessor. Though ultimate and effective control may be an impossible task given the unique capacities of the human labor input, it did not prevent generations of managers, and their consultants, from striving to develop such a system. Nowhere has the law of unintended and unanticipated consequences (Merton, 1957; Portes, 2000) operated with such predictable regularity. A classic example lies with the development of scientific management.

ORGANIZATIONAL CONFLICT AND SCIENTIFIC MANAGEMENT

Scientific management can be viewed as one of the first and best-known attempts to deal systematically with the problem of labor control and recalcitrance. Much of the conflict and tension at the beginning of the twentieth century can be linked to the perception by owners that the considerable residual discretion afforded the factory workers produced inefficiency and relatively low rates of productivity. The system of scientific management, under the direction of Frederick Winslow Taylor (1911), was explicitly designed to address this "labor problem" in a comprehensive fashion. For Taylor, the key to establishing an efficient and productive workplace required the possession and control of knowledge about the methods of production. He was also interested in addressing what he described as "soldiering"—the individual and collective withholding of maximum work effort.

Worker control over production knowledge and know-how placed owners at a serious disadvantage. Skilled workers and foremen, rather than the owners, determined the organization and pace of production. The owners had to depend on these employees to organize production in what was hoped to be the most efficient manner. However, there were no independent and reliable means for determining whether, in fact, output was reaching an optimal level. In this context, as others have noted (see Goldman & Van Houten, 1988), the knowledge of workers was a potent source of power. Though workers depended upon owners for employment, owners depended on the craft knowledge of workers for production to proceed. Shifting the balance of power decisively in favor of owners required eliminating this residual dependence on worker knowledge. Taylor (1911) viewed this as one of the fundamental objectives of scientific management.

Taylor (1911) believed that the application of scientific principles would allow the discovery of the "one best way" to complete any given task. The "one best way" meant that every production process could be reduced to tasks involving basic physical motions and requirements and that human labor could be assigned these narrowly defined tasks as parts are fitted into a machine. Labor would then conform to the existing scientifically determined tasks already in place, rather than determining its structure. In this way, the organization would operate as a harmonious, well-oiled machine.

Scientific management represented an engineering solution to a human problem. If human organizations of production could be conceptualized as machines, then machine design principles could be applied to organizing the division of labor. The primary challenge was the humans who populate the machine, possessing properties that engineers find least attractive—temperament, resistance, friction, and nonuniformity. Taylor's (1911) science of management was aimed at minimizing the conflict and tension generated by this variable and unpredictable factor of production.

The horizontal differentiation of tasks built into the labor as machine parts paradigm also entailed a vertical dimension. Taylor (1911) noted that, in contrast to earlier systems of management where "practically the whole problem is up to the workman," under scientific management "fully one-half of the problem is up to the management" (p. 38). While the 50–50 split can be viewed as an "equal division" quantitatively, there is a clear qualitative division. Vertically, there are the mental labor exercised by management and the manual labor exercised by workers. The managers conceive. The workers execute. Of course, this perpetual organizational principle of hierarchy would generate further conflict.

The application and implementation of scientific management principles produced a predictable response from human labor. Much of this is documented in a remarkable study of scientific management that was published in 1915 by Robert Hoxie (1966), who was appointed special investigator for the United States Commission on Industrial Relations. He included in his study the official "trade union" position and its specific objections to scientific management. On the question of the meaning of scientific management, labor argued,

"Scientific management" thus defined is a device employed for the purpose of increasing production and profits; and tends to eliminate consideration for the character, rights and welfare of employees. It looks upon the worker as a mere instrument of production and reduces him to a semiautomatic attachment to the machine or tool. It does not take all the elements into consideration but deals with human beings as it does with inanimate machines. . . . "Scientific management" is undemocratic, it is a reversion to industrial autonomy which forces the workers to depend upon the employers' conception of fairness and limits the democratic safeguards of the workers . . . It allows the worker ordinarily no voice in hiring or discharge, the setting of the task, the determination of the wage rate or the general conditions of employment. (pp. 15, 18)

The reaction of labor to the system of scientific management—manifested in turnover, absenteeism, sabotage, low levels of commitment, and collective resistance—prompted revisions in managerial strategies of control. These revisions required a different conceptualization and set of assumptions about the human factor. However, the dynamic tension between human capacities and organizational systems of control, apparent from the earliest attempts to establish the factory system, is a constant force at every historical turn. In his study of the origins of modern management, Pollard (1965) concluded, "it is doubtful whether, within the context of the present structure of society and industry, the dilemmas of its beginnings have been resolved even today" (p. 208).

THE HAWTHORNE EXPERIMENTS AND HUMAN RELATIONS

The Hawthorne experiments represent one of the most influential pieces of research in the history of social science—with wide-ranging implications for organizational human relations (see Mayo 1933, 1945). This was a period of considerable interest in developing more harmonious industrial relations between labor and management and in enhancing productivity levels. The Hawthorne researchers were originally interested in gauging the impact of physical conditions—such as lighting, work layout, work pace—on output and productivity among various work teams. However, the reported paradoxical results of the research—with productivity and output rising regardless the physical conditions, suggested the social dynamics that we now associate with the "Hawthorne effect." (The Hawthorne results have been subjected to considerable critique and revision directed at the unreliability of the data as well as the conclusions reached. For example, see Jones 1992.)

The findings reported from the Hawthorne studies confirmed the existing sociological work on primary groups most closely associated with Charles Cooley (1962). Cooley wrote, "They are primary in several senses but chiefly in that they are fundamental in forming the social nature and ideals of individuals . . . . The individual will be ambitious but the chief object of his ambition will be some desired place in the thought of others" (pp. 23–24). Individuals in primary work groups are able to interact, communicate, discursively establish norms, and coordinate behavior informally. These bonds of solidarity can combine to generate a kind of "synergy" promoting higher than expected levels of human effort. In other cases, as several of the less publicized experiments have indicated, these informal bonds can also galvanize opposition to the interests of management (Katz & Kahn, 1978). The role of informal work groups in all organizations and their abilities to influence behavior and shape organizational performance have produced a vast literature on the use of informal groups to reduce organizational conflict and enhance productivity (Bacharach & Lawler, 1980; Cohen & Bailey, 1997; Guzzo & Dickson, 1996; Roethlisberger & Dickson, 1939).

Armed with the research results from Hawthorne, human relations theory became a core organizational theoretical perspective and managerial strategy acknowledging the inherent complexities of human organization and suggesting methods to minimize potential resistance and conflict. Much greater attention was given to the presumably inherent human needs for social interaction and communication. Management texts place a heavy emphasis on the practical application of human relations assumptions. Understanding needs and promoting communication can reduce conflict and foster compliance, as expressed, for example, in a typical textbook chapter titled "Satisfying Human Needs" (Chung & Megginson, 1981): "Studying human needs is important for understanding organizational behavior, because it explains the internal causes of behavior . . . to manage, direct, and coordinate human behavior in organizations, we need to predict it." Other texts focus on the "communication problem" (Scanlan & Keys, 1979):

> When communications are neglected or overlooked, the organization is depriving itself of some very important benefits . . . . Failure to communicate this information may result in damaging and lowering of morale, not only of a few individuals, but also of the entire organization . . . if properly communicated, enables the employees to feel that they are integral parts of the organization; that is, that they are working *with* it, not just *for* it. (p. 252)

The relationship between human needs and management strategy was further developed with the application of Abraham Maslow's (1943) work on the human needs hierarchy. If the Hawthorne experiments can be viewed as the single most influential workplace study, Maslow's need hierarchy represented the single most influential personality theory. Combining a theory of motivation with a model of human development, Maslow argued that human behavior, over the life span, was directed first toward the satisfaction of simple, or lower-order, needs (e.g., physiological and safety needs) and then, later, the more complex or higher-order needs (e.g., social, ego, and self-actualization needs). Self-actualization, which played a particularly important role in organization and management theory, involved the need to realize one's full potential and capacity as a human being. Presumably, this need could not be realized under standard conditions prevailing in most organizations. Potential sources of conflict—worker alienation and job dissatisfaction—resulting from inadequate organizational structures, work tasks, and managerial authority deprived workers of the opportunity to fulfill this highest order need. The full organizational implications of Maslow's model, and the structural sources of need fulfillment, were perhaps best exemplified in the work of Douglas McGregor (beginning with his 1966 article "The Human Side of Enterprise") and the juxtaposition of "Theory X" and "Theory Y" managerial approaches.

The managerial application of Maslow's (1943) theoretical ideas involved the restructuring and redesign of job tasks and authority structures to enhance levels of variety, autonomy, and participation. McGregor (1966), for example, suggested greater decentralization and delegation, job enlargement, consultative management, and employee-determined performance targets. It is important to emphasize that these workplace reforms would not have been considered were it not for organizational tensions and conflicts prompting reflection and revisions in organization theory and management practice.

A distinction has been made between *human relations theory,* which did not necessarily call into question the scientific management–based organization of production and tasks, and *human resources theory,* which advocated structural reforms to meet ego and self-actualization needs (Tausky, 1970). However, both perspectives offer practical suggestions for reducing tension, conflict, and recalcitrance stemming from the coordination of the human factor. Both assume that managerial strategies can simultaneously satisfy the various needs of workers and advance administrative objectives for efficiency. Human relations theory assumes a human desire for association, while human resource theory assumes a drive for self-actualization (Argyris, 1964; Likert, 1961; McGregor, 1966). Each of these managerial approaches continues to have a significant impact on the structure and processes in most organizations (Pfeffer, 1994). Both were also incorporated into the Japanese-style management reforms (e.g., Toyotaism) popular in the 1980s as a means to gain the consent of workers and address productivity problems (Boswell, 1987; Dohse, Jurgens, & Malsch, 1985; Lincoln & Kalleberg, 1985).

An important qualifier must be added to any discussion of internally initiated organizational restructuring designed to satisfy human needs and elicit consent. That is, managerial discretion over organizational structures and processes is significantly constrained by external or environmental pressures that lie outside the immediate control of management. What has now come to be known as the "open-systems," "environmental," or "resource dependence" model of organizations (Aldrich, 1979; Burns & Stalker, 1961; Lawrence & Lorsch, 1967; Mintz & Schwartz, 1985; Pfeffer & Salancik, 1978; Useem, 1996) posits pressures deriving from market competition, external constituents, buyers, sellers and suppliers, and regulatory agencies. The interorganizational network in which most organizations conduct their businesses dictates the implementation of particular personnel, managerial, and technological strategies that contribute to organizational conflict and tension. These pose a particular challenge for negotiation, resolution, and compromise given that the parties that must be satisfied are "external" and reside outside the formal management and administrative structure of the organization.

In the midst of the humanistic approaches to organizations, and the recognition of environmental constraints, organization theory and practice remained seduced by the compelling attraction of formal structure and instrumental rationality. Thus, the bureaucratic model coexisted, albeit in stressful fashion, alongside new managerial and organizational developments. We can now consider more closely the relationship between bureaucratic organization and conflict and change.

BUREAUCRATIC THEORY AND SOURCES OF CONFLICT

One way to address organizational conflict is to create formal procedures that can guide and facilitate organizational behavior and interactions. This can reduce confusion about role expectations, clarify chains of command, and prescribe appropriate methods for completing tasks and advancing organizational goals. The rational bureaucratic approach to organizations is incorporated conceptually and practically in almost every organization. It is designed to bring rationality and predictability to a human endeavor that routinely defies both.

Embedded in the theory of rational bureaucracy, most closely associated with the work of Max Weber (1947), are three central principles: formalization, instrumentalism, and rational legal authority. *Formalization* is the centerpiece of bureaucracy. It refers to the degree to which rules, procedures, regulations, and task assignments exist in written form. Written documentation indicating the procedures for acting, deciding, and communicating represent the formalization of organizational activity. These written directives exist prior to the entry of people into positions within the organization. They are designed to direct and regulate organizational behavior after one has been slotted into a formal position.

The concept of *instrumentalism* conveys the notion that the organization is like a tool or machine designed to achieve a particular purpose. The formal internal structure—positions, procedures, rules, interaction patterns—is regarded as the instrument that directs and ensures the realization of the larger organizational mission. The explicit formal relationship between the structures and tasks, and goals or objectives, makes bureaucracy a rational organizational instrument.

Weber (1947) emphasized the third central principle, *rational legal authority*, as the most efficient means to gain the compliance of human members. This was contrasted with commanding authority on the basis of tradition (e.g., authority residing in a family name) or charisma (e.g., authority stemming from extraordinary personality or leadership traits). "Legitimate authority" rests on the formal position of the authority figure (therefore legal) in the organizational hierarchy coupled with the belief that these authority relations represent the best means to achieve organizational ends (therefore rational).

It is generally acknowledged that these aspects of bureaucracy are designed to implement a regiment of predictable control and potentially reduce the level of organizational contention. However, bureaucratic structures, characterized as they are by hierarchy and formal constraints, will themselves inevitably produce "latent conflict" (Pondy, 1967) and unintended consequences (Blau, 1955; Gouldner, 1954; Merton, 1957; Selznick, 1957). We shall consider several more specific bureaucratic sources of conflict that have been widely observed and analyzed in organizations.

The first was originally posed as a theoretical problem (Gouldner, 1954; Parsons, 1947), but it has practical implications for organizational harmony. It pertains directly to Weber's (1947) argument about rational legal authority. In Weber's model, the exercise of authority (by those who command) in bureaucratic organizations was legitimate (accepted by those who obey) because it is derived from a formal position (e.g., manager, supervisor) filled on the basis of technical competence (e.g., credentials, knowledge, demonstrated skill, experience). An obvious and real source of conflict in any organization can be found where subordinates do not regard the exercise of authority as legitimate due to the demonstrated absence of technical competence by those in formal positions of authority. Organizational members are then faced with the dilemma of whether they should comply with the directives from a superior purely because the person occupies a formal position of authority, or must that person also demonstrate superior knowledge? If the two characteristics are not joined and those in authoritative positions demonstrate less technical competence than their subordinates, each group has a legitimate claim to exercise authority over the other. This can generate instability and conflict. Gaining the willing compliance of workers may also be problematic because a normative foundation for the exercise of authority—superior knowledge—is being violated.

The notion of "legitimate authority" acknowledges that humans are not bureaucratically programmed automatons but that they have the capacity to subjectively evaluate the authority structure and engage in opposition and resistance. For example, workers can decide that their bosses are not technically competent, that particular methods are not the best way to achieve some goal, or that the goals of the organization conflict with their goals. In all of these cases, the mechanistic bureaucratic model breaks down and other arrangements are required to gain cooperation and compliance.

A second source of bureaucratic conflict, most lucidly identified in the work of Alvin Gouldner (1954, 1955), was discovered during his extensive fieldwork in an industrial mining and manufacturing enterprise. Gouldner was interested in the relationship between the constituency responsible for proposing an organization's bureaucratic rules and the extent to which members comply with the rules. His analysis assumed organizational members do not have the same political and economic interests or goals. More specifically, workers were likely to have different interests than management on most work-related issues. Therefore, bureaucratic rules and regulations should be examined to see whether they represent, or conflict with, the interests of the different parties in the organization. This analytical framework yielded Gouldner's well-known "patterns of industrial bureaucracy"—mock bureaucracy, representative bureaucracy, and punishment-centered bureaucracy—that remain widely applicable.

Mock bureaucracy referred to rules that no party in the organization had a direct interest in and which were, therefore, rarely enforced and routinely violated. Gouldner (1954, 1955) reported on the "no-smoking" rule as one example of mock bureaucracy. Neither managers nor workers had an interest in the prohibition against smoking. The rule was implemented to satisfy the requirements of an external third party—the company insuring the factory against fire damage.

Representative bureaucracy referred to rules that all parties had an interest in and, consequently, were followed closely and were strongly enforced. In the mining facilities, rules and regulations pertaining to safety practices inside the mines were followed to the letter. Both workers and managers had an interest in minimizing workplace injuries and accidents.

Punishment-centered bureaucracy denoted the rules that one group imposes on another. Gouldner (1954, 1955) cited rules that penalize workers for absenteeism and tardiness. Management imposed these rules on the workers. Workers did not share a concern with these matters and believed they had the right to occasionally miss a day of work or arrive late for personal reasons. As would be expected, this form of bureaucracy generated the greatest tension and conflict, and it was the most highly contested. We also most closely associate this form with the term *bureaucracy*. People in organizations who do not believe that those people on whom they depend will fulfill their role obligations create punishment-centered bureaucratic rules. Thus, a lack of trust generates these rules. Therefore, organizations plagued by conflicting interests and low levels of trust are likely to be the most bureaucratically punishment centered.

A third observation, also provided by Gouldner (1960), is worth noting; that is, organizational harmony is often the result of selective nonenforcement of bureaucratic rules. In the manufacturing facility, Gouldner observed what he called an "indulgency pattern" under which managers frequently allowed workers to bypass various rules and requirements. Workers would routinely arrive at work late, take coffee breaks, and socialize on the job in direct violation of written rules and procedures. Gouldner's explanation for nonenforcement by management highlighted a critical factor facilitating organizational harmony—the ability of supervisors to anticipate the consequences of rigid rule enforcement. The strident exercise of supervisory authority would prompt worker resentment and create workplace tension. This would make it difficult to gain the cooperation of workers generally, and more specifically in assisting with tasks that might occasionally lie outside their immediate job responsibility. Therefore, supervisors settled on a posture of tolerance and indulgence. Supervisors had to exercise flexibility *with* workers if they were to expect flexibility *from* workers. This "norm of reciprocity" (Gouldner,

1960) is a critical ingredient in the analysis of organizational conflict and cooperation. The question is whether it can truly operate in a hierarchical organizational structure where one party possesses greater resources than the other.

A fourth major limitation on the applicability of rational bureaucratic principles lies at the center of a literature most closely associated with the works of Herbert Simon, James March, and Richard Cyert (Cyert & March, 1992; March & Simon, 1958; Simon, 1997). The work of Herbert Simon and his colleagues represented one of the most influential efforts to link the abstract principles of the rational model with concrete administrative decision making. Simon's primary objection to rational bureaucratic theory related to the lack of sufficient attention to the human factor and, more specifically, the way humans go about making decisions in organizations.

Simon was best known for developing, with James March, the concept of "bounded rationality" (March & Simon, 1958). March and Simon argued that the humans could not really be expected to make rational optimal decisions given three significant limitations. That is, humans are limited in (a) the amount of information they can access and process, (b) the number of possible alternatives they are able to entertain, and (c) their abilities to predict the consequences of their actions. These constraints limit rational decision making. They also open the door to a wide range of competing courses of action based on the particular type of information one decides to collect, the alternatives various individuals and groups are willing to entertain given their organizational interests, and the abilities to anticipate or admit to negative unintended consequences of a policy proposal.

Gortner's (1977) analysis of administrative decision making posed the problem:

> One of the most important factors that must be considered when discovering the limitations of rationality in decision-making is that of the personal, or psychological, factors that influence the decision maker. . . . The most common types of psychological barriers can be grouped into five general categories: (1) the determination of thought by position in social space; (2) the projection of values and attitudes; (3) over-simplification; (4) cognitive nearsightedness; and (5) identification with outside groups. (pp. 115–116)

As the analysis of organizational decision making has evolved, there has been a growing acknowledgement that the human factor is subject to cognitive influences that preclude the rational calculation of a single optimal course of action (e.g., "projection of values and attitudes," "oversimplification," and "cognitive nearsightedness") and that these are often closely correlated with one's position in the structurally differentiated organization (e.g., "the determination of thought by position in social space" and "identification with outside groups"). The net result is difference, debate, conflict, and competition among organizational members. This is clearly recognized in recent literature on organizational negotiation and conflict resolution (Bazerman & Neale, 1992; Neale & Bazerman, 1991). Subsequent theoretical work done by Simon (1997) and his associates, Cyert and March (1992), also attempted to deal with these challenges by introducing the notion of organizations as coalitions made up of individuals and parties with divergent interests and goals.

The human limitations on rational decision making coupled with the contested nature of top-down bureaucratic organizational decisions and policy—both stemming from the fundamental organizational tensions related to the human factor and the differentiation of tasks and interests—are among the factors stimulating the development of alternative organizational structures. This leads us to a consideration of less bureaucratically configured organizational systems.

THE POSTBUREAUCRATIC PARADIGM AND ORGANIZATIONAL HARMONY

Formal bureaucratic organizational models are increasingly viewed as antithetical to productive and efficient organizational process, the need for organizations to be more flexible and adaptive in relation to their environment, and the increasingly knowledge-based labor processes requiring greater cooperation and collaboration. Together, these forces create tensions and conflicts within bureaucratic organizations that prompt alternative paradigms and managerial practices. Postbureaucracy is clearly the trend in both the practical world of management and the theoretical world of organizational studies (Barzelay, 1992; Clegg, 1990; Heckscher & Donnelon, 1994). It is also an underlying element in other more recent organizational developments including post-Fordism, lean production, and flexible specialization (Castells, 1996; Harrison, 1994; Piore & Sabel, 1984; Sayer & Walker, 1992; Womack, Jones, & Roos, 1990).

Heckscher (1994) outlined the main features of postbureaucracy. In contrast to bureaucratic theory, organizational efficiency and harmony in this model are based not on formalization, instrumentalism, or rational legal authority but rather on dialogue, persuasion, and trust. Based on the preceding discussion, this would suggest a reduced need for formal authority and punishment-centered bureaucratic rules. Consensual participatory decision making carries the day.

Practices supporting the postbureaucratic organization include information sharing and dissemination; organizational behavior and action guided not by formal roles and job descriptions but by professional principles; interaction, communication, and decision making driven by problems and projects rather than top-down directives; and evaluation and reward based on peer input and negotiated standards of performance.

Taken together, Heckscher's (1994) ideal type postbureaucracy rested on what he called the "master concept" which is

an organization in which everyone takes responsibility for the success of the whole. If that happens, then the basic notion of regulating relations among people by *separating* them into specific predefined functions must be abandoned . . . organizational control must center not on the management of tasks, but the management of relationships . . . they are essentially structures that develop *informed consensus* rather than relying on hierarchy and authority. (p. 24)

The postbureaucratic organization proposes replacing one method of control—formal structural differentiation of functions and authority—with another, structures that develop "informed consent." This poses a central organizational tension: In the absence of formal bureaucratic control and coordination, organizational members are given wide latitude to pursue a variety of goals. Control in this model is regained through collective peer pressure and obligations stemming from team membership. Social integration takes precedence over differentiation and specialization. In such nonbureaucratic organizational settings, "organizational culture" (Schein, 1992) does the heavy lifting in the management of individual behavior and social relationships. More specifically, organizations require "strong cultures," which are "based on intense emotional attachment and the internalization of 'clearly enunciated company values' that often replace formal structures . . . . The ideal employees are those who have internalized the organization's goals and values—its culture—into their cognitive and affective make-up, and therefore no longer require strict and rigid external control" (Kunda, 1992, p. 10). These modes of "normative control" (Etzioni, 1961) are designed to contain the ever-present latent conflict inherent in all organizations.

CURRENT TRENDS AND FUTURE DIRECTIONS

A number of recent contributions to the analysis of organizational conflict, which do not fall neatly into the broad organization theory categories outlined above, are considered in this final section. We will review the perspectives that focus on the microfoundations of conflict, the role of "dignity" in generating organizational tension and conflict, and the deployment of subtle modes of resistance.

Microfoundations of Organizational Conflict

Bowles and Gintis (1990), two neo-Marxist theorists who traditionally focused on broader forms of social class conflict, developed a model that rests on the microfoundation (rather than macrofoundation) of conflict, embedded in the struggle over individual work effort between workers (labor) and owners (capital). Their analysis assumed that labor (e.g., workers, employees) has a desire to minimize work effort, while capital (e.g., owners, employers) seeks to maximize work effort. The traditional method for extracting work effort and discouraging lollygagging is the threat of dismissal. The problem from the perspective of owners, however, is that the amount of effort employees expend is difficult to gauge effectively and reliably. This is increasingly the case as work becomes less manual and more mental, less the production of physical objects and more the production and organization of knowledge. Employers can attempt to measure work effort through greater supervision, bureaucratic monitoring, and surveillance. However, as the underlying premise of this chapter would suggest, humans subjected to this regime of oversight have the capacity to assess this organizational arrangement subjectively. They may assume that it represents a pronounced lack of trust by employers, and this may produce greater hostility and resentment. Added to the potentially negative impact on worker morale are the "hard" costs associated with layers of additional supervisory management (what David Gordon, 1996, called "guard labor") and technological monitoring devices. A new dilemma is generated: Do the hard (e.g., personnel, technology) and soft (e.g., employee morale, organizational climate) costs nullify the gains derived from the enhanced detection of shirking? For economists such as Bowles and Gintis, the additional hard costs produce inefficiencies and nonoptimal outcomes that can only be addressed by examining and reconfiguring the microfoundational relations between labor and capital, in particular, the different interests workers and owners have in the expending of work effort. One solution to this conflict—workers' ownership and control—would give workers an interest in efficiency and productivity. Workers would self-monitor their own efforts and have an interest in also monitoring the efforts of their coworkers. This would presumably produce greater harmony and productivity without the heavy costs of bureaucratic surveillance and worker distrust.

Worker Dignity and Conflict

More recently, Randy Hodson (2001) advanced the concept of "dignity" as a key entry point into workplace relations and organizational conflict. Hodson suggested that all humans have an inherent dignity that is developed through social action, as an inalienable trait carried into the organization by the human factor of production. More specifically, "workers from all walks of life struggle to achieve dignity and to gain some measure of meaning and self-realization at work. The achievement of dignity at work thus depends on creative and purposive activity on the part of workers" (Hodson, p. 4). Dignity is something that all humans desire and seek to realize in the various spheres of social participation. It entails self-worth, self-respect, and enjoying the respect of others. In the context of work and organization, it is assumed that the realization of dignity is potentially problematic, prompting active strategies for achieving and protecting dignity. Organizational conflict in this formulation stems from organizational arrangements and managerial practices that threaten dignity and that generate employee actions in defense of dignity.

Hodson (2001) did not presume an inherently antagonistic relationship between workers and owners that would yield perpetual organizational conflict. Rather, his theoretical scheme and empirical analysis was built around ethnographic case studies of a wide range of workplace settings that could produce a wide range of outcomes. He did presume that most workers take pride in and seek meaning from their work and that they are willing to expend considerable work effort as a result. Various workplace conditions, however, make this difficult and can prompt reactions that can conflict with managerial dictates. Among these workplace conditions generating conflict, Hodson identified mismanagement and abuse, overwork, challenges to autonomy, and contradictions of employee involvement.

The first two conditions—mismanagement and abuse, and overwork—are most common in work settings characterized by unilateral managerial power and control. *Mismanagement* denotes a chaotic and disorganized workplace that results from irresponsible, incompetent, and poorly trained management. Workers are challenged under these conditions by inadequate direction, insufficient provision of needed resources, and poor communication. An *abusive* workplace is characterized by the arbitrary, capricious, and inappropriate exercise of power over employees. In both of these cases—mismanagement and abuse—it is less the actual work tasks than the subjective perception by employees of delinquent management practices that represents an affront to dignity and elicits the behavioral response.

Overwork is closely associated with the classic Marxist concept of exploitation. It is manifested in the intensification of labor, the speedup, an accelerated pace of production, and the maximization of the extraction of work effort. It is most common in organizations where productivity and profit depend upon quantitatively measurable output.

The third workplace condition—*challenges to autonomy*—is most common in organizational settings where employees possess more advanced craft skills, or professional credentials, that would lead them to expect the exercise of discretion in the labor process. When management encroaches on employee control over decision making in these settings, efforts to reestablish autonomy and control are a common behavioral response.

The fourth and final workplace condition—*contradictions of employee involvement*—is especially relevant in the current climate of alternative nonbureaucratic, team-based modes of organizational restructuring. The rhetoric of workers' participation, control, and ownership frequently conflicts with the true intentions of management or the actual organization of the labor process. The distinction between expectation and reality gives rise to employee strategies aimed at bridging the gap.

Hodson (2001) analyzed not only the range of conditions that might give rise to organizational conflict but also the behavioral responses of workers to these conditions. Actions taken to "safeguard dignity" are resistance, organizational citizenship, developing independent meaning system, and group relations. These can be regarded as tactics aimed at restoring dignity in the face of unfavorable working conditions. The most significant for the study of organizational conflict is resistance.

Resistance is not only the most common response, but it can also take a variety of both active and passive modes (Hodson, 1995). Actively, employees can engage in direct conflict through sabotage, strikes, walkouts, and confrontations with management and other employees. Passively, employees can withhold their effort and commitment, bypass unpleasant requirements, or engage in noncooperative behavior.

There is now an emerging literature dealing with informal and unorganized forms of resistance in organizations (Davis & McAdam, 2000; Jermier, Knights, & Nord, 1994). Morrill, Zald, and Rao (2003) described "covert political conflict" as the means by which "subordinate groups express their political grievances against superiors, displaying tacit, if not explicit, coordination and various forms of group solidarity. By contrast, organizational elites and superiors typically deploy formally structured instruments of control as they engage in political struggles with subordinates" (p. 392). Differential access to the formal means of social control suggests that subordinates resort to informal covert techniques that can include material and personal sabotage, theft, noncooperation, strategic inaction, and symbolic disrespect or escape. Future studies of organizational conflict are well advised to include and acknowledge these employee strategies that do not necessarily involve formal or interpersonal encounters between conflicting parties.

CONCLUSION

The history of organizational conflict can be analyzed with a metatheoretical framework that identifies the constant and overarching challenges facing all organizations. These challenges, or tensions, stem from the unique capacities of the human factor of production and the differentiation of organizational roles. These two factors not only contribute to the galvanization of resistance and conflict, but they are also a constant preoccupation of organization theories. As permanent features of all human organization, they must be addressed in both theory and practice. This can be clearly demonstrated by a careful review of the historical evolution of organization theory and management practice. Theories based on assumptions about human motivation and needs, and the requisite structural arrangements, inform the implementation of management strategies.

As human action renders the strategy problematic, produces unintended consequences, or provokes challenges and resistance, new organization theories are developed and applied. The new theories and practices meet with the same fate as their predecessors.

Though conflict is often viewed as a dysfunctional aspect of organizations, particularly by those interested in preserving the status quo and maintaining predictable control, it is, in fact, as Marx might have said, the "motor of history." In this case, the engine of change compels organizational owners and managers continually to develop alternative techniques that acknowledge the human factor and that may advance positive and progressive change.

The tension, conflict, and change framework advanced in this chapter is based on the fundamental sociological tenet that situates human behaviors within a social-structural context. While the unique capacity of humans provides the raw material for organizational social dynamics, it is when individuals are embedded in organizational structures—that constrain, control, and differentiate—that the likelihood of tension and conflict increase; that is, we would expect to find various forms of organizational conflict regardless of the particular individual, psychological, or personality characteristics of the population. The big question for the field of organizational conflict is the extent to which conflict stems from the individual traits transported into the organization by organizational members, or whether it is based on behaviors that emerge out of the organization's social structure. Ideally, both levels of analysis must be incorporated into conceptual models and empirical investigations.

REFERENCES

Aldrich, H. (1979). *Organizations and environment*. Englewood Cliffs, NJ: Prentice Hall.

Argyris, C. (1964). *Integrating the individual and the organization*. New York: Wiley.

Bacharach, P., & Lawler, E. L. (1980). *Power and politics in organizations*. San Francisco: Jossey-Bass.

Barzelay, M. (1992). *Breaking through bureaucracy*. Berkeley, CA: University of California Press.

Bazerman, M. H., & Neale, M. A. (1992). *Negotiating rationally*. New York: Free Press.

Bendix, R. (1956). *Work and authority in industry: Ideologies of management in the course of industrialization*. New York: Wiley.

Blau, P. (1955). *The dynamics of bureaucracy*. Chicago: University of Chicago Press.

Boswell, T. (1987). Accumulation innovations in the American economy: The affinity for Japanese solutions to the current crisis. In T. Boswell & A. Bergeson (Eds.), *America's changing role in the world system* (pp. 95–126). New York: Praeger.

Bowles, S., & Gintis, H. (1990). Contest exchange: New microfoundations for the political economy of capitalism. *Politics and Society, 18*, 165–222.

Braverman, H. (1974). *Labor and monopoly capital: The degradation of work in the twentieth century*. New York: Monthly Review Press.

Brehm, S. S., & Brehm, J. W. (1981). *Psychological reactance: A theory of freedom and control*. New York: Academic Press.

Burns, T., & Stalker, G. M. (1961). *The management of innovation*. London: Tavistock Publications.

Castells, M. (1996). *The rise of the network society*. Malden, MA: Blackwell.

Chung, K. H., & Megginson, L. C. (1981). *Organizational behavior: Developing managerial skills*. New York: Harper & Row.

Clawson, D. (1980). *Bureaucracy and the labor process: The transformation of U.S. industry 1860–1920*. New York: Monthly Review Press.

Clegg, S. R. (1990). *Modern organizations: Organization studies in the postmodern world*. Newbury Park, CA: Sage.

Cohen, S. G., & Bailey, D. E. (1997). What makes teams work: Group effectiveness research from the shop floor to the executive suite. *Journal of Management, 23*, 239–263.

Cooley, C. H. (1962). *Social organizations: A study of the larger mind*. New York: Schocken.

Cyert, R. M., & March, J. G. (1992). *A behavioral theory of the firm* (2nd ed.). New York: Blackwell.

Davis, G. F., & McAdam, D. (2000). Corporations, classes, and social movements after managerialism. *Research in Organizational Behavior, 22*, 193–236.

Dohse, K., Jurgens, U., & Malsch, T. (1985). From "Fordism" to "Toyotaism"? The social organization of the labor process in the Japanese automobile industry. *Politics and Society, 14*(2), 115–146.

Edwards, R. (1979). *Contested terrain: The transformation of the workplace in the twentieth century*. New York: Basic Books.

Etzioni, A. (1961). *A comparative analysis of organizations*. New York: Free Press.

Goldman, P., & Van Houten, D. R. (1988). Bureaucracy and domination: Managerial strategy in turn-of-the-century American industry. In F. Hearn (Ed.), *The transformation of industrial organization* (pp. 46–67). Belmont, CA: Wadsworth Publishing.

Gordon, D. M. (1996). *Fat and mean: The corporate squeeze of working Americans and the myth of managerial "downsizing."* New York: Free Press.

Gortner, H. F. (1977). *Administration in the public sector*. New York: Wiley.

Gouldner, A. (1954). *Patterns of industrial bureaucracy*. Glencoe, IL: Free Press.

Gouldner, A. (1955). *Wildcat strike*. Yellow Springs, OH: Antioch Press.

Gouldner, A. (1960). The norm of reciprocity: A preliminary statement. *American Sociological Review, 25*, 161–178.

Gutman, H. (1975). *Work, culture and society in industrializing America*. New York: Knopf.

Guzzo, R. A., & Dickson, M. W. (1996). Teams in organizations: Recent research on performance and effectiveness. *Annual Review of Psychology, 47*, 307–338.

Harrison, B. (1994). *Lean and mean: The changing landscape of corporate power in the age of flexibility*. New York: Basic Books.

Harvey, D. (1982). *The limits to capital*. Cambridge, MA: Blackwell.

Heckscher, C. (1994). Defining the post-bureaucratic type. In C. Heckscher & A. Donnelon (Eds.), *The post-bureaucratic organization* (pp. 14–62). Thousand Oaks, CA: Sage.

Heckscher, C., & Donnelon, A. (Eds.). (1994). *The post-bureaucratic organization.* Thousand Oaks, CA: Sage.

Hodson, R. (1995). Worker resistance: An underdeveloped concept in the sociology of work. *Economic and Industrial Democracy, 16*(1), 79–110.

Hodson, R. (2001). *Dignity at work.* New York: Cambridge University Press.

Hoxie, R. F. (1966). *Scientific management and labor.* New York: A. M. Kelley.

Jaffee, D. (2001). *Organization theory: Tension and change.* New York: McGraw-Hill.

Jermier, J. M., Knights, D., & Nord, W. R. (1994). *Resistance and power in organizations: Agency, subjectivity, and the labor process.* New York: Routledge.

Jones, S. R. G. (1992). Was there a Hawthorne effect? *American Journal of Sociology, 98,* 451–468.

Katz, D., & Kahn, R. L. (1978). *The social psychology of organizations.* New York: Wiley.

Kunda, G. (1992). *Engineering culture: Control and commitment in a high-tech corporation.* Philadelphia: Temple University Press.

Lawrence, P., & Lorsch, J. (1967). *Organization and environment: Managing differentiation and integration.* Homewood, IL: R. D. Irwin.

Likert, R. (1961). *New patterns of management.* New York: McGraw Hill.

Lincoln, J. R., & Kalleberg, A. L. (1985). Work organization and workforce commitment: A study of plants and employees in the U.S. and Japan. *American Sociological Review, 50,* 738–760.

Littler, C. (1982). *The development of the labor process in capitalist societies.* Exeter, NH: Heinemann.

March, J., & Simon, H. (1958). *Organizations.* New York: Wiley.

Marglin, S. A. (1974). What do bosses do? *Review of Radical Political Economy, 6,* 33–60.

Maslow, A. H. (1943). A theory of human motivation. *Psychological Review, 50,* 370–396.

Mayo, E. (1933). *The human problems of an industrial civilization.* New York: Macmillan.

Mayo, E. (1945). *The social problems of an industrial civilization.* New York: Ayer.

McGregor, D. (1966). The human side of enterprise. In W. G. Bennis & E. H. Schein (Eds.), *Leadership and motivation: Essays of Douglas McGregor* (pp. 3–20). Cambridge, MA: MIT Press.

Merton, R. (1957). *Social theory and social structure.* New York: Free Press.

Mintz, B., & Schwartz, M. (1985). *The power structure of American business.* Chicago: University of Chicago Press.

Montgomery, D. (1979). *Workers' control in America: Studies in the history of work, technology, and labor struggles.* New York: Cambridge University Press.

Morrill, C., Zald, M. N., & Rao, H. (2003). Covert political conflict in organizations: Challenges from below. *Annual Review of Sociology, 29,* 391–415.

Neale, M. A., & Bazerman, M. H. (1991). *Cognition and rationality in negotiation.* New York: Free Press.

Parsons, T. (1947). Introduction. In A. M. Henderson & T. Parsons (Eds.), *Max Weber: Theory of social and economic organization* (pp. 58–60). New York: Oxford University Press.

Pfeffer, J. (1994). *Competitive advantage through people: Unleashing the power of the workforce.* Boston: Harvard Business School Press.

Pfeffer, J., & Salacik, G. R. (1978). *The external control of organizations: A resource dependence perspective.* New York: Harper & Row.

Piore, M. J., & Sabel, C. F. (1984). *The second industrial divide: Possibilities for prosperity.* New York: Basic Books.

Pollard, S. (1965). *The genesis of modern management.* Cambridge, MA: Harvard University Press.

Pondy, L. (1967). Organizational conflict: Concepts and models. *Administrative Science Quarterly, 12*(2), 296–320.

Portes, A. (2000). The hidden abode: Sociology as the analysis of the unexpected. *American Sociological Review, 65,* 1–18.

Roethlisberger, F. J., & Dickson, W. (1939). *Management and the worker.* Cambridge, MA: Harvard University Press.

Sayer, A., & Walker, R. (1992). *The new social economy: Reworking the division of labor.* Cambridge, MA: Blackwell.

Scanlon, B., & Keys, J. B. (1979). *Management and organizational behavior.* New York: John Wiley.

Schein, E. (1992). *Organizational culture and leadership* (2nd ed.). San Francisco, CA: Jossey-Bass.

Selznick, P. (1957). *Leadership in administration.* New York: Harper & Row.

Simon, H. (1997). *Administrative behavior: A study of decision-making processes in administrative organizations* (4th ed.). New York: Free Press.

Tausky, C. (1970). *Work organizations: Major theoretical perspectives.* Itasca, IL: F. E. Peacock.

Taylor, F. W. (1911). *The principles of scientific management.* New York: Norton.

Thompson, E. P. (1963). *The making of the English working class.* New York: Vintage.

Useem, M. (1996). *Investor capitalism: How money managers are changing the face of corporate America.* New York: Basic Books.

Weber, M. (1947). *Max Weber: The theory of social and economic organization* (A. M. Henderson and T. Parsons, Trans.). New York: Free Press.

Womack, J., Jones, D., & Roos, D. (1990). *The machine that changed the world.* New York: Rawson Associates.

II

Interpersonal and Group Levels of Analysis

3

Communication Processes and Conflict Management

MARA OLEKALNS
Melbourne Business School, University of Melbourne

LINDA L. PUTNAM
Department of Communication, Texas A&M University

LAURIE R. WEINGART
David A. Tepper School of Business, Carnegie Mellon University

LAURIE METCALF
Department of Communication, University of Arkansas

Communication is central to the experience and management of conflict. What people say and how they say it signals their approach to resolving conflicts of interests. It is through communication that people express their desires, recognize differences, and attempt to resolve those differences. While there is a rich tradition of research on conflict in organizational settings, the focus on the role of communication has developed in the last 20 years. Putnam and Poole (1987) wrote one of the first reviews of this literature, noting that "communication constitutes the essence of conflict in that it undergirds the formation of opposing issues, frames perceptions of the felt conflict, translates emotions and perceptions into conflict behaviors, and sets the stage for future conflicts" (p. 552). However, they also noted that studies of communication in conflict were relatively scarce at that time. Now, 20 years later, we revisit this literature. Our goal in this chapter is to review the advances in the arena of communication and conflict, assess progress made, and consider the potential for future contributions.

A communication approach necessarily focuses on the messages that people send while negotiating or resolving conflict. In this review, we identify and elaborate on two distinct approaches to understanding the role of communication in conflict resolution. These approaches reflect two separate but interwoven domains within which researchers have studied the role of interaction in managing and resolving differences. The first domain examines the role of communication in *conflict management*. This domain focuses on how conflict styles reflect the broad strategic approaches that individuals adopt and that shape the messages they send to the other party. The second domain examines the role of communication in *negotiation*. This domain focuses on the negotiation context, particularly such factors as negotiators' goals, power, and culture influence communication. Implicit in both domains is the assumption that exogenous factors (e.g., conflict styles, power, outcome goals, and culture) shape the broad approach or strategy that individuals adopt and that this strategy, in turn, shapes what negotiators say to each other.

Some of this research reflects a cognitive orientation that casts communication as a goal-oriented activity in which messages signal tactics, strategies, and broad intentions to the other party. However, messages also contain an emotional component. Consequently, our review incorporates research that examines how emotion affects an individual's communicative behaviors and how expressed emotion affects the other party. The analysis of emotions represents an important new direction in conflict and negotiation research, one that goes beyond the strategic intent of messages to examine the accompanying emotional tone. Sociofunctional theories of emotion, which suggest that emotion serves as an important signaling function, imply that emotional expressions will affect individuals' willingness to reach settlement (Bodtker & Jameson, 2001; Davidson & Greenhalgh, 1999; Morris & Keltner, 2000; Putnam 1994).

Looking back, our review of the conflict management and negotiation domains focuses on research that analyzes communication rather than self-reported behavior. Although self-reports contribute to our understanding of how behavior is linked to conflict management, they represent a holistic approach to behavior that assumes that styles remain stable over time (e.g., Putnam, 1990). A focus on what individuals say in disputes and negotiations enables a more fine-grained analysis that incorporates the dynamic nature of interaction. It allows us to track subtle changes in behavior that can have a significant impact on a negotiator's ability to resolve conflicts or make deals successfully.

Looking forward, we focus on how technology is changing the way we make deals and resolve disputes. Increasingly, e-mail and instant messaging provide alternative ways to communicate. Individuals can buy and sell goods and other services online and, when deals go bad, may manage disputes via online mediation services. Our knowledge of the effects of moving from face-to-face to computer-mediated interactions is still in its infancy, as is our understanding of how we might use technology to improve conflict management. In our final section, we review research focusing on the role of technology in conflict management and negotiation. Drawing on this literature, we identify emotional expressions and the impact of cultural differences on negotiation as key areas for future research on the relationships among technology, communication, and conflict.

CONFLICT MANAGEMENT STYLES AND STRATEGIES

In this section, we examine the work on conflict styles and communication behaviors. Given the breadth of the literature on conflict styles, we focus on only those studies that treat styles as strategies or as dynamic choices for engaging in conflict situations. These studies employ measurement scales that use message behaviors as items or include scenarios about conflicts that demonstrate how styles change during a conflict episode. We also review studies that employ the dual concern model to code strategic behavior in negotiations. Therefore, the studies on conflict styles and strategies included in this review focus on the interconnections of intentions, strategic choice, and actual communication behaviors.

Conflict Styles

Initially defined as a mode, an intention, or a habitual way of handling conflict, a style is an individual's preference for handling conflicts that is determined by the individual's concern for either self or others (Blake & Mouton, 1964; Filley, 1975; A. Rahim, & Bonoma, 1979; Thomas, 1976). Typically, researchers focus on five styles—integrating, forcing, smoothing, avoiding, and compromising—based on the two dimensions of cooperativeness (concern for other people) and assertiveness (concern for self). Integrating entails the intention to confront the conflict directly, to collaborate, and to engage in problem solving while forcing or competing relies on position power and competitiveness to address a conflict. Individuals who prefer smoothing are likely to accommodate to others, while parties who prefer to avoid often withdraw from the scene, either physically or psychologically. Compromise refers to a preference to meet parties halfway, or split the difference. Although linked to behaviors, conflict styles were assumed to be relatively stable across situations.

The Dual Concern Model

The conflict style approach was elaborated by Pruitt (1983; Pruitt & Carnevale, 1993) in the development of the dual concern model. This model
shifted the focus from generalized predispositions to strategic choice.
More specifically, the dual concern model provided a social psychological
approach to strategic choice based on the dual aspirations of maximizing
own versus others' outcomes. Hence, the dual concern model is a descriptive theory that aims to predict strategy use from the combination of both
concern for self and concern for other. It operates from the presumption
that concern about your own outcome is not in direct opposition to concern about the other party's outcomes (see Fig. 3.1).

Each strategy in the dual concern model is associated with a distinct set
of behaviors: (a) *inaction* (low concern for self and other)—doing nothing,
ignoring the topic, failure to confront, changing the subject; (b) *yielding*
(low concern for self, high concern for other)—glossing over differences,
obliging, and playing down the conflict; (c) *contending* (high concern for
self, low concern for other)—verbal dominance, repetition of goals, and
arguing persistently for one's needs; and (d) *problem solving* (high concern
for self and other)—effective use of persuasive influence, statements of
willingness to collaborate, and statements indicating movement toward
resolution. Compromise is excluded from the dual concern model because
it surfaces as a "lazy" approach to problem solving that involves a half-
hearted attempt to satisfy both parties' interests (Pruitt, 1983).

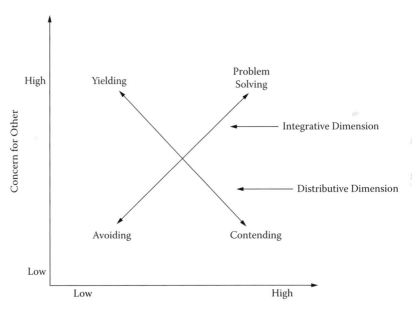

FIGURE 3.1. Dual concern model (Pruitt, 1983).

Choosing Styles

Both the conflict styles and dual concern models are clear regarding when particular styles are used: Individuals typically choose a style/strategy based on the emphasis that they give to achieving their own or the other's goals. They differ in whether these preferences are stable across time (e.g., conflict styles) or whether they are sensitive to changes in the conflict context (e.g., dual concern model). Research suggests that the choice of a conflict style is influenced by individual, dyadic, and organizational factors; however, those factors that relate to the underlying relationship between the parties yield the strongest link between communication and choice of conflict strategies (Putnam & Poole, 1987). From this perspective, S. R. Wilson and Putnam (1990) named identity and relational goals as two critical factors that shape people's choice of strategies. In this section, we expand on how these goals affect the choice of conflict styles.

Identity Goals.   Identity goals reflect an individual's concern for maintaining one's own and the other person's sense of self. These goals are reflected in an individual's efforts to manage his or her face, that is, the concern or respect that this person shows for maintaining his or her own and the other person's self-esteem (Goffman, 1967). This variable is especially interesting in that it captures both individual and cultural differences in the use of conflict styles.

Strong parallels between identity concerns and the concern for self and others suggest that individuals who desire to maintain the other party's face will choose less confrontational styles than those who focus on maintaining their own face. In support of this argument, Oetzel, Myers, Meares, and Lara (2003) showed that employees who express concern for the other person's face are more likely to use integrating, smoothing, and compromising strategies than are individuals who focus on protecting, restoring, or saving their own face. These results parallel findings from studies of social motives; namely, concern for the other person facilitates the use of integrative styles (De Dreu, Weingart, & Kwon, 2000).

Face concerns are evident as we move from individualistic to collectivistic cultures. One consequence is that people in collectivistic cultures prefer other-focused strategies, especially avoiding (Brew & Cairns, 2004; Ting-Toomey et al., 1991; Tjosvold & Sun, 2002). Consistent with this argument, managers from China, Korea, and the Middle East score higher on avoiding as a preferred style than do managers from the United States and Australia (Brew & Cairns, 2004; Elsayed-Ekhouly & Buda, 1996; Kirkbride, Tang, & Westwood, 1991; Kozan & Ergin, 1999; Ting-Toomey et al., 1991). A recent meta-analysis further supports this argument (Holt & DeVore, 2005). Several authors contend that such differences stem from the relative emphasis that cultures place on preserving the other party's face (Ting-Toomey & Kurogi, 1998). Oetzel and Ting-Toomey (2003), for example, reported that preservation of face accounts for most of the variance in the use of dominating and integrating. However, recent research on generational differences in preferred styles suggests that these patterns may be changing. When asked to rate a young coworker's reactions to an older worker's criticism, older Chinese adults endorsed accommodating rather than problem solving whereas younger Chinese adults preferred problem solving (Zhang, Harwood, & Hummert, 2005). Thus, cultural context plays an important role in determining how organizational members interpret and respond to conflict situations.

A different perspective on face management surfaces in the research on emotional expression in conflicts. According to politeness theory, language that threatens the other party also attacks face (B. H. Drake & Moberg, 1986). One example of such language is the expression of negative emotions, such as anger (Brown & Levinson, 1987). When disputants express anger, they are more likely to reach early impasse, create hostile relationships, and achieve poorer outcomes (Allred, 1999; Allred, Mallozzi, Matsui, & Raia, 1997; Barry, 1999; Friedman et al., 2004; Pillutla & Murningham, 1996). Moreover, anger begets anger, and these sequences of reciprocated anger predict impasse (Friedman et al., 2004). When combined with contempt, anger feeds attribution processes that perpetuate stereotypes, increase intergroup conflict (Betancourt, 1990), and decrease the likelihood that disputants will find an acceptable outcome (Brett, Olekalns, Friedman, Goates, Anderson, & Lisco, 2007). One interpretation of these findings is that in a heated emotional context, the expression of negative emotions such as anger and contempt act as face attack (Brett et al., 2007) and shift disputants' goals from trying to reach a settlement to wanting to retaliate against or punish the other party (Pillutla & Murninghan, 1996).

Relational Goals. Relational goals also affect an individual's choice of conflict styles. A key dimension of relationships is how power is distributed across parties. When power is unevenly distributed, as is the case in supervisor–subordinate relationships, our assumption is that the less powerful party would show greater concern for the other person and less concern for self. However, this assumption does not appear to be the case. In actuality, perceived power in superior–subordinate conflicts interacts with anticipated resolution to influence style choice. Basically, when employees anticipate resolving a conflict, they use integrating or compromising strategies, regardless of whether they perceive power as balanced or imbalanced and view their own role as low or high powered (Powell & Hickson, 2000). Moreover, supervisors are most effective in resolving conflicts with subordinates when they use either problem solving or a combination of problem solving and forcing (Van de Vliert, Huismans, & Euwema, 1995). These studies suggested that power is a less salient factor in the selection of conflict styles than face management. Instead, they implied that, at least in an organizational context, the choice of style is governed more by the desire to reach a settlement than by whether the conflict is with superiors, subordinates, or peers (Phillips & Cheston, 1979;

Putnam & Wilson, C. E., 1982; A. Rahim, 1983, M. A. Rahim, 1986; Richmond, Wagner, & McCroskey, 1983).

Combining Styles

Because the dual concern model assumes that the choice of a style is strategic (rather than dispositional), it suggests that individuals combine or change approaches in order to reach an agreement. The literature indicates that conflict styles can be combined either sequentially (over time) or simultaneously (at the same time) to improve outcomes.

Sequential Combinations. The dual concern model considers the perceived feasibility of a given strategy, that is, the extent to which a strategy is capable of achieving the concerns that give rise to it and the costs anticipated from using it (Pruitt, 1983). If a potential strategy seems infeasible, then parties shift to the next best approach, based on the perceived common ground between the parties, level and firmness of each party's aspirations, faith in one's own problem-solving ability, and readiness for problem solving. In this section we review three factors that trigger changes in conflict strategies over time: compliance versus noncompliance with requests, likelihood of settlement, and gender.

First, the degree of compliance or noncompliance with an initiated strategy influences the choice of follow-up approaches. In two separate studies, researchers examined the use of a contending strategy over time. Supervisors who initially used collaborative strategies switched to contending when faced with subordinates who did not comply with initial requests (Conrad, 1991). Second, parties shifted their strategies when reaching an agreement seemed less likely to them. Those disputants who typically began conflict encounters with problem-solving approaches shifted to inaction and finally to contending when agreements were not reached (McCready & Roberts, 1996). Nicotera (1994) reinforced this finding in a Markovian analysis of written responses to conflict episodes. In this study, the emotional valence of the conflict moderated shifts from contending to problem solving and vice versa. Third, shifts in the use of conflict strategies differed depending on the gender composition of a dyad. Coding strategic choice during three 5-minute time periods of a conflict episode, Papa and Natalle (1989) observed that male/male dyads employed high levels of *contending* across the three intervals while male/female dyads relied on *compromising* in the first two time periods and contending in the last segment. Female/female dyads shifted from problem solving and contending in the first two periods to *compromising* toward the end of the conflict. Thus, organizational members shifted in strategy use from initial to follow-up stages of conflict management, based on whether the other party accepted or rejected their initial approaches, the perceived likelihood of success of a strategy, and the gender of their partners.

Simultaneous Combinations. Van de Vliert's conglomerated model presented an alternative approach for characterizing how multiple strategies emerged (Van de Vliert et al., 1995). He argued that the five conflict styles did not occur in isolation. Instead, they functioned as "conglomerated behaviors" that occurred in combination as individuals worked toward maximizing effectiveness. Working within this framework, Van de Vliert et al. (1995; Van der Vliert, Nauta, Giebels & Janssen, 1999; Van de Vliert et al., 2004) demonstrated that problem solving was typically combined with forcing. This combination resembled the "firm flexibility"[1] principle derived from the dual concern model (Pruitt, 1981), which suggested that contention promoted the information search necessary for problem solving. Therefore, combining problem solving with forcing proved highly effective in resolving conflicts with subordinates (Van de Vliert et al., 1995), specifically forcing followed by problem solving resulted in the best substantive and relational outcomes (Van de Vliert et al., 1999). In more recent research, Van de Vliert, Ohbuchi, Van Rossun, Hayashi, and Van der Vegt (2004) examined the cultural specificity of these conglomerated behaviors. In a questionnaire study of Japanese employees, forcing combined with accommodating emerged as the most effective way to handle conflicts with superiors.

Contributions and Limitations of Conflict Style and Strategy Research

Conflict style research is one of the first areas in conflict studies that is directly related to the use of communicative behaviors. This work moved the field beyond relying on cooperative versus competitive behaviors to other motivations and choices for handling conflicts. The dual concern model tied these orientations to specific strategies that embraced both concern for self and concern for other. This work led to the first coding of communicative behaviors and efforts to tie intentionality to conflict tactics. The majority of the conflict style research, however, continues to rely on self-report instruments rather than coding actual behaviors. While one self-report measure (DUTCH) correlated positively with independent observations and ratings of conflict-handling styles (e.g., problem solving, forcing, yielding, and avoiding; De Dreu, Evers, Beersma, Kluwer, & Nauta, 2001), other studies found that self-report instruments often serve as weak predictors of the actual use of communicative behaviors in conflict situations. Gayle (1991) reported only 17% agreement between scores on the OCCI (organizational communication conflict instrument) and messages coded from conflict episodes. When scores on style instruments

---

[1] *Firm flexibility* refers to being firm with respect to interests but flexible regarding the means of achieving those interests.

predict initial behaviors, they often fail to identify follow-up sequences of style use (Conrad, 1991). Other studies reveal that the five styles fail to capture the full range of approaches to conflict management in organizations (Morrill & Thomas, 1992; Nicotera, 1993, 1994; Sternberg & Soriano, 1984) and may function as attitudes rather than as predispositions for behavior (Moberg, 2001). The question thus remains as to whether self-report instruments for assessing conflict styles reflect actual communicative behaviors in organizations.

UNDERSTANDING NEGOTIATION PROCESSES

Compared with conflict style research, negotiation research has a stronger foundation in measuring disputants' behaviors directly, through coding videotaped or audio-taped interactions. A large segment of this research links strategy and tactical choices to negotiators' outcome goals (S. R. Wilson & Putnam, 1990). Typically, these goals focus on whether bargainers aim to maximize individual or joint outcomes. These different outcome goals form the basis for one of two approaches to negotiation, distributive or integrative, respectively. A distributive approach to negotiation focuses on claiming value or dividing resources. An integrative approach, in turn, also centers on creating value for both parties via problem solving. The two approaches map onto the concern for self and concern for other distinction in the dual concern model (Pruitt & Rubin, 1986), with yielding and contending representing the extremes of a distributive dimension and problem solving and avoiding representing the extremes of an integrative dimension (Thomas, 1976; see Fig. 3.1). With these distinctions in mind, negotiation researchers study the role of strategic behaviors in bargaining through coding communication. As one of the first researchers to develop a coding scheme based on negotiator tactics, Pruitt and his colleagues used the dual concern model to classify actual negotiation behaviors. Their research set the stage for studies of communication in bargaining (Pruitt, 1983; Pruitt & Carnevale, 1993).

In this section, we focus on research that examines negotiators' communication, that is, on studies of what bargainers say and how they respond to the other party. We summarize empirical work in which researchers transcribe and code what negotiators say into tactics and broader strategies (Weingart, Olekalns, & Smith, 2004). In doing this, we identify three levels that researchers employ to analyze the communication of negotiators: the frequency with which individuals choose integrative or distributive strategies; how those strategies form sequences within dyads or groups—that is, the immediate actions and reactions of negotiators; and how strategies aggregate and evolve over time to establish a dominant orientation in the negotiation. Moreover, we consider how these patterns affect the quality of negotiated outcomes and how external factors such as negotiators' goals, culture, and emotion shape strategy choices.

Individual Level: Analyses of the Frequencies of Strategy Use

A frequency approach examines the amount or total use of different types of negotiation strategies during a given negotiation. Researchers interested in knowing which behaviors negotiators use typically count the number of times a specific strategy or tactic is employed, control for (divide by) the total number of communicative behaviors, and compare the (relative) frequencies across tactics, groups, or experimental conditions.

Researchers who employ a frequency approach typically characterize integrative and distributive processes as mutually exclusive (Putnam, 1990). This distinction allows researchers to focus on the links between inputs to a negotiation and each bargainer's use of strategies. One input factor that dominates research on strategy frequencies is outcome goals. As negotiators make choices to maximize their own aims or their joint gains, the frequency with which they use integrative or distributive strategies is likely to reflect their individualistic or cooperative outcome goals, respectively. In this section, we review the literature that links outcome goals to strategy use, and then we examine the more recent streams of research that connect culture and emotion to negotiation strategy.

Outcome Goals and Strategy Use. In experimental research, a negotiator's goals often arise explicitly from the instructions (or incentives) that participants receive or implicitly from the differences in negotiators' characteristics (e.g., culture, personality). Whether goal differences are established explicitly or implicitly, the effect is to establish a dominant strategic orientation that is typically cooperative or competitive.

Goals that predispose a negotiator to adopt a cooperative orientation increase the frequency with which negotiators use integrative strategies, such as information exchange, concessions, and process management (Hyder, Prietula, & Weingart, 2000; Lewis & Fry, 1977; O'Connor, 1997; Olekalns & Smith, 2003b; Pruitt & Lewis, 1975; Schulz & Pruitt, 1978; Weingart, Bennett, & Brett, 1993; Weingart, Hyder, & Prietula, 1996). Negotiators who embrace a cooperative orientation are also more likely to express support for the other party (Olekalns & Smith, 1999). Moreover, a cooperative orientation mitigates the effects of unequal power, resulting in more cooperative and less competitive behavior (Giebels, De Dreu & Van de Vliert, 2000). However, some of these relationships may be moderated by the level of trust present in the negotiating relationship: When trust is low, negotiators with cooperative goals often reduce the level and accuracy of information exchange (De Dreu, Giebels, & Van de Vliert, 1998; Olekalns & Smith, 2005). In contrast, when goals encourage a competitive orientation, negotiators are more likely to use such strategies as argumentation, substantiation, demands, and threats (Carnevale & Lawler, 1987; Hyder et al., 2000; Lewis & Fry, 1977; Olekalns & Smith, 2000; Pruitt & Lewis, 1975; Schulz & Pruitt, 1978).

Strategies, Goals, and Outcomes. Negotiation studies that focus on the individual also examine the impact of communication processes on bargaining outcomes. For negotiators with individualistic goals (e.g., maximizing own outcomes), this research reveals that a bargainer's approach to information exchange influences self and joint outcomes. A *willingness* to exchange information moves negotiators from impasse into the settlement zone, and once negotiators are in the settlement zone, the *nature* of the information that they exchange determines the amount of joint gain. The degree to which negotiators defend their claims, attack the other party, or make threats or demands distinguishes between resolved and unresolved disputes. High levels of argumentation and use of contentious tactics result in impasse (Olekalns & Smith, 2000; Roloff, Tutzauer, & Dailey, 1989). In contrast, negotiators who engage in information exchange are able to reach agreement, although the quality of that agreement stems from the nature of the information. When the interaction continues to center on arguments and positions, negotiators typically realize low joint gains (Hyder et al., 2000; Olekalns & Smith, 2000; Olekalns, Smith, & Walsh, 1996; Putnam & Wilson, 1989; Roloff et al., 1989). However, negotiators may obtain high joint gains when they exchange information about their underlying needs and the relative importance of issues (Olekalns & Smith, 2000; Olekalns et al., 1996; Weingart et al., 1996; Weingart, Thompson, Bazerman, & Carroll, 1990).

The relationship between communicative behaviors and bargaining outcomes is moderated by the negotiators' goals. Research that tests the effects of explicitly and implicitly derived goals shows that although these goals influence a negotiator's strategic choice, they do not directly affect a bargainer's ability to obtain high joint gains (Adair et al., 2004; O'Connor, 1997; Olekalns & Smith, 2003a, 2003b). For example, in the studies that explicitly manipulated outcome goals via instructions (e.g., motivational orientation), the level of priority information exchange was positively associated with high joint gains *only* under a cooperative orientation; it was unrelated to the level of joint gains under an individualistic orientation (O'Connor, 1997; Olekalns & Smith, 2003a). In contrast, high joint gains under an individualistic orientation were associated with the use of positional information and multi-issue offers (Olekalns & Smith, 2003a). Whereas cooperative dyads benefit from direct information exchange (perhaps because they trust the validity of the information and care about the other party), individualistic dyads attain better outcomes by relying on indirect forms of information exchange (via offers and clear statements of positions on issues).

However, a study that examined dispositional differences in goals reported contradictory results (Olekalns & Smith, 2003b). When both negotiators had a proself (e.g., individualistic) orientation, high joint gains were associated with the *underutilization* of multi-issue offers, whereas with a prosocial (e.g., cooperative) orientation, high joint gains were linked to frequent use of process management strategies and positional information

(Olekalns & Smith, 2003b). These contradictory findings imply that implicitly (via social value orientation) and explicitly (via instructions) established goals may not exert the same influence on the negotiators' behaviors. One interpretation of this finding is that explicitly established goals provide clearer behavioral cues to negotiators and focus them on the most efficient way to achieve their goals.

Culture, Emotion, and Strategy Choice. Exogenous factors other than social motives also influence the frequency with which negotiators choose cooperative or competitive strategies. One of these factors, *culture*, parallels the research on social motives and influences the use of strategic behaviors (for a review of the literature on cross-cultural negotiation, see De Dreu and Gelfand, chapter 1, this volume). Frequently, cultures are differentiated along the dimension of individualism versus collectivism. One feature of this dimension is the emphasis placed on personal versus group outcomes, respectively. Negotiators from collectivist cultures are more likely than those from individualist cultures to show a preference for smoothing, compromising, and using ambiguous language. Conversely, negotiators from individualist countries are more likely to interrupt the other party, to say no frequently, to make extreme offers, and to view the use of exaggerating opening offers and hiding bottom lines as appropriate (Adler, Graham, & Gehrke, 1987; Graham, 1985; Graham, Kim, Lin, & Robinson, 1988; Kirkbride et al., 1991; Volkema, 1998). In addition, several studies show that a bargainer's role (buyer vs. seller) also influences strategy use in diverse cultures (Cai, Wilson, & Drake, 2000; Drake, 2001; Graham et al., 1988). Cai et al. (2000) reported that, in collectivist dyads, sellers lead buyers to ask more questions and to ask about priorities, whereas in mixed dyads, collectivist buyers influence individualist sellers to use distributive tactics and make single offers, thus resulting in low joint profits and lack of reciprocity.

Beyond individualism and collectivism, cultural differences often appear in the negotiators' communication styles. Research in this area focuses on direct and indirect communication styles linked to high- and low-context cultures. Basically, individuals from high-context cultures, typically eastern nations, rely on indirect cues, nonverbal messages, and implicit communication to convey meanings while communicators from low-context cultures, typically western nations, employ direct language to convey messages (Hall, 1976). Negotiators from high-context cultures tend to rely on exchanging offers to convey information about their preferences and priorities, whereas those from low-context cultures rely on direct statements of preferences and priorities (Adair, Okumura, & Brett, 2001).

This literature, however, focuses on the individual messages and tactic choices without considering the explicit or implicit emotional content in these strategies. However, other research reflected an increasing interest in the role of emotion in negotiation (Barry, Fulmer, & Van Kleef, 2004).

Past studies revealed that the presence of either positive or negative affect influenced the type and frequency of negotiator behaviors. When manipulated prior to the negotiation, having a positive as opposed to a negative or neutral mood relates to using few contentious tactics, more problem solving behaviors, more concessions, and greater willingness to reach a compromise (Baron, 1990; Carnevale & Isen, 1986; Druckman & Broome, 1991; Forgas, 1998; Hollingshead & Carnevale, 1990; Isen & Patrick, 1983). The use of negative affect, in turn, increases the use of contentious tactics (Baron, 1990) and leads to greater variety in the expression of ideas (Baron, Fortin, Frei, Hauver, & Shack, 1990).

Dyad Level: Analysis of Sequences

A second way of characterizing the negotiation process is to view integrative and distributive processes as interdependent components of a single approach (Putnam, 1990). This orientation acknowledges that most negotiations involve both competitive and cooperative elements and that negotiators attempt to satisfy the dual goals of maximizing joint and personal gains (Lax & Sebenius, 1986; Walton & McKersie, 1965). Consequently, one of the key tasks facing negotiators is to blend integrative and distributive strategies judiciously as the negotiation progresses. This model of negotiation draws attention to how bargainers structure or organize their interactions (e.g., Diez, 1986; Smith, Olekalns, & Weingart, 2005; Taylor & Donald, 2003), in particular how the two negotiators sequence their use of strategies. This section explores the relationship between strategy sequences and outcomes.

Structure of Strategy Sequences. Negotiation researchers describe three kinds of strategy sequences—reciprocal, transformational, and complementary (Brett, Weingart, & Olekalns, 2004; Olekalns & Smith, 2000). *Reciprocal sequences* capture those occasions in which negotiators match each other's strategies exactly, for example, a sequence in which priority information from one party is matched by priority information from the other party. *Transformational sequences* describe patterns in which negotiators mismatch strategies by pairing a cooperative and a competitive strategy, for example, one negotiator offers priority information and the other responds with a threat. Finally, *complementary sequences* have some components of matching and mismatching. They pair broadly similar strategies (cooperative or competitive) but they mismatch the specific behavior. For example, a demand elicits a threat.

Reciprocity is a two-edged sword for negotiators. On the one hand, reciprocal cooperation, which assists in value creation, is difficult to maintain. The frequency and duration of reciprocal cooperation is increased when individuals are given tactical knowledge (especially regarding integrative tactics) before they negotiate (Weingart, Prietula,

Hyder, & Genovese, 1999) or when they adopt a cooperative orientation (Olekalns & Smith, 2003a; Weingart et al., 1993). On the other hand, reciprocal use of contentious tactics or aggressive arguments blocks cooperative behaviors (e.g., Brett, Shapiro, & Lytle, 1998; Olekalns & Smith, 2000; Putnam & Jones, 1982a, 1982b; Weingart et al., 1999). In the same way that negotiators need to sustain cooperative sequences, bargainers need to disrupt contentious sequences. Negotiators can accomplish this process through using strategies that mismatch the other party's contentious moves or responding with a cooperative move or with a two-part message that combines contentious with cooperative tactics (Brett et al., 1998). This finding attests to the power of transformational sequences to move negotiators to a productive bargaining pattern (see also, Olekalns & Smith, 2000).

Sequences and Negotiated Outcomes.   Paralleling the studies on frequency-outcome relationships, a small body of research examines the relationship between strategy sequences and outcomes. Sequence-outcome research also focuses on the role of context and information management in reaching negotiated agreements and in shaping the quality of these outcomes. It extends the frequency-outcome research by showing that sequential patterns are not simply adding structure to the strategies that negotiators use; but rather, they make a unique contribution to how the bargaining unfolds and ends.

Different patterns of sequences distinguish between resolved and unresolved negotiations. Compared with dyads that settle, impasse dyads are characterized by two distinct patterns: the frequency of competitive reciprocity (Putnam & Folger, 1988; Putnam & Jones, 1982b) and strategic inflexibility (Olekalns & Smith, 2000). Competitive reciprocity is evident in the matching of defensive tactics such as substantiation, commitment, and retraction. Strategic inflexibility surfaces in the pairing of these defensive strategies with offensive strategies such as threats, attacks, and rejections to create complementary competitive sequences (Putnam & Jones, 1982b) and in a greater emphasis on the use of both competitive and complementary sequences (Olekalns & Smith, 2000). The observation that impasse dyads are more likely to match strategies and less likely to mismatch strategies (use transformational sequences) implies that tight communication structures, particularly the inability to blend cooperative and competitive strategies, result in impasse.

Research on strategy sequences also adds to our understanding of how joint gains are realized. Negotiators who reciprocate positional information obtain lower joint gains than do those who reciprocate priority information and trade-offs (Olekalns & Smith, 2000; Weingart et al., 1990). Low joint gains also characterize outcomes for negotiators who engage in asymmetric information exchange, specifically sequences in which concessions and proposal modifications elicit information (Olekalns & Smith,

2000, 2003a, 2003b; Weingart et al., 1990). This type of asymmetric information exchange is less effective than reciprocal information exchange because it represents a looser communication structure, making it more difficult to extract meaning from the interaction (Putnam & Jones, 1982b). Thus, as the effectiveness of information exchange increases, so does the level of joint gains. A small number of studies further suggested that negotiators' goals influence the kinds of sequences linked to high joint gains (Olekalns & Smith, 2003a, 2003b). Overall, these findings indicate that high joint gains are linked to not only the type of information used but also how effectively it is exchanged.

Finally, negotiators also claim value in distributive bargaining situations that have no integrative potential. Donohue (1981) demonstrated that negotiators who claim the smaller share of the resource pool and feel blamed for the bargaining situation are more likely to respond to the other party by displaying agreement. They are also more likely than their opponents to accept rather than to reject offers. This agreeableness reduces their abilities to claim value for themselves.

Other Research on Sequences of Strategy Use. Research on culture in negotiation also examines sequential behaviors. For example, mixed culture dyads who use direct integrative sequences (e.g., explicit information exchange) obtain higher joint gains that do dyads from high-context cultures (Adair, 2003). Both cultures, however, must recognize and reciprocate these strategies to achieve high joint gains. When only one culture makes this adaptation, the negotiation results in low joint gains: Adair et al. (2001) reported that while Japanese negotiators adapt to the U.S. style of giving explicit information, U.S. negotiators fail to understand and adapt to the indirect styles of their Japanese counterparts; thus, these mixed-culture, mixed-context dyads obtain low joint gains.

Research on emotion in negotiation also considers sequential behaviors in negotiations. Van Kleef, De Dreu, and Manstead (2004a, 2004b) examined the impact of expressed emotions on the other party's behaviors. These authors reported that expressions of anger elicit concessions from the other party, in part, because they test the other party's limits. This finding paralleled Thompson and her coworkers' (Thompson, Medvec, Seiden, & Kopelman, 2001) argument that an expression of extreme negative emotions (e.g., anger, indignation, or impatience) may break an impasse, signal concessions to the other party, and communicate intensity and sincerity. It was also consistent with Putnam and S. R. Wilson's (1989) finding that threats, communicated within a cooperative context, improve joint outcomes. When contrasted with the impact of emotions in conflict situations, these findings imply that the communicative functions of similar emotions differ depending on whether they are expressed in the emotionally charged context of disputes or the more emotionally neutral context of deal making.

Negotiation Level: Analysis of Bargaining Phases

Analyzing strategy sequences centers on the immediate actions and reactions of the negotiators. Even though these analyses incorporate a temporal element to understanding the negation process, the focus is short term. Phase research also adopts a temporal perspective but investigates how bargaining strategies aggregate over longer periods of time. Similar to the work on behavioral sequences, a negotiator's actions can either maintain or challenge the strategic approach that dominates in the interaction (Olekalns & Weingart, 2003).

Phase models of the negotiation process blend cooperative and competitive strategies. They differ from the research on sequential patterns by casting integrative and distributive bargaining as critical activities at different points during the negotiation process (Holmes, 1992; Putnam, 1990; Walton & McKersie, 1965). Negotiation theorists and researchers have adopted two distinct approaches to capture how negotiation strategies aggregate over time, both falling within the phase model perspective. From one phase model perspective, sometimes referred to as "stages" of negotiation, negotiators must complete a series of tasks in one phase/ stage before shifting to the next one; thus, task-completion triggers phase changes. *Episodic models* provide an alternative view, one which captures moment-to-moment changes in negotiation behaviors. These models define an episode as an uninterrupted sequence of the same strategies with phases shifting through an interruption in the prolonged use of a strategic pattern (Baxter, 1982; Holmes, 1992; Olekalns, Brett, & Weingart, 2003). These models fit within a broader literature on stages and interruptions of sequential patterns in group processes (Gersick, 1989; Jett & George, 2003; Okhuysen & Eisenhardt, 2002).

Stage models imply a gradual transition from one dominant strategy to another. Typically, researchers who adopt this approach segment negotiations into equal time periods and analyze changes in strategy use over these time segments. Several studies demonstrate that strategy use varies over time or across negotiation phases. The patterns that emerge indicate that the precise nature of these phases is also context dependent. For example, when in distributive negotiations, bargainers increase the frequency of messages to each other over time and increase the number of offers that they make immediately before their deadlines (Lim & Murnighan, 1994). In mixed-motive negotiations, the pattern is somewhat different in that negotiators move back and forth between integrative and distributive approaches over time (Olekalns et al., 1996; Olekalns et al., 2003). Overall, these studies revealed the time sensitive nature of strategy use.

Three studies examined the distribution of strategies across negotiation phases and the effects of these phases on joint gains. These studies showed that integrative agreements emerge from increases in flexibility and problem solving tactics over time, whereas distributive agreements evolve from the use of power struggles and contentious tactics (Olekalns

& Smith, 2000; Olekalns et al., 1996; Putnam, S. R. Wilson & Turner, 1990). Through adding culture to the mix, Natlandsmyr and Rognes (1995) reported that individualistic (Norwegian) negotiators increased the pattern of multi-issue offers over time and also obtained higher joint gains. Collectivist (Mexican) negotiators, who maintained a steady use of single-issue offers, in turn, obtained lower joint gains. Use of differential sequences across phases also influences joint gains. As Adair and Brett (2005) observed, dyads who shifted from persuasion to priority information exchange in the first of four phases and who reciprocated priority information in the second phase obtained high levels of joint gains.

In *episodic models,* negotiations may be punctuated by abrupt transitions in strategy use. Such transitions may reflect efforts to realign the negotiators' strategies or they may indicate a fundamental transformation in how negotiators understand and represent the conflict (McGinn, Lingo, & Ciano, 2004; Putnam, 2004). Consistent with this view, analyses of international and other large-scale negotiations demonstrate that progress to a settlement is often punctuated by a series of discrete and highly salient events. These events may result from changes in either the negotiating context or the negotiation process. Ripe moments in international conflicts identify points in time when, for a number of external reasons, resolution is more likely (Zartman, 1992). The procedural parallel of this type of transition is a *turning point,* which describes a significant change in the negotiation process that moves the negotiation either forward, increasing the likelihood of a settlement, or backward, impeding a settlement (Coleman, 2000; Druckman, 1986, 2001; Druckman, Husbands, & Johnston, 1991).

In dyadic negotiations, a similar pattern occurs in how negotiators shift their strategies over time. Abrupt shifts in strategies occur when negotiators encounter a temporary impasse, that is, when negotiators recognize that they are at risk of further escalating a conflict (Harinck & De Dreu, 2004). Under these circumstances, negotiators may consciously redirect the process by making a specific intervention. That is, they may explicitly suggest a new way of proceeding with the negotiation. Such process interventions, which redirect strategy, are highly effective in shifting negotiators to a more constructive process (Brett et al., 1998). Finally, as an analogue of Druckman's work (1986, 2001), research revealed that dyadic negotiations are similarly punctuated by both positive and negative turning points. Moreover, the emergence of positive turning points is associated with the development of trust over time whereas the emergence of negative turning points is linked to decreases in trust over time (Olekalns & Smith, 2005).

ONLINE CONFLICT MANAGEMENT

A communication perspective on conflict management would not be complete without considering the role of technology as a medium for negotiating and resolving conflict. Advances in communication technology over the past twenty years have been revolutionary. In like manner, the research on technology and communication has grown, thus, revealing a marked change from the days when e-mails and the World Wide Web were in their infancy and negotiation decision support systems were rudimentary.

Research on the relationship between computer mediated communication and conflict management has its roots in the effects of written and oral communication media on successful conflict resolution and deal making. Dating back to the 1970s, researchers compared the relative efficacy of written, telephone, and face-to-face negotiations (Short, 1974; Turnbull, Strickland, & Shaver, 1976; Wichman, 1970). A unifying theme in these studies was that communication becomes more ambiguous and contention escalates when communication cues are filtered out through the media. Media richness, the ability of the communication medium to convey visual and verbal cues (Daft & Lengel, 1986), is central in discovering how computer mediated communication helps or hinders conflict management. This section reviews research that compares different communication media and the ways that conflicting styles and negotiation strategies are adapted to media that filter out visual and verbal cues. The conclusion of this section speculates on the challenges that computer-mediated communication poses for disputants and negotiators alike.

Media richness affects negotiators' choice of strategies both in conflict episodes and in negotiations. A comparison among face-to-face, video-conferencing, telephone, and computer-mediated communication reveals that face-to-face disputants are more likely to collaborate, are less likely to compete, and have greater desire for future interactions than do bargainers who use only telephone and computer-mediated interactions (Purdy, Nye, & Balakrishnan, 2000). Videoconferencing, though, compares favorably with face-to-face communication and may be considered a reasonable substitute for it (Purdy et al., 2000). However, videoconferencing reduces the abilities of negotiators to identify accurately the other party's collaborative moves, thus indicating that even small losses in social cues can impact negotiation. Offsetting this shortcoming is the finding that visual communication influences bargaining styles and reduces equivocality about negotiation orientations, thus fostering integrative bargaining (Sheffield, 1995).

Similar patterns emerge in group situations in which participants are more likely to use negative (rather than positive) conflict management strategies in computer-mediated communication than when they are working face to face (Zornoza, Ripoll, & Peiró, 2002). However, these effects may be transitory: Group members that use computer-mediated communication express more process and relational conflicts early in their interactions than do those employing other media, but these differences diminish over time (Hobman, Bordia, Irma, & Chang, 2002). This finding suggests that, as individuals become more comfortable with a new form of communication, they are able to overcome its apparent shortcomings. Moreover, computer-mediated communication may provide an escape route when conflicts flare up. Using a confederate to escalate conflict, Dorado, Medina, Munduate, Cisneros, and Euwema (2002) reported that escalatory behavior elicits avoiding in computer-mediated communication but leads to contending in face-to-face disputes.

Computer-mediated communication also affects information exchange. For example, compared with face-to-face negotiation, computer-mediated communication increases anonymity, reduces information exchange, and leads to lower joint profits (Arunachalam & Dilla, 1995). Valley, Moag, and Bazerman (1998) observed that groups who rely on asynchronous, text messages, such as e-mail, are less likely than face-to-face groups to be open with each other, to work together collaboratively, and to achieve mutually beneficial outcomes. Negotiators in computer-mediated situations also use few words, informal tones, and slow speed, making text-based bargaining systems less efficient and less easy to comprehend than face-to-face communication (Sheffield, 1995). These effects may be due to the particular features of e-mail communication. Friedman and Currall (2003) argued that using a series of intermittent, one-way messages with long-time delays in feedback promotes the bundling of multiple arguments and excessive attention to only one or two ways of interpreting a message. This process, in turn, intensifies emotions, reduces cooperation, and leads to conflict escalation. Comparisons between e-mail and other message systems demonstrated that e-mail conflicts could spiral out of control and produce antisocial behaviors (Kiesler, 1997; Orcutt & Anderson, 1977).

Even though computer-mediated communication may restrict information flow, it offers a set of tools to detect deception (Zhou, Burgoon, Nunamaker, & Twitchell, 2004). For example, patterns of language dominance in computer-mediated settings differentiate deceivers and truth tellers (Zhou, Burgoon, Zhang, & Nunamaker, 2004). The use of text-coding programs, such as LIWC (Linguistic Inquiry and Word Count), shows that deceivers make fewer self- or other-references and use more negative emotion words than do nondeceivers (Newman, Pennebaker, Berry, & Richards, 2003). These findings offer hope to negotiators who experience information asymmetry and potential deception (Murnighan, Babcock, Thompson, & Pillutla, 1999). The ability of a negotiating partner to detect deception offers negotiators a level of confidence that will reduce the risks associated with increasing trust, promoting collaboration, and improving outcomes.

Computer-mediated communication influences conflict management in three other areas—culture, emotion, and dispute resolution. In culture research, computer-mediated interactions both exacerbate and mitigate the effects of culture on face-to-face negotiations. For example, comparisons among cultures characterized as high (Japan) or low (United States) in uncertainty avoidance reveal that Japanese managers are affected by limited information and ambiguity when participating in eBay auctions.

Compared with U.S. buyers, Japanese buyers show a higher participation rate and are willing to pay more when the product information is available as a picture rather than as a verbal (text) description (Vishwanath, 2003). Consistent with a greater concern for face, Koreans are not only more likely than U.S. participants to accompany SPAM with an apology; they also view SPAM as more credible when an apology occurs (Park, Lee, & Song, 2005). Even though these findings did not focus on negotiation or conflict resolution, they suggested the potential for computer-mediated communication to magnify the cultural differences in negotiation. Conversely, the ability to spend time processing information and composing responses may offset the disadvantages that come with negotiating in a nonnative language.

Emotion plays a big role in the analysis of computer-mediated communication. Given that mediated communication can filter cues, it seems logical that disputants would be more careful in expressing emotions in this context rather than in face-to-face interactions. Research, however, reveals the opposite pattern in that individuals significantly overestimate their abilities to convey emotions via e-mail. Disputants often think they are more competent in cueing the other party than they actually are (Kruger, Epley, Parger, & Ng, 2005). Research suggested that the value of expressing emotions is limited, especially if the tone of the interaction is already negative. Thompsen and Foulger (1996) demonstrated that the use of direct emotional expressions could reduce the perception of flaming, but only when disputants have low levels of hostility. More recently, Walthier and D'Addario (2001) revealed that individuals give greater weight to the verbal content of messages than they do to the expression of emotions. However, if either the verbal content or the emotions express negativity, this orientation dominates interpretation of the entire message. Given the potential for emotional language to escalate disputes and slow resolution (Brett et al., 2007; Friedman et al., 2004), a critical area for future research is investigating how disputants can signal their emotions and intentions to the other party effectively.

A third area in which technology influences negotiation is work on dispute resolution. Since computer-mediated communication typically reduces social cues, parties are left trying to infer the other disputant's intentions based on their words alone (Friedman & Currall, 2003; Kiesler, Seigel, & McGuire, 1984; Ramirez, Walther, Burgoon, & Sunnafrank, 2002). Individuals appear to recognize this pattern and engage in higher levels of uncertainty reduction (Tidwell & Walther, 2002). The impact of such behaviors, however, is not clear. Although Moore, Kurtzberg, Thompson, and Morris (1999) noted that sharing basic personal information via e-mail improved negotiators' outcomes, negative impressions and low trust may still abound in the world of computer-mediated communication. Compared with participants in face-to-face negotiations, individuals who engage in computer-mediated bargaining perceive both the negotiation and the other party more negatively (Fischer-Lokou & Guéguen, 2001; Fischer-Lokou, Guéguen, & Lépy, 2004). Moreover, individuals in computer-mediated interactions begin the process with low trust and then gradually build over time to the levels that are comparable with those found in face-to-face interactions (J. M. Wilson, Straus, & McEvily, 2006). Research further shows that whereas inflammatory remarks can substantially slow the trust-building process, empathic accuracy assists in developing online trust (Feng, Lazar, & Preece, 2004; Reinig & Mejias, 2004). These findings have important implications for both conflict resolution and negotiation. In both cases, trust is critical to the kinds of behaviors necessary for problem solving. This research highlights the need to better understand not only how communication assists in building online trust but also how this process shapes negotiators' willingness to employ collaborative strategies.

Effects of Negotiation/Group Support Systems on Conflict

To counter the shortcomings of both face-to-face and mediated communication, researchers have produced a wide array of negotiation, mediation, and decision support systems (Nyhart & Samarasan, 1989; Shell, 1995; Wheeler, 1995). These negotiation support systems (NSS) aid in preparing and evaluating negotiation options (e.g., NEGOPLAN; Kersten, Michalowski, Szpakowicz, & Koperczak, 1991; and NEGOTEX; Rangaswamy, Eliashberg, Burke, & Wind, 1989) or in restructuring the dynamics of the negotiation process (e.g., Nagel & Mills, 1990; PERSUADER; Sycara, 1991). These systems simulate the negotiation problem, calculate risk and uncertainty, introduce options, and help parties assess preferences (Nyhart & Samarasan, 1989). Some software programs play the role of a mediator who assists both parties in communicating with each other (e.g., MEDIATOR; Kolodner & Simpson, 1989).

Advocates of NSS claim that these programs facilitate agreement, improve solution quality, and enhance problem-solving skills (Shell, 1995). Research, however, reveals mixed results. In terms of outcomes, Rangaswamy and Shell (1997) reported that NSS dyads reach higher Pareto optimal agreements than do face-to-face teams, but other studies show no differences between NSS and face-to-face groups in obtaining integrative settlements (Miranda & Bostrom, 1993–1994), engaging in productive conflicts (Poole, Holmes, & Desanctis, 1991), and increasing negotiation quality or satisfaction (Zigurs, Reitsma, Lewis, Hubscher, & Hayes, 1999). In studies of group conflict, teams who use group decision support systems (GDSS) employ more avoidance behaviors, more voting tactics, less interpersonal conflicts, and lower amounts of issue conflict than do control groups, even though the two conditions do not differ in outcomes (Miranda & Bostrom, 1993–1994; Poole et al., 1991). Overall, NSS serves a useful function in clarifying procedures and deciphering complex technical tasks, but research leads to mixed results regarding its promise to improve negotiated outcomes.

As an emerging area, the study of communication technology and conflict management needs to move away from comparing different types of media. Media per se extend beyond the physical features of particular technologies into the ways that negotiators determine appropriate options and interpret the strategies that bargainers use (DeSanctis & Poole, 1994). The negotiation process literature suggests potential avenues for investigation. For example, researchers might track the sequences, patterns, and phases of bargaining when using communication technologies. Specifically, several threads of conversation can run concurrently in the use of instant messaging and this written, synchronous medium may affect patterns of communication in conflict management. Researchers also need to investigate the ways that bargainers combine different media in negotiations, as scholars have done with trade negotiations that employ telephone, computer-mediated, and face-to-face interactions and discussions (Firth, 1995). Finally, future research on negotiation support systems needs to move beyond design and explore the conditions under which the software systems would be an asset or a hindrance to effective negotiations.

CONCLUSION

In general, scholars have gained numerous insights about the role of communication in conflict management and negotiation. Yet, there is still much to be done. The inherent difficulties in studying communication processes act as a barrier to the rapid growth of knowledge in this field (Weingart, 1997; Weingart, Olekalns, & Smith, 2004). Yet, as this review shows, understanding the complex relationships between antecedent factors and the choice of conflict styles and negotiation tactics is central to improving dispute resolution and reaching effective negotiated agreements.

There are many opportunities for expanding theory and knowledge in this field. Despite the increase in the number of studies that examine antecedent factors, research on the types and ways that context shapes negotiated behaviors is limited. Although researchers incorporate a range of antecedent conditions (e.g., face concerns, power, culture, outcome goals, emotion), scholars have not developed a systematic approach to the study of contextual factors. That is, scholars include a wide array of different context variables that might influence conflict management, but they do not build on a theoretical model of their interrelationships. Consequently, researchers cannot draw any broad conclusions about the ways that external factors affect behavioral choices. The absence of a theoretical framework that identifies and unifies context variables contributes to this problem.

This issue explains why seemingly identical variables exert different effects on the same behavior and outcomes. In particular, identical goals (to maximize own or joint outcomes) have different effects on negotiation behaviors and outcomes. For example, when researchers manipulate goals explicitly through instructions, they influence *both* behavior and outcomes, but when they are established implicitly through disposition or culture, they tend to affect only behavior. This finding raises the broad question as to whether other contextual factors have different effects on behavior and outcomes, depending on whether the research design introduces them explicitly or they surface implicitly through other antecedent variables. Examples of such variables include situational power versus power distance and high- versus low-context communication patterns. Another example is the finding that implicit cues influence behavior in the absence of clear external ones, but when external cues are present, these factors dominate research findings (Olekalns & Weingart, 2003). The explanatory power of this relationship remains unclear.

Moreover, research on the behavior–outcomes relationships reveals slightly different findings in the conflict management and negotiation domains. Whereas the conflict management literature focuses on the intangible consequences of strategy use, such as disputant satisfaction, negotiation research centers on the fine-grained analyses of strategy patterns and substantive outcomes. Whereas conflict management studies focus on the effectiveness of strategies for managing disputes, negotiation research asks how communication strategies contribute to the equality of a settlement. Because research in the two domains is asymmetrical, negotiation studies could benefit from focusing on the relationship between behaviors and intangible outcomes while conflict management research could benefit from concentrating on the relationship between behaviors and the quality of settlements.

Finally, both domains would benefit from exploring the complex relationships between context, communication, and outcomes. To our knowledge, a limited number of studies address these relationships in negotiation and only two studies consider these complex relationships in dispute resolution (Friedman et al., 2004; Pinkley, Brittain, Neale, & Northcraft, 1995). Knowledge of these relationships is increasingly important given that context appears to contribute to outcomes more significantly than does limiting the quality or nature of settlements. These findings suggest the need for a contingent model of strategic choice (e.g., Carnevale, 2006).

Many studies included in this review center on individuals and their strategic choices for managing conflicts. However, recognizing that individuals act in dyads or groups suggests that scholars should focus on patterns of behavior and the temporal aspects of negotiation and conflict management. This focus shifts analyses from the individual to the dyad or the negotiation/conflict episode as a whole. Again, an asymmetrical pattern typifies research in the negotiation and the conflict management domains. On the whole, negotiation researchers concentrate on the dyad and immediate patterns of action–reaction (strategy sequences), whereas conflict management researchers examine how an entire conflict episode unfolds. This difference in context may emanate from studying negotiation in laboratory settings as opposed to studying conflict management in the field. Examining interaction sequences may be easier in the lab than in the field while tracking conflict episodes may be natural for field investigations.

Finally, research on the role of technology in negotiation and dispute resolution focuses largely on the relative efficacy of various media; hence, it lags behind studies of face-to face negotiation and dispute resolution. Linking the use of technology to communication patterns (e.g., sequences and phases) introduces the idea of using technology to manage conflict in productive ways. For example, researchers could pose the questions: Can technology help negotiators sustain cooperative cycles and prevent contentious ones over time? Or, can technology be used to structure the expressions of emotion in ways that assist negotiators in reaching resolution to a conflict?

This chapter aimed to review the progress in the field of communication and conflict over the last 20 years. Certainly, the number of studies examining the role of communication in negotiation and conflict management has grown. However, the development of research trends in the field seems somewhat haphazard in nature. This pattern may reflect, in part, the lack of a clear theoretical framework to guide research as well as the different interests of negotiation and conflict management scholars. In particular, while scholars in both domains address similar broad questions, their focus on the relationships between communication and conflict is asymmetrical. A more complete picture of these relationships would occur if researchers addressed these asymmetries. The greatest knowledge gaps in this work center on the temporal aspects of negotiations; thus, an important direction for future research is to link the evolution of strategies over time to emotional expressions and link the use of technology to communication structuring over time. We concluded by looking to the future and recognizing that, increasingly, communication would occur through media other than face-to-face interactions. Understanding how culture, emotion, and trust play out in the online world is critical to the effective use of communication in resolving disputes and making deals.

REFERENCES

Adair, W. L. (2003). Integrative sequences and negotiation outcome in same- and mixed-culture negotiations. *International Journal of Conflict Management, 14* (3–4), 273–296.

Adair, W., Brett, J., Lempereur, A., Okumura, T., Shikhirev, P., Tinsley, C., et al. (2004). Culture and negotiation strategy. *Negotiation Journal, 20,* 87–111.

Adair, W., & Brett, J. M. (2005). The negotiation dance: Time, culture, and behavioral sequences in negotiation. *Organizational Science, 16*(1), 33–51.

Adair, W., Okumura, T., & Brett, J. (2001). Negotiation behavior when cultures collide: The U.S. and Japan. *Journal of Applied Psychology, 86,* 371–385.

Adler, N. J., Graham, J. L., & Gehrke, T. S. (1987). Business negotiations in Canada, Mexico, and the United States. *Journal of Business Research, 15,* 411–429.

Allred, K. G. (1999). Anger and retaliation: Toward an understanding of impassioned conflict in organizations. In R. J. Bies, R. J. Lewicki & B. H. Sheppard (Eds.), *Research on negotiation in organizations* (Vol. 7, pp. 27–58). Greenwich, CT: JAI Press.

Allred, K. G., Mallozzi, J. S., Matsui, F., & Raia, C. P. (1997). The influence of anger and compassion on negotiation performance. *Organizational Behavior and Human Decision Processes, 70*, 175–187.

Arunachalam, V., & Dilla, W. N. (1995). Judgment accuracy and outcomes in negotiations: A causal modeling analysis of decision-aiding effects. *Organizational Behavior and Human Decision Processes, 61*, 289–304.

Baron, R. A. (1990). Environmentally induced positive affect: Its impact on self-efficacy, task performance, negotiation, and conflict. *Journal of Applied Social Psychology, 20*, 368–384.

Baron, R. A., Fortin, S. P., Frei, R. L., Hauver, L. A., & Shack, M. L. (1990). Reducing organizational conflict: The role of socially-induced positive affect. *International Journal of Conflict Management, 1*, 133–152.

Barry, B. (1999). The tactical use of emotion in negotiation. In R. J. Bies, R. J. Lewicki, & B. H. Sheppard (Eds.), *Research on negotiation in organizations* (Vol. 7, pp. 93–121). Greenwich, CT: JAI Press.

Barry, B., Fulmer, I. S., & Van Kleef, G. (2004). I laughed, I cried, I settled: The role of emotion in negotiation. In M. J. Gelfand & J. M. Brett (Eds.), *The handbook of negotiation and culture: Theoretical advances and cross-cultural perspectives* (pp. 71–94). Palo Alto, CA: Stanford University Press.

Baxter, L. A. (1982). Conflict management: An episodic approach. *Small Group Behavior, 13*, 23–42.

Betancourt, H. (1990). An attributional approach to intergroup and international conflict. In S. Graham & V. Folkes (Eds.), *Attribution theory: Application to achievement, mental health, and interpersonal conflict* (pp. 205–220). Hillsdale, NJ: Lawrence Erlbaum Associates.

Blake, R. R., & Mouton, J. S. (1964). *The new managerial grid.* Houston, TX: Gulf Publishing Company.

Bodtker, A. M., & Jameson, J. K. (2001). Emotion in conflict formation and its transformation: application to organizational conflict management. *International Journal of Conflict Management, 12*, 259–275.

Brett, J., Olekalns, M., Friedman, R., Goates, N., Anderson, C., & Lisco, C. (2007). Sticks and stones: Language, structure and on-line dispute resolution. *Academy of Management Review, 50*, 85–100

Brett, J. M., Shapiro, D. L., & Lytle, A. L. (1998). Refocusing rights- and power-oriented negotiators toward integrative negotiations: Process and outcome effects. *Academy of Management Journal, 41*, 410–424.

Brett, J. M., Weingart, L. R., & Olekalns, M. (2004). Baubles, bangles and beads: Modeling the evolution of negotiating groups over time. In M. A. Neale, E. A. Mannix, & S. Blount (Eds.), *Research in managing groups and teams: Time in groups* (Vol. 6, pp. 39–64). New York: Elsevier Science.

Brew, F. P., & Cairns, D. R. (2004). Styles of managing interpersonal workplace conflict in relation to status and face concern: A study with Anglos and Chinese. *International Journal of Conflict Management, 15*, 27–56.

Brown, P., & Levinson, S. (1987). *Politeness: Some universals in language usage.* Cambridge, U.K.: Cambridge University Press.

Cai, D. A., Wilson, S. R., & Drake, L. E. (2000). Culture in the context of intercultural negotiation: Individualism-collectivism and paths to integrative agreements. *Human Communication Research, 26,* 591–671.

Carnevale, P. (2006). *The structure of integrative agreement: The agreement circumplex.* Paper presented at the International Association of Conflict Management Conference, Montreal, Canada.

Carnevale, P. J., & Isen, A. M. (1986). The influence of positive affect and visual access on the discovery of integrative solutions in bilateral negotiation. *Organizational Behavior and Human Decision Processes, 37,* 1–13.

Carnevale, P. J. D., & Lawler, E. J. (1987). Time pressure and the development of integrative agreements in bilateral negotiations. *Journal of Conflict Resolution, 30,* 636–659.

Coleman, P. T. (2000). Fostering ripeness in seemingly intractable conflict: An experimental study. *International Journal of Conflict Management, 11,* 300–317.

Conrad, C. (1991). Communication in conflict: Style-strategy relationships. *Communication Monographs, 58,* 135–155.

Daft, R. L., & Lengel, R. H. (1986). Organizational information requirements, media richness and structural design. *Management Science, 32,* 554–571.

Davidson, M. N., & Greenhalgh, L. (1999). The role of emotion in negotiation: The impact of anger and race. In R. J. Bies, R. J. Lewicki, & B. H. Sheppard (Eds.), *Research on negotiation in organizations* (Vol. 7, pp. 3–26). Stamford, CT: JAI Press.

De Dreu, C. K. W., Evers, A., Beersma, B., Kluwer, E. S., & Nauta, A. (2001). A theory-based measure of conflict management strategies in the workplace. *Journal of Organizational Behavior, 22,* 645–668.

De Dreu, C. K. W., Giebels E., & Van de Vliert, E. (1998). Social motives and trust in integrative negotiation: The disruptive effects of punitive capability. *Journal of Applied Psychology, 83,* 408–422.

De Dreu, C. K. W., Weingart, L. R., & Kwon, S. (2000). Influence of social motives on integrative negotiations: A meta-analytic review and test of two theories. *Journal of Personality and Social Psychology, 78,* 889–905.

Desanctis, G., & Poole, M. S. (1994). Capturing the complexity in advanced technology use: Adaptive structuration theory. *Organizational Science, 5,* 121–147.

Diez, M. A. (1986). Negotiation competence: A conceptualization of the rules of negotiation interaction. In D. G. Ellis & W. A. Donohue (Eds.), *Contemporary issues in language and discourse processing.* Hillsdale, NJ: Lawrence Erlbaum Associates.

Donohue, W. A. (1981). Development of a model of rule use in negotiation. *Communication Monographs, 48,* 106–120.

Dorado, M. A., Medina, F. J., Munduate, L., Cisneros, I. F. J., & Euwema, M. (2002). Computer-mediated negotiation of an escalated conflict. *Small Group Research, 33,* 509–524.

Drake, B. H., & Moberg, D. J. (1986). Communicating influence attempts in dyads: Linguistic sedatives and palliatives. *Academy of Management Review, 11,* 567–584.

Drake, L. E. (2001). The culture-negotiation link: Integrative and distributive bargaining through an intercultural communication lens. *Human Communication Research, 27,* 317–349.

Druckman, D. (1986). Stages, turning-points, and crises: Negotiating military base rights, Spain and the United-States. *Journal of Conflict Resolution, 30,* 327–360.

Druckman, D. (2001). Turning points in international negotiation—A comparative analysis. *Journal of Conflict Resolution, 45,* 519–544.

Druckman, D., & Broome, B. J. (1991). Value differences and conflict resolution: Familiarity or liking? *Journal of Conflict Resolution, 35,* 571–593.

Druckman, D., Husbands, J. L., & Johnston, K. (1991). Turning-points in the INF negotiations. *Negotiation Journal, 7,* 55–67.

Elsayed-Ekhouly, S. M., & Buda, R. (1996). Organizational conflict: A comparative analysis of conflict styles across cultures. *International Journal of Conflict Management, 7,* 71–81.

Feng, J. J., Lazar, J., & Preece, J. (2004). Empathy and online interpersonal trust: A fragile relationship. *Behaviour and Information Technology, 23,* 97–106.

Filley, A. (1975). *Interpersonal conflict resolution.* Glenview, IL: Scott, Foresman.

Firth, A. (1995). Talking for change: Commodity negotiating by telephone. In A. Firth (Ed.), *The discourse of negotiation: Studies of language in the workplace* (pp. 183–222). Kidlington, U.K.: Pergamon Elsevier Science Ltd.

Fischer-Lokou, J., & Guéguen, N. (2001). Impact of a mediator, mutual representation of the negotiators and decision making in a dyad: Evaluation in the case of computer-mediated communication. *Studia Psychologica, 43,* 13–21.

Fischer-Lokou, J., Guéguen, N., & Lépy, N. (2004). Effects of communication on information networks versus face-to-face on the reciprocal representation of negotiators/Effets de la communication par réseaux informatiques versus en face-à-face sur la representation réciproque des négociateurs. *Bulletin de Psychologie, 57,* 525–533.

Forgas, J. P. (1998). On feeling good and getting your way: Mood effects on negotiator cognition and bargaining strategies. *Journal of Personality and Social Psychology, 74,* 565–577.

Friedman, R., Anderson, C., Brett, J., Olekalns, M., Goates, N., & Lisco, C. C. (2004). The positive and negative effects of anger on dispute resolution: Evidence from electronically mediated disputes. *Journal of Applied Psychology, 89,* 369–376.

Friedman, R. A., & Currall, S. C. (2003). Conflict escalation: Dispute exacerbating elements of e-mail communication. *Human Relations, 56,* 1325–1347.

Gayle, B. M. (1991). Sex equity in workplace conflict management. *Journal of Applied Communication Research, 19,* 152–169.

Gersick, C. J. G. (1989). Marking time: Predictable transitions in task groups. *Academy of Management Journal, 32,* 274–309.

Giebels, E., De Dreu, C. K. W., & Van de Vliert, E. (2000). Interdependence in negotiation: Effects of exit options and social motive on distributive and integrative negotiation. *European Journal of Social Psychology, 30,* 255–272.

Goffman, E. (1967). *Interaction ritual: Essays in face-to-face behavior.* Chicago: Aldine.

Graham, J. L. (1985). The influence of culture on the process of business negotiations: An exploratory study. *Journal of International Business Studies, 16,* 81 96.

Graham, J. L., Kim, D. K., Lin, C., & Robinson, M. (1988). Buyer-seller negotiations around the Pacific Rim: Differences in fundamental exchange processes. *Journal of Consumer Research, 15,* 48–54.

Hall, E. T. (1976). *Beyond culture.* New York: Anchor Press.

Harinck, F., & De Dreu, C. K. W. (2004). Negotiating interests or values and reaching integrative agreements: The importance of time pressure and temporary impasses. *European Journal of Social Psychology, 34,* 595–611.

Hobman, E. V., Bordia, P., Irmer, B., & Chang, A. (2002). The expression of conflict in computer-mediated and face-to-face groups. *Small Group Research, 33,* 439–465.

Hollingshead, A. B., & Carnevale, P. (1990). Positive affect and decision frame in integrative bargaining: A reversal of the frame effect. *Academy of Management Proceedings,* 385–389.

Holmes, M. E. (1992). Phase structures in negotiation. In L. L. Putnam & M. E. Roloff (Eds.), *Communication and negotiation* (pp. 83–105). Newbury Park, CA: Sage.

Holt, J. L., & DeVore, C. J. (2005). Culture, gender, organizational role, and styles of conflict resolution: A meta-analysis. *International Journal of Intercultural Relations, 29,* 165–196.

Hyder, E. B., Prietula, M. J., & Weingart, L. R. (2000). Getting to best: Efficiency versus optimality in negotiation. *Cognitive Science, 24,* 169–204.

Isen, A. M., & Patrick, R. (1983). The effect of positive feelings on risk-taking: When the chips are down. *Organizational Behavior and Human Performance, 31,* 194–202.

Jett, Q. R., & George, J. M. (2003). Work interrupted: A closer look at the role of interruptions in organizational life. *Academy of Management Review, 28,* 494–507.

Kersten, G., Michalowski, W., Szpakowicz, S., & Koperczak, Z. (1991). Restructurable representations of negotiation. *Management Science, 37,* 1269–1290.

Kiesler, S. (1997). Preface. In S. Kiesler (Ed.), *Culture of the Internet*. Hillsdale, NJ: Lawrence Erlbaum Associates.

Kiesler, S., Seigel, J., & McGuire, T. W. (1984). Social psychological aspects of computer-mediated communication. *American Psychologist, 39,* 1123–1134.

Kirkbride, P. S., Tang, S. F. Y., & Westwood, R. I. (1991). Chinese conflict preferences and negotiating behavior: Cultural and psychological influences. *Organizational Studies, 12,* 365–386.

Kolodner, J. L., & Simpson, R. L. (1989). The MEDIATOR: Analysis of an early case-based problem solver. *Cognitive Science, 13,* 507–549.

Kozan, M. K., & Ergin, C. (1999). The influence of intra-cultural value differences on conflict management practices. *International Journal of Conflict Management, 10,* 249–267.

Kruger, J., Epley, N., Parker, J., & Ng, Z. W. (2005) Egocentrism over e-mail: Can we communicate as well as we think? *Journal of Personality and Social Psychology, 89,* 925–936.

Lax, D., & Sebenius, J. (1986). *The manager as negotiator*. New York: Free Press.

Lewis, S. A., & Fry, W. R. (1977). Effects of visual access and orientation on the discovery of integrative bargaining alternatives. *Organizational Behavior and Human Performance, 20,* 75–92.

Lim, S. G. S., & Murnighan, K. (1994). Phases, deadlines and the bargaining process, *Organizational Behavior and Human Decision Processes, 58,* 153–171.

McCready, V., & Roberts, J. E. (1996). A comparison of conflict tactics in the supervisory process. *Journal of Speech & Hearing Research, 39,* 191–199.

McGinn, K. L., Lingo, E. L., & Ciano, K. (2004). Transitions through out-of-keeping acts. *Negotiation Journal, 20,* 171–184.

Miranda, S. M., & Bostrom, R. P. (1993–1994). The impact of group support systems on group conflict and conflict management. *Journal of Management Information Systems, 10,* 63–95.

Moberg, P. J. (2001). Linking conflict strategy to the five-factor model: Theoretical and empirical foundations. *International Journal of Conflict Management, 12,* 47–68.

Moore, D. A., Kurtzberg, T. R., Thompson, L. L., & Morris, M. (1999). Long and short routes to success in electronically-mediated negotiations: Group affiliations and good vibrations. *Organizational Behavior and Human Decision Processes, 77,* 22–43.

Morrill, C., & Thomas, C. K. (1992). Organizational conflict management as disputing process: The problem of social escalation. *Human Communication Research, 18,* 400–428.

Morris, M. W., & Keltner, D. (2000). How emotions work: The social functions of emotional expression in negotiations. *Research in Organizational Behavior, 22,* 1–50.

Murnighan, J. K., Babcock, L., Thompson, L., & Pillutla, M. (1999). The information dilemma in negotiations: Effects of experience, incentives, and integrative potential. *International Journal of Conflict Management, 10,* 313–339.

Nagel, S. S., & Mills, M. K. (1990). *Multi-criteria methods for alternative dispute resolution: With microcomputer software applications.* New York: Quorum Books.

Natlandsmyr, J. H., & Rognes, J. (1995). Culture, behavior, and negotiation outcomes: A comparative and cross-cultural study of Mexican and Norwegian negotiators. *International Journal of Conflict Management, 6,* 5–29.

Newman, M. L., Pennebaker, J. W., Berry, D. S., & Richards, J. M. (2003). Lying words: Predicting deception from linguistic styles. *Personality and Social Psychology Bulletin, 29,* 665–675.

Nicotera, A. M. (1993). Beyond two dimensions: A grounded theory model of conflict-handling behavior. *Management Communication Quarterly, 6,* 282–306.

Nicotera, A. M. (1994). The use of multiple approaches to conflict: A study of sequences. *Human Communication Research, 20,* 592–621.

Nyhart, J. D., & Samarasan, D. K. (1989). The elements of negotiation management: Using computers to help resolve conflict. *Negotiation Journal, 5,* 43–62.

O'Connor, K. (1997). Motives and cognitions in negotiation: A theoretical integration and an empirical test. *International Journal of Conflict Management, 8,* 114–131.

Oetzel, J., Myers, K. K., Meares, M., & Lara, E. (2003). Interpersonal conflict in organizations: Explaining conflict styles via face-negotiation theory. *Communication Research Reports, 20,* 106–115.

Oetzel, J. G., & Ting-Toomey, S. (2003). Face concerns in interpersonal conflict: A cross-cultural empirical test of the face negotiation theory. *Communication Research, 30,* 599–624.

Okhuysen, G. A., & Eisenhardt, K. M. (2002). Integrating knowledge in groups: How formal interventions enable flexibility. *Organization Science, 13,* 370–386

Olekalns, M., Brett, J. M., & Weingart, L. R. (2003). Phases, transitions and interruptions: Modeling processes in multi-party negotiations. *International Journal of Conflict Management, 14,* 191–211.

Olekalns, M., & Smith, P. L. (1999). Social value orientations and strategy choices in competitive negotiations. *Personality & Social Psychology Bulletin, 25,* 657–668.

Olekalns, M., & Smith, P. L. (2000). Negotiating optimal outcomes: The role of strategic sequences in competitive negotiations. *Human Communication Research, 24*, 528–560.

Olekalns, M., & Smith, P. L. (2003a). Social motives in negotiation: The relationship between dyad composition, negotiation processes and outcomes. *International Journal of Conflict Management, 14*, 233–254.

Olekalns, M., & Smith, P. L. (2003b). Testing the relationships among negotiators' motivational orientations, strategy choices, and outcomes. *Journal of Experimental Social Psychology, 39*, 101–117.

Olekalns, M., & Smith, P. L. (2005). Moments in time: Meta-cognition, trust, and outcomes in dyadic negotiations. *Personality and Social Psychology Bulletin, 31*, 1696–1707.

Olekalns, M., Smith, P. L., & Walsh, T. (1996). The process of negotiating: Strategies, timing and outcomes. *Organizational Behavior and Human Decision Processes, 67*, 61–77.

Olekalns, M., & Weingart, L. R. (2003, June). *Think globally, act locally: Towards an adaptive model of dyadic negotiations in organizations.* Paper presented at the 16th annual meeting of the International Association for Conflict Management, Melbourne, Australia.

Orcutt, J. D., & Anderson, R. E. (1977). Social interaction, dehumanization, and the "computerized other." *Sociology and Social Research, 61*, 380–396.

Papa, M. J., & Natalle, E. J. (1989). Gender, strategy selection, and discussion satisfaction in interpersonal conflict. *Western Journal of Speech Communication, 53*, 260–272.

Park, H. S., Lee, H. E., & Song, J. A. (2005). "I am sorry to send you SPAM": Cross-cultural differences in use of apologies in e-mail advertising in Korea and the U.S. *Human Communication Research, 31*, 365–398.

Phillips, E., & Cheston, R. (1979). Conflict resolution: What works? *California Management Review, 21*, 76–83.

Pillutla, M. M., & Murnighan, J. K. (1996). Unfairness, anger, and spite: Emotional rejections of ultimatum offers. *Organizational Behavior and Human Decision Processes, 68*, 208–224.

Pinkley, R. L., Brittain, J., Neale, M. A., & Northcraft, G. B. (1995). Managerial third-party dispute intervention: An inductive analysis of intervener strategy selection. *Journal of Applied Psychology, 80*, 386–402.

Poole, M. S., Holmes, M., & Desanctis, G. (1991). Conflict management in a computer-supported meeting environment. *Management Science, 37*, 926–953.

Powell, L., & Hickson, M. (2000). Power imbalance and anticipation of conflict resolution: Positive and negative attributes of perceptual recall. *Communication Research Reports, 17*, 181–190.

Pruitt, D. G. (1981). *Negotiation behavior.* New York: Academic Press.

Pruitt, D. G. (1983). Strategic choice in negotiation. *American Behavioral Scientist, 27*, 167–194.

Pruitt, D. G., & Carnevale, P. J. (1993). *Negotiation in social conflict.* Pacific Grove, CA: Brooks/Cole.

Pruitt, D. G., & Lewis, S. A. (1975). Development of integrative solutions in bilateral negotiations. *Journal of Personality and Social Psychology, 31*, 621–630.

Pruitt, D. G., & Rubin, J. Z. (1986). *Social conflict: Escalation, stalemate, and settlement.* New York: Random House.

Purdy, J. M., Nye, P., & Balakrishnan, P. V. (2000). The impact of communication media on negotiated outcomes. *International Journal of Conflict Management, 11,* 162–187.

Putnam, L. L. (1990). Reframing integrative and distributive bargaining: A process perspective. *Research on Negotiation in Organizations, 2,* 3–30.

Putnam, L. L. (1994). Challenging the assumptions of traditional approaches to negotiation. *Negotiation Journal, 10,* 337–346.

Putnam, L. L. (2004). Transforming moves as critical moments in negotiations. *Negotiation Journal, 20,* 275–295.

Putnam, L. L., & Folger, J. P. (1988). Communication, conflict and dispute resolution: The study of interaction and the development of conflict theory. *Communication Research, 15,* 349–359.

Putnam, L. L., & Jones, T. S. (1982a). Reciprocity in negotiations: An analysis of bargaining interaction. *Communication Monographs, 49,* 171–191.

Putnam, L. L., & Jones, T. S. (1982b). The role of communication in bargaining. *Communication Monographs, 49,* 262–282.

Putnam, L. L., & Poole, M. S. (1987). Conflict and negotiation. In F. M. Jablin, L. L. Putnam, K. H. Roberts, & L. W. Porter (Eds.), *Handbook of organizational communication* (pp. 549–599). Newbury Park, CA: Sage.

Putnam, L. L., & Wilson, C. E. (1982). Communicative strategies in organizational conflicts: Reliability and validity of a measurement scale. In M. Burgoon (Ed.), *Communication yearbook 6* (pp. 629–652). Newbury Park, CA: Sage.

Putnam, L. L., & Wilson, S. R. (1989). Argumentation and bargaining strategies as discriminators of integrative outcomes. In M. A. Rahim (Ed.), *Managing conflict: An interdisciplinary approach* (pp. 549–599). Newbury Park, CA: Sage.

Putnam, L. L., Wilson, S. R., & Turner, D. B. (1990). The evolution of policy arguments in distributive and integrative bargaining contexts. *Argumentation, 4,* 129–152.

Rahim, A. (1983). A measure of styles of handling interpersonal conflict. *Academy of Management Journal, 26,* 368–376.

Rahim, A., & Bonoma, T. V. (1979). Managing organizational conflict: Model for diagnosis and intervention. *Psychological Reports, 44,* 1323–1344.

Rahim, M. A. (1986). Referent role and styles of handling interpersonal conflict. *Journal of Social Psychology, 126,* 79–86.

Ramirez, A., Jr., Walther, J. B., Burgoon, J. K., & Sunnafrank, M. (2002). Information-seeking strategies, uncertainty, and computer-mediated communication toward a conceptual model. *Human Communication Research, 28,* 213–228.

Rangaswamy, A., Eliashberg, J., Burke, R., & Wind, J. (1989). Developing marketing expert systems: An application to international negotiations. *Journal of Marketing, 53,* 24–49.

Rangaswamy, A., & Shell, G. R. (1997). Using computers to realize joint gains in negotiations: Toward an "electronic bargaining table." *Management Science, 43,* 1147–1163.

Reinig, B. A., & Mejias, R. J. (2004). The effects of national culture and anonymity on flaming and criticalness in GSS-supported discussions. *Small Group Research, 35,* 698–723.

Richmond, V. P., Wagner, J. P., & McCroskey, J. C. (1983). The impact of perceptions of leadership style, use of power, and conflict management style on organizational outcomes. *Communication Quarterly, 31,* 27–36.

Roloff, M. E., Tutzauer, F. E., & Dailey, W. O. (1989). The role of argumentation in distributive and integrative bargaining contexts: Seeking relative advantage but at what cost? In M. A. Rahim (Ed.), *Managing conflict: An interdisciplinary approach* (pp. 109–120). New York: Praeger.

Schulz, J. W., & Pruitt, D. G. (1978). The effects of mutual concern on joint welfare. *Journal of Experimental Social Psychology, 14*, 480–492.

Sheffield, J. (1995). The effect of communication medium on negotiation performance. *Group Decision and Negotiation, 4*, 159–179.

Shell, G. R. (1995). Computer-assisted negotiation and mediation: Where are we and where are we going? *Negotiation Journal, 11*, 117–121.

Short, J. A. (1974). Effects of medium of communication on experimental negotiation. *Human Relations, 27*, 225–234.

Smith, P. L., Olekalns, M., & Weingart, L. R. (2005). Markov chain models of communication processes in negotiation. *International Negotiation, 10*, 97–113.

Sternberg, R. L., & Soriano, L. J. (1984). Styles of conflict resolution. *Journal of Personality and Social Psychology, 47*, 115–126.

Sycara, K. P. (1991). Problem restructuring in negotiation. *Management Science, 37*, 1248–1268.

Taylor, P. J., & Donald, I. (2003). Foundations and evidence for an interaction-based approach to conflict negotiation. *International Journal of Conflict Management, 14*, 213–232.

Thomas, K. (1976). Conflict and conflict management. In M. D. Dunnette (Ed.), *Handbook of industrial and organizational psychology* (pp. 889–935). Chicago: Rand McNally.

Thompsen, P. A., & Foulger, D. A. (1996). Effects of pictographs and quoting on flaming in electronic mail. *Computers in Human Behavior, 12*, 225–243.

Thompson, L., Medvec, V. H., Seiden, V., & Kopelman, S. (2001). Poker face, smiley face, and rant 'n' rave: Myths and realities about emotion in negotiation. In M. A. Hogg & R. S. Tinsdale (Eds.), *Blackwell handbook of social psychology: Group processes* (pp. 139–163). Malden, MA: Blackwell Publishers.

Tidwell, L. C., & Walther, J. B. (2002) Computer-mediated communication effects on disclosure, impressions, and interpersonal evaluations: Getting to know one another a bit at a time. *Human Communication Research, 28*, 317–348.

Ting-Toomey, S., Gao, G., Trubisky, P., Yang, Z., Kim, H. S., Liu, S., et al. (1991). Culture, face maintenance, and styles of handling interpersonal conflict: A study of five cultures. *International Journal of Conflict Management, 2*, 275–296.

Ting-Toomey, S., & Kurogi, A. (1998). Facework competence in intercultural conflict: An updated face-negotiation theory. *International Journal of Intercultural Relations, 22*, 187–225.

Tjosvold, D., & Sun, H. F. (2002). Understanding conflict avoidance: Relationship, motivations, actions, and consequences. *International Journal of Conflict Management, 13*, 142–164.

Turnbull, A. A., Strickland, L., & Shaver, K. G. (1976). Medium of communication, differential power, and phrasing of concessions: Negotiating success and attributions to the opponent. *Human Communication Research, 2*, 262–270.

Valley, K. L., Moag, J., & Bazerman, M. H. (1998). A matter of trust: Effects of communication on the efficiency and distribution of outcomes. *Journal of Economic Behavior Organization, 34*, 211–238.

Van de Vliert, E., Huismans, S. E., & Euwema, M. C. (1995). Managing conflict with a subordinate or a superior: Effectiveness of conglomerated behavior. *Journal of Applied Psychology, 80*, 271–281.

Van de Vliert, E., Nauta, A., Giebels, E. & Janssen, O. (1999). Constructive conflict at work. *Journal of Organizational Behavior, 20*, 475–491.

Van de Vliert, E., Ohbuchi, K., Van Rossum, B., Hayashi, Y., & Van der Vegt, G. S. (2004). Conglomerated contending by Japanese subordinates. *International Journal of Conflict Management, 15*, 192–207.

Van Kleef, G. A., De Dreu, C. K., & Manstead, A. S. (2004a). The interpersonal effects of anger and happiness in negotiation. *Journal of Personality and Social Psychology, 86*, 57–76.

Van Kleef, G. A., De Dreu, C. K., & Manstead, A. S. (2004b). The interpersonal effects of emotions in negotiations: A motivated information processing approach. *Journal of Personality and Social Psychology, 87*, 510–528.

Vishwanath, A. (2003). Comparing online information effects: A cross-cultural comparison of online information and uncertainty avoidance. *Communication Research, 30*, 579–598.

Volkema, R. J. (1998). A comparison of perceptions of ethical negotiation behavior in Mexico and the United States. *International Journal of Conflict Management, 9*, 218–233.

Walthier, J. B., & D'Addario, K. P. (2001). The impacts of emoticons on message interpretation in computer-mediated communication. *Social Science Computer Review, 19*, 324–347.

Walton, R. E., & McKersie, R. B. (1965). A behavioral theory of labor negotiations: An analysis of a social interaction system. Ithaca, NY: Cornell University Press.

Weingart, L. R. (1997). How did they do that? The ways and means of studying group processes. In L. L. Cummings & B. M. Staw (Eds.), *Research in organizational behavior* (Vol. 19, pp. 189–239). Greenwich, CT: JAI Press.

Weingart, L. R., Bennett, R. J., & Brett, J. M. (1993). The impact of consideration of issues and motivational orientation in group negotiation process and outcome. *Journal of Applied Psychology, 78*, 504–517.

Weingart, L. R., Hyder, E., & Prietula, M. J. (1996). Knowledge matters: The effect of tactical descriptions on negotiation behavior and outcomes. *Journal of Personality and Social Psychology, 70*, 1205–1217.

Weingart, L., Olekalns, M., & Smith, P. L. (2004). Quantitative coding of negotiation processes. *International Negotiation, 9*, 441–456.

Weingart, L. R., Prietula, M. J., Hyder, E., & Genovese, C. (1999). Knowledge and the sequential processes of negotiation: A Markov chain analysis of response-in-kind. *Journal of Experimental Social Psychology, 35*, 366–393.

Weingart, L. R., Thompson, L. L., Bazerman, M. H., & Carroll, J. S. (1990). Tactical behavior and negotiation outcomes. *International Journal of Conflict Management, 1*, 7–31.

Wheeler, M. (1995). Computers and negotiation: Backing into the future. *Negotiation Journal, 11*, 169–175.

Wichman, H. (1970). Effects of isolation and communication on cooperation in a two-person game. *Journal of Personality and Social Psychology, 16*, 114–120.

Wilson, J. M., Straus, S. G., & McEvily, B. (2006). All in due time: The development of trust in computer-mediated and face-to-face teams. *Organizational Behavior and Human Decision Processes, 99*, 16–33.

Wilson, S. R., & Putnam, L. L. (1990). Interaction goals in negotiation. *Communication Yearbook, 13*, 374–406.

Zartman, I. W. (1992). International environmental negotiation: Challenges for analysis and practice. *Negotiation Journal, 8*, 113–123.

Zhang, V. B., Harwood, J., & Hummert, M. L. (2005). Perceptions of conflict management styles in Chinese intergenerational dyads. *Communication Monographs, 72*, 71–91.

Zhou, L., Burgoon, J. K, Nunamaker, J. F., & Twitchell, D. (2004). Automating linguistics-based cues for detecting deception in text-based asynchronous computer-mediated communication. *Group Decision and Negotiation, 13*, 81–106.

Zhou, L., Burgoon, J. Z., Zhang, D., & Nunamaker, J. F. (2004). Language dominance in interpersonal deception in computer-mediated communication. *Computers in Human Behavior, 20*, 381–402.

Zigurs, I., Reitsma, R., Lewis, C., Hubscher, R., & Hayes, C. (1999). Accessibility of computer-based simulation models in inherently conflict-laden negotiations. *Group Decision and Negotiation, 8*, 511–533.

Zornoza, A., Ripoll, P., & Peiró, J. M. (2002). Conflict management in groups that work in two different communication contexts: Face-to-face and computer-mediated. *Communication Small Group Research, 33*, 481–508.

4

Conflict and Group Decision Making: The Role of Social Motivation

BIANCA BEERSMA
University of Amsterdam

DONALD E. CONLON AND
JOHN R. HOLLENBECK
Eli Broad College of Business, Michigan State University

Group decision making has become a crucial aspect of organizational performance (Hackman, 1998; Ilgen, 1999). Within organizations, a great variety of decision-making groups and teams exists—management teams, command-and-control teams, cross-functional project teams, self-managed work teams, as well as computer-assisted teams in which members are located in different countries or continents. All of these teams have one thing in common: Inevitably, conflicts arise regarding divergent ideas, interests, or values held by individual team members. However, based on current knowledge, it is hard to give a conclusive answer to the question of how conflict and different methods for managing conflict affect a groups' ongoing processes and decision making.

Gaining insight into the factors that influence conflict and conflict management in decision-making groups, as well as into how conflict and conflict management in turn affect group processes and decision-making performance, is thus important from both a theoretical and applied perspective. In this chapter, we will focus especially on the role of social motives—preferences for distributions of outcomes between oneself and one's team members (McClintock, 1976)—which, as we will see, constitute a major driving force of conflict behaviors and influence group decision making.

In Figure 4.1, we present an overview of the chapter. Our goal is to review research on the effects of social motives on group conflict and decision making, aiming to clarify how social motives influence whether conflicts benefit or, in contrast, harm group processes and decision-making performance. To do so, we will start by defining the major concepts used in this chapter. Then, we will give an overview of the various dispositional and situational antecedents of social motives. After that, we will describe the effects of social motives on negotiation found by studies in the negotiation research tradition and the factors that moderate these effects. This will be followed by a review of research about the effects of social motives and the factors that moderate these effects that has been conducted in the group decision-making research tradition. We will end the chapter by discussing questions that need future research and suggesting possible directions for further empirical work.

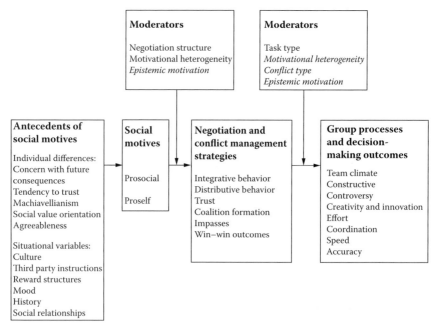

FIGURE 4.1. Overview of the concepts reviewed in this chapter and relationships between them. *Note:* Under each concept, specific operationalizations are listed. Moderators that are suggested to play a role in this chapter, but which have not been empirically investigated yet, are in italics.

CONFLICT AND GROUP DECISION MAKING: THE ROLE OF SOCIAL MOTIVES

In the literature about group decision making, the words *group* and *team* are often used interchangeably, and many different definitions of what groups and teams are have been offered over the years (e.g., Guzzo & Dickson, 1996; Kerr & Tindale, 2004; Levine & Moreland, 1998; Levine & Thompson, 1996). Although there are exceptions, most authors converged on the idea that it seems wiser to be inclusive than exclusive and, therefore, to use a broad definition of what a team or group is (Levine & Moreland, 1998). In line with Guzzo and Dickson and Hackman (1987), we define a decision-making team or group as a number of individuals who view themselves and are viewed by others as a social entity and who are *interdependent* because they perform a task together which has a specified output (e.g., solutions or decisions).

This interdependence, which is the defining characteristic of a team, is mixed motive in nature (Schelling, 1960). This means that two different motivations are present in any team: the *proself* motivation to achieve a high utility or outcome for oneself, and the *prosocial* motivation to achieve a high utility or outcome for the team as a whole. Which of these motives should take precedence often creates a dilemma for group members (Kelley & Thibaut, 1978). As an example, imagine a team in which some members have to work overtime in order to finish an important presentation for a customer. In this case, a proself motivation would lead a team member to go home early and let others finish the job, whereas a prosocial motive would lead this team member to stay late and make sure the presentation is ready before the customer arrives. The dilemma of choosing between the prosocial and the proself motives can be resolved by personal dispositions of team members and situational demands which lead team members to put more weight on either of the two motives at any moment (De Dreu, Weingart, & Kwon, 2000; Liebrand, Jansen, Rijken, & Suhre, 1986; Van Lange, 1999; Van Lange & Kuhlman, 1994; Weingart, Bennett, & Brett, 1993). Moreover, over time, team members may resolve some of the tension between the two motives, for example, by demonstrating "enlightened self-interest," the realization that, oftentimes, one's own interests will be best served if one takes into account the interests of others. This can prompt them to adopt some "middle position" between a purely proself and a purely prosocial motivational orientation. Even then, situations will occur in which prosocial tendencies predominate or in which proself tendencies prevail. For now, it is important to note that we should not assume that members of a given team are always prosocial or proself motivated. Rather, their motives are flexible to a large extent. Nevertheless, throughout this chapter, we will show that the social motives team members adopt have a strong and consistent influence on their conflict management strategies and further team processes and decision-making outcomes. Therefore, comparing the effects of prosocial and proself motives serves an important analytical function.

Many scholars argued (e.g., see De Dreu et al., 2000; Kelley & Thibaut, 1978) and showed (e.g., see Van Lange, 1999; Weingart et al., 1993) that different social motives trigger different "mindsets," or "mental models"—that is, a proself motive causes individuals to frame and define the task situation differently than a prosocial motive. Individuals who adopt a prosocial motive tend to transform the team situation into a cooperative game, in which harmony, fairness, and collective success are important. When evaluating behavior in mixed-motive situations, Liebrand et al. (1986) found that prosocially motivated individuals attach more significance to a morality dimension than to a potency dimension. That is, prosocial individuals define the situation as a choice between morally appropriate and inappropriate alternatives. In contrast, individuals who hold a proself motivation tend to transform the team situation into a competitive game in which power, independence, and personal success are key. They evaluate behavior in mixed-motive situations in terms of a potency dimension; they tend to see cooperative behavior as weak, and independent and competitive thinking as strong and smart.

Whether group members adopt a prosocial or a proself motivation is an important determinant of the way in which conflicts are addressed. We define group conflict as the process that begins when one or more group members experience tension because of perceived differences with other members (De Dreu, Harinck, & Van Vianen, 1999). These conflicts can focus on the distribution of scarce resources, differences in opinion, or value differences, and they can be centered on task-related or socioemotional issues. The research on the effects of social motivation on conflict and group decision making that we review in this chapter has concentrated in two areas that are not tightly integrated. The first area is that of small-group negotiation, and the second area is that of group decision making in a broader sense. The first research tradition is characterized by the use of well-controlled laboratory experiments focusing on decision making *within* a conflict situation. In the second area of research, both laboratory and field studies are conducted. Rather than examining decision making within the context of conflict directly, in many of these studies, conflict is seen as an input factor, influencing more distal decision-making processes and outcomes. After discussing the sources of different social motives in groups, we will first discuss the work on decision making that has been done in the field of negotiation and then proceed to work on group decision making in a broader sense. We will also discuss moderators of the effects of social motives that have been identified in both research traditions. After our analysis, we will focus on questions that await further research.

ANTECEDENTS OF SOCIAL MOTIVES

As previously argued, team members can have different social motives; they can either predominantly focus on the interests and outcomes of the group as a whole or predominantly focus on their own interests and outcomes. These social motives have been demonstrated to have a critical influence on the way in which conflicts are managed in groups (cf., De Dreu et al., 2000; Deutsch, 1973; Tjosvold, 1998). Before discussing these effects of social motivation in detail, we will first discuss the diverse sources of social motives in teams by looking at how several team input variables relate to the social motivation of team members.

Individual Differences

Several dispositional variables have been found to affect individuals' prosocial and proself orientations. Dispositional *concern with future consequences* (Messick & Brewer, 1983) as well as individuals' *tendency to trust* (Yamagishi & Sato, 1986) has been shown to make people more inclined to adopt a prosocial motive. On the other hand, *Machiavellianism*, a person's tendency to deceive and manipulate others for personal gain (Christie & Geis, 1970), has been shown to be related to adopting a proself motivation.

Much research has concentrated on *social value orientation* (McClintock, 1972), a stable individual difference variable. In this approach, individuals' tendencies to make either prosocial or proself choices are measured using so-called decomposed games. An individual is confronted with a number of choices between distributions of resources for him- or herself and an unknown other that reflect a more prosocial or a more proself oriented motivation. Differences in social value orientation, as established with this measure, have been found to be a strong predictor of behaviors in a variety of contexts, such as making cooperative versus egoistic choices in social dilemma games (Van Lange & Kuhlman, 1994), commuting to work by car (a proself choice) or by public transport (a more prosocial choice; Van Lange, Van Vugt, Meertens, & Ruiter, 1998), donating to public goods (Van Lange, 1999), and self-sacrifice in relationships (Van Lange, Agnew, Harinck, & Steemers, 1997; for reviews, see Kelley & Thibaut, 1978; Rusbult & Van Lange, 1996).

Van Lange, Otten, De Bruin, and Joireman (1997) were interested in where social value orientations originate. They found that, compared with people with a proself orientation, prosocials exhibited greater levels of secure attachment and grew up with more sisters. According to Van Lange, Otten, et al. (1997), this indicated that the development of different social value orientations was at least partially rooted in different patterns of social interaction in early childhood and young adulthood. Furthermore, they found that the prevalence of prosocials increases from early adulthood to middle adulthood and old age, whereas the prevalence of proselfs decreases. Because Van Lange, Otten, et al. employed a cross-sectional research design, they could not infer whether this effect was due to cohort differences, selective mortality in the group of proselfs, or the shaping of social value orientations in the direction of a prosocial motivation as age increases.

Other determinants of social motives are the individual group members' personalities in a broader sense. The leading approach to dispositional differences between individuals is the five factor model (FFM), a robust taxonomy of personality (Costa & McCrae, 1992). The five factors are extroversion, agreeableness, emotional stability, conscientiousness, and openness to experience. The trait of agreeableness is intrinsically interpersonal in nature (McCrae & Costa, 1989). Group members high on *agreeableness* tend to be friendly, trusting, warm, tolerant, and eager to help others and to be helped in return (Costa & McCrae). This trait seems clearly related to team members' social motivation; it may be expected that groups with a high level of agreeableness are more prosocially motivated than groups with a lower level of this trait (cf. Barrick, Stewart, Neubert, & Mount, 1998; Moynihan & Peterson, 2001). Indeed, Wagner (1995) found that highly agreeable individuals were more likely to be rated as cooperative group members by their peers. Likewise, Graziano, Jensen-Campbell, and Hair (1996) found that, even in tasks that were designed to elicit conflict, agreeable individuals perceived less conflict and saw their opponents as more positive than those lower in agreeableness, indicating that they approached the conflict in a more prosocial manner.

Situational Variables

Apart from dispositional differences, situational variables play an important role in determining the social motives of team members. The social motive one adopts may in large part depend on one's ethnic or organizational culture. Following Hofstede (1980) and Triandis (1989), collectivistic and individualistic cultures are often distinguished. In the predominantly used measure of individualism–collectivism, the IndCol, a horizontal and vertical dimension is distinguished (Singelis, 1994). In horizontal collectivism, people have an interdependent self-construal (e.g., a low need for distinction and uniqueness), and status differences are not very important. In vertical collectivism, the need for distinction and uniqueness are also low, but relative status is valued and important. In horizontal individualism, people want to be unique and distinct but they are not especially interested in having a higher status. Finally, in vertical individualism, people want to be distinguished and have a higher status than the others (Triandis & Gelfand, 1998). Probst, Carnevale, and Triandis (1999) found that scores on the "vertical individualism" scale of the IndCol, which contains items such as "winning is everything," are correlated to a proself motive. As may be expected, they also found positive correlations between the collectivism subscales and a prosocial motive. Although a criticism of the previously mentioned studies might be that their results seem tauto-logical (e.g., individualistic individuals have a stronger proself motive and collectivistic individuals have a stronger prosocial motive), their value lies in demonstrating that social motives are rooted in cultural differences.

Organizational culture, in the sense of the norms and values that are communicated to teams, is important in shaping team members' social motives as well. Instructions by superiors have been demonstrated to increase either team members' prosocial or their proself motivation. If managers communicate to group members that it is important that they should be concerned with each others' welfare, members are likely to adopt a more prosocial orientation (e.g., see Pruitt & Lewis, 1975; Wein-gart et al., 1993). A study by Deutsch (1958) demonstrated that the effects of communication by supervisors or third parties on the emergence of social motives can be quite strong even if these communications are sub-tle and implicit. Participants in a laboratory study who engaged in a deci-sion-making task with someone else and who were told that this other person was their partner engaged in more constructive behavior than participants to whom the other person was described as an opponent.

Related to the effects of supervisor communications, the reward struc-ture under which teams function plays an important role. Whereas team rewards, in which the rewards that one team member receives are posi-tively correlated with his or her group members' rewards, induce a pro-social motive, individual-based incentive structures, in which payment depends on how well a team member does individually, tend to induce a proself motive (e.g., see Beersma et al., 2003; Schulz & Pruitt, 1978).

Group members' moods have also been shown to affect social motiva-tion. A review by Barry, Fulmer, and Van Kleef (2004) showed that, in the context of integrative negotiation, positive moods seem to increase prosocial motivation, whereas negative moods decrease prosocial motiva-tion. For example, Carnevale and Isen (1986) increased participants' posi-tive affect by having them read funny cartoons. This reduced the use of contentious tactics in a bargaining task and increased joint gain. Kramer, Newton, and Pommerenke (1993) found similar results. Participants who experienced a positive mood because they had watched a humorous video before the negotiation achieved higher joint outcomes than partici-pants that had watched an affect neutral video. Baron's (1990) results also seemed to indicate that a positive mood increases prosocial motivation. Although his participants negotiated against a confederate whose behav-ior was preprogrammed and, thus, negotiation performance could not be assessed, he found that participants who had been exposed to a pleas-ant odor made more concessions during negotiation. This can be seen as a possible indication that they cared more about the other party's inter-ests. Likewise, Forgas (1998) gave participants a small gift (some candy) and found that they treated their counterparts in a negotiation task more constructively than participants who had not received a gift. These effects were mediated by positive mood. Finally, Allred, Mallozzi, Matsui, and Raia (1997) showed that participants who experienced a negative mood (i.e., they were angry because they had been led to believe that their counterpart behaved in a way that negatively affected them) had lower regard for their counterpart's interests and ultimately achieved lower joint outcomes. The previously mentioned research showed both emotions, which are specifically directed at the other party, and more general moods affect social motivation.

A team's history and social relationships within the team can affect social motivation as well. Unfortunately, much research on social motives in teams has largely ignored the fact that, in real life, team members often have an ongoing relationship with a history and future together. Although this history and future may affect whether team members adopt primarily prosocial or proself positions, most often, team conflict and decision making are studied either in the lab, with ad hoc teams lacking a shared history or future, or cross-sectionally in the field, which also excludes the possibility of investigating the effects of the team history and future. Evidence points to the fact that a team's past and future matter. For example, Ben-Yoav and Pruitt (1984) showed that knowing one will interact with a group member in the future renders conflict-management tactics more constructive. Finally, Fry, Firestone, and Williams (1983) showed that existing relationships between conflict parties make the conflict interaction less hostile.

SOCIAL MOTIVES AND TEAM DECISION MAKING

The preceding overview showed that social motives can be triggered by a whole array of different sources. We discussed dispositional differences and features of the situation in which a team finds itself, including past or anticipated future experiences. In the following, we will come to the core purpose of this chapter: to examine the relationships between social motives, conflict, and team decision making. We will argue that in decision-making situations, at any given time team members tend to adopt motivational positions that are prosocial or proself. Whether group members adopt a prosocial or a proself motive is a crucial determinant of how conflict will be managed and, in turn, of how it will affect team decision making. In the following, we describe studies from two research areas that have traditionally been independent, despite the common implications they have for team decision making. The first is research on group negotiation, which has mainly employed laboratory experiments to investigate the effects of social motives on conflict and decision making in teams. The second area is that of research on team decision making, in which both lab and field research have addressed the question of how social motives and conflict affect team decision making.

LITERATURE ON GROUP NEGOTIATION

The Role of Social Motives in Negotiation Processes and Outcomes

Research on the effects of social motives on group negotiation and deci-sion making has concentrated mainly on two-party (*dyadic*) negotiations. Fortunately, there are also some studies that have focused on larger teams, and these are relevant to the purpose of this chapter. Within the negotia-tion tradition, typically, ad hoc groups of participants are assembled in the laboratory, one or more of the "sources" of social motives previously discussed are either measured or manipulated, and groups perform a negotiation simulation.

In such a simulation, group members receive information about the negotiation case and the issues at stake. To measure the quality of group decision making, researchers examine negotiation outcomes. Each member receives a "profit schedule" in which he or she can see how much each possible agreement is worth. In a typical negotiation simulation, individual pay-offs are negatively correlated, such that when one party does better, others do worse. However, negotiators' outcomes often are not perfectly diametrically opposed. Instead, like real-life negotiations, the simulations have integrative potential, in that one party's gains do not equal others' losses. Thus, parties can achieve high outcomes when they trade off losses on unimportant issues for gains on more important ones.

Negotiating team members can choose from a range of so-called *inte-grative behaviors* including the exchange of information about preferences and priorities, trading off losses on issues that are relatively unimportant for gains on more important issues (i.e., *logrolling*), and the cooperative creation of value, and *distributive behaviors* including competitive claim-ing, the use of threats and punitive capabilities, and the communication of persuasive arguments and positional commitments (i.e., statements of "final offers"; Pruitt & Carnevale, 1993). Integrative behaviors are more likely to lead to effective decision making than distributive behaviors. In addition to this, team negotiations have the interesting feature that the outcome preferences of the individual team members can be structured asymmetrically, such that multiple parties may share the same interests on more than one issue, such that one faction of parties with similar pref-erences on multiple issues may face another faction with opposing prefer-ences on these issues. For negotiators facing such a situation, forming a coalition, i.e. "any subset of a group that pools its resources or unites as a single voice to determine a decision for the entire group" (Murnighan & Brass, 1991), can be a lucrative option.

In the following we will give an overview of negotiation studies that have investigated the impact of social motives on group decision mak-ing. In a lab study by Beersma and De Dreu (1999) on three-person nego-tiations, social motive was manipulated by reward structure (i.e., *team* rewards for high joint profits in the prosocial and *individual* rewards for high individual profits in the proself condition). Results indicated that prosocially motivated groups more often were able to achieve an integrative agreement than groups which' members had a proself motive. Moreover, negotiations of prosocial groups ended in a costly impasse less often than those of proself groups. The effect of social motive on negotiation could be explained by higher levels of trust and more integrative and less distributive behavior in prosocial teams.

A study by Weingart et al. (1993) was another example of research on the effects of social motives on group decision making in a negotiation context. Apart from examining the effects of social motives, Weingart et al. also examined the interaction between social motives and agenda setting (e.g., the way in which issues were considered). In negotiations, parties can consider the issues either one by one or together, as a package. Although the first option, called "sequential negotiation," is a popular one in many real-life negotiations (Thompson, Mannix, & Bazerman, 1988), this procedure is likely to lead to suboptimal decision making in negotiations with integrative potential. When parties negotiate about each issue on the agenda one by one, they tend to overlook the possibility to trade off losses on issues that yield lower outcomes for gains on issues that yield higher outcomes, and, therefore, miss the opportunity of forming integrative agreements. However, simultaneous consideration of issues may also have its drawbacks in groups. Because team negotiations are more complex compared with dyadic negotiations, as more parties' interests and preferences need to be addressed, considering issues simultaneously may be too complicated for group members, leading to suboptimal decisions as well.

The results of Weingart et al. (1993) revealed that proself teams considering issues sequentially obtained lower profits than teams in all other conditions, which did not differ from one another. An examination of the negotiation processes of a number of teams that had participated in their experiment showed that prosocial teams overcame the limitations associated with sequential processing of issues by developing norms of reciprocity. Whereas sequential issue consideration made the development of package deals by explicit logrolling impossible, prosocial team members would still reciprocate concessions on one issue with concessions on other issues, even if the reciprocation were delayed. Although these findings need to be interpreted with caution because they were based on post hoc explanations and few cases, they do lead us to conclude that a prosocial motive may not only be highly functional in team negotiations, but that it can also overcome the influence of other variables that would otherwise hinder the negotiation process. In the next section, we will address in more detail studies that examined the influence of structural variables that may moderate the effects of social motives on conflict management and decision making in negotiation.

Moderators of the Effects of Social Motives on Negotiation Processes and Outcomes

One structural variable that may influence the effects of social motives on negotiation is the preference structure of the negotiation task. Research has often investigated so-called symmetrically structured negotiations, in which each negotiating party meets with the same number of group members that have opposite as well as compatible preferences (e.g., preferences on each of the negotiation issues are different among factions and all factions have the same size). However, negotiations may also be structured in such a way that a subset of team members has compatible interests, which are opposed to the interests of the remaining group members, such that a majority with compatible interests faces a minority with different interests. These asymmetrically structured negotiations make the possibility of forming coalitions that exclude one or more others from an agreement very salient (Beersma & De Dreu, 2002). Another structural variable that may impact the social-motives decision-making relationship is the nature of the decision rule team members adopt to determine when an agreement is valid or not. Finally, the number of team members with a prosocial motivation and a proself motivation may affect the social-motives decision-making relationship because teams are not always homogeneous with regards to social motives. We review studies that addressed these variables next.

In asymmetrical task structures, where some group members' interests are aligned, forming coalitions to serve one's own interests becomes salient. However, whether team members can actually form coalitions depends on whether their decision rule requires unanimity or a majority. The majority rule makes coalitions legitimate. The unanimity rule, in contrast, makes coalitions unnecessary; any one member has veto power. In some situations, this may result in distributive power play, where team members use their veto power to block agreements proposed by other parties that they feel do not serve their interests enough.

Beersma and De Dreu (2002) predicted that whether this power play would indeed occur would depend on the team members' social motive. Specifically, in asymmetrical tasks, in which a majority with aligned preferences exists, those excluded from the majority faction would be likely to use distributive tactics including the use of their veto power to prevent disadvantageous agreements but only when they have a proself motivation. Because this distributive power play could be expected to deteriorate negotiation outcomes, decision quality would be especially low when an asymmetrical structure was combined with unanimity rule and a proself motive. In an experiment, preference structure (symmetrical vs. asymmetrical) was manipulated by using different types of profit schedules. Decision rule was manipulated by informing participants in the unanimity-rule condition that *all three team members had to agree* on a decision in order for it to take effect, whereas participants in the majority-rule condition were informed that a decision could be implemented when a *majority* (that is, *two out of three* team members) favored this decision (cf. Mannix, Thompson, & Bazerman, 1989). As in the study by Beersma and De Dreu (1999), social motive was again manipulated using reward structure. Results indicated that when the negotiation task was asymmetrically structured, teams engaged in more distributive and less integrative behavior. Also, in an asymmetrical (but not symmetrical) task structure, unanimity rule resulted in low joint outcomes when teams had a proself rather than prosocial motive.

The results of Beersma, Kooij, Ten Velden, and De Dreu (2007) were in line with this. Rather than manipulate social motivation, they measured team members' agreeableness, and found that on an asymmetrical negotiation task, teams low in agreeableness showed poor decision making (e.g., low negotiation outcomes) under the unanimity rule. Summarizing, the results of these studies show that team members' social motives interact with structural variables and that social motives become even more important in decision-making situations where there is a risk of distributive power play.

Unfortunately, in the work reviewed thus far, all members of one team were given the same motivation, resulting in homogenously prosocial or homogeneously proself teams. This yields only limited insight into the processes and consequences caused by social motives in teams, because in real-life teams motivational heterogeneity may be the rule rather than the exception. It can be argued that in teams which members have mixed social motives, team members will reciprocate each others' behavior, and therefore, the team will converge to the social motive of the majority within the team. Thus, the more prosocial (as opposed to proself) team members are, the more likely they will use integrative strategies, and the less likely they will use distributive strategies. Alternatively, based on the findings from experimental gaming research (Kelley & Stahelski, 1970), one might argue an "asymmetrical contagion" effect of proself motivation, such that having proself members in a team will have a disproportionate effect on the negotiation processes because the behavior of even one selfishly motivated member will put the other team members on the defensive, forcing them to respond with distributive behavior. If this is the case, teams with at least one proself member will use integrative behaviors less and distributive behaviors more than teams in which there are no proself members.

Although few studies have examined the possible consequences of motivational heterogeneity in dyads (e.g., see Schei & Rognes, 2003), research has only begun to investigate the effects of mixed social motives in teams. As a case in point, Weingart, Brett, and Olekalns (2003) examined the processes that occur in motivationally diverse teams. They compared four person teams with zero, one, two, three, or four prosocially motivated members (with any remaining team members holding a proself motive). They found that teams consisting of all prosocial members engaged in distributive strategies less than teams with one or more pro-self members, supporting the "asymmetrical contagion" argument previously discussed. Apparently, in teams with at least one proself member, the other team members respond distributively—regardless of their initial social motive. For integrative behavior, however, Weingart et al. (2003) found that the more prosocial members in a team, the more integrative information exchange took place. Unfortunately, no data regarding decision quality were reported. Therefore, conclusions as to whether the distributive strategies in teams with one or more proself members had a negative effect on negotiation performance and as to whether the information exchange in the teams with more prosocials had a positive effect cannot be drawn.

Integrating the Weingart et al. (2003) study with the study by Beersma and De Dreu (2002), Ten Velden, Beersma, and De Dreu (2007) examined motivational heterogeneity in teams negotiating under a unanimity or majority rule. They argued that the positions that prosocial and proself team members held were more crucial in determining negotiation processes and team decision making than the sheer number of prosocial or proself members. Even when teams contain only one proself team member, the motivation of this team member can have a disproportionate effect on the team processes and decision making, but only if this team member is empowered. One way in which a team member can be empowered by the structural features of the negotiation is by the decision rule that a team uses. In an asymmetrically structured negotiation, a negotiator's interests can either be aligned with those of other parties or not; and in the latter case, this negotiator holds a minority position. In this case, the decision rule that a team uses determines whether minority or majority members are empowered. Because unanimity rule gives the right to veto to all team members, a minority member is relatively powerful under this decision rule. Whether he or she will use this power to influence the negotiation processes for his or her own benefits is likely influenced by his or her social motive. Proself negotiators will probably use their veto powers to block unfavorable decisions by the majority, whereas prosocial minorities are less likely to do so. Therefore, Ten Velden et al. predicted that under unanimity rule, more decision blocking by the minority, leading to less optimal decision making would occur when the minority had a proself motive.

Whereas unanimity rule empowers minority members, majority rule empowers the majority because it enables them to exclude a minority from the agreement. Again, whether team members would use this power will depend on their social motives, such that under majority rule, majorities consisting of all proself negotiators will engage in less problem solving behavior than prosocial or mixed majorities, resulting in more unevenly distributed outcomes.

Results from this study confirmed the general prediction that it is not the number of prosocial and proself negotiators in a team that determines processes and outcomes, but rather under unanimity rule, the social motive of the minority member plays a crucial role, whereas under majority rule, the social motive of the majority members plays a crucial role. Thus, more distributive agreement blocking was found under unanimity rule for teams that had a proself minority member rather than a prosocially motivated minority member. This resulted in lower joint negotiation outcomes, reflecting suboptimal decision making. Interestingly, having a proself minority lowered the collective negotiation outcomes of the entire team, but under only unanimity rule (Ten Velden et al., 2007).

However, under majority rule, the social motive of the majority members determined processes and outcomes. Specifically, teams with prosocial majorities showed more problem-solving ability than teams with proself majorities and teams with mixed majorities (e.g., one prosocial and one proself majority member). As expected, this resulted in negotiation decisions in which outcomes were distributed much more unequally over team members in teams with proself majorities than in teams with mixed or prosocial majorities.

Taken together, studies that took the moderating role of negotiation structure and decision rule into account showed that social motives play an especially important role in decision-making situations in which there is a risk of destructive power play, such as in asymmetrical negotiations. The results of the first few studies that started to investigate the effects of mixed social motives in teams look promising, in that they show that the effects of the number of proself and prosocial team members are moderated by the interest positions these prosocials and proselfs take and by the decision rule.

Summary of the Findings of Negotiation Research

Our overview of the effects of social motives on team decision making in the context of negotiation leads to an unequivocal conclusion. Results show that a prosocial motive leads to better decision making at the group level of analysis. Teams whose members are prosocially motivated develop more trusting relationships and engage in more integrative behaviors. Perhaps the most important finding of this line of research is that prosocial motivation also leads teams to optimal decisions (e.g., integrative outcomes). Studies on the factors that moderate the effects of social motives showed that these effects are even more pronounced in situations in which team members are prone to destructive power play, such as in asymmetrical negotiations. Finally, the effects of the social motives of specific (empowered or powerless) team members on group processes and decision-making quality are reliably predicted.

Skeptics might argue that the use of joint negotiation outcomes as an operationalization of decision quality paints a one-sided picture. After all, in a negotiation, what constitutes effective decision making can be argued to depend on the motive of the negotiator. Prosocial negotiators might find an integrative agreement yielding high joint outcomes very effective, but proself negotiators might favor an agreement in which they do well for themselves, albeit at the costs of others. As a counterargument, it seems highly unlikely that the organizations in which negotiating teams function would not see integrative outcomes yielding optimal group outcomes as the best possible decisions these teams can make, certainly when we keep in mind that nonintegrative solutions leave "money on the table" and do not use the resources available to negotiators optimally.

Furthermore, one might argue that the negotiation tasks used in the studies previously presented are "rigged" so as not to be zero sum, whereas the real world is often marked by zero sum games. However, there are good reasons to doubt this position. Many real-life negotiation situations do have integrative potential, but negotiators fail to realize this because of premature judgment, assuming that the negotiation situation is a "fixed pie" and searching for a single answer without considering inventing issues to add to the negotiation agenda (Fisher & Ury, 1981; Pruitt & Carnevale, 1993; Thompson & Hastie, 1990). Fortunately, research by Neale and Northcraft (1986) showed that experienced negotiators are less susceptible to this view of negotiations as a zero-sum game and that they realize the integrative possibilities that many real-life negotiation situations possess.

Interestingly, taking a closer look at the negotiation studies reviewed here reveals that even from an individualistic point of view, prosocial negotiators often do better than proself negotiators. Attempts at claiming too much of the negotiation pie for oneself often meet with resistance on the part of team members which often leads to a costly impasse. Even if one has a proself motive, following an integrative strategy and arriving at an integrative outcome is, on average, a lucrative option.

Even if we accept that joint negotiation outcomes are indeed valid operationalizations of decision quality, we might still ask whether the different "sources" of social motives in teams (e.g., dispositional differences, situational variables) all affect negotiation processes and decision quality in the same way. In reply to this, a meta-analysis of 28 negotiation studies by De Dreu et al. (2000) showed that different sources of social motivation are functionally equivalent; when a certain variable triggers a prosocial motive, conflict management is more constructive than when it triggers a proself motive, and no differences between dispositional and situational variables were observed. However, there is one caveat to these results. Of the 28 studies in the meta-analysis, most involved dyads and only two employed teams as the unit of analysis. However, as we have no theoretical reasons to assume that different sources of social motives would not be functionally equivalent in team negotiations, and the results of the studies described here do not imply otherwise, we conclude that the meta-analytic findings are likely to generalize to team negotiations.

LITERATURE ON TEAM DECISION MAKING

The Role of Social Motives in Decision-Making Processes and Outcomes

Group negotiation is one area in which research has been conducted on conflict and group decision making. Although this research has taught us a lot about the effects of social motives on conflict management processes and team decision making, the operationalization of team decision making used in this area of research is rather limited. Studies have almost exclusively focused on negotiation outcomes. In real-life groups, there is, of course, much more to decision making than only the specific outcomes of a situation in which the team members were confronted with conflicting interests. After dealing with conflict, teams have to return to their everyday tasks and perform effectively. The question of interest is therefore whether and how conflict affects team decision making in a broader sense, that is, not only during the conflict episode itself. As our focus is especially on the influence of social motives during conflict, we are specifically interested in those studies that examined the influence of social motives on the relationship between conflict and team decision making.

A first question is whether social motivation affects conflict management processes in broader decision-making settings as it has been shown to do in negotiation. Studies that have examined the influence of team members' agreeableness (an individual difference) on team outcomes suggest that this is indeed the case. Barrick et al. (1998) conducted a study among 51 work teams and found that teams with a particularly disagreeable member and teams with a low average team score on agreeableness experienced more conflict, were less cohesive, and performed less effectively according to their supervisors than teams that did not have such a disagreeable person in the team or had a higher average agreeableness score. These findings can be understood by looking at studies on the effects of agreeableness on individual conflict management strategies. For example, Graziano et al. (1996), as well as Jensen-Campbell, Graziano, and Hair (1996), found that individuals high on agreeableness preferred constructive negotiation and disengagement strategies above strategies based on power. The opposite was true for individuals low on agreeableness. Moberg (2001), who also focused on how individuals manage conflict, distinguished four conflict management strategies: nonconfrontation (handling conflict indirectly by minimizing differences, avoidance, or withdrawal), confrontation (handling conflict directly by facing or discussing issues straightforwardly), compromising (handling conflict by conceding and problem solving), and control (handling conflict directly by competing, contending, or dominating). He found that agreeableness was positively related to compromising and negatively related to control, providing more evidence that agreeableness leads to more constructive conflict management.

The study by Barrick et al. (1998) on teams together with the evidence on individual conflict management that can be derived by the studies of Moberg (2001) and Graziano and colleagues (Graziano et al., 1996; Jensen-Campbell et al., 1996) led us to conclude that social motivation affects conflict management processes in decision-making teams as it does in negotiation teams. However, this research does not answer the question of how social motives during conflict exactly influence teams' decision-making effectiveness.

Many scholars have suggested that a prosocial approach to conflict benefits group decision making in the long run. For example, Rubin, Pruitt, and Kim (1994) speculated that such a prosocial approach would lead to positive conflict experiences like achieving integrative agreements, and thereby enhance interpersonal relations, increase team members' feelings of self-efficacy, and decrease the likelihood of future conflict. Their arguments are consistent with the results of studies on teams in organizations, showing positive correlations between cooperative attitudes, constructive conflict management, and group functioning.

An impressive line of studies by Tjosvold and colleagues (for an overview, see Tjosvold, 1998), consistently shows that when group members adopt a prosocial motive, they engage in more constructive conflict management. Specifically, Tjosvold argues and shows that a prosocial orientation to conflict fosters "constructive controversy," a process in which team members express their divergent ideas and opinions and try to integrate these into an optimal decision. Evidence for this perspective comes from a laboratory experiment by Tjosvold and Deemer (1980), in which 66 dyads discussed a work-distribution issue. Results showed that dyads discussing the case in a prosocial context with a confederate who emphasized mutual benefits reached integrative decisions more often than dyads discussing the case in a proself context with a confederate who emphasized that each of the parties should try to prevail. Likewise, Tjosvold, Wedley, and Field (1986) showed that constructive controversy was significantly correlated to managers' self-described successfulness of decision-making experiences. Thus, the higher the constructive controversy, the more successful the decisions were. Moreover, Tjosvold, Dann, and Wong (1992) demonstrated that perceiving cooperative goal interdependence led individuals to engage in constructive controversy, and to focus on good customer service, work efficiently, and make progress on their tasks. Furthermore, research by Tjosvold and De Dreu (1997) showed that Dutch employees who indicated that they engaged in constructive controversy had better interpersonal relationships than employees who did not engage in constructive controversy. The process of constructive controversy was also related to higher ratings of efficiency and to more confidence in future collaboration. Finally, in a study on 61 self-managing teams, Alper, Tjosvold, and Law (2000) showed that teams employing constructive controversy felt that they were more effective in handling conflicts and received higher performance ratings from their management than teams that did not.

Jehn and Shah's (1997) study on friendship and acquaintance groups also speaks to the positive effects of prosocial motivation on group performance. Groups of friends were found to perform better on both motor and cognitive tasks than groups of acquaintances. Moreover, this effect was mediated by higher levels of cooperation as rated by independent judges and commitment to the group as rated by group members, in the friendship groups relative to the groups of acquaintances. As social relationships are a well-known determinant of social motives (Ben-Yoav & Pruitt, 1984; Fry et al., 1983), from these results we might again conclude that the stronger the prosocial motivation in the group, the better the group's performance.

Further evidence that hints in the direction of positive effects of a prosocial motive on conflict management and team decision making comes from a study by Eisenhardt (1989). In a study of top management teams of eight microcomputer firms, she found that teams which approached conflicts by a process of "consensus with qualification" showed higher speed of decisions, a performance aspect that was crucial in the high-velocity environments in which the studied firms operated. A closer look at "consensus with qualification" shows that this process is characterized by (a) attempts to reach consensus by involving all team members in the decision and (b) if consensus is not reached right away, the CEO or the member responsible for the specific decision area making the decision. Interestingly, this process is a cooperative process in principle. Only when a decision cannot be reached by integrating team members' ideas, is a decision forced by the relevant team member. Slow teams were characterized by less active conflict management. One member of a "slow" team cited in Eisenhardt's study lamented the problems associated with veto power that caused slow and inadequate resolution of conflict. Relating this to the work on team negotiations discussed earlier, we might tentatively conclude that the "slow" teams experienced problems related to conflict because of their proself motives. Because these motives were not formally assessed in Eisenhardt's work, this remains to be investigated, however.

The findings of Korsgaard, Schweiger, and Sapienza (1995) also point toward positive effects of a prosocial orientation on team decision making. In their experiment with 20 intact management teams of a Fortune 500 company, they instructed team leaders to show either high or low consideration for members' input and to either change or not change their decision based on team member input. They found that both consideration and team member input into the decision led to higher ratings of procedural fairness. Furthermore, procedural fairness was positively related to decision commitment, member attachment to the team, and trust in the leader. Finally, and most importantly, teams whose members perceived higher procedural justice made better strategic decisions as evaluated by two independent judges. From this, Korsgaard et al. conclude that procedures that enhance perceptions of procedural fairness improve cooperation and commitment to decisions without sacrificing decision quality. This is interesting in light of findings within the field of group negotiation by Beersma and De Dreu (2003), who showed that procedural fairness is a crucial mediator of the effects of prosocial motives on decision quality in negotiation. Apparently, when team leaders and members approach decision making in a prosocial way, this enhances procedural fairness perceptions and thereby decision quality.

Other findings that might lead us to conclude that a prosocial motive has positive effects on conflict management and team decision making come from a study by Amason (1996). The results of his study of 53 top management teams in the United States showed that conflict could benefit decision quality as long as positive, cognitive disagreement in the teams was not accompanied by dysfunctional affective conflict. According to Amason, a cooperative context would reduce the tendency for cognitive disagreements to arouse affective conflict.

Janssen, Van de Vliert, and Veenstra's (1999) findings also attest to the importance of a cooperative context in determining the conflict–performance relationship in teams. In their study, members of management teams rated the extent to which they perceived cooperative interdependence in their team. They also rated task conflict, person conflict, integrative and distributive conflict behavior, decision quality, and the affective acceptance of the decisions that were made. Results revealed that a cooperative context was especially important in the case where teams experienced high levels of both task and person conflict. Specifically, when person conflict arose alongside task conflict, it was vital that team members perceived cooperative interdependence. High levels of perceived interdependence resulted in less distributive and more integrative conflict behavior relative to when cooperative interdependence was perceived as low. Also, under circumstances of high task conflict combined with high person conflict, perceptions of positive interdependence were related to high decision quality and high affective acceptance of decisions. Janssen et al. concluded that, when person conflict interferes with task conflict, team members need to perceive a cooperative context in order to engage in cooperative conflict behavior, which eventually enables them to perform well.

Related to this, Simons and Peterson (2000) conducted a study in which they collected data about conflict and decision making from 70 top management teams of U.S. based hotel companies. Their data show that, in top management teams in which there was low interpersonal trust, task conflict was dealt with in a more aggressive way than in teams characterized by high trust. Also, in the former, low-trust teams, task conflict was more often related to dysfunctional relationship conflict. They also found that in those top management teams in which members raised their voices to one another, task conflict was more strongly related to relationship conflict than in teams where this as not the case. As low levels of trust and elevating one's voice are probably related to, or indicative of, insufficiently cooperative, prosocial ties in the team, this again points to the possibility that conflicts can help decision making as long as team members are prosocially motivated when dealing with the conflict. De Dreu and Weingart (2003) also discussed this possibility in their meta-analysis on fifteen studies of work teams in which conflict, job satisfaction, or team performance were measured. Perhaps task conflict can help teams perform well, as long as there is a prosocial climate that guarantees psychological safety (Edmondson, 1999) and norms of openness (Jehn & Shah, 1997).

Although mostly cross-sectional in nature, and thus inconclusive about both causality and long-term consequences, the previously mentioned work suggested that a prosocial motivation during conflict and negotiation fosters group consensus and stimulates further group functioning. Interestingly, other research, reviewed in detail in chapter 5 of this book, has suggested that a proself, rather than a prosocial, approach to negotiation benefits group performance. For example, research by Nemeth and her colleagues (for an overview, see Nemeth & Staw, 1989) suggested that a certain level of proself motivation during conflict may be functional for groups, in that it stimulates creativity and innovation. Individuals in brainstorming groups perform better and generate more creative ideas when competition and winning are rewarded (Munkes & Diehl, 2003). Moreover, work on devil's advocacy (a situational determinant of proself motivation) and groupthink has shown that groups make less reasoning errors, are more innovative, and reach better decisions when conflict is induced and independence is valued, compared with situations in which consensus is maintained and harmony is promoted (e.g., De Dreu & West, 2001; Janis & Mann, 1977; Schulz-Hardt, Jochims, & Frey, 2002; Schweiger, Sandberg & Rechner, 1989). These disparate literatures reviewed above thus indicate that when individual group members are attempting to "win" and strive to outperform each other by coming up with better ideas, this will serve the long-term needs of the group and benefits collective performance. If group members focus on their own input and performances, rather than on achieving consensus and maintaining harmony, the group is more creative and reaches better decisions.

Thus, the above studies on team decision making have not provided a conclusive answer to the question of when and why different social motives benefit or hinder group decision-making effectiveness. In the following, we will review research pointing to various moderators of the social motives during conflict–decision-making relationship.

Moderators of the Effects of Social Motives on Decision-Making Processes and Outcomes: Recent Studies and Suggestions for Future Research

Our above review showed that neither a prosocial nor a proself motivational orientation is uniformly advantageous for group decision making. To answer the question of how social motives during group conflict exactly affect subsequent decision-making performance, in this section we will take a closer look at characteristics of the teams' tasks. We will start by reviewing recent studies that have investigated how the effects of social motives during conflict and negotiation on further team performance are moderated by the characteristics of the team task, and we will conclude this section by suggesting possible avenues of research in this new area of study.

Research by Beersma, Hollenbeck, et al. (2003) showed that different aspects of team performance on a decision-making task can be distinguished, and that the effects of a prosocial versus a proself orientation on team performance are contingent on the different aspects of task performance. They found that in a command-and-control simulation task, a prosocial orientation helped teams enhance their decision-making accuracy, but it reduced the speed with which decisions were made. A proself orientation, on the other hand, was found to benefit speed but to inhibit accuracy. This can be explained by the fact that in order to perform accurately, teams need to coordinate by sharing information with one another, building on this information, and helping one another to make the right decisions. A prosocial orientation helps teams to do so. However, the same coordination that helps teams to perform accurately also comes at the cost of the team's speed. When speed is critical, teams whose members have a proself motive are at a clear advantage because these team members do not bother to lose time by coordinating and helping one another, but rather try to work for their own interests as fast as they can. Thus, which social motive is more functional for team performance may depend on which aspect of performance is more important, speed versus accuracy. This in turn depends on the boundary conditions under which the team is operating (e.g., type of market, number of competitors, difficulty of the task, and cost associated with errors).

The preceding findings point to the intriguing possibility that whether a prosocial or proself orientation to conflict helps or hinders subsequent team decision making may depend on the characteristics of the decision-making task the team has to perform. Consistent with theorizing on person–task fit (Hollenbeck et al., 2002; Kristof, 1996, Muchinsky & Monahan, 1987), Beersma and De Dreu (2005) proposed that there needs to be a fit between the task requirements and the dominant behavioral tendencies within the group for groups to perform well (cf. Peterson & Nemeth, 1996).

Tasks differ in the extent to which they require divergence or convergence between group members. Team decision-making tasks with a strong focus on creativity, as for example brainstorming tasks, require high levels of divergent performance, whereas team decision-making tasks with a strong focus on single solutions, such as planning and execution tasks, require high levels of coordination and convergent performance (Hackman, Jones, & McGrath, 1967; McGrath, 1984). Because individuals with a prosocial motivation value harmony, inclusiveness, and coordination, they may do much better on the convergent performance aspects of a task than on the divergent performance aspects. Individuals with a proself motivation, in contrast, value independence, personal success, and critical attitudes, and this fits better with divergent performance. Put differently, groups whose members have a prosocial motivation during conflict may perform subsequent decision-making tasks better than groups whose members have a proself motivation when the tasks require convergent activity, but worse when the tasks require divergent activity.

In two experiments, Beersma and De Dreu (2005) found support for this contingency idea. In the first study, the social motives of three-person teams were manipulated using incentives, and post-negotiation performance was measured by having teams engage in a task that had both convergent and divergent aspects (e.g., producing advertisement slogans). Results revealed that whereas a prosocial motive during negotiation stimulated convergent post-negotiation performance (e.g., producing useful slogans giving much information), a proself motive during negotiation stimulated divergent post-negotiation performance (e.g., producing innovative, original slogans). In a second experiment, Beersma and De Dreu (2005) tested whether social motives independently affect decision making, or whether this is only the case when team members' social motives have been acted upon in a conflict-evoking task. They manipulated social motives and whether teams negotiated prior to a decision-making task. Teams engaged either in a convergent planning task, in which they had to come up with one solution to a specified problem, or in a divergent creativity task, in which they had to come up with a variety of different ideas. Results showed that a prosocial motive stimulated performance on the convergent task, but decreased performance on the divergent task only when teams negotiated prior to the team task. A proself motive during negotiation had the opposite effect; it stimulated performance on the divergent task and harmed performance on the convergent task. The answer to the question of whether having prosocial and proself motives during conflict helps or hinders group decision making thus seems to be that it depends on whether the teams' task requires convergence or divergence.

Interestingly, in an experiment, Goncalo and Staw (2006) replicated the finding that a proself orientation stimulates creativity in divergent tasks. They primed participants with either individualistic or collectivistic orientations, concepts that are strongly related to proself and prosocial motives. They found that in a brainstorming task, groups that had been primed with an individualistic orientation generated more ideas and more highly creative ideas, but only if they had received instructions to think divergently (e.g., "be creative") instead of convergently (e.g., "be practical").

Although the above studies give us some insight into the effects of social motives during conflict on group decision making, there are a number of questions awaiting further research. For one, future studies should examine in more detail which *mediating processes* are responsible for the contingent effects of social motives during negotiation and post-negotiation task type on team performance. It is important to note that Beersma and De Dreu's (2005) results showed that social motives affected group decision making only when the group experienced a task that led them to experience conflict. Social motives by themselves had no effect on decision making.

In line with this, Beersma, Hollenbeck, et al. (2007) found that team agreeableness affected team decision-making accuracy only in a command and control simulation task when teams had experienced a negotiation situation and not when decisions were made by the experimenter. This effect might have occurred because proself teams tend to engage in contending behavior during conflicts, characterized by persuasive arguments, and by using positional commitments, threats, and bluffs. Prosocial teams, on the other hand, engage in problem solving, characterized by information exchange, listening, and mutual concern. Contentious, forcing behavior might set the stage for independent, divergent thinking in post-negotiation tasks, whereas problem solving might set the stage for collaboration and convergent thinking.

Although Beersma and De Dreu (2005) measured negotiation behavior in their studies, they did not find evidence for mediation of the effects of social motives on team decision making by these behaviors. Therefore, it might be not so much a team member's own social motive that affects his or her behavior in a decision-making task but rather his or her experiences with the team members. When teams engage in a conflict-inducing task, members are fully exposed to each others' social behavior (directed by their social motives), and this experience may set them up for either good coordination (when they experienced prosocial team members) or high individual effort (when they experienced proself team members). This idea of norm formation that affects processes and performance in subsequent group tasks is supported by findings of Bettenhausen and Murnighan (1985). In their experiment, groups of five people interacted in four subsequent decision-making tasks in which they had to distribute outcomes across the group members. Bettenhausen and Murnighan compared the outcome distributions of these groups with those that participated in an earlier experiment (Murnighan & Szwajkowski, 1979), in which group members interacted in the same tasks, but were unable to see each other or communicate verbally. Comparing the results across these two studies showed that in the interacting groups, the patterns of outcome distribution established in the first sessions became regularities over time. So, through group interaction, team members' expectations seemed to converge toward either cooperation or competition. This was not the case in the noninteracting groups.

That group norms exert a powerful influence on decision making is also exemplified by a study by Postmes, Spears, and Cihangir (2001). They found that groups that had engaged in a consensus-norm invoking task (making a poster) performed more poorly on a subsequent decision-making task than groups that had engaged in a critical-norm invoking task (engaging in a group discussion). Their results also showed that this effect was group-based; when members were asked to make an individual decision after the first task, no performance differences between conditions were found. From this work, we might thus conclude that norm formation could be one reason why social motives during group negotiation affect performance in a subsequent task.

The possibility that experiences with others' behaviors, motives, and expectations about how other group members will behave might play a crucial role is also shown by the aforementioned study by Beersma, Hollenbeck, et al. (2007). In their study, teams first engaged in a team command-and-control simulation task under either prosocial (team reward) or proself (individual reward) conditions. In a second task, all teams transferred to a team reward structure. Before making the transition to the new structure, a decision had to be made regarding the distribution of team roles, and this was decided either by team negotiation, a possible conflict-inducing state, or by the experimenter. Results showed that teams with a prosocial history demonstrated more accurate performance when the role-allocation was made for them, whereas teams with a proself history showed more accurate performance when they negotiated the decision. According to Beersma, Hollenbeck, et al. the difference between the actual, experienced process relative to what team members expected was the critical determining factor in terms of how conflict affects further performance. Whereas in the negotiation condition, no differences between previously proself and previously prosocial groups were found in actual negotiation processes, previously prosocial teams expected the negotiation to be cooperative and were unpleasantly surprised by the level of conflict they were facing. Previously proself teams, however, expected fierce competition and were relieved to see the conflict was not as harsh as they expected.

One topic that future research should investigate is the extent to which expectations and experiences of group members' social motives drive the effects on team decision making. For example, an intriguing question is: Does knowledge about group members' social motives already begin to influence the decision-making strategies a team member opts for, even when no actual interaction has taken place yet, or is interaction necessary for the effects of social motives to occur? Related to this, future studies could examine the mechanisms by which knowledge about group members' social motives gets transferred within groups—do team members learn about each others' social motives by verbal cues or by more subtle nonverbal cues?

Another relevant question is how *heterogeneity of social motives in teams* affects team decision making. In the studies previously described on the effects of social motives during negotiation on decision making, members within a team were always given the same social motive. However, as we also discussed in the section on negotiation studies, group members often enter a decision-making process with different social motives, resulting in motivational heterogeneity. Kelley and Stahelski (1970) already showed that those identified as high on prosocial motives when confronted with those high on proself motives shifted toward a more proself motivation, whereas individuals identified as high on proself motives tended to stick to their orientation and "exploited" more prosocial individuals (see also Chatman & Barsade, 1995; Steinel & De Dreu, 2004). The findings by Weingart et al. (2003), discussed earlier in this chapter, are in line with this.

This suggests asymmetrical contagion of social motivation: Proself motives tend to be more contagious than prosocial ones. As an aside, this is one of the major propositions of structural adaptation theory (SAT; see Ellis, Hollenbeck, Ilgen, Humphrey, & Li, 2006; Johnson et al., 2006; Moon et al., 2004). According to SAT, it is easier for individuals and groups to move to a more chaotic, less ordered structure than to a more ordered one. Like physical systems, social systems are differentiated by their degree of complexity, and more energy is required to maintain the structure of complex systems than simpler ones. In terms of complexity, structures that embody high levels of interdependence and mutual adjustment between individuals are more complex relative to those where each individual is an independent decision-making agent concerned only with his or her own outcomes. Thus, as a proself context requires less organization and coordination than a prosocial one, SAT would predict that having a proself minority in an otherwise prosocial group would make the group as a whole shift to a proself motive. It is interesting to investigate whether this process could undermine the positive effects of prosocial motivation on convergent tasks and, likewise, whether having a proself minority in an otherwise prosocial group may benefit performance on divergent tasks because of the same process. Studies examining this question could also vary the extent to which certain group members are empowered by the group's decision procedures and rules (cf. Ten Velden et al., 2007) to examine whether power position affects the influence of different team members' social motives.

We also believe that studying the impact of conflict types on further group decision making is a topic that deserves attention. In the experimental studies on the effects of conflict on further decision making that have been conducted so far, a conflict of interests or negotiation-type conflict task has been used to induce conflict (cf. Beersma & De Dreu, 2005; Beersma, Hollenbeck, et al., 2007). According to McGrath (1984), two types of conflict can be distinguished: (a) conflicts over interests and over points of view or (b) cognitive conflict. Likewise, Druckman and colleagues (Druckman, Rozelle, & Zechmeister, 1976; Druckman & Zechmeister, 1973) distinguished between three types of conflict: (a) conflicts over interests, (b) intellective conflicts (conflicts about "who is right" in which the topic over which there is a conflict could ultimately be objectively verified), and (c) evaluative conflicts (conflicts over "who is right" in which the topic over which there is a conflict is a matter of taste or opinion). Some scholars argued that the type of conflict does not matter in determining its effects on decision making. For example, Tjosvold (1998) argued that for future group functioning, it does not matter whether a conflict is cognitive or interest based, what matters is how the team members deal with it.

However, research by Harinck, De Dreu, & Van Vianen (2000) showed that conflict-management strategies change as a function of the conflict type. Specifically, in conflicts of interests, group members used more integrative behaviors, like logrolling, and in intellective and evaluative conflicts, they used more contentious, forcing behaviors. Future research needs to integrate these findings with the results of Beersma and De Dreu (2005), who found that the type of decision-making task interacts with the social motives group members had during conflict to determine their decision-making performances. Do social motives play a role in cognitive conflicts at all, and if so, how? Is cognitive conflict more "useful" to enhance future group decision making than conflict of interests, and if so, why? The question of how different conflict types affect further decision making and what the role of social motivation is in this is definitely an intriguing one that deserves more research attention.

Another direction for future studies is to examine more facets of group dynamics than decision making alone. Apart from affecting decision making, social motives are likely to also influence the "softer outcomes" of working in groups, such as well-being and health (Dijkstra, Van Dierendonck, & Evers, 2005; Giebels & Janssen, 2005) or job satisfaction (Guerra, Martínez, Munduate, & Medina, 2005). In their meta-analysis, De Dreu and Weingart (2003) found a negative relation between conflict and satisfaction. What we do not know yet is how this relation comes about—does conflict impact job satisfaction or does job satisfaction lead to conflict—and whether it is moderated by team members' social motives during the conflict. Studies should therefore investigate the effects of social motives during conflict on "soft" outcomes.

Finally, the studies on the contingency between social motives and task types discussed so far were all laboratory studies with ad hoc student teams. A question for future research is whether the results of these studies can be *generalized to intact organizational teams*. To examine whether the contingency theory presented here applies to intact work groups that collaborate over longer periods, longitudinal field studies should be conducted. Over a longer time span, effects might be reduced, as a study by Brodbeck and Greitemeyer (2000) exemplified. In their study, ad hoc groups suffered from process losses in their first and second task trials, but these process losses were substantially reduced or even eliminated when subsequent task trials were included. This might also be the case with the effects of social motives during group conflict or negotiation on performance; over time, effects might be diminished. Alternatively, these effects might become entrenched and exert even stronger influence over performance as time goes by due to a norm formation process, (cf. Bettenhausen & Murnighan, 1985). Future work should investigate these questions.

CONCLUSION

We have reviewed studies on conflict and group decision making, focusing on social motivation, a variable that has a crucial impact on conflict dynamics and decision-making performance in teams. First, we reviewed studies that demonstrated that social motivation has different sources. We then reviewed work from the negotiation literature, which showed that within this area of research, prosocial motives have been shown to lead to more constructive behavior and more optimal decision making than proself motives. Furthermore, the effects of social motives in negotiation were shown to be moderated by the negotiation structure and by motivational heterogeneity in the team.

We then reviewed research on more distal team decision making, showing that although some researchers argue for the beneficial effects of a prosocial motive on team decision making, others argue for the beneficial effects of proself motives in teams. This led us to studies on potential moderators of the relationship between social motives during conflict on the one hand and decision making on the other hand. We argued that whether a prosocial or proself motive helps or hinders team decision making is contingent on whether the team's task has mainly convergent or mainly divergent aspects. Although some studies have started to demonstrate the validity of this contingency model, many questions remain unanswered. We hope that the areas for future research we suggested will inspire researchers to proceed investigating the fascinating area of conflict and team decision making still further.

REFERENCES

Allred, K. G., Mallozzi, J. S., Matsui, F., & Raia, C. P. (1997). The influence of anger and compassion on negotiation performance. *Organizational Behavior & Human Decision Processes, 70*, 175–187.

Alper, S., Tjosvold, D., & Law, K. S. (2000). Conflict management, efficacy, and performance in organizational teams. *Personnel Psychology, 53*, 625–642.

Amason, A. C. (1996). Distinguishing the effects of functional and dysfunctional conflict on strategic decision making: Resolving a paradox for top management teams. *Academy of Management Journal, 39*, 123–148.

Baron, R. A. (1990). Environmentally induced positive affect: Its impact on self-efficacy, task performance, negotiation, and conflict. *Journal of Applied Social Psychology, 20*, 368–384.

Barrick, M. R., Stewart, G. L., Neubert, M. J., & Mount, M. K. (1998). Relating member ability and personality to work-team processes and team effectiveness. *Journal of Applied Psychology, 83*, 377–391.

Barry, B., Fulmer, I., & Van Kleef, G. A. (2004). I laughed, I cried, I settled: The role of emotions in negotiation. In M. J. Gelfand, & J. M. Brett (Eds.), *The handbook of negotiation and culture* (pp. 71–94). Palo Alto, CA: Stanford University Press.

Beersma, B., & De Dreu, C. K. W. (1999). Negotiation processes and outcomes in prosocially and egoistically motivated groups. *International Journal of Conflict Management, 10*, 385–402.

Beersma, B., & De Dreu, C. K. W. (2002). Integrative and distributive negotiation in small groups: Effects of task structure, decision rule and social motive. *Organizational Behavior and Human Decision Processes, 87*, 227–252.

Beersma, B., & De Dreu, C. K. W. (2003). Social motives in integrative negotiation: The mediating influence of procedural fairness. *Social Justice Research, 16*, 217–239.

Beersma, B., & De Dreu, C. K. W. (2005). Conflict's consequences: Effects of social motives on post-negotiation creative and convergent group functioning and performance. *Journal of Personality and Social Psychology, 89*, 358–374.

Beersma, B., Hollenbeck, J. R., Conlon, D. E., Humphrey, S. E., Moon, H., & Ilgen, D. R. (2007). *Adaption to reward structure changes in teams: The effects of team role negotiation on processes and outcome.* Manuscript submitted for publication.

Beersma, B., Hollenbeck, J. R., Humphrey, S. E., Moon, H., Conlon, D. E., & Ilgen, D. R. (2003). Cooperation, competition, and team performance: Towards a contingency approach. *Academy of Management Journal, 46*, 572–590.

Beersma, B., Kooij, H. J. M., Ten Velden, F. S., & De Dreu, C. K. W. (2007). *Effects of agreeableness in small group negotiations.* Manuscript in preparation.

Ben-Yoav, O., & Pruitt, D. G. (1984). Accountability to constituents: A two-edged sword. *Organizational Behavior and Human Decision Processes, 34*, 283–295.

Bettenhausen, K., & Murnighan, J. K. (1985). The emergence of norms in competitive decision-making groups. *Administrative Science Quarterly, 30*, 350–372.

Brodbeck, F., & Greitemeyer, T. (2000). A dynamic model of group performance: Considering the group members' capacity to learn. *Group Processes and Intergroup Relations, 3*, 159–182.

Carnevale, P. J. D., & Isen, A. M. (1986). The influence of positive affect and visual access on the discovery of integrative solutions in bilateral negotiation. *Organizational Behavior and Human Decision Processes, 37*, 1–13.

Chatman, J. A., & Barsade, S. G. (1995). Personality, organizational culture, and cooperation: Evidence from a business simulation. *Administrative Science Quarterly, 40*, 423–443.

Christie, R., & Geis, F. L. (1970). *Studies in Machiavellism.* New York: Academic Press.

Costa, P. T., & McCrae, R. R. (1992). *Revised NEO personality inventory.* Odessa, FL: Psychological Assessment Resources.

De Dreu, C. K. W., Harinck, S., & Van Vianen, A. (1999). Conflict and performance in groups and organizations. In C. Cooper & I. Robertson (Eds.), *International Review of Industrial and Organizational Psychology* (pp. 369–414). Chichester, U.K.: Wiley.

De Dreu, C. K. W., & Weingart, L. R. (2003). Task versus relationship conflict, team performance, and team member satisfaction: A meta-analysis. *Journal of Applied Psychology, 88*, 741–749.

De Dreu, C. K. W., Weingart, L. R., & Kwon, S. (2000). Influence of social motives on integrative negotiation: A meta-analytic review and test of two theories. *Journal of Personality and Social Psychology, 78*, 889–905.

De Dreu, C. K. W., & West, M. A. (2001). Minority dissent and team innovation: The importance of participation in decision making. *Journal of Applied Psychology, 86*, 1191–1201.

Deutsch, M. (1958) Trust and suspicion. *Journal of Conflict Resolution, 2,* 265–279.

Deutsch, M. (1973). *The resolution of conflict: Constructive and destructive processes.* New Haven: Yale University Press.

Dijkstra, M. T. M., Van Dierendonck, D., & Evers, A. (2005). Responding to conflict at work and individual well-being: The mediating role of flight behavior and feelings of helplessness. *European Journal of Work and Organizational Psychology, 14,* 119–135.

Druckman, D., Rozelle, R., & Zechmeister, K. (1976). Conflict of interest and value dissensus: Two perspectives. In D. Druckman (Ed.), *Negotiations* (pp. 105–131). Thousand Oaks, CA: Sage.

Druckman, D., & Zechmeister, K. (1973). Conflict of interest and value dissensus: Propositions in the sociology of conflict. *Human Resources, 26*(4), 449–466.

Edmondson, A. (1999). Psychological safety and learning behavior in work teams. *Administrative Science Quarterly, 44,* 350–383.

Eisenhardt, K. M. (1989). Making fast strategic decisions in high-velocity environments. *Academy of Management Journal, 12,* 543–576.

Ellis, A. P. J., Hollenbeck, J. R., Ilgen, D. R., Humphrey, S. E., & Li, A. (2006). *Centralizing and decentralizing teams: The asymmetrical nature of structural adaptation in work groups.* Manuscript submitted for publication.

Fisher, R., & Ury, W. (1981). *Getting to yes: Negotiating agreement without giving in.* Boston: Houghton Mifflin.

Forgas, J. P. (1998). On feeling good and getting your way: Mood effects on negotiator cognition and bargaining strategies. *Journal of Personality and Social Psychology, 74,* 565–577.

Fry, W. R., Firestone, I. J., & Williams, D. L. (1983). Negotiation process and outcome of stranger dyads and dating couples: Do lovers lose? *Basic and Applied Social Psychology, 4,* 1–16.

Giebels, E., & Janssen, O. (2005). Conflict stress and reduced well-being at work: The buffering effect of third-party help. *European Journal of Work and Organizational Psychology, 14,* 137–155.

Goncalo, J. & Staw, B. (2006). Individualism-collectivism and group creativity. *Organizational Behavior and Human Decision Processes, 100,* 96–109.

Graziano, W. G., Jensen-Campbell, L. A., & Hair, E. C. (1996). Perceiving interpersonal conflict and reacting to it: The case for agreeableness. *Journal of Personality and Social Psychology, 70,* 820–835.

Guerra, J., Martínez, I., Munduate, L., & Medina, F. (2005). A contingency perspective on the study of the consequences of conflict types: The role of organizational culture. *European Journal of Work and Organizational Psychology, 14,* 157–176.

Guzzo, R. A., & Dickson, M. W. (1996). Teams in organizations: Recent research on performance and effectiveness. *Annual Review of Psychology, 47,* 307–338.

Hackman, J. R., (1987) Assessing the behavior and performance of teams in organizations: The case of air transport crews. In D. B. Fishman & D. R. Peterson (Eds.), *Assessment for decision* (pp. 283–313). New Brunswick, NJ: Rutgers University Press.

Hackman, J. R. (1998). Why teams don't work. In R. S. Tindale & L. Heath (Eds.), *Theory and research on small groups: Social psychological applications to social issues* (Vol. 4, pp. 245–267). New York: Plenum Press.

Hackman, J. R., Jones, L. E., & McGrath, J. E. (1967). A set of dimensions for describing the general properties of group-generated written passages. *Psychological Bulletin, 67*, 379–390.

Harinck, F., De Dreu, C. K. W., & Van Vianen, A. E. M. (2000). The impact of conflict issues on fixed-pie perceptions, problem solving, and integrative outcomes in negotiation. *Organizational Behavior and Human Decision Processes, 81*, 329–358.

Hofstede, G. (1980). *Culture's consequences: International differences in work-related values.* Newbury Park, CA: Sage.

Hollenbeck, J. R., Moon, H., Ellis, A. P. J., West, B. J., Ilgen, D. R., Sheppard, L., et al. (2002). Structural contingency theory and individual differences: Examination of external and internal person-team fit. *Journal of Applied Psychology, 87*, 599–606.

Ilgen, D. R. (1999). Teams embedded in organizations. *American Psychologist, 54*, 129–139.

Janis, I. L., & Mann, L. (1977). *Decision making: A psychological analysis of conflict, choice, and commitment.* New York: Free Press.

Janssen, O., Van de Vliert, E., & Veenstra, C. (1999). How task and person conflict shape the role of positive interdependence in management teams. *Journal of Management, 25*, 117–142.

Jehn, K. A., & Shah, P. P. (1997). Interpersonal relationships and task performance: An examination of mediating processes in friendship and acquaintance groups. *Journal of Personality and Social Psychology, 72*, 775–790.

Jensen-Campbell, L. A., Graziano, W. G., & Hair, E. C. (1996). Personality and relationships as moderators of interpersonal conflict in adolescence. *Merrill Palmer Quarterly, 42*, 148–164.

Johnson, M. D., Hollenbeck, J. R., Humphrey, S. E., Ilgen, D. R., Jundt, D. K., & Meyer, C. J. (2006). Cutthroat cooperation: Asymmetrical adaptation of team reward structure. *Academy of Management Journal, 49*, 103–120.

Kelley, H. H., & Stahelski, A. J. (1970). Social interaction basis of cooperators' and competitors' beliefs about others. *Journal of Personality and Social Psychology, 16*, 66–91.

Kelley, H. H., & Thibaut, J. W. (1978). *Interpersonal relations: A theory of interdependence.* New York: John Wiley & Sons.

Kerr, N. L., & Tindale, R. S. (2004). Group performance and decision making. *Annual Review of Psychology, 55*, 623–655.

Korsgaard, M. A., Schweiger, D. M., & Sapienza, H. J. (1995). Building commitment, attachment, and trust in strategic decision-making teams: The role of procedural justice. *Academy of Management Journal, 38*, 60–84.

Kramer, R. M., Newton, E., & Pommerenke, P. L. (1993). Self-enhancement biases and negotiator judgment: Effects of self-esteem and mood. *Organizational Behavior and Human Decision Processes, 56*, 113–133.

Kristof, A. L. (1996). Person–organization fit: An integrative review of its conceptualizations, measurement, and implications. *Personnel Psychology, 49*, 1–49.

Levine, J. M., & Moreland, R. L. (1998). Small groups. In D. Gilbert, S. Fiske, & H. Lindsey (Eds.), *Handbook of social psychology* (Vol. 2, pp. 415–469). Boston: McGraw-Hill.

Levine, J. M., & Thompson, L. (1996). Conflict in groups. In T. Higgins & A. W. Kruglanski (Eds.), *Social psychology: Handbook of basic principles* (pp. 745–776). New York: Guilford Press.

Liebrand, W. B., Jansen, R. W., Rijken, V. M., & Suhre, C. J. (1986). Might over morality: Social values and the perception of other players in experimental games. *Journal of Experimental Social Psychology, 22*(3), 203–215.

Mannix, E. A., Thompson, L. L., & Bazerman, M. H. (1989). Negotiation in small groups. *Journal of Applied Psychology, 74*, 508–517.

McClintock, C. (1976). Social motives in settings of outcome interdependence. In D. Druckman (Ed.), *Negotiations: Social psychological perspective* (pp. 49–77). Beverly Hills, CA: Sage.

McClintock, C. G. (1972). Social motivation—A set of propositions. *Behavioral Science, 17*, 438–454.

McCrae, R. R., & Costa, P. T. (1989). The structure of interpersonal traits: Wiggins's circumplex and the five-factor model. *Journal of Personality and Social Psychology, 56*, 586–595.

McGrath, J. E. (1984). *Groups: Interaction and performance.* Englewood Cliffs, NJ: Prentice-Hall.

Messick, D. M., & Brewer, M. B. (1983). Solving social dilemma's: A review. In L. Wheeler & P. Shaver (Eds.), *Review of personality and social psychology* (Vol. 4, pp. 11–44). Beverly Hills, CA: Sage Publications.

Moberg, P. J. (2001). Linking conflict strategy to the five-factor model: Theoretical and empirical foundations. *International Journal of Conflict Management, 12*, 47–68.

Moon, H. K., Hollenbeck, J. R., Humphrey, S. E., Ilgen, D. R., West, B., Ellis, A. P. J., et al. (2004). Asymmetric adaptability: Dynamic team structures as one-way streets. *Academy of Management Journal, 4*, 681–695.

Moynihan, L. M., & Peterson, R. S. (2001). A contingent configuration approach to understanding the role of personality in organizational groups. *Research in Organizational Behavior, 23*, 327–378.

Muchinsky, P. M., & Monahan, C. J. (1987). What is person-environment congruence? Supplementary versus complementary models of fit. *Journal of Vocational Behavior, 31*, 268–277.

Munkes, J., & Diehl, M. (2003). Matching or competition? Performance comparison processes in an idea generation task. *Group Processes and Intergroup Relations, 6*, 305–320.

Murnighan, J. K., & Brass, D. (1991). Intraorganizational coalitions. In R. Lewicki, B. Sheppard, & M. Bazerman (Eds.), *Research on negotiation in organizations* (Vol. 3, pp. 283–306). Greenwich, CT: JAI Press.

Murnighan, J. K., & Szwajkowski, E. (1979). Coalition bargaining in four games that include a veto player. *Journal of Personality and Social Psychology, 37*, 1933–1946.

Neale, M. A., & Northcraft, G. B. (1986). Experts, amateurs, and refrigerators: Comparing expert and amateur negotiators in a novel task. *Organizational Behavior and Human Decision Processes, 38*, 305–317.

Nemeth, C. J., & Staw, B. M. (1989). The tradeoff of social control and innovation in groups and organizations. *Advances in Experimental Social Psychology, 22*, 175–210.

Peterson, R. S., & Nemeth, C. J. (1996). Focus versus flexibility: Majority and minority influence can both improve performance. *Personality and Social Psychology Bulletin, 22*, 14–23.

Postmes, T., Spears, R., & Cihangir, S. (2001). Quality of decision making and group norms. *Journal of Personality and Social Psychology, 80*, 918–930.

Probst, T., Carnevale, P. J., & Triandis, H. C. (1999). Cultural values in intergroup and single-group social dilemmas. *Organizational Behavior and Human Decision Processes, 77,* 171–191.

Pruitt, D. G., & Carnevale, P. J. (1993). *Negotiation in social conflict.* Pacific Grove, CA: Brooks/Cole.

Pruitt, D. G., & Lewis, S. (1975). Development of integrative solutions in bilateral negotiation. *Journal of Personality and Social Psychology, 31,* 621–633.

Rubin, J. Z., Pruitt, D. G., & Kim, S. H. (1994). *Social conflict: Escalation, stalemate, and settlement* (2nd ed.). New York: McGraw-Hill, Inc.

Rusbult, C. E., & Van Lange, P. A. M. (1996). Interdependence processes. In E. T. Higgins & A. W. Kruglanski (Eds.), *Social psychology: Handbook of basic principles* (pp. 564–596). New York: Guilford Publications.

Schei, V., & Rognes, J. K. (2003). Knowing me, knowing you: Own orientation and information about the opponent's orientation in negotiation. *International Journal of Conflict Management, 14,* 43–59.

Schelling, T. C. (1960). *The strategy of conflict.* Cambridge, MA: Harvard University Press.

Schulz, J. W., & Pruitt, D. G. (1978). The effects of mutual concern on joint welfare. *Journal of Experimental Social Psychology, 14,* 480–491.

Schulz-Hardt, S., Jochims, M., & Frey, D. (2002). Productive conflict in group decision making: Genuine and contrived dissent as strategies to counteract biased information seeking. *Organizational Behavior and Human Decision Processes, 88,* 563–586.

Schweiger, D. M., Sandberg, W. R., & Rechner, P. L. (1989). Experiential effects of dialectical inquiry, devil's advocacy, and consensus approaches to strategic decision making. *Academy of Management Journal, 32,* 745–772.

Simons, T. L., & Peterson, R. S. (2000). Task conflict and relationship conflict in top management teams: The pivotal role of intragroup trust. *Journal of Applied Psychology, 85,* 102–111.

Singelis, T. M. (1994). The measurement of independent and interdependent self-construals. *Personality and Social Psychology Bulletin, 20,* 580–591.

Steinel, W., & De Dreu, C. K. W. (2004). Social motives and strategic misrepresentation in social decision making. *Journal of Personality and Social Psychology, 86,* 419–434.

Ten Velden, F. S., Beersma, B., & De Dreu, C. K. W. (2007). Majority and minority influence in group negotiation: The moderating influence of social motivation and decision rules. *Journal of Applied Psychology, 92,* 259–268.

Thompson, L., & Hastie, R. (1990). Social perception in negotiation. *Organizational Behavior and Human Decision Processes, 47,* 98–123.

Thompson, L. L., Mannix, E. A., & Bazerman, M. H. (1988). Group negotiation: Effects of decision rule, agenda, and aspiration. *Journal of Personality and Social Psychology, 54,* 86–95.

Tjosvold, D. (1998). Cooperative and competitive goal approach to conflict: Accomplishments and challenges. *Applied Psychology: An International Review, 46,* 285–342.

Tjosvold, D., Dann, V., & Wong, C. (1992). Managing conflict between departments to serve customers. *Human Resources, 45,* 1035–1053.

Tjosvold, D., & De Dreu, C. K. W. (1997). Managing conflict in Dutch organizations: A test of the relevance of Deutsch's cooperation theory. *Journal of Applied Social Psychology, 27,* 2213–2227.

Tjosvold, D., & Deemer, D. K. (1980). Effects of controversy within a cooperative or competitive context on organizational decision making. *Journal of Applied Psychology, 65,* 590–595.

Tjosvold, D., Wedley, W. C., & Field, R. H. (1986). Constructive controversy, the Vroom-Yetton model, and managerial decision-making. *Journal of Occupational Behaviour, 7,* 125–138.

Triandis, H. C. (1989). The self and social behavior in differing cultural contexts. *Psychological Review, 96,* 506–520.

Triandis, H. C., & Gelfand, M. J. (1998). Converging measurement of horizontal and vertical individualism and collectivism. *Journal of Personality and Social Psychology, 74,* 118–128.

Van Lange, P. A. M. (1999). The pursuit of joint outcomes and equality in outcomes: An integrative model of social value orientation. *Journal of Personality and Social Psychology, 77,* 337–349.

Van Lange, P. A. M., Agnew, C. R., Harinck, F., & Steemers, G. E. M. (1997). From game theory to real life: How social value orientation affects willingness to sacrifice in ongoing close relationships. *Journal of Personality and Social Psychology, 73,* 1330–1344.

Van Lange, P. A. M., & Kuhlman, D. M. (1994). Social value orientations and impressions of partner's honesty and intelligence: A test of the might versus morality effect. *Journal of Personality and Social Psychology, 67,* 126–141.

Van Lange, P. A. M., Otten, W., De Bruin, E. M. N., & Joireman, J. A. (1997). Development of prosocial, individualistic, and competitive orientations: Theory and preliminary evidence. *Journal of Personality and Social Psychology, 73,* 733–746

Van Lange, P. A. M., Van Vugt, M., Meertens, R. M., & Ruiter, R. A. C. (1998). A social dilemma analysis of commuting preferences: The roles of social value orientation and trust. *Journal of Applied Social Psychology, 28,* 796–820.

Wagner, J. A., III. (1995). Studies of individualism-collectivism: Effects on cooperation in groups. *Academy of Management Journal, 38,* 152–172.

Weingart, L. R., Bennett, R. J., & Brett, J. M. (1993). The impact of consideration of issues and motivational orientation on group negotiation process and outcome. *Journal of Applied Psychology, 78,* 504–517.

Weingart, L. R., Brett, J. M., & Olekalns, M. (2003). *Conflicting social motives in negotiating groups.* Manuscript submitted for publication.

Yamagishi, T., & Sato, K. (1986). Motivational bases of the public goods problem. *Journal of Personality and Social Psychology, 50,* 67–73.

5

Dissent as a Facilitator: Individual- and Group-Level Effects on Creativity and Performance

STEFAN SCHULZ-HARDT, ANDREAS
MOJZISCH, AND FRANK VOGELGESANG
Georg-August-University Goettingen

For most people the word *conflict* has a negative connotation: Conflict indicates that a "normal," harmonious state is disturbed, that something is wrong, and that things are not as they should be. Consequently, conflict is something that has to be avoided, that has to be resolved or, at best, that has to be managed. In this chapter, we will try to show that a particular type of conflict, namely conflict brought about by being confronted with dissenting opinions, can be productive in that it stimulates creativity and performance.

This chapter is divided into four sections. In the first section, we highlight the notion that conflict brought about by dissenting opinions facilitates creativity and performance by reporting particular illustrative studies from this field of research. In the second section, we outline the psychological processes that mediate the facilitative effect of dissent on creativity and performance. In this section, we also draw a distinction between minority and majority dissent. In the third section, we address the question of how organizations can use dissent systematically to enhance creativity and performance. In the final section, we summarize what we know about the role of dissent for individual creativity and group decision-making quality so far and highlight some questions that would be fruitful to investigate in the future.

DISSENT AND CONFLICT: DO THEY FACILITATE CREATIVITY AND PERFORMANCE?

In this section, we will consider three lines of evidence indicating that dissent stimulates creativity and performance. When we speak of "dissent," we mean any situation where a person is confronted with one or more other persons' opinions, and at least one of these opinions is different from his or her own opinion. Hence, if one had not already made up one's mind about an issue, and if one were now confronted with two persons' opinions on that issue that contradict each other, this would not be a case of dissent according to our definition (e.g., for a treatment of such situations, see Erb & Bohner, 2001). However, if one already had an opinion on that particular issue, the situation would constitute a case of dissent because necessarily at least one of the other persons' opinions contradicts one's own opinion. In contrast, if these two persons had the same opinion as one has, we will call this "consent."

First Example: Dissent and Perspective Taking

Imagine you are a member of a management board and have to decide whether the contract of a manager should be extended or not. While having lunch at the cafeteria, you start a conversation about this issue with another member of the management board. It soon turns out that both of you agree on extending the manager's contract. In the evening, you discuss this issue with another member of the management board in your company's fitness center. This time, the member of the management board is in favor of letting the manager go—that is, she contradicts your opinion. What do you think—in which of these two situations would you be better able to accurately understand the other person's reasoning and underlying motives? Would you better understand the one who agrees or the one who disagrees with you?

This question was addressed in a seminal experiment conducted by Tjosvold and Johnson (1977). In the first part of the experiment, participants were asked to read a moral dilemma. The dilemma involved a school principal who had to decide whether to allow a student newspaper, which students appreciated but parents disliked, to continue. Participants were asked to indicate what course of action the school principal should take. Later on, they discussed the moral dilemma with another ostensible participant who was actually a confederate of the experimenter. The confederate was trained to consistently present arguments that reflected his or her primary interest, which, in this case, was to maintain social order through respect for rules, the law, authority, and the status quo. In the *no-controversy condition*, the confederate took the same position as the participant as to how the moral dilemma should be solved. In the *controversy condition*, the confederate took the position opposite from the participant.

The dependent variable was the accuracy with which participants understood the perspective of the confederate, that is, his or her primary interest in maintaining social order. This was operationalized by asking the participants after the discussion to indicate how the confederate would reason on another moral dilemma. Specifically, participants were asked to pick from a list of 11 arguments those 4 the confederate would most probably use to support his position. Wanting to maintain social order characterized 3 of the 11 arguments. To the extent that the participants were able to identify those three arguments as being the ones the confederate would use, they were considered to understand the confederate's perspective. The main finding was that participants in the controversy condition were significantly more likely to identify those three arguments than participants in the no-controversy condition were. Subsequent studies expanded this finding by showing that dissent particularly has these facilitative effects on cognitive perspective taking and understanding of the other's position if an atmosphere of "constructive controversy" is given—that is, open debate and constructive criticism are highly valued (e.g., Tjosvold, 1982; Tjosvold & Deemer, 1980; Tjosvold & Field, 1985; Tjosvold, Johnson, & Lerner, 1981). In sum, dissent—at least when the context allows free expression of it—seems to lead to more accurate cognitive perspective taking than consent does. In other words, dissent can help us to understand someone else.

Second Example: Dissent and Individual Creativity

Whereas accuracy in person perception helps us to understand and get along with others in an organization, we would not expect this variable to be as strongly linked to performance measures as, for example, team performance in organizations. A variable that is more closely linked to such performance measures is creativity. We speak of creativity if people generate new, original ideas and novel problem solutions. Does dissent affect creativity?

An intriguing study by Nemeth and Kwan (1985) shed light on this topic. Participants were asked to judge a series of 20 slides for color and brightness. In fact, all of these slides were blue in color. However, in the *majority condition*, prior to their judgments participants were informed that 80% of previous participants had judged these slides as "green" and 20% of participants had judged them as "blue." In the *minority condition*, participants were told that 20% of previous participants had judged these slides as "green" and 80% of participants had judged them as "blue." Hence, dissent came from either a majority or a minority of previous participants. In the *control condition*, no information about disagreeing judgments of previous participants was given. In both experimental conditions, each participant was paired with one confederate who answered first and judged the slide to be "green" on all 20 trials. Hence, the judgment of the confederate should have been viewed as either a minority or a majority judgment. Following this judgment session, participants were asked for word associations to the words *blue* and *green*.

The results of this study, illustrated in Figure 5.1, proved to be striking. First, participants exposed to an opposing minority judgment gave more associations than participants in the majority and the control conditions. Second, and even more important, participants exposed to the opposing minority judgment gave more creative word associations than participants in the other two conditions. For example, a response of a participant in the control or the majority dissent condition to the word *blue* might be *sky*. In contrast, the responses of participants faced with disagreement from a minority to *blue* might be *jazz* or *jeans*. Other studies by Nemeth and her colleagues (Nemeth, Brown, & Rogers, 2001; Nemeth, Connell, Rogers, & Brown, 2001) corroborated this basic finding by showing that minority dissent stimulates creative ideas and solutions to a given problem. Further studies from this research program showed that minority dissent can also facilitate memory performance (Nemeth, Mayseless, Sherman, & Brown, 1990) as well as resistance against conformity pressures (Nemeth & Chiles, 1988).

Even more striking, there is evidence showing that the productive effect of a dissenting minority occurs regardless of whether or not the dissenting minority is correct. In a seminal study, Nemeth and Wachtler (1983) used an *embedded figure task*, asking participants to find all comparison figures that contained a standard figure. Specifically, participants were shown a series of slides with a standard figure on the left and six comparison figures on the right. One comparison figure was very easy. When alone, participants named only this easy comparison figure as containing the standard figure. Depending on the experimental condition, in each

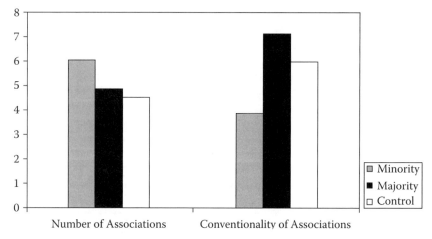

FIGURE 5.1. Number of associations and mean conventionality of associations in the study by Nemeth and Kwan (1985).

session either two (minority condition) or four of the six participants (majority condition) were confederates who said the standard figure was embedded both in the easy comparison figure and in one other figure. Again, depending on the experimental condition, this answer was either correct or incorrect. Consistent with the results previously described, participants exposed to minority dissent were more likely to find novel correct solutions than participants exposed to majority dissent or participants in the control condition. Thus, minority dissent enhanced not only creativity but also performance (more correct solutions compared with the other conditions). Importantly, this finding held true regardless of whether the minority was correct or incorrect.

Third Example: Dissent and Group Decision Quality

So far, the reported facilitative effects of dissent were located at the individual level: Individuals became more accurate in understanding other persons' positions after having been exposed to dissent, and individuals showed higher creativity and better performance after having been confronted with dissenting minority opinions. Since dissent characterizes a relation between two or more persons—does dissent also have beneficial effects on creativity and performance if the persons with different opinions have to perform together as a group?

A direct test of this hypothesis was recently conducted by Schulz-Hardt, Brodbeck, Mojzisch, Kerschreiter, and Frey (2006). In this study, Schulz-Hardt et al. used a *hidden profile task* to investigate whether dissent in group members' prediscussion preferences has a beneficial effect on group decision quality. So-called "hidden profiles" are dual- or multiple-alternative group decision tasks in which the information about the decision alternatives is distributed among the group members such that no member can detect the best alternative on the basis of his or her individual information set. To understand this type of task better, it is necessary to distinguish between shared and unshared information (Stasser & Titus, 1985). Whereas shared information is known to all group members prior to discussion, unshared information is held by only one group member. In a hidden profile, shared and unshared information have different decisional implications (i.e., favor different alternatives), and the alternative implied by the unshared information is the correct one. Hidden profiles are particularly important in group decision making because, faced with a hidden profile, groups can uncover a superior decision alternative that none of their members supported individually. Hence, hidden profiles represent a class of situations that can result in innovative and superior decisions by groups. Unfortunately, groups predominantly fail to solve hidden profiles (for overviews, see Brodbeck, Kerschreiter, Mojzisch, & Schulz-Hardt, 2007; Mojzisch & Schulz-Hardt, 2006; Stasser & Birchmeier, 2003).

Schulz-Hardt et al. (2006) constructed a personnel selection case with four decision alternatives for three-person groups, with three equally attractive suboptimal alternatives and one superior alternative (the correct solution). For the sake of simplicity, let us assume that, in the light of the total information, Candidate C is the best candidate, whereas Candidates A, B, and D are equally inferior (in the real experiment, this distribution was rotated). However, because information was distributed in a hidden profile manner, for each member Candidate C was less attractive than the three other candidates on the basis of the individual prediscussion information. In the experimental design, a hidden profile condition without dissent (*homogeneity*, e.g., all group members preferred the same suboptimal candidate prior to discussion) was contrasted with four dissent conditions: *pure minority dissent* (two members preferred the same and the third member preferred a different suboptimal candidate prior to discussion), *pure full-diversity dissent* (all three members preferred different suboptimal candidates prior to discussion), *minority dissent with proponent* (two members preferred the same suboptimal candidate and the third member preferred the correct candidate prior to discussion), *full-diversity dissent with proponent* (two members preferred different suboptimal candidates, the third member preferred the correct candidate prior to discussion). In an additional *control condition*, group members received the complete information set prior to discussion (no hidden profile).

In the experiment, participants first had to read and evaluate their individual information about the candidates. After they had indicated their preference for one of the candidates, three-person groups were formed according to the experimental conditions previously listed. The groups then had to discuss the case and make a group decision for one of the candidates. It should be emphasized that groups were explicitly informed that each member had only a subset of the whole information, that these subsets were partially different, that a best solution existed on the basis of the full information, and that making the correct decision would be rewarded.

In accordance with the previous literature (e.g., Kelly & Karau, 1999; Lavery, Franz, Winquist, & Larson, 1999; Stasser & Titus, 1985), the groups were overall not very successful in solving the hidden profile. Whereas all groups made the correct decision if the group members had full information prior to discussion (no hidden profile), only 35% of the groups with a hidden profile distribution of information chose the correct candidate. Among these, consent groups (e.g., groups with homogeneous prediscussion preferences for a suboptimal candidate) had the lowest solution rates, namely only 7%. As Figure 5.2 illustrates, these solution rates were significantly higher in groups with pure minority or pure full-diversity dissent; about 27% of these groups solved the hidden profile. In other words, although in the latter groups all three members preferred suboptimal candidates at the beginning, the fact that they had dissent among

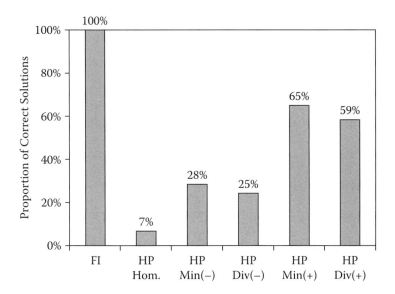

FIGURE 5.2. Proportion of correct group decisions dependent on dissent in the study by Schulz-Hardt et al. (2006). FI = Full information, HP = Hidden profile, Hom. = Homogeneity, Min(–) = Pure minority dissent, Div(–) = Pure full-diversity dissent, Min(+) = Minority dissent with proponent, Div(+) = Full-diversity dissent with proponent.

their individual preferences allowed them to make better decisions than consent groups where all three members preferred the *same* suboptimal candidate. When groups with dissent among their members' prediscussion preferences contained a proponent of the best candidate, there was an even higher likelihood that the hidden profile was uncovered as compared with dissent groups in which all members entered discussion with a suboptimal preference—about 62% of the proponent groups solved the hidden profile.

In sum, the results of the Schulz-Hardt et al. (2006) study showed that, in cases where the best choice is not evident at the beginning, group decision quality benefits from dissent (for related findings, see also Brodbeck, Kerschreiter, Mojzisch, Frey, and Schulz-Hardt, 2002). Wanous and Youtz (1986) reported similar effects of dissent on the quality of group problem solving. Additionally, Sniezek and Henry (1989) demonstrated dissent to be beneficial to the accuracy of group judgments. Not surprisingly, the benefit obtained from dissent is larger if at least one of the members with dissenting opinions favors the best solution at the beginning of the discussion. However, the Schulz-Hardt et al. (2006) study showed that dissent also facilitates decision quality if *none* of the dissenting individual preferences is correct. In other words, under conditions of dissent, three blinds together might be able to see.

DISSENT AND CONFLICT: HOW DO THEY FACILITATE
CREATIVITY AND PERFORMANCE?

The exemplary findings reported in the previous section demonstrate that, if one intends to facilitate creativity and performance, dissent works. The question that arises then is *how* does it work? In other words, what are the psychological processes that mediate these facilitative effects of dissent? In addition, not all types of dissent may lead to the same processes. As previously illustrated, minority dissent has different consequences for creativity and performance than majority dissent does, and, thus, different processes may operate for minority versus majority dissent. In what follows, we will first outline that dissent has an activating effect on information processing and information exchange in general. Next, we will outline the effects of pure minority versus majority dissent on individual information processing as related to creativity and performance. Afterwards, we turn to the question of how the simultaneous occurrence of minority and majority dissent in interacting groups affects these processes as well as creativity and performance at the group level.

The Activating Role of Dissent in General

The most basic psychological effect of dissent is activation: If we experience dissent, this increases intensity of information processing at the individual level and discussion intensity at the group level. The intensity of individual information processing is high if many thoughts and ideas are generated on a topic and if the information about it gets deeply elaborated. Discussion intensity in a group is high if much information on a topic is exchanged and discussed in the group.

At the individual level, the intensifying effect of dissent for information processing is a concrete manifestation of one of the basic principles of social cognition, namely that people allocate attention and cognitive resources selectively and that one of the criteria for selectively allocating cognitive resources is inconsistency between one's belief or opinion and a message from another person (e.g., Ditto, Scepansky, Munro, Apanovitch, & Lockhart, 1998; Edwards & Smith, 1996). This is a highly functional principle of human cognition because cognitive resources are scarce. If something we hear is consistent with our opinion, there is no direct need to scrutinize it intensively. If, however, something contradicts our belief or opinion, we should invest cognitive resources, because this inconsistency indicates that either our opinion or the incoming information (e.g., about the opinion of another person) might be wrong (Edwards & Smith).

This activating effect of dissent for individual information processing becomes evident, for example, in information search: In a study by Mojzisch, Schulz-Hardt, Lüthgens, Kerschreiter, and Frey (2007), five-person groups discussed a decision case with two alternatives. Consent and dissent groups were formed by either composing groups of five individuals with the same individual preferences or building groups with a minority or majority faction. After their discussion, participants had the opportunity to acquire additional information about the topic. Members of former dissent groups requested more additional pieces of information than members of former consent groups did. Similar effects became evident in a study by Levine and Russo (1995). In the studies by Tjosvold and his colleagues, reported in the previous section, people who were confronted with someone who disagreed with them were more interested to get further information about the other person's thoughts than people who where confronted with agreement (Tjosvold & Johnson, 1978). This higher receptivity to and interest in additional information can explain why people understand the perspective of dissenters better than the perspective of those with whom they agree.

On the level of the group, the equivalent to intensified information processing is intensified discussion. Groups with dissent among their members conduct more intensive discussions than groups without dissent. More specifically, groups with prediscussion dissent among their members (e.g., where members enter the discussion with different opinions or choice preferences) discuss a decision problem longer (Brodbeck et al., 2002), exchange more information (Parks & Nelson, 1999), repeat exchanged information more often (Schulz-Hardt et al., 2006), and generate more arguments about a decision problem (Smith, Tindale, & Dugoni, 1996) than groups without prediscussion dissent. Although this mechanism might not be very surprising, since dissent requires more intensive discussion to come to a consensual solution than consent does, it has important consequences: As Schulz-Hardt et al. (2006) showed, intensified discussion is the primary reason dissent groups are more likely than consent groups to talk about and subsequently choose superior solutions that no group member has preferred before. Thus, better performance in dissent groups can be simply due to the fact that discussion in these groups is much more intensive than discussion in consent groups.

Exposure to Minority Versus Majority Dissent: Effects on Individuals

As already outlined in the first section, different subtypes of dissent seem to be differently facilitative of creativity and performance. The research program by Nemeth and her colleagues provided convincing evidence that exposure to minority dissent is more likely to enhance individual creativity and performance than exposure to majority dissent is. To understand why this is the case, we have to look at the different psychological processes resulting from minority versus majority dissent.

In her theory of minority influence, Nemeth (1986) predicted that both minority and majority dissent induce cognitive activity, but that these activities differ in direction. Specifically, majority dissent is proposed to induce information processing that focusses on the position of the majority. Due to this focus-inducing nature of majority dissent, this information processing style is called "convergent" thinking. By contrast, minority dissent is assumed to induce thought processes in multiple directions. In other words, people who are exposed to minority dissent focus neither on their own nor on the majority position, but also take positions and alternatives into account that are proposed neither by themselves nor by the minority. This information processing style is called "divergent" thinking.

A study by Nemeth and Kwan (1987) nicely illustrated these different styles. Participants in groups of four were shown a series of letter strings with the middle three letters in capitals (e.g., tDAMp) and were asked to write down the first three-letter word that they noticed. All participants named the word formed by the three capital letters from left to right (e.g., DAM). After five slides were shown, participants in the experimental conditions were given bogus feedback on the judgments of the three other participants. In the *majority condition*, participants were led to believe that the other three participants noticed the word formed by the backward sequencing of the capital letters. In our example, the experimenter thus would have said, "MAD, MAD, MAD, DAM." In the *minority condition*, participants were led to believe that only one of the other participants noticed the word formed by the backward sequencing. In our example, the experimenter thus would have said, "MAD, DAM, DAM, DAM." Because all participants first noticed the word formed by the three capital letters from left to right (i.e., used the forward sequencing strategy), dissent came hence from either a majority or a minority of the other participants. In the *control condition*, participants received no feedback.

Subsequently, participants saw a series of 10-letter strings (with the first five being identical to the ones presented before and the last five being new) and were asked to write down *all* of the words they could form from the letters. Compared with the control condition with no feedback, participants exposed to majority dissent made significantly more use of the backward sequencing strategy, but they did that at the expense of using the forward sequencing strategy. Thus, these participants focussed on the majority strategy (convergent thinking) without the overall number of correct solutions being affected. In contrast, participants exposed to minority dissent made use of all possible strategies—forward sequencing, backward sequencing, and mixed sequencing of letters (which had previously been proposed neither by themselves nor by the minority). Hence, compared with the majority and the control condition, participants under minority dissent showed higher flexibility in the usage of strategies (divergent thinking) and found more solutions that were correct.

These results not only illustrated the different information processing styles induced by minority and majority dissent, but also showed that, as a consequence of these styles, exposure to minority dissent facilitates the generation of novel thoughts and solutions, whereas exposure to majority dissent hinders the generation of novel ideas. Hence, creativity almost exclusively benefits from minority dissent, whereas it should even suffer from majority dissent. This is exactly what the study by Nemeth and Kwan (1985), reported in the previous section, found.

In contrast to creativity, individual performance can also benefit from majority dissent. However, these benefits are restricted to situations where the majority perspective itself is correct or implies high performance. In accordance with this, Peterson and Nemeth (1996) showed that majority dissent facilitates performance (compared with a control condition without dissent) if the majority's strategy enhances performance and if no flexible use of strategies is required. If, however, a flexible use of strategies is required for good individual performance, only minority dissent is beneficial. The latter superiority of minority dissent is further underlined by the fact that minority dissent stimulates individual performance even if the solution proposed by the minority is wrong (Nemeth & Wachtler, 1983), or even if the solution proposed by a dissenting minority on a previous problem cannot be transferred to a current problem by means of simple analogy transfer (Martin & Hewstone, 1999).

Taken together, majority dissent is beneficial to individual performance only if a direct application of what the majority proposes leads to success. At the same time, the great danger of majority dissent is uncritical conformity with incorrect majority positions (e.g., Asch, 1951; Janis, 1982). In contrast, minority dissent initiates a multidirectional search for solutions and, thus, stimulates individual performance even if the solution proposed by the minority is incorrect or not directly applicable.

Minority and Majority Dissent: Effects Within Groups

So far, our consideration of differential minority versus majority dissent effects has been restricted to *unidirectional* influence and its effects at the level of the *individual*. *Unidirectional* means that the person is confronted with dissent from a minority or a majority—for example, by being given background information about the distribution of opinions in a particular group or population, or by reading or listening to a statement that contradicts her opinion and that supposedly comes from a minority or majority—without having an opportunity to exert reciprocal influence on the source of dissent. When the dissent episode is over, subsequent individual processes are measured. This unidirectional, individualistic perspective is dominant in social psychological dissent research.

Whereas this clear isolation of influence types may be beneficial from a sociocognitive process perspective, its value for gaining insights into dissent effects in organizations may be limited to the extent that such isolated dissent situations are the exception rather than the rule in organizations. Because dissent in organizations usually is to be found in groups (e.g., boards, staff groups, committees, units, development teams), we cannot have one type of influence without the other. If we facilitate minority dissent in a group in order to stimulate divergent thinking among the majority, from the perspective of the minority, we also have majority dissent. Furthermore, both factions do not exert isolated influence on each other but rather interact with each other, and this interaction might change the nature of the influence processes. This leads us to two questions: First, do we still observe divergent thinking and enhanced creativity among majorities (due to minority dissent) and convergent thinking among minorities (due to majority dissent) after both factions have interacted with each other? Second, what is the net effect of both influence types at the group level? If majorities become more flexible and creative and minorities become more rigid and convergent, do these two counterdirectional effects eliminate each other, or is there still a flexibility enhancing effect of dissent evident at the group level?

Studies of simultaneous majority and minority influence in interacting groups are far less frequent in the literature than studies on individual level effects of majority and minority influence. Unfortunately, some of the few studies in interacting groups do not even fully qualify for an answer to the questions previously posited, for example, because confederates were used as minorities (e.g., Van Dyne & Saavedra, 1996), or because dependent variables were reported only for majority members but not for minority members (e.g., Smith et al., 1996). The essence of these studies is that minority dissent stimulates divergent thinking and cognitive flexibility also among majority members in interacting groups, but they do not tell us whether the minorities have to pay the price in terms of more convergent, conventional thinking, and they also do not tell us whether the net effect of both types of influence at the group level is still in favor of flexibility, creativity, and performance.

With regard to the first question (information processing among minorities and majorities during or after mutual interaction), a preliminary answer can be obtained from studies by Gruenfeld and her colleagues. Gruenfeld (1995), as well as Gruenfeld and Preston (2000), analyzed U.S. Supreme Court decisions in cases of nonunanimous support and found that the statements of members of the majority faction (who had been exposed to minority dissent) were characterized by higher integrative complexity than those of the minority faction (who had been exposed to majority influence). High integrative complexity means considering an issue divergently from multiple perspectives, whereas low integrative complexity means convergently focussing on a single perspective. Since such differences need not necessarily reflect different information processing styles but, instead, could also be an impression management strategy (the minority argues very consistently for the sake of persuasion), Gruenfeld, Thomas-Hunt, and Kim (1998) conducted a laboratory experiment with students simulating court discussions. On the basis of individual judgments about the case, groups with minority and majority factions were formed. After having made a majority-vote decision, members of both factions either were asked to write down their personal thoughts about the case and assured strict confidentiality or were instructed to write a rationale for the public record. Compared with initial statements given before the discussion, the statements of majority members (who had been exposed to minority dissent) increased in integrative complexity, whereas those of the minority members (exposed to majority dissent) were characterized by decreased integrative complexity. This held true for both the public and the private condition, indicating that the differences in integrative complexity reflect differences in information processing style (rather than public impression management strategies).

So far, these results seem to fit perfectly with Nemeth's ideas: Minority dissent facilitates divergent thinking (increased integrative complexity), whereas majority dissent induces convergent thinking (reduced integrative complexity). There is, however, one remarkable difference with respect to the minority members: Whereas Nemeth (1986) predicted that minority members should focus on the perspective of the majority, the low integrative complexity in the studies of Gruenfeld and colleagues indicated a focus on their *own* perspective. Thus, we have convergence among the minority members, but in a different direction than predicted.

Some clarification can be obtained from the previously mentioned Mojzisch, Schulz-Hardt, Lüthgens, et al. (2007) study. As outlined, five-person groups that either were unanimous or consisted of a majority and a minority faction discussed a decision case with two alternatives. Afterwards, group members had the opportunity to individually search for additional information. For each participant, half of the information was in favor of their preferred alternative and the other half of the information was in favor of the opposite alternative. Majority members conducted an almost balanced information search among the two alternatives (which is a divergent information search strategy; see also Nemeth & Rogers, 1996). Similar to the members of unanimous groups, minority members in dissent groups who had resisted the majority influence during group discussion exhibited a clear confirmation bias—that is, they selectively requested information supporting their previous decision and thus focused on their *own* position—which is in line with the findings of Gruenfeld and colleagues. However, if the minority members converted to the majority position, they selectively searched for information in favor of the majority position—which is in line with the predictions of Nemeth (1986). Taken together, the evidence suggests that after simultaneous minority and majority influence in dissent groups, majorities exhibit increased divergent thinking, whereas minorities tend to converge to their own position—and this can be the majority position if the minority has converted.

With regard to the second question, namely whether the net effect of more divergence among majorities and more convergence among minorities is still in favor of cognitive flexibility and divergent thinking at the group level, we have obtained conclusive evidence in our own research program. Somewhat similar to Mojzisch, Schulz-Hardt, Lüthgens, et al. (2007), in a study by Schulz-Hardt, Frey, Lüthgens, and Moscovici (2000) three- and five-person groups discussed a decision case with two alterna-tives. After an initial discussion, this time the groups (instead of the indi-vidual group members) had the opportunity to select expert statements on the decision problem, half of which supported the decision alterna-tive favored by the majority in the group and half of which favored the opposite alternative. In an individual control condition, a confirmation bias (i.e., a preference for supporting information) emerged. Whereas this bias was even more pronounced among consent groups (i.e., groups with all members favoring the same alternative), it was roughly eliminated in three-person groups with a majority and a minority faction and in five-person groups with a three-person majority and a two-person minority. Additional analyses showed that this difference between consent and dis-sent groups could not be reduced to a simple aggregation of individual tendencies (if each group member exhibits a confirmation bias, the confir-mation bias of the minority runs counter to the confirmation bias of the majority and, thus, information search is automatically less biased toward the alternative favored by the majority). Rather, consent was shown to *intensify* the confirmation bias compared with what would have occurred if each member had made individual information requests (biased toward his or her preferred alternative) and these individual requests had been summed up in the group. At the same time, dissent *debiased* information search over and above what would be expected on the basis of the mem-bers' individual information requests. Schulz-Hardt, Jochims, and Frey (2002) obtained similar results.

These findings were conceptually replicated and extended in the Schulz-Hardt et al. (2006) study, mentioned in the first section. In the context of real interacting groups discussing a hidden profile case, con-sent groups were shown to focus their discussion on information that all members had already known before (shared information) and that sup-ported the speaker's preferred alternative. This bias was significantly reduced in groups with prediscussion dissent. In other words, discussion in dissent groups was more divergent than discussion in consent groups. Furthermore, this enhanced divergence in discussion was shown to par-tially mediate the facilitative effects of dissent on uncovering the correct decision alternative. Thus, in addition to enhanced discussion intensity, more discussion divergence in dissent groups (i.e., a greater openness to new and inconsistent information) is another reason for the superiority of dissent groups in the detection of solutions that no group member has detected before. Figure 5.3 illustrates these relations.

To summarize, studies on simultaneous minority and majority influ-ence in interacting groups support the idea that minority dissent facili-tates flexibility and divergent thinking among majority members. The minority members are those who have to pay the price in terms of more convergent, less flexible individual processes. In contrast to Nemeth's assumption, the minorities in interacting groups converge on their *own* position. Both processes do not seem to outweigh each other at the group

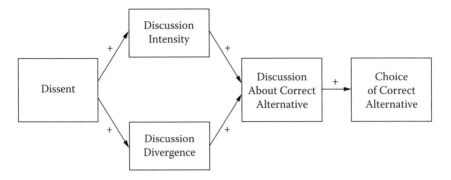

FIGURE 5.3. The two paths from dissent to enhanced group decision quality.

level; instead, increased flexibility and less bias (in favor of one's own position and one's own prior knowledge) result for the group. Together with increased discussion intensity, this increased flexibility allows dissent groups to detect innovative, superior solutions.

DISSENT AND CONFLICT: HOW CAN WE USE THEM TO FACILITATE CREATIVITY AND PERFORMANCE?

Now that we know *that* dissent enhances creativity and performance and that particularly *minority* dissent is beneficial to creativity and performance, and now that we also know *how* these processes are brought about, the question is what organizations can do to systematically *use* dissent as a stimulator for creativity and performance. We will organize our answer around three key aspects, namely establishing dissent, facilitating the expression and transformation of dissent, and mimicking dissent through dialectical decision procedures.

Establishing Dissent

As we have already outlined, dissent in organizations usually can be found in groups such as boards, staff groups, committees, units, or development teams—to name just a few. Thus, if organizations intend to utilize dissent in order to enhance creativity and performance, the most direct way to do so is to compose teams that are heterogeneous with regard to group members' initial opinions. When (a) a team is composed exclusively for a particular judgmental, decision-making, or problem-solving task, (b) the primary aim is to come up with the best solution or ideas (rather than making a rapid decision or maximizing satisfaction), and (c) the individual opinions of potential team members are known in advance, dissent should be a criterion for group formation. This often requires extra effort for group formation because socialization in organizations pushes the members toward homogeneity (Schein, 1968) and, thus, the "natural" group composition is often homogeneous rather than heterogeneous (Janis, 1982).

This general principle of forming groups with different opinions among their members leads to two questions, namely: (a) Is more dissent better than less dissent or is a minimum amount of dissent sufficient to fully realize the beneficial effects of dissent? (b) How can we use this principle if the initial opinions of potential members are previously unknown or if the team is formed for multiple tasks (so that dissent on each particular task cannot be achieved directly)?

With regard to the first question, empirical findings are rare because the amount of dissent in groups has seldom been systematically varied. In two studies from our own research group, three-person decision-making groups with a majority–minority distribution of initial preferences were compared with full-diversity groups, that is, groups with each member favoring a different alternative at the beginning (Brodbeck et al., 2002; Schulz-Hardt et al., 2006). In a full-diversity group, each member is a minority confronted with a heterogeneous majority. Hence, facilitative minority influence should be maximized in this condition, with little or no majority pressures occurring (at least not at the beginning). However, whereas full diversity led to superior decision quality in the Brodbeck et al. study, Schulz-Hardt et al. found minority dissent groups to be equally successful compared with full-diversity dissent groups (and either superior to consent groups). A plausible (yet so far untested) interpretation of these inconsistent findings is that full-diversity dissent is superior to minority dissent only in cases where the best solution is very difficult to detect (as it seems to be the case in the Brodbeck et al. study).

In spite of this inconsistency, from a practical point of view there are two reasons one should generally prefer more compared with less dissent if the aim is to maximize creativity and solution quality. On the one hand, even if dissenting opinions exist at the beginning of a group session, not all dissenters express their dissent and, thus, more prediscussion dissent makes it more likely that at least some of the dissenting opinions will be expressed. On the other hand, groups not only benefit from the creativity and flexibility enhancing effect of dissent. Rather, at least in problem-solving tasks, groups do also benefit from the fact that the more diverse their members' initial opinions, the greater are the chances that at least one of the group members favors the best (or near best) solution right from the beginning, and as we have outlined, if the group contains such a proponent for the best solution, solution quality in the group is significantly enhanced. Thus, if only creativity and solution quality are concerned, organizations should try to maximize dissent when forming groups.

The second question concerned what organizations can do if prediscussion opinions are unknown before the team is formed or if the team is supposed to work together over a series of tasks (e.g., a personnel selection committee having to make a series of personnel selection decisions) so that prediscussion dissent cannot be realized for every task. An opportunity in situations like these is to form teams that are diverse with regard to other aspects and to use such aspects that are known to be correlated with dissent. For example, diversity of group members' functional background has consistently been shown to be facilitative of team performance, presumably because it facilitates dissent and task-related conflict (for an overview, see Williams & O'Reilly, 1998; a new integrative perspective is given by van Knippenberg, De Dreu, and Homan, 2004; see also chapters 7 and 8, this volume, for a more detailed treatment of diversity in groups). Hence, by forming teams of specialists from different areas, organizations not only make sure that diverse knowledge can be used for the task, they also enhance the likelihood that dissenting opinions bearing the potential of stimulating creativity and performance will prevail in the team.

Facilitating the Expression and Transformation of Dissent

For organizations to benefit from dissent, two conditions are necessary: On the one hand, the existing dissent has to be expressed, and on the other hand, the recipients have to properly react on this dissent. With regard to the first condition, particularly minorities in organizations often withhold diverging views (Stanley, 1981). This can be due to formal or informal communication barriers (Baron & Greenberg, 1989), evaluation apprehension (Gallupe, Bastianutti, & Cooper, 1991), or conformity pressures within the group (Janis, 1982). However, unless expressed, dissent is useless. For example, in the study by Schulz-Hardt et al. (2000), groups with a minority member who, rather than consistently advocating his or her dissenting opinion, converged to the majority position, exhibited the same confirmation bias in information acquisition as consent groups did.

With regard to the second condition, even if dissent is expressed, the recipients might fail to react on it due to ignorance, lack of motivation, or lack of capacity or skills. In these cases, dissent is not transformed into beneficial outcomes. Therefore, organizations should be interested in realizing conditions that facilitate the expression and transformation of dissent. Four factors seem to be particularly important with respect to this, namely a unanimity decision rule, participation, dialectical leadership, and critical norms.

First, the expression of dissent as well as the transformation of dissent is facilitated if the group works under a unanimity rule, that is, for a solution to be accepted, all group members have to agree to this solution. If all members have to agree, minorities know that their opinions matter. Moreover, majorities have to pay attention to minority statements under a unanimity rule, because both factions have to reach a consensus. In contrast, under a majority rule majorities can simply overrule minorities, which makes their dissent almost useless (Miller, 1985). Consequently, groups working under a unanimity rule have been shown to express more disagreement as well as to exchange more arguments and opinions than groups working under a majority rule (Nemeth, 1977). In addition, the former are more satisfied with their decision and report greater confidence about the correctness of their decision than the latter (Nemeth, 1977). However, although more disagreement and more opinion exchange under a unanimity rule should imply more creativity, more divergence, and higher quality of problem solutions, systematic empirical tests of this link are still lacking.

Second, both the expression and the transformation of dissent are facilitated if participation is a given. The more the group members are used to being heard when important decisions are made and being able to influence these decisions through expressing their own opinion, the more each group member will be motivated to express a dissenting opinion if he or she disagrees with the prevailing opinion in the group. Furthermore, participation also supports the transformation of dissent into outcomes that are beneficial to the organization. For example, De Dreu and West (2001) argued that creative thinking instigated by dissent is a necessary yet not sufficient condition for innovation to occur. The reason is that product and process innovations not only require creative ideas but also a careful selection of the most promising ideas as well as a solid implementation of the ones chosen, and both processes are facilitated by participation. In two field studies with self-managed teams in a postal service and with cross-functional teams from different public and private organizations, De Dreu and West demonstrated that measures of self-reported minority dissent in the team were positively correlated with supervisor ratings of the corresponding team's innovativeness only when participation in the team was high. Thus, without participation, dissent is not transformed into innovation.

Third, facilitating the expression and transformation of dissent in groups requires a leadership style that we call "dialectical." By this, we mean that the leader is open to dissent and even encourages thoughts and ideas that run counter to the solution and to decision alternatives or ideas that are currently favored in the group. As shown by Peterson (1997), as well as Peterson, Owens, Tetlock, Fan, and Martorana (1998), decision making in top management teams in organizations as well as elite groups in politics does not suffer if leaders clearly advocate their own position. On the contrary, high decision quality is associated with strong leaders who actively structure the group process and who take a firm stand on the issue at hand. However, the critical point is whether such leaders are still open to dissent. Leaders who explicitly or implicitly communicate intolerance against counterarguments and criticism systematically suppress the expression of dissent and destroy the acceptance of contrary positions in the group. In contrast, if the leader is open to dissent and encourages a controversial debate during group meetings, high-quality decision making is associated with this leadership style (Peterson, 1997; Peterson et al., 1998).

Finally, the expression of dissent as well as its transformation into outcomes that are beneficial to the organization benefits from a "critical norm." This means a common understanding in the group (or even in the whole organization) that independence and critical thought are essential components of the group's (or the organization's) collective work (cf. Postmes, Spears, & Cihangir, 2001). If group members have internalized such a common understanding, they should feel free to express dissent if they disagree with proposals or solutions favored in the group. Groups with a critical norm should be characterized by high degrees of task reflexivity (West, 1996), that is, a tendency to critically reflect the team's task-related objectives, strategies, and procedures on a regular basis. As demonstrated by De Dreu (2002), dissent is particularly associated with team effectiveness and innovation if the team's task-related reflexivity is high. Furthermore, acceptance of dissent occurring in the group should be higher among the other group members if a critical norm prevails in the group, and this acceptance facilitates interest in the dissenting position, accurate perspective taking, and incorporation of the dissenter's arguments by the recipients of dissent (Tjosvold et al., 1981). Finally, in groups with a critical norm, dissenters should not be seen as disloyal. As shown by Dooley and Fryxell (1999), dissent enhances decision quality in teams only if loyalty is attributed to the dissenters. In sum, a critical group norm is a precondition for many processes that facilitate the expression of dissent as well as its transformation into beneficial outcomes. In contrast, if the group is characterized by a norm that praises harmony at all costs, the members are likely to fall prey to a pattern that is called "groupthink" (Janis, 1982)—a collective concurrence-seeking tendency that avoids dissent by means of self-censorship and mindguarding, as well as subtle and overt pressures on dissenters, and that is supposed to lead to faulty decision making.

Mimicking Dissent

As already mentioned, it is not always possible to make sure that "authentic" dissent occurs, that is, dissent being expressed because the corresponding person truly disagrees with something that is proposed in the group. For example, a managerial board might experience that right from the beginning of a meeting all members of the board have the same preference with regard to a product launch decision. In this case, the only way to ensure authentic dissent would be to (temporarily) exchange board members or bring in new members to the board—which is hardly realizable in a managerial board.

In situations like this, an opportunity to achieve dissent is to use so-called "dialectical" decision techniques (for an overview, see Katzenstein, 1996). Dialectical decision techniques are procedures that contrive dissent by enforcing a controversial debate independent of the actors' real opinions. The most popular of these techniques are "devil's advocacy" and "dialectical inquiry." Devil's advocacy means that a single group member or a subgroup is assigned the role of the devil's advocate, which has the task of criticizing as substantially as possible a proposal made by the group. Dialectical inquiry differs from devil's advocacy in that, after a proposal has been made, the opposite faction in the group not only criticizes this proposal but also comes up with a complete counterproposal, and a dialectical debate between the two factions emerges about both proposals.

Dialectical decision techniques have been shown to enhance the accuracy of individual judgments as well as the quality of group decisions, particularly in strategic decision making (e.g., Schweiger, Sandberg, & Ragan, 1986; Schweiger, Sandberg, & Rechner, 1989; Schwenk, 1982; for a meta-analysis, see Schwenk, 1990). Thus, it seems possible to capture at least some of the beneficial effects of authentic dissent by mimicking dissent through dialectical techniques. This raises the question of how the beneficial effects of contrived dissent (dialectical techniques) compare with those of authentic dissent reported in the previous sections.

Unfortunately, only very few studies so far have directly compared the effects of authentic dissent and dialectical techniques. Nemeth, Brown, and Rogers (2001) confronted their participants with a dissenting opinion that presumably came either from an authentic minority or from a devil's advocate; in a control condition no dissent occurred. Of these two forms of dissent, only authentic dissent significantly increased the number of issue relevant thoughts generated by the participants. Similarly, in a study by Nemeth, Connell, et al. (2001), quantity and quality of solutions were affected only by authentic dissent, not by a devil's advocate, and these effects were independent of whether the devil's advocate was said to truly believe in the position advocated or whether the other group members expected this person to argue against her true conviction. Nemeth, Brown, and Rogers (2001) came up with an even more striking result: Whereas authentic dissent increased *divergent* thinking (thoughts in support of vs. opposed to one's own judgment were balanced) compared with the control condition, contrived dissent increased cognitive *convergence* (dominance of thoughts in favor of one's own judgment).

One of our own studies also revealed a superiority of authentic dissent over contrived dissent, but with slightly more favorable results for the latter. Schulz-Hardt et al. (2002) used the group information search paradigm previously described: In three-person groups, managers discussed an investment decision case. Half of the groups had homogeneous prediscussion preferences (authentic consent), whereas the other half consisted of a majority and a minority faction (authentic dissent). In each condition, half of the groups used the devil's advocacy procedure (with the role of the devil's advocate being randomly assigned), whereas the other half received no such instructions. The main dependent variable was the confirmation bias in the group information search. Whereas groups lacking both types of dissent selectively searched for information in favor of the alternative preferred in the group (a convergent search strategy), both types of dissent facilitated the consideration of information that was in support of the opposite alternative (e.g., a more divergent information search). However, authentic dissent had a much stronger effect than contrived dissent.

It would be premature to interpret the partially divergent results of these studies with regard to contrived dissent as the dependent variables were different (thought generation vs. information search) and as Nemeth and her colleagues collected data at the individual level, whereas Schulz-Hardt et al. (2002) compared authentic and contrived dissent at the group level. However, the latter difference offers an interesting (although yet completely untested) possibility: In the Schulz-Hardt et al. study, all of the group members (including the devil's advocate) contributed to the results. In contrast, Nemeth, Brown, and Rogers (2001) measured only responses of those group members who were not the devil's advocate. Thus, the results (being more favorable for devil's advocacy in the Schulz-Hardt et al. study than in those of Nemeth, Brown, and Rogers study) would interlock smoothly if the devil's advocates especially benefited from devil's advocacy. This, of course, would be a substantial difference between contrived dissent and authentic dissent, since in the latter case the ones who are *exposed* to minority dissent (rather than *advocating* it themselves) seem to benefit more.

Whereas such considerations are speculative, the results of the few comparative studies are consistent in demonstrating that contrived dissent is less effective than authentic dissent in stimulating divergent thinking, creativity, and performance. Consequently, dialectical techniques are an option if authentic dissent is not available (or is considered to be too expensive—see also the final section), but if organizations have a real choice between designing heterogeneous teams with regard to members' prediscussion opinions or using dialectical decision techniques, the former seems to be more promising than the latter.

CONCLUSION

Dissent, Creativity, and Performance: What Have We Learned So Far?

As outlined in the previous sections, conflict need not always be negative and dysfunctional. More specifically, if task-related conflict results from dissenting opinions being voiced, this type of conflict can be beneficial to both individual and collective creativity and performance. We have shown that dissent in general (i.e., independent of the type of dissent) has an activating effect by intensifying individual information processing and group discussion. Furthermore, exposure to minority and majority dissent has been shown to result in partially different consequences for individual information processing: In cases of unidirectional influence, majority dissent induces convergent thinking toward the majority, whereas minority dissent leads to divergent thinking toward all sides of an issue. As a consequence, majority dissent stimulates individual performance if the majority position is correct and is directly applicable. In contrast, minority dissent facilitates performance independent of the correctness of the minority position and independent of whether this position can be directly applied as a solution to a problem. Furthermore, minority dissent rather than majority dissent stimulates creativity and the detection of novel problem solutions. In interacting groups, both types of influence are necessarily intertwined. Group interaction seems to leave minority dissent effects on the majority largely unaffected but seems to change the nature of majority dissent effects on the minority: If the minority resists the majority influence, convergent information processing toward its own position rather than the majority position seems to be the consequence. At the group level, the net effect of both types of dissent is less bias (toward common, supportive information) and, thus, more divergence in group information exchange and information search. Both the higher discussion intensity and the higher divergence brought about by dissent facilitate the detection of new, superior solutions by the group.

While having focused on the positive effects of dissent on creativity and performance, we do not want to conceal that dissent also has costs that have to be taken into account: For example, making a decision takes longer if dissent is given (Brodbeck et al., 2002; Parks & Nelson, 1999). Furthermore, divergence of opinions in a group can lower group cohesiveness (Terborg, Castore, & DeNinno, 1976) and slow down the implementation of a common decision (Hambrick, Cho, & Chen, 1996). However, many of these problems should diminish if our recommendations from the third section are put into practice. For example, dissent should not reduce group cohesiveness if all members have internalized a critical norm, so that dissent simply means adherence to this norm. For some negative side effects of dissent still present, other chapters in this book show how to successfully deal with them (e.g., chapters 3 and 5).

Taken together, dissent has so far been shown to have facilitative effects on individual as well as collective creativity and performance. Hence, rather than suspect that something might be wrong if we experience dissent, we should habitually become suspicious about dissent *being absent*. At least if the primary aim is to either come up with the best solution possible or generate novel ideas of high quality and quantity, consent and harmony can be dangerous, whereas dissent will most likely prove helpful.

Dissent, Creativity, and Performance: What Might We Learn in the Future?

As we have outlined, solid evidence about facilitative effects of dissent on individual- and group-level creativity and performance has accumulated particularly in the last 20 years of research, and significant progress in understanding how these effects are brought about has been made. Nevertheless, important theoretical and practical issues regarding these facilitative effects of dissent are still poorly understood. We finish our chapter by outlining some important theoretical and practical questions for future research in this area. We start with theoretical issues and then turn to more practical questions concerning the effective design of and facilitating conditions for dissent effects in organizations.

Mediators of the Differential Minority Versus Majority Dissent Effects. As we have previously outlined, minority dissent induces divergent thinking, whereas majority dissent leads to convergent thinking. What we do *not* yet know is *how* minority versus majority dissent brings about these different information-processing styles. Nemeth (1986) discussed two possible explanations: On the one hand, majority dissent should induce more stress among the recipients than minority dissent does. Because high stress leads to a focussing of attention, the recipients of majority dissent exhibit convergent processing (focus on one perspective, namely that of the majority). In contrast, the moderate stress induced by minorities should stimulate a widened focus of attention, that is, divergent processing. On the other hand, people exposed to dissent should immediately assume that a majority is right and a minority is wrong. Therefore, people exposed to majority dissent focus on the presumed truth, namely the majority perspective. In contrast, if people experience that a minority consistently advocates a dissenting opinion, they ask themselves how someone can be so sure about something that is so wrong—which should stimulate an open reappraisal of the situation. However, as of yet no considerable attempts have been made to empirically test any of these two hypothesized mediations or any other explanations—so this obviously is a central topic in need of investigation.

The Role of Behavioral Styles. If minority dissent induces divergent thinking among the majority members by making them wonder how someone can be so sure about something that must be wrong, then the premise of this is that the minority is *consistent* in advocating its dissenting opinion. In other words, divergent thinking induced by minority dissent requires or is at least substantially facilitated by consistency over time. Interestingly, the behavioral style of the minority is a central variable in another theory of minority influence, namely conversion theory (Moscovici, 1980), and consistency has been shown to be the most important feature of successful minorities. Since research on this theory is only very loosely related to creativity and performance, we have not discussed it in this chapter. In sharp contrast to that, research on convergent versus divergent thinking induced by majorities versus minorities has largely ignored the role of consistency or other behavioral styles of the minority (for an exception, see Nemeth et al., 1990). As a consequence, we do not know whether minorities have to exhibit some consistency in order to induce divergent thinking, or whether simply presenting a dissenting minority opinion is sufficient to induce this processing style. We also do not know whether other behavioral styles of the minority (e.g., flexibility) are beneficial to triggering this effect. However, knowledge on such effective behavioral styles would help us to design dissent effectively in organizations.

Differentiating between Different Forms of Exposition to Dissent.   As previously outlined, the distinction between different *sources of* dissent (minority vs. majority) is central to dissent research. In contrast, another distinction has hardly been systematically investigated yet, namely that between different forms of *exposition to* dissent. In dissent research, very different forms of exposition to dissent are used. Sometimes (e.g., Nemeth & Rogers, 1996), people receive only abstract information about how opinions are distributed in their population (e.g., they hear that 18% of their reference group has an opposing opinion to their own) or in a particular group (e.g., one of the five persons actually performing the experimental task disagrees with them). In other studies (e.g., Levine & Russo, 1995), the participants receive similar information as in the latter case, and additionally they anticipate that they will have a subsequent interaction (e.g., a group discussion) with these other persons. Again, in other studies (e.g., Nemeth, Brown, & Rogers, 2001), people are actually confronted with the persons expressing this dissent and interact with them. At the moment, all of these different expositions to dissent are treated as if they were the same or, at least, differences between them did not have to be considered. However, type of exposition to dissent might bring about substantially different dissent effects. For example, Mojzisch, Schulz-Hardt, Kerschreiter, and Frey (2007) directly compared the first two of the aforementioned types of exposition. One of their findings was that people who were just given feedback about two other persons' decisions and learned that these persons favored a different alternative than they did (majority dissent) exhibited an information search strategy focussing on the majority position. In contrast, if they expected to interact with this majority, their information search focussed on their own position. Hence, the anticipation of interaction with a majority may induce self-defensive processes that are lacking if no such interaction is anticipated (see also the differences between dissent effects in previous sections). Systematically exploring such differential effects of different expositions to dissent would not only contribute to our theoretical understanding of dissent effects but also help us to find out how people should be exposed to dissent in organizations in order to maximize positive effects on creativity and performance.

How to Improve the Effects of Contrived Dissent.   As we have argued, authentic dissent cannot always be realized, and even if it can be realized, it can also have costs in terms of low group cohesiveness or slow implementation of solutions found by a group. Thus, using contrived dissent (e.g., dialectical decision techniques) can be an alternative in such situations. Unfortunately, as we have shown, the facilitative effect of contrived dissent on creativity and performance seems to be lower than the corresponding effect of authentic dissent. Given that this finding generalizes across different task types—which also has to be systematically investigated in the future—we have to find out what we can do to improve the effects of contrived dissent. One possibility is that making effective use of techniques such as devil's advocacy or dialectical inquiry is not as self-evident as has been assumed so far—groups might need some training or time of experience before the full effect of such techniques pays off. In a recent study, Greitemeyer, Schulz-Hardt, Brodbeck, and Frey (2006) found a dialectical procedure (a so-called "advocacy system") to facilitate the exchange of unshared information in groups and thereby debias group discussion. However, this effect became evident only in the third and, even more so, the fourth trial (which was the final one). Similarly, Schweiger, Sandberg, and Rechner (1989) found two dialectical techniques to work better in the second compared with the first trial. So exploring such effects of training or experience could prove fruitful to further research on contrived dissent.

The aforementioned topics represent areas of creativity- and performance-related dissent research that have as yet hardly been investigated. This, of course, does not mean that the topics having been more in the focus of empirical research (reported in the previous sections) are understood well enough to not require further research. For example, some facilitators of the relation between dissent and beneficial outcomes have already been identified, and all of these moderators (unanimity decision rule, participation, dialectical leadership style, and critical norms) are relevant to and can be influenced by organizations. Although this constitutes a fruitful basis for organizational design measures, a whole number of possible moderating variables are still relevant to organizations and are awaiting solid empirical investigation. For example, Ng and Van Dyne (2001) showed that individualistic and collectivistic orientations affect reactions to minority influence. Since organizational culture is often linked to such individual value orientations among their members (by both influencing them and being influenced by them), it could be a relevant moderator of facilitative effects of dissent on creativity and performance. Furthermore, people in organizations are not exposed to single moderators at a time but rather deal with the simultaneous interplay of all moderators we have reported so far (and also of additional ones we have not reported). Thus, we need to learn how these moderators interact with each other in affecting dissent effects on creativity and performance. For example, does a critical norm substitute for the effects of dialectical leadership? Or can dialectical leadership only be effective if critical norms are prevalent to some extent?

In sum, research on dissent effects on individual as well as group creativity and performance has made encouraging progress, particularly over the last 20 years. Nevertheless, it is still a long way to go to a comprehensive understanding of how dissent works and how it can be utilized in organizations. We hope that this chapter will be successful in giving some ideas and some inspiration for the next steps on this way.

REFERENCES

Asch, S. E. (1951). Effects of group pressure upon the modification and distortion of judgments. In H. Guetzkow (Ed.), *Groups, leadership and men: Research in human relations* (pp. 177–190). Oxford, U.K.: Carnegie Press.

Baron, R. A., & Greenberg, J. (1989). *Behavior in organizations: Understanding and managing the human side of work* (3rd ed.). Boston: Allyn & Bacon.

Brodbeck, F. C., Kerschreiter, R., Mojzisch, A., Frey, D., & Schulz-Hardt, S. (2002). The dissemination of critical, unshared information in decision-making groups: The effects of pre-discussion dissent. *European Journal of Social Psychology, 32*, 35–56.

Brodbeck, F. C., Kerschreiter, R., Mojzisch, A., & Schulz-Hardt, S. (2007). Improving group decision making under conditions of distributed knowledge: The information asymmetries model. *Academy of Management Review, 32*, 459–479.

De Dreu, C. K. W. (2002). Team innovation and team effectiveness: The importance of minority dissent and reflexivity. *European Journal of Work and Organizational Psychology, 11*, 285–298.

De Dreu, C. K. W., & West, M. A. (2001). Minority dissent and team innovation: The importance of participation in decision making. *Journal of Applied Psychology, 86*, 1191–1201.

Ditto, P. H., Scepansky, J. A., Munro, G. D., Apanovitch, A. M., & Lockhart, L. K. (1998). Motivated sensitivity to preference-inconsistent information. *Journal of Personality and Social Psychology, 75*, 53–69.

Dooley, R. S., & Fryxell, G. E. (1999). Attaining decision quality and commitment from dissent: The moderating effects of loyalty and competence in strategic decision-making teams. *Academy of Management Journal, 42*, 389–402.

Edwards, K., & Smith, E. E. (1996). A disconfirmation bias in the evaluation of arguments. *Journal of Personality and Social Psychology, 71*, 5–24.

Erb, H.-P., & Bohner, G. (2001). Mere consensus effects in minority and majority influence. In C. K. W. De Dreu & N. K. De Vries (Eds.), *Group consensus and minority influence: Implications for innovation* (pp. 40–59). Oxford, U.K.: Blackwell.

Gallupe, R. B., Bastianutti, L. M., & Cooper, W. H. (1991). Unblocking brainstorms. *Journal of Applied Psychology, 76*, 137–142.

Greitemeyer, T., Schulz-Hardt, S., Brodbeck, F. C., & Frey, D. (2006). Information sampling and group decision making: Effects of an advocacy decision procedure and task experience. *Journal of Experimental Psychology: Applied, 12*, 31–42.

Gruenfeld, D. H. (1995). Status, ideology, and integrative complexity on the U.S. Supreme Court: Rethinking the politics of political decision making. *Journal of Personality and Social Psychology, 68*, 5–20.

Gruenfeld, D. H., & Preston, J. (2000). Upending the status quo: Cognitive complexity in U.S. Supreme Court justices who overturn legal precedent. *Personality and Social Psychology Bulletin, 26*, 1013–1022.

Gruenfeld, D. H., Thomas-Hunt, M. C., & Kim, P. (1998). Cognitive flexibility, communication strategy, and integrative complexity: Public and private reactions to majority and minority status. *Journal of Experimental Social Psychology, 34*, 202–226.

Hambrick, D., Cho, T., & Chen, M. (1996). The influence of top management team heterogeneity on firms' competitive moves. *Administrative Science Quarterly, 41*, 659–684.

Janis, I. L. (1982). *Groupthink* (Rev. 2nd ed.). Boston: Houghton Mifflin.

Katzenstein, G. (1996). The debate on structured debate: Toward a unified theory. *Organizational Behavior and Human Decision Processes, 66*, 316–332.

Kelly, J. R., & Karau, S. J. (1999). Group decision making: The effects of initial preferences and time pressure. *Personality and Social Psychology Bulletin, 25*, 1342–1354.

Lavery, T. A., Franz, T. M., Winquist, J. R., & Larson, J. R., Jr. (1999). The role of information exchange in predicting group accuracy on a multiple judgment task. *Basic and Applied Social Psychology, 21*, 281–289.

Levine, J. M., & Russo, E. (1995). Impact of anticipated interaction on information acquisition. *Social Cognition, 13*, 293–317.

Martin, R., & Hewstone, M. (1999). Minority influence and optimal problem solving. *European Journal of Social Psychology, 29*, 825–832.

Miller, C. E. (1985). Group decision making under majority and unanimity decision rules. *Social Psychology Quarterly, 48*, 51–61.

Mojzisch, A., & Schulz-Hardt, S. (2006). Information sampling in group decision making: Sampling biases and their consequences. In K. Fiedler & P. Juslin (Eds.), *Information sampling and adaptive cognition* (pp. 299–325). Cambridge, U.K.: Cambridge University Press.

Mojzisch, A., Schulz-Hardt, S., Kerschreiter, R., & Frey, D. (2007). *Interactive effects of knowledge about others' opinions and anticipation of discussion on confirmatory information search.* Manuscript submitted for publication.

Mojzisch, A., Schulz-Hardt, S., Lüthgens, C., Kerschreiter, R., & Frey, D. (2007). *Social influence in freely interacting groups: Information acquisition after group discussions.* Manuscript in preparation.

Moscovici, S. (1980). Towards a theory of conversion behavior. In L. Berkowitz (Ed.), *Advances in experimental social psychology* (Vol. 13, pp. 209–239). New York: Academic Press.

Nemeth, C. J. (1977). Interactions between jurors as a function of majority vs. unanimity decision rules. *Journal of Applied Social Psychology, 7*, 38–56.

Nemeth, C. J. (1986). Differential contributions of majority and minority influence. *Psychological Review, 93*, 23–32.

Nemeth, C. J., Brown, K., & Rogers, J. (2001). Devil's advocate vs. authentic dissent: Stimulating quantity and quality. *European Journal of Social Psychology, 31*, 707–720.

Nemeth, C. J., & Chiles, C. (1988). Modeling courage: The role of dissent in fostering independence. *European Journal of Social Psychology, 18*, 275–280.

Nemeth, C. J., Connell, J. B., Rogers, J., & Brown, K. S. (2001). Improving decision making by means of dissent. *Journal of Applied Social Psychology, 31*, 48–58.

Nemeth, C. J., & Kwan J. L. (1985). Originality of word associations as a function of majority vs. minority influence. *Social Psychology Quarterly, 48*, 277–282.

Nemeth, C. J., & Kwan, J. L. (1987). Minority influence, divergent thinking, and detection of correct solutions. *Journal of Applied Social Psychology, 17*, 788–799.

Nemeth, C. J., Mayseless, O., Sherman, J., & Brown, Y. (1990). Exposure to dissent and recall of information. *Journal of Personality and Social Psychology, 58,* 429–437.

Nemeth, C. J., & Rogers, J. (1996). Dissent and the search for information. *British Journal of Social Psychology, 35,* 67–76.

Nemeth, C. J., & Wachtler, J. (1983). Creative problem solving as a result of majority vs. minority influence. *European Journal of Social Psychology, 13,* 45–55.

Ng, K. Y., & Van Dyne, L. (2001). Individualism–collectivism as a boundary condition for effectiveness of minority influence in decision making. *Organizational Behavior and Human Decision Processes, 84,* 198–225.

Parks, C. D., & Nelson, N. L. (1999). Discussion and decision: The interrelationship between initial preference distribution and group discussion content. *Organizational Behavior and Human Decision Processes, 80,* 87–101.

Peterson, R. S. (1997). A directive leadership style in group decision making is both virtue and vice: Evidence from elite and experimental groups. *Journal of Personality and Social Psychology, 72,* 1107–1121.

Peterson, R. S., & Nemeth, C. J. (1996). Focus versus flexibility: Majority and minority influence can both improve performance. *Personality and Social Psychology Bulletin, 22*(1), 14–23.

Peterson, R. S., Owens, P. D., Tetlock, P. E., Fan, E., & Martorana, P. (1998). Group dynamics in top management teams: Groupthink, vigilance and alternative models of organizational failure and success. *Organizational Behavior and Human Decision Processes, 73,* 272–305.

Postmes, T., Spears, R., & Cihangir, S. (2001). Quality of decision making and group norms. *Journal of Personality and Social Psychology, 80,* 918–930.

Schein, E. H. (1968). Organizational socialization and the profession of management. *Industrial Management Review, 9,* 1–15.

Schulz-Hardt, S., Brodbeck, F. C., Mojzisch, A., Kerschreiter, R., & Frey, D. (2006). Group decision making in hidden profile situations: Dissent as a facilitator for decision quality. *Journal of Personality and Social Psychology, 91,* 1080–1093.

Schulz-Hardt, S., Frey, D., Lüthgens, C., & Moscovici, S. (2000). Biased information search in group decision making. *Journal of Personality and Social Psychology, 78,* 655–669.

Schulz-Hardt, S., Jochims, M., & Frey, D. (2002). Productive conflict in group decision making: Genuine and contrived dissent as strategies to counteract biased information seeking. *Organizational Behavior and Human Decision Processes, 88,* 563–586.

Schweiger, D. M., Sandberg, W. R., & Ragan, J. W. (1986). Group approaches for improving strategic decision making: A comparative analysis of dialectical inquiry, devil's advocacy, and consensus. *Academy of Management Journal, 29,* 51–71.

Schweiger, D. M., Sandberg, W. R., & Rechner, P. L. (1989). Experiential effects of dialectical inquiry, devil's advocacy, and consensus approaches to strategic decision making. *Academy of Management Journal, 31,* 745–772.

Schwenk, C. R. (1982). Effects of inquiry methods and ambiguity tolerance on prediction performance. *Decision Sciences, 13,* 207–221.

Schwenk, C. R. (1990). Effects of devil's advocacy and dialectical inquiry on decision making: A meta analysis. *Organizational Behavior and Human Decision Processes, 47,* 161–176.

Smith, C. M., Tindale, S. R., & Dugoni, B. L. (1996). Minority and majority influence in freely interacting groups: Qualitative versus quantitative differences. *British Journal of Social Psychology, 35*, 137–150.

Sniezek, J. A., & Henry, R. A. (1989). Accuracy and confidence in group judgment. *Organizational Behavior and Human Decision Processes, 43*, 1–28.

Stanley, J. D. (1981). Dissent in organizations. *Academy of Management Review, 1*, 13–19.

Stasser, G., & Birchmeier, Z. (2003). Group creativity and collective choice. In P. B. Paulus & B. A. Nijstad (Eds.), *Group creativity* (pp. 85–109). New York: Oxford University Press.

Stasser, G., & Titus, W. (1985). Pooling of unshared information in group decision making: Biased information sampling during discussion. *Journal of Personality and Social Psychology, 48*, 1467–1478.

Terborg, J. R., Castore, C. H., & DeNinno, J. A. (1976). A longitudinal field investigation of the impact of group composition on group performance and cohesion. *Journal of Personality and Social Psychology, 34*, 782–790.

Tjosvold, D. (1982). Effects of the approach to controversy on superiors' incorporation of subordinates' information in decision making. *Journal of Applied Psychology, 67*, 189–193.

Tjosvold, D., & Deemer, D. K. (1980). Effects of controversy within a cooperative or competitive context on organizational decision making. *Journal of Applied Psychology, 65*, 590–595.

Tjosvold, D., & Field, R. H. (1985). Effect of concurrence, controversy, and consensus on group decision making. *Journal of Social Psychology, 125*, 355–363.

Tjosvold, D., & Johnson, D. W. (1977). Effects of controversy on cognitive perspective-taking. *Journal of Educational Psychology, 69*, 679–685.

Tjosvold, D., & Johnson, D. W. (1978). Controversy within a cooperative or competitive context and cognitive perspective-taking. *Contemporary Educational Psychology, 3*, 376-386.

Tjosvold, D., Johnson, D. W., & Lerner, J. (1981). The effects of affirmation and acceptance on incorporation of an opposing opinion in problem-solving. *Journal of Social Psychology, 114*, 103–110.

Van Dyne, L., & Saavedra, R. (1996). A naturalistic minority influence experiment: Effects on divergent thinking, conflict, and originality in work-groups. *British Journal of Social Psychology, 35*, 151–168.

van Knippenberg, D., De Dreu, C. K. W., & Homan, A. C. (2004). Work group diversity and group performance: An integrative model and research agenda. *Journal of Applied Psychology, 89*, 1008–1022.

Wanous, J. P., & Youtz, M. A. (1986). Solution diversity and the quality of group decisions. *Academy of Management Journal, 29*, 149–159.

West, M. A. (1996). Reflexivity and work group effectiveness: A conceptual integration. In M. A. West (Ed.), *Handbook of work group psychology* (pp. 555–579). Chichester, U.K.: Wiley.

Williams, K. Y., & O'Reilly, C. A., III. (1998). Demography and diversity in organizations: A review of 40 years of research. In B. M. Staw & L. L. Cummings (Eds.), *Research in organizational behavior* (Vol. 20, pp. 77–140). Greenwich, CT: JAI Press.

6

Conflict, Diversity, and Faultlines in Workgroups

KAREN A. JEHN
Leiden University

KATERINA BEZRUKOVA
Rutgers University

SHERRY THATCHER
Eller College of Management, University of Arizona

A growing body of research in organizational psychology has, in recent years, addressed the interplay among conflict, group composition (social category and informational diversity), and the effectiveness of organizational teams. This chapter will review and compare dispersion theories of group composition (e.g., heterogeneity) and alignment theories (e.g., faultline theory) as they explain group conflict (task conflict, relationship conflict, and process conflict). We do this by reviewing the typology of conflict types and focus, in addition to task and relationship conflict, on process conflict in workgroups. We then distinguish between dispersion theories of group composition (e.g., heterogeneity) and alignment theories (e.g., faultlines). We also delineate between the bases of group composition; that is, we distinguish diversity and alignment based on social category characteristics (e.g., race, gender, and age) and information-based characteristics (e.g., work experience and education). We propose that a better understanding of the various types of group diversity possible in teams and the links to conflict will help clarify past inconsistencies and provide theoretical guidance to future research. We conclude by discussing three future directions for research: (a) faultline activation within groups, (b) group culture as an important context variable that influences the group composition–conflict relationships, and (c) faultline measurement issues.

Conflict Types

Reviews of group composition research have noted conflict as a main group process that is affected by the diversity of group members (cf. Lau & Murnighan, 1998; Pelled, 1996; Williams & O'Reilly, 1998). Research on organizational conflict has focused mainly on two types of conflict related to group composition, relationship and task conflict (Amason, 1996; Jehn, Northcraft, & Neale, 1999; Kabanoff, 1991; Kramer, 1991; Pelled, 1996). These are based on, and subsume, past typologies of conflict that delineate cognitive/emotional and substantive/affective aspects (for a thorough review of the history and evolution of conflict typologies, see Jehn & Bendersky, 2003).

Relationship conflicts are disagreements and incompatibilities among group members about issues that are *not* task related but that focus on personal issues. Relationship conflicts frequently reported are about social events, gossip, clothing preferences, political views, and hobbies (Jehn, 1997). This type of conflict often is associated with animosity and annoyance among individuals within a group (Amason, 1996; Amason & Schweiger, 1997; Pelled, 1996). Relationship conflicts can cause extreme negative process problems such as lack of coordination, cooperation, and cohesion (Brewer, 1995, 1996; Labianca, Brass, & Gray, 1998). These conflicts deplete energy and effort that could be expended toward task completion and consolidation around mutual goals (Amason & Mooney, 1999; Northcraft, Polzer, Neale, & Kramer, 1995). It has been shown that relationship conflict has negative effects and is responsible for outcomes such as increased turnover, high rates of absenteeism, decreased satisfaction, low levels of perceived performance, poor objective performance, lack of creativity, and low commitment (Amason, 1996; Baron, 1991; cf. De Dreu & Weingart, 2003; Jehn, 1995; Jehn, Chadwick, & Thatcher, 1997; Pelled, 1996; Simons & Peterson, 2000).

Task conflicts are disagreements among group members' ideas and opinions about the task being performed, such as disagreements regarding an organization's current strategic position or determining the correct data to include in a report. Task conflict, which is focused on content-related issues, can enhance performance quality (Jehn et al., 1999). For example, critical debate among members and open discussion regarding task issues can increase group performance because members are more likely to offer and evaluate various solutions, thus reaching optimal decisions and outcomes (Amason, 1996; Cosier & Rose, 1977; Schweiger, Sandberg, & Rechner, 1989). However, conflict in any form can create an uncomfortable environment, decreasing individuals' perceptions of team-work and their satisfaction (Amason & Schweiger, 1997). In fact, a recent review by De Dreu and Weingart (2003) indicated that the positive effects of task conflict are the exception rather than the rule.

There are many group-related activities, some having to do with the actual task and others having to do with the process of doing the task or delegating resources and duties. Therefore, recent works (e.g., Behfar, Mannix, Peterson, & Trochin, 2005; Jehn & Mannix, 2001) examined process conflict as a separate conflict type compared with task conflict. *Process conflicts* are about logistical and delegation issues such as how task accomplishment should proceed in the work unit, who is responsible for what and how things should be delegated (Jehn, 1997; Kramer, 1991). Jehn (1997) delineated between task and process conflict based on findings of an ethnographic study of work groups. While process conflict may seem closely related to task conflict in that the issues are related to task strategy and accomplishment, process conflict operates more like relationship conflict in its connection to performance and satisfaction in groups. *Who* does something often includes discussion about values and abilities that can feel personal, especially when related to material and human resources. Process conflict remains the least examined and understood of the three types of conflict; however, we believe that it is a critical process in work-groups and suggest that more studies on intragroup conflict include pro-cess conflict, in addition to task and relationship conflict. We base our main discussion of diversity on these three types of conflict; however, later in the chapter, we propose that future research should examine a more com-prehensive typology of conflict as well as different profiles of workgroup conflict that may be influenced by the diversity of group members.

CONTRASTING DISPERSION AND ALIGNMENT THEORIES

We separate theories of group composition into two types: theories of dispersion and theories of alignment. This, we believe, will assist theoreti-cians and researchers in being able to better specify the differences in con-ceptualizations of group composition that influence workgroup conflict.

Overview of Dispersion Theories of Group Composition

Group composition research based on dispersion theories focuses on how individual characteristics are distributed within a group (McGrath, 1998; Milliken & Martins, 1996; Moreland & Levine, 1992). For example, heterogeneity (or group diversity) research examines the dispersion of individual demographic characteristics and the influence this has on a number of outcomes. Dispersion models have predicted group processes such as conflict through mechanisms explained by self-categorization theory, social identity theory, the similarity attraction paradigm, and a cognitive resource perspective. Self-categorization theory posits that individuals classify themselves and others into familiar categories in order to make predictions about subsequent interactions. These categorization groupings (e.g., female or engineer) are also used in defining an individual's social identity (Turner, 1987). Individuals categorize themselves and others into in-groups and out-groups and then base part of their social identity on the characteristics of their in-group (Tajfel & Turner, 1986). These categorization processes are likely to give rise to stereotypes, prejudice, and out-group discrimination that can further lead to conflict (e.g., Jehn et al., 1999; Pelled, Eisenhardt, & Xin, 1999). The similarity attraction paradigm argues that people are attracted to others who are similar to themselves (Byrne, 1971). Diversity researchers have used the similarity attraction paradigm to describe how demographic characteristics provide a means of determining similarity, leading to communication that is more frequent and a desire to remain in the group (Lincoln & Miller, 1979). In addition, the similarity attraction paradigm also suggests that individuals will apply negative assumptions to those with whom they are dissimilar (Byrne, 1971). Finally, a cognitive resource perspective suggests that diversity facilitates a more complex problem-solving process, that is, a higher quality of decision making from different experiences and perspectives that group members bring to their team (Gruenfeld, Mannix, Williams, & Neale, 1996).

While dispersion theories of group composition base predictions of group processes and outcomes on the degree to which members are different based on demographic characteristics (e.g., race, gender, and tenure), they fall short of taking into account the interdependence among multiple forms of diversity. The heterogeneity concept captures the degree to which a group differs on only one demographic characteristic (e.g., male) while often ignoring other demographic characteristics (e.g., Asian; McGrath, 1998). Even when dispersion researchers take into account more than one demographic characteristic by examining social category diversity, thus combining the effects of age, gender, and race diversity, for instance, they use an additive model and aggregate the effects of the single-characteristic dispersion model (for an exception, see Alexander, Nuchols, Bloom, & Lee, 1995). Although these aggregate dispersion models are able to tell you the degree to which a group is demographically different on race *and* gender *and* age, these models are not able to reflect adequately the degree of interdependence between these characteristics. For example, we are unable to tell if all the Asians in a group are also women. This limitation is overcome in alignment-based theories.

Overview of Alignment Theories of Group Composition

In contrast to dispersion theories, alignment theories of group composition take into account the simultaneous alignment of multiple demographic characteristics across members. One such alignment theory is faultline theory. Faultlines are defined as hypothetical dividing lines that split a group into relatively homogeneous subgroups based on the group members' demographic alignment along one or more attributes (adapted from Lau & Murnighan, 1998). While the original theory specifically discusses demographic alignments made up of characteristics such as age, sex, race, and job tenure or status (Lau & Murnighan, 1998, p. 326), other non-demographic characteristics (e.g., personality and values) can also contribute to active subgroup formation within a larger group. Alignment theories base predictions of group processes on the reasoning that the compositional dynamics of multiple attributes (e.g., alignment and coalition formation) has a greater effect on process than separate demographic characteristics (e.g., Lau & Murnighan, 1998; Thatcher, Jehn, & Zanutto, 2003). For example, Hambrick, Li, Xin, and Tsui (2001) argued that "compositional gaps" that occur along *multiple demographic dimensions* (e.g., age and education) may accentuate distinct managerial coalitions and influence group functioning of international joint ventures. Thus, the effects of diversity are likely to be a complex function of aligned demographic characteristics, and we need a more sophisticated consideration of demographic alignment to understand its potential effects (Lau & Murnighan, 1998).

In Table 6.1, we present four theoretical sources of work that we consider the main set of alignment theories from organizational, sociological, and social psychological literatures: group faultlines (e.g., Lau & Murnighan, 1998), factional groups (Hambrick et al., 2001; Li & Hambrick, 2005), multiform heterogeneity (Blau, 1977; Kanter, 1977), and cross-categorization (e.g., Brewer, 2000; Hewstone, Rubin, & Willis, 2002). For each of these theories we discuss the focal unit regarding composition (e.g., demographics and identity) and the forms of group composition discussed by the theory that relate to dispersion or alignment.

Alignment Theories in Organizational and Sociological Research. Faultline theory proposes that the compositional dynamics of multiple attributes and their alignment has a greater effect on group processes and outcomes than separate demographic characteristics (e.g., Lau & Murnighan, 1998; Thatcher et al., 2003). For instance, Cramton and Hinds (2004) theorized about how the alignment of compositional diversity and geographic distribution creates tension between subgroups emerging from faultlines. In a study of the formation of breakaway organizations, Dyck and Starke (1999) found that faultlines were strengthened with increased competition between the breakaway group and the status quo supporters.

In the second perspective (factional groups; Table 6.1), Hambrick et al. (2001; Li & Hambrick, 2005) argued that "compositional gaps" that occur along multiple demographic dimensions (e.g., age and values) in factional groups may accentuate managerial coalitions and influence group functioning and effectiveness of international joint ventures. A compositional

TABLE 6.1
Comparing Theoretical Bases of Dispersion and Alignment

Theoretical basis	Group faultlines	Factional groups	Multiform heterogeneity	Cross-categorization
Disciplinary foundation	Organizational behavior	Organizational behavior	Sociology	Social psychological
Focal unit	"Demographic characteristics"	"Demographic dimensions"	"Parameters of social structure"	"Social identity"
Group Composition				
Dispersion: similarity	Homogeneous	Demographically similar	Inclusive: all parameters same	Inclusive
Dispersion: difference	Heterogeneous	Demographically dissimilar	Exclusive: all parameters different	Exclusive
Alignment: high	Faultlines	Factional groups/ compositional gaps	Consolidated: high correlation	Convergent
Alignment: low	Weak/medium faultlines	Weak factional groups/homo- geneous factions	Low correlation	Cross-categorization

gap is the difference between managerial coalitions on one or more dimensions that are of potential importance to the group's functioning. It separates a group into two distinctly different factions where a faction is relatively homogeneous, or tightly clustered around its own central tendency (Hambrick et al., 2001; Li & Hambrick, 2005). Studies of international joint venture (IJV) management groups showed that subgroups forming within groups based on demographics are inherently coalitional and are likely to reduce identification with the whole team and negatively impact group functioning and IJV effectiveness (Earley & Mosakowski, 2000; Hambrick et al., 2001).

Thirdly, the multiform heterogeneity literature is deeply rooted in sociological tradition and has stressed the importance of focusing on the multiple parameters of social structure (e.g., sex and race; Table 6.1). Multiform heterogeneity refers to overlapping groups and subgroups generated by differences in sex, race, national background, and religion (Blau, 1977). Highly correlated parameters strengthen in-group bonds and reinforce group barriers, whereas low correlation between them indicates the intersection of parameters, which promotes group integration. We now contrast these approaches with the main social psychological approach.

Alignment Theories in Social Psychological Research. The question of multiple group membership has been a long-standing and pervasive problem in social psychology and much research has been done within the cross-categorization paradigm. Cross-categorization typically refers to the crossing of two dichotomous social dimensions, resulting in four groups (double in-group, two mixed groups, and double out-groups; Migdal, Hewstone, & Mullen, 1998). In other words, cross-categorization is based on horizontal crosscutting categories, where "others" can be simultaneously classified as in-group or out-group members on multiple dimensions (Hewstone et al., 2002). When categories are crosscut, they partially overlap. "Take, for example, gender and age; instead of considering only females versus males or young versus elderly, in crossed categorization situations perceivers attend to both of these dimensions and respond to composite groups such as young females, young males, elderly females and elderly males. In terms of in-group/out-group relations, we have four groups that are similar and different from the perceiver in distinct ways. If our perceiver is a young female, then other young females are *double in-group members*, young males and elderly females are *partial group members* and elderly males are *double out-group members* [italics added]" (Crisp, Hewstone, & Rubin, 2001, p. 76). *Crosscutting identities* are like multiple identities that can be either formal (e.g., committees and work groups) or informal (e.g., common-interest groups and demographic characteristics).

Within the group context, the effects of cross-categorization depend on the extent to which categories are inclusive (all members are similar) or exclusive (all members are different) and convergent or crosscutting (Brewer, 2000). The two later possibilities perhaps, are the most interesting for our discussion of alignment and we compare the faultline and cross-categorization approaches in the following text and Table 6.2. According to the cross-categorization paradigm, the more the two bases

---

TABLE 6.2
Comparing Faultline and Cross-Categorization Approaches

	Faultlines	Cross-categorization
Focal unit	Demographic characteristics	Identities
Social dimension	Potential and active identities	Active identities
Nature of categories	Social Informational	Not considered
Number of characteristics considered	Numerous	Two
Outcomes	Individual and team-level	Individual

of categorization are *convergent* (e.g., in-group/out-group distinctions on one category overlap perfectly with in-group/out-group distinction on a second category, e.g., as if gender and nationality perfectly align), the stronger the intergroup bias will be. Brewer (2000) provided an example of convergence for a first two-group categorization (A and B) and a second two-group categorization (1 and 2). If these groups converge, then all members of group A are also members of group 1, while all members of group B are also members of group 2 (a strong faultline), and strong intergroup differentiation and intergroup bias will be expected. In the *crosscutting categorization*, membership in A versus B and membership in 1 versus 2 is orthogonal (Brewer, 2000). Individuals may fall into any one of four classifications based on the overlapping categories: A1, A2, B1, B2 (a moderate or weak faultline condition). The basic assumption of cross-categorization is that overlapping memberships reduce the psychological distance between in-groups and out-groups. Overall, cross-cutting social identities contribute to cooperative intergroup contact by increasing intra-category differentiation and decreasing perceived intergroup differences (Ensari & Miller, 2001; Major, Quinton, McCoy, & Schmader, 2000).

Demographic attributes are often correlated with nested identities (e.g., White male senior executives) and with each other (e.g., female and ethnic minority maids), thus reinforcing the salience of attributes (Ashforth & Johnson, 2001). While faultline literature has considered both potential (focusing on objective characteristics of alignment) and active identities (perceived differences across subgroups formed by faultlines), cross-categorization literature often considers only active identities (see Table 6.2). For instance, Haslam and Ellemers (2005) suggested that group members who share a certain identity perceive themselves less differently than do members who do not share the identity. In general, alignment theories in social psychology have focused more on identity salience and paid less emphasis to objective demographic categories.

Another difference between alignment theories in organizational and social psychology is that while both cross-categorization and faultline hypotheses predict increased intergroup bias when multiple categories perfectly align, cross-categorization falls short in taking into account the *nature* of these categories (Table 6.2; Eurich-Fulcer & Schofield, 1995). In contrast, some research on faultlines delineated between social category and informational characteristics and predicted either positive or negative effects based on the nature of the faultlines (see the next section). Furthermore, social psychological studies that have gone beyond single in-group/out-group categorization have still used individual-level attitudes and behaviors to test intergroup-level theory. Faultlines studies, in contrast, consider not only individual-, but also group-level outcomes in an intergroup context (Table 6.2). Thus, although the ideas of the multiple identity complexity and alignment have entered the theoretical realm in social psychology (e.g., Brewer & Pierce, 2005; Roccas & Brewer, 2002), conceptualizations and operationalizations to understand such alignments and how they relate to conflict in groups has been limited. This is what we specifically address in the model presented in the remainder of this chapter by incorporating aspects of the dispersion and alignment theories reviewed to predict the various types of conflict. We now consider specifically the nature of the dispersed or aligned characteristics of group members; that is, the social category or informational diversity within the group.

Social Category Diversity and Informational Diversity

Research on the implications of diversity has been mixed. Negative effects of diversity have been attributed to conflict that arises from perceived differences among team members (e.g., Tsui, Egan, & Xin, 1995), which interferes with performance (e.g., Pelled, 1996). Positive effects of diversity have been explained using the argument of cognitive resource diversity suggesting that the breadth of perspectives that diverse group members embrace enhances performance (e.g., Ancona & Caldwell, 1992; Gruenfeld et al., 1996). These competing theoretical arguments, along with inconsistent empirical results, have led to a lack of consensus regarding a valid conceptual framework for understanding diversity.

One response to this has been for researchers to classify diversity variables based on similar attributes, such as social category diversity and informational diversity (Jehn et al., 1997; Jehn et al., 1999; Milliken & Martins, 1996; Polzer, Milton, & Swann, 2002). *Social category characteristics* (also described as "relations oriented;" Jackson, Joshi, & Erhardt, 2003) are observable attributes, such as racial/ethnic background, nationality, sex, and age, that are likely to induce responses such as in-group biases and conflict (Cummings, Zhou, & Oldham, 1993; Jehn et al., 1997; Jehn et al., 1999). *Informational characteristics* are underlying attributes of individuals (e.g., work experience and education) which, although not immediately detectable, are important in the completion of a task (Jehn et al., 1997; Jehn et al., 1999; Thatcher & Jehn, 1998; Tsui, Egan, & O'Reilly, 1992). Researchers suggested that these two types of diversity may differentially impact group processes due to their job relatedness (Pelled et al., 1999; Webber & Donahue, 2001). Jehn and colleagues (Jehn et al., 1997; Jehn et al., 1999) found empirical evidence that social category heterogeneity resulted in increased relationship conflict and informational heterogeneity was positively associated with task conflict. As other researchers argued (Rink & Ellemers, 2006; Van Knippenberg, De Dreu, & Homan, 2004), we believe that the distinction between social category and information diversity incorporates previous distinctions of visible versus nonvisible diversity (Tsui & Gutek, 1999) and surface-level diversity versus deep-level diversity (Harrison, Price, Gavin, & Florey, 2002; Mohammed & Angell, 2004; Phillips & Loyd, 2005). Social category diversity (or heterogeneity) is dispersion across members of a group on social category characteristics that are easily observed by others and used for categorization purposes. While social category heterogeneity may not be relevant to a given task, it does shape people's perceptions and behaviors through mechanisms of categorization and prejudice (Pelled, 1996).

Informational heterogeneity refers to the differences in knowledge bases and perspectives that members of a group possess (Jehn et al., 1999). A cognitive resource perspective suggests that diversity will have positive implications on workgroup outcomes because the group will have access to a wider array of views, skills, and information (Gruenfeld et al., 1996). Educational background, functional background, and industry experience are linked to the set of skills one employs when undertaking a task. For example, different functional backgrounds suggest that an extended resource pool exists based on nonoverlapping knowledge and expertise from which a team can draw to solve problems (Bunderson, 2003; Lovelace, Shapiro, & Weingart, 2001). However, various backgrounds can also lead to a fundamentally different understanding of what is to be completed for the task. For example, an individual with a philosophy background may perceive the format of a memo very differently than someone with an engineering background. Integrating these skill differences is important if members are to work together effectively as a unit. In addition, they are less visible and, therefore, less prone to interpersonal prejudice and stereotyping than social category demographic characteristics.

Social Category Versus Informational Faultlines

The rationale described for distinguishing between social category and informational heterogeneity can be applied to faultlines as well. In fact, we believe this is necessary given the inconsistencies found in the few studies that have examined faultlines and conflict. For instance, all of the published empirical papers to date examining the effect of faultiness on conflict (Lau & Murnighan, 2005; Li & Hambrick, 2005; Thatcher et al., 2003) predicted that faultlines will increase conflict per Lau and Murnighan's (1998) original theory. However, the results are mixed. In fact, both Thatcher et al. (2003) and Lau and Murnighan (2005) found that faultlines actually *decreased* relationship conflict. Only Li and Hambrick (2005) found the proposed positive relationship between faultlines and relationship conflict; and none of these articles found an association with task conflict. We propose that distinguishing between the bases of faultlines will result in more accurate predictions of group processes such as conflict and will therefore improve the explanatory power of models of group diversity. Thus, social category faultlines are hypothetical dividing lines that split a group into subgroups based on social category demographic characteristics (e.g., age, race, and gender). Informational faultlines are hypothetical dividing lines that create subgroups based on informational demographic characteristics (e.g., work experience or tenure). This extended Lau and Murninghan's (1998) original conceptualization of faultlines as it differentiated between the effects of different bases for subgroup formation (alignments along informational or social category characteristics) on group processes.

Whereas Lau and Murninghan (1998) based the idea of faultlines on social identity, self-categorization, and coalition theories, we feel that a cognitive resource perspective should be added when conceptualizing informational-based faultlines. A cognitive resource perspective suggests that diversity in job related or informational characteristics (e.g., tenure or education) offers greater cognitive resources to the group than others (Tziner & Eden, 1985). We believe that the *nature* of the faultline subgroups is crucial to the future functioning of groups. Subgroups formed along social category characteristics such as race, gender, or age may set in motion mechanisms such as stereotyping and prejudice (Messick & Mackie, 1989). Subgroups that form based on informational faultlines, on the other hand, are more likely to result in a detached information perspective, which increases flexibility of group members' thoughts (De Dreu & West, 2001; Nemeth, 1986) and facilitates effective pooling of information and integrating of alternative perspectives (Gruenfeld et al., 1996). Such informational splits can operate in workgroups as "healthy divides" that stimulate effective decision-making processes (Gibson & Vermeulen, 2003) effectively utilizing the teams' cognitive resources. In the following section, we further explain the differences that social category and informational diversity and faultlines have on the various types of workgroup conflict.

A MODEL COMPARING THE EFFECTS OF HETEROGENEITY AND FAULTLINES ON CONFLICT

To show the differences between dispersion and alignment theories of group composition, we present a model delineating the mechanisms by which social category and informational heterogeneity and faultlines influence the various types of conflict. Table 6.3 provides a summary of our propositions presented in the following section.

Social Category Heterogeneity, Faultlines, and Relationship Conflict

Dispersion theories predict that groups heterogeneous on social category characteristics are likely to experience frustration, discomfort, hostility, and anxiety that can result in higher levels of relationship conflict (Jehn, 1997; Tajfel & Turner, 1986). For example, studies have shown that diverse social category characteristics increase relationship conflict within groups (Alagna, Reddy, & Collins, 1982; Jehn et al., 1997; Pelled,

TABLE 6.3
Summary of Propositions

Group Composition	Conflict
Proposition 1: Social Category Heterogeneity Social Category Faultline	high RC[1] **high RC**[2]
Proposition 2: Social Category Heterogeneity	low TC
Proposition 3: Social Category Faultline	high TC
Proposition 4: Social Category Heterogeneity Social Category Faultline	high PC **high PC**
Proposition 5: Informational Heterogeneity	high RC
Proposition 6: Informational Faultline	low RC
Proposition 7: Informational Heterogeneity Informational Faultline	high TC **high TC**
Proposition 8: Informational Heterogeneity	high PC
Proposition 9: Informational Faultline	low PC

[1]RC = Relationship Conflict; TC = Task Conflict; PC = Process Conflict.
[2]Variables in bold reflect that the effects of Faultlines will be stronger than the effects of
    Heterogeneity.

1996). Specifically, Jehn et al. (1997), in a study of project teams, examined individual demographic differences and found that members in visibly diverse groups experienced more relationship conflicts than members in groups that were visibly similar. Moreover, messages may suffer distortion (Asante & Davis, 1985; Cox, 1993) with the potential to cause conflict because attempts to share viewpoints across demographic boundaries may be thwarted. Heterogeneity on the dimensions of sex and ethnicity has also been found to be related to more interpersonal tension, lower levels of friendliness, and lower levels of satisfaction (Alagna et al., 1982; O'Reilly, Caldwell, & Barnett, 1989; Pfeffer & O'Reilly, 1987; Riordan & Shore, 1997; Tsui, Egan, & O'Reilly, 1992; Wagner, Pfeffer, & O'Reilly, 1984; Wharton & Baron, 1987; Wiersema & Bird, 1993).

Alignment theories suggest that strong subgroupings can lead to political issues and covert relationship conflict within the group (Lau &

Murnighan, 1998). Based on coalition theory (Caplow, 1956; Komorita & Kravitz, 1983; Murnighan, 1978), we suggest that if social category demographic attributes align, similar members will interact with each other more often and, therefore, will be likely to form coalitions (Pool, 1976; Stevenson, Pearce, & Porter, 1985). Furthermore, the existence of coalitions based on social categories is likely to amplify the salience of in-group/out-group membership causing strain and polarization between subgroups (Hogg, Turner, & Davidson, 1990). The "us versus them" mentality of subgroups formed based on social category faultlines makes it easy for one subgroup to blame the other subgroup for mistakes (Hogg, 1996). It also leads to power differentials allowing a subgroup to dominate discussion and prevent the participation of others (Gillespie, Brett, & Weingart, 2000; Johnson & Johnson, 1994). Tension and personal attacks within a group resulting from these processes can cause further frustration among group members (e.g., Amason & Schweiger, 1994; Jehn, 1994). These group processes are likely to intensify relationship conflict.

Based on the preceding discussion, both social category heterogeneity and social category faultlines will likely result in high levels of relationship conflict; however, we expect that social category faultlines will have stronger effects on relationship conflict than will social category heterogeneity. From the cross-categorization perspective (e.g., Brewer, 2000; Hewstone et al., 2002; Vanbeselaere, 2000), we suggest that members in such heterogeneous groups may possess crosscutting social identities which contribute to cooperative contact by reducing bias toward out-group members, whereas members in groups with strong social category faultlines will have no overlap between in-group and out-group membership and, thus, no bias reduction (Ensari & Miller, 2001). We believe that members in groups with social category faultlines may exhibit stronger intragroup bias due to additional identification with subgroups. This intergroup bias may encourage more negative stereotyping and animosity among individuals in groups with social category faultlines than among those in groups heterogeneous on social category characteristics. Thus,

- *Proposition 1:* While individuals in groups with high levels of social category heterogeneity and social category faultlines will both experience high levels of intragroup relationship conflict, social category faultlines will have a stronger effect on relationship conflict than will social category heterogeneity.

Social Category Heterogeneity, Faultlines, and Task Conflict

Social category membership provides a particularly salient basis for categorizing members into in-groups and out-groups based on personal characteristics that may promote hostile interactions among members of heterogeneous groups (Jehn et al., 1999; Pelled et al., 1999)—this is the personal-based relationship conflict discussed in proposition 1. However, we propose that the process as it relates to task conflict is less direct, given that the characteristics that people differ on are not obviously task related (Jackson et al., 2003; Pelled, 1996). Rather than open and direct hostilities based on prejudices and stereotypes, we believe the effect on task conflict is more passive. Members of social categorically diverse groups may dislike and distance members who belong to other social categories (Byrne, 1971). Individuals who feel that they are distant may also feel alienated and withhold task-related contributions to the group (Milliken & Martins, 1996), or they may not take seriously task-related comments of group members who belong to other social categories. For example, researchers found that members of diverse groups in age and race communicated less frequently and more formally than members of homogeneous groups regarding the task (Hoffman, 1985; Zenger & Lawrence, 1989). Moreover, the processes through which people seek and attain confirmation of their thoughts and feelings about the self (self-verification; Swann, Polzer, Seyle, & Ko, 2004) may be impaired when members feel alienated and isolated. Swann et al. (2004) further proposed that divergent thinking, a precondition for task conflict to arise, may not occur when members cannot verify their personal views. We suggest that members of groups that are heterogeneous on social category characteristics, therefore, will experience low levels of task conflict.

- *Proposition 2:* Individuals in groups with high levels of social category heterogeneity will experience low levels of intragroup task conflict.

When groups have *social category faultlines*, on the other hand, members of emerging subgroups might more freely express the divergent opinions as they feel support from their subgroup members (Lau & Murnighan, 1998) and verification of their self-views (Swann et al., 2004). Also, they may have a strong tendency toward conformity to the opinion, idea, or perspective favored by their own subgroup (Baron, Kerr, & Miller, 1993) and a need to distinguish their views from the other subgroup's (Brewer, 2000; Hogg et al., 1990). These processes may cause group members to exhibit intense polarization around ideas and thoughts across subgroups (Ancona, 1990). We further argue that in common-goal groups with social category faultlines, subgroup members are likely to voice support for their particular position or opinion as they strive to integrate these opinions into their view of the group tasks. Thus, in groups with strong social category faultlines, we propose that there will be high levels of task conflict due to polarization around divergent opinions.

- *Proposition 3:* Individuals in groups with strong social category faultlines will experience high levels of intragroup task conflict.

Social Category Heterogeneity, Faultlines and Process Conflict

Dispersion theories suggest that members of groups that are heterogeneous on social category characteristics may face "interpretive barriers" resulting from members' different language systems, life experiences, or values acquired from varying socialization experiences (Dougherty, 1992). These differences are likely to emphasize the differences in conventions for social interaction and shape views about how one should approach a task (Jehn et al., 1999). For example, female members may rely on conventions that are typical to their particular networks of relationships to interpret actions needed to proceed with work, whereas male members may use interpretations representative of their own conventions (Von Glinow, Shapiro, & Brett, 2004). The two interpretive systems may not necessarily coincide, and differing interpretations of what actions to take to get work done may affect a group's ability to coordinate task progress (Behfar et al., 2005). This is likely to promote disagreements over procedural and administrative features of the task and result in process conflict (Jehn & Chatman, 2000; Jehn et al., 1999).

Similarly, alignment theories propose that members across subgroups formed by social category faultlines might also have different "thought worlds" (Dougherty, 1987) and different interpretations about how work should be done in a group. Members of such groups may further feel that their priorities and work approaches are not aligned within a group, and thus, they may spend more time "staking out" territory and viciously arguing who does what, when, and how (Behfar et al., 2005). A faultline that breaks a group into subgroups may inhibit boundary-spanning activities, creating distinct subgroup networks and leading to less coordination of interdependent but differentiated subgroups within a group (e.g., Edmondson, 1999; Miles & Perreault, 1976). Under these circumstances, developing a shared approach to task accomplishment in groups with strong social category faultlines will be difficult and process conflict will be likely to surface.

Groups with high levels of social category heterogeneity and groups with strong social category faultlines are both predicted to experience high levels of process conflict; however, we expect faultlines to have stronger effects than heterogeneity. Members of groups with strong social category faultlines may support certain ways of doing work favored by their respective subgroups, at the same time displaying prejudice and intolerance toward opinions of members of another subgroup. Heterogeneous groups, in turn, may have a number of divergent viewpoints but without support from others, individuals may not vigorously compete and argue their points of view. Thus, while heterogeneous groups and groups with strong social category faultlines will both experience challenges in coordinating their tasks, groups with strong faultlines will disagree over process-related issues in a more competitive way than will heterogeneous groups. This leads us to

- *Proposition 4:* While individuals in groups with high levels of social category heterogeneity and social category faultlines will both experience high levels of intragroup process conflict, social category faultlines will have a stronger effect on process conflict than will social category heterogeneity.

Informational Heterogeneity, Faultlines, and Relationship Conflict

We propose that informational heterogeneity will increase relationship conflict. In groups with a high dispersion of informational characteristics, it is necessary to communicate with people different from yourself. As with social category characteristics, different experiences and socialization backgrounds can elicit stereotypes (Pelled, 1996). For example, you often hear of people saying, "All accountants are picky." In Strauss' (1964) classic case study of cross-functional interactions, resentment and annoyance characterized communication between engineers and purchasing agents. Just as social category (or visible) types of heterogeneity such as gender and race can trigger relationship conflict, group heterogeneity with respect to functional background, tenure, and other less visible characteristics can also incite relationship conflict (Pelled, 1996).

- *Proposition 5:* Individuals in groups with high levels of informational heterogeneity will experience high levels of intragroup relationship conflict.

However, given expectancy effects emerging from alignment we propose the opposite relationship between *informational faultlines* and relationship conflict (informational faultlines will decrease relationship conflict—see Table 6.3). Unlike social category characteristics, attributes that make up information-based heterogeneity and faultlines are less visible and less prone to interpersonal prejudice and stereotyping. However, because they are directly applicable to the work context, they play an important role in developing expectations about behaviors of others in the workplace. Expectancy-violation theory, in part, suggests that the violations of category-based expectations (or the experience of unexpectedness) may influence affective reactions and promote negative evaluations of out-group members (Bettencourt, Dill, Greathouse, Charlton, & Mulholland, 1997). Therefore, because members of informationally *heterogeneous* groups can be simultaneously classified as in-group or out-group members based on multiple dimensions (Hewstone et al., 2002), they may construct inconsistent expectations leading to violations and, thus, negative affect. In contrast, in groups with informational *faultlines*, the fact that members of another subgroup have *different* functional backgrounds would be consistent with the fact that they also have *different* levels of education and work experiences. Because of subgroup formation, members are aware of their differences and *expect* to be different along informational lines. This elicits less uncertain and ambiguous environments in which members are more likely to accept their informational differences and cooperate (Rink & Ellemers, 2006). As such, they may exert more effort toward regulating task-focused group processes rather than fighting over relationship-related issues.

- *Proposition 6:* Individuals in groups with strong informational faultlines will experience low levels of intragroup relationship conflict.

Informational Heterogeneity, Faultlines, and Task Conflict

Members of *informationally heterogeneous* groups are assumed to have different training and socialization experiences (Lovelace et al., 2001; Mortensen & Hinds, 2001). Research further suggested that debates and disagreements about group tasks often arise from differences in knowledge and experiences (Tziner & Eden, 1985; Wittenbaum & Stasser, 1996). The presence of different perspectives is likely to manifest itself as intragroup task conflict (Pelled et al., 1999). As such, group members in informationally heterogeneous groups will engage in debate about divergent viewpoints and discuss their disagreements over group tasks (Jehn et al., 1997). For example, Pelled (1996) found that functional background and educational diversity were related to conflicts that focused on the task or content of ideas.

In the case of *informational faultlines*, subgroup members align along informational characteristics and tend to exhibit similar viewpoints within each subgroup and display different opinions across subgroups. This is due to different approaches to problem solving caused by differences in training and experiences (Bantel & Jackson, 1989; Gruenfeld et al., 1996; Pelled, 1996). Literature on minority influence suggests that information sharing in diverse groups depends on the extent to which group members are provided with social support (cf. Allen & Levine, 1971; Bragg & Allen, 1972). When a group has strong informational faultlines, its members may find support and validation for their knowledge (e.g., opinions, assumptions, and information) in their subgroups due to mutual liking, shared experiences, and perceived similarity of aligned members (Phillips, Mannix, Neale, & Gruenfeld, 2004). In groups with strong informational faultlines, members may freely express their ideas and actively engage in open discussion of divergent perspectives across subgroups because they have support from within their own subgroup (Lau & Murnighan, 1998; Phillips, 2003; Swann et al., 2004). We therefore argue that individuals in such groups will experience high levels of conflict over task-related issues.

We expect informational faultlines to be a better predictor of intragroup task conflict than informational heterogeneity. Based on interindividual–intergroup discontinuity research (e.g., Insko et al., 1998; Schopler, Insko,

Graetz, Drigotas, & Smith, 1991; Wildschut, Insko, & Gaertner, 2002), we argue that members in groups with informational faultlines may disagree over various ideas or perspectives in a more confident and convincing way than do individuals in informationally heterogeneous groups. Interindividual–intergroup discontinuity is the tendency of intergroup relations to be more competitive and less cooperative than interindividual relations (Insko et al., 1998; Schopler et al., 1991). Heterogeneous groups may have a number of divergent viewpoints but without support from others, individuals may not actively share their point of view (Wit & Kerr, 2002). This is consistent with past work showing that individual (minority) influence can be attributed to the individual's personality and easily disregarded while influence from more than one person (even if deviant) is seen as more credible and reliable (Wood, Lundgren, Ouellette, Busceme, & Blackstone, 1994). Thus, we propose that these subgroup-supported divergent opinions enter into the discussion and are strongly supported by the subgroup and just as strongly opposed by the opposing subgroup. Groups with strong informational faultlines may have more intense conflicts over tasks because each subgroup rallies around one particular point of view (Lau & Murnighan, 2005). These subgroup differences and intrasubgroup alignment may encourage more intense discussion and debate over task-related issues in groups with informational faultlines than in informationally heterogeneous groups.

- *Proposition 7:* While individuals in groups with high levels of informational heterogeneity and informational faultlines will both experience high levels of intragroup task conflict, informational faultlines will have a stronger effect on task conflict than will informational heterogeneity.

Informational Heterogeneity, Faultlines, and Process Conflict

Dispersion theories suggest that members of informationally heterogeneous groups tend to rely on working methods particular to their backgrounds (Bantel & Jackson, 1989; Gruenfeld et al., 1996) and display different views about how one should approach a task (Jehn et al., 1999). Members' differing expertise and a broad array of information, knowledge, and skills add to the variety of opinions about how to do the work. This affects a group's ability to coordinate task progress (Behfar et al., 2005) and often results in disagreements over procedural issues (Jehn et al., 1999). For instance, research has demonstrated that heterogeneous groups on informational characteristics experienced more difficulty defining how to proceed with their task than did homogeneous groups (Jehn, 1997; Watson, Kumar, & Michaelson, 1993).

- *Proposition 8:* Individuals in groups with high levels of informational heterogeneity will experience high levels of intragroup process conflict.

We propose the opposite relationship between informational fault-lines and process conflict (informational faultlines will decrease process conflict—see Table 6.3). Alignment theories suggest that members across subgroups formed by informational faultlines are aware of their differences and *expect* to be different along informational lines. Although they might have different beliefs about how work should be done in a group, members of such groups are likely to be effective in dealing with logistical problems. When there are consistent expectations, there is less confusion about who is responsible for what and how task accomplishment should proceed in the work unit. This certainty allows members to accept their expected informational differences (Rink & Ellemers, 2006) and exert more effort toward coordinating task accomplishment.

- *Proposition 9:* Individual in groups with strong informational fault-lines will experience low levels of intragroup process conflict.

In sum, we again refer the reader to Table 6.3, which summarizes our propositions about social category and informational heterogeneity and faultlines on task, relationship, and process conflict. However, it is not as straightforward as this table suggests given that both demographic dispersion and alignment can occur simultaneously. In addition, informational and social category characteristics co-occur in individuals and thus in groups. To integrate the dispersion and alignment concepts in groups, for instance, we must consider the effects of having a social categorically diverse (dispersed) yet informationally aligned group such that subgroups occur along educational and functional lines but may crosscut across gender and race (social category). Will this type of group experience high levels of both task conflict (attributed to informationally based faultlines) and relationship conflict (attributed to social-categorical dispersion) or will one type of group composition dominate the other with regard to its effects on group conflict? For example, the group may capitalize on informationally based faultlines and experience high levels of task conflict and low levels of relationship conflict. To make it even more complicated, different demographic characteristics *within* a type of faultline may *differentially* contribute to group dynamics as group context may lead to reliance on one faultline base. For example, group norms about competence and recognition may encourage seniority-salient faultlines, whereas norms supporting diversity may be more likely to promote gender- or race-salient faultlines. We discuss this and other future research directions below.

FUTURE RESEARCH DIRECTIONS

The ways that faultlines affect various types of conflict within groups and organizations are only beginning to be investigated. There are a number of future research directions that can be pursued to further our knowledge of this relationship. Future research on faultlines should investigate issues of faultline measurement such as whether faultline distance (the level of divergence between two subgroups) should be evaluated in addition to faultline strength (the degree to which each subgroup is relatively homogeneous), potential moderators such as group identity and task type, and issues of context such as virtual teams. This work may also be extended by considering additional conflict types (e.g., creative conflict and political conflict; Jehn & Conlon, 1999) and examining conflict profiles (e.g., proportional composition of conflict types within a group; see Jehn & Chatman, 2000). Rather than try to describe all of our thoughts for future research for the faultlines–conflict relationships, we will focus on describing three such promising areas in detail: faultline activation, group/organizational culture, and measurement challenges.

Faultline Activation

Similar to the geological concept of faults in the Earth's crust, faultlines in groups can be inactive and go unnoticed without any changes in group processes for years (Lau & Murnighan, 1998). Although faultlines are dormant, they can become active, causing the group to split into subgroups. While potential faultlines are often based on the objective demographics of group members, active faultlines exist when the members perceive and behave as if they are two separate groups. Current research on faultlines has generally focused on potential faultlines by assuming that demographic (e.g., gender and race) or contextual (e.g., physical distance and organizational member) characteristics represent sources of identification for individuals in groups (e.g., Li & Hambrick, 2005; Thatcher et al., 2003). There are two potential areas for future investigation. One is to determine whether the demographic and contextual characteristics used in previous research are relevant attributes that trigger faultline activation. A second potential area is to determine whether other attributes are more likely to trigger faultlines (e.g., parental status or love of baseball). Finally, we might examine the extent to which faultline activation is more likely to occur over time rather than in a single moment of time.

The degree to which demographic characteristics act as triggers for faultline activation is related to research on identity saliency. According to Lau and Murnighan (1998), faultlines can lead to salient subgroups that then become a basis for social identification and categorization. Once group members start identifying themselves with a particular subgroup, the negative outcomes of categorization (e.g. negative stereotyping and prejudice) are likely to lead to coalition formation and conflict (Thatcher & Jehn, 1998). However, because individuals have multiple identities, the salience of a particular identity depends on the context in which individuals operate (Hogg & Terry, 2000). For example, a group of three men and three women has a potential faultline based on gender. If all six individuals view their genders as salient identities, then there is an active faultline.

However, not all potential faultline situations are activated; that is, while the demographics of the group members suggest the potential for fault-lines, the members may never actually feel or behave as separate groups leading to little or no animosity across subgroups.

When individuals have salient identities, they are more likely to think of themselves along the lines of that particular identity. For example, if gender is a salient identity to a female worker, then she is more likely to perceive workplace issues from the point of view of a female. Thus, one possible approach to understanding faultline activation is to examine identity saliency as a moderator of potential faultiness and conflict. How-ever, even if the salience of gender is not initially important to the group members, the potential faultline may develop into an active faultline. For instance, if this group is tasked to review a sexual harassment initiative, the potential faultline may become activated as the male subgroup and female subgroup view this initiative from opposing angles.

Another approach to investigating faultlines would be to ask group members if any issues or identities are the cause of faultline activation. For example, something as trivial as the love for baseball could create a perceived in-group and out-group within the larger group. All problems or issues that this group then faces could then be perceived through the in-group/out-group lens. It will be interesting to see whether the nature of faultline activation is more often a result of demographic/contextual characteristics or whether it is based on relatively innocuous differences. If, in fact, trivial differences are important in activating faultlines, then managers may be able to counteract this by proactively engaging in some group identification efforts.

A third approach is to view faultline activation as a longitudinal process. Characteristics that are visible and have had historic social implications for role behavior (e.g., gender) may be the impetus for initial faultline devel-opment. Based on evolutional psychology, gender is the most influential difference between humans because it appeared earliest in human society (Kurzban, Tooby, & Cosmides, 2001). People easily registered the differ-ences in gender and developed cognitive adaptations to encode the gender dimension preferentially. As members get to know one another, other char-acteristics (e.g., race and age) may solidify the faultlines if the characteris-tics align with gender faultlines. Finally, we would expect that nonvisible groupings (e.g., organizational tenure and educational background), where aligned, would continue to support subgroup alignment. Viewing faultline activation as a longitudinal process suggests that interventions may occur at various points in time to reduce the strength of faultline alignment.

Group and Organizational Culture

Another future direction we discuss is the role that group and organi-zational cultures play on the relationship between faultlines and conflict.

Understanding group and organizational culture is an important avenue for future research because these cultures may determine whether
faultlines become active as well as influence the dimensions on which
faultlines may become activated. The essential core of culture consists of
traditional ideas, their attached values, and the extent to which a group
accepts these ideas and values (Kroeber & Kluckhohn, 1963). There
are different levels of analysis from which to study culture, as culture
can exist at societal, national, and regional levels (DiMaggio & Powell,
1983). Within organizations, culture can exist at an organizational, business unit, department, or group level (Chatman & Jehn, 1994; Mannix,
Thatcher, & Jehn, 2001).

Group culture is defined as the extent to which group members have
consensus on values, norms, and appropriate behaviors related to work
(adapted from Chatman & Jehn, 1994; Mannix et al., 2001; Rousseau, 1990).
Group culture can reflect preferred ways to perform individual and group
tasks such as being innovative, task oriented, or career oriented (Jehn,
1994; Jehn et al., 1997; O'Reilly, Chatman, & Caldwell, 1991). Two primary
concerns become relevant when researchers conceptualize group culture:
(a) the extent to which members care about the group culture (culture
strength) and (b) the extent to which these cultures differ across content
(culture content; Flynn & Chatman, 2001; Mannix et al., 2001). The norms
and behaviors supported by group cultures vary widely across groups in
an organization (Bettenhausen & Murnighan, 1991; Jehn, 1994). Thus, it
would be interesting to examine how different group cultures (e.g., values
about career advancement or diversity initiatives) shape the way in which
group faultlines affect performance. In fact, past research on diversity suggests that strong group cultures may be "a powerful way for managers to
use informational and social influence processes to encourage solidarity
rather than divisiveness" (Williams & O'Reilly, 1998). Similarly, we might
expect that group cultures that value career advancement and diversity
might suppress faultline activation.

Organizational culture can be defined as a common set of shared
meanings or understandings about an organization (Reichers & Schneider, 1990). As in our discussion of group culture, the impact of organizational culture comes from the content and the strength of the shared
meanings. Previous research has found that organizational culture affects
group-level actions (O'Reilly, Williams, & Barsade, 1998; Thomas & Ely,
1996). O'Reilly et al. (1998) found that organizational cultures that supported ethnic diversity reported positive effects on performance. Similarly, Thomas and Ely (1996) found that organizations that have cultures
in which diversity is viewed as an opportunity to learn rather than as a
legal requirement tend to perform better. Thus, as in the case with group
cultures, we might expect that organizational cultures supporting career
advancement and diversity might suppress faultline activation. Finally,
we argue that it is not merely the content or strength of the organizational
culture that influences group-level relationships; it is the resulting impact

of shared group culture *and* organizational culture (cultural consistency) that influences the relationship between group faultlines and conflict. We believe that cultural consistency is important because it can create extremely positive effects (in the case where the group and organizational cultures align) or extremely negative effects (in the case where group and organizational cultures do not align). Thus, we would expect that in culturally consistent environments, faultline activation would be suppressed whereas in culturally inconsistent environments, faultlines are not only more likely to be activated but the resulting activation will create more negative types of conflict.

Measurement Challenges

Recently, a few attempts to measure faultlines have been made. Shaw (2004) developed an SPSS-based program to measure internal and cross-subgroup alignments along categorical attributes for up to six-member groups. Gibson and Vermeulen (2003) proposed a measure of subgroup strength to capture overlapping demographics among members of a group. Thatcher et al. (2003) and Bezrukova, Jehn, Zanutto, and Thatcher (2005) described the measures of faultline strength and distance that have a number of advantages: They simultaneously allow continuous and categorical variables, can fit an unlimited number of attributes, can handle groups of unlimited size, and are flexible enough to allow for different weights of the attributes. Zanutto, Bezrukova, and Jehn (2005) described an SAS-based code, which should make faultline calculations accessible and facilitate more empirical research. However, there continue to be challenges in developing the faultline measure.

One of the first challenges is being able to measure actual faultlines as well as potential faultlines. One solution is to develop a measure that asks group members to report on the dimensions on which subgroups exist. The potential dimensions may differ for every group subjecting this form of measurement to bias and error. In addition, it may be more meaningful to then focus on the strength of the faultline (is the split very strong) rather than the nature of the faultline (e.g., gender or race). A second challenge is determining the best approach for rescaling faultline dimensions so that they have the same meaning. For example, what does one difference in race equal to in terms of years? Past measurements have looked at the standard deviation of continuous variables in order to calculate "equal difference," but other approaches may be equally compelling.

CONCLUSIONS

This chapter was intended to uncover the nuances of group composition that play a critical role in influencing intragroup conflict in organizational workgroups by contrasting group composition theories of dispersion and alignment. We proposed that a particular alignment across group members and the resulting demographically motivated subgroups are what make a difference in predicting the various types of conflict, more so than the dispersion, or heterogeneity, of demographic characteristics. This alignment may not necessarily cause dysfunctional processes, as has been suggested (e.g., Lau & Murnighan, 1998; Thatcher, et al., 2003), but rather it may promote effective decision-making processes via the various types of conflict. Consequently, we theorized about the *nature* of alignment, and specifically about the type of diversity responsible for the alignment (social category vs. information based), which determines to what degree members of a group will experience task, relationship, or process conflict (or a combination of the three). The delineation of the processes behind social category and information-based splits as related to conflict should help managers to handle effectively the dynamics of diverse groups and researchers to further the specification of the complex processes resulting from various profiles of group composition.

REFERENCES

Alagna, S., Reddy, D., & Collins, D. (1982). Perceptions of functioning in mixed sex and male medical training groups. *Journal of Medical Education, 57,* 801–803.

Alexander, J., Nuchols, B., Bloom, J., & Lee, S. Y. (1995). Organizational demography and turnover: An examination of multiform and nonlinear heterogeneity. *Human Relations, 48,* 1455–1480.

Allen, V. L., & Levine, J. M. (1971). Social support and conformity: The role of independent assessment of reality. *Journal of Experimental Social Psychology, 7*(1), 48–58.

Amason, A. C. (1996). Distinguishing the effects of functional and dysfunctional conflict on strategic decision making: Resolving a paradox for the top management teams. *Academy of Management Journal, 39,* 123–148.

Amason, A. C., & Mooney, A. C. (1999). The effects of past performance on top management team conflict in strategic decision making. *International Journal of Conflict Management, 10,* 340–359.

Amason, A. C., & Schweiger, D. M. (1994). Resolving the paradox of conflict, strategic decision making, and organizational performance. *International Journal of Conflict Management, 5,* 239–253.

Amason, A. C., & Schweiger, D. M. (1997). The effects of conflict on strategic decision making effectiveness and organizational performance. In C. K. W. De Dreu & E. Van de Vliert (Eds.), *Using conflict in organizations* (pp. 101–115). Thousand Oaks, CA: Sage Publications, Inc.

Ancona, D. G. (1990). Outward bound: Strategies for team survival in the organization. *Academy of Management Journal, 33,* 334–365.

Ancona, D. G., & Caldwell, D. (1992). Bringing the boundary: External activity and performance in organizational teams. *Administrative Science Quarterly, 37,* 634–665.

Asante, M., & Davis, A. (1985). Black and white communications: Analyzing workplace encounters. *Journal of Black Studies, 16*(1), 77–93.

Ashforth, B. E., & Johnson, S. A. (2001). Which hat to wear? The relative salience of multiple identities in organizational contexts. In M. A. Hogg & D. J. Terry (Eds.), *Social identity processes in organizational contexts* (pp. 31–48). Philadelphia: Psychology Press.

Bantel, K. A., & Jackson, S. E. (1989). Top management and innovation in banking: Does the composition of the top team make a difference? *Strategic Management Journal, 10,* 107–124.

Baron, R. A. (1991). Positive effects of conflict: A cognitive perspective. *Employee Responsibilities and Rights Journal, 4,* 25–36.

Baron, R. M., Kerr, N., & Miller, N. (1993). *Group process, group decision, group action.* Buckingham, U.K.: Open University Press.

Behfar, K. J., Mannix, E. A., Peterson, R. S., & Trochin, W. M. K. (2005). *A multifaceted approach to intra-group conflict: Issues of theory and measurement.* Chicago: Northwestern University.

Bettencourt, B. A., Dill, K. E., Greathouse, S., Charlton, K., & Mulholland, A. (1997). Evaluations of ingroup and outgroup members: The category-based expectancy violation. *Journal of Experimental Social Psychology, 33,* 244–275.

Bettenhausen, K., & Murnighan, J. K. (1991). Developing and challenging a group norm: Interpersonal cooperation and structural competition. *Administrative Science Quarterly, 36,* 20–35.

Bezrukova, K., Jehn, K., Zanutto, E., & Thatcher, S. M. B. (2005). *Do workgroup faultlines help or hurt? The role of distance and shared identity on individual outcomes.* New Brunswick, NJ: Rutgers University.

Blau, P. (1977). *Inequality and composition: A primitive theory of social structure.* New York: Free Press.

Bragg, B. W., & Allen, V. (1972). The role of the public and private support in reducing conformity. *Psychonomic Science, 29*(2), 81–82.

Brewer, M. B. (1995). Managing diversity: The role of social identities. In S. E. Jackson & M. N. Ruderman (Eds.), *Diversity in work teams: Research paradigms for a changing workplace* (pp. 47–68). Washington, DC: American Psychological Association.

Brewer, M. B. (1996). When contact is not enough: Social identity and intergroup cooperation. *International Journal of Intercultural Relations, 20,* 291–303.

Brewer, M. B. (2000). Reducing prejudice through cross-categorization: Effects of multiple social identities. In S. Oskamp (Ed.), *Reducing prejudice and discrimination* (pp. 165–183). Mahwah, NJ: Lawrence Erlbaum Associates.

Brewer, M. B., & Pierce, K. P. (2005). Social identity complexity and outgroup tolerance. *Personality & Social Psychology Bulletin, 31*(3), 428–437.

Bunderson, S. (2003). Team member functional background and involvement in management teams: Direct effects and the moderating role of power centralization. *Academy of Management Journal, 46,* 458–474.

Byrne, D. (1971). *The attraction paradigm.* New York: Academic Press.

Caplow, T. (1956). A theory of coalitions in the triad. *American Sociological Review, 21,* 489–493.

Chatman, J., & Jehn, K. (1994). Assessing the relationship between industry characteristics and organizational culture: How different can you be? *Academy of Management Journal, 35,* 522.

Cosier, R., & Rose, G. (1977). Cognitive conflict and goal conflict effects on task performance. *Organizational Behavior and Human Performance, 19,* 378–391.

Cox, H. (1993). Encouraging creativity. *Business and Economic Review, 40,* 26–28.

Cramton, C. D., & Hinds, P. J. (2004). Subgroups dynamics in internationally distributed teams: Ethnocentrism or cross-national learning? In B. Staw & R. Kramer (Eds.), *Research in Organizational Behavior* (p. 26). Oxford, U.K.: Elsevier Science, Inc.

Cummings, A., Zhou, J., & Oldham, G. (1993). *Demographic differences and employee work outcomes: Effects of multiple comparison groups.* Paper presented at the annual meeting of the Academy of Management, Atlanta, GA.

De Dreu, C. K. W., & Weingart, L. R. (2003). Task versus relationship conflict, team performance, and team member satisfaction: A meta-analysis. *Journal of Applied Psychology, 88,* 741–749.

De Dreu, C. K. W., & West, M. (2001). Minority dissent and team innovation: The importance of participation in decision making. *Journal of Applied Psychology, 86,* 1191–1201.

DiMaggio, D. J., & Powell, W. W. (1983). The iron cage revisited: Institutional isomorphism and collective rationality in organizational fields. *American Sociological Review, 48,* 147–160.

Dougherty, D. (1987). *New products in old organizations: The myth of the better mousetrap in search of the beaten path.* Unpublished doctoral dissertation, Sloan School of Management, MIT, Cambridge, MA.

Dougherty, D. (1992). Interpretive barriers to succeful product innovation in large firms. *Organization Science, 3*(2), 179–202

Dyck, B., & Starke, F. A. (1999). The formation of breakaway organizations: Observations and a process model. *Administrative Science Quarterly, 44,* 792–822.

Earley, P. C., & Mosakowski, E. (2000). Creating hybrid team cultures: An empirical test of transnational team functioning. *Academy of Management Journal, 43*(1), 26–49.

Edmondson, A. (1999). A safe harbor: Social psychological conditions enabling boundary spanning in work teams. In R. Wageman (Ed.), *Research on managing groups and teams* (Vol. 2, pp. 179–199). Stamford, CT: JAI Press, Inc.

Ensari, N., & Miller, N. (2001). The out-group must not be so bad after all: The effects of disclosure, typicality, and salience on intergroup bias. *Journal of Personality and Social Psychology, 83*(2), 313–329.

Eurich-Fulcer, R., & Schofield, J. W. (1995). Correlated versus uncorrelated social categorizations: The effect on intergroup bias. *Personality & Social Psychology Bulletin, 21*(2), 149–159.

Flynn, F. J., & Chatman, J. A. (2001). Strong cultures and innovation: Oxymoron or opportunity? In C. Cooper, C. Early, J. Chatman, & W. Starbuck (Eds.), *Handbook of organizational culture* (pp. 263–288). Chichester, U.K.: John Wiley & Sons, Ltd.

Gibson, C., & Vermeulen, F. (2003). A healthy divide: Subgroups as a stimulus for team learning behavior. *Administrative Science Quarterly, 48,* 202–239.

Gillespie, J. J., Brett, J. M., & Weingart, L. R. (2000). Interdependence, social motives, and outcome satisfaction in multiparty negotiation. *European Journal of Social Psychology, 30,* 779–797.

Gruenfeld, D. H., Mannix, E. A., Williams, K. Y., & Neale, M. A. (1996). Group composition and decision making: How member familiarity and information distribution affect process and performance. *Organizational Behavior and Human Decision Processes, 67*, 1–15.

Hambrick, D., Li, J. T., Xin, K., & Tsui, A. S. (2001). Compositional gaps and downward spirals in international joint venture management groups. *Strategic Management Journal, 22*(11), 1033–1053.

Harrison, D. A., Price, K. H., Gavin, J. H., & Florey, A. T. (2002). Time, teams, and task performance: Changing effects of surface- and deep-level diversity on group functioning. *Academy of Management Journal, 45*, 1029–1045.

Haslam, S. A., & Ellemers, N. (2005). Social identity in industrial and organizational psychology: Concepts, controversies, and contributions. *International Review of Industrial and Organizational Psychology, 20*, 39–118.

Hewstone, M., Rubin, M., & Willis, H. (2002). Intergroup bias. *Annual Review of Psychology, 53*, 575–604.

Hoffman, E. (1985). The effect of race-ratio composition of the frequency of organizational communication. *Social Psychological Quarterly, 48*, 17–26.

Hogg, M. A. (1996). Social identity, self-categorization, and the small group. In E. Witte & J. Davis (Eds.), *Understanding group behavior: Vol. 2: Small group processes and interpersonal relations* (pp. 227–253). Mahwah, NJ: Lawrence Erlbaum Associates.

Hogg, M. A., & Terry, D. J. (2000). Social identity and self-categorization processes in organizational contexts. *Academy of Management Review, 25*, 121–140.

Hogg, M. A., Turner, J. C., & Davidson, B. (1990). Polarized norms and social frames of reference: A test of self-categorization theory of group polarization. *Basic and Applied Social Psychology, 11*, 77–100.

Insko, C. A., Schopler, J., Pemberton, M. B., Wieselquist, J., McIlraith, S. A., Currey, D. P., et al. (1998). Future consequences and the reduction of interindividual-intergroup discontinuity. *Journal of Personality and Social Psychology, 75*, 695–711.

Jackson, S. E., Joshi, A., & Erhardt, N. L. (2003). Recent research on teams and organizational diversity: SWOT analysis and implications. *Journal of Management, 29*(6), 801–830.

Jehn, K. A. (1994). Enhancing effectiveness: An investigation of advantages and disadvantages of value-based intragroup conflict. *International Journal of Conflict Management, 5*, 223–238.

Jehn, K. A. (1995). A multimethod examination of the benefits and detriments of intragroup conflict. *Administrative Science Quarterly, 40*, 256–282.

Jehn, K. A. (1997). A qualitative analysis of conflict types and dimensions in organizational groups. *Administrative Science Quarterly, 42*, 520–557.

Jehn, K. A., & Bendersky, C. (2003). Intragroup conflict in organizations: A contingency perspective on the conflict-outcome relationship. In B. Staw & R. Kramer (Eds.), *Research in organizational behavior* (Vol. 25, pp. 187–242). Oxford, U.K.: Elsevier Science, Inc.

Jehn, K. A., Chadwick, C., & Thatcher, S. M. B. (1997). To agree or not to agree: The effects of value congruence, individual demographic dissimilarity, and conflict on workgroup outcomes. *International Journal of Conflict Management, 8*(4), 287–306.

Jehn, K. A., & Chatman, J. A. (2000). The influence of proportional and perceptual conflict composition on team performance. *International Journal of Conflict Management, 11*(1), 56–74.

Jehn, K., & Conlon, D. (1999). *Diversity in punk rock bands: Conflict and performance.* Paper presented at the International Association for Conflict Management Conference, Spain.

Jehn, K. A., & Mannix, E. (2001). The dynamic nature of conflict: A longitudinal study of intragroup conflict and group performance. *Academy of Management Journal, 44,* 238–251.

Jehn, K. A., Northcraft, G., & Neale, M. (1999). Why differences make a difference: A field study of diversity, conflict, and performance in workgroups. *Administrative Science Quarterly, 44,* 741–763.

Johnson, D. W., & Johnson F. P. (1994). *Joining together: Group theory and group skills.* Boston: Allyn and Bacon.

Kabanoff, B. (1991). Equity, equality, power, and conflict. *Academy of Management Review, 16,* 416–441.

Kanter, R. (1977). *Men and women of the corporation.* New York: Basic Books.

Komorita, S. S., & Kravitz, D. A. (1983). Coalition formation: A social psychological approach. In P. B. Paulus (Ed.), *Basic group processes* (pp. 1979–2003). New York: Springer-Verlag.

Kramer, R. M. (1991). Intergroup relations and organizational dilemmas: The role of categorization processes. In L. L. Cummings & B. M. Staw (Eds.), *Research in organizational behavior* (Vol. 13, pp. 191–227). Greenwich, CT: JAI Press.

Kroeber, A. L., & Kluckhohn, C. (1963). *Culture: A critical review of concepts and definitions.* New York: Random House.

Kurzban, R., Tooby, J., & Cosmides, L. (2001). Can race be erased? Coalitional computation and social categorization. *PNAS, 98*(26), 15387–15392.

Labianca, G., Brass, D. J., & Gray, B. (1998). Social networks and perceptions of intergroup conflict: The role of negative relationships and third parties. *Academy of Management Journal, 41*(1), 55–67.

Lau, D., & Murnighan, J. K. (1998). Demographic diversity and faultlines: The compositional dynamics of organizational groups. *Academy of Management Review, 23,* 325–340.

Lau, D., & Murnighan, J. K. (2005). Interactions within groups and subgroups: The dynamic effects of demographic faultlines. *Academy of Management Journal, 48, 645–659.*

Li, J., & Hambrick, D. C. (2005). *Factional groups: A new vantage on demographic faultlines, conflict, and disintegration in work teams.* Hong Kong: Hong Kong University of Science and Technology.

Lincoln, J. R., & Miller, J. (1979). Work and friendship tries in organizations: A comparative analysis of relational networks. *Administrative Science Quarterly, 24,* 181–199.

Lovelace, K., Shapiro, D. L., & Weingart, L. R. (2001). Maximizing cross-functional new product teams' innovativeness and constraint adherence: A conflict communications perspective. *Academy of Management Journal, 44,* 779–783.

Major, B., Quinton, W. J., McCoy, S. K., & Schmader, T. (2000). Reducing prejudice: The target's perspective. In S. Oskamp (Ed.), *The Claremont symposium on applied social psychology: Reducing prejudice and discrimination* (pp. 211–237). Mahwah, NJ: Lawrence Erlbaum Associates.

Mannix, E. A., Thatcher, S., & Jehn, K. A. (2001). The dynamic nature of conflict: A longitudinal study of intragroup conflict and group performance. *Academy of Management Journal, 44*, 238–251.

McGrath, J. E. (1998). A view of group composition through a group-theoretic lens. In M. A. Neale, E. A. Mannix, & D. H. Gruenfeld (Eds.), *Research on managing groups and teams* (Vol. 1, pp. 255–272). Stamford, CT: JAI Press.

Messick, D. M., & Mackie, D. M. (1989). Intergroup relations. *Annual Review of Psychology, 40*, 45–81.

Migdal, M. J., Hewstone, M., & Mullen, B. (1998). The effects of crossed categorization on intergroup evaluations: A meta-analysis. *British Journal of Social Psychology, 37*(3), 303–324.

Miles R. H., & Perreault, W. D. (1976). Organizational role conflict: Its antecedents and consequences. *Organizational Behavior and Human Performances, 17*, 19–44.

Milliken, F., & Martins, L. (1996). Searching for common threads: Understanding the multiple effects of diversity in organizational groups. *Academy of Management Review, 21*, 402–433.

Mohammed, S., & Angell, L. C. (2004). Surface- and deep-level diversity in workgroups: Examining the moderating effects of team orientation and team process on relationship conflict. *Journal of Organizational Behavior, 25*, 1015–1039.

Moreland, R. L., & Levine, J. M. (1992). The composition of small groups. In E. J. Lawler, B. Markovsky, C. Ridgeway, & H. A. Walker (Eds.), *Advances in group processes* (Vol. 8, pp. 237–280). Greenwich, CT: JAI Press.

Mortensen, M., & Hinds, P. J. (2001). Conflict and shared identity in geographically distributed teams. *International Journal of Conflict Management, 12*, 212–238.

Murnighan, J. K. (1978). Models of coalition behavior: Game theoretic, social psychological and political perspectives. *Psychological Bulletin, 85*, 1130–1153.

Nemeth, C. J. (1986). Differential contributions of majority and minority influence. *Psychological Review, 93*, 23–32.

Northcraft, G. B., Polzer, J. T., Neale, M. A., & Kramer, R. M. (1995). Diversity, social identity, and performance: Emergent social dynamics in cross-functional teams. In S. E. Jackson & M. N. Ruderman (Eds.), *Diversity in work teams: Research paradigms for a changing workplace* (pp. 69–96). Washington, DC: American Psychological Association.

O'Reilly, C. A., Caldwell, D., & Barnett, W. (1989). Work group demography, social integration, and turnover. *Administrative Science Quarterly, 34*, 21–37.

O'Reilly, C. A. III, Chatman, J. A., & Caldwell, D. F. (1991). People and organizational culture: A profile comparison approach to assessing person-organization fit. *Academy of Management Journal, 34*, 487–516.

O'Reilly, C. A., III, Williams, K. Y., & Barsade, S. (1998). Group demography and innovation: Does diversity help? In D. H. Gruenfeld (Ed.), *Composition: Research on managing groups and teams* (Vol. 1, pp. 183–207). Stamford, CT: JAI Press, Inc.

Pelled, L. H. (1996). Demographic diversity, conflict, work group outcomes: An intervening process theory. *Organization Science, 7*, 615–631.

Pelled, L. H., Eisenhardt, K. M., & Xin, K. R. (1999). Exploring the black box. An analysis of work group diversity, conflict and performance. *Administrative Science Quarterly, 44*, 1–28.

Pfeffer, J., & O'Reilly, C. A. (1987). Hospital demography and turnover among nurses. *Industrial Relations, 26*, 158–173.

Phillips, K. W. (2003). The effects of categorically based expectations on minority influence: The importance of congruence. *Society for Personality and Social Psychology, 29*(1), 3–13.

Phillips, K. W., & Loyd, D. L. (2005). *When surface and deep-level diversity meet: The effects of dissenting group members.* Chicago: Northwestern University.

Phillips, K. W., Mannix, E. A., Neale, M. A., & Gruenfeld, D. H. (2004). Diverse groups and information sharing: The effects of congruent ties. *Journal of Experimental Social Psychology, 40,* 497–510.

Polzer, J. T., Milton, L. P., & Swann, W. B., Jr. (2002). Capitalizing on diversity: Interpersonal congruence in small work groups. *Administrative Science Quarterly, 47*(2), 296–324.

Pool, J. (1976). Coalition formation in small groups with incomplete communication networks. *Journal of Personality and Social Psychology, 34*(1), 82–91.

Reichers, A., & Schneider, B. (1990). Climate and culture: An evolution of constructs. In B. Schneider (Ed.), *Organizational climate and culture.* San Francisco: Jossey-Bass.

Rink, F., & Ellemers, N. (2006). *The cost and benefits of work, style, diversity, and informational diversity on work process and work outcomes in task groups: A multimethod study.* Leiden, the Netherlands: Leiden University.

Riordan, C. M., & Shore, L. M. (1997). Demographic diversity and employee attitudes: An empirical examination of relational demography within work units. *Journal of Applied Psychology, 82*(3), 342–358.

Roccas, S., & Brewer, M. B. (2002). Social identity complexity. *Personality and Social Review, 6,* 88–106.

Rousseau, D. (1990). Normative beliefs in fund-raising organizations: Linking culture to organizational performance and individual responses. *Group & Organization Studies, 15,* 448.

Schopler, J., Insko, C. A., Graetz, K. A., Drigotas, S. M., & Smith, V. A. (1991). The generality of the individual-group discontinuity effect: Variations in positivity-negativity of outcomes, players' relative power, and magnitude of outcomes. *Personality and Social Psychology Bulletin, 17,* 612–624.

Schweiger, D. M., Sandberg, W., & Rechner, P. (1989). Experiential effects of dialectical injury, devil's advocacy, and consensus approaches to strategic decision making. *Academy of Management Journal, 32,* 745–772.

Shaw, J. B. (2004). The development and analysis of a measure of group "faultlines." *Organizational Research Methods, 7*(1), 66–100.

Simons, T. L., & Peterson, R. S. (2000). Task conflict and relationship conflict in top management teams: The pivotal role of intragroup trust. *Journal of Applied Psychology, 85,* 102–111.

Stevenson, W. B., Pearce, J. L., & Porter, L. W. (1985). The concept of "coalition" in organizational theory and research. *Academy of Management Review, 10,* 256–268.

Strauss, G. (1964). Work-flow frictions, interfunctional rivalry, and professionalism: A case study of purchasing agents. *Human Organization,* 137–149.

Swann, W. B., Polzer, J. T., Seyle, D. C., & Ko, S. J. (2004). Finding value in diversity: Verification of personal and social self-views in diverse groups. *Academy of Management Review, 29*(1), 9–27.

Tajfel, H., & Turner, J. C. (1986). The social identity theory of intergroup behavior. In S. Worchel & W. G. Austin (Eds.), *Psychology of intergroup relations* (pp. 7–24). Chicago: Nelson-Hall.

Thatcher, S. M., & Jehn, K. A. (1998). A model of group diversity profiles and categorization processes in bicultural organizational teams. In D. H. Gruenfeld (Ed.), *Composition: research on managing groups and teams: Vol. 1* (11th ed., pp. 11–20). Stamford, CT: JAI Press, Inc.

Thatcher, S. M. B., Jehn, K. A., & Zanutto, E. (2003). Cracks in diversity research: The effects of faultlines on conflict and performance. *Group Decision and Negotiation, 12,* 217–241.

Thomas, D. A., & Ely, R. J. (1996). Making differences matter: A new paradigm for managing diversity. *Harvard Business Review, 74*(5), 79–91.

Tsui, A. S., Egan, T. D., & O'Reilly, C. (1992). Being different: Relational demography and organizational attachment. *Administrative Science Quarterly, 37,* 549–577.

Tsui, A. S., Egan, T. D., & Xin (1995). Diversity in organizations: Lessons from demography research. In M. M. Chemers & S. Oskamp (Eds), *The Claremont symposium on applied social psychology: Vol. 8: Diversity in organizations: New perspectives for a changing workplace* (pp. 191–219). Thousand Oaks, CA: Sage Publications, Inc.

Tsui, A. S., & Gutek, B. A. (1999). *Demographic differences in organizations: Current research and future directions.* Lanham, MD: Lexington Books.

Turner, J. C. (1987). *Rediscovering the social group: A self-categorization theory.* Oxford, U.K.: Basil Blackwell.

Tziner, A., & Eden, D. (1985). The effects of crew composition on crew performance: Does the whole equal the sum of its parts? *Journal of Applied Psychology, 70,* 85–93.

Vanbeselaere, N. (2000). The treatment of relevant and irrelevant outgroups in minimal group situations with crossed categorizations. *The Journal of Social Psychology, 140,* 515–26.

Van Knippenberg, D., De Dreu, C. K. W., & Homan, A. C. (2004). Work group diversity and group performance: An integrative model and research agenda. *Journal of Applied Psychology, 89,* 1008–1022.

Von Glinow, M., Shapiro, D. L., & Brett, J. M. (2004). Can we talk, and should we? Managing emotional conflict in multicultural teams. *Academy of Management Review, 29*(4), 578–592.

Wagner, W. G., Pfeffer, J., & O'Reilly, C. A. (1984). Organizational demography and turnover in top management groups. *Administrative Science Quarterly, 29*(1), 74–92.

Watson, W. E., Kumar, K., & Michaelsen, L. K. (1993). Cultural diversity's impact on interaction process and performance: Comparing homogeneous and diverse task groups. *Academy of Management Journal, 36,* 590–602.

Webber, S., & Donahue, L. (2001). Impact of highly and less job-related diversity on work group cohesion and performance: A meta-analysis. *Journal of Management, 27,* 141–162.

Wharton, A., & Baron, J. (1987). So happy together? The impact of gender segregation on men at work. *American Sociological Review, 52,* 574–587.

Wiersema, M., & Bird, A. (1993). Organizational demography in Japan: Group heterogeneity, individual dissimilarity, and top management team turnover. *Academy of Management Journal, 36,* 996–1025.

Wildschut, T., Insko, C. A., & Gaertner, L. (2002). Intragroup social influence and intergroup competition. *Journal of Personality and Social Psychology, 82,* 975–992.

Williams, K., & O'Reilly, C. A. (1998). Demography and diversity in organizations: A review of 40 years of research. In B. M. Staw & L. L. Cummings (Eds.), *Research in organizational behavior* (Vol. 20, pp. 77–140). Oxford, U.K.: Elsevier Science, Inc.

Wit, A. P., & Kerr, N. L. (2002). "Me versus just us versus us all" categorization and cooperation in nested social dilemmas. *Journal of Personality and Social Psychology, 83,* 616–637.

Wittenbaum, G. M., & Stasser, G. (1996). Management of information in small groups. In J. L. Nye & A. M. Brower (Eds.), *What's social about social cognition? Social cognition research in small groups* (pp. 3–28). Thousand Oaks, CA: Sage.

Wood, W., Lundgren, S., Ouellette, J. A., Busceme, S., & Blackstone, T. (1994). Minority influence: A meta-analytic review of social influence processes. *Psychological Bulletin, 115,* 327.

Zanutto, E., Bezrukova, K., & Jehn, K. (2005). *Measuring group faultline strength and distance.* Philadelphia: University of Pennsylvania.

Zenger, T. R., & Lawrence, B. S. (1989). Organizational demography: The differential effects of age and tenure distributions on technical communication. *Academy of Management Journal, 32,* 353–376.

7

Workplace Aggression and Conflict: Constructs, Commonalities, and Challenges for Future Inquiry

JANA L. RAVER AND JULIAN BARLING
Queen's University

In recent years, scholars and practitioners alike have shown a great interest in understanding various negative acts in the workplace. These negative acts include behaviors such as making offensive remarks, threatening others, isolating an individual so he or she has difficulty working, harshly criticizing others, making obscene gestures, giving someone the "silent treatment," failing to transmit information, physical assault, and theft from other employees, among others. Scholars have recognized that despite the seemingly endless list of negative acts, these behaviors possess many commonalities. As such, constructs such as *workplace aggression*—e.g., behaviors by individuals to harm others with whom they work (Neuman & Baron, 1996)—have been proposed to encompass a wide array of negative acts at work. Workplace aggression and its relationship with conflict at work is the focus of this chapter.

A review of the recent literature on workplace aggression reveals that there is little grounding within the organizational conflict literature (for notable exceptions, see Andersson & Pearson, 1999; Aquino, 2000; Keashly & Nowell, 2003; Zapf & Gross, 2001). This is unfortunate because decades of research and theory on conflict and conflict resolution can offer valuable insights into this emerging body of research. What has emerged in recent years are two parallel literatures that often address similar questions about antecedents, processes, and outcomes of negative interpersonal relations at work. We argue that one could learn a great deal from greater cross-fertilization between these areas of research.

The purpose of this chapter is to review the nature of workplace aggression, to explore its overlap with conflict in organizations, and to provide several avenues for future inquiry based upon insights that can be gleaned from the integration of these two literatures. We begin with a review of construct definitions from the literature on the "dark side of the workplace" (e.g., workplace aggression and related constructs), highlighting their similarities and differences. We then examine the extant literature on the antecedents and consequences of workplace aggression. Following this, we detail commonalities and distinctions between the literatures on workplace aggression and conflict, and based upon this review, we conclude with several challenges for future inquiry on workplace aggression and conflict.

DEFINING WORKPLACE AGGRESSION AND RELATED CONSTRUCTS

A large number of constructs that capture an array of aggressive, deviant, counterproductive, hostile, abusive, bullying, harassing, and/ or uncivil actions at work have been proposed over the past 10–15 years. This construct proliferation has led to a confusing state of affairs in which many scholars are studying virtually identical employee behaviors but are using different terminology (Spector & Fox, 2005). This is not unusual for new constructs in the organizational sciences. As noted by Reichers and Schneider (1990), new fields of research must go through a first stage of introducing and elaborating upon constructs, as well as developing measures and exploring correlates. The second stage is characterized by researchers evaluating and augmenting the body of knowledge, including the investigation of mediators and moderators. Research on workplace aggression and related constructs is currently at this stage. Much of the published research has focused upon correlates, yet research on more complex questions is beginning to emerge. Reichers and Schneider (1990) noted that it is only during the third stage that scholars begin to use a common set of terminology and consolidate the existing research findings. One goal of the current chapter is to help move scholarship on workplace aggression to the next stage.

In an attempt to distinguish clearly between the "dark side of the workplace" constructs, we provide definitions for many of the most frequently studied constructs in this literature (see Table 7.1). We also summarize distinctions between these constructs across several dimensions (see Table 7.2). Several excellent reviews devoted to these constructs and the ways in which they differ exist (see Bennett & Robinson, 2003; Fox & Spector, 2005; Kidwell & Martin, 2005; O'Leary-Kelly, Duffy, & Griffin, 2000; Robinson & Greenberg, 1998); thus, we only briefly describe these distinctions and refer readers to these sources for additional detail. However, none of the prior construct reviews included conflict at work. This is an important

TABLE 7.1
Definitions of "Dark Side of the Workplace" Constructs

Construct label	Definition
Workplace Aggression	Any form of behavior directed by one or more persons in a workplace toward the goal of harming one or more others in that workplace (or the entire organization) in ways the intended targets are motivated to avoid. (Neuman & Baron, 2005, p. 18; see also Greenberg & Barling, 1999; Neuman & Baron, 1996, 1998)
Counterproductive Work Behavior	Volitional acts that harm or intend to harm organizations and their stakeholders (e.g., clients, coworkers, customers, and supervisors). (Spector & Fox, 2005, pp. 151–152; see also Fox, Spector, & Miles, 2001; Sackett, 2002; Spector & Fox, 2002)
Employee Deviance	Voluntary behavior [of organizational members] that violates significant organizational norms and in doing so threatens the well-being of an organization, its members, or both (Robinson & Bennett, 1995, p. 556; see also Bennett & Robinson, 2000; Robinson & Bennett, 1997)
Revenge	An action in response to some perceived harm or wrongdoing by another party that is intended to inflict damage, injury, discomfort, or punishment on the party judged responsible (Aquino, Tripp, & Bies, 2001, p. 53; see also Bies & Tripp, 2005; Bies, Tripp, & Kramer, 1997; Bradfield & Aquino, 1999)
Organizational Retaliatory Behavior	A subset of . . . negative [workplace] behaviors . . . used to punish the organization and its representatives in response to perceived unfairness (Skarlicki & Folger, 1997, p. 435; see also Folger & Skarlicki, 2005; Skarlicki, Folger & Tesluk, 1999)
Workplace Violence	Workplace violence refers only to instances [of aggression] involving direct physical assaults (Neuman & Baron, 1998, p. 393; see also Baron & Neuman, 1996; LeBlanc & Barling, 2005; LeBlanc & Kelloway, 2002).
Workplace Bullying	A person is bullied . . . when he or she feels repeatedly subjected to negative acts in the workplace, acts that the victim may find it difficult to defend themselves against (Einarsen, Raknes, & Matthiesen, 1994, p. 383; see also Hoel, Rayner, & Cooper, 1999; Leymann, 1996; Rayner & Keashly, 2005)
Emotional Abuse	Repeated hostile verbal and nonverbal behaviors (excluding physical contact) directed at one or more individuals over a period of time such that the target's sense of self as a competent worker and person is negatively affected (Keashly & Harvey, 2005, p. 205; see also Keashly, 1998; Keashly & Jagatic, 2003; Keashly, Trott, & MacLean, 1994)
Workplace Incivility	Low-intensity deviant behavior with ambiguous intent to harm the target, in violation of workplace norms for mutual respect. Uncivil behaviors are characteristically rude and discourteous, displaying a lack of regard for others (Andersson & Pearson, 1999, p. 457; see also Cortina, Magley, Williams, & Langhout, 2001; Pearson, Andersson, & Porath, 2005)
Abusive Supervision	Subordinates' perceptions of the extent to which supervisors engage in the sustained display of hostile verbal and nonverbal behaviors, excluding physical contact (Tepper, 2000, p. 178; see also Tepper, Duffy, & Shaw, 2001; Zellars, Tepper, & Duffy, 2002)
Conflict	The process that begins when one party perceives that the other has negatively affected, or is about to negatively affect, something that he or she cares about (Thomas, 1992, p. 653) Three features shared by definitions of conflict: (a) Interdependence among parties, (b) perception by at least one of the parties that there is some degree of opposition or incompatibility among the goals of the parties, and (c) some form of interaction between the parties (Putnam & Poole, 1987)

TABLE 7.2
Summary of "Dark Side of the Workplace" Constructs and Their Distinctions

Construct label	Nature of behavior	Nature of actor	Nature of target	Actor–Target power differential	Motive	Duration of behavior	Violation of norms	Outcome(s) of behavior
Workplace Aggression	Full range of behaviors & severity	Org. insider at any level	Individual, org. (as a social collective), or stakeholders	None required	Intent to harm target	Episodic	Not required	Negative outcomes for targets
Counterproductive Work Behavior	Full range of behaviors & severity	Org. insider at any level	Individual, org., or stakeholders	None required	Intent to harm target or purposeful action that resulted in harm	Episodic	Not required	Negative outcomes for targets and org.
Employee Deviance	Full range of behaviors & severity	Org. insider at any level	Individual, org., or stakeholders	None required	Intent to harm target or purposeful action that resulted in harm	Episodic	Required	Negative outcomes for targets, but may have positive consequences
Revenge	Full range of behaviors & severity	Org. insider at any level	Individual, org., or stakeholders	None required	Intent to harm target	Episodic	Not required	Negative outcomes for targets, but may have positive consequences
Organizational Retaliatory Behavior	Full range of behaviors & severity	Org. insider at any level	Individual, org., or stakeholders	None required	Intent to harm target	Episodic	Not required	Negative outcomes for targets, but may have positive consequences
Workplace Violence	Physical and severe behaviors only	Anyone	Anyone	None required	Harm to target must be inflicted, not merely intended	Episodic	Not required	Negative outcomes for targets
Workplace Bullying	Full range of behaviors & severity (but rarely physical)	Org. insider at any level	Individual only	Required—may be formal or informal power	No intent to harm required (target's perspective)	Persistent/long term	Not required	Negative outcomes for targets
Emotional Abuse	Full range of behaviors & severity except physical contact	Org. insider at any level	Individual only	Required—may be formal or informal power	No intent to harm required (target's perspective)	Persistent/long term	Not required, but a standard of conduct violated	Negative outcomes for targets
Workplace Incivility	Mild severity only; physical contact excluded	Org. insider at any level	Individual only	None required	Ambiguous intent to harm (target's perspective)	Episodic	Required	Negative outcomes for targets
Abusive Supervision	Full range of behaviors & severity except physical contact	Org. insider and must be target's superior	Individual only	Required—formal position power	No intent to harm required (target's perspective)	Sustained	Not required	Negative outcomes for targets
Conflict	Full range of behaviors & severity	Anyone	Anyone	None required	No intent to harm required	May be episodic or sustained	Not required	May have positive or negative outcomes for each party

Note: These construct characteristics are summarized based upon the publications referenced in Table 7.1.

omission; thus, we include "conflict" in Table 7.1 and Table 7.2. Through-out the remaining sections of this chapter, we elaborate upon insights that can be gained by integrating scholarship on aggression and conflict.[1]

Conceptual Distinctions between "Dark Side of the Workplace" Constructs

The first dimension described in Table 7.2 is the *nature of the behavior* and is based on Buss' (1961) typology of aggression and Robinson and Bennett's (1995) distinction between minor versus serious acts. Specifically, aggressive acts can be (a) physical versus verbal (e.g., physical assault vs. verbal insults), (b) actively enacted versus passively withheld (e.g., lying to harm someone vs. passively withholding needed information), and (c) directly adminis-tered to target versus indirectly administered through others or through something the target values (e.g., yelling in someone's face vs. spreading rumors or failing to support the target's ideas; Buss, 1961). Robinson and Bennett (1995) demonstrated that acts of employee deviance vary from relatively minor (e.g., spreading rumors) to severe (e.g., physical assault). As seen in Table 7.2, most of the constructs include behaviors that span the full range of possible acts, including physical, verbal, active, passive, direct, indirect, minor, and severe. However, this is not the case for abusive super-vision, emotional abuse, and incivility, which specifically exclude physical contact. Workplace bullying does not specifically exclude physical contact but it is rare. With regard to severity, incivility focuses upon mild acts only, while violence focuses primarily upon physical and severe acts.

The next three columns in Table 7.2 distinguish between each of the con-structs in terms of the actor, the target, and the relationship between them. The *nature of the actor* details whether the actor is located within or outside of the organization, and whether he/she has a relationship with the tar-get. Most of the constructs include acts committed by any organizational member, while abusive supervision requires that the actor be the target's superior (Tepper, 2000), and workplace violence can be enacted by perpetra-tors inside or outside the organization (LeBlanc & Barling, 2005). The *nature of the target* is based, in part, on Robinson and Bennett's (1995) discovery of an interpersonal versus organizational dimension along which deviant acts vary, yet also recognizes that targets can include stakeholders of the organization (e.g., customers and suppliers). The constructs can be grouped into two main categories on this dimension (see Table 7.2): those that focus

---

[1] There are other "dark side" constructs that have been discussed in the literature but are not covered in the current review (e.g., organizational misbehavior, orga-nizationally motivated aggression, antisocial behavior, dysfunctional behavior, social undermining, and victimization). We focus upon behavioral constructs that have appeared with high frequency in journals relevant to I/O psychology. Read-ers should refer to construct reviews and edited volumes for additional detail (e.g., Bennett & Robinson, 2003; Fox & Spector, 2005; Griffin & Lopez, 2005; Kidwell & Martin, 2005; O'Leary-Kelly, Duffy, & Griffin, 2000; Robinson & Greenberg, 1998).

on *actors* engaging in negative acts that target individuals, the organization as a whole, or stakeholders; and those that are studied from *targets'* perspectives and thus include only individual targets in the definitions. Workplace aggression includes organization-targeted acts, yet these acts must be directed against the organization as a social collective because it is not possible to aggress against an inanimate object (Neuman & Baron, 2005). The *power differential between the actor and the target* indicates whether the construct definition stipulates that there is a difference in power (formal or informal) between them. Although most of the constructs do not require power differentials, abusive supervision requires that the actor have formal position power over the target, and both bullying and emotional abuse require that targets have difficulty defending themselves against the actor, even if the actor holds no formal power over them.

The *motive for the behavior* describes whether the behavior is driven by an underlying motive, particularly "intent to harm." Constructs studied from the target's perspective exclude intent because it is difficult for targets to know the actor's actual intent, and there are practical constraints on including it (e.g., if bullying definitions included actor intent, no grievances or legal remedies could be pursued unless the bully admitted intent to harm). In contrast, workplace aggression, organizational retaliatory behavior, and revenge require that the actor intend to harm the target. Counterproductive work behavior (CWB) and deviance include both behaviors intended to harm and purposeful (nonaccidental) behaviors that inadvertently result in harm.

The final three columns describe details regarding the behaviors that constitute each of the constructs and their outcomes. *Duration of the behavior* indicates whether the behaviors must persist across time or if they may be episodic in nature. Workplace bullying and emotional abuse involve persistent negative acts, and abusive supervision has been described as "sustained" negative acts (Tepper, 2000), while the other constructs in Table 7.2 can be episodic. *Violation of norms* indicates whether the construct definition requires that significant organizational norms be violated. Only employee deviance and workplace incivility require that organizational norms be violated. Finally, *outcomes of the behavior* describes whether the construct stipulates a particular outcome as a result of the behavior, and if so, the nature of that outcome. Most of the constructs have negative effects for targets, but employee deviance (Kidwell & Martin, 2005; Warren, 2003), revenge (Bies & Tripp, 2005), and retaliatory behaviors (Folger & Skarlicki, 2005) can have positive consequences as well (e.g., sanctioning). CWB by definition is contrary to organizations' legitimate interests (Sackett, 2002), and therefore is presumed to have negative consequences for individuals and for the organization as a whole.

Empirical Overlap between "Dark Side of the Workplace" Constructs

Table 7.2 lists conceptual differences between the "dark side" constructs; however, many of these distinctions have been ignored in their operationalizations. Thus, there is strong empirical overlap between these constructs such that scholars seem to be studying a highly similar set of behaviors in most cases but just relying on different conceptual definitions and labels, as numerous examples show. Spector and Fox (2005) demonstrated how the three measures of employee deviance, workplace aggression, and retaliatory behavior have several, virtually identical items. Also, measures of "mild" constructs (e.g., incivility; Cortina, Magley, Williams, & Langhout, 2001) contain items that are highly similar to the "mild" items in measures that assess a full range of acts (e.g., workplace aggression; Glomb, 2001; Neuman & Keashly, 2003). There are also cases where the construct of interest has been operationalized by borrowing items or entire scales from similar constructs (e.g., Robinson & O'Leary-Kelly's, 1998, antisocial behavior measure used to assess aggression; Douglas & Martinko, 2001). Furthermore, some constructs have intent to harm as part of their definitions, yet we are not aware of any research that has assessed intent as part of these constructs' measures. Intent is implied conceptually but not assessed empirically. Similarly, deviance and incivility include norm violation as part of their definition, yet their measures do not actually assess whether the behaviors violate norms, and are thus more likely to be measuring CWB than deviance. The empirical overlap between constructs, and the implications of this overlap are even more apparent because research has demonstrated nearly identical correlates across constructs.

Current Focus upon Workplace Aggression

We adopt Neuman and Baron's (2005) conceptualization of *workplace aggression* (or simply *aggression*) as a construct that encompasses most negative interpersonal acts at work that are described in various "dark side" constructs. It has the advantage of including all possible acts that intend to harm others in the workplace, these acts can be enacted by any organizational member and be experienced by any other organizational member (or social collective), and there is no necessity for target–actor power differentials, norm violations, or sustained negative acts to qualify as aggression. Another advantage of focusing on workplace aggression is that aggression does not impose a value judgment regarding the outcomes of such behaviors for the organization, whereas CWB does. Yet another advantage is that it does not require that organizational norms be violated, yet deviance does. The workplace aggression construct can be (and has been) studied equally well from the perspectives of targets or actors (e.g., Baron, Neuman, & Geddes, 1999; Glomb, 2002), which is not the case of either CWB or deviance because they are studied from the actor's perspective. Workplace aggression encompasses revenge, organizational retaliatory behaviors, and workplace violence; it also encompasses bullying, emotional abuse, abusive supervision, and in many cases, workplace incivility. CWB and employee deviance include acts that are *not* part of workplace aggression (e.g., noninterpersonal acts), but CWB and deviance also include many acts that are interpersonally aggressive (Neuman & Baron, 2005).

Two controversial and related issues—the intent to harm and the interpersonal nature of the construct—must be confronted in defining workplace aggression. Intent to harm is part of the definition, yet many well-intentioned behaviors inadvertently cause harm (Neuman & Baron, 2005). In this regard, we follow the broader social scientific literature on human aggression that includes intent to harm in the definition of aggression, thereby excluding acts that accidentally harm others but including intentional acts of harm that are not successfully carried out (e.g., Anderson & Bushman, 2002). We acknowledge that this remains a source of debate because it fails to recognize the divergent perspectives and goals of the actors involved (Felson & Tedeschi, 1993; Mummendry & Otten, 1993), and suggest that when workplace aggression is studied from the target's perspective, intent may be conceptually implied without being empirically assessed.

The definition of workplace aggression that we adopt is also interpersonal in nature (Anderson & Bushman, 2002), and excludes acts intended to harm inanimate objects. It is possible for employees to intend to harm the organization as a social collective that represents many individuals or upper management (Neuman & Baron, 2005). In contrast, when the goal is to research acts not directed toward any other individual or social group (e.g., unethical decision making, lying about hours worked, putting forth minimal effort, or breaking equipment), it is more appropriate to study these acts under the rubric of CWB or employee deviance.

In sum, workplace aggression is an overarching construct for being able to explore the dark side of employees' interpersonal relations. We return to Table 7.1 and Table 7.2 to explore the overlap between workplace aggression and conflict in the sections below, but we first review the extant empirical literature on workplace aggression.

EMPIRICAL RESEARCH ON WORKPLACE AGGRESSION

The empirical research on workplace aggression and related constructs has emerged along two distinct paths: examinations of (a) the predictors of enacting aggression and (b) the outcomes of experiencing aggression. Several recent studies have now moved beyond examining correlates and focused on mediated or moderated models of the antecedents and/or consequences of aggression. A summary of the key findings in each of these areas follows.

Predictors of Enacting Workplace Aggression

Research has highlighted several situational factors and individual difference variables that predict propensity to enact workplace aggression. With regard to situational predictors, some antecedents reflect features of the job or organizational context, whereas others are more appropriately considered as employees' responses to the social context (cf. Neuman & Baron, 1998). Specifically, job and organizational context factors that predict enacting aggression include job-related stressors (Chen & Spector, 1992; Fox & Spector, 1999; Miles, Borman, Spector, & Fox, 2002; Spector & Fox, 2005), organizational change (Baron & Neuman, 1996), absence of charismatic leadership (Hepworth & Towler, 2004), poor leader–member exchange relationship quality (Townsend, Phillips, & Elkins, 2000), workplace surveillance (Greenberg & Barling, 1999), and organizational or group norms that support aggression (Glomb & Liao, 2003; Robinson & O'Leary-Kelly, 1998). There is also some evidence that levels of violence in the larger community predict workplace aggression (Dietz, Robinson, Folger, Baron, & Schulz, 2003). Predictors of aggression that reflect employees' responses to their social context include perceptions of injustice (Greenberg & Barling, 1999; Skarlicki & Folger, 1997; Skarlicki, Folger, & Tesluk, 1999), state negative emotions (Fitness, 2000; Fox, Spector, & Miles, 2001; Glomb, 2002; Lee & Allen, 2002; Spector & Fox, 2005), and having been the target of aggression (Glomb, 2001; Raver, 2004).

Individual difference variables that predict engaging in aggression include dispositional hostility (trait anger; Douglas & Martinko, 2001; Hepworth & Towler, 2004), type A personality (Baron et al., 1999; Holmes & Will, 1985), attributional style (Douglas & Martinko, 2001; Martinko & Zellars, 1998), negative affectivity (Skarlicki et al., 1999), lack of self-control (Hepworth & Towler, 2004), history of enacting aggression (Greenberg & Barling, 1999; Jockin, Arvey, & McGue, 2001), positive attitudes toward revenge (Douglas & Martinko, 2001), and substance and/or alcohol abuse (Greenberg & Barling, 1999; Jockin et al., 2001). Measures to assess employees' propensity to engage in aggression (James, McIntyre, Glisson, Green, & Patton, 2005), revenge (Sommers, Schell, & Vodanovich, 2002), and CWB (Lanyon & Goodstein, 2004) have also been validated.

Research has begun to explore interactions among these predictors of aggression. For example, Skarlicki and Folger (1997) showed interactions among distributive, procedural, and interactional justice that predicted retaliation, which were further qualified by negative affectivity and agreeableness (Skarlicki et al., 1999). Greenberg and Barling (1999) found that situational (e.g., procedural justice) and individual (e.g., alcohol consumption) factors interacted to predict aggression against coworkers and subordinates (see Colbert, Mount, Harter, Witt, & Barrick, 2004). Research also showed some support for the notion that control over the environment moderates the effects of job stressors on CWB (Fox, Spector, & Miles, 2001). Inness, Barling, and Turner (2005) recently investigated both individual difference and situational predictors of aggression in people working two jobs. They showed that situational variables (e.g., interactional justice and abusive supervision) explained proportionally more of the variance in enacting aggression at each job than did individual differences (e.g., self-esteem and history of aggression). The context-specific nature of these findings is consistent with results from a recent meta-analysis on the antecedents of workplace aggression (Hershcovis et al., 2007).

Only a few studies have explored more basic psychological processes involved in workplace aggression incidents. Bradfield and Aquino (1999) proposed and found attributions of blame as antecedents to enacting revenge, as mediated by revenge cognitions; offense severity influenced blame attributions. Aquino, Tripp, and Bies (2001) also found that blame was an antecedent to revenge, but the relationship was moderated by the victim–offender relative and absolute status. Finally, Fox et al. (2001) proposed a tested an integrative model in which state negative affect mediated the effects of justice perceptions on interpersonal and organizational CWB.

Outcomes of Experiencing Workplace Aggression

Research from the target's perspective has demonstrated that experiencing workplace aggression is associated with psychological outcomes, physiological outcomes, negative job attitudes, and negative work-related behaviors (for reviews, see Keashly & Harvey, 2005; Spector & Bruk-Lee, chapter 9, this volume). Psychological outcomes associated with experiencing aggression include depression (Tepper, 2000); anxiety (Keashly, Trott, & MacLean, 1994; Tepper, 2000); stress, helplessness, and frustration (Ashforth, 1997); low self-esteem (Ashforth 1997; Vartia, 1996); emotional exhaustion (Tepper, 2000); poor general psychological well-being (Cortina et al., 2001; LeBlanc & Kelloway, 2002; Mikkelsen & Einarsen, 2001; Zapf, Knorz, & Kulla, 1996); fear (Barling, Rogers, & Kelloway, 2001); and low life satisfaction (Tepper, 2000). Physiological outcomes include somatic complaints (Duffy, Ganster, & Pagon, 2002; Mikkelsen & Einarsen, 2001), low overall health satisfaction (Cortina et al., 2001), and poor psychosomatic well-being (LeBlanc & Kelloway, 2002). Negative job attitudes include low job satisfaction (Cortina et al., 2001; Keashly et al., 1994; Tepper, 2000), low commitment to the organization (Ashforth, 1997; Duffy et al., 2002; LeBlanc & Kelloway, 2002; Tepper, 2000), perceptions of injustice (Tepper, 2000; Zellars et al., 2002), and low job involvement (Ashforth, 1997). Research on behavioral outcomes has shown that targets of aggression report greater intentions to leave the organization (Ashforth, 1997; Cortina et al., 2001; Keashly et al., 1994; Keashly, Harvey, & Hunter, 1997; Leymann, 1996; Rayner & Hoel, 1997; Tepper, 2000) and are likely to engage in problem drinking (Richman, Rospenda, Flaherty, & Freels, 2001; Richman et al., 1999; Rospenda, Richman, Wislar, & Flaherty, 2000). Evidence regarding other behaviors associated with aggression is starting to emerge, and there is evidence that targets of aggression engage in counterproductive work behaviors (Duffy et al., 2002; Raver, 2004) and have high levels of work–family conflict (Raver, 2004; Tepper, 2000).

Evidence on moderators and mediators of these outcomes of aggression is emerging. For example, Duffy et al. (2002) assessed experiences of aggression and social support from supervisors and coworkers, to determine whether social support buffers the negative effects of aggression. They found that receiving support and aggression from the same source (e.g., supervisors) actually made negative outcomes *more* likely. Tepper (2000) demonstrated that justice perceptions mediate the relationship between abusive supervision and negative personal outcomes; these negative personal outcomes were accentuated when targets had low job mobility. Finally, Raver (2004) proposed and tested a more comprehensive model of behaviors associated with experiencing aggression, including interpersonal justice perceptions and state negative affect as mediators, and job characteristics, target characteristics, and perpetrator characteristics as moderators of the effects.

Now that we have delineated the conceptual and empirical nature of the "dark side of the workplace constructs," explained our current focus upon workplace aggression, and detailed the current status of empirical research on workplace aggression, we turn to a consideration of the overlap between workplace aggression and conflict in organizations.

DEFINING CONFLICT AND EXPLORING ITS RELATIONSHIP WITH WORKPLACE AGGRESSION

In their review, Putnam and Poole (1987) concluded that there are three shared aspects of most conflict definitions: (a) interdependence among parties, (b) perception by at least one of the parties that there is some degree of opposition or incompatibility among the goals of the parties, and (c) some form of interaction between the parties. Thomas (1992) integrated these features into a synthesized definition of conflict, which we adopt in this chapter: "The process that begins when one party perceives that the other has negatively affected, or is about to negatively affect, something that he or she cares about" (p. 653).

Several similarities and distinctions are apparent based upon the definitions of workplace aggression and conflict (Table 7.1) and the distinctions detailed in Table 7.2. With regard to similarities, both conflict and aggression involve an interaction between two or more parties who are interdependent in some way. Also, both constructs refer to a situation where at least one party perceives he or she is at odds with the other. As such, conflict and aggression may be unilateral, bilateral, or multilateral. In addition, both aggression and conflict can be manifest through the enactment of a wide variety of different behaviors. Finally, in organizational settings, the parties involved in conflict and aggression are similar; one party is typically an organizational member at any level, and the other party is an individual, the organization, or a stakeholder. With regard to differences between workplace aggression and conflict, aggression conceptually entails *intent to harm*, whereas conflict does not. In addition, aggression entails *negative actions* that the target is motivated to avoid, whereas conflict may be task oriented with no relationship-oriented conflict involved. Finally, aggression may be enacted as a discrete action or it may be enacted as part of an ongoing exchange, whereas conflict typically implies a *process* of exchanges between parties.

In sum, *conflict* is a broader term that encompasses workplace aggression. In other words, workplace aggression may be construed as a particular form of conflict at work. However, not all conflict involves aggression. If workplace aggression is indeed a form of conflict at work, it is possible to draw from theoretical, methodological, and practical insights from the organizational conflict literature to inform and advance our knowledge of workplace aggression.[2,3]

WHY THE DISCONNECT? EXPLORING THE DISTINCTIONS BETWEEN THE WORKPLACE AGGRESSION AND CONFLICT LITERATURES

If workplace aggression is a form of conflict at work, why has there been so little cross-fertilization between these areas of research? Why is there not greater representation of workplace aggression research within journals (e.g., *International Journal of Conflict Management*) and professional associations (e.g., International Association for Conflict Management; Conflict Division of the Academy of Management) devoted to conflict? In this section, we begin to explore some of the reasons behind the disconnect between workplace aggression and conflict in organizations.

Nature of Outcomes

The literature on workplace aggression emerged largely in the early 1990s in response to increasing concerns regarding employee violence and several widely publicized incidents of workplace homicides (e.g., U.S. Postal Service). Violence is a severe and infrequent form of workplace aggression; yet

---

[2] Note that aggression is not the same thing as an escalated conflict. Aggression can exist without escalation. For example, an individual might engage in an act of aggression without any provocation or escalatory sequences (e.g., *predatory aggression* rather than *dispute-related aggression*; Felson & Tedeschi, 1993). Escalation can also exist without aggression. For example, a negotiation party might begin to use more severe tactics such as threats to get what he wants (e.g., time pressure or pursuing alternative deals), yet there may be no interpersonal ill will or intent to harm the other party. Thus, while escalation and aggression are related, and there are many cases where escalatory conflict spirals do result in aggression (for additional detail, see Pruitt, chapter 8, this volume), these constructs are not identical.

[3] We do not intend to imply that all studies on workplace aggression are studies of organizational conflict. As noted by Bies and Tripp (2005), the term *conflict* may be too broad of a label for the specific phenomena that scholars in this area are investigating. We agree that it can be useful to maintain narrower construct labels to more clearly define the construct of interest. However, we believe that studies of workplace aggression fit within the domain of organizational conflict and that scholars in both areas would benefit from greater attention to insights that can be gained through greater cross-fertilization.

as research in this domain proceeded, it became clear that less severe forms of aggression occur far more regularly at work. Scholars drew from research and theory on human aggression in many domains (e.g., social psychology, family violence, and criminology) and began to explore the factors that predict workplace aggression (Barling, 1996; Baron & Neuman, 1996; Neuman & Baron, 1996). A second stream of literature that developed simultaneously, predominantly in Europe, focused on workplace bullying (or mobbing) and its negative consequences for employees who are subjected to aggressive acts over a period of time (Einarsen et al., 1994; Leymann, 1996). These include posttraumatic stress disorder, job loss, and even permanent exclusion from the job market (e.g., Davenport, Schwartz, & Elliott, 2002; Leymann, 1996). Because these studies show that experiencing aggression has negative effects, there have been few discussions of how workplace aggression may have positive outcomes. A few authors have argued that although aggression may harm the direct target, there may be second-order positive effects for others in the social context or for the organization (e.g., Bies & Tripp, 2005; Bies, Tripp, & Kramer, 1997; Warren, 2003). Still, most research on workplace aggression continues to focus on negative outcomes.

In contrast, conflict can produce positive benefits and there has been a strong emphasis upon constructive aspects of conflict in organizations (De Dreu & Van de Vliert, 1997). Managers and practitioners have long been encouraged to stimulate "functional" conflict in their organizations, such as task-related debates and discussions to motivate change (e.g., Robbins, 1978). Although it is recognized that conflict can have negative outcomes, particularly if based upon personality disagreements (discussed in more detail in the following section), one of the most important recent contributions of the conflict literature has been to enhance understanding of the conditions under which conflict exerts positive outcomes (e.g., De Dreu, 1997; Jehn, 1995; Jehn & Mannix, 2001).

Task Versus Relationship Focus

One distinction between the conflict and aggression literatures deals with the nature of the incompatibility between the parties. Conflict scholars distinguish between conflicts about people's relationships (i.e., *relationship conflict*) and conflicts about the task (i.e., *task conflicts*; Amason, 1996; De Dreu & Weingart, 2003; Jehn, 1995, 1997; Pinkley, 1990; Wall & Nolan, 1986). Relationship conflict has been proposed to be negative for the parties and the group context in which they occur, whereas task conflict can stimulate a productive and innovative group and thus have positive consequences. The positive effects of task conflict have been questioned in a recent meta-analysis (De Dreu & Weingart, 2003), yet the available evidence supports the distinction between task- and relationship-based conflict.

In contrast, aggression involves the intent to harm another party, which the other party is motivated to avoid, and thus aggression is a form of relationship conflict by definition. In practice, however, workplace aggression may not always appear to be a relationship conflict because people can harm others through indirect forms of aggression (Buss, 1961), such as by openly disagreeing with their ideas, critiquing their work, or trying to block their goal progress. Thus, what may appear to be a task conflict on the surface may actually mask aggressive behavior. We return to this issue when considering future research questions.

Focus upon Cognition Versus Affect

The aggression literature has long emphasized emotions as both antecedents to and consequences of aggression, and as processes that mediate a range of outcomes associated with experiencing aggression. In particular, anger has long been a core focus in aggression research (Anderson & Bushman, 2002; Fitness, 2000; Glomb, 2002), so much so that aggression has been considered as a fundamental part of the experience of anger (Rubin, 1986), and trait anger (hostility) has consistently been shown to predict workplace aggression (Douglas & Martinko, 2001; Hershcovis et al., 2007). Attention to cognitions in workplace aggression has focused largely upon perceptions of injustice (e.g., Skarlicki & Folger, 1997; Skarlicki et al., 1999). Much less research has addressed other cognitions such as attributions, beliefs, intent, goals, or blame (for exceptions, see Aquino, Tripp, & Bies, 2001; Bradfield & Aquino, 1999).

The opposite is true in attempts to understand conflict and conflict resolution, where research has benefited from an emphasis on cognition and there has been less of an emphasis upon emotions. Within the cognitive tradition, negotiations are viewed as a cognitive decision-making task in which negotiators construct mental representations of the conflict situation, issues and their opponents (Neale & Bazerman, 1991; Thompson, 1990). Based within this tradition, there has been a strong emphasis upon cognitive constructs including heuristics and cognitive biases (e.g., Bazerman, 1998), conflict frames (e.g., Pinkley, 1990), mental models (e.g., Bazerman, Curhan, Moore, & Valley, 2000), and metaphors (Gelfand & McCusker, 2002), among others. Indeed, this emphasis upon cognitions during conflicts has been cited as one of the key factors essential for deciphering the "black box" of conflict processes (Dirks & Parks, 2003). However, emotions are emerging more prominently in recent studies of interpersonal conflict (e.g., Van Kleef, De Dreu, & Manstead, 2004).

Dynamic Versus Static Perspectives on Social Exchange

With few exceptions (Glomb, 2001, 2002), the conceptual and empirical literatures on workplace aggression depict people as *either* perpetrators *or* targets of aggression (Fox & Spector, 2005). Not surprisingly, there has also been virtually no empirical attention on how dyadic aggression spirals make one party a perpetrator at one moment, yet a target at the next moment (for theory on this, see Andersson & Pearson, 1999). This simplistic division of people as either actors or targets ignores the evidence from the broader literature on human aggression showing that aggression most frequently emerges from ongoing social exchanges (e.g., *dispute-related aggression*; Felson & Tedeschi, 1993).

In contrast, research and theory on conflict and conflict resolution have long recognized the existence of dynamic exchanges between parties. For example, negotiation research commonly adopts methodologies for studying exchanges of offers and counteroffers as they occur throughout negotiations or disputes. Conflict studies from a communication perspective have explored how conflicts are perpetuated through dialogue between parties. Research on conflict escalation has also evidenced this tendency toward dynamic perspectives (Pruitt, chapter 8, this volume).

Level of Analysis and Methodological Techniques

Research on workplace aggression has predominantly been conducted at the individual level, despite the existence of more than one party in aggressive exchanges, and emerging evidence that aggression is a meaningful group-level construct with outcomes that are masked by an exclusive individual-level focus (cf. Glomb & Liao, 2003; Glomb et al., 1997; Raver & Gelfand, 2005; Robinson & O'Leary-Kelly, 1998). Although aggression research implicitly refers to another party involved in the incident, there have been few attempts to involve a second party to understand dyadic processes, much less group processes. We thus know little about how multiple parties' perspectives and roles may be influencing the dynamics of aggression, or about how the social context influences aggression.

In contrast, research on conflict has been conducted at the *intra*personal, dyadic, group, intergroup, organizational, interorganizational, and cross-national levels. Conflict research methodologies are extremely diverse, including dyadic negotiation experiments, surveys of team conflict, discourse analysis, and case studies of interorganizational conflicts. One factor that distinguishes these methods from aggression research is the emphasis on assessing *dyadic* or *group* processes. For example, there is a large amount of research on *group* outcomes of task and relationship conflict, yet no comparable body of work on aggression at the group level exists. Conflict research has often recognized that the behaviors of one person in isolation of the social context in which he/she operates is not sufficient to understand the conflict at hand.

Summary

Although workplace aggression is conceptually a form of conflict at work, a substantial empirical divide remains between the constructs. We argue, however, that this discussion regarding the divide between the constructs actually provides several insights regarding opportunities for future research, especially on workplace aggression.

TOWARD A RAPPORT? OPPORTUNITIES FOR RESEARCH ON WORKPLACE AGGRESSION AND CONFLICT

Several recommendations for workplace aggression research have appeared in earlier reviews, and we reiterate the need to establish common terminology and measures for studying workplace aggression (Bies & Tripp, 2005; Neuman & Baron, 2005; Spector & Fox, 2005) and to improve survey methodologies for studying aggression while also preserving participants' anonymity (Fox & Spector, 2002; Spector & Fox, 2005). Nonetheless, our current focus is to discuss opportunities for research that derive specifically from parallels between the conflict and aggression literatures. We identify several avenues for research on workplace aggression below.

Greater Attention to Cognitive Constructs

There are several ways in which cognitive constructs can be integrated into the study of workplace aggression and we focus on attributions, cognitive biases, and conflict frames.

Cognitive Appraisals: Harm, Intent and Blame. Appraisals of whether one was harmed, whether the harm was inflicted intentionally, and who might be to blame are fundamental considerations in social psychological theorizing about conflict and aggression (Alicke, 2000; Allred, 2000; Baron, 1990; Festinger, Abel, & Sarat, 1980; Schlenker, Britt, Pennington, Murphy, & Doherty, 1994). These cognitive appraisal processes have also been detailed in theoretical models of workplace aggression (e.g., Bies et al., 1997; Folger & Skarlicki, 1998; Martinko, Gundlach, & Douglas, 2002; Martinko & Zellars, 1998; Neuman & Baron, 1996, 2005), and calls for research on cognitive appraisals appeared in early literature reviews (Neuman & Baron, 1998). It is surprising, therefore, that empirical assessments of experienced harm and perceived intent are virtually nonexistent in workplace aggression research, and only a few have studies assessed blame (e.g., Aquino et al., 2001; Bradfield & Aquino, 1999). Attributional ambiguity is the norm when one experiences a personal affront, and it is critical to determine one's understanding of *why* something occurred because appraisals determine subsequent behaviors (Allred, 2000).

In their model of blame, Tedechsi and Felson (1994) proposed that targets first determine whether the actor intended to cause them harm. If intended harm is perceived, the target then makes a judgment regarding whether the intent was justifiable (e.g., whether harm could not have been avoided); if the harm was not perceived as justifiable, blame would then be attributed. An alternative path toward attributing blame occurs when the target perceives that the actor should have foreseen that their actions would cause harm. If the target determines that the harm was foreseeable, blame will be attributed even if intent was not seen.

Within the workplace aggression literature, Bies, Tripp, and colleagues (Aquino et al., 2001; Bies & Tripp, 2005; Bies et al., 1997) argued that the process of establishing blame is critical to the sense-making process that determines whether revenge will be enacted for a perceived transgression. They noted further that blame attributions can become biased through several mechanisms such as overattributing negative acts to other's internal dispositions rather than situational features, rumination about the negative acts, and using self-serving perceptions of the nature of the exchange between parties (Bies et al., 1997).

In sum, theoretical models within the conflict and the aggression literatures suggest that attention to such cognitive processes is critical for a more comprehensive understanding of the mechanisms through which people choose to enact aggression. Future research on workplace aggression that includes the cognitive appraisals of actors engaging in aggressive acts, and those of targets who must appraise the situation before enacting a response, is critical in this regard.

Cognitive Biases.   One important advance in the cognitive tradition in negotiation in recent years has been the study of judgment biases that negotiators rely upon due to limited information processing capabilities (Bazerman, 1998; Bazerman & Carroll, 1987; Thompson, 1990). Although such heuristics are efficient, they also lead to systematically biased information processing, which can impair dispute resolution. These cognitive biases include *fixed pie perceptions* of negotiations (e.g., the belief that what is good for me must be bad for you; Thompson & Hastie, 1990), a *devaluation of partners' concessions* (Ross & Stillenger, 1991), and *self-serving* or *egocentric* perceptions of the conflict (Thompson & Loewenstein, 1992; Babcock & Loewenstein, 1997), among others (for a review, see Bazerman et al., 2000). These biases prevent negotiation partners from seeing integrative solutions and as such, maintain conflict.

Cognitive biases have not yet been studied in the realm of workplace aggression, and we believe that this could be a fruitful avenue of inquiry. For example, with regard to self-serving biases, there is substantial evidence that people have overly inflated views of themselves, which limit the likelihood of dispute resolution (De Dreu, Nauta, & Van de Vliert, 1995; Loewenstein, Issacharoff, Camerer, & Babcock, 1993). With regard to workplace aggression, self-serving biases may be one underlying reason why ambiguous personal affronts are often perceived as intentional (e.g., I don't deserve this type of treatment; You must be jealous). Fixed pie perceptions may also prevent the de-escalation of dispute-related aggression spirals—such as if both parties perceive that their interests are equal and opposite and they have absolutely nothing in common, it may be difficult or impossible to find an integrative solution. The devaluation of concessions may be another mechanism underlying the inability to de-escalate aggression spirals. For example, if one party attempts to forgive the other (Bradfield & Aquino, 1999) or talk rationally about the issue, the other party will likely devalue the concession and be suspicious of the "real" motives behind the action. Thus, the study of cognitive biases could provide aggression scholars with a better understanding of the "black box" of processes that predict spirals of aggression and also provide the basis for practical interventions to help reduce such biases.

Conflict Frames.   One component of cognitive appraisal deals with how parties *frame* the conflicts in which they are involved. Conflict frames reflect the underlying nature of the conflict, reflect who is involved, and reflect what their concerns are. Pinkley (1990) identified three frames through which disputants conceptualize a conflict situation: (a) *relationship versus task*—such as the degree to which disputants focus on the ongoing relationship versus material aspects of a dispute, (b) *emotional versus intellectual*—such as the extent to which disputants focus upon affective components versus objective actions and behaviors that occur, and (c) *cooperate versus win*—such as whether disputants view both parties as responsible and aim to maximize benefits to both parties vs. their own gain, even at the expense of their partner. Pinkley and Northcraft (1994) demonstrated that these frames differentially predict negotiation outcomes. We suggest that conflict frames will also explain how people react to perceived injustices and whether they respond with aggression. For instance, examination of cooperate versus win frames may help understand why only some targets of aggression retaliate. Also, disputants with relationship versus task frames may be equally likely to enact aggression after a triggering event, yet may choose different aggressive acts (e.g., interpersonal aggression for relationship frames, organizational aggression for task frames).

Dynamic Social Interactionist Perspectives on Aggression

As previously noted, there has been little recognition in the organizational literature that aggressive episodes emerge as part of a social interaction in which one might be a target of aggression at one moment, and a perpetrator of aggression at the next. One theoretical exception to this is Andersson and Pearson's (1999) model, which adopted a social interactionist perspective (Felson & Tedeschi, 1993; Tedeschi & Felson, 1994) to explain the escalation of workplace aggression from minor acts of incivility, to coercive actions (e.g., actions taken with the intent of harming another person), to more severe acts of aggression and violence. They argued that minor incivilities are often exchanged between colleagues, resulting in interactional injustice, negative affect, and desire for reciprocation. Subsequently, reciprocation may lead to a "tipping point" if one's social identity is damaged, at which point coercive actions begin and quickly escalate. They also argued that incivility spirals between two people might spawn secondary incivility spirals among others in the workplace, thereby creating organizations characterized by such negative exchanges. This theory is important because it portrays the dynamic nature of workplace aggression, suggests mechanisms through which aggressive norms develop throughout work groups, and illustrates the foundations of aggression within relatively minor social conflicts or uncivil exchanges at work. Two avenues for future inquiry stem from this perspective, namely investigations of conflict resolution strategies and multiparty investigations of aggression.

Conflict Resolution Strategies. Research on conflict resolution strategies used by targets of aggression is one avenue for future research based on a dynamic social interactionist perspective. For example, Zapf and Gross (2001) found that workplace bullying began with conflictual exchanges, which escalated to the point where victims could no longer defend themselves. To resolve the conflict, targets most frequently began with a collaborative strategy, which is typically recommended as the most effective strategy for long-term conflict resolution (Thomas, 1992), yet it was ultimately ineffective. Targets then began to use a range of different conflict resolution strategies, eventually settling on avoidance as the preferred strategy because they chose to leave the organization. Similarly, Aquino (2000) argued that victims might unwittingly contribute to their own victimization by using ineffective conflict resolution techniques, particularly by using avoidance and accommodating strategies. Interestingly, the use of the accommodating and collaborating styles was even more ineffective for those low in status (Aquino, 2000). These findings corroborated Keashly and Nowell's (2003) argument that a collaborating strategy may be particularly ineffective when in a low-power situation and that low-power individuals in prolonged affective conflicts may be most likely to use accommodating and avoiding strategies, which may inadvertently maintain their victim status.

Further research is needed to better understand the strategies that *are* effective for preventing future aggression, particularly given the existing evidence that the best way for targets of bullying to stop the aggression has been to leave their jobs (Zapf & Gross, 2001). To provide useful information to organizations about how to deal with bullying, researchers need to identify conflict resolution strategies that de-escalate aggression. Insights from practitioners who deal with relationship conflicts (notably marital or family problems) may be helpful.

Multi-Party Investigations of Workplace Aggression. Existing research on target's reports of the processes involved in aggressive exchanges provides an important beginning, but it is not possible to garner a comprehensive perspective on the nature of the aggression through targets' reports alone. Targets often portray perpetrators as having hostile or abusive personalities, and even if correct, it is likely that perceptual biases (such as those previously described) influenced the target's reports of the other party's actions. For example, Ayoko, Callan, and Härtel (2003) found that more than half of the employees surveyed in a governmental agency perceived their supervisors as bullies. While this may be the case, we see only one side of the story from targets' reports. At the dyadic or group levels, research investigating aggression from *multiple* parties' perspectives as part of an ongoing exchange would be most useful.

In particular, longitudinal research that adopts a multiparty perspective on aggressive exchanges and that assesses members' personality characteristics would help explain the development of aggression. For example, it is possible to administer personality measures to work group members, followed by a longitudinal study in which each group member is asked to keep a diary of his or her perceptions of all "conflict-related" events that occur in the group. Alternatively, surveys that assess group members' experiences and observations of aggression in their group could be administered on a regular basis over time. Given the high frequency of aggressive acts that employees report (Baron & Neuman, 1996; Raver, 2004; Salin, 2001), it is likely that aggressive exchanges will naturally emerge during the period of the study. Project groups would be an excellent setting, since they make it possible to examine the emergence of aggression among previously unacquainted members, and personality can be assessed prior to any interactions. Social network approaches to multiparty perspectives on aggression (e.g., Mouttapa, Valente, Gallaher, Rohrbach, & Unger, 2004) would also be beneficial. Research on marital relationships has shown the benefits that can be derived from multiparty investigations of conflict and aggression. Such research has provided support for the escalating nature of conflict and aggression (Fincham & Beach, 1999; Murphy & O'Leary, 1989), and it might offer an established methodology for understanding the process of interpersonal relationships (e.g., Gottman & Krokoff, 1989).

Attention to the Overlap Between Task and Relational Issues in Aggression

Greater empirical attention to the distinction between task and relationship issues is needed in both conflict and aggression research. A recent meta-analysis demonstrated that task conflict is associated with negative team performance and low team member satisfaction (De Dreu & Weingart, 2003), despite arguments to the contrary (e.g., Jehn, 1995, 1997). This is one place where the aggression literature may be useful for informing conflict research. Specifically, aggression may be enacted indirectly by harshly critiquing one's work or by placing obstacles in the way of others' goal attainment (Buss, 1961). However, as most frequently operationalized, this would qualify as a task conflict even if the motive behind it is aggressive. Moreover, people who are disadvantaged or insulted by a task-related disagreement may see the act as intended to harm them and blame the other party, regardless of the other party's actual motive. As previously described, perceived intent and blame justify aggressive acts of revenge (Bies et al., 1997), and aggressive exchanges are relationship conflicts by definition. By paying greater attention to the perceived motives behind conflicts (based upon targets' attributions), it may be possible to gain a clearer picture of the conditions under which task conflict will lead to positive outcomes.

Workplace Aggression at Higher Levels of Analysis

Despite the conflict literature's strong emphasis on group or team contexts, research on workplace aggression in groups is only beginning to emerge. The evidence thus far reveals that group contexts influence individuals' levels of aggression enacted and that they also make the negative effects of experiencing aggression even more detrimental. With regard to enacting aggression, individuals' levels of aggression are influenced by the levels enacted by group members (Robinson & O'Leary-Kelly, 1998), even after controlling for individual differences known to influence aggression (Glomb & Liao, 2003). With regard to experiences of aggression, research on sexual harassment, a type of aggressive behavior at work (e.g., Barling et al., 2001; Neuman & Baron, 1996; O'Leary-Kelly, Paetzold, & Griffin, 2000), explored individual and group outcomes. Glomb et al. (1997) argued that sexual harassment is an organizational stressor that may be either discretionary (e.g., transmitted to individuals differentially) or *ambient* (e.g., pervade a group and be potentially available to all group members; Hackman, 1992). They introduced the construct *ambient sexual harassment* (ASH), a group-level phenomenon reflecting the general or ambient level of sexual harassment in a work group, and they demonstrated that ASH predicts negative personal outcomes for group members, even after controlling for individual experiences of harassment. Raver and Gelfand (2005) demonstrated that ASH was associated with team-level outcomes including high levels of conflict, low levels of cohesion, and poor team financial performance. They also provided a multilevel theoretical model, which outlined several group- and organizational-level antecedents, processes, and consequences of ASH.

Based upon this evidence on how interdependent work contexts influence the levels and outcomes of aggression, future research must continue to investigate the nature and outcomes of workplace aggression within dyads and larger groups (e.g., units and organizations). In doing so, one important question is *how* aggression emerges as a construct that characterizes the group as a whole. Future research should explore the ambient and shared nature of workplace aggression and the mechanisms through which information about aggression is communicated, understood, and observed in work groups. Consistent with Raver and Gelfand's (2005) model, research is also needed to explore the group- and organizational-level performance outcomes associated with experiences of workplace aggression, as well as cross-level relationships and moderators.

Expanding the Range of Emotions and Integrating with Cognition

In reviewing research on emotions, Kumar (1989) concluded that different emotions have different effects on conflict resolution, such that anger/hostility tends to encourage aggressive actions, anxiety/threat tends to encourage withdrawal approaches, and positive emotions encourage helpfulness and cooperative conflict resolution approaches. Within the aggression literature, perhaps due to consistent link between anger and aggression (Hershcovis et al., 2007), much attention has been focused on anger as an antecedent to aggression, with considerably less attention to other emotions (for exceptions, see Fox et al., 2001; Miles et al., 2002). Yet anger is by no means the only possible emotional antecedent to aggression. For example, having a coworker point out one's error to a supervisor might result in anxiety or shame, rather than or in addition to anger, which may result in indirect or passive forms of aggression such as withdrawing support toward that coworker (cf., Folger & Skarlicki, 2005). Different emotions are associated with different behavioral responses (Kumar, 1989), thus future research must systematically examine a broader range of emotions in aggressive exchanges, along with their associated behavioral intentions and behaviors. It is also important to integrate research on emotions with the emphasis upon cognitive appraisals (previously described) such that theoretical models that include *both* cognitive and emotional appraisals are advanced and tested.

Aggression in Cross-Cultural and Diverse Contexts

There is no question that cross-cultural research has become an essential part of the conflict and negotiation literature, where cross-national investigations have revealed how the cultural context influences negotiators' biases, goals, communication, and outcomes, among other factors (Gelfand & Brett, 2004; Gelfand & Dyer, 2000). Conflict research has also been sensitive to within cultural diversity, including investigations of how group diversity influences the nature of conflict in groups, and subsequent outcomes (for a review, see Dirks & Parks, 2003). In contrast, workplace aggression research has not evidenced much attention to how aggression is influenced by cross-cultural and within-cultural diversity. This is an important avenue for future research.

Cross-Cultural Differences in Aggression. National culture is likely to influence the reasons for aggression and the forms aggression takes. Commonly cited triggers for aggression include goal obstruction; violation of rules, norms, or promises; and status or power derogation (Bies & Tripp, 2005). Given that norms and the emphasis upon status vary considerably across nations (Gelfand, Nishii, & Raver, 2006; Schwartz, 1994), triggers based upon norm violations and insults to one's status should vary cross-culturally. The nature of aggressive acts is also likely to differ due to cultural constraints on the appropriateness of various behaviors, and aggression against "different" people may be more likely in nations with norms that constrain variability (Gelfand, Nishii, & Raver, 2006). Initial evidence on cross-cultural differences in aggression is emerging (Blader, Chang, & Tyler, 2001; Bond, 2004), but much more is needed.

One form of workplace aggression that has been studied a great deal outside of North America is workplace bullying (Einarsen, Hoel, Zapf, & Cooper, 2003). Unfortunately, many North American scholars have failed to attend to workplace bullying research in their literature reviews (for a notable exception, see Keashly & Jagatic, 2003). We strongly urge scholars to draw from international research on the phenomenon of interest, rather than limiting reviews to North American studies. In addition, an important avenue for future inquiry is to pursue a cross-national study on workplace bullying. To date, it has been difficult to compare studies from different nations due to a lack of agreement about the terminology, measures, and criteria for determining whether bullying has occurred (Neuman & Keashly, 2003). Studying multiple nations in one study would permit comparisons and answer important questions about cross-cultural differences in the antecedents, nature, and consequences of workplace aggression.

Within-Cultural Diversity and Aggression. Workplace aggression research has also largely neglected the study of within-cultural diversity, particularly with regard to who becomes the target and what forms of aggression individuals from different demographic groups (e.g., gender, race, age, and nationality) experience. Theory and research on stigma has long recognized that individuals who are different from others in the context can become stigmatized and, thus, experience derogation, social isolation, or abuse because of their "spoiled identities" (Goffman, 1963). Recent evidence suggested that individuals who are demographically dissimilar are likely to *enact* deviant behaviors (Liao, Joshi, & Chuang, 2004), but we are not aware of research that has drawn from theory on stigma to predict whether demographically dissimilar group members will become *targets* of aggression. Relational demography research on this would be beneficial.

There has also been a surprising lack of attention to how many employees experience forms of workplace aggression in conjunction based upon their identity group memberships (e.g., race and gender; Tajfel, 1982; Tajfel & Turner, 1979). Specifically, although sexual and ethnic harassment are forms of workplace aggression (Barling et al., 2001; Neuman & Baron, 1996; O'Leary-Kelly, Paetzold, & Griffin, 2000), they have been studied in isolation, rather than in conjunction with each other or with generalized aggression (for exceptions, see Barling et al., 2001; Raver & Nishii, 2006). Research on multiple forms of aggression in conjunction is needed; our paucity of knowledge about the additive or interactive effects of different forms of aggression is of particular concern given the fact that workplace diversity is very much a reality and that many women and racial/ethnic minorities are subjected to sexual harassment and/or ethnic harassment in addition to other forms of workplace aggression.

It is well-established that males are more physically aggressive than females (Hyde, 2005), but physical forms of aggression at work are rare (Baron & Neuman, 1996); hence, most studies on workplace aggression have found few gender differences in the enactment of workplace aggression (Hershcovis et al., 2007). If future research is to explore differences in workplace aggression across gender (and racial) groups, it is important to also examine when these differences occur and which psychological mechanisms explain the differences. For example, emerging theory suggests that women are more likely than men to have relational self-construals (RSC) activated in relational contexts (e.g., negotiation) and that RSC activation can encourage subtle forms of aggression if one's attempts to establish a positive relationship with a partner are thwarted (Gelfand, Major, Raver, Nishii, & O'Brien, 2006). Research that explores this and other reasons for *when* and *why* demographic group differences in workplace aggression emerge will be a valuable addition.

Methodological Sophistications

One final avenue for future inquiry is for scholars to expand the range of methodologies used to study workplace aggression. To date, the range of methodologies has been limited, with most research using cross-sectional surveys of the correlates of experiencing (e.g., Cortina et al., 2001; LeBlanc & Kelloway, 2002) or enacting (e.g., Aquino et al., 2001; Fox et al., 2001) aggression, surveys with predictors and outcomes at two points in time (e.g., Tepper, 2000), or surveys assessing retrospective accounts of aggression (e.g., Bradfield & Aquino, 1999). Employee surveys at one or two points in time have been advantageous for studying this phenomenon that is difficult to replicate in the lab; however, this methodology should not be the only tool in our toolkit. The study of workplace aggression has advanced to the point where multiple methodologies are needed to allow us to triangulate upon theoretically grounded results.

Investigations using alternative methodologies would advance research on workplace aggression, including (a) experimental studies that prioritize testing causal theories, (b) scenario studies that permit tests of causality while still pertaining to the work context, (c) longitudinal studies that assess the dynamic development of aggression across time from multiple parties' perspectives, and (d) qualitative studies that explore uncharted territory on workplace aggression. Although ethical considerations limit the use of aggression in experiments, it may be possible to use confederates to implement minor aggressive acts such as giving dirty looks, purposefully withholding information, or speaking in a rude manner. Adapting experimental methodologies from the conflict resolution literature (e.g., multi-issue negotiation scenarios) is another way to explore the emergence of aggression in a more controlled laboratory environment where each party's cognitions, emotions, and behaviors can be readily assessed. Scenario studies are one alternative to experiments, which maintain internal validity for causal theory testing while having a focus upon workplace-based situations and also reducing ethical concerns. Policy capturing, a type of scenario study that uses a within-subjects design to assess judgments regarding different scenarios (e.g., Rotundo & Sackett, 2002), would be useful for evaluating how situational features influence target's appraisal of aggressive situations at work. As previously described, longitudinal research is critical; if we continue to rely on cross-sectional designs for research on workplace aggression, discerning the sequence through which conflict spirals out of control to become aggression and even violence will remain beyond our grasp. Finally, qualitative methods such as open-ended diaries or interviews would be helpful, particularly for exploring issues that have not been previously investigated (e.g., mechanisms through which aggressive norms get communicated in groups and group members' different interpretations of the same aggressive acts in their group). Ideally, scholars will begin to use several of these methods to triangulate upon their research questions of interest.

CONCLUSION

The aim of this chapter has been to demonstrate the nature of workplace aggression and its overlap with conflict in organizations, and to provide several avenues for future inquiry based upon insights that can be gleaned from the integration of these two literatures. In doing so, we have seen how research and theorizing on conflict and conflict resolution has reached a more mature stage than that of workplace aggression and how our understanding of workplace aggression would benefit from a greater appreciation of insights from the literature on conflict and conflict resolution. Doing so, we believe, will help move research on workplace aggression to the third stage of the construct life cycle (Reichers & Schneider, 1990).

REFERENCES

Alicke, M. D. (2000). Culpable control and the psychology of blame. *Psychological Bulletin, 126*, 556–574.
Allred, K. G. (2000). Anger and retaliation in conflict: The role of attribution. In M. Deutsch & P. T. Coleman (Eds.), *The handbook of conflict resolution: Theory and practice* (pp. 236–255). San Francisco: Jossey-Bass.
Amason, A. C. (1996). Distinguishing the effects of functional and dysfunctional conflict on strategic decision making: Resolving a paradox for top management groups. *Academy of Management Journal, 39*, 123–148.
Anderson, C. A., & Bushman, B. J. (2002). Human aggression. *Annual Review of Psychology, 53*, 27–51.

Andersson, L. M., & Pearson, C. M. (1999). Tit for tat? The spiraling effect of incivility in the workplace. *Academy of Management Review, 24,* 452–471.

Aquino, K. (2000). Structural and individual determinants of workplace victimization: The effects of hierarchical status and conflict management style. *Journal of Management, 26,* 171–193.

Aquino, K., Tripp, T. M., & Bies, R. J. (2001). How employees respond to personal offense: The effects of blame attribution, victim status, and offender status on revenge and reconciliation in the workplace. *Journal of Applied Psychology, 86,* 52–59.

Ashforth, B. E. (1997). Petty tyranny in organizations: A preliminary examination of antecedents and consequences. *Canadian Journal of Administrative Science, 14,* 126–140.

Ayoko, O. B., Callan, V. J., & Härtel, C. E. J. (2003). Workplace conflict, bullying, and counterproductive work behaviors. *International Journal of Organizational Analysis, 11,* 283–301.

Babcock, L., & Loewenstein, G. (1997). Explaining bargaining impasse: The role of self-serving biases. *Journal of Economic Perspectives, 11,* 109–125.

Barling, J. (1996). The prediction, psychological experience, and consequences of workplace violence. In G. VandenBos & E. G. Bulatao (Eds.), *Violence on the job: Identifying risks and developing solutions* (pp. 29–49). Washington, DC: American Psychological Association.

Barling, J., Rogers, A. G., & Kelloway, E. K. (2001). Behind closed doors: In-home workers' experience of sexual harassment and workplace violence. *Journal of Occupational Health Psychology, 6,* 255–269.

Baron, R. A. (1990). Conflict in organizations. In K. R. Murphy & F. E. Saal (Eds.), *Psychology in organizations: Integrating science and practice* (pp. 197–216). Hillsdale, NJ: Lawrence Erlbaum.

Baron, R. A., & Neuman, J. H. (1996). Workplace violence and workplace aggression: Evidence on their relative frequency and potential causes. *Aggressive Behavior, 22,* 161–173.

Baron, R. A., Neuman, J. H., & Geddes, D. (1999). Social and personal determinants of workplace aggression: Evidence for the impact of perceived injustice and the Type A behavior pattern. *Aggressive Behavior, 25,* 281–296.

Bazerman, M. H. (1998). *Judgment and managerial decision making* (4th ed.). New York: Wiley.

Bazerman, M. H., & Carroll, J. S. (1987). Negotiator cognition. In B. M. Staw & L. L. Cummings (Eds.), *Research in organizational behavior* (Vol. 9, pp. 247–288). Greenwich, CT: JAI Press.

Bazerman, M. H., Curhan, J. R., Moore, D. A., & Valley, K. L. (2000). Negotiation. *Annual Review of Psychology, 51,* 279–314.

Bennett, R. J., & Robinson, S. L. (2000). Development of a measure of workplace deviance. *Journal of Applied Psychology, 85,* 349–360.

Bennett, R. J., & Robinson, S. L. (2003). The past, present, and future of workplace deviance research. In J. Greenberg (Ed.), *Organizational behavior: The state of the science* (pp. 247–281). Mahwah, NJ: Lawrence Erlbaum.

Bies, R. J., & Tripp, T. M. (2005). The study of revenge in the workplace: Conceptual, ideological, and empirical issues. In S. Fox & P. E. Spector (Eds.), *Counterproductive work behavior: Investigations of actors and targets* (pp. 65–81). Washington, DC: American Psychological Association.

Bies, R. J., Tripp, T. M., & Kramer, R. M. (1997). At the breaking point: Cognitive and social dynamics of revenge in organizations. In R. Giacalone & J. Greenberg (Eds.), *Antisocial behavior in organizations* (pp. 18–36). Thousand Oaks, CA: Sage.

Blader, S. L., Chang, C. C., & Tyler, T. R. (2001). Procedural justice and retaliation in organizations: Comparing cross-nationally the importance of fair group process. *International Journal of Conflict Management, 12,* 295–311.

Bond, M. H. (2004). Culture and aggression: From context to coercion. *Personality and Social Psychology Review, 8,* 62–78.

Bradfield, M., & Aquino, K. (1999). The effects of blame attributions and offender likeableness on forgiveness and revenge in the workplace. *Journal of Management, 25,* 607–631.

Buss, A. H. (1961). *The psychology of aggression.* New York: John Wiley & Sons.

Chen, P. Y., & Spector, P. E. (1992). Relationships of work stressors with aggression, withdrawal, theft, and substance use: An exploratory study. *Journal of Occupational and Organizational Psychology, 65,* 177–184.

Colbert, A. E., Mount, M. K., Harter, J. K., Witt, L. A., & Barrick, M. R. (2004). Interactive effects of personality and perceptions of the work situation on workplace deviance. *Journal of Applied Psychology, 89,* 599–609.

Cortina, L. M., Magley, V. J., Williams, J. H., & Langhout, R. D. (2001). Incivility in the workplace: Incidence and impact. *Journal of Occupational Health Psychology, 6,* 64–80.

Davenport, N., Schwartz, R. D., & Elliott, G. P. (2002). *Mobbing: Emotional abuse in the American workplace* (2nd ed.). Ames, IA: Civil Society Publishing.

De Dreu, C. K. W. (1997). Productive conflict: The importance of conflict management and conflict issue. In C. De Dreu & E. Van De Vliert (Eds.), *Using conflict in organizations* (pp. 9–22). Thousand Oaks, CA: Sage.

De Dreu, C. K. W., Nauta, A., & Van de Vliert, E. (1995). Self-serving evaluations of conflict behavior and escalation of the dispute. *Journal of Applied Social Psychology, 25,* 2049–2066.

De Dreu, C., & Van de Vliert, E. (1997). *Using conflict in organizations.* Thousand Oaks, CA: Sage.

De Dreu, C. K. W., & Weingart, L. R. (2003). Task versus relationship conflict, team performance, and team member satisfaction: A meta-analysis. *Journal of Applied Psychology, 88,* 741–749.

Dietz, J., Robinson, S. L., Folger, R., Baron, R. A., & Schulz, M. (2003). The impact of community violence and an organization's procedural justice climate on workplace aggression. *Academy of Management Journal, 46,* 317–326.

Dirks, K. T., & Parks, J. M. (2003). Conflicting stories: The state of the science of conflict. In J. Greenberg (Ed.), *Organizational behavior: The state of the science* (pp. 283–324). Mahwah, NJ: Lawrence Erlbaum.

Douglas, S. C., & Martinko, M. J. (2001). Exploring the role of individual differences in the prediction of workplace aggression. *Journal of Applied Psychology, 86,* 547–559.

Duffy, M. K., Ganster, D. C., & Pagon, M. (2002). Social undermining in the workplace. *Academy of Management Journal, 45,* 331–351.

Einarsen, S., Hoel, H., Zapf, D., & Cooper, C. L. (Eds.). (2003). *Bullying and emotional abuse in the workplace: International perspectives in research and practice.* London/New York: Taylor & Francis.

Einarsen, S., Raknes, B. I., & Matthiesen, S. B. (1994). Bullying and harassment at work and their relationships to work environment quality: An exploratory study. *European Journal of Work and Organizational Psychology, 4*, 381–401.

Felson, R. B., & Tedeschi, J. T. (1993). *Aggression and violence: Social interactionist perspectives.* Washington, DC: American Psychological Association.

Festinger, W. L. F., Abel, R. L., & Sarat, A. (1980). The emergence and transformation of disputes: Naming, blaming, claiming. *Law & Society Review, 15*, 630–654.

Fincham, F. D., & Beach, S. R. H. (1999). Conflict in marriage: Implications for working with couples. *Annual Review of Psychology, 50*, 47–77.

Fitness, J. (2000). Anger in the workplace: An emotion script approach to anger episodes between workers and their superiors, coworkers, and subordinates. *Journal of Occupational Behavior, 21*, 147–162.

Folger, R., & Skarlicki, D. P. (1998). A popcorn metaphor for employee aggression. In R. W. Griffin, A. O'Leary-Kelly, & J. M. Collins (Eds.), *Monographs in organizational behavior and industrial relations: Vol. 23. Dysfunctional behavior in organizations: Part A. Violent and deviant behavior* (pp. 43–81). Greenwich, CT: JAI Press.

Folger, R., & Skarlicki, D. P. (2005). Beyond counterproductive work behavior: Moral emotions and deonic retaliation versus reconciliation. In S. Fox & P. E. Spector (Eds.), *Counterproductive work behavior: Investigations of actors and targets* (pp. 83–105). Washington, DC: American Psychological Association

Fox, S., & Spector, P. E. (1999). A model of work frustration-aggression. *Journal of Organizational Behavior, 20*, 915–931.

Fox, S., & Spector, P. E. (2002). An emotion-centered model of voluntary work behavior: Some parallels between counterproductive work behavior and organizational citizenship behavior. *Human Resource Management Review, 12*, 269–292.

Fox, S., & Spector, P. E. (2005). *Counterproductive work behavior: Investigations of actors and targets.* Washington, DC: American Psychological Association.

Fox, S., Spector, P. E., & Miles, D. (2001). Counterproductive work behavior (CWB) in response to job stressors and organizational justice: Some mediator and moderator tests for autonomy and emotions. *Journal of Vocational Behavior, 59*, 291–309.

Gelfand, M. J., & Brett, J. (Eds.). (2004). *The Handbook of Negotiation and Culture.* Stanford, CA: Stanford University Press.

Gelfand, M. J., & Dyer, N. (2000). A cultural perspective on negotiation: Progress, pitfalls, and prospects. *Applied Psychology: An International Review, 41*, 62–99.

Gelfand, M. J., Major, V. S., Raver, J. L., Nishii, L. H., & O'Brien, K. M. (2006). Negotiating relationally: The dynamics of the relational self in negotiations. *Academy of Management Review, 31*, 427–451.

Gelfand, M. J., & McCusker, C. (2002). Metaphor and the cultural construction of negotiation: A paradigm for theory and research. In M. Gannon & K. L. Newman (Eds.) *Handbook of cross-cultural management* (pp. 292–314). New York: Blackwell.

Gelfand, M. J., Nishii, L. H., & Raver, J. L. (2006). On the nature and importance of cultural tightness-looseness. *Journal of Applied Psychology, 91*, 1225–1244.

Glomb, T. M. (2001). *Workplace aggression: Antecedents, behavioral components, and consequences.* Unpublished manuscript.

Glomb, T. M. (2002). Workplace anger and aggression: Informing conceptual models with data from specific encounters. *Journal of Occupational Health Psychology, 7,* 20–36.

Glomb, T. M., & Liao, H. (2003). Interpersonal aggression in work groups: Social influence, reciprocal, and individual effects. *Academy of Management Journal.*

Glomb, T. M., Richman, W. L., Hulin, C. L., Drasgow, F., Schneider, K. T., Fitzgerald, L. F., et al. (1997). Ambient sexual harassment: An integrated model of antecedents and consequences. *Organizational Behavior and Human Decision Processes, 7,* 309–328.

Goffman, E. (1963). *Stigma: Notes on the management of spoiled identity.* Englewood Cliffs, NJ: Prentice-Hall.

Gottman, J. M., & Krokoff, L. J. (1989). Marital interaction and satisfaction: A longitudinal view. *Journal of Consulting and Clinical Psychology, 57,* 47–52.

Greenberg, L., & Barling, J. (1999). Predicting employee aggression against coworkers, subordinates and supervisors: The roles of person behaviors and perceived workplace factors. *Journal of Organizational Behavior, 20,* 897–913.

Griffin, R. W., & Lopez, Y. P. (2005). "Bad behavior" in organizations: A review and typology for future research. *Journal of Management, 31,* 988–1005.

Hackman, J. R. (1992). Group influences on individuals in organizations. In M. D. Dunnette & L. M. Hough (Eds.), *Handbook of industrial organizational psychology.* Palo Alto, CA: Consulting Psychologists Press.

Hepworth, W., & Towler, A. (2004). The effects of individual differences and charismatic leadership on workplace aggression. *Journal of Occupational Health Psychology, 9,* 176–185.

Hershcovis, S. M., Turner, N., Barling, J., Arnold, K. A., Dupre, K. E., Inness, M., LeBlanc, M. M. et al. (2007). Predicting workplace aggression: A meta-analysis. *Journal of Applied Psychology, 92, 228–238.*

Hoel, H., Rayner, C., & Cooper, C. L. (1999). Workplace bullying. *International Review of Industrial and Organizational Psychology, 14,* 195–230.

Holmes, D. S., & Will, M. J. (1985). Expressions of interpersonal aggression by angered and non-angered persons with Type A and Type B behavior patterns. *Journal of Personality and Social Psychology, 40,* 723–727.

Hyde, J. S. (2005). The gender similarities hypothesis. *American Psychologist, 60,* 581–592.

Inness, M., Barling, J., & Turner, N. (2005). Understanding supervisor-targeted aggression: A within-person, between-jobs design. *Journal of Applied Psychology, 90,* 731–739.

James, L. R., McIntyre, M. D., Glisson, C. A., Green, P. D., & Patton, T. W. (2005). A conditional reasoning measure for aggression. *Organizational Research Methods, 8,* 69–99.

Jehn, K. (1997). Affective and cognitive conflict in work groups: Increasing performance through value-based intragroup conflict. In C. K. W. De Dreu & E. Van de Vliert (Eds.), *Using conflict in organizations* (pp. 87–100). Thousand Oaks, CA: Sage.

Jehn, K., & Mannix, E. (2001). The dynamic nature of conflict: A longitudinal study of intragroup conflict and group performance. *Academy of Management Journal, 44,* 238–251.

Jehn, K. A. (1995). A multimethod examination of the benefits and detriments of intragroup conflict. *Administrative Science Quarterly, 40,* 256–282.

Jockin, V., Arvey, R. D., & McGue, M. (2001). Perceived victimization moderates self-reports of workplace aggression and conflict. *Journal of Applied Psychology, 86,* 1262–1269.

Keashly, L. (1998). Emotional abuse in the workplace: Conceptual and empirical issues. *Journal of Emotional Abuse, 1,* 85–117.

Keashly, L., & Harvey, S. (2005). Emotional abuse in the workplace. In S. Fox & P. Spector (Eds.), *Counterproductive work behavior: Investigations of actors and targets* (pp. 201–235). Washington, DC: American Psychological Association.

Keashly, L., Harvey, S., & Hunter, S. (1997). Emotional abuse and role state stressors: Relative impact on resident assistants' stress. *Work and Stress, 11,* 35–45.

Keashly, L., & Jagatic, K. (2003). By any other name: American perspectives on workplace bullying. In S. Einarsen, H. Hoel, D. Zapf, & C. Cooper (Eds.), *Bullying and emotional abuse in the workplace: International perspectives on research and practice* (pp. 31–61). London: Taylor & Francis.

Keashly, L., & Nowell, B. (2003). Conflict, conflict resolution, and bullying. In S. Einarsen, H. Hoel, D. Zapf, & C. Cooper (Eds.), *Bullying and emotional abuse in the workplace: International perspectives on research and practice* (pp. 339–358). London, UK: Taylor & Francis.

Keashly, L., Trott, V., & MacLean, L. M. (1994). Abusive behavior in the workplace: A preliminary investigation. *Violence and Victims, 9,* 341–357.

Kidwell, R. E., Jr., & Martin, C. L. (2005). *Managing organizational deviance.* Thousand Oaks, CA: Sage.

Kumar, R. (1989). Affect, cognition and decision making in negotiations: A conceptual integration. In M. A. Rahim (Ed.), *Managing conflict: An integrative approach* (pp. 185–194). New York: Praeger.

Lanyon, R. I., & Goodstein, L. D. (2004). Validity and reliability of a pre-employment screening test: The counterproductive behavior index (CBI). *Journal of Business and Psychology, 18,* 533–553.

LeBlanc, M. M., & Barling, J. (2005). Understanding the many faces of workplace violence. In S. Fox & P. E. Spector (Eds.), *Counterproductive work behavior: Investigations of actors and targets* (pp. 41–63). Washington, DC: American Psychological Association.

LeBlanc, M. M., & Kelloway, E. K. (2002). Predictors and outcomes of workplace violence and aggression. *Journal of Applied Psychology, 87,* 444–453.

Lee, K., & Allen, N. J. (2002). Organizational citizenship behavior and workplace deviance: The role of affect and cognitions. *Journal of Applied Psychology, 87,* 131–142.

Leymann, H. (1996). The content and development of mobbing at work. *European Journal of Work and Organizational Psychology, 5,* 165–184.

Liao, H., Joshi, A., & Chuang, A. (2004). Sticking out like a sore thumb: Employee dissimilarity and deviance at work. *Personnel Psychology, 57,* 969–1000.

Loewenstein, G., Issacharoff, S., Camerer, C., & Babcock, L. (1993). Self-serving assessments of fairness and pretrial bargaining. *Journal of Legal Studies, 22,* 135–59.

Martinko, M. J., Gundlach, M. J., & Douglas, S. C. (2002). Toward an integrative theory of counterproductive workplace behavior: A causal reasoning perspective. *International Journal of Selection and Assessment, 10,* 36–50.

Martinko, M. J., & Zellars, K. L. (1998). Toward a theory of workplace violence and aggression: A cognitive appraisal perspective. In R. W. Griffin, A. O'Leary-Kelly, & J. M. Collins (Eds.), *Monographs in organizational behavior and industrial relations: Vol. 23. Dysfunctional behavior in organizations: Part A. Violent and deviant behavior* (pp. 1–42). Greenwich, CT: JAI Press.

Mikkelsen, E. G., & Einarsen, S. (2001). Bullying in Danish work-life: Prevalence and health correlates. *European Journal of Work and Organizational Psychology, 10*, 393–413.

Miles, D. E., Borman, W. E., Spector, P. E., & Fox, S. (2002). Building an integrative model of extra role work behaviors: A comparison of counterproductive work behavior with organizational citizenship behavior. *International Journal of Selection and Assessment, 10*, 51–57.

Mouttapa, M., Valente, T., Gallaher, P., Rohrbach, L. A., & Unger, J. B. (2004). Social network predictors of bullying and victimization. *Adolescence, 39*, 315–335.

Mummendry, A., & Otten, S. (1993). Aggression: Interaction between individuals and social groups. In R. B. Felson & J. T. Tedeschi (Eds.), *Aggression and violence: Social interactionist perspectives* (pp. 145–167). Washington, DC: American Psychological Association.

Murphy, C. M., & O'Leary, K. D. (1989). Psychological aggression predicts physical aggression in early marriage. *Journal of Consulting and Clinical Psychology, 57*, 579–582.

Neale, M. A., & Bazerman, M. H. (1991). *Cognition and rationality in negotiation.* New York: Free Press.

Neuman, J. H., & Baron, R. A. (1996). Aggression in the workplace. In R. A. Giacalone & J. Greenberg (Eds.), *Antisocial behavior in organizations* (pp. 37–67). Thousand Oaks, CA: Sage.

Neuman, J. H., & Baron, R. A. (1998). Workplace violence and workplace aggression: Evidence concerning specific forms, potential causes, and preferred targets. *Journal of Management, 24*, 391–419.

Neuman, J. H., & Baron, R. A. (2005). Aggression in the workplace: A social-psychological perspective. In S. Fox & P. E. Spector (Eds.), *Counterproductive work behavior: Investigations of actors and targets* (pp. 13–40). Washington, DC: American Psychological Association.

Neuman, J. H., & Keashly, L. (2003). *Development of a measure of workplace aggression and violence: The workplace aggression research questionnaire (WAR-Q).* Unpublished manuscript.

O'Leary-Kelly, A. M., Duffy, M. K., & Griffin, R. W. (2000). Construct confusion in the study of antisocial work behavior. *Research in Personnel and Human Resources Management, 18*, 275–303.

O'Leary-Kelly, A. M., Paetzold, R. L., & Griffin, R. W. (2000). Sexual harassment as aggressive behavior: An actor-based perspective. *Academy of Management Review, 25*, 372–388.

Pearson, C. M., Andersson, L. M., & Porath, L. (2005). Workplace incivility. In S. Fox & P. E. Spector (Eds.), *Counterproductive work behavior: Investigations of actors and targets* (pp. 177–200). Washington, DC: American Psychological Association.

Pinkley, R. L. (1990). Dimensions of conflict frame: Disputant interpretations of conflict. *Journal of Applied Psychology, 75*, 117–126.

Pinkley, R. L., & Northcraft, G. B. (1994). Conflict frames of reference: Implications for dispute processes and outcomes. *Academy of Management Journal, 37*, 193–205.

Putman, L. L., & Poole, M. S. (1987) Conflict and negotiation. In F. M. Jablin, L. L. Putnam, K. H. Roberts, & L. W. Porter (Eds.), *Handbook of organizational communication: An interdisciplinary prospective* (pp. 549–599). Newbury Park, CA: Sage.

Raver, J. L. (2004). *Interpersonal aggression at work: A model of behavioral outcomes, psychological mediators, and contextual moderators.* Unpublished doctoral dissertation, University of Maryland, College Park, MD.

Raver, J. L., & Gelfand, M. J. (2005). Beyond the individual victim: Linking sexual harassment, team processes, and team performance. *Academy of Management Journal, 48*, 387–400.

Raver, J. L., & Nishii, L. H. (2006). Interactive effects of gender harassment and ethnic harassment on targets. In S. Kaplan, J. Bradley, & J. L. Raver (Chairs), *Modern-day sexism at work: Forgotten, but not gone.* Symposium conducted at the Society for Industrial and Organizational Psychology annual conference, Dallas, Texas.

Rayner, C., & Hoel, H. (1997). A summary review of literature relating to workplace bullying. *Journal of Community and Applied Social Psychology, 7*, 181–191.

Rayner, C., & Keashly, L. (2005). Bullying at work: A perspective from Britain and North America. In S. Fox & P. E. Spector (Eds.), *Counterproductive work behavior: Investigations of actors and targets* (pp. 271–296). Washington, DC: American Psychological Association.

Reichers, A. E., & Schneider, B. (1990). Climate and culture: Life cycles of constructs. In B. Schneider (Ed.), *Organizational climate and culture* (pp. 5–39). San Francisco: Jossey-Bass.

Richman, J. A., Rospenda, K. M., Flaherty, J. A., & Freels, S. (2001). Workplace harassment, active coping, and alcohol-related outcomes. *Journal of Substance Abuse, 13*, 347–366.

Richman, J. A., Rospenda, K. M., Nawyn, S. J., Flaherty, J. A., Fendrich, M., Drum, M. L., et al. (1999). Sexual harassment and generalized workplace abuse among university employees: Prevalence and mental health correlates. *American Journal of Public Health, 89*, 358–363.

Robbins, S. P. (1978). "Conflict management" and "conflict resolution" are not synonymous terms. In P. B. DuBose (Ed.), *Readings in management* (pp. 247–257). Englewood Cliffs, NJ: Prentice Hall.

Robinson, S. L., & Bennett, R. J. (1995). A typology of deviant workplace behaviors: A multidimensional scaling study. *Academy of Management Journal, 38*(2), 555–572.

Robinson, S. L., & Bennett, R. J. (1997). Workplace deviance: Its definition, its manifestations, and its causes. *Research on Negotiation in Organizations, 6*, 3–27.

Robinson, S. L., & Greenberg, J. (1998). Employees behaving badly: Dimensions, determinants, and dilemmas in the study of workplace deviance. In C. L. Cooper & D. M. Rousseau (Eds.), *Trends in organizational behavior* (Vol. 5, pp. 1–30). New York: John Wiley & Sons.

Robinson, S. L., & O'Leary-Kelly, A. M. (1998). Monkey see, monkey do: The influence of work groups on the antisocial behavior of employees. *Academy of Management Journal, 41*, 658–672.

Rospenda, K. M., Richman, J. A., Wislar, J. S., & Flaherty, J. A. (2000). Chronicity of sexual harassment and generalized workplace abuse: Effects on drinking outcomes. *Addiction, 95,* 1805–1820.

Ross, L., & Stillenger, C. (1991). Barriers to conflict resolution. *Negotiation Journal, 7,* 389–404.

Rotundo, M., & Sackett, P. R. (2002). The relative importance of task, citizenship, and counterproductive performance to global ratings of job performance: A policy-capturing approach. *Journal of Applied Psychology, 87,* 66–80.

Rubin, J. (1986). The emotion of anger: Some conceptual and theoretical issues. *Professional Psychology: Research and Practice, 17,* 115–124.

Sackett, P. R. (2002). The structure of counterproductive work behaviors: Dimensionality and relationships with facets of job performance. *International Journal of Selection and Assessment, 10,* 5–11.

Salin, D. (2001). Prevalence and forms of bullying among business professionals: A comparison of two different strategies for measuring bullying. *European Journal of Work and Organizational Psychology, 10,* 425–441.

Schlenker, B. R., Britt, T. W., Pennington, J., Murphy, K. R., & Doherty, K. (1994). The triangle model of responsibility. *Psychology Review, 101,* 632–652.

Schwartz, S. H. (1994). Beyond individualism/collectivism: New cultural dimensions of values. In U. Kim, H. C. Triandis, C. Kagitiçibasi, S. Choi, & G. Yoon (Eds.), *Individualism and collectivism: Theory, method, and applications.* Thousand Oaks, CA: Sage.

Skarlicki, D. P., & Folger, R. (1997). Retaliation in the workplace: The roles of distributive, procedural, and interactional justice. *Journal of Applied Psychology, 82,* 434–443.

Skarlicki, D. P., Folger, R., & Tesluk, P. (1999). Personality as a moderator in the relationship between fairness and retaliation. *Academy of Management Journal, 42,* 100–108.

Sommers, J. A., Schell, T. L., & Vodanovich, S. J. (2002). Developing a measure of individual differences in organizational revenge. *Journal of Business and Psychology, 17,* 207–222.

Spector, P. E., & Fox, S. (2002). An emotion-centered model of voluntary work behavior: Some parallels between counterproductive work behavior and organizational citizenship behavior. *Human Resource Management Review, 12,* 269–292.

Spector, P. E., & Fox, S. (2005). The stressor-emotion model of counterproductive work behavior. In S. Fox & P. E. Spector (Eds.), *Counterproductive work behavior: Investigations of actors and targets* (pp. 151–174). Washington, DC: American Psychological Association.

Tajfel, H. (1982). *Human groups and social categories: Studies in social psychology.* Cambridge, U.K.: Cambridge University Press.

Tajfel, H., & Turner, J. (1979). An integrative theory of intergroup conflict. In W. G. Austin & S. Worchel (Eds.), *The social psychology of intergroup relations* (pp. 33–47). Monterey, CA: Brooks/Cole.

Tedeschi, J. T., & Felson, R. B. (1994). *Violence, aggression, & coercive actions.* Washington, DC: American Psychological Association.

Tepper, B. J. (2000). Consequences of abusive supervision. *Academy of Management Journal, 43,* 178–190.

Tepper, B. J., Duffy, M. K., & Shaw, J. D. (2001). Personality moderators of the relationship between abusive supervision and subordinates' resistance. *Journal of Applied Psychology, 86*, 974–983.

Thomas, K. W. (1992). Conflict and negotiation processes in organizations. In M. D. Dunnette & L. M. Hough (Eds.), *Handbook of industrial and organizational psychology: Vol. 3.* (2nd ed., pp. 651–717). Palo Alto, CA: Consulting Psychologists Press.

Thompson, L. L. (1990). Negotiation behavior and outcomes: Empirical evidence and theoretical issues. *Psychological Bulletin, 108*, 515–532.

Thompson, L. L., & Hastie, R. (1990). Social perception in negotiation. *Organizational Behavior and Human Decision Processes, 47*, 98–123.

Thompson, L., & Loewenstein, G. (1992). Egocentric interpretations of fairness and interpersonal conflict. Decision processes in negotiation [Special issue]. *Organizational Behavior and Human Decision Processes, 51*, 176–197.

Townsend, J., Phillips, J. S., & Elkins, T. J. (2000). Employee retaliation: The neglected consequences of poor leader-member exchange relations. *Journal of Occupational Health Psychology, 5*, 457–463.

Van Kleef, G. A., De Dreu, C. K. W., & Manstead, A. S. R. (2004). The interpersonal effects of emotions in negotiations: A motivated information processing approach. *Journal of Personality and Social Psychology, 87*, 510–528.

Vartia, M. (1996). The sources of bullying—psychological work environment and organizational climate. *European Journal of Work and Organizational Psychology, 5*, 203–214.

Wall, V., & Nolan, L. (1986). Perceptions of inequity, satisfaction, and conflict in task-oriented groups. *Human Relations, 39*, 1033–1052.

Warren, D. E. (2003). Constructive and destructive deviance in organizations. *Academy of Management Review, 28*, 622–632.

Zapf, D., & Gross, C. (2001). Conflict escalation and coping with workplace bullying: A replication and extension. *European Journal of Work and Organizational Psychology, 10*, 497–522.

Zapf, D., Knorz, C., & Kulla, M. (1996). On the relationship between mobbing factors and job content, social work environment, and health outcomes. *European Journal of Work and Organizational Psychology, 5*, 215–237.

Zellars, K. L., Tepper, B. J., & Duffy, M. K. (2002). Abusive supervision and subordinates' organizational citizenship behavior. *Journal of Applied Psychology, 87*, 1068–1076.

8

Conflict Escalation in Organizations

DEAN G. PRUITT
Institute for Conflict Analysis and Resolution
George Mason University

Escalation occurs when a party to a conflict first uses a contentious (aggressive) tactic or employs heavier contentious tactics than before. (Parties to a conflict may be individuals, small groups, departments, or entire organizations.) Escalation must be distinguished from conflict, which is a state of mind involving a perceived divergence of interest, a perceived difference of opinion, or a feeling of annoyance about another party's actions (Pruitt & Kim, 2004). Escalation is one way of dealing with conflict. There are other ways, including problem solving, yielding, and inaction (Pruitt & Kim, 2004).

Some scholars (e.g., Walton, 1969) talk about "escalation of relationships," in which there is increased antagonism between parties. However, I will call this "deterioration" of relationships and speak of "distressed" rather than "escalated" relationships. Escalation and deterioration of relationships are intimately related, as will be seen in a later section.

Escalation in organizations can take many forms, some quite subtle. Buss's (1961) three-dimensional typology of aggression (physical verbal, direct indirect, active passive) is a useful way of sorting out these varieties, a modification of which as seen in Table 8.1.

Unlike escalation in other settings (e.g., marriage and international relations), escalation within organizations is generally frowned on by powerful higher ups, who are likely to punish it, especially if it is directed at them. Hence, escalation will commonly take either legitimate forms or forms that cannot easily be traced to their source. This means that passive and indirect approaches are often seen in organizations (Neuman

245

TABLE 8.1
Examples of Eight Types of Workplace Escalation*

		Direct	Indirect
Physical	Active	Homicide Assault Angry displays Obscene gestures Unfriendly, cold behavior Firing an employee Prosecuting strikers Violence against strikers	Theft Sabotage Defacing property Consuming needed resources Hiding needed resources
	Passive	Going on strike Quitting Chronic lateness Work slowdown Failing to help Failing to transmit memos Avoiding target Failing to provide a raise Locking out employees	Delaying work to make target look bad Failing to protect target's welfare
Verbal	Active	Threats Yelling Insults and sarcasm Angry displays Hostile comments Using derogatory tone of voice Criticism or blame Negative performance evaluation	Taking company to court Filing a grievance Whistle blowing Denouncing organization to the press Transmitting damaging information Grumbling Talking behind target's back Attacking target's protégé
	Passive	Failing to return phone calls Giving target the silent treatment Refusing target's requests Damning with faint praise	Failing to transmit information Failing to warn of impending damage Failing to defend target Failing to refer clients to target

*Modified from Neuman and Baron (1997, p. 40)

& Baron, 1997). For example, Geddes (1994) found that subordinates who were given negative feedback reported that they had engaged in avoidance, slowdowns, and sabotage but not physical aggression. Greenberg (1990) found that across the board pay reductions often led to theft.

This chapter will first discuss the impact of escalation on individuals and organizations. Then, it will turn to escalation sequences, in which progressively heavier tactics are used over time. Escalation usually takes the form of retaliation, a contentious response to annoyance from another party. Hence, a long section will be devoted to the conditions that affect the likelihood and extent of this phenomenon. That section will be followed by a discussion of the structural changes that occur if escalation becomes a persistent part of the relationship between two parties. The penultimate section will suggest some methods for avoiding or coping with severe escalation. At the end of the chapter, some suggestions for future research on escalation will be made.

IMPACT OF ESCALATION

Escalation sometimes has positive consequences for individuals and organizations. Selective escalation helps reveal the relative importance to each party of the issues in the conflict, thus promoting the development of logrolling solutions. In addition, the shock value of escalation can encourage information gathering, problem solving, rethinking of faulty activities or policies, and hence, needed social change (Bies, Tripp, & Kramer, 1997; Skarlicki & Folger, 2004). Furthermore, the fear of escalation can keep managers in line (Bies et al., 1997).

However, escalation (especially severe escalation) is often harmful to organizations. Many of the behaviors listed in Table 8.1 are directly harmful, for example, work slowdown, theft, and sabotage. Escalation can also lead to ill feeling and breakdown in working relationships. Escalation tends to crowd out problem solving by encouraging strategic rather than integrative thinking, by producing hostility to the other party's welfare, and by impeding creative thinking (Carnevale & Probst, 1998). This encourages one-sided, win–lose decisions that fail to balance the multiple interests that must be served for good organizational functioning (Brett, Shapiro, & Lytle, 1998). In addition, fear of escalation can cause conflict avoidance: important issues are swept under the rug. This is especially likely to occur in workgroups where people are interdependent and trust is low (Tjosvold, Leung, & Johnson, 2000). Prior escalation can encourage such fear.

ESCALATION SEQUENCES

There are two types of escalation sequences: unilateral and bilateral. In unilateral sequences, only one party escalates. A trivial example is when the chair of a meeting that has gone astray first suggests "Let's get back to the topic," then demands "Come on guys, talk about the topic," and finally gets angry and bangs a fist on the table. The organizational change consultant who finds resistance to his or her recommendations may reach a higher level of escalation. At first, he or she calls meetings and puts pressure on employees, then issues threats, and finally complains to upper management.

In a laboratory experiment on unilateral escalation sequences, Mikolic, Parker, and Pruitt (1997) studied reactions to persistent annoyance by having confederates of the experimenter withhold supplies needed by the participants to complete a project. The data were based on a content analysis of telephone message to the confederates. Most participants tried to get the supplies by means of the following orderly progression of tactics: requests, demands, angry statements, threats, harassment, and abuse. Participants stopped escalating at different points along this progression. Some made only requests; others requests and then demands; still others, requests, then demands, then angry statements, and so on. Groups, on the whole, escalated farther than individuals—following the same orderly progression of tactics.

In bilateral escalation sequences, the parties escalate in tandem. An example can be seen in Ury, Brett, and Goldberg's (1988) description of the labor-management conflict at a Kentucky coalmine, in the period between 1978 and 1980.

> (In this two-year period) the miners had engaged in twenty-seven wildcat strikes. Management had responded by firing miners and taking the union to court for a breach of contract. In the end, 115 miners had gone to jail for a night. This not only failed to stop the strikes but led to a wave of bomb threats, sabotage, and theft. Miners started bringing guns in their cars when they came to work. (p. 101)

Bilateral escalation sequences usually develop through conflict spirals entailing repeated retaliation and counterretaliation, or defense and counterdefense. Thus, an employee might criticize a management policy, provoking disciplinary action such as failure to receive a raise. Annoyed by this treatment, he or she might then talk to the press, being fired as a result.

RETALIATORY ESCALATION

The most common type of escalation involves retaliation aimed at punishing an annoying other. An "actor" punishes an apparent "offender." The actor may be responding to annoyance to self or to another party with whom the actor identifies.

The two kinds of escalation sequences described earlier often involve retaliation. Unilateral escalation in response to persistent annoyance, such as was seen in the Mikolic et al. (1997) study, involves an increasingly harsh series of retaliatory actions by the actor. Bilateral escalation often involves alternating retaliatory moves: A retaliates in response to annoyance from B, then B retaliates in response to A's retaliation, and so on.

The motivation for retaliation can be one or more of the following (partly based on Skarlicki & Folger, 2004): as an expression of anger, to deter further annoyance from the offender, to show the offender or a third party that one is not weak, to serve the cause of justice, or to prop up social norms. Often, there is an element of evening up the score. The actor feels "one down" because of the offender's prior action and seeks to restore his or her status, sense of power, or material well-being by responding aggressively.

The rest of this section will discuss conditions that enhance or diminish the likelihood and extent of retaliation. Conditions that encourage retaliation are assumed to make escalation sequences more likely and more extensive, while those that discourage retaliation are assumed to have the opposite effect. Some conditions involve the actor's attributions and perceptions. Others involve temporary features of the situation, characteristics of the actor, the actor's relationship with the offender, and the nature of the community in which actor and offender are embedded.

Attributions of Responsibility

Retaliation is more likely and more extensive if the offender is seen as responsible for the annoyance, that is, as taking action that was "both controllable and intentional, without significant mitigating circumstances" (Martinko & Zellars, 1998). Evidence for this effect comes from a study of marriage by Bradbury & Fincham (1992) in which people who saw their spouses as responsible for a problem in their marriage were especially likely to make hostile and rejecting comments when they discussed that problem with their spouses. Attributions of responsibility were also prominent in student explanations of incidents in which they "decided to get even" with someone at work (Bies & Tripp, 1996).

Allred (1999) added to these findings the plausible hypothesis that retaliation is more likely if the offender *does not* see him- or herself as responsible for the annoyance. If the offender accepted this responsibility, he or she would probably apologize or make amends, which should ward off retaliation by the actor.

In attributing responsibility to an offender, actors often overlook the possibility that the offender is retaliating for something the actor did previously. They retaliate further on the mistaken assumption that the offender started the fight. This self-serving assumption makes it easier for actors to retaliate because they fault the offender entirely rather than faulting themselves or the two of them jointly.

If a conflict spiral ensues and this misattribution continues, the phenomenon is sometimes called "biased punctuation" (Bies et al., 1997; Kramer, 2004) An objective observer would see the escalation sequence as A→O→ A→O→A→O→A (where A is the actor's contentious behavior, O is the offender's contentious behavior, and the arrows denote causation). But the actor punctuates the sequence differently, (A,O→A,O→A,O→A), seeing the offender as the originator of each turn in the spiral and ignoring his or her own input. This justifies what the actor is doing and may well be the driving force behind the escalation. If the offender also engages in biased punctuation (A→O,A→O,A→O,A)—as often happens—there are two driving forces, and the escalation sequence is likely to be more severe and to last longer than would otherwise be the case.

Perceptions of Illegitimacy

Retaliation is also more likely and more extensive if the offender is seen as acting illegitimately, that is, as disregarding rules, breaking promises, or violating fairness norms (Bies et al., 1997). There is a rich research tradition concerning the violation of fairness (also called justice) norms.

A distinction can be made between three kinds of fairness norms: distributive justice (one's outcomes are commensurate with one's merit or effort), procedural justice (decision making about one's outcomes is consistent, unbiased, accurate, and correctable), and interactional justice (one's views are solicited, one's outcomes are honestly explained, and one is treated sensitively and with respect). Violations of each kind of fairness norm have been shown to produce retaliation (distributive justice; Adams, 1965; procedural justice; Lind & Tyler, 1988; interactional justice; Greenberg, 1990; Lind, 1999).

In a study that looked at the three kinds of fairness norms together, Skarlicki and Folger (1997) asked factory workers about their company's policies in all three realms and about their coworkers' retaliatory behavior in the form of damaging equipment, wasting time or materials, calling in sick when well, spreading rumors, and the like. Retaliation was most pronounced in companies that were seen as violating all three kinds of norm. However, companies that were seen as according their workers either procedural or interactional justice were able to violate the norm of distributive justice with relative impunity.

Temporary Features of the Situation That Affect the State of the Actor

Retaliation is sometimes encouraged by a cognitive deficit that erodes attention to standards of conduct or the capacity to think ahead. Sources of such a deficit include stress, fatigue, and cognitive overload (Baron, 2004). Time pressure can also produce such a deficit, as shown in an experiment by Yovetitch and Rusbult (1994). Participants were asked how they would act in various situations where a person they knew engaged in annoying behavior (e.g., a romantic partner saying during an argument "I'd be better off without you"). Those who were given little time to respond were more likely to endorse a harsh response, such as yelling at or refusing to talk to the offender, than those who were given ample time.

Heavy alcohol consumption (three or more drinks) has a related effect by focusing attention on the annoyance and away from the little voice that tells one that retaliation may be illegitimate or may get one into trouble (Steele & Josephs, 1990; Taylor & Leonard, 1983). Indeed, alcohol has such a profound effect on retaliation that it contributed to 64% of the homicides in Philadelphia between 1948 and 1952 (Wolfgang & Strohm, 1956).

Anger from a prior unrelated annoyance can make people irritable and prone to retaliate (Berkowitz, Cochran, & Embree, 1981; Pederson, Gonzales, & Miller, 2000), a phenomenon sometimes called "displaced aggression." For example, "after a severe 'dressing-down' by a supervisor concerning one issue, an individual may aggress strongly against a coworker who offers mild criticism on a totally unrelated matter" (Baron, 2004, p. 40).

Autonomic arousal also promotes retaliatory behavior. In an experiment on this effect (Zillmann, Katcher, & Milavsky, 1972), participants were either provoked or not provoked by a confederate and then either aroused by strenuous physical exercise or not so aroused. When they eventually had an opportunity to retaliate by giving electric shocks to the confederate, the combination of provocation and arousal produced a disproportionate level of shock. Similar effects have been found for arousal produced by injection of a stimulant, loud noise, and competitive activity (Baron, 1977).

By contrast, recent pleasurable experiences, such as humor or mildly erotic stimulation, have been shown to diminish retaliatory behavior. Thus, Baron (1976) annoyed male motorists by having the car ahead of them fail to start up when a traffic light turned green. At the same time, a female confederate crossed the road in plain view of the motorist. When the confederate was dressed normally, 90% of the motorists retaliated against the car ahead by blowing their horn. However, when she was dressed as a clown (humor) or in "a very brief and revealing outfit" (mildly erotic stimulation), only about half of them did so. It may be that the latter two conditions put the motorists in a good mood, which was incompatible with an aggressive response. There are other possible explanations for these findings, but more highly controlled laboratory experiments have confirmed that nonhostile forms of humor (Baron & Ball, 1974) and mildly erotic stimulation (Baron & Bell, 1977) discourage retaliation.

Aggressive cues (anything that reminds people of aggression) tend to encourage retaliation and hence escalation. These include aggressive people (models), aggressive words, and aggressive objects. This effect partly explains how a "culture of aggression" is perpetuated in an organization. Aggressive cues encourage aggression, which provides more aggressive cues.

More research is needed on the impact of a delay after experiencing annoyance. Some scholars (e.g., Baron, 2004; Berkowitz, 1993) argue that a delay produces dysphoric rumination that encourages retaliation while others (e.g., Walton, 1969) contend that a delay allows a cooling off period, which diminishes retaliation.

Actor Characteristics

Individual Differences.   Overall, men retaliate more heavily than women do, especially in the physical realm (Eagly & Steffen, 1986; Martinko & Zellars, 1998). However, there is some evidence that women are more annoyed by perceived unfairness, so there may be a special exception in this case. In the unilateral escalation study described earlier (Mikolic et al., 1997), women viewed the confederates who deprived them of the resources as more unfair and escalated further in their comments to these confederates than did men.

Research also suggests a number of personality characteristics that are related to the tendency to retaliate. One example is the hostile attribution bias—a tendency to assume that annoying behavior from others is done with hostile intent. Dodge and associates (Dodge & Coie, 1987; Dodge & Crick, 1990) showed that this bias is predictive of retaliatory behavior. For example, in the Dodge and Coie (1987) study, teachers put primary school boys into three categories: often initiating aggression, often retaliating aggressively, or neither. Unlike the other two groups, the retaliators were found to see hostile intent in videotaped incidents of accidental annoyance.

Type A individuals—people who are hard driving, competitive, and time urgent—have also been shown to engaged in more retaliation than type B individuals—people who are easy going (Baron, Neuman, & Geddes, 1999; Carver & Glass, 1978). In the Carver and Glass (1978) experiment, undergraduates were first insulted about their progress on a puzzle and then had a chance to shock the insulter. Type A individuals employed more shock than did type B individuals.

Folklore to the contrary, no relationship has been found between low self-esteem and readiness to retaliate (Baumeister, Smart, & Boden, 1996). However, certain kinds of people with high self-esteem show that tendency—those whose self-esteem is unstable so that they occasionally experience periods of self-doubt (Kernis, Grannemann, & Barclay, 1989) and those with narcissistic (inflated and grandiose) views of themselves (Bushman & Baumeister, 1998). In the Bushman and Baumeister (1998) study, undergraduates at various levels of measured narcissism were given strikingly unfavorable evaluations of essays they had written and then had a chance to blast the evaluator with noise. Those who were higher in narcissism gave louder and, hence, more punitive blasts, an effect that was not found when positive evaluations of the essays were given. The mechanism for both these effects is probably one of ego threat. People with unstable high self-esteem and narcissists suffer especially uncomfortable self-doubts when others assert superiority over them or put them down. Hence, they lash out to protect their self-esteem.

Two personality traits—high need for social approval (Dengerink, 1976) and empathy with others (Rusbult, Verette, Whitney, Slovik, & Lipkus, 1991)—encourage underreaction and, hence, reduce the extent of escalation.

Group Characteristics. Personality effects such as those just described are important in interpersonal interaction, but they tend to wash out in intergroup and interorganizational settings, where several people with different personalities make collective decisions. In such settings, group characteristics are much more important.

As mentioned earlier, groups tend to escalate farther in response to persistent annoyance than do individuals (Mikolic et al., 1997). In addition, some kinds of groups are more prone to escalation than others. For example a culture of honor, requiring retaliation in the face of personal slights, is seen in some parts of the world. Strong evidence of this cultural trait has been found for White men from the U.S. South (Nisbett & Cohen, 1996). Such cultures are also found in U.S. inner cities (Anderson, 1999) and in many prisons (Toch, 1969).

Group mobilization is often an antecedent of escalation. Mobilization means that group members become aware of their common identity and grievances and develop group solidarity. Leaders typically emerge in the process of mobilization. Gurr (1996) found that mobilization often occurs when ethnic groups come into conflict. The early days of unionization followed a similar path, with workers becoming mobilized in workplace after workplace. Mobilized groups are particularly prone to retaliate when their group is attacked or one or more members of their group are harmed.

Relationships Between the Parties

Retaliation, and hence escalation, is less severe to the extent that there are bonds between the actor and the defender. The bonds in question include kinship, friendship, common group identity, perceived similarity, positive attitudes, and dependence. The importance of friendship was shown by Ransford (1968) in a survey of African Americans immediately after the first Watts riots. Respondents who reported having social contact with Whites were much less likely to say that they were willing to use violence to get African American rights than those who did not report such contact. The importance of dependence was shown in a laboratory experiment on negotiation by Ben-Yoav and Pruitt (1984). Participants who were dependent on the other negotiator for future cooperation were less likely to employ contentious tactics than those who were not so dependent.

The opposite side of this coin is that the absence of bonds makes retaliation, and hence escalation, more severe. Thus, in a survey of Israeli citizens, Struch and Schwartz (1989) found that respondents who saw ultraorthodox Jews as very different in behavior and appearance from their own group were especially likely to endorse punitive actions to keep the ultraorthodox in line.

The effect of bonds is often masked by the fact that bonds encourage interaction, which encourages conflict. But the existence of bonds means that this conflict is more likely to be handled by problem solving and less likely to escalate. This paradox was seen in an experiment on two-person groups by Back (1951). High group solidarity (e.g., strong bonds) was created in three different ways: increasing the attraction between group members, enhancing the importance of the group task, and heightening the prestige of the group in the experimenter's eyes. A fourth condition involved low group solidarity. When the groups discussed a controversial topic, the highly solidary groups argued more vigorously than the less solidary group, but they also made a greater effort to reach agreement.

Negative attitudes, hostility, and disrespect tend to encourage retaliation and hence escalation. Research on marital functioning suggested that this effect is mediated by distrust, leading to a tendency to see the other as responsible for unpleasant events and hence as deserving retaliation. For example, Bradbury and Fincham (1992) found that in distressed marriages, wives tended to blame their husbands for their marital problems—to see the spouse as "behaving intentionally and with selfish motivation" (p. 620). This blame was related, in turn, to "negative reciprocity" in conversations—responding to the husband's hostile and rejecting remarks with similar remarks.

In sound marriages, on the other hand, one finds "accommodation," where annoyance from the partner produces mild reactions because the partner's behavior is assumed to be inadvertent or due to mitigating circumstances (Bradbury & Fincham, 1992; Rusbult et al., 1991). In a related questionnaire study of dating couples (Murray & Holmes, 1997), positive images of the partner were associated with avoidance of conflict spirals.

Characteristics of the Broader Community

Individuals are imbedded in workgroups, workgroups in departments, departments in organizations, and organizations in states or countries. At every level, there is a broader community that can influence the way conflict is handled and how much escalation there will be. For example, outside support in a controversy—approval from members of the broader community—tends to encourage an unwillingness to concede and a readiness to fight back, leading to escalation (Pruitt & Kim, 2004).

Community members can also discourage or try to reverse escalation, and this is particularly common within organizations. Communities often maintain and enforce conflict-limiting norms aimed at reducing the harshness of tactics used by community members. Indeed, Gurr (1996) argued, on the basis of many case studies of ethno-political conflict, that weakened enforcement of such norms often leads to revolts by ethnic minorities who have strong, shared grievances.

Communities may also provide third-party services, both formal and informal, to help solve conflicts that might otherwise escalate. Some organizations have ombudsmen (Kolb, 1989) or outside consultants (Walton, 1969) to provide such services. Superiors have traditionally not been much interested in serving as mediators (Kolb & Sheppard, 1985), though this may be changing as executives attend the many conflict management workshops available today, they are often well placed to mediate. As organizations become more complex and decentralized, emergent mediators are becoming more common, that is, people who "operate at the boundaries between different parts of the organization" and talk informally to both sides in a controversy (Kolb, 1989, p. 107).

Community structure is also important. Heavily escalated reactions to annoyance from other groups are much less likely when there are *crosscutting*, as opposed to *overlapping*, bonds (Coleman, 1957). In a heavily crosscutting structure, important members of most subgroups have bonds with members of most other subgroups. In a heavily overlapping structure, subgroup members are only bonded to other members of their own subgroup. When conflict arises between two groups in a heavily crosscutting community, group members who are bonded to members of the other group will be reluctant to escalate. They will also try to dampen the conflict by urging moderation, criticizing leaders who are seeking to incite intergroup hostility, refuting inflammatory rumors, and trying to mediate the conflict. In heavily overlapping communities, such individuals are not available, and escalation is much more likely.

The importance of crosscutting for preventing severe escalation was seen in a study by Varshney (2002). Three Indian cities that experienced repeated and severe Hindu–Muslim conflict over a 45-year period were compared with three matched cities that did not experience much conflict. The latter cities contained strong civic associations—trade unions, political parties, professional associations, business groups—that embraced members of both ethnic groups, while the former did not. Furthermore, whenever signs of conflict arose, members of these associations became active in combating escalation.

Common group membership is an especially important bond in organizations. It motivates problem solving because of the desire to preserve the common group and it facilitates communication, which makes problem solving possible. Likert's (1961) "linking pin" approach to organizational decision making is an example of a crosscutting structure. Critical members of each department (the linking pins) become members of an interdepartmental (crosscutting) committee with decision-making powers.

STRUCTURAL CHANGES AND PERSISTENT ESCALATION

Most escalation dissipates over time. However, heavy escalation sometimes persists, continuing month after month or reasserting itself regularly whenever there is minor conflict. Persistent, heavily escalated conflict is sometimes called "intractable conflict" (Coleman, 2000).

Two main dynamics underlie intractable conflict. Conflict spirals account in part for this phenomenon, with the parties alternating, ad infinitum, in reacting harshly to each other's unacceptable behavior. However, the main source of intractable conflict lies in structural changes—enduring transformations to the parties, their relationship, and/or the surrounding community—that result from heavy escalation and encourage further heavy escalation (Pruitt & Kim, 2004). What happens is that some of the conditions that were discussed in the prior section are exacerbated by heavy escalation and do not return to their former state (Pruitt & Kim, 2004; Pruitt & Olczak, 1995).

An example of a structural change is that escalation can encourage group mobilization on one or both sides of a conflict. People become more identified with their group, solidarity increases, and militant leaders gain a wider audience, urging hostile action against the opposing group. The result is more escalation, and *more persistent* escalation because such transformations are not easily reversed.

Another example is the deterioration of relationships that often accompanies escalation. Negative attitudes and perceptions, hostility and distrust set in, and bonds between the parties are destroyed. The antagonists stop identifying with each other, drop their membership in common groups, and sever their dependence on each other. Communication between them breaks down. Again, such transformations tend to endure, which encourages persistent escalation.

When the parties to a conflict are groups, the destruction of bonds is called "community polarization"—a movement away from crosscutting structure and toward overlapping structure (Pruitt & Kim, 2004). As escalation continues, community polarization often deepens, with formerly neutral individuals and groups taking sides with one or the other antagonist. Potential mediators disappear, norms that protect each side from the other's aggression are viewed as outdated, and the antagonists find increasing social support for escalated behavior against each other. Communities often have difficulty finding their way back from such heavy polarization, and escalation becomes a permanent feature of the landscape.

Perhaps the most ominous kind of structural change in intergroup conflict is the development of militant subgroups that have an agenda of defeating or destroying the opponent. An example would be the revival of the Irish Republican Army (IRA) in 1970, which occurred after a series of clashes between nationalists and unionists in Northern Ireland. This group of about 500 men developed the goal of ejecting the British government from Northern Ireland and used guerilla tactics in an effort to accomplish this goal. Similar groups were organized on the other side of the conflict. The result was a heavily escalated conflict that lasted for more than 25 years and in which more than 3,700 people were killed out of a population of 1.5 million (Moloney, 2002).

A similar but less lethal structural change occurred in 1970 on the author's campus after a clash between students and campus police (Pruitt & Gahagan, 1974; Pruitt & Kim, 2004). A strike committee of about 400 students was organized. The goals of this committee were to close down the

campus and thereby force the administration to make a number of concessions including abolishing ROTC and stopping military-funded research.
In addition to urging students to stop attending classes, the strike committee occupied the administration building and turned on the fire hoses.
The administration responded by suspending students and summoning
the city police onto the campus. At one point, a crowd of students who
emerged from a strike committee "war council" began throwing ice and
stones at the police, who charged into the crowd injuring and arresting
a number of students. Organization of the strike committee produced a
heavily escalated conflict that persisted for only a few weeks. However,
the basic dynamics were similar to those that produced the much longer
conflict in Northern Ireland.

AVOIDING AND COPING WITH SEVERE ESCALATION

Conflict is not the culprit. It is a normal part of organizational life,
resulting from the division of labor and differences in specialties. Nor
is escalation, per se, the culprit. Mild escalation helps the parties identify critical issues and motivates them to engage in problem solving and
accept needed change. Rather, the culprit is severe escalation that disrupts
organizational functioning, dries up creativity, and produces structural
changes that keep escalation going.

The fear of severe escalation sometimes motivates people to avoid talking about conflicts. This is unfortunate. Nontrivial conflicts need to be
brought out into the open and resolved through win–win agreements
(Tjosvold & Fang, 2005). Such agreements are beneficial to the organization as a whole as well as to the units involved in the agreement. But how
can conflict be confronted without sparking injurious escalation? A partial answer can be derived from some of the principles mentioned earlier
and some new principles.

When conflict is brewing, it is important to avoid conditions that
encourage escalation. For example, cognitive deficits should be avoided—
everybody should get enough sleep, heavy alcohol consumption should
be prohibited. In addition, people should be kept in a good mood, and
aggression-prone individuals should be screened out. Aggressive cues
should also be avoided. Treaties should not be negotiated in rooms that
are decorated with murals of the Trojan War.

When it is necessary to take actions that annoy people (e.g., criticism,
discipline, and discharge of popular employees), one should strive for
legitimacy and the basic elements of fairness. People should be rewarded
in accordance with their merit. Fair procedures should be used, involving
careful fact gathering, consistent criteria, unbiased decision making, and
avenues for appeal. The people impacted by the actions should have a
chance to defend themselves, and the decisions should be fully explained
in a way that shows respect for and sensitivity to the target of the action.

If an employee must be punished, it is essential to clearly link the punishment to the offender's actions. Otherwise, biased punctuation may set in, with the offender viewing the episode as starting with an arbitrary administrative action rather than with his or her own misdeeds.

It is also important to organize for effective conflict management. Ury et al. (1988) suggested that if there is tension between two groups, negotiators should be appointed in both groups, and mediators should be chosen from the broader community. These people should be trained in their roles and should get to know each other. This will allow the organization to move quickly when escalation is looming to prevent the development of conflict spirals and structural changes. Organizations often fail to reward people for serving as mediators (Kolb, 1989), but it is important to do so if escalation is to be avoided. Organizing for conflict management also involves building crosscutting bonds. Cross-departmental lunches, company picnics, and the like are a good idea, but cross-departmental groups that meet regularly and have some real power are likely to be more effective.

Another approach to tension between two groups is to run problem-solving workshops (Fisher, 1997; Kelman, 1992). This involves (a) locating second-level people in each group who are interested in resolving the conflict and (b) involving them in meetings to analyze what has happened and develop plans for alleviating the situation. Sometimes there is a "reentry problem," such that these individuals are reabsorbed into the old escalation-prone system when they return to their home base. If so, it may be possible to run a workshop involving the entire home base, using the large-group intervention methods developed by Bunker and Alban (1997).

Timing is critical when structural changes are imminent and conflicts threaten to spiral out of control (Pruitt & Kim, 2004). Thus, Varshney (2002) argued that, when conflict is looming, community leaders must move fast to quell rumors about atrocities and to silence militant factional leaders. Strategic apology is also sometimes useful (Ohbuchi, Kameda, & Agarie, 1989). In the conflict on the author's campus, the strike committee was organized a few days after campus police beat two students in full view of hundreds of others. The result was severe escalation and weeks of turmoil. This escalation might well have been avoided if the university president had immediately apologized for the beatings and disciplined the offending police officers (Pruitt & Kim, 2004).

If directly involved in a conflict spiral, one should avoid retaliation because that will perpetuate the spiral. But it is also important to avoid conceding, as that rewards the adversary's aggressive behavior (Brett et al., 1998). Instead, some form of problem solving makes most sense.

If intractable conflict develops despite efforts at conflict management, third parties need to be alert for a "ripe" moment in which both sides see themselves as in a stalemate or are suffering enough to consider changing their approaches (Pruitt, 2005; Zartman, 1989, 2000). Alternatively, if third parties are powerful, they may create a ripe moment by putting pressure on both sides to stop the escalation (Fisher & Keashly, 1990). When a ripe moment arises, it may be possible to arrange for the parties to discuss their differences directly. If that is not possible, third parties can serve as intermediaries to reassure each side of the other's readiness to de-escalate and to help both sides develop ideas for solving the basic problems (Pruitt, 2003; Pruitt & Kim, 2004). Another approach at the point of ripeness is to persuade one party to take a unilateral conciliatory initiative to enhance the other party's trust (Osgood, 1962; Pruitt & Kim, 2004). Ripeness theory has been developed in the context of international conflict and civil war, but it seems fully applicable to organizational settings.

If all else fails, it is sometimes possible to reduce the parties' interdependence so that they no longer have to deal with each other. Individuals can be transferred or fired, counterpart workgroups can be shuffled, or departments can report to a different supervisor.

GAPS IN THEORY AND RESEARCH

Theory and research on escalation are not as well developed as in many other subfields of social science. Hence, it is especially important to identify gaps in this body of knowledge. Three kinds of gaps will be addressed: gaps in empirical research, gaps in theory, and gaps in knowledge about how to apply escalation theory to organizations.

Gaps in Empirical Research

In writing this chapter, I tried where possible to draw on well-designed, empirical research. Doing so was not a problem in the section on retaliatory escalation, which is mainly based on psychological studies of aggression, perceived fairness, and marital dysfunction. However, I had to rely on untested theory in most of the rest of the chapter. That theory has its roots in case material and practitioner experience and is by no means idle speculation. However, it needs to be tested with well-designed empirical studies.

The following are some of the most pressing empirical challenges:

1. *Examining* the impact of group mobilization and its elements (in-group identity, recognition of common grievances, group solidarity, and the emergence of leadership) on retaliation for annoyance to the group or its members
2. *Testing* the hypothesis that crosscutting (as opposed to overlapping) bonds between groups discourage the escalation of community conflict. Varshney's (2002) study of Hindu–Muslim conflict in three

matched pairs of Indian cities made an excellent beginning at testing this hypothesis. However, his sample of cases should be expanded and statistical methods should be used. It is also important to gather more process information in order to understand how crosscutting bonds produce this effect, if indeed they do.

3. *Assessing* whether the conditions that encourage retaliation (e.g., attribution of responsibility, autonomic arousal, highly unstable self-esteem, group mobilization, and crosscutting) also encourage unilateral and bilateral escalation sequences. In looking at bilateral escalation sequences, or conflict spirals, such studies should compare three circumstances: the presence of these conditions on both sides of the conflict, their presence on only one side, and their presence on neither side.

4. *Testing* the assumption that escalation-induced structural changes (e.g., heightened hostility and distrust, community polarization, and the development of militant subgroups) underlie intractable conflict

5. *Examining* the effectiveness of the various prophylactics and remedies proposed in the just prior section (e.g., appointing and training potential negotiators and mediators, problem solving workshops, strategic apology, and third-party intervention at a ripe moment). Theory and practitioner experience have almost entirely outrun empirical research in the realm of practice.

Gaps in Theory Development

Four gaps in escalation theory seem particularly noteworthy. To fill these gaps will require imaginative thought followed by empirical test. The gaps are as follows:

1. *Conflict spirals* do not always produce continued escalation. Sometimes the harshness of tactics increases for a while and then levels off with a conflict spiral still going on. For example, after escalating from quiet expressions of displeasure to shouting and threats, two boys may begin a fistfight in which they exchange blows with a constant level of force for a period. Theory is needed about the processes underlying this leveling off and the conditions that produce it.

2. *Useful theory* about the structural changes that contribute to intractable conflict exists. However, little is known about the conditions under which these transformations occur. Do they occur at a time when escalation becomes so severe that it passes over a point of no return (see Pruitt, 1969)? Or are there other contributing conditions, such as the prior existence of potential group leadership?

3. *Ripeness theory* is quite useful for explaining de-escalation in a number of international and ethno-political conflicts (e.g., Zartman, 1989; Pruitt, 1997). However, this theory is considerably less

adept at *predicting* de-escalation. For example, we know that high costs on both sides cause some highly escalated conflicts to end quickly (e.g., the Nagorno–Karabakh War; see Mooradian & Druckman, 1999), but they have a much delayed effect on others (e.g., the Israeli–Palestinian conflict since 2000). What conditions account for this difference? How can ripeness theory be made more predictive (for initial efforts to answer these questions, see Zartman, 2000; Pruitt, 2005)?

4. *Ripeness theory* is also deficient in identifying the mechanisms by which ripeness produces movement toward de-escalation. Somehow, the structural changes that produce persistent escalation are reversed or outbalanced, but it is not clear just how this works? Coleman (1997) suggested that "unfreezing" occurs, and Pruitt (2005) proposed that leaders gather new information. However, these ideas are quite preliminary.

Gaps in Applying Escalation Theory to Organizations

Most escalation theory has been developed in realms other than organizational behavior, and it is not always clear how to extend this theory into the latter realm. Three empirical questions arise from this unclarity:

1. Is it true, as hypothesized earlier, that passive and indirect forms of escalation are more common within organizations than in other settings, such as relations between organizations?
2. If passive and indirect forms of escalation are especially common within organizations, it should be harder for victims to trace escalation to its source than in other settings. If so, there should be less retaliation within organizations than in other settings. This implies, in turn, that conflict spirals should be less likely to develop. Can this derivation be verified empirically?
3. The last and most important question is a broad one: Do the propositions of escalation theory that have been developed in other settings apply equally to organizations? The answer to this question is clearly "yes" for some propositions because they have been cross validated (or in a few cases initially tested) in organizations. Thus, Bies and Tripp (1996) showed that attributions of responsibility encourage retaliation in organizations, as they do in other settings. All three forms of injustice (distributive, procedural, and interactional) are found to be related to escalation in organizations (see Adams, 1965; Greenberg, 1990; Lind & Tyler, 1988) as well as other settings. Type A (in comparison with type B) individuals are more likely to retaliate in organizational settings (Baron, Neuman, & Geddes, 1999) as well as in the laboratory. However, most escalation theory still needs to be tested in organizational settings.

REFERENCES

Adams, J. S. (1965). Inequity in social exchange. In L. Berkowitz (Ed.), *Advances in experimental social psychology* (Vol. 2, pp. 267–299). New York: Academic Press.

Allred, K. C. (1999). Anger and retaliation: Toward an understanding of impassioned conflict in organizations. In R. J. Bies, R. J. Lewicki, & B. H. Sheppard, (Eds.), *Research on negotiation in organizations* (Vol. 7, pp. 27–58). Stamford, CT: JAI.

Anderson, E. (1999). *Code of the street: Decency, violence, and the moral life of the inner city.* New York: W. W. Norton.

Back, K. W. (1951). Influence through social communication. *Journal of Abnormal and Social Psychology, 46,* 9–23.

Baron, R. A. (1976). The reduction of human aggression: A field study of the influence of incompatible reactions. *Journal of Applied Social Psychology, 6,* 260–274.

Baron, R. A. (1977). *Human aggression.* New York: Plenum.

Baron, R. A. (2004). Workplace aggression and violence: Insights from basic research. In R. W. Griffin & A. M. O'Leary-Kelly (Eds.), *The dark side of organizational behavior* (pp. 23–61). San Francisco: Jossey-Bass.

Baron, R. A., & Ball, R. L. (1974). The aggression-inhibiting influence of nonhostile humor. *Journal of Experimental Social Psychology, 10,* 23–33.

Baron, R. A., & Bell, P. A. (1977). Sexual arousal and aggression by males: Effects of type of erotic stimuli and prior provocation. *Journal of Personality and Social Psychology, 35,* 79–87.

Baron, R. A., Neuman, J. H., & Geddes, D. (1999). Social and personal determinants of workplace aggression: Evidence for the impact of perceived injustice and the type A behavior pattern. *Aggressive Behavior, 25,* 281–297.

Baumeister, R. F., Smart, L., & Boden, J. M. (1996). Relation of threatened egotism to violence and aggression: The dark side of high self-esteem. *Psychological Review, 103,* 5–33.

Ben-Yoav, O., & Pruitt, D. G. (1984). Accountability to constituents: A two-edged sword. *Organizational Behavior and Human Performance, 34,* 283–295.

Berkowitz, L. (1993). *Aggression: Its causes, consequences, and control.* New York: McGraw-Hill.

Berkowitz, L., Cochran, S. T., & Embree, M. C. (1981). Physical pain and the goal of aversively stimulated aggression. *Journal of Personality and Social Psychology, 40,* 687–700.

Bies, R. J., & Tripp, T. M. (1996). Beyond distrust: "Getting even" and the need for revenge. In R. M. Kramer & T. R. Tyler (Eds.), *Trust in organizations* (pp. 246–260). Thousand Oaks, CA: Sage.

Bies, R. J., Tripp, T. M., & Kramer, R. M. (1997). At the breaking point: Cognitive and social dynamics of revenge in organizations. In R. A. Giacolone & J. Greenberg (Eds.), *Antisocial behavior in organizations* (pp. 18–36). Thousand Oaks, CA: Sage.

Bradbury, T. N., & Fincham, F. D. (1992). Attributions and behavior in marital interaction. *Journal of Personality and Social Psychology, 63,* 613–628.

Brett, J. M., Shapiro, D. L., & Lytle, A. L. (1998). Breaking the bonds of reciprocity in negotiations. *Academy of Management Journal, 41,* 410–424.

Bunker, B. B., & Alban, B. T. (1997). *Large group interventions.* San Francisco: Jossey-Bass.

Bushman, B. J., & Baumeister, R. F. (1998). Threatened egotism, narcissism, self-esteem, and direct and displaced aggression: Does self-love or self-hate lead to violence? *Journal of Personality and Social Psychology, 75*, 219–229.

Buss, A. H. (1961). *The psychology of aggression.* New York: Wiley.

Carnevale, P. J., & Probst, T. M. (1998). Social values and social conflict in creative problem solving and categorization. *Journal of Personality and Social Psychology, 74*, 1300–1309.

Carver, C. S., & Glass, D. C. (1978). Coronary-prone behavior pattern and interpersonal aggression. *Journal of Personality and Social Psychology, 36*, 361–366.

Coleman, J. S. (1957). *Community conflict.* New York: Free Press.

Coleman, P. T. (1997). Redefining ripeness: A social-psychological perspective. *Journal of Peace Psychology, 3*, 81–103.

Coleman, P. T. (2000). Intractable conflict. In M. Deutsch & P. T. Coleman (Eds.), *The handbook of conflict resolution: Theory and practice* (pp. 428–450). San Francisco: Jossey-Bass.

Dengerink, H. A. (1976). Personality variables as mediators of attack-instigated aggression. In R. G. Geen & E. C. O'Neal (Eds.), *Perspectives on aggression* (pp. 61–98). New York: Academic Press.

Dodge, K. A., & Coie, J. D. (1987). Social-information-processing factors in reactive and proactive aggression in children's peer groups. *Journal of Personality and Social Psychology, 53*, 1146–1158.

Dodge, K. A., & Crick, N. R. (1990). Social information-processing bases of aggressive behavior in children. *Personality and Social Psychology Bulletin, 16*, 8–22.

Eagly, A. H., & Steffen, V. J. (1986). Gender and aggressive behavior: A meta-analytic review of the social psychological literature. *Psychological Bulletin, 100*, 309–330.

Fisher, R. J. (1997). *Interactive conflict resolution.* Syracuse, NY: Syracuse University Press.

Fisher, R. J., & Keashly, L. (1990). A contingency approach to third party intervention. In R. J. Fisher (Ed.), *The social psychology of intergroup and international conflict resolution* (pp. 234–238). New York: Springer-Verlag.

Geddes, D. (1994). *The relationship between negative feedback and increased organizational aggression.* Paper presented at the meeting of the Academy of Management, Dallas, Texas.

Greenberg, J. (1990). Employee theft as a reaction to underpayment inequity: The hidden cost of pay cuts. *Journal of Applied Psychology, 75*, 561–568.

Gurr, T. R. (1996). Minorities, nationalists, and ethnopolitical conflict. In C. Crocker & F. Hampson (Eds.), *Managing global chaos: Sources of and responses to international conflict* (pp. 53–78). Washington, DC: United States Institute of Peace Press.

Kelman, H. C. (1992). Informal mediation by the scholar/practitioner. In J. Bercovitch & J. Z. Rubin (Eds.), *Mediation in international relations* (pp. 64–96). New York: St. Martins.

Kernis, M. H., Grannemann, B. D., & Barclay, L. C. (1989). Stability and level of self-esteem as predictors of anger arousal and hostility. *Journal of Personality and Social Psychology, 56*, 1013–1022.

Kolb, D. M. (1989). Labor mediators, managers, and ombudsmen: Roles mediators play in different contexts. In K. Kressel, D. G. Pruitt, & Associates, *Mediation research* (pp. 91–114). San Francisco: Jossey-Bass.

Kolb, D. M., & Sheppard, B. H. (1985). Do managers mediate or even arbitrate? *Negotiation Journal, 1,* 379–388.

Kramer, R. M. (2004). The "dark side" of social context: The role of intergroup paranoia in intergroup negotiations. In M. J. Gelfand & J. M. Brett (Eds.), *The handbook of negotiation and culture* (pp. 219–237). Stanford, CA: Stanford University Press.

Likert, R. (1961). *New patterns of management.* New York: McGraw-Hill.

Lind, E. A. (1999). Social involvement, justice judgments, and the psychology of negotiation. In Bies, R. J., Lewicki, R. J., & Sheppard, B. H. (Eds.), *Research on negotiation in organizations* (Vol. 7, pp. 125–139). Stamford, CT: JAI.

Lind, E. A., & Tyler, T. R. (1988). *The social psychology of procedural justice.* New York: Plenum.

Martinko, M. J. & Zellars, K. L. (1998). Toward a theory of workplace violence and aggression: A cognitive appraisal perspective. In R. W. Griffin, A. O'Leary-Kelly, & J. M. Collins (Eds.), *Dysfunctional behavior in organizations: Violent and deviant behavior* (pp. 1–42). Stamford, CT: JAI Press.

Mikolic, J. M., Parker, J. C., & Pruitt, D. G. (1997). Escalation in response to persistent annoyance: Groups versus individuals and gender effects. *Journal of Personality and Social Psychology, 72,* 151–163.

Moloney, E. (2002). *A secret history of the IRA.* New York: Norton.

Mooradian, M., & Druckman, D. (1999). Hurting stalemate or mediation? The conflict over Nagorno-Karabakh, 1990–95. *Journal of Peace Research, 36,* 709–727.

Murray, S. L., & Holmes, J. G. (1997). A leap of faith? Positive illusions in romantic relationships. *Personality and Social Psychology Bulletin, 23,* 586–604.

Neuman, J. H., & Baron, R. A. (1997). Aggression in the workplace. In R. A. Giacalone & J. Greenberg, *Antisocial behavior in organizations* (pp. 37–67). Thousand Oaks, CA: Sage.

Nisbett, R. E., & Cohen, D. (1996). *Culture of honor: The psychology of violence in the South.* Boulder, CO: Westview.

Ohbuchi, K., Kameda, M., & Agarie, N. (1989). Apology as aggression control: Its role in mediating appraisal of and response to harm. *Journal of Personality and Social Psychology, 56,* 219–227.

Osgood, C. E. (1962). *An alternative to war or surrender.* Urbana, IL: University of Illinois Press.

Pederson, W. C., Gonzales, C., & Miller, N. (2000). The moderating effect of trivial triggering provocation on displaced aggression. *Journal of Personality and Social Psychology, 78,* 913–947.

Pruitt, D. G. (1969). Stability and sudden change in interpersonal and international affairs. *Journal of Conflict Resolution, 13,* 18–38.

Pruitt, D. G. (2003). *Communication chains in negotiation between organizations.* (Occasional Paper #3). Istanbul, Turkey: Sabanci University, Istanbul, Turkey. http://www.sabanciuniv.edu/ssbf/conf/eng/docs/occ_paper/finding_integrative_agreements.pdf

Pruitt, D. G. (2005). *Whither ripeness theory?* (Working Paper #25). Fairfax, VA: Institute for Conflict Analysis and Resolution, George Mason University. http://www.gmu.edu/departments/ICAR/wp_25_pruitt.pdf

Pruitt, D. G., & Gahagan, J. P. (1974). Campus crisis: The search for power. In J. T. Tedeschi (Ed.), *Perspectives on social power* (pp. 349–392). Chicago: Aldine.

Pruitt, D. G., & Kim, S. H. (2004). *Social conflict: Escalation, stalemate, and settlement* (3rd ed.). New York: McGraw-Hill.

Pruitt, D. G., & Olczak, P. V. (1995). Beyond hope: Approaches to resolving seemingly intractable conflict. In B. B. Bunker, & J. Z. Rubin, & Associates, *Conflict, cooperation and justice: Essays provoked by the work of Morton Deutsch* (pp. 59–92). San Francisco: Jossey-Bass.

Ransford, H. E. (1968). Isolation, powerlessness and violence: A study of attitudes and participation in the Watts riot. *American Journal of Sociology, 73,* 581–591.

Rusbult, C. E., Verette, J., Whitney, G. A., Slovik, L. F., & Lipkus, G. A. (1991). Accommodation processes in close relationships: Theory and preliminary empirical evidence. *Journal of Personality and Social Psychology, 60,* 53–78.

Skarlicki, D. P., & Folger, R. (1997). Retaliation in the workplace: The roles of distributive, procedural, and interactional justice. *Journal of Applied Psychology, 82,* 434–443.

Skarlicki, D. P., & Folger, R. (2004). Broadening our understanding of organizational retaliatory behavior. In R. W. Griffin & A. M. O'Leary-Kelly (Eds.), *The dark side of organizational behavior* (pp. 373–402). San Francisco: Jossey-Bass.

Steele, C. M., & Josephs, R. A. (1990). Alcohol myopia: Its prized and dangerous effects. *American Psychologist, 45,* 921–933.

Struch, N., & Schwartz, S. H. (1989). Intergroup aggression: Its predictors and distinctness from in-group bias. *Journal of Personality and Social Psychology, 56,* 364–373.

Taylor, S. P., & Leonard, K. E. (1983). Alcohol and human physical aggression. In R. G. Geen & E. Donnerstein (Eds.), *Aggression: Theoretical and empirical reviews: Vol. 2. Issues in research* (pp. 77–101). New York: Academic Press.

Tjosvold, D., & Fang, S. S. (2005). Manager as mediator: Developing a conflict-positive organization. In M. S. Herrman (Ed.), *The Blackwell handbook of mediation: A guide to effective negotiation.* Oxford, U.K.: Blackwell.

Tjosvold, D., Leung, K., & Johnson, D. W. (2000). Cooperative and competititve conflict in China. In M. Deutsch & P. T. Coleman (Eds.), *The handbook of conflict resolution: Theory and practice* (pp. 475–495). San Francisco: Jossey-Bass.

Toch, H. (1969). *Violent men: An inquiry into the psychology of violence.* Chicago: Aldine.

Ury, W., Brett, J. M., & Goldberg, S. (1988). *Getting disputes resolved.* San Francisco: Jossey-Bass.

Varshney, A. (2002). *Ethnic conflict and civic life: Hindus and Muslims in India.* New Haven, CT: Yale University Press.

Walton, R. E. (1969*). Interpersonal peacemaking: Confrontations and third-party consultation.* Reading, MA: Addison-Wesley.

Wolfgang, M., & Strohm, R. B. (1956). The relationship between alcohol and criminal homicide. *Quarterly Journal of Studies on Alcohol, 17,* 411–425.

Yovetitch, N. A., & Rusbult, C. E. (1994). Accomodative behavior in close relationships: Exploring transformation of motivation. *Journal of Experimental Social Psychology, 30,* 138–164.

Zartman, I. W. (1989). *Ripe for resolution: Conflict resolution in Africa* (2nd ed.). New York: Oxford.

Zartman, I. W. (2000). Ripeness: The hurting stalemate and beyond. In P. C. Stern, & D. Druckman (Eds.). *Conflict resolution after the Cold War* (pp. 225–250). Washington, DC: National Academy Press.

Zillmann, D., Katcher, A. H., & Milavsky, B. (1972). Excitation transfer from physical exercise to subsequent aggressive behavior. *Journal of Experimental Social Psychology, 8,* 247–259.

9

Conflict, Health, and Well-Being

PAUL E. SPECTOR AND VALENTINA BRUK-LEE
University of South Florida

The impact of interpersonal conflict in the workplace is not limited to outcomes of organizational relevance, such as performance; it also has serious detrimental effects on the health and well-being of employees. In fact, conflict has been shown to be associated with employee depression, negative emotional states, psychosomatic complaints, life dissatisfaction, burnout, and psychiatric morbidity (e.g., Dormann & Zapf, 1999; Spector, Dwyer, & Jex, 1988). A diary study by Bolger, DeLongis, Kessler, and Schilling (1989) showed that interpersonal conflicts were considered the most upsetting stressor by a sample of married couples who were asked to report work and nonwork sources of stress. C. S. Smith and Sulsky (1995) reported that 25% of a large sample of employees from a wide range of occupations listed interpersonal issues as the most vexing stressors at work. In addition, negative social interactions with others at work accounted for three fourths of all work situations that employees described as detrimental (Schwartz & Stone, 1993). It is not surprising then that interpersonal conflict in the workplace is consistently cited as a leading source of stress for employees across cultures, age groups, and occupations. Consequently, occupational stress research has experienced a recent shift in focus from commonly studied role and workload variables to stress resulting from the social work environment, namely interpersonal conflict.

The occupational stress literature differentiates between two main types of variables labeled "stressors" and "strains." Stressors are the perceived or objective environmental characteristics that may elicit a response from an employee, while strains refer to the negative responses employees may experience resulting from stressors. Hence, interpersonal conflict is categorized as a social stressor that may result in psychological, behavioral, and physiological strains. This social stressor may be conceptualized as "a dynamic process that occurs between parties as they experience negative emotional reactions to perceived disagreements and interference with the attainment of their goals" (adapted from Hartwick & Barki, in press).

THE CURRENT STATE OF CONFLICT, HEALTH, AND WELL-BEING RESEARCH

One of the most basic limitations to this topic is that there is no consensus on the definition of conflict, and often researchers fail to be precise in what they mean by conflict in their studies. In fact, researchers often omit a definition of conflict as measured in their studies or provide definitions that are unique to their own work. For example, conflict has been described as a "relationship in which a sequence of conditions and events moves toward aggressive behavior and disorder" (Ware & Barnes, 1992, p. 213) or as a "situation in which two individuals disagree about issues, actions, or goals and joint outcomes become important" (Gordon, 1999, p. 275) among many other definitions. Without a concise, widely agreed upon definition, research progress is slowed because results cannot always be generalized from one study to another.

What is needed is more conceptual and empirical work to clearly explicate what is meant by conflict. For example, researchers are not always clear whether conflict is an exchange in which two parties engage in behaviors directed toward one another or a unidirectional phenomenon in which one person does something to another passive recipient. The latter approach fails to distinguish conflict from other forms of interpersonal behavior at work such as bullying (Rayner & Keashly, 2005) or incivility (Pearson, Andersson, & Porath, 2004). Certainly, one can define *conflict* as a general phenomenon that subsumes others that are more specialized. However, there might well be differences between a case in which a person is the passive recipient and a case in which a person is an active participant in an equal exchange, even though the specific behaviors the person experiences, such as critical and insulting remarks, may be the same. Empirical work is needed to explore both types of phenomena in parallel to see if one is more damaging than the other is. Some researchers have argued that conflict is a bidirectional phenomenon (Fink, 1968; Hartwick & Barki, in press), and other terms might better refer to the unidirectional. The term *social stressor* is a more general concept that can subsume both.

There is also a need to break conflict into its component parts. Some of that work has been done; for example, Barki and Hartwick (2001) distinguished various components of the conflict process, including disagreement, interference, and emotional response. They also divided conflict into types, according to its focus on personal issues versus work tasks. Work is needed to further explore these and possibly other components/ types of conflict.

Given the lack of a consensus definition, it is not surprising that well-established, psychometrically sound measures are in short supply. Often, measures are created for the purpose of a particular study, and evidence for the reliability and validity of the scales is deficient or not presented. Sometimes, there is an incomplete explication of the link between the conceptual definition of conflict and the measure being used. Other times, there may be overlap between the measure of conflict and other variables. For example, the interpersonal conflict at work scale (ICAWS; Spector & Jex, 1998) is a four-item, summated rating scale. Although the ICAWS has been shown to have reasonable psychometric properties, some of the item content overlaps with measures of incivility or bullying in that they ask about things that are done to the individual that might or might not be part of a bidirectional exchange (e.g., "people do nasty things to me at work"). Other measures may provide an incomplete picture of conflict, such as Jehn's (1995) eight-item scale that focused mostly on disagreement and that might not clearly distinguish conflict from merely having different views. Lastly, some conflict measures were created for use in specific settings and samples and are, thus, limited in their application to diverse settings.

Additional scale development work is needed to provide scales for general workplace use that have good content validity in covering the various aspects of conflict, clearly distinguishing conflict from other related constructs. It seems important to distinguish personal from task conflict, unidirectional versus bidirectional interactions between people, and conflict from just disagreement. The development of sound measures will help encourage continued work.

Similarly, De Dreu and Weingart (2003) pointed out that a widely accepted conceptualization of personal well-being is missing, which raises concerns regarding the operationalization of our research criteria. Further, there have been few studies on physical strains other than rather minor physical symptoms, such as headache and stomach upset, thus limiting our understanding of the effects of conflict on health itself. The latter is more difficult as serious health disorders can take a long time to develop and can arise from a complex interaction of many factors. However, strong circumstantial evidence suggests interpersonal conflict is a stressor that contributes to health.

With these limitations in mind, we propose a model in which we incorporate what we do know about the effects of conflict on health and well-being and propose areas for further empirical and theoretical investigation.

INTERPERSONAL CONFLICT AND THE JOB STRESS MODEL

Two main streams of research emerge from the conflict literature. One is focused on the styles of conflict management and resolution while the other is focused on measuring the occurrence of interpersonal conflict at work. The latter stream is consistent with job stress research, which assesses the experience of conflict at work and its consequences on health and well-being. For the purpose of this chapter, the implications of conflict in the workplace on employee health and well-being will be reviewed using a stress model perspective. Although the conflict literature has traditionally differentiated between task and relationship conflict (see Jehn, 1994, 1995), research on conflict and well-being has largely ignored this distinction. We venture to say that this may be due to the lack of integration of the business and occupational stress literatures on this topic. Consequently, empirical support for the impact of conflict on well-being comes from studies that overall operationalize it as relationship conflict. Thus, we have limited our proposed model to relationship conflict until future research elucidates the process whereby task conflict may impact health and well-being.

As seen in Figure 9.1, Spector's (1998) emotion-centered model of job stress depicted a process whereby social stressors lead to negative emotion and to subsequent strains. According to the model, employees monitor their work environments, observing conditions and events as they unfold. Some events are perceived as job stressors that elicit an emotional reaction and subsequent strains. Attributions are particularly important in determining the particular emotional response to a situation and, therefore, may play a role in conflict. Perrewé and Zellars (1999) suggested that internal attributions lead to guilt and shame, whereas external attributions lead to anger. Thus, external attributions would be more likely to lead to conflict because anger is more likely to lead a person to treat someone in a way that would cause conflict. The stress process is not entirely unidirectional as causal processes can occur in both directions; for example, strains can affect emotions, perceptions, and the environment itself. Also, personality (e.g., locus of control, negative affectivity, and type A) and both actual and perceived control moderate the process.

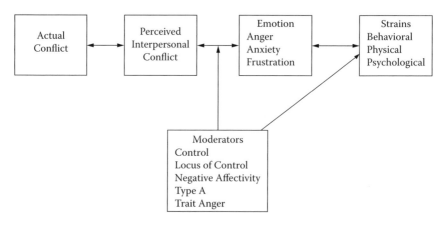

FIGURE 9.1. Emotion-centered model of job stress.

INTERPERSONAL CONFLICT AND STRAINS

As depicted in the job stress model presented in Figure 9.1, interpersonal conflict is linked to a variety of negative emotional states, including anger, anxiety, and frustration. This relationship has been repeatedly supported by occupational stress studies for a variety of stressors including interpersonal conflict (Spector & Jex, 1998). Furthermore, anger, annoyance, and frustration were the most frequently cited emotions reported in a study of young engineers ranking conflict as a leading stressor (Keenan & Newton, 1985). Similarly, Narayanan, Menon, and Spector (1999a) reported that these three negative affective states as well as anxiety were associated with stressors that included interpersonal conflicts at work for all three occupational groups in their sample. Further, the most frequently cited emotional reactions by an American sample reporting interpersonal conflicts in a cross-national study were frustration, annoyance, and anger, in descending order (Narayanan, Menon, & Spector, 1999b). Work frustration and anxiety were also reported to be significant positive correlates of conflict at work in a longitudinal study by Spector and O'Connell (1994).

Spector et al. (1988), in a study with multiple data sources, presented further evidence of the affective outcomes of interpersonal conflict. Data were obtained from incumbent self-reports and supervisor reports. Incumbents reported conflict to be positively correlated with anxiety and frustration. Interestingly, cross-source data using the supervisors' reports of incumbent conflict showed a significant positive correlation with incumbent reported anxiety and frustration. Finally, meta-analytic findings also support a positive mean correlation in the mid-.30s between conflict and anxiety and between conflict and frustration (Spector, 1997; Spector & Jex, 1998).

The aforementioned studies indicated that this social stressor may elicit a variety of negative emotional states and, therefore, suggested that the specific emotional reaction that is experienced as a result of conflict is not what matters, but rather, it is the experience of overall negative affect that may require closer attention. Consequently, Fox, Spector, and Miles (2001) used the job-related affective well-being scale to obtain a negative emotion score derived from the responses to 15 items measuring various negative emotional states. The results supported a significant positive correlation ($r = .49$) between conflict and negative emotion, thus, indicating that the variety of negative affective states resulting from conflict at work can be studied by using a measure of overall negative emotions. In a study that tested a model of voluntary work behaviors, Spector, Fox, Goh, and Bruursema (2003) replicated these findings. Furthermore, Lee (2003) showed that conflict both with coworkers and with supervisors was related to a measure of overall negative emotions ($r = .23$ and .30, respectively) for a sample of full-time working adults from a variety of occupations. The correlations remained significant even when using cross-source data, such that peer reports of conflict were correlated with self-reports of negative emotion, thus dispelling the argument that correlations are due to common method bias.

Perrewé and Zellars (1999) developed a model that described in more detail the connection between stressors in general and emotions that can help explain reactions to interpersonal conflict. When conflicts occur, an individual will appraise the situation and make attributions about the cause. It is quite likely that people who are having conflicts with others will appraise the situation as at least somewhat threatening and anxiety provoking. They will see the cause of the conflict as the other individual rather than themselves, and they will assume that the other person was able to control and avoid the conflict in the first place. Under conditions in which the stressor is both controllable and external, anger is the most likely emotion to be experienced.

Clearly, there is strong support for the negative affective outcomes of interpersonal conflict in the workplace. Due to research linking the experience and expression of anger to cardiovascular disease (Greenglass, 1996; Julkunen, 1996), the emotional reactions resulting from conflicts in the workplace are of critical importance to employee health. Furthermore, the experience of negative emotional states has been shown to suppress human immune function (O'Leary, 1990) and increase the production of cortisol and catecholamines (Frankenhaeuser & Johansson, 1986).

Depression is a psychological strain that has been widely reported in studies of interpersonal conflict at work. Dormann and Zapf (1999, 2002) found that increased social stressors, as indicated by conflict, led to higher levels of depressive symptoms in two studies. The earlier study was a three wave longitudinal study, which showed that social stressors in all three waves of data were positively related to depression ($r = .14$ to .26). The latter study provided support for Mohr's (1986) stress model and indicated a direct and mediated path between conflict and depressive symptoms. Bolger et al. (1989) concluded that interpersonal conflicts accounted for more than 80% of the variance in daily mood, which was assessed by a measure of anxiety, hostility, and depression. They concluded that it was the most important stressor influencing psychological distress. The positive relationship between conflict and depression also received support in a study with young working adults (Frone, 2000). The study differentiated between conflict with supervisors and with coworkers based on Fiske's (1992) model of social relations. The results indicated that conflict with coworkers was positively related to depression ($r = .31$), which was assessed by various dimensions of depressive symptoms, including depressed mood, feelings of hopelessness and worthlessness, and sleep disturbance. Heinisch and Jex (1997) reported a similar correlation between conflict and depression in a study of the moderating effects of gender and personality on the stress-depression relationship. Furthermore, meta-analytic findings of 13 studies supported a positive correlation between conflict and depression in the mid-.30s (Spector & Jex, 1998). The link between depression and cardiovascular disease raises concerns regarding the potential indirect impact that conflict can have on employee physical health (e.g., Wei & O'Connor, 2002).

Interpersonal conflicts in the workplace have also been associated with increased somatic complaints, which are self-reports of physical symptoms that may include headaches, gastrointestinal problems, and faintness among others. Data from a diary study conducted by Hahn (2000) showed that participants reported more health symptoms following a conflict. Specifically, participants with an internal locus of control were more likely to report health symptoms after the occurrence of a conflict. Furthermore, Spector and Jex (1998) reported a correlation of .26 between the physical symptoms inventory (PSI) and a measure of interpersonal conflict at work. Similarly, Frone (2000) found that when employees reported experiencing more conflict with their coworkers, they also reported higher levels of somatic symptoms as measured by a physical symptoms checklist.

A variety of other strains such as burnout, life dissatisfaction, and psychiatric morbidity has also been reported in response to this social stressor. Burnout refers to a feeling of emotional exhaustion that may result from the experience of stressors. Rainey (1995) tested a model of stress with a sample of sports officials and found that interpersonal conflict was the best predictor of burnout. The implications of these findings are important given the fact that burnout is associated with health symptoms and a predictor of changes in cholesterol and triglycerides levels (Shirom, Westman, Shamai, & Carel, 1997). In addition, Appelberg, Romanov, Honkasalo, and Koskenvuo (1991) conducted a study on the occupational and psychological factors associated with conflict at work using the Finnish twin cohort. The results for both males and females indicated that employees reporting more conflict at work were also more dissatisfied with their lives and experienced more daily stress. However, Romanov, Appelberg, Honkasalo, and Koskenvuo (1996) reported an even more alarming finding in a longitudinal study using the same Finnish sample. The researchers collected epidemiological follow-up data in addition to health, education, psychosocial, sleep, and personality information. The follow-up data included suicidal deaths, hospitalization, and free medication due to psychiatric diagnoses. The results showed that employees who reported interpersonal conflicts at work in the prior six months had a higher risk for psychiatric morbidity even after controlling for social class, mental instability, personality, alcohol consumption, health status, mental instability, marital status, and conflict with spouse. Although the results cannot establish causality, the researchers believe that "the extent to which interpersonal conflict at work can weaken an individual's ability to solve his or her emotional problems and eventually lead to mental disease seems to be a crucial topic for future research and interventions in the occupational field" (Romanov et al., 1996, p. 169).

Another stream of research reporting psychiatric illnesses, including posttraumatic stress disorder, as outcomes of extreme escalated conflict is found in the European literature. "Mobbing" refers to a persistent escalating process of conflict in which a power differential exists between the parties (Zapf & Einarsen, 2004). It is the duration and repeated nature of this conflict situation that differentiates it from the everyday conflict (Leymann, 1996). Thus, conflict is viewed as an extreme social stressor resulting in serious health outcomes. Mobbing behaviors range from verbal aggression to physical violence and are thought to be a top-down problem, which may reflect poor organizational leadership. Perpetrators may engage in different types of mobbing, of which one is dispute related and refers to escalated interpersonal conflict. Various studies have demonstrated the health implications that escalated conflict may pose. For instance, mobbing victims reported more psychosomatic symptoms than nonvictims (Zapf, 1999), depressive symptoms (Einarsen & Mikkelsen, 2003), and posttraumatic stress disorder symptomatology (Leymann & Gustafsson, 1996).

PERSONALITY AND CONFLICT

Individual differences play an important role in the stress process whereby conflict affects employee health and well-being. Personality variables that have been associated with conflict include negative affectivity, trait anxiety, trait anger, type A, and locus of control.

Trait Anxiety/Negative Affectivity

Trait anxiety refers to a tendency, which is mostly limited to the psychosocial environment, to perceive situations as threatening (Spielberger, 1979). Watson and Clark (1984) expanded this construct to include additional negative emotional states and labeled it "negative affectivity" (NA). One would expect a direct relationship between trait anxiety/NA and interpersonal conflict at work. That is, employees higher in trait anxiety/NA would perceive more incidents of conflict. This is, in fact, what the stress research has found. Meta-analytic findings indicate an average correlation of .33 for six studies assessing negative affectivity and conflict at work (Spector & Jex, 1998). In a study testing the moderating effects of NA on the stressor/strain relationship, Heinisch and Jex (1997) reported similar findings. Chen and Spector (1991) also reported a positive relationship between NA and interpersonal conflict. Furthermore, Fox et al. (2001) indicated a significant correlation of .30 between trait anxiety and a measure of conflict at work. Although the cross-sectional nature of these studies may raise questions regarding the relationship between personality and perceptions of conflict at work, Spector and O'Connell (1994) provided further supporting evidence in a longitudinal study. A two-wave design was conducted in which personality data were collected at Time 1 for a cohort of college students and conflict data were collected at Time 2 approximately a year after graduation and entering the workforce. Here again, the results support a positive relationship between trait anxiety/ NA and stressors including interpersonal conflict, such that employees reporting a higher level of NA also reported more conflict at work.

Thus, it has been argued that the relationship between trait anxiety/ NA and conflict exists due to the highly anxious person's tendency to perceive his or her surroundings as stressful. Therefore, it would be expected that in addition to the direct relationships previously reviewed, studies would also report moderating effects of personality on the stress process. However, research looking at the moderating effects of trait anxiety/NA on the stress process as it pertains to social stressors is very limited. A diary study on interpersonal stressors by Bolger and Zuckerman (1995) found that participants high in NA reported greater negative reactivity to conflicts. Trait anxiety was also found to be a moderator of the relationship between interpersonal conflicts and counterproductive work behaviors, a type of behavioral strain (Fox et al., 2001). As expected, trait anxiety enhanced the relationship between the social stressor and strain.

Trait Anger

Spielberger (1979) defined trait anger as a proneness to perceive a variety of situations as provoking anger. Very few studies in organizational research investigated this personality variable; however, it seems that individuals high in trait anger may be more reactive to the experience of interpersonal conflict at work. For example, Fox and Spector (1999) and Fox et al. (2001) found significant positive correlations between a measure of trait anger and conflict. Further, Fox et al. (2001) reported a moderator effect of trait anger on the social stressor/strain relationship. Specifically, the relationship between interpersonal conflict and counterproductive work behaviors was stronger for individuals higher in trait anger. Given the association of trait anger to cardiovascular disease (Booth-Kewley & Friedman, 1987) and to conflict, trait anger's role in the stress process warrants further research.

Type A

Type A personality has been commonly studied in conjunction with research on cardiovascular disease (T. W. Smith, 1992). Friedman and Rosenman (1974) described the type A person as having a sense of time urgency and as being competitive, hostile, and impatient. Two dimensions of the type A personality have received particular attention: impatience/irritability and achievement striving (Edwards, Baglioni & Cooper, 1990). The first refers to an individual's proneness to experience anger and frustration when having to wait, while the latter refers to a predisposition to work toward goal achievement. Given the fact that a high type A tends to overreact to uncontrollable stressors (Glass & Carver, 1980a, b) and that the social work environment can have multiple influences outside of one's control, it is likely that he or she will report more social stressors. Although not many studies have investigated the association between type A and interpersonal conflict, there is some evidence for a correlation. Spector and O'Connell (1994) showed that employees higher in type A impatience/irritability, assessed when they were students, reported experiencing more conflict in their work after graduation. These results are promising given the time lapse (12–15 months) between the collection of personality and conflict data. As with trait anger, more evidence is necessary to establish the link between type A and conflict, as well as its possible moderator effects on the relationship between conflict and employee health and well-being.

Locus of Control

Perhaps one of the most widely researched personality variables in the job stress literature is locus of control. Rotter (1966) defined it as a general belief that external forces or one's own actions control outcomes. Individuals who perceive a lack of control over rewards and outcomes in their lives are labeled "externals," whereas those who believe their actions can influence outcomes are "internals." Control beliefs can be specific to situations, such as work or interpersonal relationships, and can affect the conflict/ strain relationship through stressor perception. Specifically, it would be expected that externals feel a lack of control over conflict situations and, thus, perceive them to be more stressful or threatening. As such, locus of control should correlate with social stressors. Predictably, Spector and O'Connell (1994) found that employees who were assessed as externals in school subsequently reported higher levels of interpersonal conflicts in their workplaces. Locus of control has also been found to be a moderator of the stressor/strain relationship with externals generally showing stronger relationships (Spector, 2003; Storms & Spector, 1987).

Nevertheless, contradictory findings have also posited stronger stressor/ strain relationships for internals, especially when there is little objective control (Kolb & Aiello, 1996). Hahn (2000) proposed that this might result from the incongruence between expected and actual situational control. A diary study assessing conflict at work and interpersonal locus of control, which refers to expectancies regarding one's control in interpersonal situations, indicated that the relationships between conflict, anger, and self-reported health were higher for internals. That is, internals reported more anger and health symptoms on days when they recorded experiencing conflicts at work. However, externals were more likely to report depressive symptoms on days when they recorded conflicts. Therefore, it seems that interpersonal locus of control may require further attention as these findings provide some interesting differences in strain reactivity to conflict by internals and externals.

PERCEIVED CONTROL AND CONFLICT

A situational variable that is important in the stress process in general and conflict in particular is control. Employee perception of control (operationalized as autonomy in doing the job) has been shown to relate to the amount of interpersonal conflict they report (Spector & Jex, 1998), although results have been somewhat variable across studies. Furthermore, employee control has been linked to a variety of strains, both physical (e.g., Bosma, Stansfeld & Marmot, 1998) and psychological (e.g., Spector et al., 1988). However, control can also play a more complex moderator role. The control–demand model (Karasek, 1979) suggested that control could buffer the effects of stressors such that having high control can reduce their impact on strains. Thus, having high control might mitigate some of the negative impact of interpersonal conflict. Unfortunately, support for this model has been mixed in part perhaps because of methodological limitations in much of the research designed to test it (Terry & Jimmieson, 1999). Behavioral responses can also be affected by control. Research has also shown that coping styles may differ across employees when faced with a stressor of an interpersonal nature depending upon their perceived level of situational control. For example, employees reported using covert coping mechanisms, such as avoidance, when they perceived little or no control over social stressors. More interestingly, covert coping mechanisms were associated with elevated blood pressure in the same sample (Theorell, Alfredsson, Westerholm, & Falck, 2000).

THE PREVALENCE OF INTERPERSONAL CONFLICT AT WORK

It is evident that interpersonal conflict, acting as a social stressor, can have very serious consequences on employee health and well-being, both physical and psychological. Various dispositional and situational variables exacerbate or buffer this process. Nevertheless, what gives this research added importance is the frequency with which interpersonal conflict is reported to occur in the workplace. In essence, if the base rate of this social stressor is low, then one can argue that it affects only a selected few in the workplace. However, what we know about the prevalence of this social stressor raises serious concerns regarding its detrimental effects.

For example, Hahn (2000) asked participants, who were representative of a full-time working sample in a variety of occupations, to record the number of conflicts they experienced at work and to describe the occurrences. Content analysis of the diary data showed that respondents recorded interpersonal stressors on 50% of their workdays.

Keenan and Newton (1985) used an open-ended method to assess stress among young engineers. Respondents completed the stress incident record (SIR) by recording critical events that they considered stressful. The incidents reported ranged widely, however; 74% of them were social in nature, such that they were caused by social interactions with superiors, subordinates, or colleagues. As expected, one of the most cited stressors was interpersonal conflict at work. Narayanan et al. (1999b) also used the SIR in a study that asked respondents from clerical, sales, and academic groups to report an incident that occurred within the past month and which they considered stressful. Interpersonal conflict was the most reported stressor for both the academic and sales groups. Gender analysis showed that women in the sales and academic groups reported interpersonal conflict as the leading stressor whereas men reported it to be the second most frequent stressor. Further, the clerical group reported conflict to be the third major source of stress among nine types.

Kandel, Davies, and Raveis (1985) studied sources of stress for women in three specific roles. In particular, the researchers examined the marital, occupational, and household roles. The occupational role was found to be one of the most stressful roles for women. A factor analysis of the data revealed seven sources of stress associated with the occupational role. Two of the sources were interpersonal in nature. Further, regression analyses indicated that interpersonal conflict was the strongest predictor of a measure of overall stress for the occupational role. Also, psychological well-being was shown to be more strongly affected by interpersonal conflicts than by any other situational characteristic, such as the noxiousness of the work environment. Pearlin (1980) also found depersonalization, one of the sources of interpersonal conflict reported in the previous study, to be the most stressful in the occupational role for a sample of women and men. Depersonalization, as measured by Kandel et al. (1985), included similar items to those found in widely used measures of interpersonal conflict at work.

Further evidence supports the notion that this stressor is among the most cited across occupations and cultures. Taylor and Daniel (1987) examined the sources of stress among a sample of soccer referees using the Soccer Official's Stress Survey and found that interpersonal conflict and peer conflict were two of the five stress factors that emerged from the data. Rainey's (1995) factor analysis of stress data gathered from a sample of baseball and softball umpires also included interpersonal conflict as one of four factors. Similarly, Stewart and Ellery (1998) examined the sources of stress among high school volleyball officials and indicated that interpersonal conflict was one of four factors that emerged from the data as significant sources of stress. In their study, items loading on the interpersonal conflict factor were individually rated as being mild to moderate and strong sources of stress.

Cross-cultural evidence for the prevalence of interpersonal conflict at work as a source of significant stress has also been found. Narayanan et al. (1999a) reported that interpersonal conflict was the third most cited source of stress in a U.S. sample and the fourth most cited source of stress in an Indian sample. Respondents in both samples consisted of clerical workers and eleven possible stressor categories were considered. In this study, role stressors traditionally studied in occupational stress were the least reported sources of stress. Liu (2002) found that Chinese faculty reported experiencing significantly more overall interpersonal conflict and conflict with supervisors than American faculty did. Furthermore, the levels of interpersonal conflict among university support staff in the two countries did not differ, providing evidence for the presence of this stressor across cultures (Liu, 2002). Consistent with these findings, Spector, Sanchez, Siu, Salgado, and Ma (2004) found that Chinese in Hong Kong and People's Republic of China reported more conflict than Americans did.

CONFLICT AND SOCIAL REGULATION

Although interpersonal conflict has been shown to have negative effects on health and well-being, there can be circumstances in which behaviors that lead to short-term conflict can be useful in the longer term. Bies, Tripp, and Kramer (1997) discussed how revenge (e.g., striking back against someone who has done something perceived as harmful) could have a social regulatory function. If an individual is treated in an unkind way, that individual might strike back, thus producing a conflict with the offending individual. The other individual might be careful in the future to avoid further acts of revenge, and thus future conflicts could be avoided. Of course, there can be instances in which an act of revenge produces an equivalent response, thus prolonging the conflict over time.

THE IMPACT OF CONFLICT ON ORGANIZATIONAL EFFECTIVENESS: PRACTICAL IMPLICATIONS

The effects of interpersonal conflict at work are not limited to employee health and well-being; they also affect organizational effectiveness through direct bottom line costs and by means of organizationally relevant variables. For example, it is estimated that organizations spend over $200 billion on work stress issues, including turnover, health care costs, and productivity (DeFrank & Ivancevich, 1998). Longitudinal research has also shown that from 60% to 90% of health care provider visits are, in some part, due to stress (Cooper & Payne, 1988). This and other studies point to the fact that the mental and physical health of employees can heavily affect the health care costs of organizations. The Health Enhancement Research Organization (HERO; 2004) reported that employees reporting persistent depression had health care costs 70% greater than their nondepressed counterparts did (¶ 8). These findings are even more dramatic for males for whom the increase in costs was 91% more than for men not at risk. Given the strong support for the relationship between conflict in organizations and employee depression, these findings are quite alarming. Furthermore, HERO findings also indicated an increase in health care expenditures of 46% for employees reporting uncontrolled stress over those not at risk.

Job satisfaction is a psychological strain traditionally studied in the occupational stress literature. Various studies have consistently shown a significant negative correlation between the experience of conflict at work and levels of overall job satisfaction. For example, Frone (2000) reported that employees who reported more conflict with supervisors also reported lower levels of overall satisfaction their jobs ($r = -.44$). Furthermore, a meta-analysis of 10 studies showed that the ICAWS correlated negatively (average $r = -.32$) with job satisfaction (Spector & Jex, 1998). Lastly, a study testing a model of voluntary behaviors looked at the mediating role of job satisfaction in the stress process and found that conflict had a direct negative relationship with a measure of overall job satisfaction (Spector et al., 2003). These results indicate that employees who report experiencing higher levels of interpersonal conflicts at work also report lower job satisfaction.

Given the key role that job satisfaction plays in turnover models, it is not surprising that increased turnover intentions are also an organizational outcome resulting from higher levels of interpersonal conflict. Given the positive relationship between turnover intentions and actual turnover, self-reports of intentions to quit are a good indicator of actual turnover (Carsten & Spector, 1987). In his study of young employees, Frone (2000) found that employees who reported more conflict with supervisors indicated higher intentions of quitting and were less committed to the organization. Rainey (1995) reported that referees who indicated higher levels of interpersonal conflict were more likely to quit their jobs. Chen and Spector (1992) also found a strong positive correlation ($r = .39$) between interpersonal conflict and intentions to quit in a large sample of employees from a variety of occupations. Furthermore, the correlation between interpersonal conflict and intentions to quit was the strongest from among various job strains (Spector & Jex, 1998). These findings are also supported by research on intragroup conflict where both task and relationship conflict result in less intention to stay with the group (Jehn, 1995).

Perhaps one of the organizational outcomes of conflict that has received the most attention is counterproductive work behavior (CWB). CWBs are behaviors aimed at hurting the organization and/or the individuals who are part of it. Numerous terms exist to refer to research in this area, such as *deviance* (Hollinger, 1986; Robinson & Bennett, 1995), *organizational retaliatory behavior* (Skarlicki & Folger, 1997), *antisocial behaviors* (Giacalone & Greenberg, 1997), and *workplace aggression* (Baron & Neuman, 1996). All of these terms share the fact that each refers to detrimental behaviors that affect an organization's productivity and coworkers' performance. Behaviors that are considered counterproductive may include coming to work late without permission, stealing things from the workplace, aggressing against a coworker or supervisor, or taking unauthorized breaks. CWBs have a bottom line impact on organizations due to the billions of dollars that are lost annually in employee absence, lost productivity, and theft. Murphy (1993) estimated the cost of a variety of counterproductive work behaviors to be between $6 and $200 billion annually.

In a study on job stressors and counterproductive behaviors, Chen and Spector (1992) found that conflict at work was positively related to a variety of CWBs. Specifically, it was associated with more interpersonal aggression ($r = .49$), increased workplace hostility and complaining ($r = .46$), more sabotage ($r = .34$), and theft ($r = .16$). Fox et al. (2001) distinguished between counterproductive behaviors aimed at the organization versus those aimed at other individuals in their test of an emotion-centered model of CWB. Their results showed direct positive relationships between conflict and both organizational and personal CWB, such that employees who reported more conflict also reported engaging in more counterproductive behaviors. Spector et al. (2003) supported these findings by using multiple sources of data, which included self and peer reports. Lee (2003) also collected data from incumbents and their peers, showing a relationship between sources of conflict and CWB targeting both the organization and other employees.

Therefore, it seems that conflict has practical implications for organizations through absence, increased health care costs, negative work attitudes, and counterproductive work behaviors. Ultimately, this social stressor is not only damaging to employees, but can play a deleterious role in the maintenance of a healthy work organization.

LIMITATIONS AND FUTURE RESEARCH DIRECTIONS

Given the previously mentioned evidence, it is clear that interpersonal conflict is a leading social stressor in organizations and, consequently, of great importance to researchers of job stress. Furthermore, its relationship with numerous health and well-being outcomes makes it a variable of critical importance. Nevertheless, a number of both conceptual and methodological limitations to the literature will require future research attention.

There are also a number of questions raised by the literature as well as research gaps, such as the role that task conflict plays in employee health and well-being. While moderate amounts of task conflict have been regarded as being functional and even desirable (see Jehn, 1995), its impact on health and personal well-being is unknown. However, there is reason to believe that task conflict can result in detriments to employee health, as does relationship conflict. For instance, to the extent that task conflict leads to relationship conflict, we can expect it to have negative outcomes for personal well-being. Simons and Peterson (2000) found that task conflict might result in relationship conflict when a misattribution of behavior occurs. This is particularly true for groups with low trust in which negative intentions are attributed to the occurrence of task conflict. This poses two interesting areas for research. First, it is clear that more research is necessary to understand the direct impact that task conflict can incur on health and well-being. Second, more research is needed to understand the spiraling

effect of one conflict type into another and, therefore, the indirect consequences that task conflict may ultimately have on personal well-being. The
latter represents a much larger challenge as it calls for theoretical development of the interrelationships between conflict types.

Another basic question that requires attention is whether the proposed
model applies to conflict that occurs at the intragroup level. Although
research has focused exclusively on relationship conflict at the interpersonal level, it is our contention that the basic process would remain
for relationship conflicts at the intragroup level. Future research could
address whether the health and well-being impact of conflict is exacerbated for people having to work in an interdependent group.

Current occupational stress studies have focused on the negative health
and well-being consequences of interpersonal conflict. While our model
proposes that conflict is detrimental to health and well-being, it is possible
that how that conflict is managed results in positive outcomes to well-
being. For example, although conflict with your coworkers may lead to
psychosomatic complaints (e.g., inability to sleep at night), effective management of that conflict may result in an increased sense of self-esteem
because you now realize you are capable of resolving interpersonal issues
with others. This distinction between the effects of conflict and the effects
of conflict after effective conflict management has not been previously
studied in the area of occupational stress. Future research could address
whether individuals engaged in conflict report different health and well-
being reactions depending upon whether the conflict was effectively
resolved. Although intuitively we would think that effective conflict management behaviors would impact the effects of conflict on employee well-
being, research is lacking empirically to address such a question, and for
that reason, for now, we have not included this link in our model.

Most studies of conflict have relied on cross-sectional, single-source
survey methods, which limit causal conclusions. There are a handful of
studies, however, that have used longitudinal and multisource designs, as
noted in our review. Additional research using these and other designs is
needed to help delineate the causal connections between interpersonal
conflict and other variables. This might involve experimental or quasi-
experimental designs in which interventions intended to reduce interpersonal conflict are introduced to see if they have an impact on conflict
and other variables expected to be the result of conflict, such as emotional
reactions. Such studies might be quite feasible if tied to team building and
conflict resolution interventions in organizations.

CONCLUSION

As our review has shown, interpersonal conflict at work has implications
for both employee and organizational well-being. For individuals excessive conflict can lead to behavioral, physical, and psychological strain. For

organizations, interpersonal conflict has the potential to affect employee absence, counterproductivity, health costs, and turnover. Organizations can enhance both their own health and that of their employees by taking proactive measures to manage interpersonal conflict among employees. This can include sound organizational practices that minimize conflict-inducing situations, such as competition for scarce resources. Another approach is to train supervisors to recognize and mediate conflicts among employees and to avoid being sources of conflict themselves.

Interpersonal conflict has been shown to be one of the most important stressors in the workplace. Recent research has represented a shift from focusing on stressors that are more related to people's functions and tasks in organizations to the social environment. Relatively little research has been conducted on how health and well-being are affected by interpersonal conflict. Certainly, this important area deserves far more attention than it has received to date.

REFERENCES

Appelberg, K., Romanov, K., Honkasalo, M. L., & Koskenvuo, M. (1991). Interpersonal conflict at work and psychological characteristics of employees. *Social Science Medicine, 32*, 1051–1056.

Barki, H., & Hartwick, J. (2001). Interpersonal conflict and its management in information system development. *MIS Quarterly, 25*, 195–228.

Baron, R. A., & Neuman, J. H. (1996). Workplace violence and workplace aggression.

Bies, R. J., Tripp, T. M., & Kramer, R. M. (1997). At the breaking point: Cognitive and social dynamics of revenge in organizations. In R. A. Giacalone & J. Greenberg (Eds.), *Antisocial behavior in organizations* (pp. 18–36). Thousand Oaks, CA: Sage.

Bolger, N., DeLongis, A., Kessler, R. C., & Schilling, E. A. (1989). Effects of daily stress on negative mood. *Journal of Personality and Social Psychology, 57*, 808–818.

Bolger, N., & Zuckerman, A. (1995). A framework for studying personality in the stress process. *Journal of Personality and Social Psychology, 69*, 890–902.

Booth-Kewley, S., & Friedman, H. S. (1987). Psychological predictors of heart disease: A quantitative review. *Psychological Bulletin, 101*, 343–362.

Bosma, H., Stansfeld, S. A., & Marmot, M. G. (1998). Job control, personal characteristics, and heart disease. *Journal of Occupational Health Psychology, 3*, 402–409.

Carsten, J. M., & Spector, P. E. (1987). Unemployment, job satisfaction, and employee turnover: A meta-analytic test of the Muchinsky model. *Journal of Applied Psychology, 72*, 374–381.

Chen, P. Y., & Spector, P. E. (1991). Negative affectivity as the underlying cause of correlations between stressors and strains. *Journal of Applied Social Psychology, 30*, 867–885.

Chen, P. Y., & Spector, P. E. (1992). Relationships of work stressors with aggression, withdrawal, theft, and substance use: An exploratory study. *Journal of Occupational and Organizational Psychology, 65*, 177–184.

Cooper, C. L., & Payne, R. (Eds.). (1988). *Causes, coping, and consequences of stress at work*. New York: John Wiley & Sons.

De Dreu, C. K. W., & Weingart, L. R. (2003). Toward a contingency theory of task conflict and performance in groups and organizational teams. In M. A. West, D. Tjosvold, and K. G. Smith (Eds.), *International handbook of organizational teamwork and cooperative working* (pp. 151–166). Chichester, UK: John Wiley.

DeFrank, R. S., & Ivancevich, J. M. (1998). Stress on the job: An executive update. *Academy of Management Executive, 12*, 55–66.

Dormann, C., & Zapf, D. (1999). Social support, social stressors at work, and depressive symptoms: Testing for main and moderating effects with structural equations in a three-wave longitudinal study. *Journal of Applied Psychology, 84*, 874–884.

Dormann, C., & Zapf, D. (2002). Social stressors at work, irritation, and depressive symptoms: Accounting for unmeasured third variables in a multi-wave study. *Journal of Occupational and Organizational Psychology, 75*, 33–58.

Edwards, J. R., Baglioni, A. J., Jr., & Cooper, C. L. (1990). Examining the relationships among self-report measures of the Type A behavior pattern: The effects of dimensionality, measurement error, and differences in underlying constructs. *Journal of Applied Psychology, 75*, 440–454.

Einarsen, S., & Mikkelsen, E. G. (2003). Individual effects of exposure to bullying at work. In S. Einarsen, H. Hoel, D. Zapf, & C. L. Cooper (Eds.), *Bullying and emotional abuse in the workplace: International perspectives in research and practice* (pp. 127–144). London: Taylor & Francis.

Fink, C. F. (1968). Some conceptual difficulties in the theory of social conflict. *Journal of Conflict Resolution, 12*, 412–460.

Fiske, A. P. (1992). The four elementary forms of sociability: Framework for a unified theory of social relations. *Psychological Review, 99*, 689–723.

Fox, S., & Spector, P. E. (1999). A model of work frustration-aggression. *Journal of Organizational Behavior, 20*, 915–931.

Fox, S., Spector, P. E., & Miles, D. (2001). Counterproductive work behavior (CWB) in response to job stressors and organizational justice: Some mediator and moderator tests for autonomy and emotions. *Journal of Vocational Behavior, 59*, 1–19.

Frankenhaeuser, M., & Johansson, G. (1986). Stress at work: Psychobiological and psychosocial aspects. *International Review of Applied Psychology, 35*, 287–299.

Friedman, M., & Rosenman, R. H. (1974). *Type A behavior and your heart*. New York: Knopf.

Frone, M. R. (2000). Interpersonal conflict at work and psychological outcomes: Testing a model among young workers. *Journal of Occupational Health Psychology, 5*, 246–255.

Giacalone, R. A., & Greenberg, J. (Eds.). (1997). *Antisocial behavior in organizations.* Thousand Oaks, CA: Sage.

Glass, D. C., & Carver, C. S. (1980a). Environmental stress and the type: A response. In A. Baum & J. E. Singer (Eds.), *Applications of personal control* (pp. 59–83). Hillsdale, NJ: Lawrence Erlbaum Associates.

Glass, D., & Carver, C. (1980b). Helplessness and the coronary-prone personality. In J. Garber & M. Seligman (Eds.), *Human helplessness, theory, and applications* (pp. 223–244). New York: Academic Press.

Gordon, J. R. (1999). *Organizational behavior: A diagnostic approach.* Upper Saddle River, NJ: Prentice Hall.

Greenglass, E. R. (1996). Anger suppression, cynical distrust, and hostility: Implications for coronary heart disease. In C. D. Spielberger, I. G. Sarason, J. M. T. Brebner, E. Greenglass, P. Laungani, & A. M. O'Roark (Eds.). *Stress and emotion: anxiety, anger, and curiosity* (Vol. 16, pp. 205–225). Washington, DC: Taylor & Francis.

Hahn, S. E. (2000). The effects of locus of control on daily exposure, coping, and reactivity to work interpersonal stressors: A diary study. *Personality and Individual Differences, 29,* 729–748.

Hartwick, J., & Barki, H. (in press). Conceptualizing the construct of interpersonal conflict. *International Journal of Conflict Management.*

Health Enhancement Research Organization. (2004). Retrieved January 3, 2005, from http://www.the-hero.org/research.htm

Heinisch, D. A., & Jex, S. M. (1997). Negative affectivity and gender as moderators of the relationship between work-related stressors and depressed mood at work. *Work and Stress, 11,* 46–57.

Hollinger, E. C. (1986). Acts against the workplace: Social bonding and employee deviance. *Deviant Behavior, 7,* 53–75.

Jehn, K. A. (1994). Enhancing effectiveness: An investigation of advantages and disadvantages of value-based intragroup conflict. *International Journal of Conflict Management, 5,* 223–238.

Jehn, K. A. (1995). A multimethod examination of the benefits and detriments of intragroup conflict. *Administrative Science Quarterly, 40,* 256–282.

Julkunen, J. (1996). Suppressing your anger: Good manners, bad health? In C. D. Spielberger, I. G. Sarason, J. M. T. Brebner, E. Greenglass, P. Laungani, & A. M. O'Roark (Eds.). *Stress and emotion: Anxiety, anger, and curiosity* (Vol. 16, pp. 227–240). Washington, DC: Taylor & Francis.

Kandel, D. B., Davies, M., & Raveis, V. H. (1985). The stressfulness of daily social roles for women: Marital, occupational and household roles. *Journal of Health and Social Behavior, 26,* 64–78.

Karasek, R. A. (1979). Job demands, job decision latitude, and mental strain: Implications for job redesign. *Administrative Science Quarterly, 24,* 285–308.

Keenan, A., & Newton, T. J. (1985). Stressful events, stressors and psychological strains in young professional engineers. *Journal of Occupational Behavior, 6,* 151–156.

Kolb, K. J., & Aiello, J. R. (1996). The effects of electronic performance monitoring on stress: Locus of control as a moderator variable. *Computers in Human Behavior, 12,* 407–423.

Lee, V. B. (2003). *The impact of different sources of interpersonal conflict on the target of counterproductive work behaviors.* Unpublished master's thesis, University of South Florida, Tampa.

Leymann, H. (1996). The content and development of mobbing at work. *European Journal of Work and Organizational Psychology, 5,* 165–184.

Leymann, H., & Gustafsson, A. (1996). Mobbing and the development of post-traumatic stress disorder. *European Journal of Work and Organizational Psychology, 5,* 251–276.

Liu, C. (2002). *A comparison of job stressors and job strains among employees holding comparable jobs in Western and Eastern societies.* Unpublished doctoral dissertation, University of South Florida, Tampa.

Mohr, G. (1986). *Measuring psychological complaints of workers*. Frankfurt am Main, Germany: Peter Lang.

Murphy, K. R. (1993). *Honesty in the workplace*. Belmont, CA: Brooks/Cole.

Narayanan, L., Menon, S., & Spector, P. E. (1999a). A cross-cultural comparison of job stressors and reaction among employees holding comparable jobs in two countries. *International Journal of Stress Management, 6*, 197–212.

Narayanan, L., Menon, S., & Spector, P. E. (1999b). Stress in the workplace: A comparison of gender and occupations. *Journal of Organizational Behavior, 20*, 63–73.

O'Leary, A. (1990). Stress, emotion, and human immune function. *Psychological Bulletin, 108*, 363–382.

Pearlin, L. L. (1980). Life-strains and psychological distress among adults: A conceptual review. In N. J. Smelser & E. H. Erikson (Eds.), *Themes of love and work in adulthood* (pp. 174–192). Cambridge, MA: Harvard University Press.

Pearson, C. M., Andersson, L. M., & Porath, C. L. (2004). Workplace incivility. In S. Fox & P. E. Spector (Eds.). *Counterproductive work behavior: Investigations of actors and targets* (pp. 177–200). Washington, DC: American Psychological Association.

Perrewé, P. L., & Zellars, K. L. (1999). An examination of attributions and emotions in the transactional approach to the organizational stress process. *Journal of Organizational Behavior, 20*, 739–752.

Rainey, D. W. (1995). Sources of stress among baseball and softball umpires. *Journal of Applied Sport Psychology, 7*, 1–10.

Rayner, C., & Keashly, L. (2005). Bullying at work: A perspective from Britain and North America. In S. Fox & P. E. Spector (Eds.). *Counterproductive work behavior: Investigations of actors and targets* (pp. 271–296). Washington, DC: American Psychological Association.

Robinson, S. L., & Bennett, R. J. (1995). A typology of deviant workplace behaviors: A multidimensional scaling study. *Academy of Management Journal, 38*, 555–572.

Romanov, K., Appelberg, K., Honkasalo, M. L., Koskenvuo, M. (1996). Recent interpersonal conflict at work and psychiatric morbidity: A prospective study of 15, 530 employees aged 24-64. *Journal of Psychosomatic Research, 40*, 169–176.

Rotter, J. B. (1966). Generalized expectancies for internal versus external control of reinforcement. *Psychological Monographs, 80*(1, Whole No. 609).

Schwartz, J. E., & Stone, A. A. (1993). Coping with daily work problems: Contributions of problem content, appraisals, and person factors. *Work and Stress, 7*, 47–62.

Shirom, A., Westman, M., Shamai, O., & Carel, R. S. (1997). Effects of work overload and burnout on cholesterol and triglycerides levels: The moderating effects of emotional reactivity among male and female employees. *Journal of Occupational Health Psychology, 2*, 275–288.

Simons, T. L., & Peterson, R. S. (2000). Task conflict and relationship conflict in top management teams: The pivotal role of intragroup trust. *Journal of Applied Psychology, 85*, 102–111.

Skarlicki, D. P., & Folger, R. (1997). Retaliation in the workplace: The roles of distributive, procedural, and interactional justice. *Journal of Applied Psychology, 82*, 434–443.

Smith, C. S., & Sulsky, L. (1995). An investigation of job-related coping strategies across multiple stressors and samples. In L. R. Murphy, J. J. Hurrell, S. L. Sauter, & G. P. Keita (Eds.), *Job stress interventions* (pp. 109–123). Washington, DC: American Psychological Association.

Smith, T. W. (1992). Hostility and health: Current status of a psychosomatic hypothesis. *Health Psychology, 11,* 139–150.

Spector, P. E. (1997). The role of frustration in antisocial behavior at work. In R. A. Giacalone & J. Greenberg (Eds.), *Anti-social behavior in organizations* (pp. 1–17). Thousand Oaks, CA: Sage.

Spector, P. E. (1998). A control theory of the job stress process. In C. L. Cooper (Ed.), *Theories of organizational stress* (pp. 153–169). Oxford, UK: Oxford University Press.

Spector, P. E. (2003). Individual differences in health and well-being. In D. A. Hofmann & L. T. Tetrick (Eds.), *Health and safety in organizations: A multilevel perspective* (pp. 29–55). San Francisco: Jossey-Bass.

Spector, P. E., Dwyer, D. J., & Jex, S. M. (1988). Relation of job stressors to affective, health, and performance outcomes: A comparison of multiple data sources. *Journal of Applied Psychology, 73,* 11–19.

Spector, P. E., Fox, S., Goh, A., Bruursema, K. (2003, April). Counterproductive work behavior and organizational citizenship behavior: Are they opposites? In J. Greenberg (Chair), *Vital but neglected topics in workplace deviance research.* Symposium conducted at the meeting of the Society for Industrial and Organizational Psychology, Orlando, Florida.

Spector, P. E., & Jex, S. M. (1998). Development of four self-report measures of job stressors and strain: Interpersonal conflict at work scale, organizational constraint scale, quantitative workload inventory, and physical symptoms inventory. *Journal of Occupational Health Psychology, 3,* 356–367.

Spector, P. E., & O'Connell, B. J. (1994). The contribution of personality traits, negative affectivity, locus of control and type A to the subsequent reports of job stressors and job strains. *Journal of Occupational and Organizational Psychology, 67,* 1–11.

Spector, P. E., Sanchez, J. I., Siu, O. L., Salgado, J., & Ma, J. (2004). Eastern versus western control beliefs at work: An investigation of secondary control, socioinstrumental control, and work locus of control in China and the US. *Applied Psychology: An International Review, 53,* 38–60.

Spielberger, C. D. (1979). *Preliminary manual for the State-Trait Personality Inventory* (STPI). Unpublished manuscript, University of South Florida, Tampa.

Stewart, M. J., & Ellery, P. J. (1998). Sources and magnitude of perceived psychological stress in high school volleyball officials. *Perceptual and Motor Skills, 87,* 1275–1282.

Storms, P. L., & Spector, P. E. (1987). Relationships of organizational frustration with reported behavioral reactions: The moderating effect of locus of control. *Journal of Occupational Psychology, 60,* 227–234.

Taylor, A. H., & Daniel, J. V. (1987). Sources of stress in soccer officiating: An empirical study. In T. Reilly, A Lees, K. Davids, & W. J. Murphy (Eds.), *Science and football: Proceedings of the first world congress of science and football* (pp. 538–544). London: E. & F. N. Spon.

Terry, D. J., & Jimmieson, N. L. (1999). Work control and employee well-being: A decade review. In C. L. Cooper & I. T. Robertson (Eds.), *International review of industrial and organizational psychology* (pp. 95–148). Chichester, U.K.: John Wiley.

Theorell, T., Alfredsson, L., Westerholm, P., & Falck, B. (2000). Coping with unfair treatment at work-What is the relationship between coping and hypertension in middle-aged men and women? *Psychotherapy and Psychosomatics, 69,* 86–94.

Ware, J., & Barnes, L. B. (1992). Managing interpersonal conflict. In J. J. Gabarro (Ed.), *Managing people in organizations* (pp. 213–226). Boston: Harvard Business School Publications.

Watson, D., & Clark, L. A. (1984). Negative affectivity: The disposition to experience aversive emotional states. *Psychological Bulletin, 96,* 465–490.

Wei, J., & O'Connor, C. M. (2002). Depression and cardiac health in women: How close is the relationships? *Women's Health in Primary Care, 5,* 393–404.

Zapf, D. (1999). Organizational, work group related and personal causes of mobbing/bullying at work. *International Journal of Manpower, 20,* 70–85.

Zapf, D., & Einarsen, S. (2004). Mobbing at work: Escalated conflicts in organizations. In S. Fox & P. E. Spector (Eds.). *Counterproductive work behavior: Investigations of actors and targets* (pp. 237–270). Washington, DC: American Psychological Association.

III

Organizational Level of Analysis

10

The Role of Third Parties/ Mediation in Managing Conflict in Organizations

BARRY M. GOLDMAN, RUSSELL CROPANZANO,
JORDAN STEIN, AND LEHMAN BENSON III
Eller College of Management, University of Arizona

Third party intervention has had a rich and important role in the management of conflict. One can think back to the story of King Solomon's wise decision when two women from his Kingdom came to him, each arguing that a baby was hers. Solomon threatened to cut the baby in half, realizing that the real mother would rather the baby live—even if given to the wrong woman—than let the baby die. Solomon's story, even if apocryphal, points to an established human tradition going back for millennia of third party conflict resolution. We hope that scholars and researchers have learned a few things in these intervening years since King Solomon's story was written. The purpose of this chapter is to investigate and integrate our current understanding of this issue as it applies to organizations.

The scope of the literature reviewed for this chapter broadly considers third party intervention in conflict situations involving organizations. However, reflecting the emphases of modern researchers and practitioners, it focuses most attention on issues related to mediation (rather than other third-party techniques, e.g., arbitration). Moreover, as noted, our focus is limited to issues relating to conflicts within organizations and, for the most part, does not examine other uses of third parties to resolve conflicts in extraorganizational situations (e.g., the legal system).

Broadly speaking, this chapter will cover the role of third parties in the conflict management process. Specifically, the chapter starts with a discussion of informal conflict resolution in organizations. Mostly, this work examines the role of managers as dispute solvers. Next, we turn our attention to discussion of the behavior and strategies as they often affect individual mediators. Then, we discuss aspects of both formal and informal dispute resolution as they may affect workplace dispute resolution. Finally, we conclude with a brief discussion of organizational approaches to formal disputing, emphasizing the case of mediation. Moreover, we discuss future directions for research as appropriate within each section.

INFORMAL CONFLICT RESOLUTION

Some decades ago, Thomas and Schmidt (1976) found that managers devoted up to a fifth of their time resolving conflicts. Despite this early recognition of its importance (Wall & Callister, 1995), research on managers acting as third parties has been surprisingly limited. Indeed, putatively comprehensive taxonomies of leadership competencies sometimes fail to include conflict management skills as an explicit category (e.g., Tett, Guterman, Bleier, & Murphy, 2000). Fortunately, some research exists that both describes how managers perform these duties and makes recommendations for honing their abilities to resolve disputes. We consider this evidence in the following section.

The Social Psychological Tradition

In the 1970s, Thibaut and Walker (1975, 1978) conducted an influential series of studies examining dispute resolution. Their early research was largely concerned with legal settings. In fact, Walker was an attorney. Similar to a courtroom trial, they divided a resolution episode into two parts—a process stage and a decision stage. During the process stage, evidence and arguments were presented. During the decision stage, a judgment was rendered. In addition, they pictured a disagreement as having two disputants (with or without representatives) along with a third party. Either the two disputants or the third party could exert control. This control could be manifest at the process stage, the decision stage, or both. Pulling these ideas together, Thibaut and Walker were able to list five strategies for third-party intervention:

1. *Bargaining:* Disputants possess both process and decision control.
2. *Mediation:* The third party possesses process control; disputants possess decision control.
3. *Arbitration:* Disputants possess process control; the third party possesses decision control. (Note that Thibaut and Walker's "arbitration" does not necessarily refer to formal labor arbitration.)

4. *Autocratic:* The third party possesses both process and decision control.
5. *Moot:* Both process control and decision control are shared by the third party and the disputants.

Thibaut and Walker's (1975, 1978) insight was that decision control was not necessary to create satisfaction among conflicting parties. Indeed, disputants were able to accept their inabilities to render their own decisions, so long as they maintained control over the process (for empirical examples, see Houlden, LaTour, Walker, & Thibaut, 1978; Walker, LaTour, Lind, & Thibaut, 1974).

There is a wealth of evidence from the experimental research tradition inspired by Thibaut and Walker (1975, 1978). For example, a considerable body of research has explored courtroom proceedings (e.g., Folger, Cropanzano, Timmermann, Howes, & Mitchell, 1996; Lind, Kurtz, Musante, Walker, & Thibaut, 1980; Sheppard, 1985). Other work has tended to examine disputant responses within legal settings, such as interactions with police officers (Tyler & Folger, 1980), mediation (Lind et al., 1990), and plea bargaining (Casper, Tyler, & Fisher, 1988; Houlden, 1981).

Thibaut and Walker (1975, 1978) influenced the organizational sciences as well. For example, their model was applied to employee participation (Rasinski, 1992; Roberson, Moye, & Locke, 1999). In addition, later research expanded Thibaut and Walker's model so that it was more applicable to business environments. We will now turn our attention to this work.

Managerial Conflict Resolution

Sheppard's (1984) Taxonomy.   In an attempt to be build a more comprehensive typology, Sheppard (1983, 1984) expanded Thibaut and Walker's (1975, 1978) list of conflict intervention phases from two to four: definition, discussion (much like the process stage), alternative selection (much like the decision stage), and reconciliation. Each of these four stages contains an additional two to five substages. Sheppard also added a more comprehensive list of controls that a third party might exercise. The four basic types of control are (a) process control, (b) content control, (c) control by request, and (d) motivational control (e.g., control over incentives). Additionally, numerous subtypes of control also exist.

The key advantage of Sheppard's (1983, 1984) model was found in its thoroughness. By expanding on the initial work of Thibaut and Walker (1975, 1978), Sheppard demonstrated that social psychological ideas of third-party intervention could be applied outside of legal settings. Moreover, Sheppard specifically articulated the different ways in which such an intervention could occur. This precision, of course, comes with a cost. The full matrix of types of controls to stages of conflict comes to 403 cells. For giving practical advice or for conducting research, this is rather unwieldy.

Therefore, empirical tests, while strongly influenced by Sheppard's work, employed simplified versions of his taxonomy.

An Abbreviated Taxonomy.   In exploring the informal tactics used by managerial third parties, researchers have distilled Sheppard's (1984) taxonomy (cf. Sheppard, 1983) into a few commonly used methods (for reviews, see Cropanzano, Aguinis, Schminke, & Denham, 1999; Folger & Cropanzano, 1998, chapter 6; Kolb, 1986; Kolb & Glidden, 1986; Lewicki & Sheppard, 1985). In general, six approaches seem to predominate, though researchers have given them different names:

- *Advising or facilitation:* The manager allows the disputants to maintain decision control. Acting as a third-party facilitator, the manager shares process control to the extent it is necessary to keep the conflicting parties talking constructively about their differences.
- *Mediation:* The third party retains process control but does not exercise decision control.
- *Adversarial or arbitration:* The manager allows the disputants to control the process but retains control over the final decision.
- *Autocratic or inquisitorial:* The manager exerts a good deal of control over both the process and the decision.
- *Providing impetus or motivational control:* The manager does not control the process or the outcome. However, the third party does provide incentives—sometimes even threats—in order to get the disputants to settle the matter themselves.
- *Avoidance or ignoring:* The manager does nothing.

Advising or facilitation.   When acting as an advisor (Kolb, 1986; Kolb & Glidden, 1986) or a facilitator (Kozan & Ilter, 1994), the manager takes the two parties aside and encourages them to engage in productive discussion. As a third party, the manager is not especially controlling. Rather, he or she exerts only limited influence on the process in order to reach an effective conclusion. Individuals report a preference for advising, as opposed to more autocratic methods. This seems to be true for both students and practicing managers (Karambayya, Brett, & Lytle, 1992). Cross-cultural surveys lead to similar conclusions. For example, Cropanzano et al. (1999) found that advising was the top-ranked conflict resolution procedure among samples from Argentina, the Dominican Republic, Mexico, and the United States. Kozan and Ilter (1994) found similar results among Turkish workers. Additionally, in a survey of undergraduates from Spain and Japan, Leung, Au, Fernández-Dols, and Iwawaki (1992) found that participants were happiest with interventions that allowed them to participate actively. However, Leung et al. were not exploring third-party conflict management per se.

While these results bode well for advising, we should be mindful of its limitations. As we have seen, research inspired by Thibaut and

Walker's (1975, 1978) work suggested that disputants willingly give up process control under certain conditions. For example, individuals are more willing to surrender process control when there is a need for speedy resolution (LaTour, Houlden, Walker, & Thibaut, 1976), when the conflict is a serious one (Bigoness, 1976; Johnson & Pruitt, 1972), and when there is a need for face saving (LaTour et al., 1976). On the other hand, LaTour et al. found that, when disputants have an established pattern of cooperation, they seem more eager to take on process control. Indeed, under certain conditions, the two conflicting parties may even forgo decision control to a third party, so long as they believe that this loss of decision control will facilitate successful resolution of their disagreement (Rubin, 1980).

Mediation.   When a manager mediates, he or she retains process control but allows the two conflicting parties to select their own resolution. Mediation is quite similar to advising, in that the disputants retain decision control. Indeed, the two are sometimes categorized together (e.g., Cropanzano et al., 1999; Folger & Cropanzano, 1998), but there is a meaningful difference in degree. Mediation implies that the third party retains relatively more control over the process; advising or facilitation implies that he or she retains relatively less.

As is true for advising, people tend to prefer mediation to methods that vest control of the outcome in a third party (Karambayya & Brett, 1989), and this is especially so when time is available and the conflicting parties must continue to work together (Lewicki & Sheppard, 1985). A general preference for mediation, as opposed to more autocratic strategies, has been observed in both Canada and the Netherlands (Leung, Bond, Carmet, Krishnan, & Liebrand, 1990; for a correction, see Leung, Bond, Carment, Krishnan, & Liebrand, 1991), as well as for Hong Kong and the United States (Leung, 1987; Leung & Lind, 1986). However, as in the case with advising, mediation may not be the most appropriate form of third-party tactic when time is limited, the matter is complex, or the need for strong authority is otherwise perceived to be needed (e.g., certain cross-cultural situations; see the following section).

Adversarial or arbitration.   When employing the adversarial method, the manager listens carefully as each party presents his or her case without interference. Subsequently, the third party issues an opinion. The tactic has been called "adversarial" by Lewicki and Sheppard (1985), "arbitration" by Kolb and Glidden (1986) and Shapiro and Rosen (1994), and "adjudication" by Karambayya and Brett (1989). Individuals prefer to retain decision control, unless there are no alternatives for reaching a settlement (Rubin, 1980). Nevertheless, the adversarial approach is generally preferred to more autocratic methods (Folger et al., 1996), and this is true in Canada and the Netherlands (Leung et al., 1990), as well as in the United States. Having said that, there do seem to be some cross-cultural differences regarding preferences for this tactic. The adversarial style comes with a built-in confrontation. In East Asian cultures, which prefer social harmony, such a technique may be liked relatively less well than it is in North America. Leung and Lind (1986) and Leung (1987) found support for this idea in studies comparing the United States and Hong Kong. Benjamin (1975) came to similar conclusions regarding Japan.

Autocratic or inquisitorial.   When taking an inquisitorial approach, the third party controls both the process and the outcome. Managers employ autocratic methods quite commonly (e.g., Bergmann & Volkema, 1994; Shapiro & Rosen, 1994; Sheppard, 1983), though the use of hierarchy is typically disliked by disputants. In business settings, various studies have found that participants prefer to retain some control over the process and, especially, over the outcome (e.g., Cropanzano et al., 1999; Karambayya & Brett, 1989; Karambayya et al., 1992; Lewicki & Sheppard, 1985). This seems to be the case in legal settings as well (Folger et al., 1996; Thibaut & Walker, 1975). Similar results have also been obtained in Hong Kong (Leung & Lind, 1986) and Turkey (Kozan & Ilter, 1994).

Providing impetus.   Analogous to a "kick in the pants" (Shapiro & Rosen, 1994), providing impetus involves low third-party process control and low third-party outcome control (Lewicki & Sheppard, 1985). However, it also involves the provision of motivational incentives to reach a settlement (Kolb & Glidden, 1986). The third party does not fix the problem, but he or she creates an atmosphere wherein it is in the disputants' best interests to achieve a settlement. In one study, Lewicki and Sheppard (1985) found that providing impetus was liked less well than mediation. Likewise, Cropanzano et al. (1999) found that, except for avoidance (discussed in the following section), providing impetus was the most unpopular tactic in Argentina, the Dominican Republic, Mexico, and the United States.

Avoidance.   Avoidance, sometimes referred to simply as "ignoring" (Leung et al., 1992), is doing nothing at all (Kolb & Glidden, 1986). People in the United States (Shapiro & Rosen, 1994) and Hong Kong (Leung, 1988) use it frequently. There is not a great deal of research on avoidance, but it tends not be evaluated favorably. This is also so in Spain, Japan (Leung et al., 1992), Canada, and the Netherlands (Leung et al., 1990, 1991). Cropanzano et al. (1999) found that avoidance was the least preferred conflict resolution option in four nations: Argentina, the Dominican Republic, Mexico, and the United States.

Elangovan's Prescriptive Model

In an attempt to organize and expand previous work, Elangovan (1995, 1998) provided managers with a set of working guidelines, assisting them in choosing the most important tactic in different situations. Elangovan recognized that supervisors require at least two pieces of information—their dispute resolution options and a set of rules for diagnosing the situation. When individuals are aware of their potential styles and have a proper understanding of critical contextual features, then they need only employ the appropriate conflict resolution procedure within the approach setting. This line of thinking is summarized in the following three figures. Figure 10.1 displays the five dispute resolution styles, Figure 10.2 shows the six diagnostic rules, and Figure 10.3 displays how applying the rules leads one to choose (hopefully) the optimal style. These latter two figures follow closely from Elangovan's original presentation.

Knowing Your Options.   Elangovan's (1995, 1998) five intervention strategies are based on the amount of control exercised by the third party (for a similar model, see Lewicki & Sheppard, 1985). Consistent with the work of Thibaut and Walker (1975, 1978), Elangovan considered two stages—process and outcome. A manager might affect control in either or both. Hence, the tactics are similar, but Elangovan provided a distinct nomenclature. These are shown in Figure 10.1:

- *Low-control strategy (LCS):* Third party has neither process nor decision control. This is similar to Thibaut and Walker's bargaining procedure.
- *Means-control strategy (MCS):* Third party has process control but not decision control. This corresponds to *mediation* (Lewicki & Sheppard, 1985), as the term was used earlier.
- *Ends-control strategy (ECS):* Third party has decision control but lacks process control. This corresponds to the adversarial or arbitration tactic that we previously discussed (Lewicki & Sheppard, 1985).

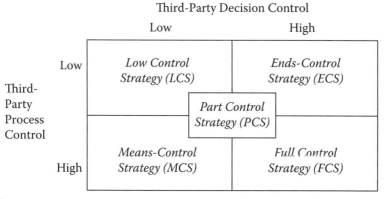

FIGURE 10.1. Thibaut and Walker's (1975, 1978) five dispute intervention strategies.

Name of Rule	Diagnostic Question
1. Dispute-Importance Rule (DI)	How important is the dispute to the effectve functioning of the organization?
2. Time-Pressure Rule (TP)	How important is it to resolve the dispute quickly?
3. Nature of Dispute Rule (ND)	Does the dispute concern the interpretation of existing rules and arrangements or the changing of existing rules and arrangement?
4. Nature of Relations Rule (NR)	What is the expected frequency of future work-related interactions between the disputants?
5. Commitment-Probability Rule (CP)	If you were to impose a settlement, what is the probability that the disputants would be committed to it?
6. Disputant-Orientation (DO)	If you were to let the disputants settle their differences, what is the probability that they would come to an organizationally compatible settlement?

FIGURE 10.2. Rules of diagnosing a situation (Elangovan, 1995, pp. 817–819).

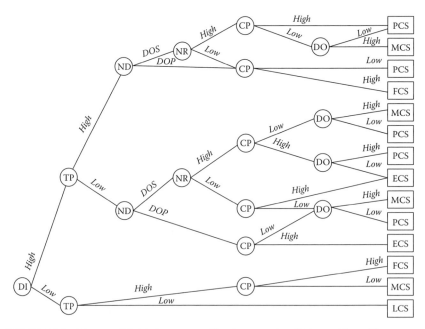

FIGURE 10.3. Managerial third-party conflict intervention (Adapted from Elangovan, 1995).

- *Full-control strategy (FCS):* Third party has both process control and decision control. This is what we earlier referred to as the "autocratic" or "inquisitorial" approach (Kolb, 1986; Lewicki & Sheppard, 1985).
- *Part-control strategy (PCS):* Third party shares both process and decision control. This is comparable to Thibaut and Walker's (1975, 1978) moot procedure. It is very roughly comparable with advising (Kolb, 1986; Kolb & Glidden, 1986), but there is an important difference. In advising, the third party shares process control, but he or she may allow the disputant to retain decision control.

It should be noted that these five strategies are "ideal types." Actual managerial interventions could well vary on a continuum that ranges from no control whatsoever to almost complete control. Many actual resolution attempts will fall somewhere between these extremes. Nevertheless, Elangovan's (1995) five approaches provided a beginning framework. We will now turn our attention to his rules for diagnosing situations.

Assessing the Situation.   As shown in Figure 10.2, Elangovan (1995) presented six rules; their applications can help one understand the relevant situational context. We have also quoted (or in some cases paraphrased) the corresponding list of diagnostic questions. Notice that the first three rules pertain directly to the dispute, while the latter three emphasize the conflicting parties.

When speaking of dispute "importance," Elangovan (1995) referred to importance for the organization's mission or effectiveness. When a dispute is important for a firm's basic operation, then the manager should take more decision control (e.g., move toward the left column of Fig. 10.1) to ensure quality. Seizing decision control could potentially compromise fairness. However, as Thibaut and Walker (1975, 1978) demonstrated, disputants tend to accept low outcome control so long as they maintain process control. Thus, for important decisions supervisory third parties should err toward allowing the disputing parties process control.

When time pressure is high, a decision needs to be made quickly. Since managerial hegemony is more efficient, at least in the short run, the third party will likely wish to sacrifice process control. If necessary, the supervisor may also need to control the decision as well (Elangovan, 1995, 1998).

Not all disputes are the same, and different problems call for different solutions. Elangovan (1995) suggested that disputes be divided into two types. *Disputes over privileges* (DOP) involve construals of existing rules or policies. There is some standard or agreement in place, but individuals interpret it differently. Hence, the challenge lies in finding a shared understanding that all parties can accept. *Disputes over stakes* (DOS) are about changes involving the setting of rules, plans, and other policies. These disagreements are less "cognitive" than DOP conflicts because the DOS disputes often involve one's values and goals. Since DOP disputes are over interpretations, the manager should retain outcome control. DOS disputes, on the other hand, can be more complex. The third party will probably not wish to forgo process control, but he or she will need to yield ends or outcome control to the conflicting parties.

The nature of the relationship between the disputants has long-term implications. If the participants are expected to work together into the future, then the third party should leave them with decision control but should retain process control. For example, mediation might be effective. Managerial control over the outcome is more viable when a long-term interaction is not anticipated.

Long-term commitment to a settlement is important. In some settings, the disputants may be committed to a unilateral decision, in other settings this will not be so. When commitment probability is low, managers should give up at least some outcome control (e.g., move toward the left column of Fig. 10.1). When commitment probability is high, then managers have more leeway in deciding whether to dominate the decision.

A final question has to do with the likelihood that conflicting parties reach an effective settlement. Elangovan (1995) termed this probability the "disputant orientation." A high disputant orientation means that the two parties have the ability and motivation to achieve an agreement on their own. A low disputant orientation indicates that this is less likely. The higher the disputant orientation (the more likely disputants are to resolve their own problems), the less control the third party should retain over the decision.

Applying the Model.   The final step in applying Elangovan's (1995) model was displayed in Figure 10.3, which is adapted from Elangovan's original figure (p. 819). Managers can ask themselves the six questions listed in Figure 10.2, maintaining the order among them. Each response moves the individual forward along the flow chart. The terminus provides what Elangovan believed to be the optimal strategy. Available evidence was limited but generally supportive of the model. Elangovan (1998) surveyed 92 supervisors in a variety of organizations. These participants were asked to recall successful and unsuccessful attempts at dispute resolution. Their attempts at third-party intervention were more successful to the extent that they followed Elangovan's perspective advice and less successful to the extent that they did not.

Future Research Needs and Critical Omissions

Our review of informal conflict resolution suggests considerable promise but also serious limitations in our current body of knowledge. Scholars have provided taxonomies of conflict management behavior (e.g., Sheppard, 1984; Elangovan, 1995). While this research was promising, there have still been relatively few rigorous empirical tests of actual mediation systems in organizations. It would be useful to have additional descriptive research. Such a program of study could describe what tactics are used and under what circumstances. It would also be useful to know more about workers' responses.

Likewise, much of the evidence to date has been collected in laboratory studies. Most of this research has been of real benefit in our understanding of mediation in organizations, but the results would benefit from more organizational field studies if for no other reason than to limit questions relating to external validity of the existing studies.

Elangovan's (1995, 1998) model provided a useful point of departure for future research. As noted, that model contains three parts (Figure 10.1, Figure 10.2, and Figure 10.3), each one of which may be empirically tested. It offers advantages over a number of other models in that it is both comprehensive and prescriptive. If research were able to verify the model substantially, it might be of real benefit to practitioners.

Now that we have spent some time discussing informal methods of conflict resolution, we would like to turn our attention to the specific tactical actions and strategic thoughts that guide actual mediator behavior.

MEDIATOR BEHAVIOR AND STRATEGY

Every mediator is an individual. As such, each employs varying tactics and strategies during the mediation process. However, the models of mediator behavior put forth in the dispute resolution literature to explain mediation share many similarities because most mediators espouse the common goal of a harmonious relationship between disputing parties. We discuss the major models of mediator behavior in the following section.

Models of Mediation

Descriptive Models.   One of the most frequently referenced descriptive models of mediator behavior is Kolb's (1983) model of third party action and cognition. Kolb outlined two models of action that a mediator could utilize during the mediation process: (a) deal making and (b) orchestration. While deal making is characterized by a forcefully and domineering third party that almost compels parties to reach settlement using his or her influence, a mediator espousing the ideals of the orchestration technique can be characterized as more of a "fly on the wall" that develops a dialogue between the parties but does not intervene unless absolutely necessary. The orchestrator may pose questions to the parties but tends not to push them toward any specific resolution (Lewicki, Weiss, & Lewin, 1992).

Normative Models.   As with descriptive models, normative models were conceived through the examination of labor disputes. However, they can be used to solve disputes outside of a unionized environment. In 1952, Jackson delineated his five-part mediator technique consisting of (a) gathering the parties together, (b) gaining confidence in the mediator, (c) establishing the true weighted importance of various issues, (d) questioning disputing parties' assumptions, and (e) determining and expanding upon areas of agreement and formulating alternative solutions. Additionally, Jackson emphasized the importance of quelling angry tempers by utilizing cooling off periods. Stevens (1963) fashioned a slightly more formal model describing stages in terms of the "contract zone" instead of focusing on the disputing parties. More specifically, this involves bargaining that is driven by the manipulation of the perceived costs. Many years later, Folberg and Taylor (1984) used concepts from the aforementioned models to develop a seven-part "megaprocess" model of mediation that was similar to Jackson's (1952) and Stevens' (1963) models with the addition of (a) a legal review process and (b) an implementation, review, and revision stage. Almost concurrently, Moore (1986) put forth a twelve-stage model that provided even greater detail as to the strategies and actions that mediators should undertake to resolve disputes. Moore suggested that a mediator should consider what strategy he or she should employ, as well as, the appropriate mediation stage design prior to engaging in action at each of the twelve stages.

What is clear from this assorted mix of models is that there is not a unanimously accepted or commanding definition of mediation or mediator behavior (Lewicki et al., 1992). While each camp of researchers' valiantly attempted to enhance and fine tune the models of dispute resolution that came before it, scholars could not agree on the appropriate number of stages in the process, the specific actions the mediator should take at each of those stages, or how social context should influence a mediator's strategy and tactics (Kolb, 1986; Rubin, 1981, 1986; Sheppard, Saunders, & Minton, 1987). Future scholarly inquiry should continue to push forward and address this daunting task.

Nevertheless, each of these aforementioned models shares similarities. Most importantly, all models embrace the ultimate goal of settlement. While arbitration shares this goal, mediation differs in that the disputing parties have decision control in the endeavor. Bush and Folger (1994) questioned these underlying assumptions that were present in all of the prior models. The authors doubted the two basic assumptions that (a) problem solving and settlement should be the ultimate goals and (b) the mediators should have process control. Instead, they advocated a mediator strategy that incorporated empowerment and recognition. They termed their strategy *transformative mediation*.

Transformative Mediation.   Transformative mediation seeks to create a better socialized community by teaching disputing parties how to take the perspective of the other group and act in a way that acknowledges this perspective. In short, transformative mediation assumes that apology is a powerful method of moving disputing parties toward settlement (Levi, 1997). While transformative mediation has an intuitive appeal, it has received scholarly criticism. Specifically, Seul (1999) took issue with the idea that the mediator should take on the role of moral developer without any consideration given to the parties' current stage of moral development. In a slightly different vein, Levi (1997) noted that, in the presence of a "bona fide" dispute, a simple "I'm sorry" may not rectify the emotional harm inflicted or moral mandate that was infringed upon (Kohlberg, 1981). Moreover, apologies may not always be sincere and disputants can use public recantations as "attitude structuring tactics" in hopes of leveraging their positions against the opponent (Pruitt, 1981). Likewise, Gaynier (2005) contended that Bush and Folgers's (1994) myopic dependence on empowerment and recognition lacked any sort of realization that resistance, conflicting interests, and mediator self-awareness all play roles in the dispute resolution process. Finally, Kressel (2000) argued that transformative mediation is not actually a novel idea at all. He noted that the "hallmarks" of this type of mediation could be seen in mediators that espouse a problem-solving style of mediation. Specifically, mediators using a problem-solving style, as in the case of divorce mediation, can be characterized as nonjudgmental about the disputants' decisions, impartial, and encouraging open and honest communication. However, comparative studies examining clearly defined models have not yet been carried out. Future research in this area would no doubt be fruitful.

To summarize, it is still unclear whether transformative mediation can produce its intended effects. Additionally, we know that mediation is not always the chosen dispute resolution tactic by both parties. Indeed, mandatory mediation is common and has its own set of implications surrounding the ability to change parties' attitudes and reach settlement.

Mediator Strategy

Given the numerous stages during mediation and the distinct and diversified subtypes of mediation, it is essential that mediators put thought into their strategies prior to sitting down with both parties. Carnevale (1986) laid out four possible strategies that could be selected by a mediator: (a) integration, which involves finding solutions based on common ground; (b) pressing, which involves encouraging parties to be less obdurate; (c) compensation, which involves giving something back to the party making concessions; and (d) inaction, which involves a laissez-faire approach to the problem (see Figure 10.4). Additionally, Carnevale (1986) outlined a model of mediator strategic choice based on five core assumptions: (a) Mediators desire an agreement between disputants; (b) mediators are able to use any of the four strategies; (c) mediators are willing and driven to take action; (d) only one strategy can be utilized at a single point in time; and (e) mediators choose a strategy based on two variables—how

Mediator's Value of Parties' Aspirations

		High	Low
Mediator's Perception of Common Ground	High	Integrate	Inaction
	Low	Compensate	Press

FIGURE 10.4. Strategic choice model of mediator behavior adapted from Carnevale (1986).

much the mediator cares about the disputants resolving their dilemma and the mediator's recognition of a common ground.

According to Carnevale's (1986) model, integration was the most desirable method due to its ability to accommodate both parties. However, in order to utilize this strategy effectively, the mediator must perceive an ample amount of common ground and recognize that both parties have high aspirations for any communal solution. The size of common ground is dependent upon the mediator's assessment of the probability that a mutually acceptable solution will be found. For example, if the disputing parties are business partners, any dispute that leads to a stoppage in business productivity could hurt both of the parties. Therefore, it is likely that the disputants will agree that they want to continue to do business together and concur that the solution should be quick and cost effective for both parties. Because both parties have similar end goals, the mediator can guide them toward resolutions that will benefit both groups.

While the compensation strategy shares the same high settlement aspirations as the integrative solution, the mediator recognizes that there is little common ground between the parties. Therefore, the best solution involves meeting one party's reservation value and compensating by other means the party that is forced to acquiesce. For example, there is a dispute between a used-car salesperson and a customer over a car that the customer purchased. The customer is angry because the car that was sold to her broke down three weeks after she purchased it and requires $500 to repair. She wants the salesperson to take back the lemon and refund the money she spent on the vehicle. However, the salesperson refuses to buy back the vehicle. The customer is angry because she does not feel that the salesperson disclosed all of the relevant information about the car's history prior to the purchase. In this situation, both parties have high aspirations, but there is little common ground to come to an integrative solution. In this case, the mediator might suggest that the salesperson pay the customer for a portion of the repairs instead of buying back the vehicle. Using this compensation strategy, the salesperson pays a small fee (meeting the reservation value), and the customer is compensated for acquiescing and keeping the car.

However, when both disputing parties have low expectations for reaching a settlement and there is little common ground between them, it may be advisable for the mediator to engage in pressing because of the likely failure of all of the other strategies due to the uncertainty that the parties can reach a mutual agreement given that their current reservation values do not overlap. In this case, "pressing" that is of the form that causes a party (or parties) to change their reservation value may lead to satisfaction with the mediation outcome (mediators should take care not to apply too much coercion because it can sometimes cause parties to reevaluate the outcome shortly after settlement). For example, mediators may set a deadline for the disputants to reach agreement, which can serve to make the disputants more flexible and lower their reservation values (Carnevale & Lawler, 1986). Moreover, they can raise questions to each party as to the basis of their reservation values.

If the mediator does decide to use the fourth strategy, inaction, it is because he or she assesses that both parties have low aspirations and a large amount of common ground. In other words, the disputants are willing to compromise on their positions and the mediator assesses that they are working toward complementary goals. In this case, the parties will most likely be able to compromise without additional direction from the mediator. Unfortunately, less experienced or unskilled mediators may gravitate toward inaction because it requires the least amount of intellectual strain. Hence, the tactic of inaction may be incorrectly chosen due to its appeal as being the easiest choice.

In addition to Carnevale's (1986) taxonomy, Kressel (2000) set forth a typology of his own with regard to mediator behavior. In the past, this typology was used to describe other types of mediation (Kressel, 1972, 1985; Kressel & Deutsch, 1977; Kressel & Pruitt, 1985; Carnevale, Lim, & McLaughlin, 1989). Although multidimensional scaling has found similar dimension in the previous research (McLaughlin, Carnevale, & Lim, 1991), Kressel (2000) further simplified earlier typologies and suggested that a three-factor structure was best to describe mediator strategy. Kressel divided mediator behavior into *reflexive, contextual,* and *substantive* strategies. Kressel's strategies were different from Carnevale's in that they depicted the more general ways by which mediators could approach a conflict situation. Specifically, reflexive interventions occur when the mediator puts in an initial effort to establish the foundation on which later dispute resolution will take place. Rapport building and neutrality are essential components of this strategy. And, Kressel emphasized that the mediator must be acceptable to both parties in order for this tactic to be truly successful. On the other hand, in contextual interventions, the mediator focuses on producing a climate that promotes problem-solving dialogue between the parties. Finally, substantive interventions spotlight the specific issues in the dispute. When using this strategy, the primary goal of the mediator is to deal with the issues by some means.

In practice, mediators may espouse all three types of strategies to varying extents. Indeed, researchers suggested that, many times, tactics are used contingently depending on the mediators' assessments of the dispute (Lim & Carnevale, 1990). Specifically, they found that mediators thought certain tactics were acceptable in some situations, but not in others. For example, substantive/press tactics were negatively associated with settlement under low levels of hostility but positively related under high levels of hostility.

Managerial Intervention. The aforementioned tactics are common among professional mediators due to the clear roles and defined limits that mediators, arbitrators, and fact finders have in managing disputes (Elkouri & Elkouri, 1979). Managers, on the other hand, have more flexibility to select one or any combination of the previously mentioned strategies. Additionally, managers often are not bound by the same constraints as are third parties (Sheppard, Lewicki, & Minton, 1986). Moreover, due to the managers' inherent closeness to the conflict, they may adopt a different set of dispute resolution tactics than a detached third party. Formal or appointed third parties are less likely to have a vested interest in the outcome of the dispute. Managers, however, are often involved in the conflict and will have to deal with the repercussions if the dispute is not resolved properly (Lewicki & Sheppard, 1985). Indeed, research found that managers utilize tactics that are distinct from the ones professional mediators employ to resolve workplace conflict (Sheppard et al., 1987).

Just as Carnevale (1986) suggested several determinants of formal third-party strategies, Pinkley, Neale, Brittain, and Northcraft (1995) examined the relevant literature and extracted situational factors that they expected to influence managerial selection: (a) dispute intervention goals of the manager (Sheppard, 1983); (b) amount of conflict (Lewicki & Sheppard, 1985); (c) time constraints (Lewicki & Sheppard, 1985) and importance of the issue (Carnevale & Conlon, 1988); (d) power balance and relationship of the conflicting parties (Karambayya & Brett, 1989); and (e) hierarchical positioning of third party (Heller, 1981).

In a related vein, we find a drawback that echoes throughout all of the aforementioned studies. Specifically, the experimenters, and not the managers, identified and categorized the situational factors posited to affect managerial strategy selection. To deal with this problem in the tactic research, Pinkley et al. (1995) used an inductive method that allowed managers to identify, categorize, and label the conflict resolution tactics that they used. Their use of multidimensional scaling provided a means of detecting and quantitatively grouping the dispute resolution strategies of managers, even when the managers were unable to conceptualize their behavior fully in terms of a specific strategic category. Their results evidenced five managerial intervention dimensions: "(1) Attention given to stated versus underlying problem; (2) disputant commitment forced versus encouraged; (3) manager versus disputant decision control; (4) manager approaches conflict versus manager avoids conflict; and (5) dispute is handled publicly versus privately" (Pinkley et al., 1995, p. 398).

In sum, Pinkley et al. (1995) supplied support for an empirically tested and inductively derived taxonomy of managerial conflict resolution tactics as described by managers. Their findings, along the previously mentioned experimenter-derived situational factors, may serve as a base for future research in this area. Undoubtedly, subsequent research endeavors are required to provide a clearer picture of the elements that drive a manager to pick a given strategy. Along those lines, we move to the intervention goals of the manager.

Dispute intervention goals of the manager.   Sheppard (1983) argued that managerial strategy is chosen based on the intervention goal with which the manager is most concerned. The author laid out four possible goals that a manager could be striving for during the dispute resolution process: efficiency, effectiveness, fairness, and disputant satisfaction. Therefore, the goal that the manager espouses will dictate, to some extent, the type of intervention strategy that should be employed. For example, if a manager is concerned only with the time efficiency of the conflict resolution, he or she may engage in pressing and attempt to coerce the parties to come to a settlement. While this strategy may be efficient, the disputants may perceive it as unfair. However, in the real world, managers often desire conflicting goals, such as settling a dispute quickly while maintaining fairness. This makes the selection of an intervention strategy arduous.

Intensity of the dispute.   If a manager detects an intense strain between the disputants, this may impact the selection of a dispute resolution technique. The manager must gauge the intensity of the conflict by means of discussion with both of the parties to decide how involved to become in the dispute. If the parties are on somewhat amicable terms, the manager may choose to let the disputants solve the problem on their own. However, if one or both parties are obdurate and refuse to negotiate, the manager may require a higher level of involvement of him- or herself (Carnevale & Conlon, 1988; Kressel & Pruitt, 1985).

Time constraints.   Most decisions are made under time constraints imposed by the pace of ongoing events, by explicit deadlines, or by others becoming impatient with the decision maker's indecisiveness (Benson & Beach, 1996). The effects of time constraints on choice are remarkably consistent: decision makers speed up execution of their decision strategies or switch to simpler strategies, sometimes speeding up after having switched (Edland & Svenson, 1993; Maule & Mackie, 1990; Payne, Bettman, & Johnson, 1988;

Smith, Mitchell, & Beach, 1982; Svenson & Benson, 1993; Svenson, Edland, & Slovic, 1990; Svenson & Maule, 1993; Wright, 1974; Zakay, 1985).

Similar effects occur when people need to solve disputes under time pressure. For instance, time pressure can produce epistemic freezing in which people become less aware of plausible alternatives during dispute resolution (Kruglanski & Freund, 1983). Time pressure can also result in a phenomenon called "closure of the mind" (De Dreu, 2003). Closure of the mind increases disputants' reliance on inadequate decision heuristics during the dispute resolution process. Time pressure can also influence the process and outcome of integrative bargaining (Carnevale & Lawler, 1986). For example, if negotiators have an individualist orientation, time pressure produces more nonagreements and poor negotiation outcomes. If negotiators adopt a cooperative orientation, negotiators achieve better negotiation outcomes.

When managers feel the need to solve disputes in a brief amount of time, they will generally engage in tactics that allow them maximum outcome control (Lewicki & Sheppard, 1985). In fact, mediated dispute resolution often occurs when one or all of the parties involved feel some sense of urgency to solve a dispute that the original parties could not solve alone. The perceived urgency may result from internal or external time constraints. The internal constraints include things like arbitrary deadlines selected by the negotiator or mediator that provide impetus for a quick settlement (Cropanzano et al., 1999). External constraints include things like shareholder meetings, court dates, and contract deadlines.

Urgency can also result from the parties involved thinking about the potential outcome of the negotiation process (the outcome can be positive, negative, or neutral). We will call this "outcome urgency." For many disputes, the parties involved must feel a sense of time urgency or outcome urgency. If procrastination is advantageous to one or all parties involved, there is little incentive to settle the dispute.

Importance of the issue.   The extent to which the organization will be negatively affected by the dispute will influence the strength of actions to be taken by the organization. For example, a complaint filed against a company with the Equal Employment Opportunity Commission (EEOC) accusing the company of racial discrimination would most likely receive a stronger and more immediate response from the company than a petty squabble between two employees about seniority for picking vacation time. When the dispute has the potential to impact the welfare of the company negatively, managers are apt to address the issue with greater urgency (Pinkley et al., 1995). Indeed, empirical research supports this idea (Lewicki & Sheppard, 1985; Sheppard et al., 1986).

Power balance between the conflicting parties.   Research has found that the relationship of the manager to the disputants is a key determinant of the intervention tactic used (Karambayya & Brett, 1989; Kipnis & Schmidt,

1983). Additionally, research suggested that the power balance between the disputants influences strategy choice (Sheppard et al., 1986). Laskewitz, Van de Vliert, and De Dreu (1994) tried to determine whether a mediator's decision to choose sides was a function of the power differential between the disputants. They found that mediators tend to side with the less powerful party only when both parties have the same abilities to sanction the mediator. When the stronger party also has more power to sanction the mediator, the mediator sides with the stronger disputant. Hence, the propensity to balance the power between both disputants is moderated by the self-interest of the mediator. Furthermore, outcomes appear to be affected by the power balance of the disputants and what the mediator asks them to consider. Specifically, Arunachalam, Lytle, and Wall (2001) found that, when the mediator suggested to the powerful party he or she should show concern for the weaker party, this reduced the powerful party's outcomes. For weaker parties, this suggestion increased the outcomes. However, no interaction was found with regard to joint outcomes. These finding would suggest that it might not always be beneficial to express concern for the other disputant, especially if you are the powerful party. But, further research should be conducted before any prescriptive suggestions are made.

Hierarchical positioning of the third party.   Based on Heller's (1971, 1981) work, there was some indication that managers high in the hierarchy are more willing to share power. However, this topic has not been thoroughly examined and much more work still needs to be done.

Future Research Needs and Critical Omissions

While a "one-size-fits-all" approach may not be appropriate when sequencing the dispute resolution system, it definitely does not seem fitting when defining the goals of the mediation process. Specifically, with the advent of transformative mediation, mediators that espouse this holistic methodology are structuring their interventions to promote a healing process that proposes not only to solve the dispute but also to morally enhance the minds of the conflicting parties by coaching them to forgive and accept. These are admirable objectives but lofty goals at the same time. Moreover, one must assume that once dueling opponents are willing to forgive and embrace the others' viewpoint. Future research should examine whether or not these are attainable objectives. Explicitly, under what circumstances is transformative mediation appropriate? Are certain disputes less likely to benefit from this technique than others are? If so, what are they? Additionally, should both formal third party mediators and managers use transformative mediation? From a theoretical perspective, fine tuning the definition of third party strategies still needs to be accomplished. For example, is transformative mediation actually a new idea, or have mediators been acting in accordance with this model all along?

There are several areas related to the effects of time constraints on the mediation process that warrant future research. One such area is the relationship between time constraints and the mediation process. For example, do the effects of time constraints differ depending on the stage of the mediation process at which the time constraint occurs?

A second area that warrants future research is the relationship between time constraints and the perspective of the parties in the dispute. As stated earlier in this manuscript, most research on mediation in the workplace has focused on the worker's perspective (e.g., McDermott, Obar, Jose, & Bowers, 2000). Future research should address the effects of time constraints on the mediation process from various perspectives including the perspectives of the employer, employee, and the legal system.

A third area for future research is the relationship between time constraints and the strategy or type of third party mediation used by the parties involved in the dispute. For instance, researchers could investigate if time constraints affect facilitation, advising, mediation, and/or arbitration in the same manner. Researchers could also investigate whether having time constraints influences the type of mediation that occurs (e.g., under severe time constraints disputants prefer arbitration to facilitation because they need resolution quickly).

From a methodological standpoint, it would be beneficial to see more qualitative research examining the most efficient and effective strategies that third parties employ in various situations. Specifically, while we know the different types of strategies that third parties utilize, we still do not know which ones work the best. Similarly, are certain goals better for a mediator to espouse than other goals? Additional qualitative research in organizational settings may help to answer these questions. No doubt, scholars will have future lines of research for years to come in the area of mediator strategy and behavior.

COMBINING FORMAL AND INFORMAL DISPUTE RESOLUTION

Thus far we have implied that formal and informal third-party dispute resolution were completely separate. While this is a reasonable strategy for purposes of explication, the reader should not be misled. Organizations often combine formal and informal strategies into a system with a well-defined progression. Firms have long been advised to sequence the different forms of resolution so that they proceed from low cost to high cost (e.g., Brett, Goldberg, & Ury, 1990; Gordon & Miller, 1984; Starke & Notz, 1981; Weiss & Hughes, 2005). The less expensive initial stages are typically less formal and more flexible; the more expensive later stages are typically more formal and structured.

There is evidence that proper sequencing can improve the effectiveness of dispute resolution systems. For one thing, it seems that the majority of complaints are resolved at the earlier and lower costs stages (e.g., Graham & Heshizer, 1979). This would seem to suggest that beginning with informal and less expensive tactics and only later moving toward more expensive procedures might well save organizations considerable money. Moreover, at least in union settings, labor/management relations are better when grievances are settled before escalation up the hierarchy (Turner & Robinson, 1972). While supportive in a general sort of way, available research on sequencing leaves many questions unanswered.

Ross and Conlon (2000) took up one interesting question. These authors compared the effectiveness of mediation–arbitration (med–arb) with arbitration-mediation (arb–med). Med–arb follows the traditional low to high cost procession. The disputants are given a mediator and a predetermined deadline. If they do not resolve their differences within this time, then the mediator becomes an arbitrator.

Med–arb has much to recommend it (Ross & Conlon, 2000), but it can be turned on its head. Saunders (1993) argued that arb–med is also a viable procedure. In any case, arb–med proceeds through three steps. In the first part, an arbitrator listens to the disputes and prepares a recommendation. However, that recommendation is not issued. Rather, the arbitrator moves to the second part, whereby he or she acts as a mediator. If this attempt at mediation remains unsuccessful, then the arbitrator presents the binding opinion to the disputants. While the conflicting parties may prefer med–arb, Ross and Conlon (2000) argued that arb–med will promote more cooperative behavior, greater information disclosure, and more agreement with mediator settlements. However, these authors further maintain that arb–med may be less advantageous than med–arb when long-range outcomes are considered.

Future Research Needs and Critical Omissions

If future research supports Ross and Conlon's (2000) propositions, it suggests that the overall cost of a *system* might vary depending on how the components are sequenced. Whether one prefers arb–med or med–arb, there seem to be some synergies that result from considering the order in which they occur. Mediation plus arbitration may not be the same as arbitration plus mediation. Thinking of dispute management procedures as part of larger units could bring additional insights to our knowledge; scholars should not limit themselves to examining each stage in isolation from the others.

Combining aspects of both formal and informal dispute resolution raises a number of interesting questions. Perhaps the most interesting is the importance of sequencing in the dispute resolution system. Ross and

Conlon's (2000) ideas as to when arb–med may be preferable over med–arb offered fresh insights into what is often viewed as a "one-size-fits-all" approach. Bendersky (2003) offered her own novel twist on the sequencing issue—that multiple approaches could be pursued at once. An empirical test of this model, if supported, may offer practical benefits.

Up until this point, we may have left the reader with the impression that workers and organizations are about equally likely to embrace disputing mechanisms. However, this is not necessarily the case (Kressel, 2000). Before we leave this section, which deals more with organizational designs on disputing mechanisms, we wanted to address organizational acceptance to mediation, as an example of dispute mechanisms. We chose mediation because it is perhaps the most common dispute resolution vehicle (it can, for example, constitute both an informal and formal dispute resolution mechanism) and it is one for which there exists important research investigating organizational reactions to it.

ORGANIZATIONAL APPROACHES TO FORMAL DISPUTING: THE CASE OF MEDIATION

Historically, claimants (employees) have been more willing to mediate than organizations (e.g., McDermott et al., 2000). According to the EEOC, workers want to mediate 87% of discrimination claims while organizations agree to it only 31% of the time (D. Grinberg, personal communication, July 21, 2004). In that context, one study found that employers were hesitant to participate for the following reasons: (a) they did not believe the case had "merit" (although it was not always clear what the organizational basis for this judgment was it did include the perception that the EEOC itself would not find a "reasonable cause" finding in the case); and (b) they perceived that EEOC mediation required monetary settlement (which, by implication, they must have disagreed with; McDermott, Jose, & Obar, 2003). In another study, lawyers for the construction industry recommended that their clients mediate in most or all disputes less than half (49.3%) of the time (Henderson, 1996). Some of the reasons industry lawyers recommended against mediation were stated as (a) the dispute involved a novel interpretation of law (something, it should be noted, that a deep pockets organization is more capable of making "novel" than most workers); (b) the credibility of a witness is an issue; or (c) the opposing party or his or her representative was considered untrustworthy or unlikely to compromise.

So why do organizations agree to mediate disputes? In this same construction industry study, some reasons for a recommendation of mediation were stated as follows: (a) desire for an ongoing relationship, (b) need for a quick resolution of disputes, (c) an essential economical alternative to litigation, and (d) desire for privacy and confidentiality. This last factor, privacy, can often be compelling. A public dispute, especially in a large, publicly traded company, can have devastating effects. It can adversely affect recruiting and worker morale, and it may spawn similar claims and may even adversely affect the stock price (e.g., Texaco).

Mediation has proven popular because, to a large degree, it works and has led to many positive perceptual outcomes. Research indicates settlement rates for mediation at around 60%–78% and user satisfaction at 75% or more (Brett, Barsness, & Goldberg, 1996; Kressel, Pruitt, & Assoc., 1989). One of the most encouraging of these findings is the satisfaction of the parties with the short-term outcomes of mediation (Pruitt, Peirce, McGillicuddy, & Syna, 1992). However, there is scant evidence of long-term success with mediation. What little evidence does exist suggests little relationship between short-term success in mediation and long-term success (Pruitt, Peirce, & McGillicuddy, 1993; Pruitt, Peirce, Zubek, McGillicuddy, & Welton, 1993). Moreover, as noted earlier, mediation has a positive effect on perceptions of justice as well. In particular, the high decision and process control inherent in mediation leads to increased perceptions of procedural justice (Ross & Conlon, 2000).

Behaviorally, besides the obvious fact that mediation reduces conflicts, there is some evidence that mediation may facilitate discussion with coworkers and restore the ability to sleep (when that is an issue; Bergmann & Volkema, 1994). An interesting question for mediation researchers is the appropriate criterion variable to measure common behavioral outcomes. Often, "settlement" has been deemed the measure. However, in certain circumstances, it may be more appropriate to measure "degree of compromise" or "willingness to recommend to others," as well as other variables (Henderson, 1996).

Future Research Needs and Critical Omissions

As previously suggested, for practical reasons alone, research is needed to better understand why organizations agree to mediate employment disputes at significantly lower rates than employees. Some possible avenues for exploration include anticipated organizational justice. That is, there is some evidence that organizations believe among other things that the federal mediators may be biased against them (McDermott et al., 2000). This suggests a violation of perceived or anticipated procedural justice may be an issue to some organizations in mediation situations (Colquitt, 2001). Moreover, as previously suggested, the benefits of mediation over litigation in terms of privacy and confidentiality is an area worthy of further research in part because it has not received much attention to date. If future research supports this reason, this can be an important leverage for mediators and others interested in this technique to use to encourage use of mediation.

Finally, most research on mediation in the workplace has focused on the worker's perspective (e.g., McDermott et al., 2000). However, the limiting factor in workplace mediation has been organizations because they participate in mediation at far lower rates than individual employees do. Research that is able to answer questions surrounding this issue will be valuable to research and practice.

CONCLUSION

Third-party dispute resolution has exploded in popularity during the last 20 years or so. It has proven itself to have many advantages over traditional court-based approaches to resolving conflicts. Yet, there is still much we do not know or fully appreciate about this phenomenon. We hope that this chapter offers some fresh insights on this important issue.

REFERENCES

Arunachalam, V., Lytle, A., & Wall, J. A. (2001). An evaluation of two mediation techniques, negotiator power, and culture in negotiation. *Journal of Applied Social Psychology, 31*(5), 951–980.

Bendersky, C. (2003). Organizational dispute resolution systems: A complementarities model. *Academy of Management Review, 28,* 643–656.

Benjamin, R. W. (1975). Images of conflict resolution and social control: American and Japanese attitudes toward the adversary system. *Journal of Conflict Resolution, 19,* 123–137.

Benson, L., III, & Beach, L. R. (1996). The effects of time constraints on the pre-choice screening of decision options. *Organizational Behavior and Human Decision Processes, 67,* 222–228.

Bergmann, T. J., & Volkema, R. J. (1994). Issues, behavioral responses, and consequences in interpersonal conflicts. *Journal of Organizational Behavior, 15,* 467–471.

Bigoness, W. J. (1976). The impact of initial bargaining position and alternative modes of third party intervention in resolving bargaining impasses. *Organizational Behavior and Human Performance, 17,* 185–198.

Brett, J. M., Barsness, Z. I., & Goldberg, S. B. (1996). The effectiveness of mediation: An independent analysis of cases handled by four major service providers. *Negotiation Journal,* 259–269.

Brett, J. M., Goldberg, S. B., & Ury, W. L. (1990). Designing systems for resolving disputes in organizations. *American Psychologist, 45,* 162–170.

Bush, R. A., & Folger, J. P. (1994). *The promise of mediation.* San Francisco: Jossey-Bass.

Carnevale, P. J. (1986). Strategic choice in mediation, *Negotiation Journal, 2*(1), 41–56.

Carnevale, P. J., & Conlon, D. (1988). Time pressure and mediator strategy in a simulated organizational dispute. *Organizational Behavior and Human Decision Processes, 42,* 111–133.

Carnevale, P. J., & Lawler, E. J. (1986). Time pressure and the development of integrative agreements in bilateral negotiations. *The Journal of Conflict Resolution, 30*(4), 636–659.

Carnevale, P. J., Lim, J. D., & McLaughlin, M. E. (1989). Contingent mediator behavior and its effectiveness. In K. Kressel & D. G. Pruitt (Eds.), *Mediation research: The process and effectiveness of third-party intervention.* San Francisco: Jossey-Bass.

Casper, J. D., Tyler, T. R., & Fisher, B. (1988). Procedural justice in felony cases. *Law and Society Review, 22,* 483–507.

Colquitt, J. (2001). On the dimensionality of organizational justice: A construct validation of a measure. *Journal of Applied Psychology, 86,* 386–400.

Cropanzano, R., Aguinis, H., Schminke, M., & Denham, D. (1999). Disputant reactions to managerial conflict resolution tactics: A comparison among Argentina, the Dominican Republic, Mexico, and the United States. *Group and Organization Management, 24,* 124–154.

De Dreu, C. K. W. (2003). Time pressure and closing of the mind in negotiation. *Organizational Behavior and Human Decisions Processes, 91,* 280–295.

Edland, A., & Svenson, O. (1993). Judgment and decision making under time pressure. In O. Svenson & A. J. Maule (Eds.), *Time pressure and stress in human judgments and decision making.* New York: Plenum.

Elangovan, A. R. (1995). Managerial third-party dispute intervention: A prescriptive model of strategy selection. *Academy of Management Review, 20,* 800–830.

Elangovan, A. R. (1998). Managerial intervention in organizational disputes: Testing a prescriptive model of strategy selection. *The International Journal of Conflict Management, 9,* 301–335.

Elkouri, F., & Elkouri, E. A. (1979). *How arbitration works.* Washington, DC: Bureau of National Affairs.

Folberg, J., & Taylor, A. (1984). *Mediation: A comprehensive guide to resolving conflicts without litigation.* San Francisco: Jossey-Bass.

Folger, R., & Cropanzano, R. (1998). *Organizational justice and human resource management.* Beverly Hills, CA: Sage.

Folger, R., Cropanzano, R., Timmerman, T. A., Howes, J. C., & Mitchell, D. (1996). Elaborating procedural fairness: Justice becomes both simpler and more complex. *Personality and Social Psychology Bulletin, 22,* 435–441.

Gaynier, L. P. (2005). Transformative mediation: In search of a theory of practice. *Conflict Resolution Quarterly, 22*(3), 397–408.

Gordon, M. E., & Miller, S. J. (1984). Grievances: A review of research and practice. *Personnel Psychology, 37,* 117–146.

Graham, H., & Heshizer, B. (1979). The effect of contract language on low-level settlement of grievances. *Labor Law Journal, 30,* 427–432.

Heller, F. A. (1971). *Managerial decision making: A study of leadership styles and power-sharing among senior executives.* London: Tavistock.

Heller, F. A. (1981). *Competence and power in managerial decision making: A study of senior levels of organization in eight countries.* New York: Wiley.

Henderson, D. A. (1996). Mediation success: An empirical analysis. *Ohio State Journal on Dispute Resolution, 11,* 105–147.

Houlden, P. (1981). Impact of procedural modifications on evaluation of plea bargaining. *Law and Society Review, 15,* 267–291.

Houlden, P., LaTour, S., Walker, L., & Thibaut, J. (1978). Preferences for modes of dispute resolution as a function of process and decision control. *Journal of Experimental Social Psychology, 14,* 13–30.

Jackson, E. (1952). *Meeting of the minds: A way to peace through mediation.* New York: McGraw-Hill.

Johnson, D. E., & Pruitt, D. G. (1972). Pre-intervention effects of mediation versus arbitration. *Journal of Applied Psychology, 56,* 1–10.

Karambayya, R., & Brett, J. M. (1989). Managers handling disputes: Third-party rules and perceptions of fairness. *Academy of Management Journal, 32,* 687–704.

Karambayya, R., Brett, J. M., & Lytle, A. (1992). Effects of formal authority and experience on third-party roles, outcomes, and perceptions of fairness. *Academy of Management Journal, 35,* 426–438.

Kipnis, D., & Schmidt, S. M. (1983). An influence perspective on bargaining with organizations. In M. Bazerman & R. Lewicki (Eds.), *Negotiating in organizations* (pp. 303–319). Beverly Hills, CA: Sage.

Kohlberg, L. (1981). *The philosophy of moral development.* New York: Harper & Row.

Kolb, D. M. (1983). *The mediators.* Cambridge, MA: MIT Press.

Kolb, D. M. (1986). Who are organizational third parties and what do they do? In R. J. Lewicki, B. H. Sheppard, & M. H. Bazerman (Eds.), *Research on negotiation in organizations.* Greenwich, CT: JAI Press.

Kolb, D. M., & Glidden, P. (1986). Getting to know your conflict options. *Personnel Administration, 31*(6), 77–90.

Kozan, M. K., & Ilter, S. S. (1994). Third party roles played by Turkish managers in subordinates' conflict. *Journal of Organizational Behavior, 15,* 453–466.

Kressel, K. (1972). *Labor mediation: An exploratory survey.* Albany, NY: Association of Labor Mediation Agencies.

Kressel, K. (1985). *The process of divorce.* New York: Basic Books.

Kressel, K. (2000). Mediation. In M. Deutsch & P. T. Coleman (Eds.), *The handbook of conflict resolution: Theory and practice.* San Francisco: Jossey-Bass.

Kressel, K., & Deutsch, M. (1977). Divorce therapy: An in-depth survey of therapists' views. *Family Process, 16,* 413–443.

Kressel, K., & Pruitt, D. G. (1985). Themes in mediation of social conflict. *Journal of Social Issues, 41,* 179–198.

Kressel, K., Pruitt, D. G., & Associates (Ed.). (1989). *Mediation research: The process and effectiveness of third party intervention.* San Francisco: Jossey-Bass.

Kruglanski, A. W., & Freund, T. (1983). The freezing and unfreezing of lay-inferences: Effects on impressionable primacy, ethnic stereotyping, and numerical anchoring. *Journal of Experimental Social Psychology, 19,* 448–468.

Laskewitz, P., Van de Vliert, E., & De Dreu, C. K. W. (1994). Organizational mediators siding with or against the powerful party. *Journal of Applied Psychology, 24*(2), 176–188.

LaTour, S., Houlden, P., Walker, L., & Thibaut, J. (1976). Some determinants of preferences for modes of conflict resolution. *Journal of Conflict Resolution, 20,* 319–356.

Leung, K. (1987). Some determinants of reactions to procedural models of conflict resolution: A cross-national study. *Journal of Personality and Social Psychology, 53,* 898–908.

Leung, K. (1988). Cross-cultural differences of conflict avoidance. *Journal of Cross-Cultural Psychology, 19,* 125–136.

Leung, K., Au, Y-F., Fernández-Dols, J. M., & Iwawaki, S. (1992). Preference for method of conflict processing in two collectivist cultures. *International Journal of Psychology, 27,* 195–209.

Leung, K., Bond, M. H., Carment, D. W., Krishnan, L., & Liebrand, W. B. G. (1990). Effects of cultural femininity on preference for method of conflict processing: A cross-cultural study. *Journal of Experimental Social Psychology, 26,* 373–388.

Leung, K., Bond, M. H., Carment, D. W., Krishnan, L., & Liebrand, W. B. G. (1991). Correction to this paper. *Journal of Experimental Social Psychology, 27,* 201–202.

Leung, K., & Lind, E. A. (1986). Procedural justice and culture: Effects of culture, gender, and investigator status on procedural preferences. *Journal of Personality and Social Psychology, 50,* 1134–1140.

Levi, D. L. (1997, November). The role of apology in mediation. *New York University Law Review, 70.*

Lewicki, R. J., & Sheppard, B. H. (1985). Choosing how to intervene: Factors affecting the use of process and outcome control in third party disputes. *Journal of Occupational Behavior, 31,* 465–502.

Lewicki, R., Weiss, S. E., & Lewin, D. (1992). Models of conflict, negotiation and third party intervention: A review and synthesis. *Journal of Organizational Behavior, 13*(3), 209–252.

Lim, R. G., & Carnevale, P. J. D. (1990). Contingencies in the mediation of disputes. *Journal of Personality and Social Psychology, 58*(2), 259–272.

Lind, E. A., Kurtz, S., Musante, L., Walker, L., & Thibaut, J. (1980). Procedure and outcome effects on reactions to adjudicated resolutions of conflicts of interest. *Journal of Personality and Social Psychology, 39,* 338–350.

Lind, E. A., MacCoun, R. J., Ebener, P. A., Felstiner, W. L. F., Hensler, D. R., Resnik, J., et al. (1990). In the eye of the beholder: Tort litigants' evaluations of their experiences in the civil justice system. *Law and Society Review, 24,* 953–996.

Maule, J., & Mackie, P. (1990). A componential investigation of the effects of deadlines on individual decision making. In K. Borchering, O. I. Larichev, & D. M. Messick (Eds.), *Contemporary issues in decision making* (pp. 449–461). Amsterdam: North-Holland.

McDermott, P. E., Jose, A., & Obar, R. (2003). *An investigation of the reasons for the lack of employer participation in the EEOC mediation program.* Retrieved April 1, 2006, from http://www.eeoc.gov/mediate/study3

McDermott, P. E., Obar, R., Jose, A., & Bowers, M. (2000). An evaluation of the Equal Employment Opportunity Commission mediation program (EEOC Order No. 9/0900/7632/2). Washington, DC: Equal Employment Opportunity Commission.

McLaughlin, M. E., Carnevale, P., & Lim, R. G. (1991). Professional mediators' judgments of mediation tactics: Multidimensional scaling and cluster analysis. *Journal of Applied Psychology, 76*(3), 465–472.

Moore, C. W. (1986). *The mediation process: Practical strategies for resolving conflict.* San Francisco: Jossey-Bass.

Payne, J. W., Bettman, J. R., & Johnson, E. J. (1988). Adaptive strategy selection in decision-making. *Journal of Experimental Psychology: Learning, Memory, & Cognition, 14,* 534–552.

Pinkley, R. L., Neale, M. A., Brittain, J., & Northcraft, G. B. (1995). Managerial third-party intervention: An inductive analysis of intervenor selection. *Journal of Applied Psychology, 80*(3), 386–402.

Pruitt, D. (1981). *Negotiation behavior.* New York: Academic Press.

Pruitt, D., Peirce, R., & McGillicuddy, L. (1993). Long-term success in mediation. *Law and Human Behavior, 17,* 313–330.

Pruitt, D., Peirce, R., McGillicuddy, L., & Syna, H. (1992). Disputant and mediator behaviors affecting short-term success in mediation. *The Journal of Conflict Resolution, 36,* 546–572.

Pruitt, D., Peirce, R., Zubek, J., McGillicuddy, L., & Welton, G. (1993). Determinants of short-term success in mediation. In S. Worchel & J. A. Simpson (Eds.), *Conflict between people and groups: Causes, processes, and resolution.* Chicago: Nelson-Hall Publishers.

Rasinski, K. A. (1992). Preference for decision control in organizational decision making. *Social Justice Research, 5,* 343–357.

Roberson, Q., Moye, N. A., & Locke, E. A. (1999). Identifying a missing link between participation and satisfaction: The mediating role of procedural justice perceptions. *Journal of Applied Psychology, 84,* 585–593.

Ross, W. H., & Conlon, D. E. (2000). Hybrid forms of third-party dispute resolution: Theoretical implications of combining mediation and arbitration. *Academy of Management Review, 25,* 418–427.

Rubin, J. Z. (1980). Experimental research on third-party intervention in conflict: Toward some generalizations. *Psychological Bulletin, 87,* 379–391.

Rubin, J. Z. (1981). *Dynamics of third party intervention: Kissinger in the Middle East.* New York: Praeger

Rubin, J. Z. (1986). Third parties in organizations: A responsive communication. In R. J. Lewicki, B. H. Sheppard, & M. A. Bazerman (Eds.), *Research on negotiation in organizations* (pp. 271–286). Stamford, CT: JAI Press.

Saunders, F. E. A. (1993). The courthouse and alternative dispute resolution. In L. Hall (Ed.), *Negotiations: Strategies for mutual gain* (pp. 43–60). Newbury Park, CA: Sage.

Seul, J. R. (1999). How transformative is transformative mediation?: A constructive-developmental assessment. *Ohio State Journal on Dispute Resolution, 15.*

Shapiro, D. L., & Rosen, B. (1994). An investigation of managerial interventions in employee disputes. *Employee Responsibilities and Rights Journal, 7,* 37–51.

Sheppard, B. H. (1983). Managers as inquisitors: Some lessons from the law. In M. H. Bazerman & R. J. Lewicki (Eds.), *Negotiating in organizations* (pp. 193–213). Beverly Hills, CA: Sage.

Sheppard, B. H. (1984). Third party conflict intervention: A procedural framework. In B. M. Staw & L. L. Cummings (Eds.), *Research in organizational behavior* (Vol. 6, pp. 141–160). Greenwich, CT: JAI Press.

Sheppard, B. H. (1985). Justice is no simple matter: Case for elaborating our model of procedural fairness. *Journal of Personality and Social Psychology, 49,* 953–962.

Sheppard, B. H., Lewicki, R. J., & Minton, J. (1986). A new view of organizations: Some retrospective comments. In R. J. Lewicki, B. H. Sheppard, & M. A. Bazerman (Eds.), *Research on negotiation in organizations* (Vol. 1, pp. 311–321). Stamford, CT: JAI.

Sheppard, B. H., Saunders, D., & Minton, J. (1987). Procedural justice from the third party perspective. *Journal of Personality and Social Psychology, 54,* 629–637.

Smith, J. F., Mitchell, T. R., & Beach, L. R. (1982). A cost benefit mechanism for selecting problem-solving strategies: Some extensions and empirical tests. *Organizational Behavior and Human Performance, 29,* 370–396.

Starke, F. A., & Notz, W. W. (1981). Pre- and post-intervention efforts of conventional versus final offer arbitration. *Academy of Management Journal, 24*, 832–850.

Stevens, C. M. (1963). *Strategy and Collective Bargaining Negotiation,* New York: McGraw-Hill.

Svenson, O., & Benson L. (1993). On experimental instructions and the inducement of time pressure behavior. In O. Svenson & A. J. Maule (Eds.), *Time pressure and stress in human judgment and decision making.* New York: Plenum.

Svenson, O., Edland, A., & Slovic, P. (1990). Choices between incompletely described alternatives under time stress. *Acta Psychologica, 75*, 153–169.

Svenson, O., & Maule, A. J. (1993). (Eds.). *Time pressure and stress in human judgment and decision-making.* New York: Plenum.

Tett, R. P., Gutterman, H. A., Bleier, A., & Murphy, P. J. (2000). Development and content validation of a "hyperdimensional" taxonomy of managerial competence. *Human Performance, 13*, 205–251.

Thibaut, J., & Walker, L. (1975). *Procedural justice: A psychological analysis.* New York: Erlbaum/Wiley.

Thibaut, J., & Walker, L. (1978). A theory of procedure. *California Law Review, 66*, 541–566.

Thomas, K. W., & Schmidt, W. H. (1976). A survey of managerial interests with respect to conflict. *Academy of Management Journal, 19*, 315–318.

Turner, J. T., & Robinson, J. W. (1972). A pilot study of the validity of grievance settlement rates as a predictor of union-management relationships. *Journal of Industrial Relations, 14*, 314–322.

Tyler, T. R., & Folger, R. (1980). Distributional and procedural aspects of satisfaction with citizen-police encounters. *Basic and Applied Social Psychology, 1*(4), 281–292.

Walker, L., LaTour, S., Lind, E. A., & Thibaut, J. (1974). Reactions of participants and observers to modes of adjudication. *Journal of Applied Social Psychology, 4*, 295–310.

Wall, J. A., Jr., & Callister, R. R. (1995). Conflict and its management. *Journal of Organizational Behavior, 21*, 515–558.

Weiss, J., & Hughes, J. (2005). Want collaboration? Accept—and actively manage—conflict. *Harvard Business Review, 93*–101.

Wright, P. (1974). The harassed decision-maker: Time pressure, distraction, and the use of evidence. *Journal of Applied Psychology, 59*, 555–561.

Zakay, D. (1985). Post-decision confidence and conflict experienced in a choice process. *Acta Psychologica, 58*, 75–80.

11

Organizational Dispute Resolution Systems

JULIE B. OLSON-BUCHANAN
Craig School of Business
California State University, Fresno

WENDY R. BOSWELL
Mays Business School
Texas A&M University

There is a range of disputes that can emerge because of individuals (and groups) working together in organizations. For example, in a given week an organization might witness disputes ranging from fairness concerns over its new need-based parking space policy, to a contested performance evaluation, to a violent confrontation between two assistant supervisors. Certainly some disputes that might occur in organizations (e.g., criminal behavior), by their very nature, can and should be addressed outside the organization in the public court system. However, the question remains as to how an organization can best manage the remaining disputes in such a way that will minimize the potential negative consequences (e.g., absences) and maximize the potential positive consequences (Coser, 1956; De Dreu, Harinck, & Van Vianen, 1999) of conflict. As the rest of the chapters in this volume illustrate, there are a host of ways by which an organization may try to achieve formally or informally these conflict management objectives.

In this chapter, we focus specifically on organizational dispute resolution (ODR) systems. We define ODR systems as any process identified in organizational policy as a sanctioned means to resolve disputes *within* the organization. This definition has considerable overlap with the term *alternative dispute resolution* (ADR) that encompasses any nonlitigation means of resolving disputes. However, we focus only on ADR *within* the organization. Also, a considerable amount of the literature uses the terms *ODR* and *grievance procedures* interchangeably. For clarity purposes, we will limit the use of the term *grievance procedure* to the multistep appeal procedures that are traditionally used in union settings.

We will focus on a number of issues related to ODR systems. In light of the careful examination of labor-management disputes in chapter 12 of this volume, we will focus primarily on nonunion settings. First, we describe the historical and current organizational use of ODR systems. Then we discuss the various purposes of ODR systems as well as the various measures of ODR effectiveness that have been proposed or examined in the literature. Next, we discuss the classic theoretical roots of ODR research and describe some of the corresponding empirical research. Then we examine the current theoretical and empirical examinations of ODR systems as they relate to the major measures of ODR effectiveness. Next we discuss the movement toward a multioption approach to dispute resolution in organizations. Finally, we conclude with a discussion of the many potential areas for future research.

HISTORICAL AND CURRENT PRACTICE OF ODR SYSTEMS IN ORGANIZATIONS

Early Practice of ODR systems

The earliest formal ODR systems were created as a result of collective bargaining agreements. Unions negotiated such systems as a way to address union contract disputes with management, while ensuring the protection of union employees from management reprisal. Before World War II, most unionized ODR systems were multistep appeal systems (typically referred to as "grievance procedures"). These grievance procedures are loosely patterned after our public court system in which the dispute is initially presented (and decided on) at lower levels and a disputant has the opportunity to appeal the decision to higher levels until the final step. Interestingly, before World War II, most grievance procedures had mediation as the final step in the process (Lewin & Peterson, 1999). Thus, a neutral, third party served to help disputants reach agreement, but did not make a binding decision. However, after World War II, there was a shift toward using ODR systems with arbitration (in which a neutral third party makes a binding decision) as the final step (Lewin & Peterson). As early as 1952, 89% of all collective bargaining agreements included a formal ODR system (U.S. Bureau of Labor Statistics, 1966), and by the mid-1970s, this percentage had grown to 98.5% (U.S. Bureau of Labor Statistics, 1977). As Peterson and Lewin (2000) noted, many scholars consider the proliferation of ODR systems "the major accomplishment of the United States system of industrial relations" (p. 395).

The ubiquity of formal ODR systems in the union setting is credited for the growth of ODR systems in nonunion settings as well. Following World War II, there was very little implementation, let alone use, of formal ODR in nonunion organizations (Slichter, Healy, & Livernash, 1960). In the 1960s and 1970s, we started to see more substantial ODR procedures adopted within firms. For example, General Electric introduced its multistep appeal system in the 1970s in response to the threat of unionization (see Ewing, 1989). It was the late 1970s and early 1980s, however, that witnessed the largest rise of nonunion ODR procedures. In 1980, Berenbeim's (1980) survey indicated that approximately two thirds of its sample of 96 non-union firms had a formal multistep appeal system in place. Ichniowski and Lewin's (1987) survey of a larger number of both union and nonunion firms suggests approximately 50% of nonunionized employees had access to a formal ODR system by the early 1980s.

Although the early research primarily focused on grievance procedures as ODR, certainly other types of ODR systems were being introduced and used in organizational settings. For example, IBM's open-door policy, in which disputants can approach any level of management with a dispute, emerged in the 1960s. Cherrington (1982) identified open-door policies as the "the most popular procedure for responding to employee complaints" (p. 596) in nonunion organizations. Similarly, Thomson (1974) identified open-door policies as the default for organizations without a formal multi-step appeal system in place. However, several researchers called into question whether typical open-door policies were truly operating as effective ODR systems in organizations (e.g., Cherrington, 1982; McCabe, 1988). The use of ombudsperson (explained more in the following section) was also being discussed in the literature (e.g., Balfour, 1984; McCabe, 1988), but it was not clear how prevalent its use was in organizations.

Current Practice of ODR systems

ODR systems in organizations have grown considerably in use and variability since the 1980s. The U.S. General Accounting Office's (1995) study of a sample of federal contractors found "almost all employers of 100 or more employees use one or more ADR approaches" (p. 3). This study found that nearly 10% in the sample had adopted nonunion multistep appeal systems (with arbitration as the final step) in particular. Similarly, approximately 16% of the nonunion firms in Colvin's (2003b) study of the telecommunications industry had multistep appeal systems with arbitration and/or peer review as the final step. Among workplaces that do adopt ODR systems, these procedures vary in basic features, such as the extent to which there is a formal, set procedure to follow, who is the final decision maker, whether employees are permitted representation, what complaints can be brought under the procedure, and what criteria are used to decide disputes (Feuille & Chachere, 1995; Feuille & Delaney, 1992). Though ODR procedures in the nonunion workplace are characterized by a high degree of variation in both occurrence and structure (Colvin, 2004a; Dibble, 1997; Feuille & Chachere), there are several common approaches in use today.

Arguably the most informal ODR for addressing workplace conflict is a policy that directs disputants to communicate with the other person(s) involved in the dispute (Olson-Buchanan & Boswell, 2002). More specifically, an individual could try to talk with the other party or parties involved to attempt to resolve a dispute. This is consistent with Costantino and Merchant's (1996) term, "negotiated alternative dispute resolution," whereby the parties "talk things over." While this is not a stand-alone ODR system, per se, it is often identified in organizational policy as the best/preferred way to handle workplace disputes before pursuing other alternatives. Similarly, it is often a first step in formal multistep appeal systems (explained further in the following section). A number of research studies suggest that negotiation is typically the first action taken (e.g., Peirce, Pruitt, & Czaja, 1993).

Other ODR-related policies direct disputants to present their case to managers, in particular. For example, an open-door policy is a popular approach that allows a considerable amount of variability in how dispute resolution is approached. In this ODR system, the individual can approach any level of management with his or her dispute. Presumably, the individual could informally appeal any decision made by a manager in the chain of command to someone at a higher level. Managerial intervention is similar, except the individual would present his or her dispute to whoever has control over a given area. So, for example, if the dispute was between two coworkers over claiming a particular client, one individual may report the problem to his or her manager who then intervenes.

Some organizations incorporate the use of mediators as either a stand-alone ODR or resource to be used in conjunction with other ODR systems. That is, disputants are encouraged or directed to resolve disputes with the assistance of a mediator. A mediator may be an employee of the organization or an external individual trained in this role that is available to organizational members. In mediation, a neutral third party (e.g., mediator) listens to and reviews information presented by the parties involved in the dispute. Though a mediator makes an informed recommendation about what should be done, the final resolution or terms of the settlement are in the "hands of the disputants" (Lewicki, Weiss, & Lewin, 1992). Thus, the objective behind mediation is to help the parties reach a settlement; that is, facilitate a resolution through problem solving (Jameson, 1999; Lewicki et al., 1992; Prein, 1987).

Similarly, an ombudsperson serves the role of helping settle a dispute, though an ombudsperson's role in resolving conflict can be more varied and often quite informal. For example, ombudspersons may counsel employees on how to resolve issues themselves, conduct formal or informal investigations of disputes, or simply serve as a support system for employees to defuse hostility and escalation of conflict (Dibble, 1997). Though an ombudsperson "typically functions outside the normal organizational hierarchy" (Dibble, 1997, p. 75), he or she is an employee of the organization, typically reporting to the CEO or Human Resource Director and, thus, is often seen as representing management's interests more so than those of employees, though this depends on the structure of the position as well as the culture of the organization.

Finally, the multistep appeal system (Dibble, 1997), made popular by union collective bargaining agreements, is still a fairly popular ODR system in use in nonunion settings today. Often called a grievance procedure, this ODR system is a formal process that is loosely modeled after the U.S. court system. Typically, an individual (e.g., a grievant) would file an initial complaint, and its merits would be considered by the lowest level within the grievance system (e.g., a supervisor). The individual could appeal the decision through several levels of the procedure. The final level varies by organization (cf., Feuille & Chachere, 1995) and can be one person (e.g., CEO or arbitrator) or a panel (e.g., peer review panel or panel of managers). For example, under a peer review procedure, employees who are peers of the complainant sit on panels that review grievances (McCabe, 1988), whereby under nonunion arbitration procedures, a neutral third-party arbitrator hears and decides employee complaints. Peer employees and arbitrators have at least the potential to be viewed by employees as more independent and neutral decision-makers than managers (Klaas & Feldman 1993; Lewin & Peterson, 1999). We see examples of arbitration procedures in nonunion as well as union settings in such diverse companies as Circuit City, Anheuser-Busch, PeopleSoft USA, Summit Products Toys, Hallmark, Ford Motor Co., Dillard's Inc., and DataLogic International. Often, through the implementation of signed arbitration agreements with employees, these companies have attempted to move workplace disputes from the courtroom into the hands of an arbitrator (typically a retired judge or lawyer) with the goal of saving companies from costly litigation as well as presumably encouraging a more amicable resolution.

Summary. As indicated, there is growing evidence of an expansion in recent decades of both the number and complexity of ODR procedures (Colvin, 2003b; Feuille & Chachere 1995; Feuille & Delaney 1992; McCabe 1988). The early, nearly exclusive use of multistep appeal systems in unionized settings has expanded to include other types of ODR systems. In addition, the last few decades have witnessed the introduction and use of a variety of ODR systems (e.g., open door, mediation) in the nonunion setting as well. In particular, a growing number of organizations provide multiple types of ODR systems, thereby allowing employees the choice of which system, if any, they would like to use to address a workplace dispute. As will be discussed in a later section, this approach is consistent with implications from both theory and empirical research.

PURPOSES AND EFFECTIVENESS MEASURES OF DISPUTE RESOLUTION SYSTEMS

Purposes

The research literature has noted several possible purposes for implementing ODR systems in nonunion organizations. These reasons include ensuring fair governance (Aram & Salipante, 1981) and fair treatment (Colvin, 2003b), minimizing the costs or threat of litigation (Aram & Salipante, 1981; Colvin, 2003a), encouraging voicing of organizational problems (Aram & Salipante, 1981), and avoiding unionization (Berenbeim, 1980). Although these various purposes may be quite diverse, several of them could easily fall under McCabe's (1988) two major goals for ODR systems: to correct the company's mistakes and to fulfill an "ethical obligation" to employees.

Effectiveness Measures

Similarly, researchers have proposed and used a number of different effectiveness measures of ODR systems. Several of these measures are organizational-level outcomes, but process measures as well as individual-level effectiveness measures are increasingly being examined and used.

Organizational Outcomes. Organizational outcome effectiveness measures can take several forms. These have included organizational measures such as higher firm productivity, fewer absences, and lower turnover rates. ODR system usage rates have also been considered a measure of effectiveness (for a review, see Peterson & Lewin, 2000). Arguably, an organization's legal costs on issues that could have been addressed in an ODR system may be a reasonable indicator of ineffectiveness. Similarly, one could argue that the extent to which the organization remains union free (relative to the industry norms) may indicate whether an ODR system effectively meets the needs of employees who might otherwise be served by a union.

Process Measures. Labor relations research has often focused on process variables as appropriate effectiveness measures of ODR systems in union contexts, but these variables are arguably important in nonunion contexts as well. Such measures would include the timeliness with which disputes are resolved, the hierarchical level at which they are resolved (lower is generally considered better), and whether the final settlements are balanced with respect to which side (e.g., employees and management) prevailed (Lewin, 1987). More recent measures would include perceived fairness of the dispute resolution system.

Individual Outcome Measures. As noted, some research has examined individual outcome measures associated with ODR system usage, such as absences, performance ratings, and employee turnover. Individual perceptions are also important effectiveness measures. These would include perceptions of fairness by individuals who have used ODR systems as well as those who have not. Similarly, measures of perceived post-ODR system consequences, both positive (e.g., justice) and negative (e.g., reprisals) would arguably be measures of whether the ODR systems do, in fact, provide fair opportunities to address disputes in organizations while protecting disputants from recrimination. Assessing the reactions of various constituent groups (e.g., managers, union officials) is also relevant, particularly since determinants of perceived ODR system effectiveness may be quite divergent across groups (cf. Boroff, 1991).

CLASSIC THEORETICAL AND CORRESPONDING EMPIRICAL RESEARCH

Classic Theoretical Approaches

The classic theoretical roots of ODR systems research stem from two main approaches: the labor economics literature that emphasized ODR systems as a form of voice in exit-voice-loyalty theory (Hirschman, 1970; Freeman & Medoff, 1984) and the labor relations literature that emphasized the concept of due process (e.g., Kuhn, 1961; Peach & Livernash, 1974) in ODR systems.

Hirschman's Exit-Voice-Loyalty Model. Hirschman (1970) argued that a business firm would learn about "an absolute or comparative deterioration of the quality of the product or service provided" (p. 4) in two major ways: exit or voice. Hirschman argued that exit, when consumers stop buying the product or service, is economic in nature because it is an indirect, anonymous signal that is gleaned from the market. On the other hand, Hirschman equated voice, when consumers communicate the deterioration to the organization, as "political action par excellence" (p. 16) because it is direct. As explained by Hirschman, while exit is straightforward (either you leave or you do not), voice is not as clear-cut as it can range "from faint grumbling to violent protest" (p. 16). Voice can be positively framed as well. For example, a restaurant customer might suggest a new or modified item as a way to retain customers. Hirschman further argued that voice is more desirable to organizations because it allows organizations to learn about the specifics of a problem directly and quickly. In addition, his theory asserted that more loyal consumers are likely to choose to voice a deterioration in the relationship with the organization. Thus, his theory essentially argued that more loyal consumers would result in economic gains for the organization because they would provide more specific information about problems so that the organization could solve them more quickly and efficiently.

Freeman and Medoff (1984) extended Hirschman's (1970) theoretical arguments to the employment context. They argued that organizations could learn about workplace problems from employees quitting (exit) or complaining about the problem in some way (voice). That is, if an employee felt a supervisor had mistreated him or her, he or she could voice the complaint directly by talking to the supervisor, or another manager, or by filing a grievance. On the other hand, an employee could choose to exit the organization by quitting his or her job. Again, employees that are more loyal would be more likely to use voice to express discontent with the organization, thereby providing the organization with the specific information needed to correct a problem. However, Freeman and Medoff argued that there are potential costs to employees for exercising voice because they may suffer reprisals for doing so, asserting that the "collective voice" of a union ODR system (e.g., grievance procedure) will serve to protect employees better. They suggested that this collective voice would also benefit the organization because it would provide an alternative to exit that, by protecting employees, would result in lower turnover rates and provide management with more useful, specific information to make needed changes. Thus, exit-voice-loyalty theory was mainly used to generate predictions of the role of ODR systems as a voice mechanism and as an alternative to exit.

Due-Process Literature. The early ODR systems research also drew heavily from scholarly discussions of "due process" or "fair and orderly procedures" (McCabe, 1988, p. 33). Davis (1957), in his seminal discussion of ODR procedures, argued that "justice which is defined as fairness according to established rules and relationships ... is a fundamental requirement in employee human relations because it gives substance and meaning to human dignity" (p. 439). A number of early scholars theorized and discussed the critical factors to achieve such due process or justice in ODR systems (e.g., Ewing, 1982; Luthans, Hodgetts, & Thompson, 1987). Accordingly, early studies, particularly in the labor relations area, examined ODR systems with respect to whether (or to what extent) they met the objective of due process by incorporating factors theorized to be related to justice or due process, such as timeliness and impartiality.

Classic Empirical Research

Given the early dominance of union-based ODR systems, most of the early empirical literature examined ODR systems in union settings (see chapter 12, this volume). As nonunion ODR systems became increasingly popular, researchers started to focus on the effectiveness of such systems, without the presence of a union (e.g., Berenbeim, 1980). Lewin's (1987) seminal article provided the first large-scale examination of this topic. Lewin examined the antecedents and consequences of grievance activity in three large, nonunion organizations over a period of four years. To that end, Lewin pulled relevant data from the firms' grievance-system activity files and employee records.

Lewin (1987) integrated several literatures to examine the effectiveness of the grievance systems at multiple levels of analysis. Drawing from previous empirical studies, he identified possible demographic correlates of appeal filing and overall appeal system usage such as sex, race, tenure, and education. Consistent with the labor relations research, Lewin examined due process-related criteria such as level at which the appeal is settled and the proportion of employee versus employer "wins." Incorporating the dominant use of the exit-voice model in labor economics research, Lewin also investigated postgrievance behavior measures such as performance ratings, absences, promotions, and turnover.

It was somewhat surprising how consistent Lewin's (1987) findings from a nonunion setting were with previous union-based research. For example, the demographic predictors (e.g., primarily male, young, and less education) of appeal-system usage in the nonunion firms were similar with what had been found in the largely union-based empirical literature. However, little is known as to why there are demographic differences in appeal system usage in either the union or nonunion setting. While some skeptics questioned whether employees would use ODR systems without the support of unions, the overall appeal filing rates were significant, albeit below what is typically found in union settings (Lewin, 1987). The ODR systems in all three firms also appeared to be effective with respect to due process factors such as the settlements' proximity to the source (83% were settled at the first or second step) and win/loss ratio (employees prevailed on average 53%).

Lewin's (1987) findings in terms of the consequences of dispute system usage were especially interesting. While previous research had examined organizational outcomes of dispute system usage (e.g., Ichniowski, 1986), this was the "first systematic evidence about the consequences for employees" (p. 487). Contrary to predictions derived from exit-voice-loyalty theory, grievance system usage was *not* associated with positive outcomes for employees. Instead, grievance system users appeared to suffer negative consequences such as lower promotions, higher turnover, and, if they appealed the dispute to a higher level, decreased performance ratings. Supervisors/managers who were parties to the dispute also appeared to have similarly negative consequences including lower promotion activity and higher turnover.

Pointing to the "disconnect" between the due process measures of effectiveness (where the dispute systems fared well) and the employee consequence measures of effectiveness (where the system users did not fare well), Lewin (1987) argued that it is clearly inappropriate to consider only traditional due process measures. In addition, Lewin called into question the utility of the exit-voice-loyalty model and instead concluded that the organizational punishment literature (e.g., Arvey & Jones, 1985) provided a better explanation for the findings. Specifically, organizational members may be "punishing" those involved in a dispute for engaging in some "deviant" behavior (e.g., filing an appeal). If, indeed, using an ODR system is considered a deviant behavior worthy of punishment, then the utility of such mechanisms to resolve disputes is clearly called into question.

Lewin's (1987) study raised a number of questions about the use of ODR systems in nonunion organizations. It was the first of a number of studies that examined the consequences of employees using ODR systems in nonunion and union organizations (Klaas & DeNisi, 1989; Lewin & Peterson, 1988). It also marked a shift from considering primarily system-level effectiveness measures to individual-level measures.

RECENT THEORETICAL APPROACHES AND EMPIRICAL DEVELOPMENTS ON ODR SYSTEMS

Theoretical Developments

The growth of ODR systems in practice, particularly in the nonunion setting, coincides with emerging theoretical and empirical research involving organizational, process, and individual measures of ODR system effectiveness. A great deal of this research still draws from the two classic theoretical approaches of due process and the exit-voice-loyalty model. A third theoretical approach, systems of complementary work practices, has also emerged. Next, we will describe these three main theoretical approaches as they are currently applied.

Due Process and Procedural Justice.   The due process approach of the 1970s and 1980s has evolved into what is known as the procedural justice literature today. Procedural justice concerns one's belief that the formal process or rules used to make decisions are fair (Leventhal, Karuza, & Fry, 1980). Procedural justice has a long history in the conflict and dispute resolution literature. Indeed, as previously noted, a well-recognized purpose for implementing ODR systems is to ensure fairness. While one goal of an ODR system may be to promote fairness by simply providing an outlet for employees to voice discontent, the system of procedures used to remedy the discontent can vary, thus impacting justice perceptions. In turn, procedural justice perceptions (or "due process") have been linked to the overall evaluation of the ODR system (e.g., Fryxell & Gordon, 1989) and thus serve as a key determinant of ODR system usage and effectiveness. Various factors have been linked to justice perceptions (further discussed in regards to ODR effectiveness in the following section), yet an important development in the literature is the role of offering a range of ODR alternatives. More specifically, through offering a range of ODR options, employees are afforded procedural choice to resolve conflict, thereby enhancing control as well as opportunities for redress. The premise is that not all disputes can be handled equally well by a single procedure, supporting the need for a multioption approach (Dibble, 1997). The research and practice of multioption systems specifically are discussed more in the following section.

Exit-Voice-Loyalty Model. The exit-voice-loyalty model has continued to serve as the theoretical basis for ODR research. Its application, however, has been refined. In particular, there has been a renewed/heightened interest in the role of loyalty. While Hirschman's (1970) original model argued that more loyal employees will elect to use voice, rather than exit, the early research (e.g., Klaas, & DeNisi, 1989; Lewin, 1987) did not explicitly address the role of loyalty. However, Boroff and Lewin (1997) and Olson-Buchanan and Boswell (2002) reintroduced this aspect of the model by explicitly measuring employee loyalty and examining its relation to voice. This is an especially important aspect of the model because it attempts to explain what individual factors might relate to the decision to voice an issue to an organization rather than exit. If the exercise of voice provides valuable information to organizations, then enhancing employee loyalty may serve to increase the likelihood of receiving this valuable information.

Complementarities Perspective. A relatively new theoretical approach in the literature is the complementarities perspective. Drawing from a systems perspective (e.g., Ichnioswki, Kochan, Levine, Olson, & Strauss, 1996; MacDuffie, 1995; Milgrom & Roberts, 1992), the basic argument is that the interplay among ODR procedures enables each individual procedure to interact with one another thereby creating an internally consistent and synergistic system of practices. For example, Bendersky (2003) proposed a model of how ODR components interact, arguing that complementarities among procedures promotes synergistic effects that lead to positive work outcomes (e.g., attitudes and productivity) by motivating individuals to resolve any type of conflict through any (and multiple) type of mechanism. A "complementary" ODR system would thus be composed of multiple components including rights-based processes (e.g., arbitration), interest-based neutrals (e.g., ombudsperson) as well as negotiated processes (e.g., encouraging disputants to resolve disputes themselves), with the limitations of each individual component "mitigated through interaction with the other components in the system" (p. 647). Consistent with the notion of procedural choice previously noted, Bendersky argued that such an approach provided employees substantial (and more appropriate) voice mechanisms, greater control over conflict resolution processes and outcomes, opportunities to address the underlying cause of the dispute, and skills to address future conflict. In turn, this should increase an individual's motivation to resolve conflict and opportunity to exert power through a "richer array" of procedures (p. 651). In contrast, a "parallel" ODR system is where there is little or no choice of voice mechanism and/or individual components are poorly integrated, thus acting independently. Bendersky asserted that, relative to a parallel system, a complementary ODR system leads to an increase in positive attitudes toward conflict, reduces conflict avoidance, and increases efforts to resolve conflict.

All three of these theoretical approaches have been used in varying forms and combinations to examine various facets of ODR systems' existence, use, and effectiveness in organizations. For the purposes of this discussion, we organized this research into three general categories: organizational-level research, procedural fairness and choice, and individual outcomes. However, several of the empirical studies do examine ODR systems on multiple levels of analysis.

Recent Empirical Research—Organizational Outcomes.   Given that nearly all unions have formal ODR systems in their bargaining contract, some of the research focus has shifted to identifying organizational characteristics that are related to the adoption of ODR systems in nonunion settings. That is, why do organizations adopt ODR and what characteristics distinguish them from organizations that do not adopt ODR systems? However, merely having an ODR in place does not mean, in fact, that organizational members use the ODR to resolve disputes. Thus, another body of literature has examined the organizational factors that relate to actual employee usage of nonunion ODR systems. Finally, another body of research has examined the relationship between ODR systems and organizational-level outcomes.

Some research suggests organizations adopt ODR systems as an attempt to avoid the negative potential outcomes associated with conflict such as turnover or litigation. To that end, drawing from the exit–voice–loyalty model, some scholars argued that higher levels of workforce human capital, reflected by higher wage and tenure levels among employees, increases a firm's incentive to adopt ODR procedures in order to reduce costly turnover (e.g., Colvin, 2003b). Similarly, other researchers (e.g., Feuille & Delaney, 1992) concluded that concerns about workplace disputes giving rise to litigation as well as the desire to avoid unionization by providing workers with a mechanism for resolving complaints are motivations for nonunion organizations to introduce ODR procedures.

In contrast, the complementarities theoretical approach suggests organizations adopt ODR systems to capture the potentially positive outcomes associated with a set of practices that enhance voice, fair treatment, and effective conflict management. This is consistent with research on high performance work systems (HPWS). Briefly, HPWS encompass a set of complementary work and HR-related practices aimed at promoting high levels of employee commitment and involvement in the workplace, with the ultimate goal to increase work quality, productivity, and customer responsiveness (Ichniowski et al., 1996). Providing for employee voice, either through employee involvement practices generally (e.g., attitude surveys and autonomous work teams) and/or ODR procedures specifically, is quite complementary to the underlying goal of HPWS to enhance the protection of employee rights (Colvin, 2003b). Indeed, empirical studies often include formal ODR systems among practices seen as indicating the presence of HPWS (e.g., Arthur 1992; Datta, Guthrie, & Wright,

2005; Huselid 1995; Pil & MacDuffie, 1996). In effect, an ODR system is complementary with the goals as well as needs of an organization that has adopted other high performance work practices.

Even with an ODR system in place, the question of whether it will be used by employees remains. There is wide variance in ODR system usage rates across industries yet little understanding of what causes this variation (Bemmels & Foley, 1996). Early work suggested differences in the use of technology or the task environment (e.g., work methods, job specialization) were related to ODR usage (e.g., Kuhn, 1961; Sayles, 1958). Yet more recent work finds little effect for such variables on grievance rates (e.g., Bemmels, 1994; Bemmels, Reshef, & Stratton-Devine, 1991), leaving the reason for industry differences unclear. Interestingly, Cappelli and Chauvin (1991) found that factors related to higher employee exit costs (e.g., higher wages relative to the external labor market and high unemployment rate) result in more frequent grieving of complaints. Thus, perhaps ODR usage is higher when there are higher barriers to exit an organization.

Other characteristics of the organization arguably play a role in the overall ODR system usage rate in an organization. The social environment, such as the prevailing culture, and norms for voicing and addressing conflict in the organization are potential factors in employees' tendency to use ODR systems (Bendersky, 1998; Peterson & Lewin, 2000). For example, some work on employee silence (e.g., Milliken, Morrison, & Hewlin, 2003) provided insight as to how the culture of the organization may relate to an individual's willingness to express problems upward. In particular, employees often remain silent out of the fear of being viewed or labeled negatively and ultimately damaging valued relationships. An organizational culture in which disputes are treated as something to be avoided at all costs may have a relatively low ODR system usage rate (Harlos, 2001), in part because employees may fear reprisal (Krefting & Powers, 1998). However, these factors have not been examined in the empirical literature.

Interestingly, the extent to which a variety of other "voice" alternatives (non-ODR systems) are available is related to lower ODR system usage. For example, Colvin (2003a) showed that multilevel appeal rates were lower in workplaces that had adopted self-managed teams. His argument was that because workers in self-managed teams are granted broader decision-making authority in the workplace, disputes can more readily be addressed informally (Cutcher-Gershenfeld, 1991). Further, a study of the Canadian goods and services industries found a link between employee involvement initiatives and lower grievance rates among union workplaces, though there was a null relationship among nonunion workplaces (Colvin, 2004b).

A great deal of research has examined the link between ODR systems and employee quit rates. This research generally takes an exit-voice-loyalty perspective (Hirschman, 1970), arguing that when employees have access to voice (e.g., grievance system), they will be less likely to react to workplace conflict by leaving an organization (Freeman, 1980). This is often an explanation for the finding that unionization ("collective voice") associates with low turnover beyond any effect union presence may have on increasing wage rates (e.g., Batt, Colvin, & Keefe, 2002; Cotton & Tuttle 1986; Freeman & Medoff, 1984; Wilson & Peel, 1991).

The empirical research on the relation between ODR systems and retention rates has been mixed. For example, a substantial amount of research has shown that employees who have access to multilevel appeal system are less likely to quit than those who do not (for a review, see Peterson & Lewin, 2000). Yet in their study in the telecommunications industry, Batt et al. (2002) failed to find a relation between nonunion ODR practices and employee-quit rates. In a related study, Delery, Gupta, Shaw, Jenkins, and Ganster (2000) found the negative relation between formal ODR systems and employee quit rates became nonsignificant when controlling for unionization.

Unfortunately, there is no empirical field study that has examined the relationship between the presence or usage of ODR systems and higher performance-related outcomes. However, laboratory evidence suggests providing an ODR system is related to higher productivity than what one would experience without access to an ODR system (Olson-Buchanan, 1996). In addition, the lower quit rates associated with the availability of voice alternatives could lead to a more tenured, highly trained workforce and ultimately enhanced productivity (Freeman & Medoff, 1984; Peterson & Lewin, 2000). However, paradoxically, research in unionized settings specifically has shown that greater workplace conflict, reflected by high grievance rates, is related to lower productivity and higher unit production costs (e.g., Cutcher-Gershenfeld, 1991; Gobeille, Katz, Kochan, & Gobeille, 1983; Ichniowski, 1986; Katz, Kochan, & Weber, 1985; Norsworthy & Zabala, 1985).

The HPWS literature provides some indirect evidence of ODR systems' positive effect on firm performance/productivity. As noted previously, ODR systems are often considered a component of HPWS, and HPWS are consistently linked to organizational effectiveness (Ichniowski et al., 1996). For example, in his study of U.S. firms, Huselid (1995) found that firms adopting high performance work practices (e.g., adoption of multilevel appeal systems) were more productive and had higher employee retention rates. Arthur (1994) similarly found in a sample of steel minimills that commitment-based work systems (e.g., multistep appeal systems) were associated with moderately higher manufacturing performance and lower turnover rates.

Recent Empirical Research—Procedural Justice and Choice.   While the organizational-level research has primarily focused on general organizational variables that relate to ODR system adoption, usage, and effectiveness, the procedural justice and procedural choice literature has focused on what features of an ODR system might relate to higher perceived fairness and subsequently, higher use. In this section, we first discuss the features of ODR systems that have been linked with perceptions of higher procedural fairness. Then we turn the discussion to focus on what factors relate to decisions about which ODR procedure, if any, to use.

A critical overall feature of the ODR system is its perceived credibility. The more effective the employees perceive the ODR system to be, the more likely they will exercise the voice option rather than quit (Boroff & Lewin 1997). Indeed, as stated by Blancero and Dyer (1996), "Perceived credibility or reputation of the (procedure) influences fairness most heavily" (p. 352) and perceived fairness perceptions "influence the likelihood to use the system" (p. 343).

In terms of specific procedural characteristics of the ODR system, a procedure that allows for an employee's input and provides consideration of that input is generally deemed more fair, even if the decision is not in the employee's favor (Folger & Greenberg, 1985; Greenberg, 2004; Klaas, 1989). Similarly, research suggested that ODR systems must not simply provide the opportunity for voicing of one's concerns, but must be remedial in nature. Klaas (1989) proposed both the expected value of the remedy and the likelihood of winning as determinants of the attractiveness of filing a grievance. Inaction to employee's voicing discontent is likely to exacerbate feelings of injustice (a "deaf-ear syndrome"; Harlos, 2001).

Other research identified the characteristics of the decision maker as an important factor. For example, Arnold and O'Connor (1999) linked expertise level of the third-party mediator to positive disputant reactions. Also, research suggested ODR procedures that feature nonmanagerial decision makers were generally used more frequently (Colvin, 2003a). The argument is that involving neutral decision makers increases employees' perceptions that the ODR procedure is procedurally fair and makes a favorable outcome more probable. Colvin termed this a "neutrality effect," which in turn led to a higher probability that employees will use a particular procedure to resolve a dispute. Indeed, neutrality of the third party has been argued as a key element to the perceived fairness of and satisfaction with the ODR system (e.g., Bingham & Pitts, 2002; Daus, 1995).

Paradoxically, both consistency and flexibility are important features of ODR system design (Hendrickson & Harrison, 1998). From a justice perceptive, consistency is a key characteristic of fair procedures (e.g., Folger & Bies, 1989; Leventhal, 1980). Yet consistency may come at the price of flexibility, and some level of discretionary judgment is typically desirable and often necessary (Howard, 1994; Sheppard, Lewicki, & Minton, 1992). This is similar to Rousseau's recent discussion of idiosyncratic terms in the employment relationship (Rousseau, 2001, 2005; Rousseau, Ho, & Greenberg, in press). Idiosyncratic deals (i-deals) are individualized, nonstandard agreements between an employee and the employer and, as such, are flexible arrangements by definition. Yet inconsistency in employment arrangements may erode trust and motivation among employees (Rousseau, 2001). Thus, the balance between flexibility and consistency appears to be a key feature in managing the employment relationship, including how disputes are addressed within organizations.

Empirical research suggests another critical feature of ODR systems is whether and how the availability of ODR procedures are communicated. Even when organizations do have ODR systems in place, a significant proportion of employees may be unaware of them (Blancero & Dyer, 1996; Jameson, 2001; van den Bos, 1999). Thus, the extent to which the organization communicates the existence of ODR alternatives will affect whether they are even considered as a viable option.

As the burgeoning literature on procedural justice and choice attests, an individual facing the task of choosing how to address his or her conflict will likely be influenced by a number of factors in deciding which ODR system (if any) to use.

First, there is some evidence that preference for certain approaches vary as a function of the nature of the conflict (e.g., Renwick, 1975) or issue of dispute (e.g., Bemmels, 1994). For example, research has distinguished between disputes that are affective versus cognitive in nature (e.g., Guetzkow & Gyr, 1954). Drawing on this distinction, a series of studies by Jehn and colleagues (e.g., Jehn, 1995, 1997; Jehn, Chadwick, & Thatcher, 1997) examined task versus relationship conflict, showing that the processes and consequences of conflict differ depending on the nature of the dispute. Several studies have found that individuals prefer various forms of arbitration strategies for addressing disputes that have some type of legal-basis such as sexual harassment, discrimination, and whistle blowing retaliation claims (e.g., Houlden, LaTour, Walker, & Thibaut, 1978; Thibaut & Walker, 1975). This would similarly suggest that individuals are more likely to pursue more nonconsensual (e.g., arbitration or multistep appeal) procedures when a dispute is perceived as more severe (e.g., Arnold & Carnevale, 1997). Consistent with this, Klaas (1989) argued that when individuals experience intense feelings of anger or injustice, they often respond spontaneously or impulsively, perhaps resulting in use of nonconsensual procedures such as filing a formal complaint (e.g., grievance). Conversely, individuals seem to prefer more consensual approaches such as negotiating with the other involved party or parties personally or involving a coworker or similar third party for "everyday interpersonal conflicts" (Peirce et al., 1993, p. 201).

The relationship between the disputants is another important factor in procedural choice. In her prescriptive conflict management framework, Jameson (1999) argued that the relationship between the individual and the other disputant (or a possible third party) is an important consideration for selecting the best ODR strategy to pursue. Factors such as level of trust, previous experiences with the disputing party, and perceived supportiveness all play a role (e.g., Ewing, 1989; Klaas, 1989; Saunders, Sheppard, Knight, & Roth, 1992). For example, Weider-Hatfield (1990) showed a positive relationship between managerial strategies (e.g., positive expectations and goal setting) and the employee's propensity to use collaborative approaches to resolve disputes with the manager. Conversely, this study found that a manager's propensity to use criticism as a communication strategy was linked to confrontational conflict management strategies on the part of the employee. Such managerial behaviors shown related to higher ODR rates include lack of consideration, monitoring, and structural emphasis on production (e.g., Bemmels, 1994; Bemmels et al., 1991; Kleiner, Nickelsburg, & Pilarski, 1995).

Finally, personal characteristics of the individual play a role. Research has explored individual differences in ethnicity, culture, gender, personality traits, and work values as predictors of ODR system preference (e.g., Chan & Goto, 2003; Leung, 1987; Leung, Bond, Carment, Krishnan, & Liebrand, 1990; Lind, Huo, & Tyler, 1994). For example, Leung et al. (1990) found a relation between cultural femininity and conflict resolution preference. In terms of multistep appeal system activity specifically, an array of personal characteristics has been examined (e.g., seniority, wage rate, and past grievance activity; Chaykowski, Slotsve, & Butler, 1992; demographics, personality, and attitudes; Bemmels et al., 1991). This research generally finds that males, Blacks, and younger and less-educated workers are more likely to file a grievance (Lewin & Peterson, 1988). Research on personality traits is less clear and "insufficient to draw any firm conclusions" (Peterson & Lewin, 2000, p. 397).

More recent work has focused on an individual's affective attachment to the organization. For example, Boroff and Lewin (1997) found that more loyal employees are unlikely to utilize the organization's formal grievance system, arguing that such employees "suffer in silence." Following up on this issue, Olson-Buchanan and Boswell (2002) showed that more loyal employees prefer more informal/consensual voice mechanisms such as discussing the conflict with the other party or a neutral third party, rather than taking the more formal route of filing a grievance. This suggests that the types of informal voice mechanisms available are especially important for gaining valuable information from more loyal employees.

Recent Empirical Research—Individual Outcomes

ODR systems are in place to provide outlets for employees to voice conflict (Feuille & Delaney, 1992; Ury, Brett, & Goldberg, 1988), with the ultimate goal of helping to address and remedy mistreatment in the workplace. Yet surprisingly little research attention has focused on whether the use of ODR systems does, in fact, relate to positive outcomes for the individuals directly involved in the disputes. This is perhaps particularly troublesome given the charge of I/O psychology to contribute knowledge and implications for the enhancement of individual well-being and effectiveness in work settings.

Most of the empirical literature on the relation between ODR use and individual outcomes is certainly discouraging. A number of studies suggest individuals experience negative outcomes as a result of ODR system usage (namely multistep appeal systems) including low performance ratings, high absenteeism, and high turnover (e.g., Boroff & Lewin, 1997; Klaas & DeNisi, 1989; Lewin, 1987; Lewin & Peterson, 1999). The general conclusion from this research is that employees are "punished" for filing a complaint, as reflected by postdispute outcomes.

A recent study by Boswell and Olson-Buchanan (2004) suggested ODR systems play a more neutral role in individual outcomes and simply experiencing the dispute could account for the outcomes noted in prior research. Specifically, Boswell and Olson-Buchanan compared individuals who experienced a dispute but did not use a formal ODR system with individuals who experienced a dispute and did use a formal ODR system. They found that, as a whole, individuals who experienced a dispute reported similarly high employee work withdrawal behaviors and turnover intent, regardless of whether a grievance was filed. This suggested the negative outcomes attributed to ODR usage in previous research, in fact, could stem from the original dispute, rather than the ODR system that was used to resolve the dispute.

Interestingly, research conducted in a laboratory setting (Olson-Buchanan, 1996) suggested that grievance systems can have *favorable* consequences. Olson-Buchanan found that participants who experienced unfair treatment and filed a grievance had *higher* job performance (measured in quality and quantity) and *lower* turnover intent relative to other participants who experienced mistreatment but did not file a grievance. That is, Olson-Buchanan showed that a laboratory-based grievance system had the potential to mitigate some of the generally negative effects of being involved in a dispute.

Research at the individual level of analysis has generally focused on consequences of using an organization's multilevel appeal system (or grievance system) with much fewer studies examining the consequences of using other ODR systems. One exception was Olson-Buchanan and Boswell's (2002) study on the effect of the "formality" of the voice mechanism used on retention-related constructs. They found that use of more informal voice mechanisms (e.g., communicating directly with the other party directly or seeking the assistance of a neutral third party) associated with lower intent to quit and less job search activity compared with more formal voice mechanisms (e.g., filing a grievance or seeking assistance from an outside agency or attorney). Interestingly, employees who used an informal voice method were no more likely to job search or intend to leave the organization than those who reported mistreatment yet chose not to voice through any means (informal or formal). This latter finding suggests that utilizing more informal ODR methods has no effect on promoting employee retention than if the employee simply did nothing (e.g., "suffered in silence," Boroff & Lewin, 1997) in response to feeling discontent.

Taken together, research at the organizational and individual level indicates that while firms *adopting* ODR procedures are likely to experience positive outcomes (e.g., lower turnover rates), there is at least some evidence that actually *using* an organization's ODR system (grievance procedures in particular) associates with negative, or at best, neutral consequences for the individual. Below we discuss a couple of approaches to ODR suggested in the literature as having potential to maximize various criteria or goals for such systems (e.g., fairness, participant satisfaction, and efficiency; Prein, 1987; Sheppard, 1984; Thomas, 1982).

Summary. The two early theoretical approaches, exit-voice-loyalty and due process (now termed *procedural justice*) continue to serve as a basis for understanding the use, effectiveness, and outcomes of ODR systems. A new theoretical approach, "complementarities," stresses the role of ODR systems in complementing other HR systems. On an organizational empirical level of analysis, there is some evidence that organizations adopt ODR systems to avoid unionization, yet other research indicates some organizations adopt ODR systems to enhance positive outcomes such as fairness. The relation between ODR system usage and effectiveness measures such as turnover or performance is not clear, due to mixed results or lack of empirical research. Several procedural justice factors have been shown to relate to ODR system usage (e.g., credibility and perceptions of the decision maker). A growing body of literature suggests individual factors play a key role in which, if any, ODR is used. Relatively little is known about the consequences of ODR system usage for the individual. While early research was discouraging in this respect, more recent research suggested ODR system usage may have neutral consequences for the individual.

MOVING FORWARD: THE MULTIOPTION APPROACH

The practice and research of ODR systems have evolved considerably over the past century. While virtually all of the early organizational ODR systems were extremely similar in design (multilevel appeal systems), today there is a plethora of various ODR system options available (Feuille & Chachere, 1995). Interestingly, not only is there a variety of ODR systems *across* firms, but more and more organizations are implementing a variety of ODR system alternatives *within* firms. For example, Colvin's (2004a) qualitative study of the manufacturing firm TRW discussed the process by which the firm adopted two ODR procedures (e.g., peer review and nonunion arbitration). Colvin's study revealed that these two procedures were quite distinct in terms of their development, operation, and usage. Interestingly, divisions within the company varied in terms of the arbitration procedure format implemented. As further support of the variety of ODR alternatives within firms, recent empirical studies (cf. Batt et al., 2002; Colvin, 2003b) showed that adopting one ODR procedure (e.g., nonunion arbitration) was positively correlated with the adoption of another (e.g., peer review); yet, like many HR practices, whether the ODR system is available for a particular employee's use may vary by organizational unit or occupational group.

This change is even starting to take place in the union sector as well. True, the structure of virtually all unionized workplaces still features "collective voice" in the form of multistep appeal systems culminating in arbitration (Eaton & Keefe, 1999). However, there is growing evidence that unions are increasingly more accepting of alternative forms of voice, such as participative decision making (e.g., Saturn; Rubinstein & Kochan, 2001) and joint labor-management committees (e.g., Kaiser Permanente; McKersie, Eaton, & Kochan, 2004).

This trend is particularly encouraging because it is consistent with what we have learned from the procedural choice literature. That is, one size does not fit all. Individuals have varying preferences for ODR systems as a function of individual differences (e.g., loyalty; Olson-Buchanan & Boswell, 2002), nature of the conflict (e.g., Bemmels, 1994), and relationship with the disputants (e.g., Ewing, 1989) as well as several other procedural factors such as the characteristics of the final decision maker (Arnold & O'Connor, 1999). Indeed, offering a variety of ODR systems is consistent with the well-supported contingency model approaches in the general conflict literature (e.g., Sheppard, 1984; Elangovan, 1995, 1998) and the conflict literature specific to the organizational context as well (e.g., Jameson, 1999).

Offering several ODR system alternatives to employees within an organization is an important step forward to ensure more desirable individual outcomes, procedural fairness, and organizational effectiveness. Yet, as will be explained more fully in the following section, the research suggests that an even more comprehensive approach is needed to enhance individual well-being and organizational functioning. That is, the *entire* conflict experience, from the start of the dispute to the relationship among the disputants after ODR use, needs to be examined more fully in the research and considered more fully in practice.

FUTURE RESEARCH DIRECTIONS AND CHALLENGES

We see future research directions as falling under one broad general theme: broadening the scope of ODR system research to fully capture the complex nature and process of conflict resolution in organizations. The research, to date, primarily focused on a narrow aspect of dispute resolution, whether it be comparing organizations with a certain ODR system with those without that system or comparing individuals who used a certain ODR system with those who did not use that particular system. We believe to truly move this field of research forward it is critical to consider the full *process* of dispute resolution in the particular context of organizations. The process of dispute resolution involves experiencing and interpreting workplace conflict, seeking remedy (or not) for that conflict, and the consequences for the organization and the individual. This is a recursive process whereby prior experiences with an ODR system have implications for later dispute situations and resolution. The general research areas and the challenges researchers face in examining these issues are discussed next.

Contributing Role of Experiencing the Dispute

It is critical that future research on the consequences of resolving disputes through an ODR system tease out the independent effects of experiencing conflict from the effects of voicing that conflict via an ODR system. Recently, Boswell and Olson-Buchanan (2004), who showed the negative consequences for filing a grievance were due at least in part to the dispute that precipitated the grievance filing, highlighted this issue. Researchers need to move beyond the traditional approach of simply comparing ODR system users to nonusers. Instead, we need to better understand the relative roles of having or not having a dispute versus using or not using a particular ODR method. Only then will we truly understand the consequences of using an organization's ODR system. A similar approach could be taken at the organizational level. Research often relies on ODR usage rates as a proxy for workplace discontent. Yet if we were to examine workplace discontent separate from voicing discontent, we would have a much better understanding of the effectiveness of ODR systems in organizations. That is, what are the organizational consequences for a high level of workplace discontent that is not pursued in an ODR system and/or pursued through other organizational voice options (e.g., climate survey)?

The Organizational Context and Its Influence on Interpreting and Responding to Disputes

Experiencing and resolving conflict within organizations is, in several ways, a particularly complex context. First, many of the disputants have ongoing relationships with each other. The desire to maintain (or recover) an ongoing work relationship may influence whether a potential conflict situation is interpreted as a dispute in the first place and which ODR system, if any, is selected to resolve it. Accordingly, whether and how the dispute is resolved may have important psychological consequences for parties to the dispute. Other consequences, such as the political repercussions for dispute resolution, would also be a consideration for many individuals. The current legal context that organizations face provides another interesting backdrop for how a dispute might be interpreted and resolved. That is, the threat of litigation or setting a dangerous precedent for other employment situations may influence how disputes are addressed within the organization. While research has identified some of these factors as being relevant to procedural choice (e.g., Jameson, 1999), more attention needs to be focused on how these factors may influence whether a dispute is identified as such, whether and how it is resolved, and the associated organizational and individual consequences.

The two previously mentioned research issues highlight the need for future research to examine the entire conflict management process, from experiencing to interpreting and ultimately responding to a dispute. Ideally, research would also take into account the role of prior experiences with an organization's ODR system as well as prior relationships among the parties involved (and changes in relationships upon using, or not using, the ODR system). Of particular value would be longitudinal research designs that take into account the temporal and complex nature of conflict resolution. Such longitudinal research would need to move beyond a single time-lag approach (e.g., Time 1–Time 2) but, rather, would need to follow individuals as they experience and seek to address multiple workplace disputes.

Broader Operationalization of Employee Voice

Hirschman's (1970) original depiction of voice was a broad continuum—everything "from faint grumbling to violent protest" (p. 16). Yet, the literature that has examined his predictions has seemingly operationalized voice as a dichotomy; specifically, grievance filing is equated with voice. Indeed, it was assumed that employees who did not choose to address a perceived dispute through a grievance procedure must be "suffering in silence" (Boroff & Lewin, 1997). Recent empirical evidence counters this assumption, demonstrating that, in fact, the overwhelming majority of non-grievance-filers pursue the resolution of their dispute through some other means (Olson-Buchanan & Boswell, 2002). Clearly, an increasingly wider range of voice options (and ODR options) is available to employees to voice their discontent or resolve disputes and, in fact, employees are using them. What are the consequences to the disputants for using these other ODR procedures?

A related question that needs to be examined further is why or how individuals choose among possible ODR systems. The procedural choice literature has identified a number of individual difference variables (e.g., gender) that relate to this question. In addition, there is some evidence that the nature of the dispute and the employee's relation with the organization (e.g., loyalty) play a role in how one may choose to resolve a dispute (Olson-Buchanan & Boswell, 2002). While we know that there are certain factors that relate to individual choice of ODR procedure, we know little about their relative importance or about how these factors may interact with one another. It would be especially useful to examine the *relative* contributions of these factors (e.g., individual differences, attitudinal, and nature of dispute) to ODR choice decisions.

Similar issues should be addressed at the organizational level of analysis. That is, what factors influence how organizations choose to address workplace disputes and/or the decision to adopt various ODR options? Continued research on organizational/HR strategies and environmental pressures for adopting (or not) different ODR systems is likely to be particularly informative in understanding why organizations choose different methods over or in concert with others.

One challenge inherent in examining a broader range of ODR options is how to assess the usage and effectiveness of certain procedures. For example, employee use of the more informal dispute resolution options (e.g., direct communication) are unlikely to be recorded by an organization, thereby preventing researchers from utilizing archival data. Researchers would thus rely on employee self-reports, which are limited by retrospective biases. Another challenge posed by incorporating a broadened operationalization of voice in research design is that employees may use *multiple* ODR options to voice any one dispute; this is likely to be increasingly the case as organizations implement more multioption approaches to ODR. Similarly, an individual may have experienced multiple incidents of conflict during the period of study, each incident perhaps voiced through different (or multiple) methods. Assuming organizational records are not available or incomplete with regards to usage and outcomes of the differing methods (across multiple disputes), researchers are left challenged with collecting quite complex data (e.g., inquiring about multiple disputes and possible use of multiple ODR options for each dispute) for each study participant. Olson-Buchanan and Boswell (2002) faced this dilemma in their study of formal and informal voice methods, choosing to have respondents focus on the most severe incident of unfair treatment in the past year to address the issue of respondents potentially experiencing multiple incidents. Similarly, research by Boswell and Olson-Buchanan (2004) focused respondents on the most severe incident but also examined only one ODR mechanism (e.g., use of the organization's grievance system). Ideally, researchers would incorporate in their measures an assessment of the multiple disputes an individual might experience and the multiple methods an individual might use to voice these disputes. Though this might add complexity to the research design, such an approach would contribute to our understanding of the use and effectiveness of different ODR methods and under what conditions.

The Role of Proactive Voice Systems

Related to the notion of broader operationalization of employee voice is the need to better understand the role of proactive voice systems. While much of the extant research has focused on resolving workplace disputes, more work is needed on systems put in place to address and possibly prevent occurrences of the incidents that led up to the use of ODR (Lewin, 1999). For example, Kaminski (1999) discussed the use of problem-solving teams, employee participation in decision making, and labor–management committees as providing employees "a genuine opportunity to influence decisions over a broad range of issues before action is taken" (p. 220). Identifying potential problems by incorporating additional voice mechanisms such as systematic employee attitude surveys and focus groups in concert with more reactive voice mechanisms such as grievance systems may be a particularly effective approach. Though there is significant research focused on participatory work structures as well as enhancing employee perceptions of justice, future research would benefit by examining how these practices integrate with ODR systems. Investigating proactive voice systems in combination with more traditional ODR systems of focus in this chapter would contribute to the theoretical models of employee voice and provide practical insight into how organizations can best manage workplace conflict.

Broader, Long-Term Examination of Consequences

Our knowledge of the individual-level consequences of ODR system usage is limited. In particular, little, if any, attention has focused on the psychological outcomes, such as psychological strain, of using or not using an ODR system to address a dispute. How might an organization develop or utilize mechanisms, such as employee assistance programs or managerial training to mitigate such outcomes? Also, how might individual responses play out over time? That is, if others notice and react to individual reactions, does this create a downward spiral of heightened negative reactions?

Similarly, at the organizational level, extant research has focused on retention related and, to a lesser extent, on firm performance outcomes, yet other indicators of effectiveness exist. The effect of ODR system adoption and/or usage on organizational climate, work culture, or firm reputation (e.g., as an employer of choice) would be interesting to explore. Of course, organizational culture may also play a role in the effectiveness of ODR systems. Bendersky (1998) argued that organizational culture plays an important role in the implementation of ODR systems but also in whether or not employees use the system. She suggested that how disputes are actually resolved within the organization (the "implicit" system) might differ from how disputes are reported to be resolved (the "explicit" system). Empirical research is needed to examine more closely the role of workplace culture and norms on ODR system adoption, usage, and effectiveness.

Organizational-level research should continue to examine what ODR procedures are most effective for the organization and under what conditions, but from a longer term perspective. As previously noted, moving beyond single time-lag studies to research aimed about how ODR systems evolve over time and the respective consequences is needed. Of course, most interesting would be longitudinal research that examines both the precursors to ODR method use (or firm adoption of ODR methods) as previously noted as well as consequences of use (or of having such methods in place). This would contribute to our understanding of ODR as a dynamic process that involves procedural choice, consequences of that choice, and implications for future dispute resolution use and reactions.

Cross-Level Research

One final general research area we would like to highlight is the need to examine ODR issues across levels of analyses. For example, the current research approach is to focus either on firm adoption of an ODR system or employee usage. Yet greater attention to how the adoption of an ODR system within a firm links to employee usage would be informative. Similarly, future research could examine ODR system effectiveness at multiple levels of analyses (e.g., for the firm, work group, or individual). This would be particularly enlightening in helping to resolve the somewhat separate research streams that have shown positive outcomes for firms adopting ODR systems (e.g., lower quit rates) but negative consequences for individuals utilizing such systems (e.g., higher turnover). Such research would require comparing across organizations but also taking into account the individual processes involved in using ODR systems.

The tendency for prior ODR research to focus on either micro issues or macro issues, in large parts, has been due to the tendency for researchers in specific disciplines to approach ODR from differing perspectives with different research questions. That is, I/O psychologists tend to be interested in individuals or groups of individuals while economists and industrial relations scholars tend to focus on the firm and/or bargaining unit. We would hope researchers continue to look to and draw from disciplines outside of their own to understand ODR systems. Interdisciplinary approaches to research are most likely to lead to a fuller understanding of the practice and effectiveness of ODR systems and provide the greatest insight on the implications for workers, organizations, and public policy.

There have also been practical considerations contributing to the micro–macro disconnect. When focused on the individual level of analysis, researchers can easily gain access to many individuals within one organization, but not across more than one organization. When organizational-level research is designed, researchers tend to focus on archival firm data (e.g., quit rates and grievance rates) and/or find it easier to identify one or a small number of respondents to report on the organization's practices and outcomes. In addition to the access issue, multilevel research in the past has been limited by the statistical techniques available to researchers. However, recent developments in this area are likely to enable future research to better assess multilevel issues. For instance, more complex statistical techniques, such as repeated-measures regression and hierarchical linear modeling (cf., Hofmann, 1997; Koslowski & Klein, 2000), are increasing in use. These techniques enable researchers simultaneously to tease out individual-, group-, and organizational-level effects. From a design standpoint, firms may be increasingly amenable to conducting research across sites in order to gain an understanding of the determinants of high versus low performing units. Focusing on the establishment level (cf. Batt et al., 2002) and individuals within a firm's various establishments is perhaps the most feasible and useful avenue to bridge the micro-macro gulf. We expect that as more multilevel data sets become available and researchers become well versed in multilevel statistical techniques, we will see more cross-level research.

In the past few decades, we have witnessed an evolution of ODR systems in both practice and theory. Though recent research has contributed much to our understanding of dispute resolution within organizations, additional work is needed to more fully understand the complex nature and process of ODR. Addressing the specific issues discussed in the chapter will be challenging, but it holds the potential to contribute important insight on conflict management in organizations.

REFERENCES

Aram, J. D., & Salipante, P. F. (1981). An evaluation of organizational due process in the resolution of employee/employer conflict. *Academy of Management Review, 6,* 197–204.

Arnold, J. A., & Carnevale, P. J. (1997). Preferences for dispute resolution procedures as a function of intentionality, consequences, expected future interaction, and power. *Journal of Applied Social Psychology, 27*(5), 371–398

Arnold, J. A., & O'Connor, K. M. (1999). Ombudspersons or peers? The effect of third-party expertise and recommendations on negotiation. *Journal of Applied Psychology, 5,* 776–786.

Arthur, J. B. (1992). The link between business strategy and industrial relations systems in American steel mini-mills. *Industrial and Labor Relations Review, 45,* 488–506.

Arthur, J. B. (1994). Effects of human resource systems on manufacturing performance and turnover. *Academy of Management Journal, 37,* 670–687.

Arvey, R. D., & Jones, A. P. (1985). The use of discipline in organizational settings: A framework for future research. *Research in Organizational Behavior, 7,* 367–409.

Balfour, A. (1984, March/April). Five types of non-union grievance systems. *Personnel, 67*–76.

Batt, R., Colvin, A. J. S., & Keefe, J. (2002). Employee voice, human resource practices, and quit rates: Evidence from the telecommunications industry. *Industrial and Labor Relations Review, 55,* 573–594.

Bemmels, B. (1994). The determinants of grievance initiation. *Industrial and Labor Relations Review, 42,* 285–301.

Bemmels, B., & Foley, J. R. (1996). Grievance procedure research: A review and theoretical recommendations. *Journal of Management, 22,* 359–384.

Bemmels, B., Reshef, Y., & Stratton-Devine, K. (1991). The roles of supervisors, employees, and stewards in grievance initiation. *Industrial and Labor Relations Review, 45,* 15–30.

Bendersky, C. (1998). Culture: The missing link in dispute systems design. *Negotiation Journal, 14,* 307–311.

Bendersky, C. (2003). Organizational dispute resolution systems: A complementarities model. *Academy of Management Review, 28,* 643–656.

Berenbeim, R. (1980). *Nonunion complaint systems: A corporate appraisal.* New York: The Conference Board.

Bingham, L. B., & Pitts, D. W. (2002). Highlights of mediation at work: Studies of the National REDRESS evaluation project. *Negotiation Journal, 18,* 135–146.

Blancero, D., & Dyer, L. (1996). Due process for non-union employees: The influence of system characteristics on fairness perceptions. *Human Resource Management, 35,* 343–359.

Boroff, K. (1991). Measuring the perceptions of the effectiveness of a workplace complaint procedure. *Advances in Industrial and Labor Relations, 5,* 207–233.

Boroff, K. E., & Lewin, D. (1997). Loyalty, voice, and intent to exit a union firm: A conceptual and empirical analysis. *Industrial and Labor Relations Review, 51,* 50–63.

Boswell, W. R., & Olson-Buchanan, J. B. (2004). Experiencing mistreatment at work: The role of grievance-filing, nature of mistreatment, and employee withdrawal. *Academy of Management Journal, 47,* 129–139.

Cappelli, P., & Chauvin, K. (1991). A test of an efficiency model of grievance activity. *Industrial and Labor Relations Review, 45,* 3–14.

Chan, D. K-S., & Goto, S. G. (2003). Conflict resolution in the culturally diverse workplace: Some data from Hong Kong employees. *Applied Psychology: An International Review, 52,* 441–461.

Chaykowski, R. P., Slotsve, G. A. & Butler, J. S. (1992). A simultaneous analysis of grievance activity and outcome decisions. *Industrial and Labor Relations Review, 45,* 724–736.

Cherrington, D. J. (1982). Grievance procedures in nonunion organizations. *Personnel management: The management of human resources* (2nd ed.). Dubuque, IA: William C. Brown.

Colvin, A. J. S. (2003a). The dual transformation of workplace dispute resolution. *Industrial Relations, 42,* 712–735.

Colvin, A. J. S. (2003b). Institutional pressures, human resource strategies, and the rise of nonunion dispute resolution procedures. *Industrial & Labor Relations Review, 56,* 375–392.

Colvin, A. J. S. (2004a). Adoption and use of dispute resolution procedures in the nonunion workplace. In D. Lewin & B. E. Kaufman (Eds.), *Advances in industrial and labor relations* (Vol. 13).

Colvin, A. J. S. (2004b). The relationship between employee involvement and workplace dispute resolution. *Relations Industrielles/Industrial Relations, 59,* 671–694.

Coser, R. L. (1956). A home away from home. *Social Problems, 4,* 3–17.

Costantino, C. A., & Merchant, C.S. (1996). *Designing conflict management systems.* San Francisco: Jossey-Bass.

Cotton, J. L., & Tuttle, J. M. (1986). Employee turnover: A meta-analysis and review with implications for research. *Academy of Management Review, 11,* 55–70.

Cutcher-Gershenfeld, J. (1991). The impact on economic performance of a transformation in workplace relations. *Industrial & Labor Relations Review, 44,* 241–260.

Datta, D. K., Guthrie, J. P., & Wright, P. M. (2005). Human resource management and labor productivity: Does industry matter? *Academy of Management Journal, 48,* 135–146.

Daus, M. W. (1995). Mediating claims of discrimination. *Dispute Resolution Journal, 50,* 51–54.

Davis, K. (1957). Grievance systems. *Human Relations in Business.* New York: McGraw-Hill.

De Dreu, C. K. W., Harinck, F., & Van Vianen, A. E. M. (1999). Conflict and performance in groups and organizations. *International Review of Industrial and Organizational Psychology, 14,* 369–414.

Delery, J., Gupta, N., Shaw, J., Jenkins, G. D., & Ganster, M. (2000). Unionization, compensation, and voice effects on quits and retention. *Industrial Relations, 39,* 625–46.

Dibble, R. E. (1997). Alternative dispute resolution of employment conflict: The search for standards. *Journal of Collective Negotiations, 26*(1), 73–84.

Eaton, A. E., & Keefe, J. H. (1999). Introduction and overview. In A. E. Eaton & J. H. Keefe (Eds.), *Employment dispute resolution and worker rights in the changing workplace* (pp. 1–26). Champaign, IL: Industrial Relations Research Association.

Elangovan, A. R. (1995). Managerial third-party dispute resolution: A prescriptive model for strategy selection. *Academy of Management Review, 20*, 800–830.

Elangovan, A. R. (1998). Managerial intervention in organizational disputes: Testing a prescriptive model of strategy selection. *The International Journal of Conflict Management, 9*, 301–335.

Ewing, D. (1982). *Do it my way or you're fired: Employee rights and the changing role of management.* New York: John Wiley.

Ewing, D. W. (1989). *Justice on the job: Resolving grievances in the nonunion workplace.* Boston: Harvard Business School Press.

Feuille, P, & Chachere, D. T. (1995). Looking fair or being fair: Remedial voice procedures in nonunion workplaces. *Journal of Management, 21*, 27–42.

Feuille, P., & Delaney, J. T. (1992). The individual pursuit of organizational justice: Grievance procedures in nonunion workplaces. In G. R. Ferris & K. M. Rowland (Eds.), *Research in personnel and human resource management* (pp. 187–232). Stamford, CT: JAI Press.

Folger, R., & Bies, R. J. (1989). Managerial responsibilities and procedural justice. *Employee Responsibilities & Rights Journal, 2*, 79–90.

Folger, R., & Greenberg, J. (1985). Procedural justice: An interpretive analysis of personnel systems. In K. Rowland & G. Ferris (Eds.), *Research in personnel and human resource management* (Vol. 3, pp. 141–183). Greenwich, CT: JAI Press.

Freeman, R. B. (1980). The exit-voice tradeoff in the labor market: Unionism, job tenure, quits, and separations. *Quarterly Journal of Economics, 94*, 643–673.

Freeman, R. B., and Medoff, J. L. (1984). *What do unions do?* New York: Basic Books.

Fryxell, G. E., & Gordon, M. E. (1989). Workplace justice and job satisfaction as predictors of satisfaction with union and management. *Academy of Management Journal, 32*(4), 851–866.

Greenberg, J. (2004). Stress fairness to fare no stress: Managing workplace stress by promoting organizational justice. *Organizational Dynamics, 33*, 352–366.

Guetzkow, H., & Gyr, J. (1954). An analysis of conflict in decision-making groups. *Human Relations, 7*, 367–381.

Harlos, K. P. (2001). When organizational voice systems fail: More on the deaf-ear syndrome and frustration effects. *Journal of Applied Behavioral Science, 37*, 324–342.

Hendrickson, C. L., & Harrison, W. (1998). Consistency vs. flexibility: The impact of employee voice in rule-based and discretionary decision procedures. *Employee Responsibilities and Rights Journal, 11*, 279–295.

Hirschman, A. O. (1970). *Exit, voice, and loyalty.* Cambridge, MA: Harvard University Press.

Hofmann, D. A. (1997). An overview of the logic and rationale of hierarchical linear models. *Journal of Management* [Special issue]. *23*, 723–744.

Houlden, P., LaTour, S., Walker, L., & Thibaut, J. (1978). Preference for modes of dispute resolution as a function of process and decision control. *Experimental Social Psychology, 14*, 13–30.

Howard, P. K. (1994). *The death of common sense: How law is suffocating America.* New York: Random House.

Huselid, M. A. (1995). The impact of human resource management practices on turnover, productivity, and corporate financial performance. *Academy of Management Journal, 38,* 635–672.

Ichniowski, C. (1986). The effects of grievance activity on productivity. *Industrial and Labor Relations Review, 40,* 75–89.

Ichniowski, C., Kochan, T. A., Levine, D., Olson, C., & Strauss, G. (1996). What works at work: Overview and assessment. *Industrial Relations, 35,* 299–333.

Ichniowski, C., & Lewin, D. (1987). Grievance procedures and firm performance. In M. Kleiner (Ed.), *Human resources and the performance of the firm* (pp. 159–193). Madison, WI: IRRA.

Jameson, J. K. (1999). Toward a comprehensive model for the assessment and management of intraorganizational conflict: Developing the framework. *The International Journal of Conflict Management, 10,* 268–294.

Jameson, J. K. (2001). Employee perceptions of the availability and use of interest-based, right-based, and power-based conflict management strategies. *Conflict Resolution Quarterly, 19,* 163–196.

Jehn, K. A. (1995). A multimethod examination of the benefits and detriments of intragroup conflict. *Administrative Science Quarterly, 40,* 256–282.

Jehn, K. A. (1997). Affective and cognitive conflict in work groups: Increasing performance through value-based intragroup conflict. In C. K. W. De Dreu & E. Van de Vliert (Eds.), *Using conflict in organizations* (pp. 87–100). London, U.K.: Sage Publications, Inc.

Jehn, K. A., Chadwick, C., & Thatcher, S. M. B. (1997). To agree or not to agree: The effects of value congruence, individual demographic dissimilarity, and conflict on workgroup outcomes. *International Journal of Conflict Management, 8,* 287–305.

Kaminski, M. (1999). New forms of work organization and their impact on the grievance procedure. In E. Eaton & J. H. Keefe (Eds.), *Employment dispute resolution and worker rights* (pp. 219–246). Champaign, IL: Industrial Relations Research Association.

Katz, H. C., Kochan, T. A., & Gobeille, K. R. (1983). Industrial relations performance, economic performance, and QWL programs: An interplant analysis. *Industrial and Labor Relations Review, 37,* 3–17.

Katz, H. C., Kochan, T. A., & Weber, M. R. (1985). Assessing the effects of industrial relations systems and efforts to improve the quality of working life on organizational effectiveness. *Academy of Management Journal, 28,* 509–526.

Klaas, B. S. (1989). Determinants of grievance activity and the grievance system's impact on employee behavior: An integrative perspective. *Academy of Management Review, 14,* 445–458.

Klaas, B. S., & DeNisi, A. S. (1989). Managerial reactions to employee dissent: The impact of grievance activity on performance ratings. *Academy of Management Journal, 32,* 705–718.

Klaas, B. S., & Feldman, D. C. (1993). The evaluation of disciplinary appeals in non-union organizations. *Human Resource Management Review, 3,* 49–81.

Kleiner, M., Nickelsburg, G., & Pilarski, A. (1995). Monitoring, grievance, and plant performance. *Industrial Relations, 34,* 169–189.

Koslowski, S. W. J., & Klein, K. (2000). A multilevel approach to theory and research on organizations: Contextual, temporal, and emergent processes. In. K. J. Klein & S. W. J. Kozlowski (Eds), *Multilevel theory, research, and methods in organizations: Foundations, extensions, and new directions* (pp. 3–90). San Francisco: Jossey-Bass, Inc.

Krefting, L. A., & Powers, K. J. (1998). Exercised voice as management failure: Implications of willing compliance theories of management and individualism for de facto employee voice. *Employee Responsibilities and Rights Journal, 11,* 263–277.

Kuhn, J. W. (1961). *Bargaining in grievance settlement: The power of industrial work groups.* New York: Columbia University Press.

Leung, K. (1987). Some determinants of reactions to procedural models for conflict reolution: A cross-national study. *Journal of Personality and Social Psychology, 53,* 898–908.

Leung, K., Bond, M. H., Carment, D. W., Krishnan, L., & Liebrand, W. B. G. (1990). Effects of cultural femininity on preference for methods of conflict processing: A cross-cultural study. *Journal of Experimental Social Psychology, 26,* 373–388.

Leventhal, G. S. (1980). What should be done with equity theory? New approaches to the study of fairness in social relationships. In Gergen, K. J., Greenberg, M. S., & Willis, R. H. (Eds.), Social exchange: Advances in theory and research (pp. 27–53). New York: Plenum Press.

Leventhal, G. S., Karuza, J., & Fry, W. R. (1980). Beyond fairness: A theory of allocation preferences. In G. Mikula (Ed.), *Justice and Social Interaction* (pp. 167–218).

Lewicki, R. J., Weiss, S. E., & Lewin, D. (1992). Models of conflict, negotiation, and third part intervention: A review and synthesis. *Journal of Organizational Behavior, 13,* 209–252.

Lewin, D. (1987). Conflict resolution in the nonunion firm: A theoretical and empirical analysis. *Journal of Conflict Resolution, 31,* 465–502.

Lewin, D. (1999). Theoretical and empirical research on the grievance procedure and arbitration: A critical review. In A. E. Eaton & J. H. Keefe (Eds.), *Employment dispute resolution and worker rights in the changing workplace* (pp. 137–186). Champaign, IL: Industrial Relations Research Association.

Lewin, D., & Peterson, R. B. (1999). Behavioral outcomes of grievance activity. *Industrial Relations, 38,* 554–576.

Lind, E. A., Huo, Y. J., & Tyler, T. R. (1994). And justice for all: Ethnicity, gender, and preferences for dispute resolution procedures. *Law and Human Behavior, 18,* 269–290.

Luthans, F., Hodgetts, R. M., & Thompson, K. R. (1987). *Social issues in business: Strategic and public policy perspectives* (5th ed.). New York: Macmillan.

MacDuffie, J. P. (1995). Human resource bundles and manufacturing performance: Flexible production systems in the world auto industry. *Industrial and Labor Relations Review, 48,* 197–221.

McCabe, D. M. (1988). *Corporate nonunion complaint procedures and systems.* New York: Praeger.

McKersie, R. B., Eaton, S. C., & Kochan, T. A. (2004). Kasier Permanente: Using interest-based negotiations to craft a new collective bargaining agreement. *Negotiation Journal, 20,* 13–36.

Milgrom, P. R., & Roberts, J. (1992). *Economics, organizations, and management.* Englewood Cliffs, NJ: Prentice-Hall.

Milliken, F. J., Morrison, E. W., & Hewlin, P. F. (2003). An exploratory study of employee silence: Issues that employees don't communicate upward and why. *Journal of Management Studies, 40*(6), 1453–1476.

Norsworthy, J. R., & Zabala, C.A. (1985). Worker attitudes, worker behavior, and productivity in the U.S. automobile industry, 1959–76. *Industrial and Labor Relations Review, 38*, 544–557.

Olson-Buchanan, J. B. (1996). Voicing discontent: What happens to the grievance filer after the grievance. *Journal of Applied Psychology, 81*, 52–63.

Olson-Buchanan, J. B., & Boswell, W. R. (2002). The role of employee loyalty and formality in voicing discontent. *Journal of Applied Psychology, 87*, 1167–1174.

Peach, D., & Livernash, E. R. (1974). *Grievance initiation and resolution: A study in basic steel.* Boston: Harvard Graduate School of Business Administration.

Peirce, R. S., Pruitt, D. G., & Czaja, S. J. (1993). Complainant-respondent differences in procedural choice. *International Journal of Conflict Management, 4*, 199–222.

Peterson, R. B., & Lewin, D. (2000). Research on unionized grievance procedures: Management issues and recommendations. *Human Resource Management, 39*(4), 395–406.

Pil, F., & MacDuffie, J. P. (1996). The adoption of high involvement work practices. *Industrial Relations, 35*, 423–455.

Prein, H. (1987). Strategies for third party intervention. *Human Relations, 40*, 699–719.

Renwick, P. A. (1975). Impact of topic and source of disagreement on conflict management. *Organizational Behavior and Human Performance, 14*, 416–425.

Rousseau, D. M. (2001). Idiosyncratic deals: Flexibility versus fairness? *Organizational Dynamics, 29*, 260–271.

Rousseau, D. M. (2005). *I-deals: Idiosyncratic deals employees bargain for themselves.* New York: M. E. Sharpe.

Rousseau, D. M., Ho, V. T., & Greenberg, J. (in press). I-deals: Idiosyncratic terms in employment relationships. *Academy of Management Review.*

Rubinstein, S. A., & Kochan, T. A. (2001). *Learning from Saturn: Possibilities for corporate governance and employee relations.* Ithaca, NY: ILR Press.

Saunders, D. M., Sheppard, B. H., Knight, V., & Roth, J. (1992). Employee voice to supervisors. *Employee Rights and Responsibilities Journal, 5*, 241–259.

Sayles, L. R. (1958). *Behavior of industrial work groups.* New York: McGraw-Hill.

Sheppard, B. H. (1984). Third party conflict intervention: A procedural framework. In B. M. Staw & L. L. Cummings (Eds.), *Research in organizational behavior, 6*, 141–190.

Sheppard, B. H., Lewicki, R. J., & Minton, J. W. (1992). *Organizational justice: The search for fairness in the workplace.* New York: Macmillan.

Slichter, S., Healy, J. J., & Livernash, E. R. (1960). *The impact of collective bargaining on management.* Washington, DC: The Brookings Institution.

Thibaut, J., & Walker, L. (1975). *Procedural justice: A psychological analysis.* Hillsdale, NJ: Lawrence Erlbaum Associates.

Thomas, K. W. (1982). Manager and mediator: A comparison of third party roles based upon conflict management goals. In G. B. Bomers & R. B. Peterson (Eds.), *Conflict management and industrial relations* (pp. 141–157).

Thomson, A. W. J. (1974). *An introduction to collective bargaining in higher education.* Ithaca, NY: The New York State School of Industrial and Labor Relations.

Ury, W. L., Brett, J. M., & Goldberg, S. B. (1988). *Getting disputes resolved: Designing systems to cut the costs of conflict.* San Francisco: Jossey-Bass.

U.S. Bureau of Labor Statistics. (1966). *Characteristics of major collective bargaining agreements* (Bulletin No. 1425-6). Washington DC: U.S. Government Printing Office.

U.S. Bureau of Labor Statistics. (1977). *Characteristics of major collective bargaining agreements* (Bulletin No. 1957). Washington DC: U.S. Government Printing Office.

U.S. General Accounting Office. (1995). *Employment discrimination: Most private sector employers use alternative dispute resolution* (GAO/HEHS-95-150, U.S). Washington, DC: Government Printing Office.

van den Bos, K. (1999). What are we talking about when we talk about no-voice procedures? On the psychology of the fair outcome effect. *Journal of Experimental Social Psychology, 35,* 560–577.

Weider-Hatfield, D. (1990). The impact of managerial communication and employee conflict-handling strategies on employees' organizational outcomes, job satisfaction, and perceived equity in the work environment. In P. J. D. Drenth & J. A. Sergeant (Eds.), *European perspectives in psychology: Work and organizational, social and economic, cross-cultural, 3,* 89–104.

Wilson, N., & Peel, M. J. (1991). The impact on absenteeism and quits of profit-sharing and other forms of employee participation. *Industrial and Labor Relations Review, 44,* 454–468.

12

Union-Management Conflict: Historical Trends and New Directions

RAY FRIEDMAN
Owen Graduate School of Management,
Vanderbilt University

LARRY HUNTER
School of Business, University of Wisconsin–Madison

YING CHEN
Vanderbilt University

Labor relations in the United States were once characterized by chaos and violence. From the "Great Uprising" of 1877 through the Great Depression of the 1930s, disputes between workers and owners and between labor and capital were addressed as much through pitched battles as through negotiation. This tragic history included deaths in notorious incidents such as Chicago's Haymarket Riot of 1886, the Homestead Strike of 1892 in Pennsylvania, the 1913 Ludlow Massacre in Colorado, and more.

Conflict resolution in labor relations was simple, if brutal: Might made right. Workers, recognizing the imbalance of power between individual workers and large companies, attempted to organize themselves into unions. Unionists found themselves locked out of workplaces, with these lockouts enforced by armies of private guards as well as regular police.

Their efforts were met with hiring blacklists, jail terms, beatings, threats from armed Pinkerton detectives, and even death. They responded with violence of their own.

Such an approach to conflict resolution proved unsustainable. With the advent of the Great Depression, labor–management conflict appeared to threaten the stability of American commerce and the system of government. The U.S. Congress and President Franklin Roosevelt responded by establishing a new set of laws and practices with the intention of increasing industrial stability and order. Most prominent among these was the 1935 National Labor Relations Act, popularly known as the Wagner Act after its sponsor, Senator Robert Wagner of New York.

U.S. labor relations, which today continue to rest chiefly on the Wagner Act, institutionalize a conflict resolution system that was designed to minimize violence and disorder, while protecting the rights of management, workers, and their chosen representatives. Some 70 years on, the institution has faced challenges in adapting to changing times. In this chapter, we will review the major elements of this system, discussing recent trends and avenues for research. In our discussion, we give special consideration to attempts to transform the system from one that resolves conflict through negotiation between parties with a rough balance of power, accompanied by careful definitions of the rights of the parties, to a system that focuses relatively more heavily on the parties' underlying interests.

HISTORICAL CONTEXT

Ury, Brett, and Goldberg (1988) observed that disputes could be resolved with reference to "power," to "rights," or to "interests." In this conceptual scheme, conflicts resolved by power are those in which economic, physical, or political strength enables one party to force a solution upon the other. In rights-based conflict resolution, the focus is on rules and law—outcomes are not determined through power struggles but rather through calm deference to rules and procedures. Conflict resolution based on interests focuses on what the parties really need and care about. Ury et al. (1988) argued that healthy dispute systems are ones that focus most on interests, less on rights, and even less on power.

Power

Different eras in American labor relations have featured a variety of approaches to conflict resolution. Beginning in about 1875, American labor relations featured intense conflict for over 60 years. Early labor organizations such as the Knights of Labor, and subsequently, the various craft unions that made up the American Federation of Labor and the broader-based industrial unions of the Congress of Industrial Organization, attempted to organize workers to fight for higher wages and better working conditions. Capitalists responded fiercely. Throughout the later 19th century, strikes by railroad workers periodically erupted in violence. Mines provided a similarly turbulent setting, as conflict between labor and management developed into armed battles in small towns surrounding coal mines in Kentucky, West Virginia, and Pennsylvania.

During the 19th and early 20th centuries, governments, both local and national, tended to enter the fray on the side of business. On the legal side, labor unions were treated by the courts as illegal conspiracies to restrain trade throughout most of the 19th century, and the Sherman Anti-Trust Act of 1890 applied to labor as well as to companies. Only with the 1914 Clayton Act did lawmakers declare that labor was not a "commodity" and that labor unions had a right to exist, but even this law made it simple for employers to seek injunctions against strikes and picketing. Business interests were supported not just by the courts but also by force: State militias and even the U.S. Army were occasionally called in to protect property rights.

Rights

The Great Depression and the New Deal of the 1930s brought about a new era in American labor relations. The National Labor Relations Act, signed into law by President Franklin D. Roosevelt in 1935, sought to establish labor peace, primarily by creating a balance of power between labor and management (Heckscher, 1996). Violence and force as the primary approaches to conflict resolution gave way to a new system of industrial relations (Dunlop, 1958).

This New Deal system relied upon a rough balance of power between the parties, giving both sides an incentive to come to the bargaining table, rather than resorting to strikes, lockouts, or violence. At the table, labor and management negotiated to establish sets of rules—embedded in fixed-term contracts—to govern the workplace. During the life of the contract, the parties attempted to resolve disputes by applying these rules. Disputes over the rules that could not be resolved directly between management and union representatives were typically solved through binding arbitration; outside neutrals were hired to hear the case, and their decisions were contractually binding on both parties. With the institutionalization of the new system, dispute resolution shifted from "power" to "rights."

This system of rights-based dispute resolution comprised four key elements. First, the system established a set of rules for determining who, if anyone, would represent workers collectively. Disputes over the legitimacy of union representation had been a source of violent disagreement between workers and management; the new system provided a set of procedural steps to determine whether collective representation was desirable, and sought to ensure that workers could choose such representation free of coercion. Second, where workers chose unions, the system included a set of practices for collective bargaining. Little other than "bargaining in good faith" was legally required, but over time, norms and experiences around labor negotiation developed. For example, the Supreme Court's 1938 Mackay decision allowed companies to permanently replace striking workers (except in unfair labor practices strikes), but from the 1940s until the 1980s both parties viewed this as a drastic step and such actions were exceptionally rare. As another example, rituals that experienced bargainers on both sides understood developed for bargaining (Friedman, 1994); these included public front stage displays of anger concurrent with private backstage discussions and deal making. A third element of the system was the mechanism for enforcing the contract that emerged out of the bargaining process—most notably grievance procedures and arbitration. Fourth, underlying the whole system was a philosophical agreement that managers had the right to make key workplace decisions. Workers did not engage in "managerial" acts such as determining company investment strategies or deciding how work was to be done.

Despite the advances created by the shift from power to rights, weaknesses in this New Deal system of industrial relations in the United States have been revealed over the past few decades (Kochan, Katz, & McKersie, 1994). The shift from power to rights was not, by design, a wholesale change. Power continued to play a large role in this system as the outcome of collective bargaining negotiations reflected the relative power of each side. On the union side, the strike was the main weapon. Management responded by preparing for threatened strikes through costly policies such as redundant production facilities and extensive buildup of inventory. Will and brinksmanship also played roles in determining the result of negotiations. Over time, determined to avoid dealing with unions, managers began to work more aggressively and openly, even illegally, to prevent their employees from organizing. Companies moved production to states and countries with weaker labor laws and unions. Strikes became less effective and less credible, and the balance of power that required both sides to sit down at the bargaining table eroded.

The New Deal system produced labor contracts featuring legalistic rules at the shop floor level. These legalistic rules provided protection to workers, and managers also found some advantages in them; many best practices in human resource management in the nonunion sector had their roots in labor agreements. For example, progressive disciplinary processes that are now standard fare in HRM textbooks had their roots in union contracts that guaranteed due process to workers, as did the existence of standardized systems for promotion and pay, complete with rewards for senior workers (Jacoby, 1985).

But over time the accumulation of rules left workplace practices rigid. Unionized companies found it difficult to adapt to new situations, and as early as the 1970s, according to Kochan et al. (1994), managerial frustration with the inefficiencies associated with rules such as narrow job definitions, seniority rights, and layoff protections began to drive companies to resist unionization more strenuously and to hasten divestment of union-ized facilities. Further, the idea that workers were supposed to be passive while management made decisions neglected the possibility that the labor force could contribute to the well-being of the company. The system did not encourage workers to share their ideas, and workers in turn made little commitment to improvements in productivity or quality.

Problems in the system were revealed sharply by foreign competition in the 1980s. Such competition impelled Americans to look more closely at their global rivals, especially in Japan and Europe, where labor-relations systems seemed to be less rule bound and adversarial than in the United States. In Japan, for example, unions appeared to be more readily accepted by management, and negotiations were less focused on conflicting interests. Japanese production systems required employees to contribute actively to the improvement of production processes (Dore, 1992); this involvement was closely linked to Japanese manufacturers' dramatic achievements in the realms of productivity and quality (MacDuffie, 1995). In Germany, to take a second example, the right of unions to exist was embedded in the national constitution, and workers' representatives were entitled to seats on the boards of directors of all large companies. These countries provided alternative models for thinking about how labor–management conflict could and should be managed in the United States.

Critics on both sides saw the rights established by the Wagner Act as antiquated, unsuited to modern circumstances. On the management side, provisions of the act designed to prevent employer-dominated unions impeded employee involvement and team-based decision making. Unions, in contrast, saw their rights to organize and represent workers rendered increasingly ineffective as capital grew more mobile and managers became ever more determined to avoid unionization. The Dunlop Commission, which President Clinton appointed and which included representatives from both sides, suggested a set of reforms aimed at modernizing labor law (Kochan, 1995), but these proposals went nowhere.

Interests

Some 40 years ago, in their influential *A Behavioral Theory of Labor Nego-tiations*, Walton and McKersie (1965) distinguished "integrative," problem-solving negotiation from "distributive," zero sum bargaining. Walton and McKersie analyzed these two processes as well as actions inside labor and management (which they dubbed "intraorganizational bargaining") and the formation of preferences ("attitudinal structuring"). Appearing at the apogee of the rights-based New Deal system, Walton and McKersie's framework—in particular, their focus on the tensions between the power-oriented tactics of distributive bargaining and those approaches that generate gains for both parties—has provided guidance to subsequent generations of analysts of labor negotiations.

The chief actors in American labor relations have continued to find it difficult to capture the joint gains that Walton and McKersie (1965) suggested would accrue to parties that were effective in integrative bargaining. The Ury et al. (1988) framework suggested a common source for these difficulties. Parties that are particularly successful in integrative bargaining are those that are able to identify and focus on their underlying interests. Such identification and focus enables the parties to achieve solutions to specific issues that cost one party relatively little but yield significant advantages to the other. Yet all four elements of conflict resolution under the New Deal system are based on the parties' power and the rights established by the law, rather than on a focus on underlying interests. The rights established by the New Deal framework are poorly matched to a 21st-century economy, and increasingly, the imbalance of power between labor and management means that solutions acceptable to both parties are harder to craft at the bargaining table. New approaches to labor–management dispute resolution in the United States, in contrast, have the virtue of drawing on conflict resolution strategies geared toward solving problems based on the parties' interests.

In the following sections, we will review existing research on the four elements of conflict resolution in the labor relations system in the United States, as well as new directions within each element. Because the practice of labor relations is embedded within legal and political systems, and business practices, that vary considerably across country boundaries, we concentrate our discussion on the United States, drawing comparisons with experiences in Canada and other countries occasionally where they help us to understand American practices.

ELEMENT 1: ORGANIZING

The first element of conflict in labor relations stems from attempts to determine the extent and form of collective representation, most fundamentally, whether or not a workplace should be unionized. Many American workplaces offer forms of dispute resolution in nonunion settings, but initiation of union representation in the United States requires a formal organizing process. At the time of the passage of the National Labor Relations Act, the introduction of this process represented a major change in approach to conflict. "Recognition strikes," in which workers walked off their jobs with their main objectives being to force management to deal with their union, had often been highly adversarial, ideologically charged, and even violent. These bitter power struggles were replaced by an election overseen by the National Labor Relations Board (NLRB), complete with rules of conduct for the campaign, and an outcome determined by a majority vote of workers in the relevant bargaining unit. The Wagner Act channeled conflict over the legitimacy of union representation into a democratic decision process; the 1947 Taft–Hartley amendments to the

Wagner Act established limits on the conduct of not just management but also labor unions during this process.

Subsequent research on the organizing process focused on two substreams: how worker attitudes and demographics affect voting behaviors, and the strategies and tactics used by unions and companies to promote or resist unionization. The first body of research investigates differences in attitudes and characteristics between union members and nonmembers and between unorganized workers who have the intention to participate in union organizing or to join a union and those who have no such intentions. The research identifies a number of factors that affect worker attitudes toward unions. For example, wages and working conditions have consistently been important factors (Farber & Saks, 1980; Haberfeld, 1995), and labor political ideology has been associated with prounion attitudes (Haberfeld, 1995; Kochan, 1979). Among these factors, two variables consistently stand out as decisive attitudinal variables, namely, job dissatisfaction and perceived union instrumentality (Barling, Fullagar, & Kelloway, 1992; Brett, 1980; Fiorito, 2003). People are more likely to join unions if they are dissatisfied with their workplace and if they see unions as able to solve the problems that they face at work. Studies have also found that prounion attitudes are strongest among low-socioeconomic-status workers (Cornfield & Kim, 1994); women, minorities, and immigrants are more likely to favor unionization than are White male workers, and are thus increasingly becoming the targets of union organizers.

The rate of union membership in the United States is today lower than at any time since the New Deal legislation was passed, having dropped from 35% of the workforce 50 years ago to 12.5% in 2004 (Mishel, Bernstein, & Allegretto, 2005). In the private sector, fewer than 10% of workers belong to unions. If the New Deal system were working effectively to resolve conflict over the extent and form of collective representation, this decline in union representation could be seen as a straightforward reflection of workers' lack of interest in unionization. Yet, some evidence suggests this view may be misguided. For example, a comprehensive survey of American workers suggested that about a quarter of American workers would like to belong to unions (Freeman & Rogers, 1999), and the same survey showed that this share would be even higher if the survey question simply replaced the word *union* with a description of activities associated with collective representation, evidently because some workers have a negative impression of unions even where they believe that bargaining as a group could enhance their welfare.

The mismatch between surveyed preferences and actual union membership indicates that the research substream focused on organizing tactics may well be important. The disconnect suggests, as Bronfenbrenner (1997) argued, that union organizing campaigns play a more important role in election outcomes than do factors such as employer tactics, bargaining unit demographics, or organizer background. To take one example, a grassroots or rank-and-file organizing strategy significantly increases the probability of a winning organizing campaign (Bronfenbrenner & Juravich, 1998; Delaney, Jarley, & Fiorito, 1995; Nissen & Rosen, 1999). This strategy includes having well-educated, young organizers meeting directly with potential union members, often in community organizations such as churches. It also includes new goals such as equal pay and child care.

In contrast to the focus on organizing tactics, other scholars attribute the decline of unions to overt company resistance (Farber, 1990; Kleiner, 2001; Fiorito, 2003) in the form of union substitution and suppression (Kochan & Katz, 1988; Wolman, 1936). Union substitution strategies include offering good compensation and fairness to workers and employee involvement programs (Kleiner, 2001). Whether or not these positive employment practices are designed with union avoidance in mind, the practices do have the effect of reducing worker dissatisfaction, thus weakening one of the main reasons workers join unions (Kochan, 1980). Examples of the union suppression strategy include firing of known union supporters, captive audience speeches by supervisors, and failing to bargain seriously over first contracts (Bronfenbrenner, 1997; Kleiner, 2001). Union suppression tactics have consistently had detrimental effects on the process of organizing and collective bargaining (Cohen & Hurd, 1998; Cooke, 1983; Freeman & Kleiner, 1990; Freeman & Rogers, 1999).

In the past three decades, it has clearly become increasingly difficult for unions to win organizing battles. One of the original purposes of the Wagner Act was to promote collective bargaining as a preferred means for resolving workplace conflict, granting workers the right to organize and protecting this right with legal support for the organizing process. But the law is now 70 years old, the provisions of the act that support the right to organize are dated, and the penalties for management for breaking the law are small (Budd, 2005). For example, while it is illegal to discharge workers for engaging in union organizing activity, the associated penalty is merely that the discharged employee receives reinstatement with full back pay—with the back pay being reduced by any earnings enjoyed by the employee in another job.

Current public policy and the relative balance of power between labor and management suggest that collective bargaining is decreasingly likely to be chosen as a vehicle for conflict resolution in the American workplace. In short, the balance of power in this element of labor relations clearly resides with management. Antiunion company campaigns are increasingly sophisticated, and further, companies have shifted large amounts of work to places where unions find it either difficult or impossible to organize workers (Budd, 2005). The extent to which this constitutes a challenge for U.S. labor relations lies somewhat in the eye of the beholder; management lobbying, for example, has contributed to the defeat of attempts at labor law reform that would make it easier for unions to organize workers. Nevertheless, a number of new approaches aimed at altering the process for resolving conflicts over organizing have emerged.

New Trends and Alternatives

Card Check.   Traditional organizing in the United States requires at least 30% of employees in a bargaining unit to sign cards saying that they are interested in a union before the NLRB will call for an election. A period of campaigning by each side follows the presentation of the cards to the NLRB, which supervises a vote at the end of this period. If over 50% of the workers vote "yes," then the union is certified as the exclusive representative of the workforce, and management is required to bargain with the union in good faith (Gold, 1998).

An alternative to this process, favored by unions, is a "card check" procedure in which employers agree to recognize the union if over 50% of the employees sign a card saying they want a union. Card check agreements avoid the often acrimonious recognition campaign. This idea is attractive to some companies, especially in service industries like hotels because the period of open campaigning can lead to very tense employee relations. Even if the union is defeated, the open campaigning of a traditional election may cost the company dearly in bad service to customers and bad employee relations. Some countries have legislation that allows recognition of unions based solely on card check without management agreement. The United Kingdom, for example, introduced a card check system in 2000. Some provinces of Canada, similarly, recognize unions based on card check (though it should be noted that several provinces have actually eliminated card check in favor of mandatory voting in the past three decades; Johnson, 2002).

The card check system works in favor of union recognition. In the United States, Eaton and Kriesky (2001) examined organizing experiences under 118 separate written agreements that include a neutrality agreement or card check provision. They found that card check agreements reduced management campaigning, as well as the use of illegal tactics such as illegal discharge of employees and illegal promises of benefits, and substantially increased the union recognition rate. Neutrality alone apparently had much less effect. Johnson (2002) found, in a study of nine Canadian jurisdictions, that mandatory votes reduce certification success rates by approximately 9% below what they would have been under card check. Riddell (2004) found that when British Columbia switched from a card check to a mandatory vote system in 1984, union success rates declined by an average of 19% during the voting regime. When the law changed again in 1993, back to a card check system, the union success rate returned to its original level.

Prerecognition Negotiation.   Estreicher (1993) argued that allowing labor and management to negotiate before a union is recognized could offer benefits to both sides. In U.S. labor law, management may not control or guide the process by which workers select a union—that could lead to "company dominated" unions. Estreicher suggested, however, that anti-union campaigning by management stems in part from fears that a union would make unreasonable demands. Discussion of issues with union leaders before an election, therefore, might lead to less overt resistance of unionization; where management did continue to campaign against the union, such campaigning would draw more on firsthand experience and less on ideology or preconceived ideas.

Saturn Corporation provided an example of how prenegotiation might work (Rubinstein & Kochan, 2001). Labor leaders from the United Auto Workers (UAW) worked with General Motors (GM) management to design this company (wholly owned by GM). Representation at Saturn started with the premise of cooperation and voluntary recognition rather than with an adversarial process; employees at the new facilities did not have to organize, campaign, or vote in order to be represented by a union. Management accepted the union from the start. Both union and management had a say in how the company was structured, and labor and management "co-manage" Saturn, from the first-level manufacturing teams up through top management level.

Corporate Campaigns. A more contentious alternative used by unions is the corporate campaign. This strategy seeks to exploit systematically the company's relationships with key stakeholders (Manheim, 2001). Through corporate campaigns, unions attempt to bring public attention to negative aspects of company behavior, in effect using this publicity to increase their power to compel the company to restrain itself during an organizing drive or a bargaining encounter (Jarley & Maranto, 1990). Corporate campaigns can build morale and commitment among union members; and they are cost effective for unions, both in terms of resources and in diminishing members' risks of job loss (Perry, 1996).

The emergence of corporate campaigns generally is traced to the tactics used by the Amalgamated Clothing and Textile Workers Union during the mid-1970s in its effort to organize selected plants of the J. P. Stevens textile company (Perry, 1987). There, the union used negative publicity to embarrass the company into accepting the union, with a strong focus on shareholders, customers, employees, and regulators. Perry (1987) found that an employer's sensitivity to adverse publicity and a union's ability to escalate a conflict "beyond the level of a simple labor dispute" were the primary determinants of union success in the 10 corporate campaigns he studied. Jarley and Maranto (1990), by contrast, argued (based on a study of 28 campaigns) that such sensitivity is not enough—corporate campaigns are most effective when used together with traditional organizing activities.

ELEMENT 2: COLLECTIVE BARGAINING

We now turn from organizing to the process of collective bargaining once a union is elected and recognized. Where unions achieve legal recognition, labor and management turn (in the New Deal system) to bargaining over the set of rules that govern the workplace. These negotiations have been the subject of a number of studies (Douglas, 1962; Friedman, 1994; Walton & McKersie, 1965). The process typically produces a fixed term (e.g., three year) contract that covers wages, benefits, and job rules. Typically, each party begins by gathering information about what its constituents want and then by presenting a "wish list" of requests to their counterparts when negotiations begin. These exercises make up one part of what Walton and McKersie (1965) termed "intraorganizational bargaining." From the union side, the wish list provides a public display of its fight for its members' needs and shows the membership that union leaders are in control of the process. This tactic enhances constituent trust in the bargainers, giving them more freedom to act during negotiations.

Despite these public displays, which create the appearance of wide gaps between the parties' demands, representatives of labor and management usually negotiate quite effectively because there are countervailing "backstage" contacts between the parties. With experience, actors on each side develop enough understanding of the ritual so that true intentions can be read through subtle signaling (Friedman, 1994). Thus, while more distributive bargaining occurs front stage, more integrative bargaining occurs backstage. That is, in public, negotiations appear to be largely win–lose and highly positional. As one union representative explained, "There is a lot of show. My guys love it. I have had arbitration cases where I will bring in 25 guys and put the show on, and they don't remember I lost the case" (Friedman, 1994, p. 87). However, behind the scenes, experienced negotiators often know that they need to explore the other side's underlying interests and try to find ways to address those interests. One lawyer explained that, when meeting in private, "I am not trying to impress my clients. In that environment, communication is much more candid" (p. 95), while another said, "Those discussions are often very helpful because the signals may not be that clear across the table; there may be a misunderstanding" (p. 96). In this way, Friedman (1994) expanded on Walton and McKersie (1965) by identifying where and when integrative and distributive negotiations take place.

Further research has provided insight into other aspects of the process. Friedman and Podolny (1992) found that boundary spanning between labor and management negotiators can be split into those who send information to the other side ("representatives") and those who receive information from the other side ("gatekeepers"). The separation of these two roles becomes more pronounced as the stresses of approaching the contract expiration date approaches.

Communications scholars have also studied interactions between negotiators. Putnam and Jones (1982), for example, found that labor negotiators tended to reciprocate each other's tactics, especially following integrative moves such as problem solving with other integrative tactics. The two sides also reciprocated distributive tactics, but in a complementary way with labor relying on offensive strategies (e.g., attacking arguments, rejections, and threats) and management employing defensive maneuvers (e.g., self-supporting arguments, demands, and commitments). When either side shifted and began using the other side's specialized tactics, especially if it formed a tight predictable pattern (e.g., attacking argument followed by threat followed by counterthreat), the negotiation was likely to end in impasse. Negotiators obtained better outcomes through effective use of complementary tactics, such as when companies responded to union *offensive* moves with *defensive* moves of their own.

At a more microlevel, Putnam and Geist (1985) found that different patterns of argumentation were used for different types of issues in the final agreement. Negotiators dropped some issues, retained some in the final contract, and transformed others. For transformed issues, negotiators often fundamentally changed the definition or approach to the issue (e.g., a problem with equitability in supporting insurance premiums became a problem with the insurance carrier and type of coverage in the package). When issues underwent this type of transformation, it was not because new information was added to the discussion, but rather because one or the other party changed the way that it constructed its arguments on the issue. For example, an issue that was transformed began with competing "policy claims," and then shifted to "declarative" claims. "Shifting types of claims allowed bargainers to build on each other's arguments, creating an integrative solution by reformulating the initial proposals" (Putnam & Geist, p. 242).

Research has also investigated broader strategies for collective bargaining. For example, one issue of central concern to both parties is the extent to which bargaining across multiple units should be done in a coordinated way. The most pronounced example of coordinated bargaining is called "pattern bargaining," which is especially strong in the automobile industry. The UAW seeks to ensure equivalent wages and working conditions among the biggest auto employers so that employee wages are not the source of competition among auto companies. Pattern bargaining has some important positive effects for unions and their leaders: It produces higher economic payoffs than other bargaining strategies (Marshall & Merlo, 2004) and reduces political conflict among union members so that leadership stability is enhanced (Budd, 1995). Most importantly, there is strong evidence that for many years pattern bargaining has been effective in terms of creating common contracts. Budd (1992) found statistically significant "spillover effects" of target settlements among the Big Three automakers, although these effects declined in the 1980s compared with the period from 1955 to 1979. Erickson (1992, 1996) also found a strong wage pattern in the automobile industry in the 1970s and described a weakening of pattern bargaining since the 1980s, probably due to increasing competition among firms both domestically and internationally. Voos (1994) argued that pattern bargaining did not end with more extensive competition in the 1990s. Rather, it shifted to a more sophisticated and subtle form, such as when cooperative agreements establishing labor–management partnerships at Inland, Bethlehem, and National Steel, in effect, "set the pattern for the industry, including U.S. Steel" (p. 20).

Existing research helps us understand how and why labor negotiations happen the way they do, but studies also suggest problems with the traditional approach to negotiation. First, while we can understand the rituals of labor negotiations, we also see that such rituals can be counterproductive if interest-based bargaining is a goal. It becomes harder to focus on interests when the parties first engage in rituals that attempt to draw attention to publicly high levels of conflict between them. The scope for integrative bargaining is limited in the traditional labor–management processes, because it must be accomplished away from the public eye, during periods of high time pressure, and without the broad support of the affected parties' constituents. Second, where one or both parties pursue centralized rather than local bargaining, perhaps as a source of leverage, conflicts may be resolved in ways that fail to address the local needs of labor and management. Centrally created rules, bargained across multiple sites, provide little of the flexibility that would enable the parties to address the specific needs of particular local facilities. Thus, conflict resolution in the collective bargaining process often misses the core interests of both sides.

Mediation, often supported by the government through the Federal Mediation and Conciliation Service, is also a well-established aspect of U.S. labor relations. Mediators can help both sides reach settlement (Kolb, 1983), but it is not clear that mediated settlements address the parties' underlying interests. Labor mediation too often focuses on avoiding an impasse, not necessarily addressing interests (Simkin, 1971).

The law requires the parties to bargain in good faith with one another, but beyond this requirement, the rights of the parties matter less than the balance of power between them. Unions' weapons include the strike and the corporate campaign (previously detailed); management may threaten to lock employees out of work or to move production away from unionized facilities to nonunion workplaces. Settlements reflect the power of the parties—which party needs the other more and which party can make more credible its threat of hurting the other side (and itself; Schelling, 1980). Over the past two decades, the share of labor negotiations that have actually resulted in strikes or lockouts has shrunk substantially. It is not clear to what extent this lack of observable strife reflects the parties' ability to resolve genuinely competing interests. It is also possible to see this relative labor peace as a product of an overwhelming shift in the balance of power toward the management side.

In sum, contemporary labor negotiations continue to feature a considerable amount of contentious, two-party distributive bargaining. New approaches, however, also characterize contemporary American labor relations, and these have a common theme: an increased emphasis on integrative, problem-solving approaches to labor–management disputes. In what follows, we review some of the more popular recent initiatives. We also note that despite the advances in research that we describe, our under-standing of the labor negotiation process in practice remains incomplete: Research has been limited by difficulty of access to actual labor negotia-tions and by a shift from research in field settings toward more laboratory-style methods (e.g., highly controlled experiments with student subjects).

New Trends and Alternatives

Interest-Based Bargaining. Recognizing the dysfunctions of traditional bargaining, some scholars examined what it would take to change the bargaining process toward one that more effectively addresses the par-ties' underlying interests. Friedman (1993) found that the extent and effec-tiveness of interest-based bargaining depended on each party's trust in its counterpart, and that such trust was especially important for the union side. The concern among union leaders is that negotiations based on infor-mation rather than power will leave unions at a disadvantage, because union staffs are typically far smaller than those of companies. Friedman (1994) also found that negotiator roles and constituent expectations could impede a shift to interests-based bargaining in labor negotiations; suc-cessful shifts to interest-based bargaining require buffering negotiators from constituent pressures and bargaining-team role presses.

Walton, Cutcher-Gershenfeld, and McKersie (1994) were more optimis-tic than Friedman (1994), citing cases in which labor and management were able to "foster" a more positive relationship, including more inter-est-based negotiations. Their case studies in the auto supply and paper industries in the 1980s and early 1990s suggested that a fostering strat-egy may emerge as an original managerial initiative but that a common alternative scenario was for such "fostering" to follow a period in which management attempts to force change aggressively, but is rebuffed by the union. However, Walton et al. noted that in some cases (e.g., International Paper's mill in Jay, Maine) management was not restrained by the union: In these cases, the deployment of power enabled management to achieve settlements that served its interests but offer relatively little to the union or workforce.

Decentralized Bargaining. Experiments with interest-based bargaining in the labor arena have been sporadic. One more substantial trend is a shift to decentralized bargaining. This is characteristic not only of the United States. Western European countries that once featured national-level bar-gaining, such as Sweden and Germany, have also seen shifts toward indus-try- and company-level negotiations, a trend that Traxler (2003) referred to as "organized decentralization." In the United States, decentralization has been taken even further: Since the 1980s, bargaining has shifted from company and industry-level negotiations to enterprise- or plant-level bar-gaining (Katz, 2004).

While decentralization is widely acknowledged, researchers have not reached a general agreement on the forces behind it. One of the most commonly agreed-upon explanations for bargaining-structure decentralization is that it results from a relative shift in power toward management, away from labor (Eaton & Kriesky, 1998; Katz, 1993). While some unions may prefer decentralization (if they prefer local bargaining or can benefit from whipsawing—playing one company off another in order to gain better contracts), unions generally find that negotiating in larger units gives them more power at the bargaining table. Companies, by contrast, prefer decentralized bargaining since smaller unions have less leverage over companies and thus cannot demand as much. Whether decentralization or centralization prevails depends on the relative power of the two parties (Eaton & Kriesky, 1998; Hendricks & Kahn, 1982). As union density has declined in the United States, companies have been able to demand more decentralized bargaining, amplifying and accelerating the redistribution of power.

Decentralization may also reflect increasingly competitive product markets and stronger demands for flexibility by employers. Competition leads employers to seek more productive work systems and to reduce labor cost (Voos, 1994). Decentralized bargaining tends to allow for more flexible labor agreements that include features such as team systems and pay for performance compensation methods (Katz, 2004; Kochan, Katz, & McKersie, 1994). Decentralization is also driven by diversification in corporate structures and fragmentation in worker interests (Katz, 1993). It is worthwhile to note that these factors may have different effects on different industries or companies. For example, case studies show that competition played an important role driving decentralization in the auto industry (Katz, MacDuffie, & Pil, 2002) but was less central to the same trend in the paper industry (Eaton & Kriesky, 1998).

Interest Arbitration.   An alternative way to resolve conflicts in the negotiations process comes from the public sector, where strikes are illegal and arbitration is often mandated by statute. Interest arbitration usually involves the selection of a neutral third party to resolve a bargaining impasse. The arbitrator hears the positions of both sides, and then makes a final and binding decision regarding the terms of the contract.

Some claim that interest arbitration plays an important role in encouraging collective bargaining by balancing the power of the two parties, by clarifying the bargaining zone, and by providing the parties with incentives to make reasonable proposals (Farber & Katz, 1979; Feuille, 1979). On the other hand, there are criticisms of interest arbitration, and the most common fall into two categories: the "chilling effect" and the "narcotic effect."

The "chilling effect" of interest arbitration stems from the concern that the parties will find it difficult to reach an agreement on their own, if either believes that the other side will make an extreme proposal and then invoke arbitration in hopes that the arbitrator will "split the difference" and make an award that favors the more extreme party. Research into the extent to which interest arbitration has this effect has yielded mixed results. One recent study found that bargaining units covered by compulsory arbitration are 8.7% to 21.7% more likely to have an impasse than bargaining units are in sectors that provide the right to strike (Hebdon & Mazerolle, 2003). Yet Farber (1981) argued that exogenous factors might affect arbitrators' decision making so the expected outcome may not be the midpoint between the two sides. Farber and Katz (1979) also argued that the uncertainty created by arbitration outcomes gives parities the incentive to negotiate and reach a settlement.

The "narcotic effect" refers to the concern that once the parties start using interest arbitration they will become increasingly dependent on it in subsequent negotiations. Here, too, empirical findings have been mixed, with some studies finding this effect (Butler & Ehrenberg, 1981; Hebdon & Mazerolle, 2003), but others failing to do so (Champlin, Bognanno, & Schumann, 1997; Chelius & Extejt, 1985).

Living Contracts.   Another trend toward more integrative approaches to conflict resolution is more radical. "Living contracts" do away with the notion of fixed rules that remain in place for the duration of a contract. Living contracts provide for an ongoing, cooperative bargaining process between labor and management that allows rules to be changed when circumstances change during the life of the contract. This approach is not pervasive, and it is relatively early to assess the promise of this trend. Where there is enough trust between labor and management, living contracts can help overcome some of the rigidities that managers and observers see in a New Deal style approach to workplace dispute resolution.

In the late 1980s, for example, living contracts between the Rochester school district and its union helped it to smooth the operation of the schools and establish a timely problem-solving mechanism (Urbanski, 2001). Since 1993, 11 major San Francisco hotels have implemented living contracts. These contracts helped the hotels compete effectively (in particular, weathering the 2001–2002 recession), enhanced workers' job security, and provided a platform for workers' skill acquisition (Korshak, 1995; Tate, 2004). Labor-management cooperation, however, is a key foundation of a living contract, and such cooperation is difficult to sustain. Many of the same San Francisco hotels that were considered prototypes for the implementation of living contracts have quite recently developed conflicts that threaten their cooperative relationships and the extension of the living contract (Tate, 2004).

ELEMENT 3: GRIEVANCES AND ARBITRATION

The "living contract" notion notwithstanding, in American labor relations a contract settlement establishes the rules of the workplace. Conflict, however, does not end with the signing of the labor contract. Throughout the life of the contract, disputes continue to arise between workers and managers. For example, employees feel that they have been improperly fired or demoted, been assigned job tasks they should not have to perform, or been paid an incorrect wage for jobs they were doing. Nearly all labor-management contracts establish processes for resolution of such disputes: most typically, grievance procedures.

American contracts and practice typically require workers to follow managerial direction except, perhaps, where they believe doing so would jeopardize their own safety. Should workers believe that managerial directions run contrary to the rights established in the labor contract, the workers might file formal grievances. Labor and management commonly set up a "three step" procedure for handling these grievances. Each step provides an opportunity to resolve the dispute: Representatives of both sides meet to examine what happened, to measure it against the contract, and to see if they can come to an agreement about what should be done next (Holly & Jennings, 1994). If low-level meetings do not lead to resolution at the first step, then the next step includes higher level managers and union officials. If the parties remain at impasse, the case may go to arbitration, where an outside third party is hired to hear the case and make a binding judgment.

Just as the NLRB election procedures offered clear advantages over the recognition strike, the grievance and arbitration processes offer advantages over strikes to resolve disputes over the interpretation of the contract. The three-step grievance process is less disruptive than strikes for settling these disputes, and most contracts have a "no strike" clause that prohibits the use of strikes (or lockouts) as a way to resolve disputes while the contract is in force. The no-strike provision ensures that conflict resolution over the life of the contract is rule based rather than power based.

The system is not perfect. Arbitration is slow, expensive, and prone to "split the difference" results. The average arbitration case costs $3,209 and takes an average of 473 days from initiation to resolution (Goldberg, 2005). Further, because arbitrators want to be hired again (and depend on the good will of both the union and the company to be hired again), they often end up compromising rather than trying to find an answer that actually meets the underlying interests of the parties or who is "right" (Bazerman, 1985).

Because dealing with grievances can be costly and time consuming for management, the simple filing of grievances may be used as a source of leverage by unions, and researchers often turn to grievance rates as an indicator of how good or bad relations are between labor and management. For example, studies of the relationships between work systems and organizational performance identify low grievance rates as part of a "transformation" toward more productive work systems (Cutcher-Gershenfeld, 1991; Ichniowski, 1986). The grievance rate is related to the cycle of negotiation; when the contract expiration date approaches, the number of grievances increases, presumably as a way for unions to gain power during negotiations (Lewin & Peterson, 1988). While the intent of the grievance process is to produce more effective dispute resolution, plants with very bad labor relations can be flooded with so many grievances that the system breaks down and nothing gets resolved.

Nor is use of the grievance procedure free of cost for workers. Studies on postgrievance outcomes have consistently found that employees who file grievances are subsequently punished by the employers; these workers receive lower performance ratings, lower wage increases, and experience lower internal mobility (Klaas & DeNisi, 1989; Lewin, 1999; Lewin & Peterson, 1988).

Given the variety of costs associated with the traditional three-step procedure, management and labor have begun to experiment with alternatives. Some are straightforward attempts to reduce the costs. But others are more elaborate: Just as interest-based negotiation has begun to make inroads into traditionally distributive bargaining settings, more collaborative approaches to solving workplace problems, based on the parties' underlying interests, have made their way into this third element of the system.

New Trends and Alternatives

Expedited Arbitration.   Expedited arbitration was first proposed by arbitrator Harold Davey in 1969 in response to a lack of arbitrators and the problems of delays and increasing costs derived from regular arbitration (Kauffman, 1992). The process is generally limited to routine, nonpolicy influencing, noncomplex cases (Sandver, Blaine, & Woyar, 1981). It is not a replacement of traditional arbitration, but rather a procedure to speed up the process and save costs by using an "express route" to deal with routine issues such as disciplinary grievances. Expedited arbitration uses a single arbitrator instead of a tribunal, has shorter periods for each stage in the arbitration process, and prohibits transcripts and briefs. No lawyers are involved, short and explicit written decisions are provided, and arbitral fees are capped.

Grievance and arbitration processes are fundamentally rights based rather than interest based. Expedited arbitration does little to shift this underlying premise, but does lower the overall cost of arbitration. Research based on 682 arbitration cases in Canada found that expedited arbitration is more commonly used in the private sector than in the public sector. Discipline and seniority cases are more likely to use expedited arbitration; dismissal cases are less likely to use it (de Berdt Romilly, 1994). While some may suggest that expedited arbitration awards are inferior to conventional arbitration awards, Thomas (2002) found that expedited arbitration with a single arbitrator is more likely to have a favorable outcome for the griever than conventional arbitration with a single arbitrator. Despite the efficiency of expedited arbitration, it has not been widely adopted. Perhaps for that reason, little research on the process has been done since the mid-1990s.

High-Involvement Work Systems. Some unionized workplaces have moved in the last two decades to adopt "high-involvement" work systems featuring enhanced employee participation and the devolution of problem solving and decision making to the shop floor. Colvin (2003) argued that there are three reasons such systems should be accompanied by lower rates of use of formal dispute resolution procedures such as grievance systems. First, these systems engender greater trust between employees and management, reducing the overall level of conflict. Second, the high-involvement system itself may change the way in which disputes are resolved, with more informal decision making and real-time negotiation. Third, decisions made in the context of employee participation may enjoy greater legitimacy and thus lead to fewer disputes. In these ways, the dispute systems should move from rights to interests, and formalized dispute systems should be less necessary.

In fact, Colvin (2003) found, in a sample of 61 unionized workplaces, that grievance rates themselves did not differ significantly between unionized workplaces which did and did not have self-managed teams, suggesting that formal conflict resolution procedures were used as frequently under high-involvement work systems as in more traditional approaches. Colvin's analysis also showed, however, that the share of grievances that were appealed was more than 20% lower in workplaces that had self-managed teams. Conflicts in these high-involvement workplaces were much more likely to be resolved at or near the workplace level, without invoking the entire dispute resolution apparatus.

The underlying idea in the high-involvement workplace is to appeal to the parties' mutual interests in keeping the firm competitive. Presumably, efficient, high-quality production or service is good both for the firm and for workers. To the extent that the parties can agree they share this interest, disputes over who does what in the workplace may be easier to resolve than disputes that rely on legalistic procedures designed to protect the parties' rights. To be fully effective in resolving conflicts, however, fully elaborated, high-involvement systems must not allow managers unilateral authority to determine the best interests of the company. High-involvement management relies on all parties bringing their own perspectives to bear on workplace challenges. Where management refuses to share its decision-making power, employees are more likely to fall back, over time, on more legalistic, rights-based processes for protecting their own interests.

ELEMENT #4: MANAGERIAL CONTROL OF BUSINESS DECISIONS

As Kochan, Katz, and McKersie (1994) noted, the New Deal system was held together in part by a shared ideology between labor and management over the range of issues amenable to collective bargaining. The Wagner Act established wages, hours, and conditions as mandatory subjects of bargaining; the law described other areas as "permissive" subjects and did not require bargaining in these areas. Thus, 20th-century American industrial relations featured little or no negotiation over company strategy, the organization of production in a plant, the introduction of new technologies, or other decisions about the direction of the company. For the most part, American unions accepted that decisions in such areas fell to managers (Kochan et al., 1994). Even as European unions were taking seats on corporate boards of directors, for example, most American unions refused such strategic engagement, fearing that they would own partial responsibility for such decisions without truly having a voice in business strategy (Hunter, 1998). Negotiation was therefore restricted to bargaining over the effects of strategic decisions: if a business decision required the company to lay off workers, for example, union leaders negotiated over the terms of the layoff, the rules governing who would be laid off, and their rights to be called back to the job.

This American model became known, perhaps counterintuitively, as "business unionism." The approach provides for little to no participation in managerial decisions. Unions have no statutory rights to bargain over these areas, in sharp contrast to the approach in many European countries, in which legal mandates for works councils and workforce representation on corporate boards of directors (or "codetermination") provide arenas for discussion and negotiation over business issues.

A few unions have seen strategic involvement as a necessity in an age of new work practices, mobile capital, global competition, and corporate restructuring. For example, even where workers have favored innovative work practices, their enthusiasm is tempered by corporate strategies that leave their jobs less secure (Hunter, MacDuffie, & Doucet, 2002). Thus, some union leaders have sought venues for engaging strategic decisions, looking for influence over the direction of the business, the allocation of resources, and the distribution of revenues, and for access to the financial information and business records upon which such decisions were based. Management does not typically seek out such cooperation, preferring to preserve its freedom to maneuver. Thus, unions must bargain over the access to information and to strategic decisions as well as over the decisions themselves.

New Trends and Alternatives

Strategic Partnerships.   Appelbaum and Hunter (2004) drew on a variety of sources to note that "strategic partnerships," in which union and management jointly determine business decisions, are relatively rare. Achieving such access seems to be less important to union leaders or members than are other more immediate and traditional bargaining concerns. Nevertheless, joint interests in company growth and success have on occasion

brought companies and their workers' unions together in strategic partnerships. In the face of intense competitive pressures, companies and
unions have found that they have common interests in seeing their companies grow. Growth can be accompanied by expansion of jobs in which
workers are represented by the union, while union cooperation can help
the company increase market share. Further, strategic partnerships may
support innovative work practices at lower levels, providing a forum for
engaging issues around their implementation.

One well-documented and much publicized strategic partnership was
the Saturn division of GM, the result of extensive cooperation between
the UAW and GM management. Rubinstein and Kochan (2001) provided
a thorough account of the development and emergence of this partnership, which was designed to provide arenas for joint decision making
between labor and management at all levels of the organization from the
shop floor to the executive suite. Decisions around investments, product
design, sourcing, plant location, design, and other important business
topics were to have union involvement; Saturn has truly been an experiment in "co-management."

Over time, the Saturn experiment proved difficult to sustain. The
model did not diffuse broadly or even to the rest of GM, nor did the UAW
embrace co-management as a strategy worth pursuing more broadly.
Co-management evoked intense debates both within and outside of the
organization (Kochan & Rubinstein, 2000), and Saturn has been slowly
dragged back toward a more traditional labor–management model, with
more extensive contractual language and focus on a narrower range of
disputes. Co-management at Saturn does continue, but it has not provided
the spark for broader diffusion of strategic engagement for which some
observers had hoped.

Saturn, however, is only one example of a strategic partnership. Other
such partnerships have been pursued by unions, including the United Steel
Workers (USW), the International Brotherhood of Electrical Workers, the
Communication Workers, and others. Appelbaum and Hunter (2004) noted
that in the steel industry, for example, partnerships have provided support
for updating practices and facing up to international competition as well as
domestic threats posed to integrated steel mills by nonunion minimills. The
International Association of Machinists and Aerospace Workers (IAMAW)
provides another example of a union that has pursued partnerships on
occasion at firms including Harley Davidson and Weyerhauser. IAMAW
partnerships feature joint decision making by labor and management, with
union input on design of business plans, joint involvement in forecasting
production costs, and negotiated approaches to work process changes. The
structures include business unit or plant-level teams that determine performance measures and steer efforts to introduce new work practices.

Strategic partnerships are the logical culmination of an interest-based
approach to labor–management conflict resolution. Currently, however,
workers and their unions have no rights backing participation at this level.

Thus, the establishment of partnerships depends either on both parties perceiving that their interests lie in such cooperation or on one side having sufficient power to force the other to cooperate. Only occasionally have unions with such power deployed it in this fashion; it is a risky strategy and the benefits are uncertain.

Corporate Boards of Directors. A different approach to union involvement in strategic or business decisions is to establish union representation on corporate boards of directors. This is one way to provide a strategic partnership more firmly grounded in rights rather than in power. In Germany, for example, the law mandates such "codetermination" in large companies. In the United States, such representation is not mandated, but may be bargained for or may accompany employee stock ownership. Throughout the 1970s and 1980s, for example, unions won the right to nominate directors in conjunction with negotiations over wage concessions and the extension of stock ownership to employees (Hunter, 1998). Unions such as the USW and IAMAW have also pursued board seats as a way of supporting their other partnership efforts.

Chrysler was the first leading American firm with union representation on the board. UAW President Douglas Fraser assumed a directorship in 1980 and was succeeded in 1984 by Owen Bieber. After several years, the UAW did not emphasize preservation of the board seat as a bargaining objective, and the corporation restructured its board, dropping Bieber in 1991. Nevertheless, experiments with board representation have continued. Appelbaum and Hunter (2004) listed over 20 leading firms with union representatives on the board. Such representatives include active unionists, workers, retired union leaders, and "neutrals" sympathetic to union ends including consultants, lawyers, and professors.

Occasionally, boards of directors have emerged as forums for labor-management dispute resolution. However, this is uncommon. Union representatives, like other board directors, are legally charged with representing shareholders' interests, and these fiduciary duties block directors from explicit representation of workers' concerns. Further, except in extreme circumstances, American boards rely more on consensus rather than on constituency representation or explicit negotiation among competing interests. Managers and most directors do not see boards as appropriate venues for resolution of differences between labor and management, and thus only topics likely to generate consensus are easily tackled at the board level.

Board representation does not ensure that the parties will work together to address joint concerns. United Airlines provides a recent example of the associated difficulties. The Airline Pilots Association (ALPA) and the IAMAW obtained one seat each on the board of directors (along with share ownership for their members) in 1994. Following the employee buyout of United, trust between top managers and the unions eroded. Collective bargaining over wages and benefits was heated and contentious, proposed mergers (e.g., one with USAirways) provided further controversy, and the company struggled. For example, in the summer of 2000, management accused ALPA members of participating in work slowdowns (ALPA spokespersons denied this), and the 2001 round of bargaining between United Airlines and the IAMAW was bitter even by industry standards. The airline's performance did not improve relative to its competitors' after the buyout (Gittell, von Nordenflycht, & Kochan, 2004). None of the parties saw this business partnership as a success story.

Nevertheless, Hunter (1998) suggested that under some circumstances board representatives can be effective in forcing discussion and resolution of issues affecting labor and management, especially when the directors themselves behave strategically, the board seats are embedded in a more comprehensive approach to labor–management cooperation, and, like other partnerships, the parties are driven to cooperation by a competitive marketplace. Wever's (1989) early case study of union involvement on the board at Western Airlines, for example, showed that a board could effectively engage labor–management issues where the union was powerful and secure, and where its leaders perceived that management either would not (or was not able to) undermine that power or security. In sum, even the rights to information and consultation associated with seats on the board do not ensure genuine involvement or strategic participation. This requires either sufficient power on the union side or both parties' commitment to interest-based problem solving.

International Union Management Conflict Resolution

This chapter has focused on U.S. practices, research, and trends. Over the past decades, as changes have occurred in the United States, many scholars have had an eye outside the United States for alternative models, in particular in Germany and Japan. The German system of "codetermination" provides for strategic engagement by requiring companies to include representatives of the workforce on their supervisory boards of directors (Frege, 2002). German law also requires companies, whether or not they are unionized, to establish "works councils" (comprising representatives of the workforce) to consider a range of issues that in the United States would be the province of management, such as the implementation of technological change. Such a system may enable resolution of employer–worker conflict that reflects both parties' interests, but by requiring extensive discussion of workplace change, it may also contribute to the inflexibility that is often associated with the German labor market (Streeck, 1997). Frege (2002) argued that more research is needed linking the inner workings of these councils to key outcomes; a question of which, if any, aspects of this system would be effective in other settings might merit research attention in the United States.

Japanese firms' processes for employee and union involvement in workplace decision making have also attracted considerable interest from western scholars (Dore, 1992; Jacoby, 2005). Japanese labor–management relations, centered on unions representing workers in single enterprises rather than across industries, provide strong support for flexibility and decision making in the resolution of conflict at the local and workplace levels. This cooperative system of union–management relations has been made possible to some extent by lifetime employment and by pay linked heavily to firm tenure. Ono (2006) noted that the journalistic coverage of the Japanese system in light of global competition and the Japanese economic slump of the 1990s suggested that the system is in decline. The extent of this decline, however, can be overstated (Jacoby, 2004; Ono, 2006).

It is worth noting that in both Japan and in Germany, as well as in nearly all other industrialized countries, the share of the workforce that belongs to unions has dropped steadily over the past two decades just as it has in the United States (Katz & Darbishire, 2000). Thus, perhaps the biggest stories in international labor–management relations will come not from these countries, but from those countries that are beginning to put increasing economic pressures on the United States, Japan, and Europe—emerging markets such as China and South and Southeast Asia. In these countries, independent and effective union representation of workers is relatively uncommon, but pressures are building as these economies grow, worker expectations rise, and booming demand has led to occasional labor shortages. In 2005, for example, factories in Guangzhou, China, faced a deficit of workers for the first time. Labor, management, and governments in these countries will face dilemmas in conflict resolution similar to those faced in the United States, western Europe, and Japan in the 20th century. Will traditional unions emerge? Will worker protests force changes in the legal structures that currently provide few protections for workers? And will the resolution of such conflicts be based chiefly on the relative power of the parties, on legal systems that carefully delineate the parties' rights, or on more flexible structures that enable both parties to find solutions that serve their respective interests?

CONCLUSION

Conflict resolution in American labor relations is no longer shaped by a rough balance of power between labor unions and management. That historic balance of power had shifted conflict management in labor relations from one that was power focused to one that was rights focused. Today, a considerably smaller share of workers is represented by unions than at the height of the New Deal system 50 years ago so that employers can more easily avoid coming to the bargaining table for negotiations over wages, hours, and working conditions. Even when companies do come to the table, it is not clear that a rights-based system is able to meet either side's interests effectively.

Relatively few workers today see their workplace conflicts resolved via the New Deal system. In part, this is a function of broader changes in the environment: a new service-based economy, an increasingly diverse workforce, and the advent of global competition. The New Deal system has been slow to respond to the challenges posed by these changes. Not surprisingly for a system whose main characteristics were established 70 years ago, its approach to conflict management has at times proven a poor fit to modern circumstances. The decline in the number of workers represented by unions is in part a function of this misfit: Management resists unionization more heavily, and workers are less likely to join unions that they do not think can be part of an effective approach to conflict resolution.

Where unions retain a foothold, labor and management continue to experiment with new ways of managing conflict. One common theme we have identified among these experiments is that they strive to develop interest-based approaches to dispute resolution. Some 40 years ago, Walton and McKersie (1965) identified integrative bargaining as a key subprocess in labor relations. Should there be a renewed interest in collective bargaining, innovations that provide a more interests-based framework for such bargaining may prove to be necessary to bring labor–management relations into the 21st century.

Future Research Directions

We see research on labor union management conflict heading in new directions over the next decades. Within the United States, the central questions are whether the New Deal system will continue to dissipate in importance and impact, and what institutions and practices might emerge to replace it. One model that has emerged for employee representation is employee network or support groups that form around particular issues (Levine & Bishop, 1999) or, more commonly, particular subsets of employees. Network groups for minority and female employees have become widespread in major corporations (Friedman, 1996; Hyde, 1993), although it appears that these groups are more often social support groups than advocacy groups (Friedman & Craig, 2004). These groups cannot bargain in the traditional sense—indeed, in the U.S. legal context, it would be illegal to do so because they represent only a portion of employees at any given company—but they do provide a way for employees to express concerns about issues that affect their subgroup of employees. Also, while traditional union–management relations focus exclusively on nonexempt employees (employees who are, technically, not "managers"), network groups have the potential to focus on managerial employees' interests and needs.

Future research is likely to be more meaningful to the extent it broadens beyond traditional "union" entities. For example, groups such as Working

Today (2006) provide legal advice, health insurance, advocacy, and other services to employees who do not have unions or even stable permanent jobs. We focused in this chapter on union–management conflict, but in the future, these kinds of entities may emerge as channels for the resolution of worker–employer conflicts.

Reconsidering the four areas of labor relations covered in this chapter, we see several of the new trends as ripe for future research attention. Research on union organizing should focus especially on card check strategies and preorganizing of newly established work sites (e.g., Saturn Corporation). Recently, for example, workers at the University of Miami struck not over substantive issues but over the right to have unions recognized after card checks rather than full-blown union election campaigns. And leaders of the Change to Win coalition, which features a number of unions that withdrew from the AFL-CIO in 2005, argued that union influence depends on successful organizing. This success depends in turn on changing the grounds on which organizing campaigns are fought, and thus, the battles over procedural issues such as the card check.

Similarly, preorganizing enables labor and management to negotiate the terms of their future relationships before a union is actually voted in by workers. Preorganizing frames the organizing debate less around each side's worst fears about the other, and more on the realities of practice, allowing for a more interest-based approach. More can be done to study the conditions and legal constraints around preorganizing and to understand the effects such agreements might have on the long-term relationship between companies and unions.

For collective bargaining, future trends suggest more attention to living contracts and decentralized bargaining. These moves toward more flexible systems of conflict resolution allow for changes over time and for differences across bargaining units. The extent to which organized labor is able to respond toward managerial demands for flexibility, yet continue to provide effective, independent representation, will be central to unions' abilities to stem the erosion in membership and to regain influence over the workplace. Similarly, grievance systems are likely to stay most relevant where they are able to address problems close to their source: the metaphorical "shop floor" (itself increasingly likely to be a call center or other service workplace). Effective conflict management will be nimble and responsive to the needs of workers and managers; researchers should study the processes and structures that evolve to meet these challenges.

Finally, at the broadest level, strategic partnerships between labor and management could increase the potential of unions to represent their membership effectively. However, strategic partnerships are relatively rare. While it is not clear if managers or union leaders can adapt themselves to this view of union–management relations, this trend is worth watching.

REFERENCES

Appelbaum, E., & Hunter, L. W. (2004). Union participation in strategic decisions of corporations. In R. Freeman, J. Hersch, & L. Mishel (Eds.), *Emerging labor market institutions for the 21st century* (pp. 265–292). Chicago: University of Chicago Press.

Barling, D., Fullagar, C., & Kelloway, E. K. (1992). *The union and its member: A psychological apporach.* New York: Oxford.

Bazerman, M. (1985). Norms of distributive justice in interest arbitration. *Industrial and Labor Relations Review, 38*(4), 558–570.

Brett, J. M. (1980). Why employees want unions. *Organizational Dynamics, 8,* 47–59.

Bronfenbrenner, K. (1997). The role of union strategies in NLRB certification election. *Industrial and Labor Relations Review, 50*(2), 195–213.

Bronfenbrenner, K., & Juravich, T. (1998). It takes more than house calls to win with a comprehensive union-building strategy. In K. Bronfenbrenner, R. A. Oswald, S. Friedman, R. L. Seeber, & R. W. Hurd (Eds.), *Organizing to win: New research on union strategies* (pp. 19–36). Ithaca, N.Y.: ILR Press

Budd, J. W. (1992). The determinants and extent of UAW pattern bargaining. *Industrial and Labor Relations Review, 45*(3), 523–539.

Budd, J. W. (1995). The internal union political imperative for UAW pattern bargaining. *Journal of Labor Research, 16*(1), 43–55.

Budd, J. W. (2005). *Labor relations: Striking a balance.* New York: McGraw-Hill/Irwin.

Butler, R., & Ehrenberg, R. (1981). Estimating the narcotic effect of public sector impasse procedures. *Industrial and Labor Relations Review, 35*(1), 3–20.

Champlin, F., Bognanno, M., & Schumann, P. (1997). Is arbitration habit-forming? The narcotic effect of arbitration use. *Labour, 11*(1), 23–51.

Chelius, J. R., & Extejt, M. (1985). The narcotic effect of impasse resolution procedures. *Industrial and Labor Relations Review, 38*(4), 629–638.

Cohen, L., & Hurd, R. W. (1998). Fear, conflict, and union organizing. In K. Bronfenbrenner, R. A. Oswald, S. Friedman, R. L. Seeber, & Hurd, R. W. (Eds.), *Organizing to win: New research on union strategies* (pp. 181–196). Ithaca, NY: ILR Press.

Colvin, A. J. S. (2003). Dual transformation of workplace dispute resolution. *Industrial Relations, 42*(4), 712–735.

Cooke, W. N. (1983). Determinants of the outcomes of union certification elections. *Industrial and Labor Relations Review, 36*(3), 402–414.

Cornfield, D. B., & Kim, H. (1994). Socioeconomic status and unionization attitudes in the United States. *Social Forces, 73*(2), 521–530.

Cutcher-Gershenfeld, J. (1991). The impact on economic performance of a transformation in workplace relations. *Industrial and Labor Relations Review, 44*(2), 241–260.

de Berdt Romilly (1994). *Law reform of the arbitration process: A comparative evaluation of conventional and expedited arbitration in the provinces of Ontario and Nova Scotia.* Unpublished dissertation, Dalhousie University, Canada.

Delaney, J. T., Jarley, P., & Fiorito, J. (1995). National union effectiveness in organizing: Measures and influences." *Industrial and Labor Relations Review, 48*(4), 613–35.

Dore, R. P. (1992). Japan's version of managerial capitalism. In T. A. Kochan & M. Useem (Eds.), *Transforming organizations* (pp. 17–27). New York: Oxford University Press.

Douglas, A. (1962). *Industrial peacemaking.* New York: Columbia University Press.

Dunlop, J. T. (1958). *Industrial relations systems.* New York: Holt.

Eaton, A. E., & Kriesky, J. (1998). Decentralization of bargaining structure: Four cases from the U.S. paper industry. *Industrial Relations/Relations Industrielles, 53*(3), 486–516.

Eaton, A. E., & Kriesky, J. (2001). Union organizing under neutrality and card check agreements. *Industrial and Labor Relations Review, 55*(1), 42–59.

Erickson, C. (1992). Wage rule formation in the aerospace industry. *Industrial and Labor Relations Review, 45*(3), 507–522.

Erickson, C. (1996). A re-interpretation of pattern bargaining. *Industrial and Labor Relations, 49*(4), 615–634.

Estreicher, S. (1993). What should be done: The case for change. Labor law reform in a world of competitive product markets. *Chicago-Kent Law Review, 69*(3), 3–46.

Farber, H. S. (1981). Splitting the difference in interest arbitration. *Industrial and Labor Relations Review, 35*(1), 70–77.

Farber, H. S. (1990). The decline of unionization in the United States: What can be learned from recent experience? *Journal of Labor Economics, 8*(1), 75–105.

Farber, H. S., & Katz, H. C. (1979). Interest arbitration, outcomes, and the incentives to bargain. *Industrial and Labor Relations Review, 33*(1), 55–63.

Farber, H. S., & Saks, D. H. (1980). Why workers want unions. *Journal of Political Economy, 88*(2), 349–69.

Feuille, P. (1979). Selected benefits and costs of compulsory arbitration. *Industrial and Labor Relations Review, 33*(1), 64–76.

Fiorito, J. (2003). Union organizing in the United States. In G. Gall (Ed.), *Union organizing: Campaigning for trade union recognition* (pp. 191–210). London: Routledge.

Freeman, R. B., & Kleiner, M. (1990). Employer behavior in the face of union organizing drives. *Industrial and Labor Relations Review, 43*(4), 351–365.

Freeman, R. B., & Rogers, J. (1999). *What workers want.* Ithaca, NY: Cornell University Press.

Frege, C. (2002). A critical assessment of the theoretical and empirical research on German Works Councils. *British Journal of Industrial Relations, 40*(2), 221–248.

Friedman, R. (1993). Bringing mutual gains bargaining to labor negotiations: The role of trust, understanding, and control. *Human Resource Management, 32*(4), 435–459.

Friedman, R. (1994). *Front stage, backstage: The dramatic structure of labor negotiations.* Cambridge, MA: MIT Press.

Friedman, R. (1996). Defining the scope and logic of minority and female network groups: Can separation enhance integration? In G. Ferris (Ed.), *Research in personnel and human resources management* (pp. 307–349). London: JAI Press.

Friedman, R., & Craig, K. (2004). Predicting joining and activism in minority employee network groups. *Industrial Relations, 43*(4), 793–816.

Friedman, R., & Podolny, J. (1992). Differentiation of boundary spanning roles: Labor negotiations and implications for role conflict. *Administrative Science Quarterly, 37*(1), 28–47.

Gittell, J. H., Von Nordenflycht, A., & Kochan, T. A. (2004). Mutual gains or zero sum? Labor relations and firm performance in the airline industry. *Industrial and Labor Relations Review, 57*(2), 163–179.

Gold, M. E. (1998). *An introduction to labor law.* Ithaca, NY: Cornell University Press.

Goldberg, S. B. (2005). How interest-based grievance mediation reforms over the long term? *Dispute Resolution Journal, 59*(4), 8–15.

Haberfeld, Y. (1995). Why do workers join unions? The case of Israel. *Industrial and Labor Relations Review, 48*(4), 656–70.

Hebdon, R., & Mazerolle, M. (2003). Regulating conflict in public sector labor relations. *Industrial Relations, 58*(4), 667–686.

Heckscher, C. (1996). *The new unionism.* Ithaca, NY: ILR Press.

Hendricks, W., & Kahn, L. (1982). The determinants of bargaining structure in U. S. manufacturing industries. *Industrial and Labor Relations Review, 35*(2), 181–195.

Holly, W., & Jennings, K. (1994). *Labor relations process.* Orlando, FL: The Dryden Press.

Hunter, L. W. (1998). Can strategic participation be institutionalized? Union representation on American corporate boards. *Industrial and Labor Relations Review, 51*(4), 557–578.

Hunter, L. W., MacDuffie, J. P., & Doucet, L. (2002). What makes teams take? Employee reactions to work reforms. *Industrial and Labor Relations Review, 55*(3), 448–472.

Hyde, A. (1993). Employee caucuses: A key institution in the emerging system of employment law. *Chicago-Kent Law Review, 69*(1), 149–193.

Ichniowski, C. (1986). The effects of grievance activity on productivity. *Industrial and Labor Relations Review, 40*(1), 75–89.

Jacoby, S. M. (1985). *Employing bureaucracy: managers, unions, and the transformation of work in American industry.* New York: Columbia University Press.

Jacoby, S. M. (2004). *The embedded corporation: Corporate governance and employment relations in Japan and the United States.* Princeton, NJ: Princeton University Press.

Jacoby, S. M. (2005). Business and society in Japan and the United States. *British Journal of Industrial Relations, 43*(4), 617–634.

Jarley, P., & Maranto, C. (1990). Union corporate campaigns: An assessment. *Industrial and Labor Relations Review, 43*(5), 505–524.

Johnson, S. (2002). Voting or card-check: How the union recognition procedure affects organizing success. *Economic Journal, 112*(479), 344–361.

Katz, H. (2004). United States: The spread of coordination and decentralization without national-level tripartism. In H. Katz (Ed.), *The new structure of labor relations* (pp. 192–212). Ithaca, NY: ILR Press.

Katz, H., MacDuffie, J. P., & Pil, F. K. (2002). Collective bargaining in the U.S. auto industry. In P. Clark, J. Delaney, & A. Frost, (Eds.), *Contemporary collective bargaining in the private sector.* Champaign, IL : Industrial Relations Research Association.

Katz, H. C. (1993). The decentralization of collective bargaining: A literature review and comparative analysis. *Industrial and Labor Relations Review, 47*(1), 3–22.

Katz, H. C., & Darbishire, O. (2000). *Converging divergences: Worldwide changes in employment systems.* Ithaca, NY: Cornell University Press.

Kauffman, N. (1992). Expedited arbitration and other innovations in alternative dispute resolution. *Labor Law Journal, 43*(6), 382–87.

Klaas, B., & DeNisi, A. (1989). Managerial reactions to employee dissent: The impact of grievance activity on performance ratings. *Academy of Management Journal, 32*(4), 705–717.

Kleiner, M. (2001). Intensity of management resistance: Understanding the decline of unionization in the private sector. *Journal of Labor Research, 22*(3), 519–540.

Kochan, T. A. (1979). How American workers view labor unions. *Monthly Labor Review, 102*(4), 23–31.

Kochan, T. A. (1980). *Collective bargaining and industrial relations.* Homewood, IL: Irwin.

Kochan, T. A. (1995). Using the Dunlop Report to achieve mutual gains. *Industrial Relations, 34*(3), 350–366.

Kochan, T., & Katz, H. (1988). *Collective bargaining and industrial relations* (2nd ed.). Homewood, IL: Irwin.

Kochan, T. A., Katz, H. C., & McKersie, R. B. (1994). *The transformation of American industrial relations* (2nd ed.). Ithaca, NY: ILR Press.

Kochan, T. A., & Rubinstein, S. (2000). Toward a stakeholder theory of the firm: The Saturn Partnership. *Organization Science, 11*(4), 367–386.

Kolb, D. (1983). *The mediators.* Cambridge, MA: MIT Press.

Korshak, S. (1995). Negotiating trust in the San Francisco hotel industry. *California Management Review, 38*(1), 117.

Levine, D. I., & Bishop, L. (1999). Computer mediated communication as employee voice: A. case study. *Industrial and Labor Relations Review, 52*(2), 213–33.

Lewin, D. (1999). Theoretical and empirical research on the grievance procedure and arbitration: A critical review. In A. E. Eaton and J. H. Keefe (Eds.), *Employment dispute resolution and worker rights* (pp. 137–86). Champaign, IL: Industrial Relations Research Association.

Lewin, D., & Peterson, R. (1988). *The modern grievance procedure in the United States.* New York: Quorum Books.

MacDuffie, J. P. (1995). Human resource bundles and manufacturing performance: Organizational logic and flexible production systems in the world auto industry. *Industrial and Labor Relations Review, 48*(2), 197–222.

Manheim, J. B. (2001). *The death of a thousand cuts. Corporate campaigns and the attack on the corporation.* Mahwah, NJ: Lawrence Erlbaum.

Marshall, R., & Merlo, A. (2004). Pattern bargaining. *International Economic Review, 45*(1), 239–255.

Mishel, L., Bernstein, J., & Allegretto, S. (2005). *The state of working America: 2004–2005.* Ithaca, NY: Cornell University Press.

Nissen, B., & Rosen, S. (1999). Community-based organizing: Transforming union organizing programs from the bottom up. In B. Nissen (Ed.), *Which direction for organized labor? Essays on organizing, outreach, and internal transformations* (pp. 59–73). Detroit, MI: Wayne State University Press.

Ono, H. (2006). *Lifetime employment in Japan: Concepts and measurement* (SSE/EFI Working Paper Series No. 624). Stockholm School of Economics: Author.

Perry, C. R. (1987). *Union corporate campaigns.* Philadelphia: University of Pennsylvania, The Wharton School.

Perry, C. R. (1996). Corporate campaigns in context. *Journal of Labor Research, 17*(3), 329–333.

Putnam, L., & Geist, B. P. (1985). Argumentation in bargaining: An analyses of the reasoning process. *Southern Speech Communication Journal, 50,* 225–245.

Putnam, L., & Jones, T. S. (1982). Reciprocity in negotiation: An analysis of bargaining interaction. *Communization Monographs, 49,* 171–191.

Riddell, C. (2004). Union certification success under voting versus card-check procedures: Evidence from British Columbia, 1978–1998. *Industrial and Labor Relations Review, 57*(4), 493–518.

Rubinstein, S., & Kochan, T. (2001). *Learning from Saturn.* Ithaca, NY: ILR Press.

Sandver, M. H., Blaine, H. R., & Woyar, M. N. (1981). Time and cost savings through expedited arbitration procedures. *The Arbitration Journal, 36*(4), 11–20.

Schelling. T. (1980). *The strategy of conflict.* Cambridge, MA: Harvard University Press.

Simkin, W. E. (1971). *Mediation and the dynamics of collective bargaining.* Washington, DC: BNA.

Streeck, W. (1997). German capitalism: Does it exist? Can it survive? *New Political Economy, 2,* 237–256.

Tate, R. (2004, September 3). Partnership of union, S.F. hotels fraying. *San Francisco Business Times.*

Thomas, M. (2002). *The effect of expedited, tripartite, and conventional arbitration on arbitration outcomes.* Unpublished dissertation, Univeristy of Toronto, Canada.

Traxler, F. (2003). Coordinated bargaining: A stocktaking of its preconditions, practices, and performance. *Industrial Relations Journal, 34*(3), 194–209.

Urbanski, A. (2001). *Reform or be reformed: A new agenda for the teacher unions.* Unpublished manuscript, Hoover Institution.

Ury, W. L., Brett, J. M., & Goldberg, S. B. (1988). *Getting disputes resolved.* San Francisco: Jossey-Bass.

Voos, P. B. (1994). An economic perspective on contemporary trends in collective bargaining. P. B. Voos (Ed.), *Contemporary collective bargaining in the private sector* (pp. 1–24). Madison, WI: Industrial Relations Research Association.

Walton, R. E., Cutcher-Gershenfeld, J., & McKersie, R. B. (1994). *Strategic negotiations: A theory of change in labor management relations.* Boston: Harvard Business School Press.

Walton, R. E., & McKersie, R. B. (1965). *A behavioral theory of labor negotiation.* New York: McGraw-Hill.

Wever, K. (1989). Toward a structural account of union participation in management: The case of Western Airlines. *Industrial and Labor Relations Review, 42*(4), 600–609.

Wolman, L. (1936). *Ebb and flow in trade unionism.* New York: National Bureau of Economic Research.

Working Today. (2006). Retrieved from http://www.workingtoday.org/index.html

13

Social Identification Processes, Conflict, and Fairness Concerns in Intergroup Mergers

DEBORAH J. TERRY
University of Queensland

CATHERINE E. AMIOT
Université du Québec à Montréal

Since the beginning of the 1990s, organizational mergers have been implemented throughout the world with the aim of improving organizations' effectiveness and competitiveness in the global economy (Daly, Pouder, & Kabanoff, 2004). Most organizational changes create stress and job insecurity, but organizational mergers represent a particularly stressful kind of change, given the large-scale nature of this change, as well as the fact that employees must relinquish an identity that was previously important to them (their premerger organization) and shift their allegiance to the newly merged organization (Cartwright & Cooper, 1992; Nadler & Tushman, 1989). To account for the fact that between 60% and 70% of mergers fail to achieve their economic aims (Devoge & Shiraki, 2000; Gunders & Alpert, 2001; KPMG, 2001), commentators have proposed that relying on a strictly economical point of view is unlikely to provide insights into why mergers so often fail. In fact, some researchers have proposed that there is much unexplained variance in predicting why mergers fail or succeed (Hitt, Ireland, & Harrison, 2001), and that human factors need to be taken into consideration to understand what goes on during organizational mergers (Cartwright & Cooper, 1992).

Different psychological approaches have been proposed to understand employees' reactions to organizational mergers (see Seo & Hill, 2005). Studies using a stress-and-coping approach have focused on variables located at the individual level of analysis, such as employees' appraisals of the merger situation and the coping strategies used to deal with it (e.g., Terry & Callan, 1997; Terry, Callan, & Sartori, 1996). The organizational fit approach implicitly recognizes the intergroup dimension of the merger by proposing that the successful integration of both organizations into an overarching, merged entity depends on the degree of fit between the values and the practices endorsed by the management of the two merging organizations (Buono, Bowditch, & Lewis, 1985; Larsson & Lubatkin, 2001). To account for the fact that conflict and rivalries are often observed during mergers, however, and for the processes by which the two merging organizations come to fit together and form one new superordinate group, an intergroup approach is warranted. Because mergers involve the imposition of a new superordinate identity on employees, while also requiring them to let go of their premerger organizational identity, mergers trigger the type of recategorization and social identification processes that are central to intergroup theories (e.g., Anastasio, Bachman, Gaertner, & Dovidio, 1997; Haunschild, Moreland, & Murrell, 1994; Terry, Carey, & Callan, 2001; van Knippenberg, van Knippenberg, Monden, & de Lima, 2002).

To provide an understanding of employee responses to an organizational merger, this chapter outlines an intergoup perspective, based on the social identity approach (Hogg & Abrams, 1988; Hogg & Terry, 2001; Tajfel & Turner, 1979). From this perspective, identification and recategorization processes (Gaertner, Dovidio, Bachman, & Rust, 1993; Hornsey & Hogg, 2000) are key factors that need to be considered in an effort to understand intergroup conflict in response to an organizational merger. These processes also need to be considered longitudinally (Cartwright & Cooper, 1992; Seo & Hill, 2005), as intergroup dynamics are in flux in the context of a merger. Results of three studies are presented. The aims of these studies were to demonstrate that intergroup rivalry and conflict does occur in the context of organizational mergers and that the nature and extent of this conflict can be predicted from a social identity perspective. The second aim of the research was to examine the effects of the beliefs about the sociostructural characteristics of the intergroup relations in the new organization and justice perceptions on employees' adjustment during this change. The third goal of the research was to investigate, in a longitudinal manner, how these social identification and justice processes operate as the merger unfolds. An intergroup perspective has considerable potential to contribute to the current literature on organizational mergers, given that reducing conflict and effectively managing organizational diversity in newly formed superordinate organizations is likely to have considerable benefits for employee well-being and morale, while it also enhances the likelihood that the merger will be successful. A focus on justice complements this approach in accounting for how employees' treatment within the new, merged organization facilitates or hinders their identification with the new, merged organization and, hence, the extent to which they adjust to the change (Tyler & Blader, 2003).

SOCIAL IDENTITY THEORY

Social identity theory (SIT; Tajfel & Turner, 1979, 1986; Turner, 1982; see also Hogg & Abrams, 1988) is a general social psychological theory of group processes and intergroup relations that addresses the social component of the self-concept, which is referred to as "social identity." By accounting for the intergroup dynamics and the antagonistic motives of the groups involved, SIT is particularly useful for understanding the intergroup competition and rivalry that emerge in mergers. Social identity—the part of the individual self-concept that derives from memberships in social groups—is a fundamental psychological variable that shapes individuals' attitudes and behaviors. Organizational identity represents an important basis for self-definition (Hogg & Terry, 2001). It has been proposed that two underlying sociocognitive processes account for group and intergroup phenomena: (a) social categorization and (b) self-enhancement. Based on categorization principles, when people define or categorize themselves as members of a self-inclusive social group (e.g., an organization), distinctions between in-group and out-group members are accentuated, and differences among in-group members are minimized (Turner, Hogg, Oakes, Reicher, & Wetherell, 1987). Self-enhancement reflects the fact that because the self is defined in terms of the group membership, people are motivated to favor their in-group over the out-group. This self-enhancement motive means that group members are motivated to acquire or to maintain a positive social identity for their in-group (Tajfel & Turner, 1979). Thus, to the extent that one's in-group is perceived as better than the out-group, the quality of a person's social identity is enhanced and becomes more positive (e.g., Amiot & Bourhis, 2005).

Central to SIT is the premise that because people are motivated to enhance their feelings of self-worth, they seek to belong to groups that compare favorably with other groups (Tajfel, 1974, 1975; Tajfel & Turner, 1979). Membership in low-status groups—groups that compare unfavorably to other groups—is unlikely to provide the basis for positive social identity. The desire for a positive social identity means that while low-status group members are motivated to acquire a more positive social identity, high-status group members are motivated to maintain both their membership in the group and the existence of the social category. These behaviors are motivated by the desire to maintain or enhance the positive contribution that the identity makes to their self-concept (Ellemers, Doosje, van Knippenberg, & Wilke, 1992; van Knippenberg, 1978; see also Zuckerman, 1979).

Laboratory studies have shown that participants assigned to a high-status group (a) show pride in their group, (b) identify strongly with the group, and (c) seek to maintain their group membership (Ellemers, van Knippenberg, de Vries, & Wilke, 1988; Ellemers, van Knippenberg, & Wilke, 1990; Sachdev & Bourhis, 1987, 1991). Similar findings have been reported in field research (Brown, Condor, Mathews, Wade, & Williams, 1986). In contrast, there is evidence that memberships in low-status groups have a negative impact on strength of identification (Ellemers et al., 1990; Ellemers, Wilke, & van Knippenberg, 1993) and self-esteem (Brown & Lohr, 1987), and that members seek to disassociate themselves from such groups (Ellemers et al., 1988).

Status Differentials and Identity-Management Strategies

Like many other intergroup contexts, mergers often involve organizations that differ in status (van Oudenhoven & de Boer, 1995); that is, one organization is likely to be more productive, resourceful, and competitive in comparison with the other (see also Terry & Callan, 1998; Terry & O'Brien, 2001; Terry et al., 2001). Whereas much of the extant work on intergroup relations in organizations assumes symmetrical relations between groups, relations between nested social groups in superordinate organizational structures (such as premerger organizations in a merged organization) and those that involve groups and social categories that extend outside the organization's boundaries are likely to differ markedly in terms of status and power.

According to SIT, members of low-status groups can use a number of strategies to improve or enhance their social identity (Hogg & Abrams, 1988; Tajfel & Turner, 1979; van Knippenberg & Ellemers, 1993). Low-status group members may engage in individual mobility. The use of this strategy reflects efforts to seek membership in a relevant high-status comparison group. This strategy is particularly likely to become relevant for low-status group members involved in a merger. Because mergers destabilize the intergroup structure and involve the creation of a new, more inclusive, superordinate organization, this new structure creates the potential to allow low-status group members to "pass" and to join a higher status group. In line with SIT, it will be possible for low-status group members to use these efforts only if the previously existent boundaries between the premerger organizational groups are open.

In contrast to this individualistic response, low-status group members may engage in group-oriented or collective strategies, which by definition are more conflictual. Social competition is one such response; it involves direct strategies to address the negative standing of the group, and to reverse the status differential that separates low- and high-status groups. Social creativity is a second collective-oriented strategy; it is a cognitive response and involves making intergroup comparisons that favor the in-group (also referred to as "in-group bias" and "in-group favoritism"). The aim of this strategy is to positively reevaluate the in-group (Hogg & Abrams, 1988). To achieve this aim, intergroup comparisons may be made on new dimensions, a modification of values assigned to comparative dimensions, or the selection of a different comparison group (Hogg & Abrams, 1988; Lalonde, 1992).

Some evidence proves that members of low-status groups engage in more in-group bias than members of high-status groups (see Brewer, 1979; cf. Hinkle & Brown, 1990; Sachdev & Bourhis, 1987, 1991), a pattern of results that is consistent with Tajfel's (1974) expectation that group differentiation is most marked when the classification is particularly salient, or in other words, personally relevant to group members. The status relevance of the dimensions or attributes on which in-group and out-group members can be judged, however, must be taken into account when making predictions concerning the effects of group status on in-group bias (see Mullen, Brown, & Smith, 1992). As previously noted, low-status group members may attain a positively valued group distinctiveness through the use of social creativity in their intergroup comparisons. One way in which this may be achieved involves the pursuit of positive in-group differentiation on dimensions that do not form the basis for the status hierarchy, or which are only peripherally related to this hierarchy. Because the status-defining and status-relevant dimensions cannot be ignored (Lalonde, 1992), members of a low-status group may well acknowledge their relative inferior status on the status-relevant dimensions. On the status-irrelevant dimensions—that is, on those not directly related to the basis for the status hierarchy—however, members of low-status groups should show positive differentiation.

In contrast to members of low-status groups, high-status group members should show in-group bias on the status-defining dimensions (Mullen et al., 1992). This is because to do so serves to verify their dominant position in the intergroup context. Thus, among high-status group members, in-group bias should be more marked on status-relevant than status-irrelevant dimensions. In fact, on the latter type of dimension, a "magnanimous" out-group bias or "reverse discrimination" effect may be evident (Mullen et al., 1992). In other words, high-status group members may be willing to acknowledge that the out-group is better than the in-group on dimensions that are clearly irrelevant to the basis for the status differentiation (see also Sachdev & Bourhis, 1987; Turner & Brown, 1978).

In-Group Bias During Organizational Mergers

The very nature of an organizational merger challenges employees' organizational identity, which serves not only to heighten the salience of the identity, but also increase the likelihood of antagonistic and conflictual intergroup perceptions and behaviors. In fact, the merger situation implies a direct confrontation between the two organizations as they both strive to optimize their own position in the new organization. The heightened salience of employees' premerger group memberships in the context of a merger is likely to mean that there is an accentuation of intergroup status differences (see Mullen et al., 1992). This accentuation of differences directly confronts members of the low-status group with the reality of their disadvantaged position in the new intergroup structure. A merger of unequal status groups can also imply that the higher status premerging organization will seek to assimilate the lower status organization and impose its own premerger identity on the new, merged organization. Doing so should directly threaten the survival of the low-status group's identity within the new, merged organization (see van Knippenberg et al., 2002; van Leeuwen, van Knippenberg, & Ellemers, 2003). Thus, low-status group members should be particularly threatened by the merger situation and, for this reason, can be expected to engage in high levels of in-group bias, particularly on the dimensions that are not central to the status differentiation. In contrast, levels of threat are likely to be lower for the employees of the high-status organization in comparison with the low-status employees. In an effort to verify their superior status in an unstable intergroup context, however, these employees are likely to engage in more in-group bias than the low-status employees on dimensions that are central to the basis for the status differential.

For both the low-status and high-status employees, levels of threat associated with the merger should be positively related to in-group bias. Among members of the low-status organization, high levels of threat are likely to be associated with efforts to attain a positive social identity through in-group bias on status-irrelevant dimensions. A similar effect— on the status-relevant, rather than the status-irrelevant, dimensions— should be evident for the members of the high-status organization. The more threatened high-status employees are about the merger situation, the more they should be motivated to reassert their superiority on status-relevant dimensions, an expectation that is predicated on the basis that a threatening intergroup context is likely to engender identity protection strategies among high-status group members (Tajfel, 1975; van Knippenberg & Ellemers, 1993).

EVIDENCE OF THREAT AND IN-GROUP BIAS DURING AN INTERGROUP MERGER

In a study of an organizational merger, Terry and Callan (1998) examined the interplay among premerger organizational status, perceived threat associated with the merger, and in-group bias. Data were collected from 1104 employees of two hospitals—a high-status metropolitan teaching hospital and a relatively low-status local area hospital. To assess in-group bias, participants indicated the extent to which they agreed that each of the two organizations (their own premerger organization and the other organization) could be described as possessing eight different characteristics. Preliminary discussions with healthcare workers indicated that three of the dimensions were status-relevant: (a) high prestige in the community, (b) challenging job opportunities, and (c) high variety in patient type. In general, the other five dimensions were regarded as being peripheral to the basis of the status differential between hospitals. These dimensions included (a) little industrial unrest, (b) good relations between staff, (c) good communication by management, (d) relaxed work environment, and (e) modern patient accommodation.

It was proposed that the employees of the low-status hospital would, overall, engage in more in-group bias than the employees of the high-status hospital, particularly on the status-irrelevant dimensions. On the status-relevant dimensions, it was expected that the employees of the high-status hospital would engage in more in-group bias than the employees of the low-status hospital. As expected, employees of the low-status hospital did engage in more in-group bias, overall, than the employees of the high-status hospital. This result was qualified by a significant interaction between status and the type of dimension (status-relevant or irrelevant). As shown in Figure 13.1, in-group bias among the low-status employees was evident only on the status-irrelevant dimensions. In contrast, on the status-relevant dimensions, they acknowledged the superiority of the high-status hospital. The opposite pattern of results was obtained for the

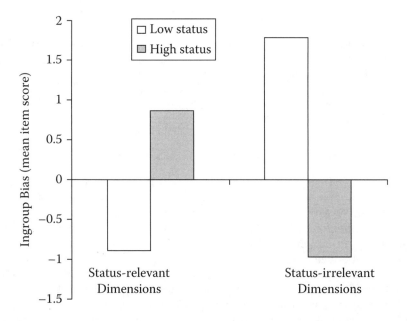

FIGURE 13.1. In-group bias on the status-relevant and status-irrelevant dimensions for employees of the low-status and high-status organizations.

high-status employees. Among these employees, there was evidence of in-group bias on the status-relevant dimensions and bias in favor of the out-group on the status-irrelevant dimensions.

As expected, employees from the low-status organization appraised the merger as more threatening than the employees of the high-status organization. Moreover, there was evidence, in line with predictions, of a positive relationship between appraised stress and intergroup differentiation on the status-irrelevant dimensions among the employees of the low-status organization, but not for the high-status employees. Thus, the more the employees of the low-status organization were threatened by the merger, the more likely they were to engage in in-group bias on the status-irrelevant dimensions. Contrary to expectations, the status-by-threat interactions were nonsignificant in the prediction of differentiation on the status-relevant dimensions.

The fact that low-status group members displayed more evidence of both threat and in-group bias could be due to the heightened salience of their relatively inferior status in the context of the merger. In such a context, they may have been particularly motivated to differentiate themselves positively from the employees of the other organization. This pattern of results accords with the social identity perspective, as does the finding that organizational status interacted with type of dimension on which the two organizations were rated. For the high-status employees, there was a tendency to rate the in-group as better than the out-group on the status-relevant dimensions, whereas the low-status employees engaged in in-group bias on the status-irrelevant dimensions. These results presumably reflected the motivation of the employees of the high-status organization to affirm their position of relative superiority in the new organization. In contrast, the low-status employees—presumably motivated by a desire to attain positive social identity—exhibited in-group bias on the dimensions not centrally relevant to the basis for the status differences among hospitals.

STATUS, LEGITIMACY, AND EMPLOYEE RESPONSES TO A MERGER

From an SIT point of view, mergers are fundamentally unstable intergroup situations. Mergers (a) create instability in the intergroup structure as they involve the recategorization of different organizational groups into one superordinate entity, (b) weaken the boundaries between the premerger organizations, and, at least to a certain extent, (c) increase the permeability between these previously distinct premerger organizations. In addition to considering the role of group status on in-group bias, subjective beliefs concerning the intergroup context are, according to SIT, critical to an understanding of intergroup relations. According to Tajfel (1974, 1975), the extent to which group members perceive their status position to be legitimately attained is an important sociostructural belief that should be an important determinant of group members' identity–management strategies. Specifically, high-status group members who perceive their current status position to be legitimate—that is, as a deserved outcome of a just procedure—are likely to react to the threat of a merger more negatively than those who view their status position as less legitimate. Dominant group members who feel that their status position is legitimate are likely to react more negatively to the possibility that the intergroup status relations may change as a consequence of the merger. This is presumably because they believe their superior status position to be deserved and that they are motivated to maintain the status distinctions between the groups (see Tajfel & Turner, 1979).

In contrast, low-status group members who perceive their status position to be a legitimate outcome of a just procedure are likely to be more accepting of a merger situation than those who perceive that it is an illegitimate reflection of the group's relative standing. The perception that their low-status position is legitimate is undesirable, and hence employees who feel this way are likely to react more positively to the merger because of the possibility that the situation may facilitate individual mobility attempts. The instability brought about by the merger is thus likely to be welcomed by these low-status group members, who are motivated to deal with their inferior status and opened to the possibilities of social mobility. On the other hand, the perception of an illegitimately low status position may engender the behavior and responses that are more typically observed in members of high-status groups. In other words, an illegitimately low group status is likely to give rise to mutual solidarity (e.g., strong in-group identification) and hence a negative reaction to the threat of an organizational merger.

Research has shown that members of groups perceiving an illegitimately low status position do display behavior that is usually observed among high-status group members, such as relatively strong in-group identification and in-group-favoring discrimination in reward allocation (Ellemers et al., 1993, Turner & Brown, 1978). There is also evidence that low-status group members are more likely to engage in collective status improvement when the situation is perceived to be illegitimate, whereas individual action (e.g., social mobility) is more likely when the status differential is perceived to be legitimate. Thus, there is some support for the proposal that low-status group members who perceive their status position to be a legitimate outcome of a just procedure are likely to be more accepting of a merger situation than those who perceive that it is an illegitimate reflection of the group's relative standing. In contrast, little empirical attention has focused on the effects of perceptions of legitimacy on the intergroup behavior and responses of members of high-status groups; however, Turner and Brown (1978) did find that members of high-status groups were most biased toward low-status groups when the status hierarchy was perceived to be unstable (which is relevant to an organizational merger) but legitimate.

To examine the interplay between relative group status and judgments about the legitimacy of the group's status position in the unstable context of an organizational merger, a study of the merger between two previously independent scientific organizations—(a) one of relatively high status, in terms of research performance, budget, and viability, and (b) one of relatively low status—was undertaken (Terry & O'Brien, 2001). First, it was proposed, once again, that members of the low-status group would show the most negative responses to the merger. Both individual outcomes (perceived threat and job satisfaction) and group-related outcomes (identification with the merged organization, common in-group identity, and intergroup anxiety) were assessed. Second, it was proposed that the employees of the low-status group would exhibit higher levels of in-group bias on dimensions not directly relevant to the basis for the status differentiation (e.g., administrative efficiency, good communication skills, professional attitudes) than the employees of the high-status organization would, but that employees of the high-status group would exhibit the most in-group bias on the status-relevant dimensions (e.g., scientific excellence, scientific diversity, project accountability). Third, it was proposed that the effects of premerger group status would be moderated by employees' perceptions of the legitimacy of the status differential between the two groups. Specifically, it was anticipated that for members of the low-status premerger group, high levels of perceived legitimacy would be related to low levels of status-irrelevant in-group bias, and more positive responses to the merger, whereas the opposite was proposed for the high-status employees—for these employees, it was anticipated that high levels of legitimacy would be associated with high levels of status-relevant in-group bias, and more negative responses to the merger.

Respondents were 120 employees of the merged organization, who ranged in age from 20 to 64 years old. The sample comprised approximately equal numbers of employees from the two premerger organizations. As expected, participants from the high-status premerger organization identified more strongly with the new organization than the employees of the low-status organization. Employees of the low-status premerger organization were also less likely to perceive a common in-group identity than employees of the high-status premerger organization, and they appraised the merger as more threatening. There was also a weak tendency for employees of the high-status organization to be more satisfied with their job than the employees of the low-status organization.

Thus, this second study replicated the finding that, overall, the employees of the low-status premerger organization are likely to react most negatively to the merger situation. There was also clear evidence of in-group bias among both groups of employees involved in the merger. Moreover, the pattern of in-group bias accorded with the predictions derived from SIT, as did the observed relations between perceived threat and in-group bias. Also, in support of SIT, the perceived legitimacy of the basis for the status differentiation between the groups was associated with more positive responses to the merger among employees of the low-status premerger organization, but with poorer responses among employees of the high-status premerger organization.

As in the Terry and Callan (1998) study, in-group bias varied as a function of whether or not the dimension was central to the basis of the status differentiation (status-relevant) between scientific organizations or more peripheral (status-irrelevant). In-group bias among the low-status employees was more marked on the status-irrelevant dimensions than on the status-relevant dimensions, whereas the opposite pattern of results was evident for the high-status employees. It was expected that threat would relate to differentiation on the status-relevant dimensions for the high-status employees and to differentiation on the status-irrelevant dimensions for the low-status employees. In line with predictions, the positive relationship between perceived threat and in-group bias on the status-relevant dimensions was significant for the employees of the high-status organization, but not for the low-status employees. In contrast, perceived threat was positively related to in-group bias on the status-irrelevant dimensions for the employees of the low-status premerger organization, but not for employees of the high-status organization.

As expected, there was consistent evidence—on a range of empirically distinct measures of employee responses to an organizational merger—that the effect of premerger organizational status was moderated by the perceived legitimacy of the status differentiation in the new organization. There were significant status-by-legitimacy interactions on each of the measures of employee responses to the merger, but not on the measures of in-group bias. In accord with SIT, the perception that the basis for the status differentiation was legitimate was associated with positive responses to the merger (in terms of scores on the measures of identification, common in-group identity, job satisfaction, and weakly, on the measure of threat) among the employees of the low-status organization, but with negative responses to the merger among the employees of the high-status group. This result was evident on in-group anxiety, common in-group identity, and perceived threat (the latter two results were relatively weak).

The consistent link between perceptions of legitimacy and acceptance of the merger among the employees of the low-status premerger organization accords with previous research (e.g., Ellemers et al., 1993; Turner & Brown, 1978). Because the perception of an illegitimately low group status is likely to give rise to mutual solidarity and collective (rather than individual) attempts to change the status quo, it should be associated with low acceptance of the merger. In contrast, the perception that a low-status position accurately reflects the group's lack of capacities (Ellemers et al., 1993) is likely to give rise to acceptance of the new organizational structure, given that it may offer options for individual mobility. For the high-status premerger group, the observed results are consistent with the expectation that dominant group members who feel that their status position is legitimate are likely to react in a negative manner to the possibility that the intergroup status relations may change. This reaction presumably occurs because they believe their superior status position to be deserved (Tajfel & Turner, 1979; see also Turner & Brown, 1978). It is not surprising that the evidence linking perceptions of legitimacy to responses to the merger among the employees of the high-status organization was relatively weak. Given that the threat associated with the merger was most marked for members of the low-status group, their responses to the situation are, hence, particularly likely to be influenced by perceptions of the sociostructural characteristics of the intergroup context.

INTERGROUP DYNAMICS OVER TIME

The Terry and Callan (1998) and Terry and O'Brien (2001) studies revealed that the instability brought about by the merger situation evoked different reactions from low- versus high-status group members; however, the experience of low- versus high-status group members over time, as the merger progressed, must also be considered. While very little longitudinal research has investigated the intergroup processes occurring in mergers over time (cf. Terry, 2003), low- versus high-status groups' motives throughout the merger are likely to change as the merger evolves. In fact, in the unstable context of a merger, members of a low-status group, who are attuned and motivated to improve their social identity, are likely to respond more favorably to the conditions of increased permeability brought about by the merger, because for them, permeability facilitates social mobility—or "passing'—into a higher status group (Tajfel & Turner, 1979; Terry et al., 2001). This *enhancement* motive among members of the low-status group is likely to be especially salient at the beginning of the merger, when perceptions of permeability and the associated opportunities provide them with an optimistic outlook on the merger (Tajfel & Turner, 1986). Whether low-status group members' initial positive reactions to the merger can be sustained throughout the merger depends in part on how much opportunities and possibilities will be concretely available to them as the merger proceeds. The tendency for low-status group members to focus on the use of social mobility at the beginning of the merger is also supported by propositions of the five-stage model of intergroup relations (Taylor & McKirnan, 1984; for empirical evidence, see Wright, Taylor, & Moghaddam, 1990). According to this model, because of the individualistic bias of our Western societies, social mobility strategies—as individual strategies—are favored as an identity-enhancement strategy and likely to be tried first. In contrast, collective or group-oriented attempts to change the intergroup situation will be used by disadvantaged groups as a later resort, only if social mobility attempts have failed and intergroup boundaries are found to be impermeable.

The unstable situation brought about by the merger, however, is likely to elicit different reactions from members of the high-status group. Because high-status group members are motivated to maintain their superiority, this instable intergroup situation involves a direct threat to the status quo and compromises their advantaged position. Becoming associated with a lower status group (e.g., the low-status merging partner) also carries the threat of having their social identity "dragged-down" by this lower status group (e.g., Hornsey, van Leeuwen, & van Santen, 2003). Because high-status group members' premerger organizational identity is likely to be quite positive (Sachdev & Bourhis, 1987), issues of identity loss inherent in mergers should be particularly strong for members of the high-status group at the beginning of the merger (Seo & Hill, 2005). High-status group members' motives for identity *maintenance* should, therefore, be particularly salient at the beginning of the merger, when feelings of novelty and uncertainty are at their peak, and they have not yet had the opportunity to assert their superiority in the new intergroup structure (e.g., Mullen et al., 1992). As the merger proceeds, and to the extent that members of the high-status group can assert their advantageous position within the new, merged group, these negative responses and feelings of threat should dissipate (Tajfel & Turner, 1986; see also Datta, Pinches, & Narayanan, 1992, and Marks & Mirvis, 1998, for discussions and evidence specific to mergers).

JUSTICE CONCERNS AND IDENTIFICATION PROCESSES

Perceptions of fairness in the merging process are also likely to be a crucial factor influencing employees' adjustment to an intergroup merger as they represent employees' beliefs about how resources and outcomes are redistributed within this new organizational entity (distributive justice), how new procedures and rules are implemented, and how employees are treated and respected within the new, merged organization (procedural justice). Research conducted during periods of organizational change has shown that when workers see themselves as being treated fairly, they are more likely to develop attitudes and behaviors in support of change (Cobb, Wooten, & Folger, 1995; Folger & Cropanzano, 1998). Furthermore, both distributive and procedural justice have been found to be important in predicting adjustment to mergers (e.g., Citera & Stuhlmacher, 2001; Cobb et al, 1995; Greenberg & Folger, 1983; Lipponen, Olkkonen, & Moilanen, 2004; Meyer, 2001).

According to Kabanoff (1991), perceptions of equity, which tap into principles of distributive justice, are crucial during mergers. Specifically, Kabanoff argued that equity should be the chief distribution principle when economic productivity is the goal and when the organizations involved differ in status. Meyer (2001) further proposed that procedural and distributive justice are not completely independent in the context of mergers. For example, equity can be used as the distribution mode when reallocating outcomes within the new, merged organization, but this can be done by ensuring that fair procedures are used and that organizational members are treated respectfully. Because equity promotes productivity, without consideration for the relationships between group members, it is important to complement this distribution mode by the use of fair and respectful procedural rules and treatment (Meyer, 2001). Combining equity with a respectful treatment of organizational members appears particularly important in the context of a merger, where relationships between members of different premerger organizations are in the process of being built (Lind & Tyler, 1988; Tyler & Blader, 2003).

In order to account for how justice concerns and social identification processes are interrelated, Tyler and Blader (2003) proposed the group engagement model (GEM). According to this model, procedures and practices within a group shape group members' degree of attachment to this group (e.g., their degree of social identity), which in turn influences their behaviors, attitudes, and values. Perceived fairness is important because it conveys identity-relevant information about the quality of one's relationships with the rest of the group. Fair procedures and treatment indicate a positive, respectful position within the group and promote pride in the group membership (see Lipponen et al., 2004; and Tyler & de Cremer, 2005, for evidence supporting these propositions during organizational mergers).

SIT and superordinate identification models (Gaertner et al., 1993; Hornsey & Hogg, 2000) concur with the GEM in considering social identification as a crucial mediating process linking characteristics of the social context (such as fairness) to intraindividual and intergroup outcomes. According to Tajfel and Turner (1979), group cognitions play a central mediating role in the relationships between group members' perceptions of the intergroup situation and different outcomes (e.g., in-group bias). Self-categorizing as a member of the new, merged organization implies that group members can relate to this new, superordinate organizational identity and that it has now become part of who they are. In their common in-group identity model, Gaertner et al. (1993) further proposed that when group members recategorize as members of the new, merged group and perceive that this group represents one rather than two distinct groups, positive intergroup and affective consequences follow. Various studies (e.g., Dovidio, Gaertner, & Validzic, 1998; Gaertner, Dovidio, & Bachman, 1996; Gaertner et al., 1993, 2000) found that identifying with a new superordinate group and perceiving the new group as inclusive of the preexisting groups mediate the relationships between the intergroup context (e.g., intergroup contact), and both in-group bias and adjustment.

A LONGITUDINAL INVESTIGATION OF STATUS, FAIRNESS, AND IDENTIFICATION OVER THE COURSE OF A MERGER

In an effort to capture the longitudinal processes involved throughout a merger, the adjustment patterns displayed by pilots involved in a merger between two airline companies were investigated over a two-year period (Amiot, Terry, & Callan, 2007). The merger involved a higher status organization (a former international carrier) and one of lower status (a domestic carrier). The merger was initiated by a government decision. When implemented, the merger followed an absorb integration pattern (Mottola, Bachman, Gaertner, & Dovidio, 1997). That is, the domestic airline was formally acquired by the international carrier, and the merged airline retained the name and many defining features of the former international carrier (see Rosson & Brooks, 2004). The acquired organization was therefore assimilated into the acquiring organization. Furthermore, the merger was implemented such that the premerger status structure was largely retained to the extent that members of the premerger organizations remained segregated and distinct in their work tasks. In fact, two years into the merger, low-status group members reported finding it more difficult to become involved in the activities and work previously done by members of the other premerger organization in comparison with members of the higher status group.

It was first hypothesized that members of the low-status group would show poorer adjustment to the merger than members of the high-status group, both in terms of perceived fairness, individual outcomes (e.g., perceived threat, job satisfaction), and group-related outcomes (e.g., in-group bias, identification with the new, merged organization). Second, it was hypothesized that patterns of adjustment would follow different routes over time for members of the low- and high-status groups (e.g., Taylor & McKirnan, 1984). More specifically, as members of the low-status group are likely to realize the implications of the merger (e.g., less permeability and social mobility than first expected, opportunities failing to materialize) and as their disadvantaged positions within the new, merged organization consolidates, their adjustment to the merger (in terms of perceived threat and job satisfaction) was expected to decline over time. Inversely, as members of the high-status group realize that the instability brought about by the merger does not threaten their advantaged positions and as their superior positions within the new, merged group can be confirmed, their adjustment to the merger should increase over time. Third, based on empirical and theoretical propositions which have stressed the role of recategorization and superordinate identification in the process of adjusting to a merger, it was expected that identification with the new, merged organization would mediate the associations between conditions of implementation (e.g., perceptions of fairness) and adjustment to the merger (e.g., in-group bias, changes in job satisfaction and in threat; see Figure 13.2).

The present analyses focus on data collected among 215 participants who completed both questionnaires. Time 1 data were collected three months after the implementation of the major changes associated with the merger, whereas the Time 2 data (collected two years later) were collected soon after the merger agreement had been formalized. The 215 participants did not differ from those who had completed only either the Time 1 (N = 662) or the Time 2 (N = 465) questionnaire. The sample consisted of 154 long-haul fleet staff (former employees of the international carrier) and 61 short-haul fleet staff (former employees of the domestic airline). Participants were employed across the full range of ranks of pilots in the

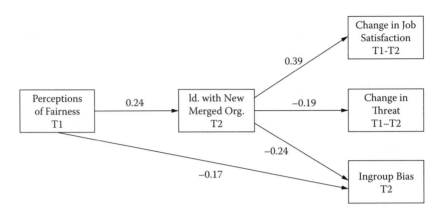

FIGURE 13.2. Test of the hypothesized model among the entire sample (*N* = 215).

organization, while a minority were flight engineers, and ages ranged from 24 to 58 (*M* = 39 years old).

While the first questionnaire included measures of perceived fairness, threat, and job satisfaction, the second questionnaire again assessed perceived status, threat, and job satisfaction, but also included measures of in-group bias, identification with the new, merged organization, and identification with the premerger organization. The perceived fairness measure included items that tapped into both distributive justice (e.g., "How equitably has the merger been implemented?") and procedural justice (e.g., "To what extent (if any) do you feel that your premerger company has been disadvantaged in the merger?"). To assess perceived threat, participants were asked to rate the merger, compared with other stressful situations they had experienced on different dimensions (e.g., stressful, disruptive, difficult). To assess in-group bias, participants indicated the extent to which they agreed that each of the two premerger organizations (their own premerger organization and the other organization) could be described as having eight different characteristics (e.g., technical expertise, friendly attitude, professional attitudes). In this study, a global in-group bias score was obtained by averaging the difference scores (in-group rating minus out-group rating) obtained for each item. While strength of identification with the new, merged organization was assessed using items tapping into this new identity (e.g., "How much do you identify with the new, merged organization?"), identification with their premerger organization was also assessed (e.g., "How much do you see yourself belonging to your premerger organization?"). Finally, job satisfaction was assessed using items such as "All things considered, how satisfied are you with your job?" Threat and job satisfaction were measured at both Times 1 and 2, and a residualized change score (Cronbach & Furby, 1970) was created so as to tap into group members' changes in these two variables over time.

First, participants agreed on the respective status position of their pre-merger organization, such that employees in the premerger, high-status (international carrier) organization rated their own premerger organization as being relatively higher in status than employees from the lower status premerger organization (domestic airline). In line with predictions, the employees of the low-status premerger organization reported poorer adjustment to the merger in comparison with high-status group members. In fact, in comparison with high-status group members, low-status group members reported lower perceptions of fairness at the very beginning of the merger (i.e., Time 1). This finding is in line with SIT, according to which members of the low-status group can become particularly aware of the injustice and the illegitimacy of their disadvantaged position within the intergroup structure when they perceive some alternatives to this situation and that their position can be improved (Tajfel & Turner, 1986; see also Platow, Wenzel, & Nolan, 2003). This might have been particularly the case at the beginning of the merger, when members of the low-status group appeared more optimistic about the opportunities offered by the merger and the intergroup structure was unstable.

Then, once the merger was implemented (e.g., two years after the begin-ning of the merging process), members of the low-status group reported lower identification with both the new, merged organization and with their premerger organization, as well as more in-group bias in comparison with members of the high-status group. The findings regarding in-group bias corroborated those from the Terry and Callan (1998) study, in reveal-ing more overall in-group bias among members of the low-status group, and also concurred with theoretical propositions made by SIT, according to which group differentiation is most marked when the social categories are particularly salient or personally relevant to group members (Tajfel, 1974). In the context of the present study, where, at Time 2, possibilities for improvement and access to new opportunities were somewhat deceiving, manifesting more in-group bias might have represented one social com-petition strategy used by low-status group members to achieve a more positive and distinct social identity. The findings concerning the identi-fication measures are in accord with SIT in that they show that an infe-rior group membership—a comparison that is likely to be heightened in a merger situation—has a negative impact on a person's social identity (e.g., Brown et al., 1986; Ellemers et al., 1993; Sachdev & Bourhis, 1987, 1991). These findings also replicated those obtained in Terry and O'Brien (2001), which revealed lower identification with the new, merged organization among members of the low-status group.

Despite these main effects of premerger organization status, and as expected, low- versus high-status group members' adjustment to the merger (on the measures of threat and job satisfaction) followed differ-ent patterns from the very beginning of the merger up to two years later. As can be seen in Figure 13.3 and Figure 13.4, members of the low-status group reported a lower level of adjustment to the merger over time (in

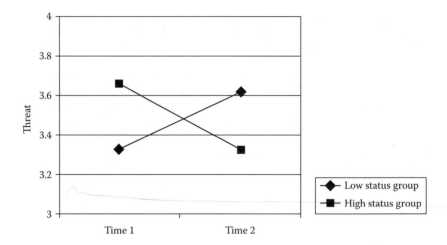

FIGURE 13.3. Mean change over time in threat among members of the low- and high-status groups.

terms of their job satisfaction more specifically), whereas members of the high-status group reported an increase in their levels of job satisfaction and a decrease in their perceptions of threat. These findings are important not only because they provide a longitudinal proof that low- versus high-group members' patterns of adjustment follow different routes throughout the merger, but they also suggest that specific motivational processes (enhancement vs. protection motives) may be involved as low- versus

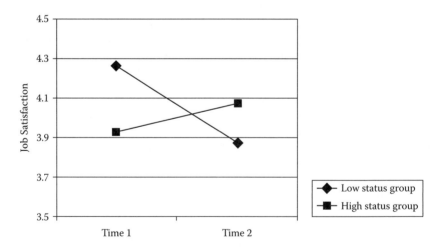

FIGURE 13.4. Mean change over time in job satisfaction among members of the low- and high-status group.

high-group members experience an organizational merger and realize the implications this change has for them as members of a specific pre-merger organization.

In fact, for members of the low-status group, the unstable context of the merger can be initially perceived as offering a certain amount of permeability and the opportunity to join a higher status group. These perceptions of permeability and social mobility might have been especially operative at the beginning of the merger, when members of the low-status group were eager to see the opportunities offered through the merger and that opportunities for "passing" were still salient. These propositions are also in line with the five-stage model of intergroup relations, which proposed that members of the low-status group should prioritize the use of social mobility (over collective strategies) as a means to improve their statuses, especially if intergroup boundaries are perceived to be permeable (Taylor & McKirnan, 1984). However, with time, members of the low-status group showed a *decrease* in their adjustment to the merger. Because the present merger was characterized by assimilation of the low-status group into the high-status group (Mottola et al., 1997), and because at Time 2, members of the low-status group came to perceive that it was difficult to have access to new opportunities, low-status group members may have come to realize, with time, that the occasions for passing and for improving their positions within the new intergroup structure were deceiving, and that the new, merged organization was in fact more representative of the higher status group. These characteristics and implications of the merger, which became clearer and more established over time, could explain why low-status group members' adjustment decreased throughout the merger.

Conversely, and as expected, members of the high-status group reported an *increase* in their adjustment to the merger over time. Whereas members of the high-status group started off the merging process by being relatively defensive, their adjustment improved throughout the merger. This pattern of findings could be explained by the fact that for members of the high-status group, the merger carried the threat of having their social identity "dragged down" by associating with a lower status group (Hornsey et al., 2003). This identity maintenance motive could have been especially prominent at the beginning of the merger, as the instability, novelty, and uncertainty of the merger was salient and likely to threaten the status quo (Seo & Hill, 2005), and when members of the high-status group did not yet have the opportunity to assert their superiority in the new intergroup structure. Yet, as the merger proceeded, and because the high-status group did come to have opportunities to assert their advantageous position within the new, merged group (i.e., the merger was characterized by assimilation and by the perpetuation of the original status differentials), these negative responses and feelings of threat decreased. These findings differed somewhat from the Terry and Callan (1998) and Terry and O'Brien (2001) studies, which found main effects for premerger status (e.g., higher threat and lower job satisfaction among members of the low- than of the high-status group). The present findings allow us to qualify and to bring more nuances to the effect that premerger organizational status has over time. Nevertheless, future research is needed to directly assess if changes in the proposed psychological processes (e.g., permeability, social mobility, perceptions of opportunities) were paralleling and underpinning the changes observed in group members' adjustment to the merger over time.

As expected, results of the path analyses conducted to test the hypothesized model (Figure 13.4) clearly showed that perceptions of fairness at Time 1 predicted an increased identification with the new, merged organization two years later (at Time 2). This identification, in turn, predicted lower in-group bias, as well as a decrease in feelings of threat and an increase in job satisfaction over time. Tests of mediation also revealed that identification with the new, merged organization was a significant mediator in the associations between perceptions of fairness and adjustment outcomes. Moderation tests further revealed that the associations of the model did not differ significantly across premerger organizations. While the model tested allows us to test the processes operating over a two-year period, these findings also allowed us to uncover the processes leading to the prediction of both intrapersonal (e.g., changes in threat and in job satisfaction) and intergroup (e.g., in-group bias) outcomes.

Changes in Social Identity and Integration of New Identities Into the Self

Despite the longitudinal contribution of this research, future research needs to directly investigate changes in social identities throughout a merger. A growing number of studies provided support for the presence of variations occurring in group members' social identities over time (e.g., Ethier & Deaux, 1994; Jetten, O'Brien, & Trindall, 2002). However, the exact processes by which group members come to increase their identification with the new, merged organization need to be examined.

Recently, we have proposed a model to account for the developmental processes whereby group members integrate novel social identities and resolve the conflicts likely to emerge between these identities within the self (Amiot, de la Sablonnière, Terry, & Smith, 2006). Theoretically, the situational, short-term changes in social identities have been accounted for by self-categorization theory (Turner et al., 1987). However, the longer term processes whereby social identities become a recurrent part of the self and by which conflicts between different social identities are reconciled within the self remain to be examined (for evidence of identity clashes during mergers, see Larsson & Lubatkin, 2001). Based on developmental theories (e.g., Harter, 1999, 2003; Mascolo & Fischer, 1998) that have proposed specific stages through which the self becomes increasingly complex over time, we have proposed three stages of social identity development and integration, which we believe could apply to the context of intergroup mergers.

The categorization stage takes place when group members are confronted with the existence of a new social group. Based on the categorization and distinctiveness principles proposed by SIT, at this stage, old and new social identities should be highly distinct and identification with the new social group is not yet possible. For instance, in the first stages of the merging process, an employee's premerger organizational identity is likely to be the only relevant and salient identity, and identification with the newly merged superordinate organization is not yet possible given the lack of exposure to this new group. Moreover, the threatening aspects of the merger (Terry et al., 2001; Terry & O'Brien, 2001), elicited both by the instability it brings to employees' work conditions and social benefits and by the risk it poses to the survival of the premerger organizational identity (van Knippenberg et al., 2002), are also likely to inhibit the integration of the new social identity in this first phase.

As the merger progresses, and as employees have increased contacts with members of the other premerger group and identities are simultaneously activated, identification with the new, merged organization becomes possible. At the second compartmentalization stage, the multiplicity of social identities is recognized, but identities are still highly distinct, unrelated, and context dependent (e.g., employees identifying strongly with their premerger organization when socializing with fellow employees from their premerger organization, but identifying with the new, merged organization when interacting with their new boss, a former member of the other premerger organization). It is only at the integration stage that a new social identity becomes incorporated and integrated within a person's sense of self. At this stage, possible conflicts between old and new identities also need to be resolved (Harter & Monsour, 1992). For the employee experiencing an organizational merger, conflicts between organizational identities could be resolved through simultaneously identifying with the premerger organization and the newly merged superordinate organization. However, this would occur only to the extent that the premerger identity is recognized as being distinct and as contributing positively to the overall merged entity (e.g., Hornsey & Hogg, 2000). Another integration strategy would occur by establishing cognitive links (i.e., finding similarities) between their premerger identification and the newly merged organization (i.e., van Knippenberg et al., 2002; van Leeuwen et al., 2003).

While longitudinal research is definitively preferable to test the proponents of this developmental model, other considerations, such as the use of appropriate statistical techniques that allow tapping into changes occurring within each individual over time and mapping the multiplicity of social identities within their overall self, are also warranted. Furthermore, both the conditions facilitating (e.g., social support) versus inhibiting (e.g., status/power differentials, threat) the integration of multiple social identities and the consequences of this integration (e.g., in-group bias vs. well-being) need to be considered so as to paint a complete portrait of the changes occurring in social identities over time.

CONCLUSIONS

Taken together, the research reviewed in the present chapter provides strong support for the utility of adopting an intergroup approach to the study of organizational mergers. More specifically, the research reveals clear evidence that the nature and extent of intergroup rivalry and conflict in the context of an organizational merger can be predicted from the social identity approach and that the relative status position of an employee's premerger organization, his or her beliefs about the nature of the intergroup relations, and the fairness involved in the merging process have an important role in predicting employees' responses to a merger situation.

Overall, the results of the present research add to a growing body of literature that has supported the importance of adopting an intergroup perspective and, more specifically, a social identity perspective, in research on employee responses to an organizational merger (see Haunschild et al., 1994; Mottola et al., 1997; Terry & Callan, 1998). Theoretically, the present research brings together propositions from different theoretical models, including SIT, justice models, and models of superordinate identification. Some work is also presented that investigated the role of these processes in a longitudinal manner, as the merger situation progressed. Such efforts are important because they provide clear evidence for the dynamic and fluctuating processes operating during such organizational changes.

The applied significance of the present research derives from the social significance of protecting the well-being of employees and the effectiveness of organizations involved in mergers. Increasingly, it is being recognized that employee responses to a merger may account for the frequent failure of this type of organizational change (e.g., Marks & Mirvis, 1998). Indeed, recent commentators pointed to the need to move beyond a consideration of financial and strategic fit in the implementation of a merger to a focus on the extent to which the two organizations can achieve "cultural fit" in the new organization. Central to whether the new partners can be effectively integrated into the new organization or, in other words, whether cultural fit can be attained, is a consideration of the intergroup dynamics that are likely to be engendered in the context of an organizational merger. The results of the present research pointed to the fact that intergroup rivalry and conflict is likely to be observed in this context, presumably because of the motivation on behalf of both groups of employees to optimize the position of their new group in the newly merged organization. In order to reduce the type of intergroup competition observed in the present research and to minimize employees' negative experiences throughout a merger, newly merged organizations should engage in efforts to encourage the development of employees' feelings of identification with their new, merged organization.

Furthermore, the present findings revealed that the merger is experienced differently by members of the low- versus the high-status group. Managers and decision makers should thus recognize the intergroup dynamics involved in a merger and ensure that mechanisms are put in place so that employees from the low-status premerger group do not feel threatened by the merger but rather, feel that they bring specific, unique, and valued contributions to a greater whole—the new, merged organization. Low-status group members' perceptions of threat could also be minimized by ensuring that their premerger identities do not become lost within the new, merged organization, but that they are alive and striving (van Knippenberg et al., 2002; van Leeuwen et al., 2003). The use of a new or an hybrid corporate visual identity (e.g., name and logo) rather than the retention of the corporate identity of the higher status premerger organization represents one example of a concrete way to achieve this goal (see Rosson & Brooks, 2004). While emphasizing the importance of the new, merged organization has been argued to decrease rivalry between the different subgroups (Gaertner et al., 1993), it also appears crucial to recognize the distinctiveness of each premerger organization within the context of a new and binding merged organization (Hornsey & Hogg, 2000; Marks & Mirvis, 1998).

REFERENCES

Amiot, C. E., & Bourhis, R. Y. (2005). Ideological beliefs as determinants of discrimination in positive and negative outcome distributions. *European Journal of Social Psychology, 35*, 581–598.

Amiot, C. E., de la Sablonière, R., Terry, D. J., & Smith, J. R. (2007). Integration of social identities in the self: Toward a cognitive-developmental model. *Personality and Social Psychology Review* (in press).

Amiot, C. E., Terry, D. J., & Callan, V. J. (2007). Status, fairness, and social identification during an intergroup merger: A longitudinal study. *British Journal of Social Psychology* (in press).

Anastasio, P., Bachman, B., Gaertner, S., & Dovidio, J. (1997). Categorization, recategorization, and common ingroup identity. In R. Spears, P. J. Oakes, N. Ellemers, & S. A. Haslam (Eds.), *The social psychology of stereotyping and group life* (pp. 236–256). Oxford, UK: Blackwell.

Brewer, M. B. (1979). Ingroup bias in the minimal intergroup situation: A cognitive-motivational analysis. *Psychological Bulletin, 86*, 307–334.

Brown, B. B., & Lohr, M. J. (1987). Peer-group affiliation and adolescent self-esteem: An integration of ego-identity and symbolic-interaction theories. *Journal of Personality and Social Psychology, 52*, 47–55.

Brown, R. J., Condor, S., Mathews, A., Wade, G., & Williams, J. A. (1986). Explaining intergroup differentiation in an industrial organization. *Journal of Occupational Psychology, 59*, 273–286.

Buono, A. F., Bowditch, J. L., & Lewis, J. W. (1985). When cultures collide: The anatomy of a merger. *Human Relations, 38*, 477–500.

Cartwright, S., & Cooper, C. L. (1992). *Mergers and acquisitions: The human factor.* Oxford, UK: Butterworth/Heinemann.

Citera, M., & Stuhlmacher, A. F. (2001). A policy-modeling approach to examining fairness judgments in organizational acquisitions. *Journal of Behavioral Decision Making, 14*, 309–327.

Cobb, A. T., Wooten, K. C., & Folger, R. (1995). Justice in the making: Toward understanding theory and practice of justice in organizational change and development. *Research in Organizational Change and Development, 8,* 243–295.

Cronbach, L. J., & Furby, L. (1970). How should we measure "change": Or should we? *Psychological Bulletin, 74,* 68–80.

Daly, J. P., Pouder, R. W., & Kabanoff, B. (2004). The effects of initial differences in firms' espoused values on their postmerger performance. *The Journal of Applied Behavioral Science, 40,* 323–343.

Datta, D., Pinches, G., & Narayanan, V. (1992). Factors influencing wealth creation from mergers and acquisitions. *Strategic Management Journal, 13,* 67–84.

Devoge, S., & Shiraki, J. (2000). People factors: The missing link in the merger success. *Compensation and Benefits Management, 6,* 26–32.

Dovidio, J. F., Gaertner, S. L., & Validzic, A. (1998). Intergroup bias: Status, differentiation, and a common ingroup identity. *Journal of Personality and Social Psychology, 79,* 109–120.

Ellemers, N., Doosje, B. J., van Knippenberg, A., & Wilke, H. (1992). Status protection in high status minority groups. *European Journal of Social Psychology, 22,* 123–140.

Ellemers, N., van Knippenberg, A., de Vries, N., & Wilke, H. (1988). Social identification and permeability of group boundaries. *European Journal of Social Psychology, 18,* 497–513.

Ellemers, N., van Knippenberg, A., & Wilke, H. (1990). The influence of permeability of group boundaries and stability of group status on strategies of individual mobility and social change. *British Journal of Social Psychology, 29,* 233–246.

Ellemers, N., Wilke, H., & van Knippenberg, A. (1993). Effects of the legitimacy of low group or individual status on individual and collective status-enhancement strategies. *Journal of Personality & Social Psychology, 64,* 766–778.

Ethier, K. A., & Deaux, K. (1994). Negotiating social identity when contexts change: Maintaining identification and responding to threat. *Journal of Personality and Social Psychology, 67,* 243–251.

Folger, R., & Cropanzano, R. (1998). *Organizational justice and human resource management: Foundations for organizational science.* Thousand Oaks, CA: Sage.

Gaertner, S. L., Dovidio, J. F., & Bachman, B. A. (1996). Revisiting the contact hypothesis: The induction of a common ingroup identity. *International Journal of Intercultural Relations, 20,* 271–290.

Gaertner, S. L., Dovidio, J. F., Bachman, B. A., & Rust, M. C. (1993). The common ingroup identity model: Recategorization and the reduction of intergroup biais. *European Review of Social Psychology, 4,* 1–26.

Gaertner, S. L., Dovidio, J. F., Nier, J. A., Banker, B. S., Ward, C. M., Houlette, M., et al. (2000). The common ingroup identity model for reducing intergroup bias: Progress and challenges. In D. Capozza & R. Brown (Eds.), *Social identity processes: Trends in theory and research* (pp. 133–148). London: Sage.

Greenberg, J., & Folger, R. (1983). Procedural justice, participation, and the fair process effect in groups and organizations. In P. B. Paulus (Ed.), *Basic group processes* (pp. 235–256). New York: Springer-Verlag.

Gunders, S., & Alpert, A. (2001). *International mergers and acquisition review: 2000–2001.* London: Deloitte and Touche.

Harter, S. (1999). *The construction of the self: A developmental perspective.* New York: Guilford.

Harter, S. (2003). The development of self-representations during childhood and adolescence. In R. R. Leary & J. P. Tangney (Eds.), *Handbook of self and identity* (pp. 610–642). New York: Guilford Press.

Harter, S., & Monsour, A. (1992). Developmental analysis of conflict caused by opposing attributed in the adolescent self-portrait. *Developmental Psychology, 28,* 251–260.

Haunschild, P. R., Moreland, R. L., & Murrell, A. J. (1994). Sources of resistance to mergers between groups. *Journal of Applied Social Psychology, 24,* 1150–1178.

Hinkle, S., & Brown, R. J. (1990). Intergroup comparisons and social identity: Some links and lacunae. In D. Abrams & M. A. Hogg (Eds.), *Social identity theory: Constructive and critical advances* (pp. 48–70). New York: Harvester Wheatsheaf.

Hitt, M. A., Ireland, D. R., & Harrison, J. S. (2001). Mergers and acquisitions: A value creating or value destroying strategy? In M. A. Hitt, R. E. Freeman, & J. S. Harrison (Eds.), *The Blackwell handbook of strategic management* (pp. 384–409). Malden, MA: Blackwell.

Hogg, M. A., & Abrams, D. (1988). *Social identifications: A social psychology of intergroup relations and group processes.* London: Routledge.

Hogg, M. A., & Terry, D. J. (2001). *Social identity processes in organizational contexts.* Philadelphia: Psychology Press

Hornsey, M. J., & Hogg, M. A. (2000). Assimilation and diversity: An integrative model of subgroup relations. *Personality and Social Psychology Review, 4,* 143–156.

Hornsey, M. J., van Leeuwen, E., & van Santen, W. (2003). Dragging down and dragging up: How relative group status affects responses to common fate. *Group Dynamics: Theory, Research, & Practice, 7,* 275–338.

Jetten, J., O'Brien, A., & Trindall, N. (2002). Changing identity: Predicting adjustment to organizational restructure as a function of subgroup and superordinate identification. *British Journal of Social Psychology, 41,* 281–297.

Kabanoff, B. (1991). Equity, equality, power, and conflict. *Academy of Management Review, 16,* 416–441.

KPMG (2001). *Merger and acquisitions integration—A business guide.* London: KPMG Consulting.

Lalonde, R. N. (1992). The dynamics of group differentiation in the face of defeat. *Personality and Social Psychology Bulletin, 18,* 336–342.

Larsson, R., & Lubatkin, M. (2001). Achieving acculturation in mergers and acquisitions: An international case survey. *Human Relations, 54,* 1573–1607.

Lind, E. A., & Tyler, T. R. (1988). *The social psychology of procedural justice.* New York: Plenum.

Lipponen, J., Olkkonen, M. E., & Moilanen, M. (2004). Perceived procedural justice and employee responses to an organizational merger. *European Journal of Work and Organizational Psychology, 13,* 391–413.

Marks, M. L., & Mirvis, P. (1998). *Joining forces.* San Francisco: Jossey-Bass.

Mascolo, M. F., & Fischer, K. W. (1998). The development of self through the coordination of component systems. In M. D. Ferrari & R. J. Sternberg (Eds.), *Self-awareness: Its nature and development* (pp. 332–384). New York: Guilford Press.

Meyer, C. B. (2001). Allocation processes in mergers and acquisitions: An organizational justice perspective. *British Journal of Management, 12,* 47–66.

Mottola, G. R., Bachman, B. A., Gaertner, S. L., & Dovidio, J. F. (1997). How groups merge: The effects of merger integration patterns on anticipated commitment to the merged organization. *Journal of Applied Social Psychology, 27,* 1335–1358.

Mullen, B., Brown, R., & Smith, C. (1992). Ingroup bias as a function of salience, relevance, and status: An integration. *European Journal of Social Psychology, 22,* 103–122.

Nadler, D. A., & Tushman, M. M. (1989). Organizational frame bending: Principles for managing reorientation. *The Academy of Management Executive, 3,* 194–204.

Platow, M. J., Wenzel, M., & Nolan, M. (2003). The importance of social identity and self-categorization processes for creating and responding to fairness. In S. A. Haslam, D. van Knippenberg, M. J. Platow, & N. Ellemers (Eds.), *Social identity at work: Developing theory for organizational practice.* New York: Psychology Press.

Rosson, P., & Brooks, M. R. (2004). M&As and corporate visual identity: An exploratory study. *Corporate Reputation Review, 7,* 181–194.

Sachdev, I., & Bourhis, R. Y. (1987). Status differentials and intergroup behaviour. *European Journal of Social Psychology, 17,* 277–293.

Sachdev, I., & Bourhis, R. Y. (1991). Power and status differentials in minority/majority relations. *European Journal of Social Psychology, 21,* 1–24.

Seo, M. G., & Hill, N. S. (2005). Understanding the human side of merger and acquisition: An integrative framework. *Journal of Applied Behavioral Science, 41,* 422–443.

Tajfel, H. (1974). Social identity and intergroup behaviour. *Social Science Information, 13,* 65–93.

Tajfel, H. (1975). The exit of social mobility and the voice of social change. *Social Science Information, 14,* 101–118.

Tajfel, H., & Turner, J. C. (1979). An integrative theory of intergroup conflict. In W. G. Austin & S. Worchel (Eds.), *The social psychology of intergroup relations.* Monterey, CA: Brooks-Cole.

Tajfel, H., & Turner, J. C. (1986). The social identity theory of intergroup behavior. In S. Worchel & W. G. Austin (Eds.), *Psychology of intergroup relations* (pp. 7–24). Chicago: Nelson-Hall.

Taylor, D. M., & McKirnan, D. J. (1984). A five-stage model of intergroup relations. *British Journal of Social Psychology, 23,* 291–300.

Terry, D. J. (2003). A social identity perspective on organizational mergers: The role of group status, permeability, and similarity. In S. A. Haslam, D. van Knippenberg, M. J. Platow, & N. Ellemers (Eds.), *Social identity at work: Developing theory for organizational practice.* New York: Psychology Press.

Terry, D. J., & Callan, V. J. (1997). Employee adjustment to a large-scale organizational change. *Australian Psychologist, 32,* 203–220.

Terry, D. J., & Callan, V. J. (1998). Intergroup differentiation in response to an organizational merger. *Group Dynamics, 2,* 67–81.

Terry, D. J., Callan, V. J., & Sartori, G. (1996). A test of a stress-coping model of adjustment to a large-scale organizational change. *Stress Medicine, 12,* 105–122.

Terry, D. J., Carey, C. J., & Callan, V. J. (2001). Employee adjustment to an organizational merger: An intergroup perspective. *Personality and Social Psychology Bulletin, 27,* 267–280.

Terry, D. J., & O'Brien, A. T. (2001). Status, legitimacy, and ingroup bias in the context of an organizational merger. *Group Processes and Intergroup Relations, 4,* 271–289.

Turner, J. C. (1982). Towards a cognitive redefinition of the social group. In H. Tajfel (Ed.), *Social identity and intergroup relations* (pp. 15–40). Cambridge, UK: Cambridge University Press.

Turner, J. C., & Brown, R. J. (1978). Social status, cognitive alternatives and intergroup relations. In H. Tajfel (Ed.), *Differentiation between social groups* (pp. 201–234). London: Academic Press.

Turner, J. C., Hogg, M. A., Oakes, P. J., Reicher, S. D., & Wetherell, M. (1987). *Rediscovering the social group: A self-categorization theory.* Oxford, UK: Blackwell.

Tyler, T. R., & Blader, S. L. (2003). The group engagement model: Procedural justice, social identity, and cooperative behavior. *Personality and Social Psychology Review, 7,* 349–361.

Tyler, T. R., & de Cremer, D. (2005). Process-based leadership: Fair procedures and reactions to organizational change. *The Leadership Quarterly, 16,* 529–545.

van Knippenberg, A., & Ellemers, N. (1993). Strategies in intergroup relations. In M. A. Hogg & D. Abrams (Eds.), *Group motivation: Social psychological perspectives* (pp. 17–23). London: Harvester Wheatsheaf.

van Knippenberg, A. F. M. (1978). Intergroup differences in group perceptions. In H. Tajfel (Ed.), *The social dimension: European developments in social psychology* (pp. 560 –578). Cambridge, UK: Cambridge University Press.

van Knippenberg, D., van Knippenberg, B., Monden, L., & de Lima, F. (2002). Organizational identification after a merger: A social identity approach. *British Journal of Social Psychology, 41,* 233–252.

van Leeuwen, E., van Knippenberg, D. & Ellemers, N. (2003). Continuing and changing group identities: The effects of merging on social identification and ingroup bias. *Personality and Social Psychology Bulletin, 29,* 679–690.

van Oudenhoven, J. P., & de Boer, T. (1995). Complementarity and similarity of partners in international mergers. *Basic and Applied Social Psychology, 17,* 343–356.

Wright, S. C., Taylor, D. M., & Moghaddam, F. M. (1990). Responding to membership in a disadvantaged group: From acceptance to collective protest. *Journal of Personality and Social Psychology, 58,* 994–1003.

Zuckerman, M. (1979). Attribution of success and failure revisited, or: The motivational bias is alive and well in attributional theory. *Journal of Personality, 47,* 245–287.

IV
Commentaries

14

On the Outside Looking In: Window Shopping for Insights Into Diversity-Driven Conflict

KRISTIN SMITH-CROWE AND ARTHUR P. BRIEF
David Eccles School of Business, University of Utah

ELIZABETH E. UMPHRESS
Mays Business School, Texas A&M University

None of us label ourselves as conflict researchers. We do, however, share an interest in organizational diversity (e.g., Umphress, Smith-Crowe, Brief, Dietz, & Watkins, 2007); and, even though organizational scholars rarely view diversity through a conflict lens, we are aware that doing so can be worthwhile (e.g., Brief, Umphress, et al., 2005). We are not alone here. For example, in their introductory chapter, De Dreu and Gelfand (this volume) reasoned principally from social identity theory (e.g., Tajfel, 1978) that diversity is a source of value-related and relationship conflicts. Also, in this volume, Jehn, Bezrukova, and Thatcher's contribution is devoted to diversity issues and conflict.

Given our common interests and outsiders' perspective, we thought it would be a potentially fruitful exercise to study the contributions in this book with an eye toward insights into diversity-driven conflicts and how to resolve them. To this end, we posed a series of questions about such conflicts and then we poured over the chapters in search of answers. This process yielded insights and perhaps even more questions, indicating the many insights yet unrealized. More broadly, it suggested to us that organizational conflict research could better inform those organizational scholars whose work does not fall into the conflict domain (e.g., those who study diversity). As outsiders, we perceive the conflict literature to be somewhat insulated; that is, it does not seem to be often employed outside of its own boundaries as a source of solutions for pressing theoretical problems. We think it should be. As the editors observed, the study of conflict focuses on a fundamental question: "How do individuals and groups manage their interdependence with one another?" (De Dreu & Gelfand, this volume). We see this question as being at the heart of organizational studies; as such, we think that organizational scholars in general, not conflict researchers in particular, are likely to gain valuable insights from the conflict literature.

In what follows, we pose some of the questions we see as being central to diversity-driven conflicts and their resolution. As the reader will see, the discussion that follows is far from exhaustive. We present rather simple ideas and questions, largely stripped of the complexities of life in organizations; we hope such simplicity stimulates others to supply richer understandings of diversity-driven conflicts and their resolution.

WHEN DOES DIVERSITY LEAD TO THE PERCEPTION OF CONFLICT?

Conflict is widely understood to be "a process that begins when an individual or group perceives differences and opposition between oneself and another individual or group about interests and resources, beliefs, values or practices that matter to them" (De Dreu & Gelfand, this volume). We know from realistic group conflict theory (e.g., Campbell, 1965; Levine & Campbell, 1972; Sherif, 1966), for example, that conflict is likely to occur when groups *perceive* that they are in competition over scarce resources. From social identity theory, we know that the *perception* of group differences coupled with a positive view of one's own group can evoke in-group/out-group conflict (Tajfel & Turner, 1986). Fundamentally, conflict begins with perception. As such, our initial inquiry was "when does diversity[1] lead to the perception of conflict?"

DeDreu and Gelfand's (this volume) definition of conflict indicates that only one party must perceive a conflict in order for it to exist. While parties potentially could become conscious of a conflict at precisely the same moment, we assume that a more likely scenario is that one party becomes aware of a conflict before the other. This scenario led us to wonder whether minority or majority parties are more likely to first perceive diversity-driven conflict. We suspect that minority group members are more likely to first detect such conflict given that majority group members sometimes fail to realize their own prejudices. Modern racists, for example, do not recognize themselves as racist despite their capacity for both hold-

---

[1] When we use the term *diversity*, we essentially are referring to differences in race, gender, sexual orientation, and the like (rather than less stigmatized and politically charged bases for diversity, e.g., organizational tenure; see Jehn, Bezrukova, & Thatcher, this volume, for a discussion of different bases of diversity).

ing subtly racist attitudes (e.g., "Blacks are pushing too hard, too fast, and into places where they are not wanted"; McConahay, 1986, pp. 92–93) and discriminating against Blacks (e.g., Brief, Buttram, Elliot, Reizenstein, & McCline, 1995). Considering their lack of insight into their own attitudes and motives, it is not difficult to imagine a modern racist expressing a racially insensitive remark without realizing the potential harm created. Such remarks could signal the existence of conflict in the minds of minority group members, despite the majority group member's ignorance of any conflict. Considering the possibility that minorities are more likely to perceive diversity-driven conflict, at least under some conditions, Olekalns, Putnam, Weingart, and Metcalf's (this volume) discussion of online conflict led us to wonder whether diversity-driven conflict might be derailed by computer-mediated communication and whether this might be a potential benefit of an often problematic medium of communication. That is, the presence of diversity may be less detectable online (e.g., due to androgynous names and communication styles). Assuming that the detection of diversity is a necessary precursor to perceiving diversity-driven conflict, ignorance of the existence of diversity could render such conflict unlikely.

Beyond the simple question of which party is more likely to first detect a conflict, we also wondered how the nature of the conflict might be affected depending on which party first becomes aware of the conflict and on the lag between when the first and second party both recognize the conflict. For instance, a woman joins an all male work group. A male member sees her as competition for a desired promotion, and he sees her sex as providing her with an unfair advantage. Weeks after joining the group, the woman realizes that the male in question has been subtly behaving as an adversary. Would the nature of such a conflict be different if the female first perceived the male as a threat or if both parties very quickly realized they were potential adversaries?

We also are led to wonder whether DeDreu and Gelfand's (this volume) definition of conflict adequately captured the full potential character of diversity-driven conflicts. Social dominance theory (Sidanius & Pratto, 1999), for instance, tells us that most types of group conflict and oppression (e.g., racism, sexism, and nationalism) can be regarded as different forms of the same basic human predisposition to form group-based social hierarchies, where valued, finite resources (e.g., money, employment, education, and healthcare) are disproportionately held by the upper echelons of the hierarchy which dominate groups at the lower levels. It is not difficult to imagine that those benefiting from such arrangements come up with rationalizations to justify the inequity (and, thus, do not perceive a conflict), while those *not* benefiting see such arrangements for what they are—resource conflicts (e.g., DeDreu & Gelfand, this volume). What is perhaps less intuitive (although it is empirically supported), is the idea put forth within social dominance theory (Sidanius & Pratto, 1999), as well as system justification theory (Jost, Banaji, & Nosek, 2004), that subordinate groups (e.g., Blacks and women) suppressed by dominant ones sometimes participate in and contribute to their own subordination (Umphress et al., 2007); that is, they too sometimes buy into the rationalizations that legitimize the inequality. From this perspective (and contrary to the widely accepted definition of conflict), groups may be seen as being in conflict without either group being consciously aware of the situation. Instead, the entire state of affairs is made palatable to both parties by the salve of a "legitimizing myth," which "provides moral and intellectual justification for the social practice that distributes social value within the social system" (Sidanius & Pratto, 1999, p. 45).

For example, Jaffee (this volume) described the development of "managerial ideology" in response to the rise of factory production. Quoting Bendix, Jaffee asserted that such an ideology neutralizes labor–management conflict by either denying or justifying the exercise of managerial authority. In other words, this managerial ideology obscures the existing conflict from view. While Jaffee was not explicit about labor and management *both* being deluded by managerial ideology, there is evidence in the diversity literature that ideology is not merely a tool of oppression, but that it also serves as a needed justification for those benefiting from favorable power differentials. Research on "White guilt," for instance, has demonstrated that when Whites are conscious of the advantages they enjoy in society merely due to their skin color, they are much more supportive of affirmative action measures (Iyer, Leach, & Crosby, 2003; Swim & Miller, 1999). That is, without a justifying ideology Whites cannot always stomach the stark reality of injustice, and, in response, they attempt to disabuse the system, endorsing a more balanced distribution of resources, such as employment.

DOES DIVERSITY-DRIVEN CONFLICT ALWAYS ARISE PASSIVELY?

To us, the view of conflict as a "process beginning with a perception" evokes an image of passivity, implying that conflict is something we wake up to one day just as we might wake up to a blue sky or snow on the ground. It is just something that happens to us. Reading Raver and Barling's (this volume) chapter on workplace aggression, however, led us to contemplate deliberately provoked conflicts. The incidents these authors described might "just happen" to victims but not to the aggressors. Unfortunately, as Raver and Barling pointed out, little is known about the connections between diversity and workplace aggression. Perhaps a place to start would be to expand on their investigation into the motives behind certain unsavory workplace behaviors. In particular, research could focus on diversity-relevant motives behind aggressive behaviors like keeping members of subordinate groups (e.g., Blacks and women) "in their place."

Pruitt's (this volume) discussion of "retaliatory escalation" suggested that conflict, in fact, may very well have to do with putting people "in their place." Describing the primary motivations behind such escalation, he included things like demonstrating strength and promoting norms. Similar to these motivations, Rudman and Fairchild (2004) suggested stereotype enforcement as the motivation behind backlash against gender deviants (or those who deviate from gender stereotypes). They found that women who dared to step outside of their roles by succeeding in male-typed activities were sabotaged by their competitors, who were fully aware of the stereotype-maintenance implication of their actions (e.g., the implication that the poor performance of the sabotaged women would preserve gender stereotypes). Moreover, the researchers found evidence that backlash resulted in implicit and state self-esteem enhancement for the saboteurs, and that gender deviant women's fear of backlash served to cow them into trying to conform to gender stereotypes by hiding any gender deviance, including successful performance in a male-typed task. The former may serve as positive reinforcement for engaging in sabotage; the latter may serve to perpetuate gender stereotypes.

Besides the motivation to maintain stereotypes, people are also motivated to seek fair distributions of resources. In fact, De Dreu and Gelfand (this volume) cited conflict over resources as a major source of conflict in organizations. As such, we suggest affirmative action programs, which have been surrounded by controversy since their inception, as a potential hornet's nest of diversity-driven resource conflict. For example, Blacks benefiting from affirmative action programs may be seen by certain White coworkers as violating distributive fairness norms (e.g., Blacks may be seen as taking more than their share of jobs in an organization). Consistent with our speculation, James, Brief, Dietz, and Cohen (2001) found that Whites high in modern racism (McConahay, 1986) demonstrated negative attitudinal reactions to affirmative action programs aimed at benefiting Blacks. Such perceptions of injustice and negative attitudes might lead these White coworkers to aggressively assert their superiority in the workplace.

WHAT TYPES OF CONFLICT FOLLOW FROM DIVERSITY?

Given the connections in the conflict literature between types of conflict and outcomes (e.g., De Dreu & Gelfand, this volume), our next question was "What types of conflict follow from diversity?" Jehn et al.'s (this volume) contribution emphasizing alignment theories of group composition concerned with the simultaneous alignment of multiple characteristics across members (e.g., faultline theory; Lau & Murnighan, 1998) provided us with a rich response. Jehn et al. recognized the difference between social category (e.g., race and sex) and informational (e.g., work experience and education) characteristics and asserted that subgroups formed along the former characteristics lead to stereotyping and prejudice, while those formed along the latter facilitate the effective pooling of information and integration of perspectives. These observations served as the basis for Jehn et al. predicting that individuals in groups with strong social category faultlines will experience high levels of intragroup relationship, task, and process conflicts. Alternatively, individuals in groups with strong informational faultlines will experience high levels of intragroup task conflict and low levels of intragroup relations and process conflicts. These propositions provide an explanation for inconsistent findings evident in the literature and alert organizational scholars *not* to construe diversity in terms of categories like race and sex as being conceptually equivalent to those based on characteristics like functional background or organizational tenure. We are dealing with apples and oranges; bravo to Jehn et al. for recognizing the difference. Too often, in our judgment, diversity researchers have ignored these differences, theoretically equating, for example, being Black and being an accountant.

WHEN MIGHT DIVERSITY-DRIVEN CONFLICT LEAD TO POSITIVE OUTCOMES?

Schulz-Hardt, Mojzisch, and Vogelgesang (this volume) argued that conflict sometimes promotes creativity and performance, providing empirical evidence from several studies supporting their claim. If conflict can be functional, then when might *diversity-driven* conflict lead to positive outcomes? Schulz-Hardt et al. offered "activation" as one explanation for the positive effects—when dissent is voiced, increased cognitive processing and group discussion takes place. Indeed, Antonio et al. (2004) found increases in complex thinking due to the presence of a racial minority in a group. We wonder, however, about the boundary conditions that might curtail the positive effects of diversity in groups. One of these conditions might be the extent to which a dissenting opinion is diversity relevant. For example, a female group member holding a dissenting opinion that the group should be less task focused and more relationship focused might choose to keep this opinion to herself for fear of confirming negative stereotypes about women in the workplace. Alternatively, should she choose to share this dissenting opinion rather than stimulating cognition and discussion, it may very well be dismissed by the men and even other women in her group as being a stereotypical female concern and not a legitimate business issue.

HOW MIGHT DIVERSITY-DRIVEN CONFLICTS BEST BE RESOLVED?

Assuming that diversity-driven conflicts are likely to emerge in organizations (cf. Sidanius & Pratto, 1999), our final question concerned their resolution. In our search for answers, we turned to Terry and Amoit's (this volume) contribution in which they discussed the implications of status for mergers. They provided the following bit of advice: Managers and decision makers should

> ensure that mechanisms are put in place so that employees from the low-status premerger group do not feel threatened by the merger but rather, feel that they bring specific, unique, and valued contributions to a greater

whole—the new, merged organization. Low-status group members' perceptions of threat could also be minimized by ensuring that their premerger
identities do not become lost within the new, merged organization, but that
they are alive and striving. (p. 407)

Could this wisdom be successfully applied to other types of "mergers"?
For instance, is this good advice for organizations trying to bring women
into largely male-occupied units or divisions, or largely White-populated
organizations trying to promote racial diversity? We see some parallels
between mergers of organizations and mergers of social groups, and we
suggest that research on the former could potentially provide very helpful
insight into the problems of the latter.

CONCLUSIONS

All in all, we found some thought-provoking answers from this volume
to the questions we posed about diversity-driven conflict. This exercise
of searching for insights into diversity-driven conflict was so stimulating
in fact that many of our "answers" really came in the form of new questions and speculation. We found that conflict research is a fertile ground
not only for insights into the problems of diversity but also for inspiring
interesting new questions.

That our reading of this volume sparked so many questions, even
in the course of our writing this brief commentary, demonstrates, we
think, the rich streams of conflict research that could be tapped should
conflict researchers turn their attention more deliberately to the problems of diversity. However, we do not mean to suggest that diversity is
the only arena into which conflict researchers could fruitfully expand.
Other central aspects of organizational life ripe for conflict researchers
to tackle include individual, group and organizational learning; worker
well-being (e.g., Spector & Bruk-Lee, this volume); a host of work-related
attitudes and affective reactions; work motivation; career outcomes;
power and politics; leadership; and organizational cultures and structures. Conflict is relevant to such a broad array of phenomena because,
as demonstrated in this volume, conflict and its resolution pervades
moment-to-moment, everyday life in organizations, influencing group
processes, communication, decision making, and interpersonal relationships in the workplace. Indeed, looking back several decades we found
precedents for conflict researchers asking and addressing broader questions (e.g., Blake, Mouton, & Sheppard, 1964; Pondy, 1967, 1969; Walton &
Dutton, 1969). It is our contention that a more broadly focused conflict
literature would be greatly beneficial to the larger community of organizational scholars.

REFERENCES

Antonio, A. L., Chang, M. J., Hakuta, K., Kenny, D. A., Levin, S., & Milem, J. F. (2004). Effects of racial diversity on complex thinking in college students. *Psychological Science, 15*, 507–510.

Blake, R. R., Mouton, J. S., & Sheppard, H. A. (1964). *Managing intergroup conflict in industry.* Houston, TX: Gulf.

Brief, A. P., Buttram, R. T., Elliot, J. D., Reizenstein, R. M., & McCline, R. L. (1995). Releasing the beast: A study of compliance with orders to use race as a selection criterion. *Journal of Social Issues, 51*, 177–193.

Brief, A. P., Umphress, E. E., Dietz, J., Burrows, J. W., Butz, R. M., & Scholten, L. (2005). Community matters: Realistic group conflict theory and the impact of diversity. *Academy of Management Journal, 48*, 830–844.

Campbell, D. T. (1965). Ethnocentric and other altruistic motives. In D. Levine (Ed.), *Nebraska symposium on motivation* (pp. 283–311). Lincoln, NE: University of Nebraska Press.

Iyer, A., Leach, C. W., & Crosby, F. J. (2003). White guilt and racial compensation: The benefits and limits of self-focus. *Personality and Social Psychology Bulletin, 29*, 117–129.

James, E. H., Brief, A. P., Dietz, J., & Cohen, R. R. (2001). Prejudice matters: Job attitudes as function of the perceived implementation of policies to advance disadvantaged groups. *Journal of Applied Psychology, 86*, 1120–1128.

Jost, J. T., Banaji, M. R., & Noseck, B. A. (2004). A decade of system justification theory: Accumulated evidence of conscious and unconscious bolstering of the status quo. *Political Psychology, 25*, 881–919.

Lau, D., & Murnighan, J. K. (1998). Demographic diversity and faultlines: The compositional dynamics of organizational groups. *Academy of Management Review, 23*, 325–340.

Levine, R. A., & Campbell, D. T. (1972). *Ethnocentrism: Theories of conflict, ethnic attitudes, and group behavior.* New York: John Wiley.

McConahay, J. B. (1986). Modern racism, ambivalence, and the Modern Racism Scale. In J. F. Dovidio & S. L. Gaertner (Eds.), *Prejudice, discrimination, and racism* (pp. 91–125). Orlando, FL: Academic Press.

Pondy, L. R. (1967). Organizational conflict: Concepts and models. *Administrative Science Quarterly, 12*, 296–320.

Pondy, L. R. (1969). Varieties of organizational conflict. *Administrative Science Quarterly, 14*, 499–506.

Rudman, L. A., & Fairchild, K. (2004). Reactions to counter-stereotypic behavior: The role of backlash in cultural stereotype maintenance. *Journal of Personality and Social Psychology, 87*, 157–176.

Sherif, M. (1966). *Group conflict and co-operation: Their social psychology.* London: Routledge & Kegan Paul.

Sidanius, J., & Pratto, F. (1999). *Social dominance: An intergroup theory of social hierarchy and oppression.* Cambridge, UK: Cambridge University Press.

Swim, J. K., & Miller, D. L. (1999). White guilt: Its antecedents and consequences for attitudes toward affirmative action. *Personality and Social Psychology Bulletin, 25*, 500–514.

Tajfel, H. (1978). *Differentiation between social groups: Studies in the social psychology of intergroup relations.* New York: Academic.

Tajfel, H., & Turner, J. C. (1986). The social identity theory of intergroup behavior. In S. Worchel & W. G. Austin (Eds.), *Psychology of Intergroup Relations* (pp. 7–24). Chicago: Nelson-Hall.

Umphress, E. E., Smith-Crowe, K., Brief, A. P., Dietz, J., & Watkins, M. B. (2007). When birds of a feather flock together and when they do not: Status composition, social dominance orientation, and organizational attractiveness. *Journal of Applied Psychology, 92,* 396–409.

Walton, R. E., & Dutton, J. M. (1969). The management of interdepartmental conflict: A model and review. *Administrative Science Quarterly, 14,* 73–84.

15

Making Sense of an Elusive Phenomenon

DEBORAH M. KOLB
Simmons School of Management

Conflict is part of the fabric of organizational life. In our daily round of interactions, we are more than likely to be involved in some form of conflict, even if we do not label it as such. Some nice examples in the context of escalation include failing to help, to return phone calls, to give out information, or talking behind another's back and refusing requests (chapter 8). Indeed, we now widely accept that conflict is embedded in the very structures of today's organizations, making the possibilities for conflict and its management almost infinite. And because it is potentially ever present, it has been an elusive phenomenon to frame and conceptualize in a systematic way. As the editors note, the absence of comprehensive treatments of the subject is striking. Certainly, there have been efforts to focus on particular dimensions—the management of conflict (De Dreu & van de Vliert, 1997), the hidden or less formal dimensions (D. M. Kolb & Bartunek, 1992), and the processes of constructive conflict (Kreisberg, 2003).

What has marked the study of conflict in the past decade or so has been fragmentation of the topic. The late Jeffrey Z. Rubin (1981) once likened the disjointed study of third parties to an elephant where different scholars notice only certain parts. A similar phenomenon has occurred in the study of organizational conflict. Foremost, have been the students of negotiation; the empirical work on this topic has been voluminous. Even though much of this work suggests an organizational context in the tasks that are studied, negotiation has been treated largely as an isolated phenomenon unhinged from other organizational processes (Barley, 1991). In a slightly different vein, the importation of alternative dispute resolution (ADR) into organizations has resulted primarily in handbooks of dispute system design with only limited inquiry into how these systems operate and fit within organizations (Lipsky, Seeber, & Fincher, 2003; Ury, Brett, & Goldberg, 1988).

What distinguishes this volume is an accomplishment to be applauded—we have a significant mass of the entire elephant in one place. The diversity of topics is exemplary—from a historical sweep of conflict theory to reviews of micro processes of negotiation to topics not heretofore represented—aggression, health, and well-being—to institutional issues such as dispute systems, labor management relations, and mergers. Despite the presence of the entire elephant, I see it as still experienced in parts. I expect there is much to learn if there were more integration across topics and levels. That is the first issue I want to raise. The second has to do with sense making and meaning. I subscribe to the view that conflict and its management is an interpretive process—that what a conflict is about shifts and changes depending on how it gets processed (D. M. Kolb & Bartunek, 1992). Even though many of the chapters take a process perspective—another welcome addition—the dynamics of how meanings shift because of processes and the relation of these shifts to conflict outcomes could be usefully expanded. Finally, this volume concerns conflict in workplace organizations. Yet, the organizational implications for how conflicts are handled, beyond a few mentions of performance and effectiveness, are missed. I want to comment on these three areas.

LET US TALK OF WHAT WE LEARN BY PARTNERING

In their classic study of organization conflict, Lawrence and Lorsch (1969) talked of the high need for both differentiation and integration in environments that are changing rapidly. Many of the chapters in this volume exemplify the kind of differentiation that has occurred in the field. In doing so, opportunities for integration that might move the field forward may have gone unrealized. I say "may" for a number of reasons. First, in their introduction (chapter 1), the editors highlighted many insights we glean across levels and topics. And second, in an interesting twist, the chapters that might be seen as "atypical," in the sense that they are not directly about negotiation, conflict resolution, or group decision making, the well *differentiated* parts of the field, do attempt to integrate some ideas about conflict, health, aggression, and dissent into existing literatures. I want to suggest a few other opportunities within the domain of the interpersonal and group level as well as between that level and the organization and institutional.

Let me give a few examples from the second part of the book. The paucity of research on emotions in the study of conflict generally, and negotiation in particular, is often noted. Considering the topic of workplace aggression (chapter 7) expands how we think about emotions. Resistance and revenge could redefine some of the ways we might think about agency in the process of escalation (chapter 8). Similarly, the study of aggression seems to lack process models whereas escalation is just that. It would also be interesting to consider how aggression changes the emotional coloration of choices in the dual concern model (chapters 1 and 3).

Chapter 9 on health and well-being has many interesting integrative implications. First, it obviously highlights how narrow some of our outcome measures typically are (chapters 3 and 4). However, it also makes us consider what other aspects of the self, psychological state for example, might play out in even highly structured negotiation tasks (J. Kolb, 1999). Further, it makes us rethink whether the neat distinctions we make among types of conflict (chapter 6), that they are task, relational, or process, might be experienced differently depending on the state of the people involved and the contexts within which the conflicts occur.

The opportunities for partnering and integration present intriguing possibilities across levels. There has been a distinct move to incorporate interest based bargaining into contemporary union management relations. The success, as chapter 12 suggested has been mixed, depending in part on the level of trust between the parties. What might the research on faultlines (chapter 6) contribute to helping parties move their constituencies in the direction of interest based bargaining? Or how might the insights in the ways minorities affect the thinking of majorities (chapter 5) contribute to the challenges in bringing along bargaining committees to commit to a different approach to bargaining? Or consider, the ways in which incorporating insights on conflict escalation (chapter 8) might be important in evaluating organizational dispute systems and their points of intervention (chapter 11). Or consider how third parties (chapter 10) might deal differently with parties bent on aggression or revenge (chapter 7). The gap between what we know from the second part of the book about microprocesses in the management of conflict and how these insights might contribute to managing conflict at the organizational and institutional level seems *ripe* for partnering and integration.

The book suggested other opportunities as well. Laid out in the history of conflict (chapter 2), we see a central dilemma in the managing of conflict—the need of organizations to control its members and the ways its members find to resist. Coming from different theoretical and methodological perspectives, studies of normative control and the oppressiveness of some corporate cultures and professional norms contribute a different perspective to our understanding about how conflict is managed (Burroway, 1979; Kunda, 1992; Morrill, 1992). Similarly, studies of resistance help us see some of the ways that organizational members incite conflict in the service of change (Meyerson, 2001). Although resistance finds its way into several parts of this book, this area could be expanded

The type of partnering I am suggesting is not a trivial matter. There are some methodological and, potentially, ideological issues that may preclude efforts at integration. Laboratory methods have dominated many of the areas covered in the book. To move into organizational contexts has typically, although not always, meant using different methods—surveys, interviews, ethnographies, and case studies. It may be a challenge, one fraught with conflict, to get scholars who work in one paradigm to agree on how to study phenomenon from an integrated perspective. It may be that integration will require more triangulation of methods. Ideology may also be an issue. A focus on conflict management focuses on the interests of leaders in the relatively smooth functioning of their organizations. We see this normative value in many of the chapters, for example, what processes lead to joint gain (chapters 3 and 4). Work on control and resistance takes a more critical stance, focusing on conflict handling, rather than management (chapter 2). These value positions may be more difficult to integrate.

THE MEANINGS (AND SHIFTING MEANINGS) OF CONFLICT IN ORGANIZATIONS

With their now classic article on *naming, blaming, and claiming*, Felstiner, Abel, and Sarat (1981) metaphorically and theoretically captured the dynamic processes of meaning in conflict. There is nothing inherent in the notion of a particular conflict. Conflicts are social events that are embedded in the structure of social relationships and that are given shape and definition as disputants take action. Depending on the audience and the forum, the same conflict can be phrased in many different ways. To use a popular example from the dispute resolution field, the same disagreement can be defined in terms of rights that are violated, interests to be worked out, or power to be exerted (Ury, Brett, & Goldberg, 1988). This perspective, sometimes called a *disputing perspective*, would expand not only our study of conflict processes, but also how we understand the outcomes. Let me use some examples from the book.

The focus on microprocesses is a welcome addition to what has been traditionally a *black box* between inputs and outcomes, especially in the study of negotiation. However, with a few exceptions, the discussion of process does not show how meanings might have changed. In chapter 3, for example, although we learn about different sequences and the relation to outcomes, how parties' understand their issues and behaviors is still a black box. Similarly, in chapter 5, we learned about how dissent affects creativity and performance but not how the majority actually takes in minority viewpoints. Putnam (2004) showed, for example, how shifts in the levels of abstraction—from specific to general, from concrete to abstract, from individual to system—change how parties understand their issues. These new understandings can lead to a redefinition of the issues, to different arguments, which in turn leaves space for different types of outcomes (chapter 12). Indeed, were we to take seriously the notion that disputes can be transformed, we might abandon our linear models in favor of more interactive ones. Then we might notice that our conflicts are rarely resolved, but are rephrased, redefined, and reprocessed, and so continue to surface again in different forms.

It is this insight that can be usefully applied in the study of third-party processes and dispute resolution systems. Akin to studies of ADR in legal and community arenas, there is a tendency to focus on particular outcomes like usage and satisfaction and on the tactics or strategies that are used (chapters 10 and 11). However, we need to pay more attention to how meaning is managed in the context of these processes. Disputes or grievances are not objective events but are negotiated over by the involved parties. As such, the subjects and remedies sought can change dramatically. Gadlin (1994) described how a complaint that came to him as ombudsman about a performance issue expanded into a larger dispute about race because of supporters who counseled the complainant. Similarly, there is an incentive in dispute systems to *normalize* disputes so they can be dealt with in ways that fit a dispute resolver's areas of expertise and capacities. The incentive to "resolve" issues at the individual level means that an issue is interpreted as being between individuals. However, the problems may be a reflection of more systemic issues and so resurface later, and/or they may be a manifestation of the conflict "splitting" where individual disputants are "blamed" for something that has its roots elsewhere in the organization (Donnellon & Kolb, 1994; Smith, 1989). Indeed, complainants may be more likely to become more aggressive in their approaches to conflict if they feel that the system has served them poorly (chapter 7). If we take seriously the challenge to move across levels in our study of conflict (chapter 1), we need to look at the ways dispute systems contribute to the ways disputes are channeled to different levels and with what consequences to complainants and organizations.

An interpretive perspective can also lead in new directions in the study of third party intervention in organizations. Although strategic choice models dominate the study of mediation (chapter 10), we need to attend more to the ways that mediators actively frame a conflict such that it leads to particular actions. This would mean that we consider the preferences and values of mediator, for say, problem solving, transformation, or other goals (Baruch-Bush & Folger, 2005), the relationships between the mediator and the parties, and the types of issues confronted. For what we know from research in other settings is that mediation is practiced in different ways by different practitioners in different settings depending on the issues, the relationship of the parties to each other and the mediator, the institutional location of mediation, the culture in which it is embedded, and the timing of it relative to other processes (Merry, 1989). If we consider these types of concerns, we can begin to compare how mediation plays out in different types of organizational contexts and how organizational cultures may influence these processes and with what consequences.

In doing so, we need to question the typologies that so neatly distinguish among third parties. Although these different forms of conflict resolution processes exist, they are not distinct in the way formalistic descriptions imply. Rather the lines between facilitation, mediation, arbitration, and adjudication, for example, are blurred. Indeed, mediation often has more in common with the procedure or processes it replaces than with the way it is practiced in other contexts (Conlon, Carnevale, & Murnighan, 1994). If that is the case, as we look to how third parties operate in organizations, we may need to take seriously the advice of the editors (chapter 1) to look at these processes over time. That means tracing the fate (and meaning) of conflicts longitudinally as they are processed using different procedures. In doing so, we need to attend to the less formal and overt means of conflict handling as well (D. M. Kolb & Bartunek, 1992).

SO WHAT? OR THE ORGANIZATIONAL CONSEQUENCES OF CONFLICT MANAGEMENT

The final issue I want to discuss brings us back to the subject of the book—organizational conflict. Factors that might influence organizational conflict and how it is expressed and managed at the individual, group, intergroup, and organizational levels (chapter 1) are given extensive treatment in this volume. The role of culture is particularly noteworthy. This is important because, as I have suggested, previous efforts tended to isolate conflict management from its organizational roots. However, we need to close the loop. How do conflict and its management impact the organization? In answering this question, it is not merely performance or turnover or other such managerial measures that we need to consider, but rather how the management of conflict influences and shapes the organizational context and culture in which future conflicts are played out (Giddens, 1984).

First, level matters. There is a tendency in organizations to individualize disputes. That is, people's understandings of a conflict often begin by focusing on individuals and dyads (Smith, 1989). Indeed, the discussion of conflict sources (chapter 1) begins at the individual level. What research has shown is that when conflicts and grievances are treated at the individual level, it means that existing systems and power relationships are more likely to remain intact (Donnellon & Kolb, 1994). To extend the discussion of level, it makes sense to consider the organizational implications of dealing with conflicts at particular levels. Second, there is some evidence in other settings that the ways conflicts are handled become *normalized*, that is, they evolve over time to be seen in ways that might be quite different from the intention. In recurring legal conflicts, for example, Galanter (1974) showed that particular relationships mean that the "haves" come out ahead. What are the organizational implications of the finding reported in chapter 11 that grievance systems in nonunion work places yields low, not high, satisfaction? Not only will the system get a negative reputation, and so will not be used, but also it might mean that other organizational consequences are more likely. To what degree does the management of conflict lead to change or does it merely duplicate existing hierarchical relationships (Kunda, 1992; D. M. Kolb & Bartunek, 1992)? Who does come out ahead?

One implication of the relative failure to consider explicitly organizational implications is that when change occurs it may go unnoticed. For example, there are some significant examples of how new approaches to collective bargaining led to a major transformation in relationships between labor and management (Eaton, McKersie, & Fonstad, 2004). At MIT, the actions of a coalition of women scientists led to more equity in working conditions and opportunities (Meyerson, 2001). It is generally accepted that conflict can lead to change, but we need to be clearer about the kinds of changes we are talking about.

Let me conclude with an example that suggests how conflict management impacts organizational practices in ways that change the context for the expression of conflict and for its potential outcomes. The example comes from an intervention study of gender, work, and family issues in the workplace (Bailyn, Kolb, & Fletcher, 1997). It is a truth generally acknowledged that, until recently, work was structured as if people had no life outside of it. This might have been a norm that fit many men very well but presents a challenge to women (and men) who have families. Conflicts over time and responsibility and schedules happen routinely in work groups and between supervisors and subordinates. People might leave the organization and/or grieve their treatment. At the same time, individuals begin to negotiate alternative work schedules. The conflict is treated at the individual level—a matter of choice even though work practices such as "face time" make it difficult for the individual to manage work and personal life. However, it can also happen that the negotiations can accumulate such that they lead to policies that enunciate flexible work arrangements. That means that future negotiations take place against a background of legitimacy as least as expressed in a policy.

However, cultural assumptions about an "ideal worker," means that people, especially those with high career ambitions, do not take advantage of the policies for fear it will negatively impact their careers, that is, until the conflict is dealt with at the group level—how can a team do its work and still let its members have a life? The potential outcome of this form of managing the conflict means that flexible work arrangements become a norm and so conflicts around them might be mitigated. It also might be because these changes happen at the group level, that decision-making structures become less centralized on other issues as well. It also may be that this process leads to more gender equity in the workplace, which might give voice to groups who have not been as vocal, and so on. I use this loose example to suggest that as we look at how conflict is managed at different levels, we need to study how these processes change the contexts within which future conflicts play out. These aspects of the management of conflict are still elusive.

REFERENCES

Bailyn, L., Kolb, D. M., & Fletcher, J. K. (1997). Unexpected connections: Considering employees' personal lives can revitalize your business. *Sloan Management Review, 38,* 11–19.

Barley, S. R. (1991). Contextualizing conflict: Notes on the anthropology of disputes and negotiations. In M. H. Bazerman, R. J. Lewicki, & B. H. Sheppard (Eds.), *Research on negotiation* (Vol. 3). Greenwich, CT: JAI Press.

Baruch-Bush, R., & Folger, J. (2005). *The promise of mediation: The transformative approach to conflict* (2nd ed.). San Francisco: Jossey-Bass.

Burroway, M. (1979). *Manufacturing consent.* Chicago: University of Chicago Press.

Conlon, D. E., Carnevale, P. J., & Murnighan, J. K. (1994). Intravention: Third party intervention with clout. *Organizational Behavior and Human Decision Processes, 57,* 387–410.

De Dreu, C. K. W., & Van de Vliert, E. (Eds.). (1997). *Using conflict in organizations.* Thousand Oaks, CA: Sage.

Donnellon, A., & Kolb, D. M. (1994). Constructive for whom? The fate of diversity disputes in organizations. *Journal of Social Issues, 50,* 139–155.

Eaton, S. C., McKersie, R. B., & Fonstad, N. O. (2004). Taking stock of the Kaiser Permanente Partnership story. *Negotiation Journal, 20,* 47–65.

Felstiner, W. R., Abel, R., & Sarat, A. (1981). The emergence and transformation of disputes: Naming, blaming, and claiming. *Law and Society Review, 15,* 631–54.

Gadlin, H. (1994). Conflict resolution, cultural differences, and the culture of racism. *Negotiation Journal, 10,* 33–44.

Galanter, M. (1974). Why the "haves" come out ahead: Speculations on the limits of legal change. *Law and Society Review, 9,* 95–160.

Giddens, A. (1984). *The constitution of society.* Berkeley: University of California Press.

Kolb, D. M., & Bartunek, J. M. (Eds.). (1992). *Hidden conflict in organizations: Uncovering behind the scenes disputes.* Thousand Oaks, CA: Sage.

Kolb, J. E. (1999). An analyst looks at negotiation. In D. M. Kolb (Ed.), *Negotiation eclectics: Essays in memory of Jeffrey Z. Rubin.* Cambridge, MA: Program on Negotiation.

Kreisberg, L. (2003). *Constructive conflict: From escalation to resolution.* Lanham, MD: Rowan and Littlefield.

Kunda, G. (1992). *Engineering culture: Control and commitment in a high-tech corporation.* Philadelphia: Temple University Press.

Lawrence, P., & Lorsch, J. (1969). *Organization and environment.* Homewood, IL: Richard D. Irwin.

Lipsky, D. B., Seeber, R., & Fincher, R. (2003). *Emerging systems for managing workplace conflict: Lessons from American corporations for managers and dispute resolution professionals.* San Francisco: Jossey-Bass.

Merry, S. M. (1989). Mediation in non industrial societies. In K. Kressel & D. G. Pruitt, (Eds.), *Mediation research.* San Francisco: Jossey-Bass.

Meyerson, D. (2001). *Tempered radicals: How people use difference to inspire change at work.* Cambridge, MA: Harvard Business School Press.

Morrill, C. (1992). The private ordering of professional relations. In D. M. Kolb & J. M. Bartunek (Eds.), *Hidden conflict in organizations Uncovering behind the scenes disputes.* Thousand Oaks, CA: Sage.

Putnam, L. L. (2004). Transformations and critical moments in negotiations. *Negotiation Journal, 20*, 275–297.

Rubin, J. Z. (Ed.). (1981). *Dynamics of third party intervention: Kissinger in the Mideast.* New York: Praeger.

Smith, K. (1989). The movement of conflict in organizations: Splitting and triangulation. *Administrative Science Quarterly, 34*, 1–20.

Ury, W. R., Brett, J. M., & Goldberg, S. B. (1988). *Getting disputes resolved: Designing systems to cut the cost of conflict.* San Francisco: Jossey-Bass.

16

Theory of Conflict in the Workplace: Whence and Whither

PETER J. CARNEVALE
Stern School of Business, New York University

> Before we inquire into origins and functional relations, it is necessary to know the thing we are trying to explain. (Asch, 1952/1987, p. 65)

This is a wonderful collection of essays that attests the depth, breadth, and vigor of the study of conflict and conflict management in organizations; it is a privilege to provide commentary. I focus here on the theories—and their historical influences and future prospects; that is, I look back in time with an eye to looking forward. Hence the *whence* and the *whither*, the former a focus on *from what place*, as in, *whence comes this splendid feast?* And the latter, whither, as in, *to what place, result, or condition*: *Whither are we wandering?*[1] If we are wandering toward more research— and we are—, this volume is a huge success. Each of the essays here is a gold mine of ideas for future studies crying out to be done. Pruitt (chapter 8, this volume), for example, lists no less that seven sets of research questions that could each be a Ph.D. thesis—each could even be a distinct career of research.

It is interesting that this volume's title starts "The psychology of . . ." because there really is more than that here. The reader will of course find here the most recent developments in psychology relevant to organizational conflicts, for example, work on motivational processes, group decision making, aggression, culture, social identification, and fairness

---

[1] The *American Heritage Dictionary of the English Language*, Fourth Edition. New York: Houghton Mifflin Company, 2000.

processes. However, we also have here important contributions that reflect state of the art scholarship in the fields of communication, creativity, organizational diversity, and health, all applied to understanding organizational conflict. There are two chapters on conflict management per se, mediation and dispute resolution systems, and chapters on two contexts of conflict that are particularly relevant to organizations, union–management conflict and mergers. And the essay on escalation, by Pruitt (chapter 8, this volume), presents a general model of conflict that is relevant to conflict no matter what, where, or whom, and an especially nice thing about escalation models is the focus on *when*: Time is by definition a primitive in escalation models. Most models of organizational conflict are static, absent the dynamic interplay of processes that evolve in time, a point nicely made by De Dreu and Gelfand (chapter 1, this volume). But the field is clearly moving toward better treatment of time as a parameter for modeling, a point I return to below.

It was Ruth (1:16) who gave us "Whither thou goest, I will go,"[2] and this is also apparent in the study of organizational conflict: The effort very much reflects the fads and fancies of the broader disciplines that are brought to bear; whither the disciplines wander—whether it be to cognition, emotion, cultural analyses, multilevel analysis, decision theory, or neuroscience models—the study of organization conflict will go as well. However, it would be a mistake to assume it is a one-way street; for example, it has taken some time for social psychology and economics to catch on to the importance of positive factors in human interaction, such as matters of fairness and respect, something that organization scholars discovered some time ago in the humanistic reaction to "scientific management," illustrated nicely here by Jaffee (chapter 2, this volume). In other words, one can see the human relations movement in organizations as having presaged the positive movement in psychology (cf. Seligman & Csikszentmihalyi, 2000).

In the study of organizational conflict, we are still largely in a taxonomic phase, with occasional efforts to move to explanation and prediction. In the study of negotiation, it is more clear, with broad agreement, that there are basic strategies—contending, concession making, problem solving—that can lead to agreement. Measures of "concession" or "tradeoff" are often clear. The comprehensive review by Goldman, Cropanzano, Stein, and Benson (chapter 10, this volume) indicated that taxonomic work in mediation has also developed nicely in recent years. And, there has been some progress on understanding the basic structure of agreement, although much work lies ahead (cf. Carnevale, 2006).

---

[2] The Bible, King James Version, Book of Ruth, 1:16: *And Ruth said, Intreat me not to leave thee, or to return from following after thee: for whither thou goest, I will go; and where thou lodgest, I will lodge: thy people shall be my people, and thy God my God: 1:17 Where thou diest, will I die, and there will I be buried: the LORD do so to me, and more also, if ought but death part thee and me.*

How significant is the term *organizational* as a qualifier of *conflict*? Of course, arenas of conflict differ from one another in terms of how negotiation works, to be sure, but there are many more similarities than differences among settings—organizational, political, and interpersonal. These similarities make it possible to develop general theories of negotiation. This means that we can learn things from one arena and generalize to another. For example, negotiations between representatives differ in some respects from negotiations between individuals who act on their own behalf, as noted by De Dreu and Gelfand (chapter 1, this volume) as well as by Beersma, Conlon, and Hollenbeck (chapter 4, this volume). These sorts of distinctions—about variables—are more fundamental than the differences between the arenas in which negotiation takes place. This means that we can borrow ideas and effects, and models, from a variety of literatures—international relations, for example, that speak to matters of organizational conflict.

WHENCE

Modern writing about organizational conflict reflects several key influences and traditions. One source of influence is *historical writing,* highly informative descriptions of actual conflict events. Indeed one of the earliest known instances of writing, in the history of writing, was a description of a conflict that was resolved via mediation (Kramer, 1963). Other examples are the highly informative descriptions of labor and industry disputes written by people close to real situations (Peters, 1955; see also Douglas, 1962; Follett, 1926), and international mediation the collection of essays put together by Campbell (1976) written by the people who were the actual participants in the 1954 Trieste negotiations involving Italy and Yugoslavia.

Sometimes historical reports and accounts inform the *popular books and manuals that provide advice* (e.g., Fisher & Ury, 1981). Often these writings are cook-bookish and full of aphorisms that in practice are difficult to apply; for example, one should be ". . . firm as a rock when necessity demands, and supple as a willow at another moment" (de Callieres, 1716/1963, p. 43). However, when does necessity demand firmness and when should one be supple? Nevertheless, these writings serve as useful foils for the modern researcher.

Often historical writings and close observations of real settings are synthesized in broad theoretical generalizations about conflict behavior. The behavioral research tradition in conflict, which is represented predominantly in this volume, seeks to develop and test predictive theory about the impact of environmental conditions on negotiator (and mediator) behavior and the impact of these conditions and behaviors on outcomes (cf. Walton & McKersie 1965). Much of the early social-psychological work, especially the laboratory experiments, tested notions presented in works such as those of Walton and Mckersie, and Stevens (1963); for example, ideas about the function of mediation, such as face saving (Pruitt & Johnson, 1970).

But the behavioral work also leans heavily on another tradition, *mathematical models* of rational behavior developed by economists and game theorists (e.g., Luce & Raiffa, 1957), and variations on that theme that combine the tools of rational analysis to examine the wide range of tactics faced by most negotiators and third parties (e.g., Raiffa, 1982; Schelling, 1960). In addition, important collaborations between economists and psychologists provided, and continue to provide, much theoretical leverage to the domain. For example, the classic work by Siegel and Fouraker (1960) inspired early studies on aspirations (Kelley, Beckman, & Fisher, 1967), which provided the foundation for the dual concern theory developed by Pruitt (1981). This theory distinguished between *self-concern*, which was reflected in the Kelley et al. notion of *resistance* and *other concern*, which has a foundation in the work on leadership style that emerged from the Ohio State Leadership Studies, that is, the notion of *consideration* (see Hollander, 1979). The essay by Beersma, Conlon, and Hollenbeck (chapter 4, this volume) nicely represents this work.

WHITHER

I began this comment with the observation that the study of organizational conflict reflects the fads and fancies of broader disciplines—social psychology, sociology, economics, and so on—and whither they wander the study of organization conflict will go as well. However, the whither will wither, in my humble opinion, if the core areas of industrial–organizational psychology are not more vigorously brought to bear on the study of organizational conflict. In particular, matters of measurement. Conflict has a lot of parts and pieces, even when we place the "organizational" boundary on it. So when we ask the Asch question—*what is it that we are trying to explain?*—there is no easy answer, a point also made in several of these essays (e.g., Spector & Bruk-Lee, chapter 9, this volume). This was apparent also in Jaffee's comments on forms of resistance in organizations: "covert political conflict" can include "material and personal sabotage, theft, noncooperation, strategic inaction, and symbolic disrespect or escape" (chapter 2, this volume). Consider these forms in conjunction with the set of behaviors identified by Raver and Barling (chapter 7, this volume): "offensive remarks, threatening others, isolating an individual so he or she has difficulty working, harshly criticizing others, making obscene gestures, giving someone the 'silent treatment,' failing to transmit information, physical assault, and theft from other employees" (p. 211).

To build a cumulative science of organizational conflict we need good measures of the parts and pieces. Moreover, there are areas that the field needs to do a better job of integrating. The traditional, core areas of industrial psychology—selection, personnel, training, performance appraisal— have not been sharply developed in the study of organizational conflict. We need a job analysis of negotiation.

In other words, a real gap in current work, especially that driven by lab-based studies of conflict, is a clear picture of the forms and character of behavior that fall under the general rubric of organizational conflict. We lack taxonomic work of conflict, basic types and forms, and the same point can be made about the structure, and discovery, of "win–win" agreements: "A large issue is how the parties come to know or be aware that they have found a creative, integrative agreement. It may ultimately be a matter of appropriate measurement that takes into consideration objective and subjective factors that are immediate as well as long term" (Carnevale, 2006, p. 431). Not to belabor the point, but we really do need measures that predict job performance when the job is negotiation, or mediation, or when the job is trying to find a good outcome in a dispute between marketing and production. There are signs of progress; for example, just to name two, the recent efforts to develop measurement tools for organizational justice processes (Donovan, Drasgow, & Munson, 1998), as well as measures of the subjective dimensions of conflict outcomes (Curhan, Elfenbein, & Xu, 2006).

Good taxonomic work is needed, as Asch suggested, prior to the analysis of functional relations. It is necessary to know the thing we are trying to explain; for one, the effects we want to explain are often not simple. Negotiation is a complex system, and this means that multiple processes interact in complex ways and with feedback. This means that a variable that has an effect in one context can have the opposite effect in another context. Schultz-Hardt, Mojzisch, and Vogelgesang (chapter 5, this volume) nicely and importantly illustrated the positive impact of dissent on creative performance, and this makes great sense especially in light of Deutsch's notion of constructive conflict (see Deutsch, Coleman, & Marcus, 2006). But when is there too much dissent? When is it destructive? Carnevale and Probst (1998) reported that conflict could inhibit creativity. Again, we lack good taxonomic work on types and forms of conflict and types and forms for creativity relevant to conflict. Steigleder, Weiss, Balling, Wenninger, and Lombardo (1980) suggested that some conflict is *aversive* and, thus, likely to produce rigidity effects.

Of course, we run the risk of too many categories and distinctions, a dizzying proliferation of distinctions; it is welcome relief to see efforts at synthesis and simplification, as when Jehn, Bezrukova, and Thatcher (chapter 6, this volume) noted, "We believe that the distinction between social category and information diversity incorporates previous distinctions of visible versus nonvisible diversity and surface-level diversity versus deep-level diversity" (p. 187).

The important matter of time in models of negotiation and conflict, mentioned by De Dreu and Gelfand (chapter 1, this volume), reflects a large and important development in the field. Time is at the center of Pruitt's discussion of escalation (chapter 8, this volume); for example, the important study by Mikolic, Parker, and Pruitt (1997) showed clearly the temporal dynamic of conflict processes, and further shows that some effects, such as gender, change across time. Olson-Buchanan and Boswell (chapter 11, this volume) made the same point about time in their call for moving the field forward, in noting that disputing in organizations is a *recursive process* "whereby prior experiences with an ODR system have implications for later dispute situations and resolution" (pp. 340–341). The same point can be made about *pattern bargaining* (Friedman, Hunter, & Chen, chapter 12, this volume). Henderson, Trope, and Carnevale (2006) reported that time perspective can organize cognitive processes in negotiation.

In an interesting analysis of organizational mergers, Terry and Amiot (chapter 13, this volume) also highlighted the importance of time: They focus on developmental processes and the emergence of novel social identities, as a three-stage process, that can facilitate resolution of conflict. Interestingly, Kelman (1999) made a similar point about emerging identities and conflict resolution in the Middle East.

There also are interesting context questions that can be raised. In their impressive review and work on groups in negotiation, Beersma et al. (chapter 4, this volume) showed that dispositional variables, such as social value orientation, could play an important role in conflict behavior. One way to extend this work is to look at groups in context. For example, Probst, Carnevale, and Triandis (1999) showed that the most competitive individuals in a group would become the most cooperative in their group when their group is in competition with another group. Will they also be the first to leave their group if their group is losing the between group competition?

The important role of the broader context of disputes is also seen at a macrolevel in the changes that have affected U.S. labor. Friedman et al. (chapter 12, this volume) note the broad changes in the environment that affect the way labor and management negotiate, for example, the advent of global competition.

One thing that is largely absent from the literature is the top-down effects of conflict in networked relationships in organizations. A nice story from the early days of research makes the point: the first attempt to get intergroup conflict by Sherif, for the Robbers Cave studies, failed.

But briefly, this happened before the Robbers Cave experiment, in the summer of 1953. In an earlier study, Sherif showed that he could produce hostile attitudes (in groups that were formed to cut across earlier established friendships) by introducing competing goals. The 1953 study was designed to test the next step, showing that these hostile attitudes could be overcome through superordinate goals. But this time around he was not able to produce the initial hostility, even though he tried hard (and in questionable ways) to do so. He considered the whole exercise a failure, since he was not able to create the conditions that would allow him to test his hypothesis. He was not interested in figuring out why creating the hostility didn't work this time around. The Robbers Cave was his second attempt to test the hypothesis. I assume it succeeded, at least in part, because in that study he did not give himself the added handicap of breaking up initial friendships in forming the groups. (H. C. Kelman, personal communication, August 8, 1998)

It turned out that in the initial effort, the two emergent leaders of the groups of kids knew each other—they had a personal relationship from their hometown—and they trusted one another; when a conflict-provoking incident occurred, they got together and talked about it and came to the conclusion that the camp counselors were responsible. They conveyed this back to their groups. In other words, the trust between the two and positive relationship between the leaders was critical, and their abilities to convey this back to their group and have it accepted was key. The important role of trust and positive relationships, especially among leaders, is a promising direction, with only a few hints in the literature of the dynamics (e.g., Nelson, 1989).

CONCLUSIONS

If organizational conflict and tension is a permanent feature of all organizational systems, as noted by Jaffee (chapter 2, this volume), this of course means that conflict scholars will never be out of work. And the work sometimes pays off. Even in the worker versus owner domain, characterized as "a history of trial and error in developing methods and techniques for managing and conceptualizing these tensions," good ideas do emerge, for example, the advent of final-offer arbitration, an idea that Carl Stevens helped along, as well as the notion of expedited arbitration noted by Friedman et al. (chapter 12, this volume). It is curious that more effort to come up with novel resolution procedures has not been tried, especially using laboratory simulation methods. A big question for the worker versus owner domain is whether the analysis of underlying processes, such as motives, cognitions, emotions, and even neuroscience models, will help the effort. The essays by Pruitt (chapter 8, this volume), Goldman et al. (chapter 10, this volume), and Olson-Buchanan and Boswell (chapter 11, this volume) suggested the affirmative. It might be worth noting in this context that the current interest in procedural justice processes might be construed as part of the "postbureaucratic" effort to "control and extract" human labor in a Machiavellian manner, which is the double-edged sword of procedural fairness noted by MacCoun (2005).

Indeed, many of our conflict and negotiation effects are *double-edged swords*. Look at the effects of *high aspirations*, which sometimes lead to no agreement, sometimes to high quality agreement; *good relationships*, which sometimes produce poor agreements; negotiation *teams*, which sometimes produce contentious responses at the same time as high quality agreements; gain and loss *frame,* which sometimes lessens the likelihood of agreement and sometimes produces high quality agreements; even cooperativeness and competitiveness as individual *dispositions* can go either way with the most competitive person in the group becoming the most cooperative in the right circumstances. All of this points to the remarkable plasticity of the human character, to use a phrase spoken by Bandura. Even conflict itself has good and bad effects, as noted by Schultz-Hardt et al. (chapter 5, this volume), as well as Deutsch et al. (2006), and others (e.g., Coser, 1956). And Pruitt (chapter 8, this volume) made the same point about escalation sometimes having positive consequences for individuals and organizations. Sometimes, our variables are triple edged, having no effects under some circumstances; for example, communication processes—such as the sight of the other—can sometimes have a positive impact and sometimes a negative impact on negotiation, and sometimes it just makes no difference, as hinted by Olekalns, Putnam, Weingart, and Metcalf (chapter 3, this volume). These authors further noted a particularly interesting aspect of communication: the advent of new communication technologies that are likely to alter the face of conflict management dramatically in the future.

If there is one thing about the study of conflict in the workplace that we can all agree on, it is that there are, today, a lot more people doing it than there was 50 years ago. And the people who are doing it come from a wide array of disciplines and countries, which means two things: the study of culture is now at the forefront, and so are efforts at cutting across disciplinary boundaries. A case in point is the recent edited volume by Carnevale and De Dreu (2006) that contained 25 chapters about method in the study of social conflict, written by scholars in political science, psychology, organization behavior, economics, law, and so on.

But there are clear exciting destinations on the horizon, and many of the essays in this volume pointed the way. For example, the work on positive psychology, civility in the workplace, and spirituality seems ripe for integration with the broader study of organizational conflict (Ashforth & Pratt, 2003). And integrating current models of decision making, such as prospect theory and the notion of framing, with models of affect and motivation is clearly a hot direction (Carnevale, 2007). Both reflect trends in the broader disciplines; for example, we now see broad efforts to integrate models of emotion with decision theory (Novemsky & Kahneman, 2005). Given the trend to brain imaging in social psychology and neuroeconomics, we can see brain-imaging studies of organizational conflict on the horizon. These are all exciting developments with great potential as the field moves forward.

REFERENCES

Asch, S. E. (1987). *Social psychology.* New York: Oxford University Press. (Original work published 1952)

Ashforth, B. E., & Pratt, M.G. (2003). Institutionalized spirituality: An oxymoron? In R. A. Giacalone & C. L. Jurkiewicz (Eds.), *The handbook of workplace spirituality and organizational performance* (pp. 93–107). Armonk, NY: M.E. Sharpe.

Campbell, J. C. (1976). *Successful negotiation: Trieste (1954).* Princeton, NJ: Princeton University Press.

Carnevale, P. J. (2006). Creativity in the outcomes of conflict. In M. Deutsch, P. T. Coleman, & E. C. Marcus (Eds.), *Handbook of conflict resolution* (2nd ed., pp. 414–435). San Francisco: Jossey-Bass.

Carnevale, P. J. (2007). Positive affect and decision frame in negotiation. *Group Decision and Negotiation.*

Carnevale, P. J., & De Dreu, C. K. W. (Eds.). (2006). *Methods of negotiation research.* Leiden, the Netherlands: Martinus Nijhoff Publishers.

Carnevale, P. J., & Probst, T. (1998). Social values and social conflict in creative problem solving and categorization. *Journal of Personality and Social Psychology, 74,* 1300–1309.

Coser, L. (1956). *The functions of social conflict.* Glencoe, IL: Free Press.

Curhan, J. R., Elfenbein, H. A., & Xu, H. (2006). What do people value when they negotiate? Mapping the domain of subjective value in negotiation. *Journal of Personality and Social Psychology, 91,* 493–512.

de Callieres, F. (1963). *On the manner of negotiating with princes* (A.F. White, Trans.). Notre Dame, IN: Notre Dame University Press. (Original work published 1716)

Deutsch, M., Coleman, P., & Marcus, E. (Eds.). (2006). *The handbook of conflict resolution: Theory and practice* (2nd ed.). San Francisco: Jossey-Bass.

Donovan, M. A., Drasgow, F., & Munson, L. J. (1998). The perceptions of fair interpersonal treatment scale: Development and validation of a measure of interpersonal treatment in the workplace. *Journal of Applied Psychology, 5,* 683–692.

Douglas, A. (1962). *Industrial peacemaking.* New York: Columbia University Press.

Fisher, R., & Ury, W. (1981). *Getting to YES: Negotiating agreement without giving in.* Boston: Houghton Mifflin.

Follett, M. P. (1926). Constructive conflict. In H. C. Metcalf (Ed.), *Scientific foundations of business administration.* Baltimore: Williams & Wilkins Co.

Henderson, M. D., Trope, Y., & Carnevale, P. J. (2006). Negotiation from a near and distant time perspective. *Journal of Personality and Social Psychology, 91,* 712–729.

Hollander, E. P. (1979). The impact of Ralph Stogdill and the Ohio State Leadership Studies on a transactional approach to leadership. *Journal of Management, 5,* 157–165.

Kelley, H. H., Beckman, L. L., & Fischer, C. S. (1967). Negotiating the division of reward under incomplete information. *Journal of Experimental Social Psychology, 3,* 361–398.

Kelman, H. C. (1999). The interdependence of Israeli and Palestinian national identities: The role of the other in existential conflicts. *Journal of Social Issues, 55,* 581–600.

Kramer, S. N. (1963). *The Sumerians.* Chicago: The University of Chicago Press.

Luce, R. D., & Raiffa, H. (1957). *Games and decisions*. New York: John Wiley.

MacCoun, R. J. (2005). Voice, control, and belonging: The double-edged sword of procedural fairness. *Annual Review of Law and Social Science, 1*, 171–201.

Mikolic, J. M., Parker, J. C., & Pruitt, D. G. (1997). Escalation in response to persistent annoyance: Groups vs. individuals and gender effects. *Journal of Personality and Social Psychology, 72*, 151–163.

Nelson, R. E. (1989). The strength of strong ties: Social networks and intergroup conflict in organizations. *Academy of Management Journal, 32*, 377–401.

Novemsky, N., & Kahneman, D. (2005). How do intentions affect loss aversion? *Journal of Marketing Research, 42*, 139–140.

Peters, E. (1955). *Conciliation in action*. New London, CT: National Foremen's Institute.

Probst, T., Carnevale, P. J., & Triandis, H. C. (1999). Cultural values in intergroup and single-group social dilemmas. *Organizational Behavior and Human Decision Processes, 77*, 171–191.

Pruitt, D. G. (1981). *Negotiation behavior*. New York: Academic Press.

Pruitt, D. G., & Johnson, D. F. (1970). Mediation as an aid to face-saving in negotiation. *Journal of Personality and Social Psychology, 14*, 239–46.

Raiffa, H. (1982). *The art and science of negotiation*. Cambridge, MA: Belknap.

Schelling, T. C. (1960). *The strategy of conflict*. Boston: Harvard University Press.

Seligman, M., & Csikszentmihalyi, M. (2000). Positive psychology: An introduction. *American Psychologist, 55*, 5–14.

Siegel, S., and Fouraker, L. E. (1960). *Bargaining and group decision making: Experiments in bilateral monopoly*. New York: McGraw-Hill.

Steigleder, M. K., Weiss, R. E, Balling, S. S., Wenninger, V. L., & Lombardo, J. P. (1980). Drivelike motivational properties of competitive behavior. *Journal of Personality and Social Psychology, 38*, 93–104.

Stevens, C. M. (1963). *Strategy and collective bargaining negotiation*. New York: McGraw-Hill.

Walton, R., and McKersie, R. (1965). *A behavioral theory of labor negotiations: An analysis of a social interaction system*. New York: McGraw-Hill.

17

Conflicts in the Study of Conflict in Organizations

DEAN TJOSVOLD
Lingnan University, Hong Kong

This impressive volume attests that researchers and professionals have begun to give conflict in organizations the theoretical attention and rigorous empirical analysis that it deserves. Through organizations, wars are waged, peace is developed, communities are built, and goods and services are produced and delivered. Less fully appreciated is that to make these organizations work requires daily, even hourly, conflict management. Indeed, in our intensifying, interconnected, cross-cultural, and fragmented world of organizations, the demands on managers and employees to deal openly and constructively with their differences are increasing. To paraphrase Kurt Lewin, there is nothing more important than a good theory about conflict management, especially theories that protagonists can apply together.

Chapters have summarized that organizational members can make good use of their conflicts to dig into issues, develop creative alternatives, select viable solutions, and gain the conviction to implement them. Conflict invigorates the problem-solving processes that are at the heart of an organization that recognizes and takes advantage of opportunities as well as deals with threats (e.g., Chen, Liu, & Tjosvold, 2005). Without problem solving, successful organizations are vulnerable; without constructive conflict, organizations cannot confront reality and develop future directions. However, chapters in this volume have also documented the staggering costs of conflict and shown how escalating conflict can split organizations.

Unfortunately, there are serious shortcomings in our research on conflict that make it much less useful than desirable. We have not very successfully given conflict management knowledge away. Indeed, surveys indicated that many employees are estranged from their managers, even

445

see them as dishonest (Hogan, Curphy, & Hogan, 1994; Kouzes & Posner, 2005). Many managers and employees appear to be skeptical about the value of our ideas and studies, even though present conflict management practices are very costly. Years ago, we did a study to estimate the dollar costs of when organizational members did not work together well and manage their conflicts (Tjosvold & Janz, 1985). The costs were many thousands of dollars a year for each employee. The costs are probably much larger today.

Applying organizational research is intellectually challenging and requires close collaboration between researchers and practitioners, but shortcomings in our research itself also interfere. Reading the chapters suggested several key conflicts in the study of conflict. These comments identify key conflicts and argue that confronting and resolving these and other conflicts can help us fulfill the promise of conflict research.

CONFLICT TO DEVELOP OUR DISCIPLINE

In the development of disciplines as in organizations more generally, conflict has a normal and potentially quite constructive role. Indeed, researchers are continually disagreeing over such issues as the value and utility of data and their sources (Kennedy, 2003). Researchers also debate such major issues as the role of values in developing science (Anderson, 2004). Like others, conflict researchers have reached agreement on ways of considering our area and conducting studies in it; however, there are also differences of opinion about various issues and approaches that can potentially alter and strengthen the field (Kuhn, 1962).

Morton Deutsch (1989) recounted that well-managed conflict contributed significantly to the very productive and influential Research Center for Group Dynamics at MIT. Kurt Lewin communicated to each person that he or she was vital to the center's mission. He led loosely organized research seminars, called the *Quasselstrippe* (or winding string), and encouraged lively, spirited debate. Near the end of these exhilarating controversies, he typically offered a deeper perspective that would integrate both the conflicting views and the people arguing them.

However, their inabilities to resolve conflicts also had costly, long-term consequences. Deutsch argued that Lewin's early death contributed to the widening rift between the "tough-minded scientist" Leon Festinger, the "soft-hearted activist" Ronald Lippit, and the people sympathetic to them and their ideas. It was not so much that their conflicts escalated into open warfare, but rather, they led to the development of separate groups and perspectives that grew apart. The unresolved conflict between science and action continues to divide contemporary social psychology and its offspring, organizational psychology and behavior.

This note identifies conflicts that I think deserve more attention and more controversies. The field is not characterized by warfare; conflicts have not escalated as much as been ignored and avoided. I also offer my own position on these conflicts not as the final word but as a means to stimulate opposing views and help us engage in full, constructive controversy.

DEFINING CONFLICT: WE HAVE TO

The most critical conflict is the definition of *conflict*. But conflict researchers generally and those who contributed to this volume in particular were not very concerned about defining *conflict*, perhaps because they assumed that there already is an accepted consensus. The Raver and Barling chapter distinguished conflict from a host of related "dark side of workplace" concepts, but they did not discuss alternative ways of defining conflict. Paul Spector and Valentina Bruk-Lee, in their chapter on health and well-being, were the exceptions in that they argued that the failure to reach a consensus on conflict is a major obstacle to our progress.

But our common definitions are misleading and have significantly disrupted our understanding. Although, as the Schulz-Hardt, Mojzish, and Vogelgesang chapter documented, researchers recently shed light on the positive face of conflict, common definitions have interfered with understanding the various ways that conflict can contribute to individual development and organizational performance.

Traditionally, conflict is defined in terms of opposing interests involving scarce resources and goal divergence and frustration (e.g., Pondy, 1967). This tradition has continued with little discussion.

Carsten De Dreu and Michele Gelfand, in their excellent introductory chapter, defined *conflict* as a "process that begins when an individual or group perceives differences and opposition between oneself and another individual or group about interests and resources, beliefs, values, or practices that matter to them" and cite Pondy (1967) as a source. This definition is an improvement over the traditional definition, but it is so general that it does not directly challenge the traditional definition of conflict as opposing interests.

In addition to obscuring the reality that people with completely compatible goals not only can but often do have conflict, conflict as opposing interests is confounded with competition defined as incompatible goals. This confounding makes it unclear whether effects theorized or found are due to conflict or to competition. We need definitions that clearly and explicitly do not assume that conflicts involve competitive, negatively related goals.

The traditional definition of opposing interests, which assumes conflict is competitive, frustrates effective operations as conflict is confused with win–lose ways to manage it. Indeed, studies that ask people to complete questionnaires that use the term *conflict* by itself typically indicate that conflicts of various kinds are negatively related to outcomes (De Dreu & Weingart, 2003). Spector and Bruk-Lee cited a number of studies using the interpersonal conflict at work scale, where one of the four items is "people do nasty things to me at work." But this item is not measuring conflict but a particular way of dealing with conflict. It is not surprising that studies using this kind of operation find that conflict seriously undermines well-being and health.

The organizational definition of conflict as opposing interests does reflect the popular assumption that conflict involves not only differences but incompatible goals and is win–lose. The Chinese term for conflict has even stronger connotations of a win–lose battle than the English term. Practically, people who assume that their conflicts are competitive are unlikely to be able to develop constructive ways of managing their conflicts (Deutsch, 1973). Our definition and research are reinforcing popular misconceptions rather than challenging them and helping people develop more realistic and useful understanding and attitudes toward conflict.

The irony is that the literature has had an unconfounded definition of conflict for several decades. Morton Deutsch's (1973) theory of cooperation and competition indicated that defining conflict as opposing interests is fundamentally flawed. Although Deutsch is one of the most prominent conflict researchers, the implications for his definition of conflict have been largely missed. There does not appear to have been enough direct, open conflict about definitions to generate questioning of traditional definitions and develop more effective ones!

Deutsch (1973) defined *conflict* as incompatible activities; one person's actions interfere, obstruct, or in some way get in the way of another's action. Incompatible activities occur in both cooperative and competitive contexts. Whether the protagonists believe their goals are cooperative or competitive very much affects their expectations, interactions, and outcomes. How they negotiate their conflicts in turn affects the extent to which they believe they have cooperative or competitive goals with each other.

TYPES OF CONFLICT: WE DO NOT HAVE TO

Recently, conflict researchers, as typified in the Karen Jehn, Katerina Bezrukova, and Sherry Thatcher chapter but also prominently throughout the literature, assumed that categorizing conflict as to its type can be very useful for understanding when conflicts can be constructive and destructive. Similarly, researchers, such as De Dreu and Gelfand in the introduction, distinguished conflict based on its source, namely, scarce resources, maintaining a positive view of the self, and the motive to have socially validated opinions. Although this categorizing may have some uses, researchers appear not to appreciate fully the serious difficulties with this approach.

Categories are arbitrary. Conflict is a very broad phenomenon; the types of conflicts and their sources are many. How can we assess whether a typology of 3 types of conflict is better than one with 5 or 12? The labels we assign these conflicts are also arbitrary. Developing an accepted, empirically developed taxonomy is a complex undertaking.

A more important difficulty is taking these categories too seriously, especially in the theorizing that conflict types or sources of conflict are more or less likely to be constructive. For example, conflicts that involve task issues are more constructive than relationship ones; conflicts based on resource scarcity are more likely to be destructive whereas those about socially validated beliefs are more apt to be constructive. The category of task conflict, for example, contains a wide variety of conflicts and they can be discussed effectively or ineffectively, as can relationship ones or process ones or whatever type of conflict. Just because people have scarce resources does not mean that they cannot approach their conflicts open mindedly and try to distribute these scarce resources fairly and efficiently (Poon, Pike, & Tjosvold, 2001; Tjosvold & Poon, 1998). Managers have demonstrated that they can use their anger to resolve issues and strengthen their relationships (Tjosvold & Su, in press). Indeed, research has not been able to show that task conflicts are reliably more constructive than relationship ones (De Dreu & Weingart, 2003).

Another objection to categories is both practical and philosophical. Practically, what value is there in telling managers and employees that relationship conflicts are not constructive? Are they supposed to make these issues disappear or simply not talk about them?

Philosophically, our research should empower people, should give them the courage and the know-how to deal with conflicts. But the idea that relationship conflicts or scarce resources are harmful can let people believe that the negative effects of conflicts are inherent in the conflicts themselves. Rather than recognize that they are making choices that affect course and consequences of conflict, they believe that the destructive conflict "just happens to them." Our research should help people confront and meet their responsibilities to manage their conflicts, not give them an excuse to avoid or escalate conflict.

Distinguishing conflicts by their type or source fits popular stereotypes about the value of rational, impersonal ways and the obstructive role of feelings in dealing with conflicts. But feelings and thinking are highly related. Even discussing academic issues involves important emotions; researchers have strong feelings about how to conduct their studies. Dealing with conflict requires an integration of our rational and emotional sides. Our research should help people confront their stereotypes and adopt more useful ways to manage their conflicts constructively. However, there is conflict over how we should conceptualize conflict management.

BEHAVIORAL STRATEGIES VERSUS SOCIAL PSYCHOLOGICAL APPROACHES TO MANAGING CONFLICT

Conflict is something people do and must act upon; even avoiding conflict often involves considerable effort and strategizing (Tjosvold & Sun, 2002). Researchers, especially communication-oriented ones, as represented in the Mara Olekalns, Linda Putnam, Laurie Weingart, and Laurie Metcalf chapter, typically have tried to identify constructive management of conflict through identifying the effects of various strategies. Experimental negotiation researchers also have examined the outcomes of various bargaining strategies.

Social psychologically oriented researchers, as represented by the Bianca Beersma, Donald Conlon, and John Hollenbeck chapter, have taken an approach that is not always clearly recognized as distinct. Beersma et al. summarized research on the effects of various motive orientations, namely, proself and prosocial, on the dynamics and outcomes of negotiation. Our own work, based on Deutsch's theory, has contrasted the effects of negotiators taking a cooperative (mutual benefit) or competitive (win–lose) approach to dealing with the conflict.

The very influential dual concerns model, summarized in the Olekalns et al. chapter, combines both approaches. It assumes that the concern for self and the concern for other combine to predict one of five strategies used in the conflict; the strategy in turn affects outcomes.

Surely motives and actions are closely related. However, behavioral strategies and social psychological approaches should be clearly recognized as distinct. I am often told, for example, that there are more than two strategies—not just a cooperative or competitive one—to deal with conflict or that a cooperative approach of compromising or being nice or never making a demand is unrealistic. But cooperative and competitive approaches communicate how the protagonists understand their relationship and intend to resolve the conflict; they are not behavioral strategies. A cooperative approach to conflict could include compromising and being nice and giving in, but not necessarily. Indeed, these strategies could be used for competitive purposes and communicate a competitive intent. Interestingly, our experimental and field studies in North America and in Asia show that openly discussing differences reinforces cooperative relationships; avoiding conflict reinforces competition (Tjosvold, Leung, & Johnson, 2006; Tjosvold & Sun, 2003).

The value of social psychological approaches has not been as widely recognized as it should be. My own disenchantment with research on strategies occurred very early. My dissertation study found that threats themselves could have quite contrasting effects depending upon the extent that they confirmed or disconfirmed the other's social face (Tjosvold, 1974). More generally, the effects of strategies depend upon how they are implemented and the conditions under which they are. A threat can be given warmly and deferentially or coldly and disrespectfully; friends can do it, as can enemies. And people have many, many strategies to deal with conflict.

Although studying behavioral strategies may appear to be a practical approach to identifying effective ways of managing conflict, social psychological approaches have the potential to develop elegant frameworks for identifying the major choices protagonists have to manage their conflict that recognize the varied conditions under which conflict is managed. No sure-fire strategy will communicate to others that you are committed to managing the conflict to strengthen cooperative goals and to resolve issues for mutual benefit. However, if you do communicate this intent, considerable research indicates that the conflict is very likely to be constructive compared with a competitive approach.

THEORIES TO ANALYZE CONFLICT ACROSS LEVELS

This volume follows the tradition of separating research based on whether the studies are micro or macro, that is, interpersonal or group level compared with the organizational level. I am not so cranky that I want to disagree with this way of organizing chapters. I have done it myself.

Indeed, De Dreu and Gelfand's introductory chapter helpfully reviewed recent research to explore how conflicts at one level affect conflicts at different levels. One of the beauties of studying conflict in organizations is that an argument between two persons is very much a part of the wider intergroup and organizational contexts. Their group membership, job demands, understanding of organizational values and relationships, and other aspects all have an impact on the conflict and its management. Indeed, a conflict within an organizational team can also be a conflict between teams. Conflict protagonists often discuss conflicts that are embedded within a larger intergroup conflict; when the senior management group, for example, makes organizational decisions, managers represent their own teams' opposing perspectives. A rivalry between executives can lead to ongoing conflict between departments.

Deutsch (2005) has recently argued that the management of internal and external conflicts is highly related. Unresolved conflicts within a person and ineffectively managed conflicts with others are mutually reinforcing (Bazerman, Tenbrunsel, & Wade-Benzoni, 1998). Similarly, competitive conflict between groups in organizations can reinforce competitive conflict within the groups (Hempel, Zhang, & Tjosvold, 2006; LaBianca, Brass, & Gray, 1998). Researchers have tended to develop and test their theories on one level; but, in addition to recognizing that organizational conflicts cross levels, we need theories of managing conflict that can be applied at various levels for a full understanding of conflict in organizations (Hempel et al., 2006).

USING OUR CONFLICTS

As with other joint undertakings, conflict researchers have conflicts but these are not obstacles. We do not want to follow the common path of conflict avoidance along with more hidden win–lose conflict.

This note has identified conflicts that deserve more attention, more conflict management. I do not mean to imply that I have the right position; there are strong arguments for different ways of resolving these conflicts. I hope my comments can promote productive dialogue. More generally, we need forums where we engage in the conflicts over the study of conflict directly, not to divide us, but to forge more effective ways to understand conflict and its management. Managers and employees need and deserve our best, united efforts to develop knowledge that they can apply to manage their increasingly complex conflicts.

REFERENCES

Anderson, E. (2004). Uses of value judgments in science: A general argument with lessons from a case study of feminist research on divorce. *Hypatia, 19*, 1–24.

Bazerman, M. H., Tenbrunsel, A. E., & Wade-Benzoni, K. (1998). Negotiating with yourself and losing: Making decisions with competing internal preferences. *Academy of Management Review, 23*, 225–241.

Chen, G., Liu, C. H., & Tjosvold, D. (2005). Conflict management for effective top management teams and innovation in China. *Journal of Management Studies, 42*, 277–300.

De Dreu, C. K. W., & Weingart, L. R. (2003). Task versus relationship conflict, team performance, and team member satisfaction: A meta-analysis. *Journal of Applied Psychology, 88*, 741–749.

Deutsch, M. (1973). *The resolution of conflict*. New Haven, CT: Yale University Press.

Deutsch, M. (1989, October 20). *Cooperation, conflict, and justice: Reflections on a career in social psychology*. Paper presented at the 50th anniversary conference/celebration of the Psychology Department of City College of the City University of New York.

Deutsch, M. (2005). *The interplay between internal and external conflict*. Paper presented at the Social Interdependence Theory Conference, Minneapolis, MN.

Hempel, P. S., Zhang, Z. X., & Tjosvold, D. (2006, June). *The interplay between internal and external conflict: Managing conflict between and within teams for trust in China*. Paper presented at the International Association for Conflict Management. Vancouver, Canada.

Hogan, R., Curphy, G. J., & Hogan, J. (1994). What we know about leadership: Effectiveness and personality. *American Psychologist, 49*, 493–504

Kennedy, G. A. (2003). Some recent controversies in the study of later Greek rhetoric. *American Journal of Philology, 123*, 296–301.

Kouzes, J. M., & Posner, B. Z. (2005). Leading in cynical times. *Journal of Management Inquiry, 14*, 357–364.

Kuhn, T. S. (1962). *The structure of scientific revolutions*. Chicago: University of Chicago Press.

LaBianca, G., Brass, D. J., & Gray, B. (1998). Social networks and perceptions of intergroup conflict: The role of negative relationships and third parties. *Academy of Management Journal, 41*, 55–67.

Lewin, K. (1951). *Field theory in social science*. New York: Harper.

Pondy, L. R. (1967). Organizational conflict: Concepts and models. *Administrative Science Quarterly, 12*, 296–320.

Poon, M., Pike, R., & Tjosvold, D. (2001). Budget participation, goal interdependence and controversy: A study of a Chinese public utility. *Management Accounting Research, 12*, 101–118.

Tjosvold, D. (1974). Threat as a low-power person's strategy in bargaining: Social face and tangible outcomes. *International Journal of Group Tensions*, 494–510.

Tjosvold, D., & Janz, T. (1985). Costing effective versus ineffective work relationships: A method and first look. *Canadian Journal of Administrative Sciences, 2*, 43–51.

Tjosvold, D., Leung, K., & Johnson, D. W. (2006). Cooperative and competitive conflict in China. In M. Deutsch, P. T. Coleman, & E. Marcus (Eds.), *The handbook of conflict resolution: Theory and practice* (pp. 671–692). San Francisco: Jossey-Bass.

Tjosvold, D., & Poon, M. (1998). Dealing with scarce resources: Openminded interaction for resolving budget conflicts. *Group & Organization Management, 23*, 237–255.

Tjosvold, D., & Su, F. S. (in press). Managing anger and annoyance in organizations in China: The role of constructive controversy. *Group & Organization Management*.

Tjosvold, D., & Sun, H. (2002). Understanding conflict avoidance: Relationship, motivations, actions, and consequences. *International Journal of Conflict Management, 13*, 142–164.

Tjosvold, D., & Sun, H. (2003). Openness among Chinese in conflict: Effects of direct discussion and warmth on integrated decision making. *Journal of Applied Social Psychology, 33*, 1878–1897.

Author Index

Page references followed by f indicate figure.
Page references followed by t indicate table.
Page references followed by n indicate footnote.

Subject Index